21283.   £30.00.

D0301778

CAMBRIDGE STUDIES IN
INTERNATIONAL AND COMPARATIVE LAW: NEW SERIES

General Editor:
SIR ROBERT Y. JENNINGS
Judge of the International Court of Justice
formerly Whewell Professor of International Law, University of Cambridge

THE APPLICATION OF THE RULE OF EXHAUSTION OF LOCAL REMEDIES IN INTERNATIONAL LAW

CAMBRIDGE STUDIES IN
INTERNATIONAL AND COMPARATIVE LAW
NEW SERIES

Tortious liability for unintentional harm in
the Common law and the Civil law
Volume I Text
Volume II Materials
by F. H. LAWSON and B. S. MARKESINIS

In preparation

The legal regime of foreign private investment in the Sudan
and Saudi Arabia: a case study of developing countries
by FATH EL RAHMAN ABDALLA EL SHEIKH

THE APPLICATION OF
THE RULE OF EXHAUSTION OF
LOCAL REMEDIES
IN INTERNATIONAL LAW

Its rationale in the international protection of individual rights

A. A. CANÇADO TRINDADE

B.A. (Minas Gerais), LL.B. (Cantab.), Ph.D. (Cantab.); Professor
of International Law at the University of Brasília
and at the Rio Branco Institute (Diplomatic Academy
of Brazil's Ministry of External Relations); formerly
Legal Officer of the United Nations Office at Geneva

CAMBRIDGE UNIVERSITY PRESS

Cambridge
London   New York   New Rochelle
Melbourne   Sydney

Published by the Press Syndicate of the University of Cambridge
The Pitt Building, Trumpington Street, Cambridge CB2 1RP
32 East 57th Street, New York, NY 10022, USA
296 Beaconsfield Parade, Middle Park, Melbourne 3206, Australia

First published 1983

Printed in Great Britain at
the University Press, Cambridge

Library of Congress catalogue card number: 82–4393

British Library Cataloguing in Publication Data
Trindade, A.A. Cançado
The application of the rule of exhaustion of
local remedies in international law.—(Cambridge
studies in international and comparative law.
New series)
1. Civil rights (International law)
I. Title
341.4   JX6053. C/

ISBN 0 521 22947 2

TM

CONTENTS

v

Contents

GENERAL EDITOR'S FOREWORD TO THE NEW SERIES

A series of *Cambridge Studies in International and Comparative Law*, under the general editors H.C. Gutteridge, H. Lauterpacht and Sir A.D. McNair, was launched in 1946 with the first edition of Professor Gutteridge's important monograph on *Comparative Law: An Introduction to the Comparative Method of Legal Study and Research*. In a general introduction to the series the editors explained that it was designed to fill certain gaps in that part of English legal literature which is concerned with international relations: and that it would involve public international law, private international law and comparative law. In fact all the subsequent volumes of a distinguished series were to do with public international law.

In the 1970s there was a gap during a time when the Syndics were persuaded that books on law should be left to commercial publishers. Happily, counsels more apt to the Press of Maitland's university have now prevailed, and the series is being revived.

The general editors of the original series said, in April 1946, that 'at present the literature of Comparative Law is scattered, fragmentary and often difficult of access'. The aim of the present volumes is precisely to make an important part of that material readily available to scholars and students, and to provide an authoritative commentary and guide to understanding it.

Cambridge   R.Y.J.
April 1981

FOREWORD

It may seem appropriate that one of the first of the new series of Cambridge Studies in International and Comparative Law should deal with the local remedies rule, since the exhaustion of local remedies is often stated to be a pre-condition of the admissibility of international claims. Dr Trindade's book seeks to show, however, that in the treaty-based regimes of human rights protection, particularly in the European Convention on Human Rights, the rule is functionally different than in the area of general diplomatic protection, being a component part of the protection system and not a preliminary barrier to it. Equipped with a rare linguistic ability and a capacity for meticulous research, Dr Trindade was awarded the degree of Doctor of Philosophy by the University of Cambridge and a Yorke Prize by its Faculty of Law for the work of which the present book is a distillation. As the person charged with the task – in the event undemanding – of research supervisor, it is a pleasure to introduce this notable addition by a Brazilian scholar to the literature of international law in general and the protection of human rights in particular.

Sidney Sussex College, Cambridge   GEOFFREY MARSTON
15 July 1982

PREFACE

The present study is an abridged version of the author's original Ph.D. dissertation (Cambridge, 1977), which consisted of two volumes, fifteen chapters, 1,728 pages, and was considerably reduced in length for publication purposes. The author wishes to thank first his Ph.D. thesis supervisor, Dr G. Marston, of Sidney Sussex College, for his patient and constant encouragement, as well as the staffs of the Squire Law Library (Cambridge), the Bibliothèque des Droits de l'Homme (Council of Europe, Strasbourg), the Peace Palace Library (The Hague), and the United Nations Library (Geneva), for various forms of assistance on different occasions.

The oral examination on the thesis was conducted on 28 November 1977 at Downing College, Cambridge, by Professor Clive Parry, LL.D., of Cambridge University, and Mr C.J. Warbrick, of Durham University, to whom the author also extends his appreciation for their encouragement and valuable suggestions concerning the publication of the work. Finally, the author wishes to thank Sidney Sussex College, in the person of Mr J.W.A. Thornely, M.A., for all the assistance throughout his happy years of research at the University of Cambridge from 1972 to 1978.

Brasília   A.A.C.T.
July 1979

Dilectissimis mihi parentibus uxori fratribus
Adriano et Otavio pueris imprimis
qui dum hoc opus perficerem floruere
ipsum dedicatum offero

INTRODUCTION

The rule of international law whereby a State should be given the opportunity to redress an alleged wrong within the framework of its own domestic legal system before its international responsibility can be called into question at international level – the rule of exhaustion of local remedies – has undergone a long evolution since the pre-history of international law. Its roots can be found in the ancient practice of private reprisals, in the requirement of prior exhaustion of local means of redress commonly applied before the taking of reprisals (in medieval times and up to the end of the seventeenth century) and in modern times, prior to the exercise of diplomatic intervention.[1]

The rule had a *preventive* character *vis-à-vis* the exercise of reprisals and of diplomatic protection, being applicable only to the relationship between a State (or a community or a prince) and foreigners, i.e., cases of a *private* origin (alien's claim for reparation for injuries suffered abroad), even if subsequently 'internationalized' by the espousal of the claim by the individual's sovereign or State. In fact, most of the specialized literature on the subject to date has been concerned with aspects of the application of the local remedies rule within the context of the law on State responsibility for injuries to aliens and the practice of diplomatic protection.

Those aspects of the rule on which much has been written seem, however, to be nowadays undergoing a constant evolution, partly stimulated by the newly emerging and distinct contexts in which it has lately been invoked. Such novel areas where the rule plays its part seem to remain to a large extent unexplored, possibly constituting *terra nova* or *incognita* of contemporary international law, in great need of closer attention and discussion. These areas do not necessarily fall within customary international law, being usually constituted by specific systems set up by treaties and other international instruments. They are usually concerned with relations between States (or less often international organizations) and individuals, and it is in this novel context that most of the present study on the local remedies rule is undertaken.

I

The majority of such instruments establish systems of *protection*, usually of certain recognized fundamental human rights. The question of the proper place of the local remedies in human rights protection presents a variety of problems to which there is no easy answer. As time passes the case-law on the local remedies rule of international organs entrusted with human rights protection grows considerably in volume as well as complexity, and still awaits a systematic treatment. Even if one tries to avoid aspects of the rule overworked in the past, examination of the rule in the new context of human rights protection cannot ignore parallel situations in general international law, because present-day instruments on human rights protection expressly refer to recognized principles of international law in their formulation of the local remedies rule in the new context. This is the point where most difficulties begin to appear.

To start with, the fundamental question to be asked, in so far as the enforcement of the international responsibility of the State is concerned, is this: is it adequate to approach the local remedies rule in distinct and newly emerging areas of international law (such as human rights protection) with the same outlook and conceptual apparatus with which the rule was approached in the framework of classical diplomatic protection?

Before trying to tackle this question, some preliminary points should be recalled. In the first half of the twentieth century, in some of the earlier international law experiments of granting a procedural status to individuals, the local redress principle received detailed treatment and found a multiplicity of particular solutions, quite distinct from its markedly preventive character *vis-à-vis* diplomatic protection as consistently reflected in State practice and general or customary international law. Would it not then be right to ask to what extent those multiple solutions were taken into account by the draftsmen of contemporary international instruments on human rights protection? By and large, earlier international experiments granting procedural status to individuals (such as, among others, the Rhine navigational system, the minorities and mandates systems under the League of Nations – the latter followed more recently by the United Nations trusteeship system) have, with one exception (the Central American Court of Justice), either not applied the local remedies rule at all, or else applied it with a marked and varying degree of flexibility, strongly suggesting that the rule is not necessarily inherent to every international experiment granting procedural status to individuals.[2]

Application of the local remedies rule in the context of human rights protection could perhaps derive some inspiration from those earlier experiments in which direct access to international organs was recognized and granted to the individuals themselves, rather than by reference to, or analogy with, State responsibility for injuries to aliens and discretionary diplomatic protection on an inter-State basis. It may be argued that international human rights protection more closely resembles instances in which States voluntarily agree, in the full exercise of their sovereignty, to open direct access to international jurisdiction to individuals themselves, whether their nationals or not, with a direct bearing on a *proper* application of the local remedies rule.[3]

What then were the reasons for the incorporation of the rule in contemporary international instruments on human rights protection, as in general international law? In the long preparatory work of the United Nations Covenants on Human Rights (1947–66), the local remedies rule was widely discussed in connection with, and as a condition for the acceptance of, the right of individual petition.[4] Under the Covenant on Civil and Political Rights as well as under the European Convention on Human Rights, the rule was adopted both as a matter of principle – to avoid domestic courts being superseded by the international organ – and for practical reasons – to avoid the international organ being 'flooded' with irrelevant complaints. There were, admittedly, limits to the application of the rule (as in, e.g., instances of undue delays).

The apparent paradox of the adoption of the rule in this new context is, accordingly, not without explanation. Unlike some of the earlier experiments (e.g., the minorities system under the League of Nations), where petitioners were generally regarded simply as a source of information, individual applicants in contemporary international instruments on human rights protection complain directly to an international organ (e.g., the European Commission of Human Rights) against a government which might well be their own. On the other hand, and perhaps for this very reason, they have to comply strictly with the local remedies rule. One may wonder whether the strengthening of the procedural status of individuals would have been at all possible without the parallel and greater restraint in the application of the rule when the instruments at issue were drafted:

3

such was indeed a paradoxical situation in which States took with one hand what they had given with the other.

Yet, it must also be pointed out that both the UN Covenants and the European Convention on Human Rights[5] envisaged the local remedies rule as directly related to the State's duty to provide effective local remedies, thus stressing that the applicant's duty to exhaust was complementary to the respondent's duty to provide local remedies.[6] The Covenant on Civil and Political Rights further provided for the 'possibilities of judicial remedy' where this latter had not yet materialized. Under the 1965 UN International Convention on the Elimination of All Forms of Racial Discrimination (concerned with discrimination affecting human collectivities), exception to the local remedies rule was expressly recognized in case of undue delays, and emphasis was shifted from the applicant's duty to exhaust, to the respondent's duty to provide, local remedies, seemingly going beyond the limits of strict individual redress, towards the ultimate goals of improving domestic judicial protection and aiming national policies at the eradication of racially discriminatory practices.

The local remedies rule in the above instruments was thus *not* conceived as a mechanically applied device, leading to systematic rejection of complaints. It may be asked to what extent this has been sufficiently recognized or understood in practice (cf. *infra*, pp. 57–212).

The distinct procedure on admissibility of human rights communications (addressed to the United Nations) devised by the UN Sub-Commission on Prevention of Discrimination and Protection of Minorities (1971) has likewise adopted with qualifications the local remedies rule: excepted from its application are cases where local remedies appear ineffective or are unreasonably prolonged.[7] The inclusion of the rule (thus qualified) may have seemed surprising in a procedure meant to apply to allegations of 'consistent patterns of gross violations of human rights'; however, if one recalls that in the UN debates on the matter much opposition to that form of supervision was raised on the ground of domestic jurisdiction,[8] it becomes apparent that again the insertion of the rule reflected a compromise, 'counter-balancing' the recognition of the right of individual petition or communication.[9]

In this investigation of the rationale of the local remedies rule in individualistic diplomatic protection and in human rights protection, attention will be focused on the relationship of the rule to the actual *enforcement* of the international responsibility of States, rather than its *birth*; thus leaving outside the present study the classical doctrinal discussion about the *nature* of the local remedies rule. Subsequent chapters will cover the conditions and extent of application of the rule, and major problems of procedure in that application,[10] with attention constantly directed to the extent to which the practice of international organs entrusted with the international protection of human rights has conformed with, or detracted from, the application of the local remedies rule in general international law.

1

THE RATIONALE OF THE RULE OF EXHAUSTION OF LOCAL REMEDIES IN DIPLOMATIC PROTECTION, AND IN HUMAN RIGHTS PROTECTION (UNDER THE EUROPEAN CONVENTION ON HUMAN RIGHTS) — THE LOCAL REMEDIES RULE IN RELATION TO THE ENFORCEMENT OF THE INTERNATIONAL RESPONSIBILITY OF STATES

I. Introduction

When the draftsmen of the European Convention on Human Rights decided to insert into Article 26 (on the exhaustion of local remedies) the qualification 'according to the generally recognized rules of international law',[1] they could hardly have imagined that the text adopted would create as many problems as it would solve. In the course of the *travaux préparatories* of Article 26, that insertion was made by a Committee of Experts only at a later stage,[2] and with the express intention of *limiting* the application of the local remedies rule to exhaustion of domestic remedies which were available and effective, and without undue delays by national courts;[3] and not with the intention of warranting a rigid interpretation and application of the rule (see *infra*, pp. 38–9).

But in so doing, the Committee of Experts established a link between the new system inaugurated by the Convention and general international law. The area of general international law within which the local remedies rule historically developed was the law of State responsibility for injuries to aliens. In that traditional context the rule used to be invoked by the 'respondent' State prior to the exercise of diplomatic protection by the State espousing the claim of its national abroad. In the system of the Convention, the rule operates as a preliminary condition of admissibility of claims, irrespective of the nationality of the claimants. Thus, however meritorious the purposes of the draftsmen of the Convention might have been, these purposes have at best not been properly understood; for this transplantation of the local redress rule from one context into a very different one has given rise to a serious problem of interpretation.

As will be seen, both the delegates of the Commission and counsel and agents for the governments concerned have, in their pleadings before the European Court, been at pains to press their own interpretation of the rule under the Convention, having in mind the reference in Article 26 to the 'generally recognised rules of international-al law'. A further complication is that there has been some inconsistency and confusion in the legal literature on the subject. Learned authors have examined the question by different or even conflicting approaches.

To be properly understood, the local remedies rule should be seen differently in the two distinct contexts of diplomatic protection and human rights protection. This is equally important for a proper interpretation of Article 26 of the Convention.[4] The starting-point of the present study is therefore an examination of the premises underlying each of the two systems of protection.

II. The rationale of the local remedies rule and basic premises of diplomatic protection

For the attribution of international responsibility to the State for the purpose of diplomatic protection, it is commonly understood that the following prerequisites ought to co-exist: an act or omission of an individual or an organ, imputable to the defendant State, in breach of an obligation under international law, and which has caused injury to the alien; and further, the injured alien must have exhausted all domestic remedies,[5] before the espousal of his claim by his State.

One of the earliest formulations of the principle was the celebrated Vattelian formula – 'Quiconque maltraite un citoyen offense indirecte-ment l'État, qui doit protéger ce citoyen.'[6] Vattel's 'orthodox' view dates from 1758, when he further stressed that 'the sovereign of the injured citizen must avenge the deed and, if possible, force the aggressor to give full satisfaction or punish him, since otherwise the citizen will not obtain the chief end of civil society, which is protection'.[7]

The classical view of the institution of diplomatic protection, seen in historical perspective,[8] derived from the then prevailing theory that only sovereign States were subjects of international law. It attracted the attention of many expert writers, shortly after Vattel,[9] but more particularly at the end of the nineteenth and beginning of the twentieth century,[10] who attempted to systematize the doctrine.

Thus the nineteenth-century writings of Halleck,[11] Phillimore,[12] Wheaton,[13] F. de Martens,[14] Brentano and Sorel,[15] and Heffter,[16] disclose important traces of Vattel's systematization of diplomatic protection when dealing with the issue of exhaustion of local remedies. On the other hand, as early as the end of the nineteenth century, doubts were raised by Pasquale Fiore[17] and Westlake[18] about the soundness of Vattel's formulation of the grounds for diplomatic protection. Nevertheless, the State's 'right and duty' to protect nationals abroad was subsequently asserted in strong terms by Fauchille,[19] Oppenheim[20] and Holland (in express reliance upon Vattel).[21]

It is significant that, in the practice of States throughout the eighteenth century, the local redress rule was clearly upheld in diplomatic practice, *before* as well as *after* the publication in 1758 of Vattel's *Le Droit des gens*.[22] There is, in fact, a great amount of evidence illustrative of the observance of the requirement of exhaustion of local remedies prior to the exercise of diplomatic protection in the nineteenth and twentieth centuries, on the part, e.g., of the British Foreign Office, the French Ministère des Affaires Étrangères, the Italian Ministero degli Esteri, the Swiss Division of Legal Affairs, the U.S. foreign policy, the Canadian Department of External Affairs, and the Ministérios de las Relaciones Exteriores of several Latin American countries.[23]

Vattel's systematization of the so-called 'right' of diplomatic protection also influenced national judicial practice, as shown by citations in pleadings and by domestic courts.[24] That influence extended to international judicial practice as well; Vattel's postulate was soon to infiltrate the jurisprudence of the International Court, as in the classical *dictum* of the Permanent Court of International Justice in the *Mavrommatis Palestine Concessions* (Jurisdiction) case (1924), that a State, by taking up the case of one of its subjects in the exercise of diplomatic protection on his behalf, is asserting its *own* right 'to ensure, in the person of its subjects, respect for the rules of international law'.[25]

Fifteen years later, the Court again stressed the 'right' of diplomatic protection, with nationality operating as the *vinculum juris*, in the *Panevezys–Saldutiskis Railway* case.[26] And, in 1928, in the *Chorzów Factory* case, the Court categorically indicated the *inter-State* basis of the system of diplomatic protection;[27] subsequently, the International Court of Justice pointed out that the rule of exhaustion of local remedies, as a principle of *customary* international law, operated a prior condition to the exercise of diplomatic protection.[28]

This, then, has been the context of application of the local remedies rule in international law: the rule applied in disputes which, though private in origin (involving an alien and a State), were subsequently 'internationalized' by the intervention of the alien's State espousing his claim for diplomatic protection, thus becoming international or inter-State disputes, sometimes brought before an international organ, the duty of exhausting local remedies remaining always upon the injured alien himself.

This characterization was properly developed in 1933 by Ténékidès, revealing traces of Vattelian thought.[29] In this system of protection by the home State, the local remedies rule operated as a rule of customary international law. The historical causes of the development of a body of law on the treatment of aliens have been reviewed by various authors;[30] within the confines of the present study, suffice it to say that the process of identification between the interests of the protecting State and those of its citizens abroad may have begun as an unconscious one, later to appear with sufficient regularity as a means of adjustment of conflicting interests (aliens and host States). Demands for redress which formerly were advanced on the basis of international comity and maintenance of friendly relations, gradually became, from the Jay Treaty of 1794 (inaugurating the modern era of international arbitration) onwards, the subject of a growing body of judicial precedents and jurisprudence on settlement of claims for indemnities for injuries to aliens.[31] It then became customary to advance such demands as 'claims of legal right', a practice further encouraged by the inclusion in treaties of provisions for the protection of nationals of each contracting party in the territory of the other.[32] Eventually this whole practice and the bulk of judicial precedents found their way into the legal treatises,[33] and 'by the middle of the nineteenth century, governments habitually treated questions of protection as legal questions and justified interposition by appeal to principles of international law and the writings of authorities. In other words, the adjustment of disputes of this character was gradually becoming institutionalized'.[34]

In 1932, Witenberg laid down the rationale of the local remedies rule in the context of diplomatic protection; as a condition of admissibility of international claims for damages to aliens, the rule found its explanation in the *subsidiary* nature of international procedures.[35] In his treatise, years earlier (1916), Borchard, as one of the most solid advocates of the 'international standard', maintained that it was up to each government to determine the justification, expediency and manner of taking up an appeal; in his classical definition of diplomatic protection, he termed it 'a complementary or reserved right invoked only when the State of residence fails to conform with this international standard',[36] but he did not hide his doubts and reservations about the foundations of the institution of diplomatic protection (e.g., the question whether it was a right as well as a duty).[37]

The subject was taken up by Charles de Visscher on two occasions before the Hague Academy of International Law: in his first Hague course (1923), he stressed that, despite the private origin of the claim for diplomatic protection, it remained a relation *between* States, with the local redress principle operating as a precondition for diplomatic intervention;[38] in his second Hague course (1935), going deeper into the problem, he observed that the local redress rule aimed at preventing diplomatic protection, operating as a precondition of admissibility of claims, thus affecting, on the procedural level, not so much the existence of responsibility itself, as the conditions for exercise of the claim.[39]

A similar approach was followed by Freeman, whose main contribution to the study of the problem was his characterization of the local remedies rule as 'a *procedural* condition precedent to diplomatic interposition'.[40] Thus, whatever view one might take of the *birth* of international responsibility,[41] its enforcement depended upon exhaustion of domestic remedies. That diplomatic protection was contingent upon local redress is clear from Eagleton's systematization of the subject: even though responsibility itself (a matter of substance) was 'not necessarily contingent upon local redress', the enforcement of that responsibility (a matter of procedure) depended upon prior exhaustion of local remedies, 'the most important rule in the application of the doctrine of State responsibility';[42] exhaustion of local remedies was a 'necessity of procedure'.[43]

Dunn justified the local redress rule on the ground of 'practical convenience';[44] but Ago ascribed a more substantial role to it, as constituting an essential condition for the configuration of a *fatto illecito internazionale perfetto*.[45]

Arbitral awards have at times expressly acknowledged that nationality constitutes the theoretical *vinculum juris* entitling the protecting State, in international law, to intervene on behalf of citizens abroad.[46] This 'orthodox' view led to Scelle's classical criticism that diplomatic protection had been conceived as a right belonging to the State to protect nationals abroad, in the exercise of a *compétence discrétionnaire* rather than a *compétence liée*; it was a protective system very limited in scope (to the benefit of certain individuals only), when what was needed was a generalization of protection to all individuals irrespective of the bond of nationality.[47]

Criticisms of this kind were also advanced by Séfériadès,[48] Brierly (four years after the *Mavrommatis* decision, *supra*, p. 8),[49] Ch. de Visscher,[50] Clive Parry (shortly after the ICJ's reassertion in the *Nottebohm* case in 1955 of the principle earlier held by the PCIJ in the *Mavrommatis* case),[51] amongst others.[52] They provided earlier indications that there were to be some fundamental differences between the traditional system of diplomatic protection and the emerging system of human rights protection (expanding after the Second World War), entailing implications for the rationale and proper application of the local remedies rule in the context of each of them (see discussion *infra*, pp. 18–56).

Diplomatic protection concerns predominantly the interests of a limited group of individuals, namely nationals abroad. The local remedies rule operates in that procedure as a condition for the exercise of the protection: its *preventive* character *vis-à-vis* the exercise of protection is manifest. The rule is in a way a 'prophylactic' device, in that, by insisting on prior settlement at local level, it reduces tension likely to arise in an inter-State dispute over injuries to nationals abroad.

But it should be born in mind that the local remedies rule is historically older than the institution of diplomatic protection: its antecedents go as far back as the medieval practice of private reprisals, which precedes by some centuries the institution of diplomatic protection as known today.[53] In the exercise of this latter, the local remedies rule serves primarily the interests of the territorial State, its basic rationale consisting in the opportunity afforded the State to remedy the wrong complained of within the framework of its domestic legal system.

But, in so doing, the local remedies rule also serves the interests of the injured alien to have prompt local redress of the wrong suffered. Indirectly this benefits the alien's State as well, and serves the general interest of the parties concerned and of international society, in having the dispute settled peacefully through the ordinary legal channels at domestic level. Accordingly, there seems to be a balance of interests[54] underlying the rule as it is applied in the framework of diplomatic protection, making it largely beneficial to all concerned.

However diminished might be the significance of diplomatic protection today,[55] it remains relevant for the alien, as it strengthens his legal position[56] in his activities abroad. On the other hand, the importance of this factor should not be pushed too far; to call for more extended diplomatic protection, when it is so difficult to provide individuals with an international right themselves to sue a foreign State,[57] would seem to beg the question.[58]

The question whether the protecting State vindicates its own right, or that of its national injured abroad, or both, touches the foundations of international law and the question of its subjects. One view (H. Lauterpacht) is that the intervening State is in substance enforcing the individual's right rather than its own exclusive right, in view of the individual's incapacity to assert it himself in the international sphere.[59] Another position (Borchard) is that the State has an interest of its own to protect its citizen abroad,[60] as a manifestation of the fact that on the plane of international law relations take place between States which exert power and control over their citizens (Anzilotti, Salvioli).[61] These two opposing views reflect the monist and dualist approaches to the relationship between municipal law and international law.[62] In practice this question is largely immaterial, since the State espouses the claim of its national within the limits in which that claim exists, i.e., on behalf of the injured individual (Guggenheim, Makarov).[63]

In municipal legal systems, where individuals are recognized as having subjective rights with remedies, the problem does not arise; and the right to reparation for injuries vests in the injured individual himself, or in his successor in interest as from the moment of the injury. This is thus essentially an international law problem, for it is at the international law level that doubts have arisen. Here the old rule of exhaustion of local remedies may help to clarify the issue.

If the right to reparation vests exclusively in the protecting State which, by taking up the case of its national, is 'in reality asserting its own rights',[64] how then is one to explain the operation of the rule of exhaustion of local remedies? Could it not be maintained that the State's rights 'could hardly be contingent upon exhaustion of local remedies by the individual'?[65] Is not the rule inconsistent with the orthodox view of diplomatic protection? The hypothesis of direct injury is promptly dismissed in the context of diplomatic protection of nationals abroad. It is the injured individual and not the intervening State who is made to exhaust local remedies in the host State as a condition prior to protection. Therefore, even if diplomatic protection is conceived as primarily an inter-State relationship, the local remedies rule demonstrates that the individual has a decisive role to play.[66]

Borchard himself admitted that the action of the protecting State 'is in large degree dependent upon the subsequent conduct of the citizen in supporting the title and right of his government to interpose on his behalf'.[67] Whatever explanation may be given to the right to reparation (whether it vests in the State, or in the individual concerned, or in both),[68] the fact remains that by the local remedies rule the territorial State is given an opportunity to redress the alleged wrong within the framework of its own domestic legal system before its international responsibility can be enforced at international level. It is the injured individual who pursues his claim before the domestic courts of the offending State, and intervention by his home State is made dependent on his unsuccessful exhaustion of local remedies. Leaving aside the *vexata questio* of the doctrine of 'injury to the State *via* its national', it would seem more accurate to find in the exercise of diplomatic protection after unsuccessful exhaustion of local remedies a procedural necessity,[69] largely explained or dictated by the decentralized structure of the international legal order itself,[70] rather than to rely on doubtful explanations found in the notion of injury to the State *via* its national.

Present trends towards a wider protection of individuals in international law (see *infra*, pp. 20–2) may gradually overcome some of the limitations *ratione personae* of traditional diplomatic protection, for example, by minimizing 'disabilities of stateless persons'.[71] Whether the rule of exhaustion of local remedies has, or should have, its place in treaties and conventions on generalized human rights protection is discussed in detail below.[72] But the primary question is not whether the local remedies rule should be transplanted from the system of diplomatic protection into that of human rights protection, but whether it should be transplanted so as to apply in the latter in the same way or to the same extent as it has applied in the former. To answer this question there must first be considered the rationale of the local remedies rule in an existing system of human rights protection.

III. The rationale of the local remedies rule and basic premises of human rights protection (under the European Convention on Human Rights)

The rule of exhaustion of local remedies under the European Convention on Human Rights[73] may be considered by comparison with corresponding treaty, and other, provisions both at global[74] and at regional[75] levels. The same applies to the State's counterpart duty to provide local remedies.[76] The present chapter deals with the system found in the European Convention on Human Rights, as the one which has produced the most concrete results to date.

Both the European Commission and the Court have pronounced on the proper interpretation of the system of protection of the European Convention as a whole. In the *Austria* v. *Italy* case (1961) the Commission approved an objective method of interpretation; the obligations undertaken by the High Contracting Parties in the Convention, the Commission stated, were 'essentially of an objective character', designed to protect the fundamental rights of individual human beings from infringement by any of the High Contracting Parties, rather than to create subjective and reciprocal rights for the High Contracting Parties themselves.[77]

Subsequently, in its judgment of 27 June 1968 in the *Wemhoff* case, it was the Court's turn to point out that the Convention was 'a law-making treaty' and that it was thus 'necessary to seek the interpretation that is most appropriate in order to realise the aim and achieve the object of the treaty, not that which would restrict to the greatest possible degree the obligations undertaken by the Parties'.[78] In the same year, in the *Belgian Linguistics* case (judgment of 23 July 1968), the Court recalled that effective human rights protection was the general aim set for themselves by the Contracting Parties through the medium of the Convention which, therefore, implied 'a just balance between the protection of the general interest of the community and the respect due to fundamental human rights while attaching particular importance to the latter'.[79]

More recently, both the Commission and the Court saw fit again to pronounce upon the question of interpretation of the basic premises of the Convention in the *S.E. Golder* v. *United Kingdom* case (1971 – 5). In its report on the case (adopted on 1 June 1973) the Commission dwelt upon the question of interpretation (with particular reference to the right of access to courts under Article 6 (1) of the Convention).[80] It reasserted the view that 'the object of the international application of the Convention is to interpret its provisions objectively, and not to interpret the Convention by references to what may have been the understanding of one Party at the time of its ratification. [...] The provisions of the Convention should not be interpreted restrictively so as to prevent its aims and objects being achieved.'[81] The Commission added: 'The decisive consideration here must be that the overriding function of this Convention is to protect the rights of the individual and not to lay down as between States mutual obligations which are to be restrictively interpreted having regard to the sovereignty of these States. On the contrary, the role of the Convention and the function of its interpretation is to make the protection of the individual effective. It is true that it represents only the "first steps" for the enforcement of human rights as the preamble says. But this fact cannot be relied upon to justify restrictive interpretations running contrary to its overall purpose.'[82] In its judgment of 21 February 1975 on the *Golder* case the Court endorsed the Commission's interpretation of the Convention in the light of its ultimate object and purpose and as a step towards the collective enforcement of human rights.[83]

Likewise, at a recent Rome colloquy marking the twenty-fifth anniversary of the European Convention, certain of the terms of the Convention were said to be 'evolutionary' concepts,[84] – a view which seems to be gaining increasing support in recent writing.[85]

As for the local remedies rule within the system of human rights protection under the Convention,[86] it is to be borne in mind that, while Article 26 of the Convention admittedly refers to general international law, Article 1 of the Convention departs from it in providing that 'the High Contracting Parties shall secure to *everyone* within their jurisdiction the rights and freedoms defined in Section 1 of this Convention'.[87] Unlike diplomatic protection or other forms of international protection of individuals, nationality does not operate here as a *vinculum juris* or prerequisite for the exercise of protection. The individual is under the Convention protected *qua* individual, not as a national of any State but as a human being.

Furthermore, the task of ensuring observance of the engagements undertaken by States Parties to the Convention was entrusted to an international body (the Commission and the Court – Article 19);[88] unlike diplomatic protection, where international law left the task of protection to the intervening State. Under the Convention, a State was not acting to defend its national interest or that of its nationals abroad; for any High Contracting Party might refer to the Commission any alleged breach of the Convention provisions by another High Contracting Party (Article 24). The basic premise was the collective guarantee entrusted to all States Parties to the Convention.

All this was stated in unequivocal terms by the Commission in its decision of 11 January 1961 in the *Austria* v. *Italy* case. In becoming a Party to the Convention, the Commission recalled, 'a State undertakes, *vis-à-vis* the other High Contracting Parties, to secure the rights and freedoms defined in Section I to every person within its jurisdiction, regardless of his or her nationality or status', and this applied not only to the State's 'own nationals and those of other High Contracting Parties but also to nationals of States not parties to the Convention and to stateless persons, as the Commission itself has expressly recognized in previous decisions'.[89]

The objective character of the obligations undertaken by the High Contracting Parties is reflected in the machinery of collective guarantee of the rights recognized in the Convention by States Parties, and in the supervision of their observance by the Convention organs pursuant to Article 19. By Article 24:

the High Contracting Parties have empowered any one of their number to bring before the Commission any alleged breach of the Convention, regardless of whether the victims of the alleged breach are nationals of the applicant State or whether the alleged breach otherwise particularly affects the interests of the applicant State. [...] It follows that a High Contracting Party, when it refers an alleged breach of the Convention to the Commission under Article 24, is not to be regarded as exercising a right of action for the purpose of enforcing its own rights, but rather as bringing before the Commission an alleged violation of the public order of Europe.[90]

Besides inter-State complaints, petitions may also come from 'any person, non-governmental organization or group of individuals claiming to be the victim of a violation by one of the High Contracting Parties of the rights set forth in this Convention, provided that the High Contracting Party against which the complaint had been lodged had recognized the competence of the Commission to receive such petitions' (Article 25).[91] Unlike diplomatic protection, the 'connecting link' here demanded by the Convention is not that of nationality, but one between the claimant (irrespective of nationality) and the injury caused to him; namely, his being a *victim*[92] of the violation complained of. Herein lies the basic distinction between individual petitions and those brought by States under Article 24. They are based upon different premises. The latter type is founded upon a right of action for the application of the collective guarantee; the former, the individual application, even though it might be presented collectively before the Commission, is not designed to serve the purpose of the collective guarantee, for here 'c'est bien la lésion qui fournit le fondement à la requête et non pas le mobile désintéressé de l'observation de la Convention *erga omnes*'.[93] This in no way detracts from the fact that, in the general framework of the Convention, the right of individual petition, possessing a judicial character,[94] rests upon the objective character of the engagements undertaken by the High Contracting Parties to the Conventions,[95] as its exercise contributes also to the fulfilment of the general interest in having the Convention respected.[96]

This can be more clearly seen because, in proceedings before the Court (to which individuals do not have access), the Commission enjoys a unique position. One of the Court's present judges describes it in this way:

It [the Commission] is not a party to the proceedings in the usual sense of the word, but it represents the public interest of the entire community of States adhering to the Convention. This community interest is best served by the protection of the individual who has suffered from a violation of the Convention. The Commission exercises procedural rights for the injured party since the injured party himself may not appear before the Court. However, the Commission does not represent the individual, but rather it represents the common interest of all member States in respecting the standards of the Conventions.[97]

It has been asserted that the *raison d'être* of the right of individual petition under the Convention is the insufficiency of the procedure of diplomatic protection.[98] But the determining factor for the standing of individuals in an international procedure is the recognition of their right to seize the international organ.[99] With regard to the European Convention, one may take the point further. It is the whole machinery under the Convention – not only the recognition of the right of individual petition but also such features as the relationship between the Commission and the Court – that remedies the insufficiencies of the traditional procedure of diplomatic protection. Judge Mosler has pointed out that 'the authority of the Commission to bring a case before the Court places the individual in a better position than if he had to rely on diplomatic protection from his own State, since the Commission need not regard political considerations which quite often influence the exercise of diplomatic protection'.[100]

The right of individual petition (Article 25, subject to optional ratification) whereby an individual becomes entitled to bring a complaint before an international organ even against his own State, may be regarded, together with the notion of collective guarantee (more salient in inter-State cases under Article 24), as constituting possibly two of the most remarkable features of the new system of protection inaugurated by the Convention.[101] The local remedies rule has been included in this new system as a condition of admissibility of human rights complaints (Articles 26 and 27 (3)). It may be asked whether the rule should here be applied in the same way as it has been in classical diplomatic protection (*supra*, pp. 7–13). This calls for a comparative study of the foundations of the two forms of protection for the purposes of application of the rule (*infra*, pp. 18–46).

IV. Diplomatic protection and human rights protection compared (for purposes of interpretation and application of the local remedies rule)

Turning now to the relationship between the systems of diplomatic protection and human rights protection, in the matter of the local remedies rule, it is possible to discern the following different approaches:

1. Historical *continuum* between the two systems;
2. Human rights protection absorbed and developed by diplomatic protection;
3. Diplomatic protection absorbed and developed by human rights protection;
4. Protection of aliens ('non-citizens') as a particularization of human rights protection;
5. Incompatibility or absence of parallelism between the two systems.

It will be convenient now to examine each of these five approaches in turn.

1. First approach: historical continuity between the two systems

A large body of opinion has found in the two systems a process of historical continuity. Some of the earlier antecedents of this process were detected in 1939 by M.G. Cohn,[102] who, in regard to a State's responsibility *vis-à-vis* its own nationals, observed that the State could not relieve itself of its international responsibility simply on the ground that the injured individuals were its own subjects.[103] Not only territorial sovereignty, but also personal sovereignty, had certain conditions and limitations. The examples afforded by the treaty of Berlin (imposing upon the Balkan countries the duty to accord certain fundamental rights 'to their own subjects' whose breach would engage their responsibility) and the minorities treaties under the League of Nations (whereby certain States contracted an international obligation to accord 'to a category of their own subjects' certain rights) demonstrated 'non seulement qu'un État peut encourir une responsabilité internationale purement formelle pour le traitement de ses propres sujets, mais aussi que, matériellement, les autres États ont un intérêt juridique à la manière dont les États se conduisent à l'égard de leurs propres sujets, ce qui peut avoir à bien des égards une grande importance aussi pour les autres États'.[104] From this it was argued that 'human rights are directly founded upon the law of nations' (*droit des gens*).[105]

In fact, the transformation of the classical *jus gentium* into the modern *jus inter gentes*, as was pointed out by Parry, continues to challenge the historical treatment of international law,[106] which has not so far produced a satisfactory explanation of the fragmentation of *jus gentium* into multiple national units. Concern with the human being as a component of groups of various political structures and geographical extensions was clearly present in the early manuscripts of the founding fathers of international law, again demonstrating that the territorial State is not and has not always been an essential factor in the evolution of international law.[107]

But it was only fairly recently that modern international law began promoting a *generalization* of the protection of the human person, which was formerly limited to certain categories of individuals (e.g., nationals abroad, members of minorities, inhabitants of territories under mandate, workers under the ILO system).[108] It was not until after the Second World War that human rights protection in international law extended to the individual *qua* individual, covering also those categories of persons (like stateless persons) who were left without protection under traditional international law. This historical process of generalized human rights protection is still largely based upon treaty obligations contracted by States, but there begin to appear indications that certain fundamental human rights may today form part of general international law. That there is a certain 'continuity' between the systems of diplomatic protection and of human rights protection is a historical fact. Doubts only begin to arise when it is suggested that human rights protection be interpreted in the light of diplomatic protection, for here difficulties arise particularly with regard to the rule of exhaustion of local remedies.

In his treatment of historical trends culminating in the establishment of the system of the European Convention on Human Rights, Hermann Mosler argues that, besides the traditional diplomatic protection of nationals abroad and the minorities system under the League, the international or minimum standard theory for alien treatment in classical international law had a further implication: the real motive for the protection of foreigners was in his submission 'to protect them as individuals',[109] even though only their States could advance a complaint in case of violation of their rights. Immediately after the Second World War, none of the general obligations for human rights protection ensuing from the peace treaties of 1947 and 1955 were mutual. They bound only one party and most of them protected only certain groups.[110] Only with the machinery of the European Convention on Human Rights was a 'uniform standard' of human rights, with fully mutual obligations, introduced. Then, for the first time 'the parties to a major Convention have obligated themselves to guarantee rights, which until now have been guaranteed by the respective State constitutions, to all persons without regard to citizenship, whether such persons be foreigners or stateless'.[111]

It might be inferred from the above that the Convention's human rights system is a new protective system, based upon new premises, even though its historical roots may be traced back to classical mechanisms under traditional international law for the protection of aliens. It might, therefore, be expected that this should have implications for a new approach to the local remedies rule in this new system of protection.

The idea that human rights protection rests upon the foundations of the rules protecting aliens has been stated by A.Ch. Kiss: not only did the individual in classical international law make an appearance, through his State, but also the list of aliens' rights corresponded *grosso modo* to the rights contained in the first part of the 1948 Universal Declaration of Human Rights[112] (a contention which has not passed unchallenged).[113] These factors might, therefore, be said to reflect an historical evolution towards an 'élargissement du contenu de la condition des étrangers', replacing the rules protecting aliens with (new) rules protecting the individuals as such, thus entailing a certain transformation of the rights themselves guaranteed to aliens by international law.[114] As for procedural mechanisms of guarantee, once human rights rules enshrined in international treaties begin to operate regularly, as a substitute for those devised for the specific protection of aliens, signatory States would be entitled to intervene on behalf of a victim of a violation of human rights even if he were not their own national. This constituted a turning point in the historical evolution from the system of diplomatic protection to that of human rights protection, as 'la protection diplomatique s'effacerait donc dans cette hypothèse devant un droit d'intervention généralisée de tous les contractants'.[115]

In his thorough treatment of this evolution Eustathiades contended that contemporary international law recognized a certain emancipation of the individual *vis-à-vis* his own State as well as a multiplication of procedures of *mise en jeu* of the international responsibility of States.[116] He observed that the individual's quality as a subject of international law, deriving from his capacity to commit an internationally wrongful act, did not imply that there was a necessary coincidence between those matters for which the international responsibility of the individual was engaged and those for which he could claim directly before an international organ. Rather than distinguish between the international wrongful act (a theory developed mainly by Ago) on the part of the State and on the part of the individual, Eustathiades preferred to consider *one* international wrongful act with collective and individual effects;[117] as for the individual concerned, he distinguished his quality as *passive* and *active* subject of international responsibility.[119]

Taking a position with some support in international practice[119] and shared by Sir Hersch Lauterpacht,[120] Eustathiades pointed out that there was 'no general prohibitive rule of a direct action of the individual upon the international plane'.[121] Wherever individual access was recognized by a treaty provision, this prevented an objection founded upon the principle of immunity of State jurisdiction; and even where such treaty provision did not exist one would not be entitled thereby to conclude that the absence reflected a general prohibitive rule.[122] There was thus no logical impossibility of a rule of international law being directly addressed to individuals, as conversely there was no logical necessity that the individual's internationally recognized rights should be guaranteed by means of a direct recourse to an international organ.[123] In this area the local remedies rule had an important role to play.

It is necessary, therefore, to distinguish between a *collective action* to enforce a State's international responsibility resulting from a breach of a treaty provision (as under Article 24 of the European Convention on Human Rights), and the traditional action of diplomatic protection of nationals abroad: the former was *not* a kind of extension of the latter.[124]

The historical evolution of the whole matter could thus be summarized: from the ancient system of private reprisals one has moved into the system of endorsement by the State (diplomatic protection),[125] and from that one has more recently evolved towards individual action (direct access or right of individual petition).[126] While formerly a State's international responsibility was enforced in relation to aliens only, being the exclusive business of the protecting State, more recently protection has been extended by treaty to individuals as such, regardless of nationality, and enforceable by all High Contracting Parties.[127]

This evolution and expansion of the scope of protection was especially important, Eustathiades observed, in view of a serious shortcoming in the system of diplomatic protection of nationals abroad:

Il existe une catégorie d'individus bien plus nombreux exposés à des violations de droits qui leur sont aujourd'hui internationalement reconnus, à savoir les nationaux qui ont subi de la part des autorités de leur propre État un tort en violation des 'droits de l'homme'. Pour eux, fait défaut même la garantie éventuelle qu'offrirait la mise en jeu de la protection diplomatique des nationaux à l'étranger.[128]

In this regard, the new system of human rights protection brought about the gradual emancipation of the individual *vis-à-vis* his own State[129] (a formulation endorsed by O'Connell and Freeman).[130]

The rule of exhaustion of local remedies, in Eustathiades's view, expressed in 1953, would be applicable in the new system of human rights protection,[131] but with some qualifications: once international organs, to which individuals were granted access, were created and enlarged by the development of international relations, they would no longer be strictly dependent upon States.[132]

In Virally's analysis, the traditional conception of international law as regulating inter-State relations rested upon a basic distinction between two spheres: that of infra-State relations under municipal law and that of inter-State relations under international law.[133] The change introduced by contemporary international protection of human rights was that it *denied* the existence of those two spheres, in directing itself towards the interests of the human person irrespective of his *statut politique*.[134]

Other writers on the subject have tended likewise to treat diplomatic protection as an historical antecedent of the new system of human rights protection,[135] leaving the impression that the heyday of diplomatic protection was past, as the historical process culminated in the emerging system of human rights protection. The difficulty with this approach is that, by stressing the historical continuity between the two systems of diplomatic protection and human rights protection, it could lead to the mistaken assumption that the latter is nowadays necessarily 'replacing' the former.

Politis observed as early as 1926 that the evolution from a lower to a higher social group[136] was accomplished 'by a series of successive stages and superimposed reforms', and the same may be said to be occurring in the 'present imperceptible passage' from inter-State relations (through the intermediary of the States) into truly international relations.[137]

It would be going too far to contend that diplomatic protection, evolved in customary international law, has been subsumed under or superseded by human rights protection, still at present largely embodied in treaty obligations. There is at present nothing to impede the co-existence of the two systems in international law, and this is what supporters of the historical approach fail to take into account. Whether such a co-existence is desirable or not, is a different matter, for there are possibilities of confusion. It is not hard to conceive, for example, of the possibility of claims for diplomatic protection from companies operating on the high seas, on the basis of principles belonging to human rights protection, which arguably were not meant to cover such claims.[138] Similarly and conversely, it is not difficult to conceive of the possibility of States relying on principles evolved under the law on State responsibility for injuries to aliens and diplomatic protection in order to evade obligations contracted under a human rights treaty.[139]

This danger seems to have been overlooked by the supporters of the approach under discussion.[140] Yet it cannot be denied that its emphasis on the historical continuity between diplomatic protection and human rights protection serves to draw attention to the particularities of the distinct contexts in which the rule of exhaustion of local remedies is made to apply.

In his perspicacious study of 1953, Eustathiades was aware that despite new developments of individual responsibility under the new human rights system, the traditional domain of State responsibility was likely to be conserved for the 'practical necessities' served, and it could not at that time be predicted that in the long run the new developments would necessarily lead to an elimination or a considerable restriction of the older domain of State responsibility. But in calling for two sets of rules (in matters of international responsibility), one applicable to the individual *qua* alien and the other to the individual *qua* individual,[141] Eustathiades did not expand much on the problem, and did not sufficiently show how that task could be accomplished. Yet his pioneering ideas call for further development, which could assist a more suitable application of the rule of exhaustion of local remedies in the new system of human rights protection; particularly since, counterbalancing the recognition to individuals of direct access to international organs,[142] the rule makes international settlement of alleged violations of human rights subsidiary[143] to the exhaustion of means of redress at local level.

2. Second approach: human rights protection absorbed and developed by diplomatic protection

In the debates on 'Diplomatic Protection of Nationals Abroad' in its sessions of 1931 and 1932, the *Institut de Droit International* (Nineteenth Commission) discussed a fundamental controversy[144] which was fatal to its work on the subject. Dumas advanced the proposition that the injured alien should have the right to claim directly before an international organ, since the notion that the basis of diplomatic protection was an injury suffered by the State in the person of its national was not sound.[145] Borchard commented that arguments of that kind would lead to the conclusion that the individual as such should have the right to claim against the State which caused him injury before an international organ without the intervention of any claimant State: he added that although he approved this proposition, it should not be examined under the heading of 'diplomatic protection of nationals abroad'. The proposition, he suggested, should be examined by a special commission of the *Institut* entrusted with the task of studying the topic, 'The access of individuals to international organs': otherwise, added Borchard, the discussion would be inopportune and would bring a new element of confusion into the basic theory on the matter.[146] In that he was followed by Charles de Visscher, who also thought that the proposition should be more appropriately examined by the other commission, whose *rapporteur* was Séfériadès.[147]

Politis strongly advocated the international personality of the individual, which, in his view, even if in some cases 'latent', had already made 'its apparition'. And he added that 'le droit isolé de l'État n'aurait pu, dans aucune de ces affaires, aboutir à une instance internationale'.[148] In that he was supported by De La Pradelle,[149] who called for the exercise of diplomatic protection 'dans un esprit juridique', devoid of political considerations.[150] De La Pradelle's subsequent interventions were to the effect of minimizing – if not nullifying – the exercise of diplomatic protection as a *right* of the State, shifting emphasis to the interest of the injured individual concerned.[151] Thus while Borchard preferred to proceed to a detailed exposition of the existing law concerning diplomatic protection, De La Pradelle and Politis chose to introduce into the discussion some new elements stressing the primary interests of the injured individual in the procedure of diplomatic protection.[152]

This basic disagreement, which remained throughout the 1931–2 discussions of the Nineteenth Commission of the *Institut*, may be shortly described as follows: Borchard, although having analytically considered the kinds of legal relations connected with the institution of diplomatic protection elsewhere,[153] defended the thesis that 'the damage caused to an individual is caused to all the collectivity' and that 'the national interest absorbs the individual interest'.[154] On the other hand, Politis and De La Pradelle espoused the opposite view, namely, that it is the individual interest that 'doit rester au premier plan'.[155] This fundamental disagreement on a matter of principle, which persisted throughout all the work of the *Institut*'s commission, was a most relevant determining factor for the outcome of the discussions: unlike on other occasions,[156] this time the *Institut* adopted no resolutions on the matter and promptly adjourned,[157] and no specific results were achieved.

Without going into the merits of that basic disagreement, there seems to be one lesson which can be drawn from those debates for the purposes of the present study. When De La Pradelle and Politis stressed the interests of the individual within the procedure of diplomatic protection, and particularly when they referred in this connection to a certain international personality of the individual which, according to them, could at that time already be perceived, they were in fact going beyond the confines of the traditional system of diplomatic protection. Dumas, as can be seen above, went as far as stating that an injured individual should have the right to claim directly to an international organ, but in so doing he was going against one of the basic premises of diplomatic protection, namely that the protection is to be undertaken by a *State*. When those jurists favoured the view that an individual's claim against the offending State should (in extreme cases, presumably) be brought directly before an international organ without the intervention of a protecting State, they were introducing a new element into the framework of diplomatic protection, however desirable or attractive the idea might theoretically have been. That element was in fact to be incorporated years later into a distinct system, namely that of human rights protection.

In this sense, Borchard was correct in stating that the idea of direct recourse to an international organ for protection of an individual's right could not be examined within the framework of the existing law of State responsibility for injuries to aliens. Although Borchard did not *expressly* state the view, he certainly implied that the basic premises of diplomatic protection were clearly distinct from those of a system designed to protect the individual *qua* individual, for such protection of an individual regardless of nationality and directly by an international organ required a separate study, focusing on the *access* of individuals to such organs and the individuals' procedural status[158] within the framework of the new system to be set up. Thus, the clearest lesson one may probably draw from the 1931–2 debates of the *Institut* seems to be that attempts to merge the elements of the human rights protection system into the system of diplomatic protection (in order to 'enrich' or 'improve' this latter)[159] are very likely to be doomed to failure.

3. Third approach: diplomatic protection absorbed and developed by human rights protection

In his First Report on International Responsibility to the UN International Law Commission (1956), *rapporteur* García Amador tackled the difficulty of the confrontation between traditional diplomatic protection and the newly emerging system of human rights protection, by initially observing that, with regard to the former, the classical antinomy remained the one between the two principles invoked, namely the 'international standard of justice' on the one hand, and the 'equality of nationals and aliens' on the other.

Although both principles pursued the same purpose (protection of the individual), they appeared in traditional theory irreconcilable.[160] However, in the light of modern developments in international law towards recognition and protection of basic human rights, García Amador argued, the distinction between nationals and aliens for purposes of protection no longer had any *raison d'être*, so that both in theory and in practice the two traditional standards of alien treatment were 'henceforth inapplicable', having apparently been 'outgrown by contemporary international law'.[161] Having hitherto been considered as 'antagonistic and irreconcilable', the two standards could well be 'reformulated and integrated into a new legal rule incorporating the essential elements and serving the main purposes of both'.[162]

The basis of this new principle lay in the 'internationalization' of human rights, to be protected irrespective of nationality; as it became immaterial whether the individual was a citizen or an alien, the two traditional standards were rendered obsolete. The two principles ('international standard of justice' and 'equality between nationals and aliens') had in the past been based upon 'the distinction between two categories of rights and two types of protection; that distinction was recognized by the first principle but denied by the second'; anyway, the distinction itself disappeared in the new system of human rights protection.[163] The new legal system of international human rights protection, García Amador submitted, far from ignoring the essential elements and basic purposes of the two traditional principles, constituted 'precisely a *synthesis* of the two principles'.[164]

This thesis was further developed by García Amador in his Second,[165] Third[166] and Fourth[167] Reports on State Responsibility for Injuries to Aliens. His revised draft on the subject (contained in the *Addendum* to his Sixth and last Report to the International Law Commission) embodied certain provisions to the effect of accomplishing the *synthesis* he so strongly advocated.[168]

In his Hague course (1958) García Amador again explained in the same line of reasoning his approach to the 'confrontation' between diplomatic protection and human rights protection,[169] and went on to consider the problem of exhaustion of local remedies in relation to the former system of protection. Although the issue was connected with that of 'imputability',[170] García Amador avoided embarking on this particular point, preferring to emphasize that:

responsibility may or may not exist, as the case may be, but unless and until the said condition [of exhaustion of local remedies] is fulfilled, the claiming State has only a sort of 'potential' right.[171] Responsibility as such may be imputable, but the duty to make reparation for the injury caused to the alien is not exigible by means of an international claim so long as the local remedies have not been exhausted. Thus, except in those cases where the injury is the result of an act or omission which implies the exhaustion of local remedies, [...] the principle will always constitute a complete bar to the exercise of diplomatic protection.[172]

García Amador's treatment of the matter clarifies a fundamental difference in the basic premises underlying the two systems of diplomatic protection and of human rights protection. In a pertinent passage he elucidates:

It should be borne in mind that the entire traditional doctrine of diplomatic protection rests on the premise that no international action whatsoever could be taken by the individual and that, after the exhaustion of local remedies, the individual was completely without recourse if the State from which he has claimed reparation denied him justice. In those circumstances the protection of the individual by the State of nationality was, for better or for worse, the only possible solution. But at present, now that States themselves have agreed voluntarily to the appearance of their nationals as direct claimants before international bodies, surely there can be no objection to a provision authorizing such persons to agree with the respondent State, as regards matters and objects of interest to these nationals exclusively, that disputes should be submitted to an international body for settlement.[173]

When the International Law Commission took up again the subject of the international responsibility of States for codification (1969) García Amador's systematization of the matter was questioned on its very principles. As observed by the new *rapporteur*, Roberto Ago, in his First Report, in considering García Amador's First Report (cf. *supra*, p. 26) in its 370th to 373rd meetings:

the great majority of the Commission took exception to the idea that an individual could be regarded as the possessor of international subjective rights, could plead international responsibility for the violation of those rights or bring claims on his own behalf in international courts. Reservations were also expressed regarding the possibility of taking the violation of a fundamental human right as a criterion in establishing international responsibility for injuries to aliens.[174]

Thus, the [new] members of the Commission, while 'fully appreciating the lofty sentiments'[175] which had inspired the former *rapporteur*, were unable to agree with him on that substantive issue. However, in so doing, it seems that they opened themselves to criticism just as much as García Amador had done. The basic disagreement here was on matters of principle, and these ultimately depended upon one's conception of international law and its subjects, corroborated by State practice, case-law and juristic interpretation.

More cogent seem to have been, in this respect, the criticisms relating to procedural law raised by Eustathiades in the debates at the International Law Commission (1013th meeting). Referring to García Amador's views[176] (*supra*, pp. 26–8), Eustathiades remarked that:

there had been a tendency to link the question of the treatment of aliens with that of the protection of human rights. [...García Amador's] work reflected the trend towards equal treatment of aliens and nationals. If the protection of aliens was henceforth to be merged with the protection of human rights, the Commission would have to provide for the necessary means of practical application, since it would no longer be a question of diplomatic protection, but of *collective guarantees* [my italics] either under the Charter or under some regional instrument. The disputes arising would then no longer be duels between two States, for no State would be able to infringe the rights of aliens, that was to say human rights, without being called to account by the community of States under the provisions for their joint international protection. In other words there would be a *collective guarantee* [my italics], under which the guilty State would be the same as under the system of diplomatic protection of aliens, but the injury would no longer concern only the State of the injured person's nationality; a community of States would be concerned and would be able to give effect to responsibility. Collective guarantees within the framework of State responsibility would therefore have to be included among the general rules and, especially, among the means of application.[177]

Thus, García Amador's systematization of the matter, however clarifying it might have been in its re-stressing of the requirement of previous exhaustion of local remedies as a *conditio sine qua non* for the exercise of diplomatic protection, in attempting to formulate a *synthesis* of the two classical opposite standards of the law on State responsibility and diplomatic protection (the international and national standards of alien treatment) it apparently tried to reconcile the irreconcilable.

4. Fourth approach: protection of aliens ('non-citizens') as a particularization of human rights protection

A new approach to the matter has lately been adopted at the United Nations. In 1973, at its 54th session, the UN Economic and Social

Council (ECOSOC) decided to request the UN Sub-Commission on Prevention of Discrimination and Protection of Minorities to consider, as a matter of priority, the problem of the applicability of existing international provisions for the protection of human rights to individuals who are not citizens of the country in which they live.[178] The initiative for this study had in fact been taken by the Sub-Commission itself, and also considered by the UN Commission on Human Rights in that same year.[179] From the start it was agreed that there was need for a survey of international human rights instruments which provided for distinctions between nationals and individuals 'who are not citizens of the State in which they live', and that the proposed survey would include 'the question of refugees and stateless persons'.[180]

At the Sub-Commission's meeting of 19 September 1973, its appointed *rapporteur*, Lady Elles, declared that it was nowadays

generally accepted in customary international law that the minimum standards of treatment must be applied to persons subject to the territorial jurisdiction of a State. That rule was based on the right of States to protect all their nationals, whether resident in their own territory or abroad. In recent years, there had been many occasions when those rules had not been applied to non-nationals, when the later had been unable to use the remedies available in the State where they were and the State of which they were nationals had been unable to take measures to protect them. Moreover, it should be remembered that no private individual could compel the State of which he was a national to take action in his behalf.[181]

Lady Elles further stated that international instruments on human rights 'either made distinctions between nationals and non-nationals or were ambiguous as to their applicability to non-nationals', and it was thus essential to ensure protection of the human rights 'of persons and groups who, for various reasons, moved – quite legally – from one country to another in order to live and, particularly, to work there'.[182]

Duly authorized by the Commission, the Sub-Commission proceeded to an investigation of the matter in 1974 (agenda item 3). The United Kingdom representative proposed (on 8 August 1974) a draft declaration on the human rights of individuals who are not citizens of the country in which they live, comprising ten Articles.[183] The draft declaration was mainly concerned with the treatment and the substantive rights to be enjoyed by so-called 'non-citizens', a term applicable to 'any individual who lawfully resides or works, on a permanent or semi-permanent basis, in a State of which he is not a citizen' (Article 1).[184] Certain minimum civil rights (Article 4) and certain minimum economic and social rights (Article 5) were recognized to 'non-citizens'[185] who at all times comply with the laws, customs and traditions of the country of residence and refrain from illegal activities prejudicial to it (Article 2).[186]

A draft resolution submitted by the representative of Uruguay (on 9 August 1974) reaffirmed the principle that the existence of certain fundamental human rights as essential attributes of the human person 'does not derive from the fact that the individual is a national or citizen of the State in which he happens to be'.[187] The draft resolution, requesting the Commission to consider the question, further declared that restrictions on the principle above, 'on the grounds of a person's nationality or citizenship, can be admissible only when based on an international norm, in keeping with the Universal Declaration of Human Rights or with general international law'.[188]

A further draft resolution was submitted (on 16 August 1974) by three members of the Sub-Commission, endorsing the contents of the draft resolution proposed by the Uruguayan representative (*supra*), and, further, retaining on its agenda the present item and designating the British representative (Lady Elles) *rapporteur* of the Sub-Commission on the subject.[189] Before the Commission of Human Rights, in the course of the discussion on the matter, it was considered that the item being taken up by the Sub-Commission should appropriately 'take into consideration particularly the status of migrant workers'.[190] On the recommendation of the Commission, the ECOSOC requested the Sub-Commission to consider the matter as one of high priority.[191] The Sub-Commission then entrusted Lady Elles, of the United Kingdom, to report on the subject.[192]

Throughout the Commission's consideration of the item (1975), the opinion was further expressed that 'in view of the growing number of persons who had, often for economic reasons, to live in a country other than their own, the situation in many cases required urgent decisions, since, among other things, the presence of a large number of foreign workers in developed countries might give rise to manifestations of racism or racial discrimination'.[193] Another point raised was that 'the principles of equality embodied in international instruments and national constitutions should be applied as far as possible', but 'a distinction had to be drawn between rights that were recognized as belonging to everyone and rights connected with a nationality, which carried national rights and obligations. Equality under labour laws and with respect to social rights was of special importance'.[194] But on 6 February 1975 the Commission decided to defer consideration of the item to its 1976 session, when it would be in a position to examine the study undertaken by the Sub-Commission's *rapporteur*.[195] Baroness Elles's study was concluded in June 1977.[196]

Lady Elles indicated in 1974 that the term 'alien' was used in the present context as meaning:

an individual over whom a State has no jurisdiction, and no link exists between the individual and the State except in so far as the individual may be within the territory of that State; 'national', 'citizen' and 'subject' will be assumed to be co-terminous. Within this term 'alien' the refugee, the stateless, the displaced or deported are all included, as well as the diplomat or member of an international organization working outside his own country, the permanent resident non-citizen, the migrant worker, the seaman within the territorial waters of a foreign State, the wife of an alien or the foreign wife of a national, the foreign news correspondent, civilians in occupied territories.[197]

Lady Elles thus spoke of protection of human rights of aliens,[198] to be secured in the light of the fundamental principles of equality and non-discrimination enshrined in the UN Charter.[199]

In the present context, she explained, 'the distinction between nationals and non-nationals is made clear by the suffering of thousands if not millions of those deprived of or persecuted because of their nationality'.[200] Even though the view had been taken that there was a necessity for an international instrument clarifying the human rights of aliens[201] in the present context, the distinction here between citizens and non-citizens seems at first sight an artificial one, in view of the basic premises underlying the system of generalized human rights protection. Lady Elles herself admitted, for example, that the UN Universal Declaration of Human Rights did not specifically mention nationality or citizenship,[202] and that the provisions of the UN Covenants on Human Rights were applicable to *all* individuals unless it could be assumed that one particular provision was aimed specifically at the protection of individuals *qua* aliens.[203] In its turn, the UN International Convention on the Elimination of All Forms of Racial Discrimination was essentially concerned with combating discrimination grounded on race or colour, rather than nationality.[204] Nevertheless, Lady Elles surveyed provisions conferring rights in UN human rights instruments, trying to distinguish rights applicable to all individuals, rights applicable to aliens and rights reserved to nationals.[205]

The use of such terms as 'protection of aliens' and 'protection of non-citizens' may suggest an analogy with the law on State responsibility for injuries to aliens and diplomatic protection. Yet this appears to be a false analogy, not warranted by the approach to the problem recently taken at the United Nations: it may be submitted that, in the present context, the protection of aliens is nothing more than a particularization of the system of international protection of human rights. That protection is entrusted to an international body, and not to intervening States. Significantly, the term 'alien' is here employed with a considerably wider meaning (see *supra*, p. 32) than in the law of State responsibility for injuries to aliens.

The situations aimed at are typically human rights situations, affecting – sometimes collectively – non-citizens as well as other categories of individuals, such as refugees, stateless persons and migrant workers. Matters pertaining to the traditional law of protection of nationals abroad were normally related to international trade, into which the individuals concerned had voluntarily engaged themselves, as pointed out by the International Court of Justice[206] and several writers.[207] Matters pertaining to the proposed system of protection of 'non-citizens' belong to an altogether different context, falling clearly within the scope of the system of generalized human rights protection.

5. Fifth approach: incompatibility or absence of parallelism between the two systems

Another approach to the 'co-existence' or 'confrontation' between the two systems of diplomatic protection and human rights protection has consisted in questioning the possibility of their compatibility with each other or of the existence of any parallelism between them. The answers generally arrived at have presented a certain variance in degree but not in nature. One may first of all distinguish the clear position whereby 'the traditional doctrine [of diplomatic protection] is incompatible with the modern conception of fundamental rights and human freedoms'[208] (O'Connell). The view has also been taken that diplomatic protection may lose some of its significance as human rights protection is developed and strengthened, but it is unlikely that the latter will supersede the former in its entirety due to the great obstacles of implementation that it will probably be faced with[209] (Castrén, Przetacznik). Accordingly, one cannot speak *at present* of a 'replacement' of diplomatic protection by a more developed remedial system of human rights protection; it has in this connection been suggested that diplomatic protection has been following, and will probably keep on following, a path of evolution *of its own*, even if that amounts to a recognition, within its own system, of certain basic human rights[210] (Berlia, P. de Visscher).

Amerasinghe's study of the problem recognizes the possibility of a place in present-day international relations for both systems, diplomatic protection and human rights protection; but in dismissing emphasis on human rights protection 'beyond the limits of the operation of the European Convention on Human Rights', he strays into the opposite extreme of calling for a much extended application of the law of alien treatment and diplomatic protection.[211] Exaggerations in this direction are rhetorical and unnecessary, as critics of diplomatic protection have not denied that aliens should be granted certain rights and, under present conditions, this proposition remains unchallenged.[212] Difficulties arise as to how wide those rights are, or should be, and under which conditions is or should the State be entitled to exercise their protection; which is the proper field of application of the local remedies rule.

With regard to the exercise of protection, to contend, for example, that diplomatic protection, as related to the principle of human rights protection, was limited to aliens and thus reflected 'a defect in the execution'[213] of that basic principle, may be a superficial way of appreciating the relationship between diplomatic protection and human rights protection. Traditional customary international law did recognize, though restrictively, protection to aliens (at least to certain aliens); and the body of law on State responsibility for injuries to aliens and the practice of diplomatic protection were for a considerable time following a line of evolution of their own, well before the basic principles embodied in the human rights system became recognized and emerged after the Second World War. It would be unlikely that the novel system would have such a drastic impact on diplomatic protection as to warrant this latter being exercised only for the execution of the basic principle of human rights protection. Even if this principle may ultimately render the institution of diplomatic protection anachronistic and obsolete[214] when human rights become effectively enforceable under international law (an unlikely and difficult hypothesis nowadays), it seems more accurate to appreciate diplomatic protection within the framework of its basic premises (cf. *supra*, pp. 7–13) and not by direct reference to the basic principle of human rights protection.

Leaving aside reliance upon the 'moral content' of principles of law[215] in this context (likely to lead to greater controversy), it is to be borne in mind that the inter-State nature of protection of individuals in international law (proper to diplomatic protection of nationals abroad) is nowadays qualified by the rise and proliferation of international organizations since the Second World War and the vast body of law and practice ensuing therefrom. While it remains true that international protection of human rights still depends ultimately to a large extent on the cooperation of individual States, the exercise or administration of that protection, unlike the law on treatment of aliens, is normally carried out by international organs.

To explain diplomatic protection as 'arising from the primitive state of international law'[216] (where individuals are left without adequate protection) would go well beyond the limits of a study of that protection, and into the realm of the historical quality of international law itself. Not only is the hypothesis of the so-called 'primitive state of international law' at present under review,[217] but also any apologetic study of one particular form of protection[218] could hardly be of much avail for an appreciation of distinct systems of protection for the purposes of a proper application of the local remedies rule.

As early as 1933, H. Lauterpacht observed that 'rules of international law on the matter of State responsibility are based on the separation of the State from the individuals and associations of which it is composed'.[219] Five years later the point was notably developed by W. Friedmann, who, witnessing the 'gradual intrusion of the State into spheres which constituted formerly a reserve of the individual' (trade and industry, or economic activity in general), observed that relations between the individual and the State were not static and were constantly evolving, producing effects upon the law of State responsibility in the sense of fostering its adaptation to changing situations.[220] A similar point was made in 1950 by Henri Rolin.[221]

Whilst in diplomatic protection the State acts allegedly 'in its own interests' (nationality as the *vinculum juris*) on an inter-governmental basis[222] (not seldom politically motivated), with citizens left unprotected *vis-à-vis* their own State,[223] in human rights protection there is allegedly a 'common interest' on the part of the Contracting States in the accomplishment of the purpose of the treaty at issue.[224]

The underlying assumption of the traditional system of diplomatic protection lay in the maintenance of a 'unified' socio-economic order among States for stable international trade; hence the identification, based on the Vattelian formulation, of private economic interests with national interests, and the individualistic espousal of claims and (discretionary) protection of interests among States of unequal power.[225] The denial of international status to individuals (enabled to act only through their own States) thus gravely over-emphasized the political undertones of inter-State relations for settlement of claims. Recognition of procedural status to individuals[226] (rendering national-ity immaterial) and of the right of individual petition could thereby cure the shortcomings of the traditional system of protection; the pursuance of rights before international organs could very much favour *peaceful* settlement at international level.[227] In the system of protection it was intrinsic in the concept of fundamental human rights that 'those rights inhere in the individual and are not derived from the State'.[228] As direct access to international organs became recognized to individuals in the new system of human rights protection, the local remedies rule was envisaged as a requirement to play a key role in the admissibility of human rights complaints.[229]

An alleged 'interaction' between diplomatic protection and human rights protection does not seem to resist closer examination and appears to be more apparent than real. While it may be true that standards for alien treatment might have historically influenced the formulation of certain fundamental human rights, and coincided to some extent with them, one cannot seemingly pursue the matter much further than that. The often acknowledged possibility that the development of an effective human rights system may well render the system of diplomatic protection superfluous or unnecessary (see *supra*, p. 23) does not seem to imply a necessary 'interaction' between the two systems leading to that result. Instead, this result, if materialized, may appear as a logical consequence of the development of two systems based upon essentially distinct premises.

As human rights protection is by its own nature more comprehen-sive, extended to aliens and nationals (and stateless persons) alike, it seems that a system directed solely to alien protection would be doomed to become superfluous. Conversely, the law on alien treatment is likely to retain its relevance, not only while human rights protection (mostly based on treaty obligations) cannot be effectively

implemented,[230] but also because of increasing international obligations in the economic area.[231]

It may then be argued, historical past left aside, not only that there is
no necessary interaction between diplomatic protection and human
rights protection today, but also that there is no necessary parallelism
in the course of their respective developments, whichever results may
be obtained in the future. Consequently, it may reasonably be argued
that there are no compelling reasons why the rule of exhaustion of
local remedies should, in the framework of human rights protection,
necessarily have the same application it has had in the system of
diplomatic protection.

The 'absence of parallelism' may be reflected in present-day
developments in the interpretation and application of the local
remedies rule in the two contexts of alien treatment (e.g., settlement
of investment disputes)[232] and of human rights protection. This
suggests that developments in the two domains may follow their own
respective courses, with no necessary parallel between them, in so far
as the incidence of the local remedies rule is concerned. This has been
the view taken in practice by the organs of the European Convention
on Human Rights. In the *Austria* v. *Italy* case (1961), for example, the
Commission recalled that 'in general international law the right to
exercise diplomatic protection and to present a claim before an
international tribunal is a right which, subject to a few exceptions, is
limited to cases of an alleged injury to a State's own nationals abroad
within the jurisdiction of another State and in violation of international law'.[233] Similarly, the Commission went on, 'the rule of the
exhaustion of domestic remedies as a condition precedent to the
exercise of diplomatic protection and the presentation of an international claim is in general international law limited to claims made by a
State in respect of an injury alleged to have been done to one of its
nationals'.[234]

After recalling the rationale of the local remedies rule, the
Commission pointed out the basic difference between the system of
diplomatic protection and that of human rights protection in the
following terms:

Whereas, in the European Convention, the High Contracting Parties have
established a system of the international protection of human rights and
fundamental freedoms for all persons within their respective jurisdictions
independently of any bond of nationality, whereas it follows that the system
of international protection provided in the Convention extends to the

nationals of the State which is alleged to have violated the law of the Convention and to stateless persons, as well as to the nationals of other States; and whereas it is manifest that the principle upon which the domestic remedies rule is founded and the considerations which led to its introduction in general international law apply not less than *a fortiori* to a system of international protection which extends to a State's own nationals as well as to foreigners; whereas, moreover, the mere fact that the system of international protection in the Convention is founded upon the concept of a collective guarantee of the rights and freedoms contained in the Convention, does not in any way weaken the force of the principle on which the domestic remedies rule is founded or the considerations which led to its introduction.[235]

Thus, although drawing attention to basic differences in the premises of diplomatic protection and human rights protection, the Commission limited itself to stating that, despite those differences, the local remedies rule was applicable in both systems of protection. Only subsequently, in a case in 1969 (see *infra*, pp. 41–4), was the Commission called upon to go deeper into the problem. But *Austria* v. *Italy* became a leading case for the issue of application under the Convention of the local remedies rule *ratione personae*: the Commission's decision made it clear that, despite a certain linguistic difficulty, the local remedies rule was to be interpreted as applying to inter-State (Article 24) as well as individual (Article 25) applications.[236] The conditions of admissibility of applications laid down in Article 27 (1) and (2) applied to individual applications alone, whereas the condition of exhaustion of local remedies enshrined in Articles 26 and 27 (3) applied to *all* applications – individual and inter-State – under the Convention.

In this connection, the Commission significantly remarked that:

Whereas, if it is true that under the generally recognized rules of international law the domestic remedies rule has no application to international claims presented in respect of non-nationals of the claimant State, it is equally true that it has no application to claims presented to international tribunals by individuals, whereas in both types of case the reason is simply that the claims themselves are inadmissible under general international law, irrespective of the exhaustion of domestic remedies, and whereas it follows that if the insertion of the words 'according to the generally recognized rules of international law' were to be taken as indicating an intention to exclude the operation of the domestic remedies rule in the case of applications brought by States under Article 24, it would equally be necessary to interpret them as excluding its operation in the case of applications brought by individual, non-governmental organization, or group of individuals under Article 25, whereas, however, it is beyond question [...] that the domestic remedies rule laid down in Article 26 of the Convention operates in the case of applications brought under Article 25; whereas by including the words 'according to the generally recognized rules of international law' in Article 26 *the authors of the Convention intended to limit the material content of the rule and not its field of application* ratione personae [my italics].[237]

Diplomatic protection and human rights protection resting upon essentially distinct premises, it would be reasonable to expect a fair and equitable application of the local remedies rule taking due account of those differences. A mechanical transplantation of the rule from the older into the newer protective system would be likely to lead to an unwarranted rigidity in its application, tending to be destructive of the very purposes of securing an effective protection of human rights. In the mechanism of diplomatic protection, exhaustion of local remedies preceded State intervention, whence the rigour with which the local redress rule has been applied in that framework. In the system of human rights protection this is certainly not the case, as the machinery is entrusted to the international authority; State sovereignty is not so easily threatened, and the local remedies rule – primarily an attribute of State sovereignty – could theoretically be more flexibly interpreted and applied.

If there were parallels between the foundations of the two systems of diplomatic protection and human rights protection, the Commission could hardly have reached the decision it did in the *Austria* v. *Italy* case. It would be a fallacy to speak of the application of the rule in individual applications in diplomatic protection, where no such thing exists, the whole system being based upon inter-State relations. And when one comes to inter-State applications, this certainly cannot mean cases of 'direct injury' to the applicant State, in which cases the local remedies rule could not possibly apply (*par in parem non habet imperium, non habet jurisdictionem*). The rule would then only apply to inter-State cases of 'indirect injury' to the State.

But while this notion, reminiscent of the Vattelian dogma, has been invoked in the system of diplomatic protection, it is kept out of the system of human rights protection. In this latter (under the European Convention), a State applies to the Commission not because it has been 'indirectly injured *via* its citizen', but by virtue of the principle of *collective guarantee* which underlies the whole system. In so doing, the State is pressing not strictly its own interests, but theoretically the general interest of the collectivity of Contracting States in securing respect for human rights (under the Convention). The political undertones remain present, but there appears to be room here for a more flexible application of the local remedies rule without hurting susceptibilities of the sovereign States concerned.

As the system of human rights protection dismisses the distinction between direct and indirect injury, it is not open to States in the present context to argue for or against the application of the local remedies rule on the basis of the alleged nature of the injury suffered. But it is possible to conceive, in the system of diplomatic protection, of States which, in the pursuit of their own interests, attempt to characterize an injury as a direct or indirect one, so as either to circumvent or to entail, respectively, the application of the rule. Reference could here be made, for example, to the oral arguments in the *Aerial Incident* case (Israel v. Bulgaria, 1959).[238]

Such arguments concerning the nature of the alleged injury seem to reflect the artificiality of the whole construction of the classical system of diplomatic protection. In principle the local remedies rule applies, but if it is established that the case is one of direct injury, it does not. The characterization of the nature of the injury thus bears direct relevance to the application of the rule in the framework of diplomatic protection. In the human rights system, it is the violation of fundamental rights of human beings that counts, and the distinction between direct and indirect injury becomes immaterial for the purposes of application of the local remedies rule: the rule applies to all complaints of human rights violations, whether they are lodged with the international organ by individual victims or by High Contracting Parties. If the complaints are lodged by individuals, the injury they suffered is the basis of their complaint and they have to claim to be victims of the acts complained of; if the complaints are lodged by States, the human rights violation remains the basis of their complaints, with the qualification that the applicant States are thereby exercising a collective guarantee of the system of protection, of which the beneficiaries are *all* persons within the jurisdiction of the High Contracting Parties. This factor seems again to suggest an absence of parallelism between the two systems of diplomatic protection[239] and human rights protection (under the Convention).

The pleadings in the *Matznetter* case (1969) before the European Court of Human Rights provide valuable indications for a comparative analysis of the application of the local remedies rule in the two systems of diplomatic protection and human rights protection. The case concerned an Austrian citizen who had been arrested and charged with various offences, including fraud. Applying to the European Commission (application n. 2178/64), Matznetter alleged *inter alia* that the length of his detention while on remand had not been 'reasonable' within the meaning of Article 5 (3) of the Convention. After the decision on admissibility of the application, the Commission and the Austrian government engaged in a legal battle in their pleadings before the Court concerning the application of the local remedies rule in such a case of detention while on remand. The Commission was of the view that domestic remedies should have been exhausted before its decision on admissibility but might still be pending at their final stage (e.g., an appeal) at the time the application was lodged with the Commission.[240] The Austrian government, on the other hand, maintained that all domestic remedies should have been exhausted at the time of the lodging of the application with the Commission.[241] This particular problem[242] opened the way for a debate on the application of the local remedies rule in the human rights system (under the Convention) as contrasted with its application in the system of diplomatic protection.

Trying to press the Austrian government's interpretation of the local remedies rule further, the agent for Austria (Mr Nettel) stated in the public hearing of 11–12 February 1969 that Article 26 of the Convention had a parallel in the exercise of diplomatic protection, in that this latter could only take place when the State complained of had had an opportunity of remedying the alleged injustice itself: the local remedies requirement (in Article 26) thus prevented the assertion of international claims. In the present case, added Mr Nettel, an international claim had been asserted against Austria before the Commission before domestic remedies had been exhausted, and that was, he argued, inadmissible.[243]

The Austrian reasoning was based upon the assumption that Article 26 of the Convention, in referring to 'generally recognized rules of international law', must thereby be interpreted and applied in the light of the law of diplomatic protection. Bearing in mind the discussion above, the assumption seemed fallacious, conflicting with past practice of the Convention organs and the preparatory work of the Convention, undermining this latter's principles and purposes, and confusing two systems (diplomatic protection and human rights protection) based upon essentially distinct premises. To take but one small point of Mr Nettel's argument, for example, he stated at a certain stage that 'not until the foreigner is deprived of his rights before a domestic court [...] may the right of diplomatic protection be invoked, or, in our case, only then can the matter be brought before the Commission'[244] (see *supra*). The false analogy in the Austrian government's argument could not be put in clearer terms, nor resist closer scrutiny: for, in the present case, in which the Austrian government was engaged as respondent party, the applicant, Otto Matznetter, born in Vienna on 21 December 1921, was not a 'foreigner', but happened to be an Austrian citizen complaining against his own government before an international machinery set up by the Convention. It would thus hardly be possible to argue by analogy with the exercise of diplomatic protection. In legal proceedings, the contending parties are, of course, pursuing their own interests; the search for soundness and truth, or otherwise, behind their contentions, is the interpreter's task.

The pleadings in the *Matznetter* case proceeded as the Commission's principal delegate, Mr Eustathiades, rejected the Austrian government's parallel of application of the local remedies rule in diplomatic protection and under the European Convention on Human Rights. In this latter, he recalled, claimants before the European Commission were private individuals themselves, and the whole system was based upon a Commission which sifted individual applications 'by persons who cannot be certain whether they have exhausted domestic remedies within the meaning of Article 26. While that Article refers to the recognized principles of international law, this does not mean that any absolute parallel exists between diplomatic protection of individual applications; all that is necessary is to prove that domestic remedies have been exhausted,[245] and it is up to the Commission to verify this point, sometimes with difficulty.[246] The Commission's principal delegate was quite categorical in concluding that the entire practice since the Commission began has 'proceeded on a different basis'[247] from diplomatic protection.

The Commission's opinion was thus clearly that human rights protection (through collective guarantee and direct access to individuals to the international organ under the Convention) could not possibly be regarded as an extension of diplomatic protection, nor could the two systems be regarded as parallel to each other and thereby calling for a similar application of the local remedies rule. The human rights system was a new one, based upon distinct premises, calling for an adequate application of the local remedies rule, with its material content limited – and not extended – by the reference made by Article 26 to the generally recognized rules of international law, in order to fulfil the principles and purposes of the new system of protection.

The agent for Austria (Mr Nettel) insisted, however, on the parallel between human rights protection and diplomatic protection, adding that the 'filter' of Article 26 should be preserved and not eliminated by a 'novel' interpretation.[248] Such an argument was quite vulnerable, as the Commission itself has in practice recognized the *subsidiary* nature of international procedures;[249] and, in the course of the instant pleadings, never suggested, by advancing its allegedly 'novel' interpretation, that Article 26 should thereby be eliminated.

In fact, it would seem unreasonable to call at the present stage for a deletion of the local remedies rule in human rights protection experiments. The *optimum* is not in harmony with the *bonum*; as the spectre of State sovereignty remains very much alive, one may well wonder whether Article 25 of the European Convention (providing for direct access to individuals before the Commission on an optional basis) would have been at all possible or viable without Article 26 (the local remedies rule). Thus, rather than the deletion of Article 26, it would appear that what is needed at present is a proper understanding of the problem and a proper understanding of the necessity of an adequate application of the rule in full accordance with the particularities of the system of human rights protection.

It seems that this was what the Commission had in mind in the pleadings in the *Matznetter* case. In this sense its interpretation could be termed as 'novel', without anything seemingly wrong with that. This is precisely the point: a novel interpretation for the application of the local remedies rule – without detracting from general international law – to a novel system of protection based upon novel premises. This view, unlike that of the Austrian government, found support in the practice of the Convention organs as well. Reference has been made to the Commission's *dicta* in the *Austria* v. *Italy* case (*supra*, pp. 37–9), with a direct bearing upon the problem presently under discussion.

There was a certain evolution from that decision (*supra*, pp. 38–9) to the Court's judgment of 10 November 1969 in the *Matznetter* case. The Court took note of the Commission's view that 'although Article 26 refers to "the generally recognised rules of international law" there was no complete parallelism between the doctrine of diplomatic protection and the new system inaugurated by the Convention, at any rate in so far as applications by private persons were concerned'.[250]

The Court's decision[251] in fact favoured the Commission's view, reiterating what it had already stated in the *Stögmüller* case (1969), namely that local remedies should certainly have been exhausted by the time of the Commission's decision on admissibility, but the same did not *ipso facto* apply invariably with regard to the time of the lodging of the application with the Commission. In cases like those of *Matznetter* and *Stögmüller* there was a certain element of a *continuing* situation.[252] And general international law, explicitly referred to by Article 26, was 'far from conferring on the rule of exhaustion the inflexible character which the government seems to attribute to it'.[253]

In fact, the Court went on to state:

in matters of detention while on remand, it is in the light of the circumstances of the case that the question is, in appropriate cases, to be assessed whether and to what extent, it was necessary, pursuant to Article 26, for the detained applicant, who had exhausted the remedies before the Commission declared his application admissible, to make later on further appeals to the national courts in order to make it possible to examine, at international level, the reasonableness of his continued detention.[254]

In a particular type of case, involving the compatibility with the Convention of internal 'legislative measures and administrative practices', the Commission has clearly drawn attention to the distinctive character of the system of human rights protection, at times opting for the non-application of the local remedies rule in such cases,[255] and has excluded the possibility of any absolute parallelism with the system of diplomatic protection. The problem is only registered in passing at this stage, as it is studied in detail in a subsequent chapter.[256] This trend, depending largely on the issues raised in each case, is of course not an instance of waiver of the local remedies rule by the parties concerned, and the dismissal of the rule in such circumstances would hardly have been possible in the system of diplomatic protection.

In a recent case in which contentions of legislative measures and administrative practices allegedly incompatible with the Convention were raised, the *Ireland* v. *United Kingdom* case (1972), one of the arguments advanced by the applicant government was that, as the application was being brought 'in respect of breaches of treaty, that is to say, to ensure the observance of the Convention, and not as measures of diplomatic protection, [...] therefore the rule of exhaustion of domestic remedies as it is to be understood in international law under Article 26 does not apply to this application'.[257] The Commission rejected the argument, observing that, by virtue of Articles 26 and 27(3) of the Convention, the local remedies rule was to apply to any application, whether from individuals (Article 25) or from States (Article 24).[258] While in the *Matznetter* case Austria pressed for a rigid application of the local remedies rule, trying to draw a parallel with diplomatic protection, in the *Ireland* v. *United Kingdom* case Ireland pressed for the exclusion of the local remedies rule on the ground that that was not a case of diplomatic protection. The two extreme positions in those two cases seem equally based on wrong assumptions. In the latter case, Ireland assumed that as diplomatic protection was not at issue and breaches of treaty were alleged, the local remedies rule thereby would not apply; this argument – just like the opposite view advanced by Austria in the *Matznetter* case – was inaccurate, as the Human Rights Convention itself provided for application of the local remedies rule.

It seems that recent legal writing on the subject begins gradually to become aware of the contextual difference of application of the rule of exhaustion of local remedies in diplomatic protection and in human rights protection. It has thus been pointed out that the application of the local remedies rule 'nel sistema classico della "protezione diplomatica" sembra incompatibile con il sistema della "garanzia collettiva" dei diritti dell'uomo instaurato dalla Convenzione'.[259] It has further been suggested that the local remedies rule as evolved in nineteenth-century practice of diplomatic protection should have its application re-examined in the present-day context of human rights protection: while in diplomatic protection it proved a beneficial requirement by minimizing tension and forcing a solution within the framework of municipal law, its transposition to the system of human rights protection has made of it a heavy burden placed upon the injured individual, also hindering the initiative of applicant States desirous to secure human rights *via* judicial action.[260]

As a general rule of international law, the local remedies rule has served some very *practical* purposes,[261] and there is nothing to suggest that it is a sacrosanct principle which could not be applied with more flexibility in the international system of human rights protection. The (geographical) limitations of this latter are perhaps greater than in diplomatic protection, in that it still largely depends on treaty stipulations (as exemplified by the European Convention on Human Rights at regional level) and it is not yet established that the rights protected have entered the realm of customary international law.

On the other hand, perhaps for this very reason, conditions for the application of the local remedies rule in human rights protection do not necessarily need to be surrounded by the same amount of uncertainty as in the scope of customary diplomatic protection. In human rights protection it always remains possible to specify those conditions of application by means of detailed rules as to the exhaustion of remedies,[262] in this way avoiding some of the uncertainties of general international law on the matter.[263] Moreover, even the relevance of the fact that diplomatic protection as part of customary international law is historically older than recent international experiments on human rights protection (still largely embodied in treaty obligations contracted by States) should not be exaggerated:[264] there already appear to be some elements (e.g., in the jurisprudence of the International Court of Justice) tending to indicate that certain basic human rights may well form part of general international law.[265]

And in addition to treaties on human rights protection, reference may also be made to mechanisms developed *within* international organizations for the same purpose. Those mechanisms (such as the one based on ECOSOC resolution 1503(XLVIII) of 1970 for dealing with communications relating to human rights violations) may well 'co-exist' with other instruments which have obtained the necessary ratifications and thus entered into force (such as, recently, the UN Covenants on Human Rights), for the reason that the former remain necessary for dealing with communications coming from countries other than those which have ratified the latter. This may well suggest an expansion of the system of human rights protection.

V. Conclusions: towards a proper understanding of the rationale of the local remedies rule within the frameworks of diplomatic protection and of human rights protection

From the above (sections II and III) it appears that the systems of diplomatic protection and of human rights protection (under the European Convention on Human Rights) are based upon essentially distinct premises. An examination of the various approaches whereby the two systems of protection have been compared reveals, first, that the 'historical approach' fails to place emphasis on the present 'co-existence' of diplomatic protection and human rights protection. This applies to an even greater extent to the approaches of the two systems as absorbing or superseding and developing each other. The so-called protection of 'non-citizens', an approach recently followed at the United Nations, appears rather as a particularization of the system of human rights protection. It is the fifth approach, namely that of an absence of parallelism between the two forms of protection, which seems, on the basis of the above study, to come closer to reality. It is this approach which has been espoused – correctly, it is submitted – by the organs of the European Convention on Human Rights. This has immediate implications for a proper understanding of the rationale of the local remedies rule, and for its interpretation and application within the frameworks of the two systems of diplomatic protection and of human rights protection.

Awareness of the contextual difference between those two systems seems necessary for a proper assessment of the local remedies rule in the distinct situations. Even though five main approaches of the correlation or confrontation of the two systems of protection have been distinguished above, it has also appeared that those five approaches could not truly be 'isolated' from each other: in fact they present points of contact; the classification is, accordingly, presented on the basis of the *preponderant* elements of each approach.

Within the context of diplomatic protection, the local remedies rule, as a condition prior to the exercise of that protection, has been credited with the 'beneficial' influences of pressing for an improvement in standards of internal administration of justice in the countries concerned,[266] and of tending to dispose of most potential international legal conflicts at domestic level.[267] Sarhan, for example, wrote with some enthusiasm that the rule was 'indispensable for the safeguard of national sovereignty' even, he added dogmatically, in experiments where individuals are recognized the right of direct recourse to an international organ.[268] This view that the local remedies rule has an intrinsic value irrespective of the domain in which it is applied is not supported by past experiments, for example under the League of Nations, recognizing procedural status to individuals in international law, in which a variety of solutions was found for the problem at issue.

Within the context of diplomatic protection, the local remedies rule is – in the words of the Greek delegate (Mr Politis) at the 1930 Hague Codification Conference – 'a guarantee for the State; it respects its independence; it makes it possible to avoid unnecessary disputes. Only those cases which are really worthy of consideration should be allowed to come before the international courts.'[269] When Head supported the rule, openly subscribing to the substantive view of it,[270] he had in mind some post-Second World War problems brought about by settlement of claims arising out of nationalization activities.[271] When Drost criticized the rule and called for its non-application, he had in mind effective international protection of human rights as he deemed it would best be pursued.[272] When Guinand, contrariwise, supported the rule (in the system of human rights protection), he seemed to have taken for granted that 'the most ancient form of human rights protection is undoubtedly that of diplomatic protection'.[273] This superficial view of the problem led him to identify in the practice of the European Commission of Human Rights an element in support of a rigid application of the local remedies rule in the human rights system under the Convention.[274] However, the practice of the Convention organs, upon careful examination, does not warrant such a conclusion and points to a different direction.

When Ténékidès, as early as 1933, criticized the local remedies rule and questioned its foundations as a rule of international law, he followed a reasoning proper to interpreters of classical diplomatic protection: the disputes in question were inter-State conflicts, and the personality of the individual was in his view 'fusionnée' in that of the protecting State. Moreover, in denying the local redress rule any utility or efficacy, any foundation in law, Ténékidès subscribed to an extreme variation of the monist theoretical position of the primacy of international law over municipal law.[275]

Other examples could be given of different positions taken on the problem at issue. A survey of specialized literature on the subject shows that authors have supported the application of the local remedies rule in the field of diplomatic protection; they have attacked the application of the rule in the field of diplomatic protection; they have defended the application of the rule in the field of human rights protection; they have contested the application of the rule in the field of humans rights protection (see *supra* for examples of all these positions).

This confusion may to some extent be due to a lack of discernment of the major issues involved in the application of the rule *within a particular context* (e.g., diplomatic protection or human rights protection). This misconception might in some cases have been deliberate, but one need not pursue this point. Rather than to contest, or support, the application of the rule, a more constructive attitude would seem to be to search for a proper and adequate application of the rule within a particular context in pursuit of clear and well-defined purposes.

It has at times been held that the local remedies rule has favoured a certain 'equilibrium' between international law and State sovereignty. Hermann Friedmann, in his study of 1933, like Ténékidès beheld in the rule not a manifestation of 'primacy' of municipal law but rather a certain 'concession' of international law to municipal law; but, unlike Ténékidès, he envisaged the rule as one of international law.[276] H. Friedmann criticized not the rule itself, but its mechanical or rigid application (which he identified with the substantive view of the rule); to him, the so-called 'exceptions' or 'limitations' to the application of the rule militated against the 'mechanical theory' and supported a 'realistic theory of the exhaustion', which admitted a certain margin of appreciation of the facts and flexibility in the application of the rule.[277] But he did not go much further than that in providing indications for the pursuit of his aim.[278]

In the traditional law of State responsibility for injuries to aliens the relevance of the local remedies rule was manifest, as a condition prior to the enforcement of international responsibility by means of the exercise of diplomatic protection. It was suggested above that the exercise of this latter, contingent upon exhaustion of local remedies, is more accurately explained as a procedural necessity rather than on the basis of debatable theories of 'injury to the State *via* its citizens'. The rationale of the local remedies rule as a pre-condition to the exercise of diplomatic protection was clearly perceived and pointed out by authors of some of the major systematizations of the subject (e.g., Eagleton,[279] Freeman,[280] Ch. de Visscher).[281] The study of the local remedies rule in the present context became somewhat incidental – not such a central issue – in the general framework of such doctrinal constructions (starting from a clear-cut distinction between responsibility in municipal law and in international law, the well-known dualist view) as those of the *fait illicite international* (Anzilotti)[282] and the *délit international complexe* (Ago).[283]

For its part, Borchard's systematization of the local remedies rule in the context of diplomatic protection placed emphasis on the clash or combination of interests underlying the operation of the rule.[284] In assuming the application and necessity of the rule, there seems to have been in this approach a certain confusion between the rule itself and the question of imputability of the alleged wrong to the State, between the moments of State responsibility and of its application by means of the exercise of diplomatic protection.[285] In that, Borchard may have misapprehended what, for example, Eagleton, Freeman, and Ch. de Visscher so clearly pointed out later; nevertheless, his treatment of the local remedies rule in the present context clarifies the different interests at stake.[286]

Most of the major works and theses on the local remedies rule in general international law have taken the rule as it evolved *within* the system of diplomatic protection, even though they did not clearly or sufficiently acknowledge or emphasize this fact.[287] It is thus not surprising to find that they did not go much beyond the point of taking note of problems entailed by the emerging human rights system and calling for reconsideration of conditions for application of the local remedies rule,[288] without indicating ways by which a proper course of development of the rule could be secured in the light of present international law trends towards more effective human rights protection.

This has probably led, for example, to a variety of terms for characterizing individual applicants within the framework of the human rights system: 'requérant',[289] 'réclamant',[290] 'demandeur',[291] 'plaideur',[292] 'partie lésée',[293] 'personne lésée',[294] and, objectionably (as reminiscent of the system of diplomatic protection), 'étranger lésé',[295] by reference to the system of the European Convention on Human Rights. In relation to this latter it would be more appropriate to refer to applicants as 'individus lésés',[296] because 'it is precisely applications from citizens wishing to establish rights *vis-à-vis* their own State under Article 26 of the Convention which are envisaged'[297] (a system thus fundamentally distinct from that of diplomatic protection).

The old and well-established practice of the local remedies rule accepted as law is studied in different chapters,[298] the same applying to legal writing and works of codification on the matter.[299] The wide but not absolute[300] acceptance of the local remedies rule may have given it a certain prominence, and, on the apparent assumption of its usefulness, it was also adopted in instruments relating to peaceful settlement of disputes.[301]

The *preventive* character of the local remedies rule in the practice of diplomatic intervention is manifest; in this context the rule has been used as 'a defence against the interference in the independence of a

State on the part of another, whatever form that interference may have taken', and it is this preventive character with regard to diplomatic interposition that, in Haesler's words, 'is inherent in the necessity for an aggrieved national to try out local means of justice first'.[302] The necessity to exhaust local remedies thus appears as 'a customary consequence of a constant attempt on the part of States to avoid interference from other States. The requirement is, therefore, a legal device for the benefit of States opposing any form of interference.'[303]

In this way it might be suggested that the approach to the rationale of the local remedies rule in the framework of diplomatic protection has been a 'negative' one, in the sense that no protection could be exercised unless and until the alien had exhausted in vain all local means of redress open to him. One is then inclined to ask whether the rationale of the rule ought necessarily to be viewed in the same perspective in the framework of human rights protection; here the rule operates as a condition of admissibility of complaints (a procedural bar or a defence, as under the European Convention on Human Rights), prescribing directly to individuals a requirement for the pursuance of their claims. Even though in both systems of diplomatic protection and human rights protection the local remedies rule operates as one of international law, is one thereby entitled to assume that the extent of application of the rule is, or should be, the same in the two systems of protection?

Might it not be argued that, in the search for a well-balanced equilibrium between international law and State sovereignty, a more rigorous application of the local remedies rule seems warranted in the system of diplomatic protection in view of this latter's inconsistencies or contingencies and its inescapably discretionary nature? In this inter-State system, where the sovereignty of States appears more vulnerable, the local remedies rule has an important role to play in preventing excesses, minimizing tensions and striving for the maintenance of the necessary balance for the preservation of an international legal order in which sovereign States continue to be regarded as its primary subjects.

The system of human rights protection would seem to present fewer inconsistencies: it is still largely a system which States 'accede' to by contracting certain well-defined treaty obligations in the full use and exercise of their sovereign will. The conditions of applicability of the local remedies rule are normally provided for in the treaty itself. The rule cannot be simply waived as in a bilateral relationship under the

law of State responsibility for injuries to aliens (e.g., the U.S.–
Mexican Claims Commissions.[304] Furthermore, it is difficult to
conceive that the great majority of human rights applications (as under
the European Convention), coming from common average citizens
complaining of their grievances, would imply any real threat or
danger to the sovereignty of the States concerned. It is clear that
international organs cannot be expected to be flooded with frivolous
complaints, and thus a sifting machinery for applications may prove
convenient or necessary at the admissibility stage, but this does not
detract from the view that, bearing the rationale of the local remedies
rule in mind, a less rigorous and more realistic application of the rule
in such a system would seem appropriate.

The rule of exhaustion of local remedies has always constituted a
major problem of implementation of the human rights system under
the European Convention. In his study of 1967, for example,
Antonopoulos noted critically that the local remedies rule, occupying
the centre of the jurisprudence under the Convention in so far as
conditions of admissibility of applications were concerned, needed to
be reconsidered for the purpose of a more adequate application in the
Convention system,[305] otherwise it would remain an 'instrument of
procedural massacre'[306] leading to systematic rejection of applications
on the ground of non-exhaustion of local remedies. Seven years later,
in 1974, Castberg deemed that the situation had improved little, as the
local remedies rule remained often 'the hurdle which the applicant has
not managed to leap'.[307] The rule seems to continue to present
unsolved problems in its application in the system of human rights
protection under the Convention.

It may be that the lack of a proper understanding of the rationale of
the rule in human rights protection, as distinct from diplomatic
protection, has accounted for some of the difficulties in practice (as
will be indicated in subsequent chapters). It may be that the insertion
of the clause 'according to generally recognized rules of international
law' in Article 26 of the Convention on the local remedies rule has led
to misunderstandings as to the proper scope of the rule and to false
analogies (deliberate or not) between the two systems of diplomatic
protection and human rights protection, thus obscuring the whole
matter to an even greater extent. For as the *travaux préparatoires* of the
Convention[308] together with the Commission's subsequent
jurisprudence[309] seem to indicate, the reference to general international
law contained in Article 26 of the Convention on the local remedies

rule was meant to draw attention to the limitations of the rule (in general international law itself)[310] and not necessarily to expand the material content of the rule under the Convention.

The problem could after all prove to be theoretically more apparent than real, as there are sufficient elements in general international law (cf. *infra*) warranting a flexible application of the local remedies rule under the Convention. Furthermore, those generally recognized rules or principles of international law, referred to by Article 26 of the Convention, are not always easily determinable, by reason of their very generality, especially when invoked with particular reference to a specific rule such as that of exhaustion of local remedies. It is difficult to avoid the impression that the inclusion of the reference to principles and rules of international law in Article 26 on the local remedies rule might have been the more comfortable way for the Convention draftsmen.[311] In practice, the problem of interpretation and proper application of the local remedies rule in human rights protection has arisen in that context.

As the two systems of diplomatic protection (in general international law) and human rights protection are based upon essentially distinct premises, the local remedies rule is arguably to be applied accordingly. Even though the organs of the Convention seem by and large to have carried out their work on the basis of the distinctive character of the system of human rights protection,[312] when one comes to application of the local remedies rule within that system difficulties and uncertainties arise, possibly in part because of the reference to general international law contained in Article 26 of the Convention on the local remedies rule (a reference also found in other human rights instruments).[313]

In the light of the above, it would seem that much of the uncertainty surrounding the provision is even unnecessary, but the fact remains that it exists, perhaps owing to the generality of the provision. In this connection it could be argued, for example, that there is nothing preventing the draftsmen of a human rights treaty from laying down specific rules governing the exhaustion of local remedies,[314] without necessarily detracting from general principles of international law on the matter. Such special or particular rules would take precedence over general rules and principles: *inclusio unius est exclusio alterius*. Such a detailed formulation of the local remedies requirement in the treaty could thus be made to reflect the distinct premises underlying human rights protection and the conferment of rights on individuals at international level. By the provision of specific rules governing the exhaustion of local remedies in the framework of human rights protection, one could reasonably expect a shift of emphasis in basic values in the application of the local redress principle towards greater recognition of the position and the rights of the individual within the human rights system. In the application of the local redress principle as a requirement serving primarily the interests of the territorial State, one could reasonably expect to have the balance tipped more in favour of the weaker party – the aggrieved individuals – within the framework of a system designed for the protection of human rights.

It could not reasonably be objected that this would *ipso facto* constitute a departure from general international law rules on the subject. The local remedies rule, after all, cannot be absolutely identified with the practice of diplomatic protection: even though largely developed under that practice, it is not its direct result. Diplomatic protection resulted from a long historical evolution whose antecedents could be traced back to the ancient practice of private reprisals. In that old practice, the local redress rule – preceding by some centuries the institution of diplomatic protection – seems to have operated as a bar or condition prior to the issuing of letters of reprisal. Subsequently, in the system of diplomatic protection, the local remedies rule operated as a *conditio sine qua non* for all exercise of that protection, but which in practice admitted certain attenuation (e.g., waiver of the rule in claims commissions in the inter-war period).[315] Nowadays, in the contemporary system of human rights protection, the rule operates as a condition of admissibility of complaints; in this system, there seems to be need for a more flexible interpretation and application of the rule.

It should not pass unnoticed, for example, as an initial step in that direction, that, subsequently to the drafting of the European Convention on Human Rights, both the UN Covenant on Civil and Political Rights[316] and the UN International Convention on the Elimination of All Forms of Racial Discrimination[317] have *expressly* provided that the local remedies rule does not apply 'where the application of the remedies is unreasonably prolonged'. This may reflect a distinctive feature of human rights protection as compared with diplomatic protection; it may further be regarded as a significant move towards a specific set of rules governing the exhaustion of local remedies in the framework of the system of human rights protection, without necessarily detracting from general principles of international law on the matter.[318] A detailed treatment of the application of the local remedies rule in human rights protection may, moreover, be rendered more necessary by some increasingly complex problems (examined *infra*, pp. 187–212, 221–8) such as, for example, those of a 'continuing situation' in violation of human rights, or of complaints of internal legislative measures and administrative practices allegedly incompatible with the provisions of a human rights treaty.

The distinct interpretation and application of the local remedies rule in human rights protection, as compared with diplomatic protection, may also be examined from the standpoint of the *duty* to provide local remedies: while the system of human rights protection embodies the State's duty to provide effective local remedies,[319] the system of diplomatic protection, on the other hand, does not throw a proper light on the matter (Tammes).[320] Furthermore, while diplomatic protection does not correspond to an international obligation to protect, human rights protection, on the other hand, may contribute towards greater recognition of fundamental rights by emphasizing, for example, the element of *adequate redress*; attention is thus shifted from the traditional prohibition of denial of justice into the obligation to provide local remedies (an obligation largely neglected in the past).[321] The denationalization of protection entailed by the human rights system not only enlarges the circle of protected persons in international law, but increases emphasis on local remedies as practical means for the enforcement of individual rights as embodied in international law.[322]

It may well be that one faces today an anomalous if not paradoxical development: in so far as protected persons are concerned, diplomatic protection, an institution of customary international law, may well gradually be reduced in scope and lose ground to human rights protection, still largely one of conventional international law, and one which appears to be gradually expanding. Minimization of this latter on the ground that it is entirely based upon treaty obligations, even if still holding largely true, should not be exaggerated, because certain fundamental human rights, as already indicated, seem to be gradually infiltrating the realm of general international law. The fact that the basic premises of diplomatic protection are distinct from those of human rights protection suggests that the rationale of the local remedies rule should be approached in distinct ways in the frameworks of the two protective systems.

Analysis of the rationale of the rule emphasizing the underlying interests, as originally proposed by Borchard within the particular context of diplomatic protection, is not necessarily adequate for the system of human rights protection. While in diplomatic protection the local remedies rule was approached in an essentially 'negative' way, preventing the exercise of protection until remedies had been unsuccessfully exhausted, there is nothing to prevent the local remedies rule being approached in a 'positive' way in the context of human rights protection, with emphasis on the element of actual redress rather than on the process of exhaustion. In this way one would look primarily for the underlying duties, rather than the underlying interests, in the operation of the rule. The complainant's duty to exhaust local remedies is thus counterbalanced by the State's duty to provide effective local redress.

A key role is thereby reserved to national courts in the application of the rule of exhaustion of local remedies in international law.[323] The operation of the local remedies rule, thus envisaged, in human rights protection need not be overwhelmed by difficulties (which might well result from confusing analogies with customary international law), for there is always the possibility of providing specific guidelines for that operation, particularly in a system still resting largely upon treaty obligations.[324] Moreover, with the growing experience of States and international organs in the field of human rights protection and the development of jurisprudence on the matter, it may well be that States become more often prepared not to insist on formal objections to admissibility of complaints, or at least not to press them so heavily as in the past. This process may be accelerated in certain areas where a general consensus can be discerned, such as, for example, in the elimination of acts and practices of racial discrimination.

The rationale of the local remedies rule, 'positively' approached in the present context, does not hinder a more flexible interpretation and application of the rule in the framework of human rights protection. It does not prevent international protection, it rather insists on local protection as part of the international system of human rights. Whether a more flexible approach of the local remedies rule has been followed, to what extent it has been followed, and how it could be pursued in the system of human rights protection, can be answered only by examining in detail the conditions and the extent of application of the local remedies rule in international human rights protection as compared to its application in general international law (Chs. 2 to 6, *infra*).

2

CONDITIONS FOR THE APPLICATION OF THE LOCAL REMEDIES RULE

Section A

Remedies to be exhausted

I. In general international law

One of the fundamental conditions for the application of the local remedies rule in international law is the determination of the local remedies to be exhausted. This is probably a direct result of the fact that under general international law the rule has been envisaged from an essentially formalistic point of view, with a consequent emphasis on existing local remedies and the individual's (the alien's) duty to exhaust them. This is not too surprising if one considers the rule as primarily an opportunity to the sovereign State to remedy the alleged wrong within the framework of its own internal legal system. Yet, speaking of 'local remedies to exhaust' presupposes the existence of those remedies, i.e., the counterpart duty of the State to provide them. This aspect of the problem seems, however, to have been somewhat overlooked by international practice and juridical activity on the subject.[1]

The expression 'local remedies to exhaust' ought thus to be regarded with caution and reservation, lest it convey the false impression that the *process of exhaustion* represents the essence of the operation of the local remedies rule in international law, thus blurring or obscuring the ultimate purpose and *raison d'être* of the rule, namely the fundamental element of *actual redress* for the wrong suffered. These preliminary words of caution are needed as a warning against the excesses of formalism in the administration of the rule. Yet an examination of its conditions of application will necessarily have to take into account the determination of the local remedies to be exhausted, as reflected in case-law, State practice and doctrine.

In general international law, it is implicit in the local remedies rule that the remedies to be exhausted include all those provided by municipal law[2] that may redress the alleged wrong, thus preventing diplomatic interposition. Such remedies must be practicable, accessible and available.[3] That the rule comprises all judicial as well as administrative remedies appears as a necessary implication of uniformity in the application of the rule, for while some countries have, in addition to ordinary courts, special administrative courts entrusted with the function of adjudicating complaints against the application of administrative law, in other countries those complaints are handled in the ordinary courts.[4] The scope of the rule thus comprises judicial and administrative remedies, i.e., all remedies of a legal nature exercisable before domestic courts performing their functions according to law. There is evidence in case-law that the remedies to be exhausted ought to be adequate[5] for the object of the claim. Likewise, local remedies must necessarily be effective in securing redress.[6] Such a test of effectiveness seems to dominate the discussion on extraordinary remedies,[7] shifting the focus of attention from the less relevant – for application of the rule – domestic law characterization of remedies as ordinary or extraordinary. Similarly, the test of essentialness of remedies seems to underlie the debate on procedural remedies.[8] That the local remedies rule is not simply a formal device of mechanical application is shown by the reliance on the standards of normal use of remedies, bearing in mind what a reasonable litigant would do in the use or exhaustion of legal means of redress at his disposal: it is normally accepted, for example, that the remedies to exhaust ought to offer fair prospects or a reasonable expectation of success.[9]

Local remedies are usually deemed to have been exhausted when a decision has been rendered (e.g., by the highest domestic court) which is final and without appeal.[10] In the process of exhaustion the conditions for the application of the local remedies rule do not necessarily appear in isolation from each other, and they may well in fact display a close interrelation with each other.[11] The emphasis laid by general international law on the claimant's duty to exhaust local remedies appears as a result of the preventive character of the local redress rule *vis-à-vis* the exercise of diplomatic protection, though it is clear that the rule conversely presupposes the State's international duty to provide local remedies. Emphasis on actual redress rather than on the process of exhaustion *per se* may apear even more imperative when fundamental human rights are at stake – a distinct context of application of the rule to which one may now turn.

II. In the practice of the European Commission of Human Rights

1 Introduction

After examining the question of the remedies to be exhausted as developed in general international law, one may now turn to an investigation of the same question in the light of the practice of the European Commission of Human Rights. This investigation will concentrate on the major problems involved in the determination of the remedies to be exhausted, before finally outlining the extent to which the practice of the Commission on the subject has to date conformed – or not – with that of other international organs and tribunals in general international law.

2. All available remedies

In the leading *Nielsen* v. *Denmark* case (1959) the Commission categorically stated that:

the rules governing the exhaustion of domestic remedies, as these are generally recognised today, in principle require that recourse should be had to all legal remedies available under the local law which are in principle capable of providing an effective and sufficient means of redressing the wrongs for which, on the international plane, the respondent State is alleged to be responsible.[12]

The *dictum* was taken up by the Commission two years later in the *X* v. *Ireland* case, where it held that, following its decision in the *Nielsen* case, the general principles governing the local remedies rule require that:

before the submission of a claim to an international tribunal, recourse should first have been had to all the legal remedies available under the local law which are capable of providing an effective and sufficient means of redressing the wrong which is the subject-matter of the international claim.[13]

Likewise, in the *Lawless* v. *Ireland* case (1958), the Commission asserted that 'the generally recognized rules of international law required the applicant to exhaust not merely the remedies in the ordinary courts but the whole system of legal remedies available in the Republic'.[14]

The Commission's adherence to these statements of principle was further confirmed by its decision in the *Syndicat National de la Police Belge* v. *Belgium* case (1971), where the Commission declared, *inter alia*, that:

aux fins d'application de l'article 26 de la Convention tout grief formulé devant elle à l'encontre d'une juridiction nationale inférieure doit avoir été invoqué auparavant, au moins en substance, devant la juridiction supérieure compétente. En effect, la règle de l'épuisement exige en principe, d'après les conceptions généralement reconnues en droit international, que soient utilisées toutes les ressources judiciaires offertes part la législation nationale, pourvu qu'elles se révèlent susceptibles de fournir un moyen vraisemblablement efficace et suffisant de redresser les griefs formulés, sur le plan international, contre l'État défendeur; il ne suffit donc pas qu'un requérant exerce les recours internes qui lui sont ouverts au sens dudit article, il doit également faire valoir devant l'autorité judiciaire supérieure les droits dont il allègue la violation.[15]

The Commission, thus recalling that under Article 26 of the Convention it may only deal with a matter after *all* domestic remedies have been exhausted, has on a great many occasions found that in the applications it examined there still were remedies to be exhausted; in the period extending from 1960 to 1974, one may refer to, for example, eighteen such decisions by the Commission in complaints brought against the Federal Republic of Germany,[16] thirteen decisions on applications lodged against the United Kingdom,[17] nine decisions on cases against Belgium,[18] seven decisions on complaints against Austria,[19] and further decisions concerning some other applications lodged against the Netherlands,[20] Sweden,[21] Luxembourg,[22] Denmark,[23] Norway,[24] and Ireland.[25]

The practice of the Commission therefore provides wide evidence in support of the view that under the European Convention on Human Rights an applicant is under the duty of previously exhausting *all* available and accessible local remedies. One may now turn to the qualifications following this broad statement of principle. In the *Austria* v. *Italy* case (1961), the Commission added, in respect of the application of the local remedies rule, that 'only the non-utilisation of an "essential" recourse for establishing the merits of a case before the municipal tribunals leads to non-admissibility of the international complaint'.[26] The Commission here introduced the indication of the 'essentialness' of the local remedies to be exhausted.

This notion was elaborated by the Commission in the *Boeckmans* v. *Belgium* case (1963) and in the *Kaiser* v. *Austria* case (1971): on both occasions the Commission, dwelling upon the question of the application of the local remedies rule, explained that 'le critère décisif à observer en la matière consiste à rechercher si le recours effectivement exercé offrait à la juridiction supérieure l'occasion d'examiner au moins en substance, et de redresser éventuellement, les violations imputées à la juridiction inférieure'.[27]

According to the practice of the Commission, the local remedies to be exhausted include all available and accessible remedies before the domestic *judicial* and *administrative* organs. In 1972 the Commission declared an application inadmissible because the applicant had failed to appeal to the Administrative Court of Appeal and had not, therefore, exhausted the remedies available to him under German law.[28] In the previous year, another application was rejected for non-exhaustion because the applicant was found not to have exhausted the remedies available to him under German law before the Administrative Courts.[29] The Commission had already indicated that such remedies could comprise recourse to administrative courts of different kinds: while, for example, in the *X* v. *Germany* case (1962) the application was rejected for non-exhaustion of local remedies before administrative courts (of first instance),[30] in the *X* v. *Ireland* case (1961) the Commission likewise rejected the complaint as inadmissible for failure of the applicant to have had previous recourse to an (administrative) Detention Commission.[31] And in an earlier case against Germany the Commission rejected the application for non-exhaustion of a remedy before the Federal Administrative Court (Bundesverwaltungsgericht).[32]

The Commission has thus clearly regarded the rule enshrined in Article 26 of the Convention as covering both judicial and administrative remedies. A member of the Commission (later its president), J.E.S. Fawcett, has proposed the following distinction between those two sorts of remedies:

Judicial remedies comprise proceedings taken in the courts including forms of appeal against their decisions. Administrative remedies, in their simplest form, cover recourse against acts of administration to higher authority in the administrative hierarchy, including perhaps the Minister himself; but more often they have a mixed character; there may be a comprehensive system of administrative courts, or special administrative tribunals or determination by a particular administrative body, which must itself act quasi-judicially or may be subject to control by proceedings in the ordinary courts.[33]

The inclusion of administrative remedies amongst the remedies to be exhausted comes as no surprise, bearing in mind not only the rationale of the local remedies rule (that of affording the State an opportunity of providing redress by its own means), but also the circumstance that many complaints are directed against administrative acts for which, on most occasions, there are no remedies available other than administrative remedies.[34] It is therefore not surprising to find the Commission requiring the exhaustion of remedies of jurisdictional character before administrative tribunals (including ordinary administrative jurisdiction as well as special administrative tribunals) and of non-jurisdictional remedies before administrative authorities (administrative remedies *stricto sensu*).[35]

Thus, *all* remedies of a judicial nature, whether they are exercisable before judicial or administrative organs, are to be exhausted. The requirement is understandable, particularly in view of the importance – perhaps growing – of administrative machinery in several countries. And in keeping with the guidelines of the practice of the Commission, the UN International Covenant on Civil and Political Rights states in Article 2(3)(b) that each State Party to the Covenant undertakes 'to ensure that any person claiming such a remedy [an effective remedy] shall have his right thereto determined by competent judicial, administrative or legislative authorities, or by any other competent authority provided for by the legal system of the State, and to develop the possibilities of judicial remedy'.[36] By the same token, administrative and other remedies which are non-judicial in character and of a discretionary nature normally fall outside the scope of application of the local remedies rule.

A striking illustration and authority for this view is found in the Commission's decision in the *De Becker* v. *Belgium* case (1958): the Commission found that in the case the applicant did not need to appeal to the Belgian *Cour de Cassation* against a judgment of the Brussels Military Tribunal, and, as to the possibility of an action for re-instatement (invoked by the Belgian government), the Commission declared that such an action 'does not seem to constitute an ordinary remedy to be exhausted according to the generally recognised rules of international law, since its purpose is to obtain a favour and not to vindicate a right'.[37]

One year earlier, in the *Greece* v. *United Kingdom* case (appl. n. 299/57, in respect of Cyprus), the Commission was faced with the United Kingdom's argument that in the case it was 'possible to address a demand for compensation by petition addressed either to the Governor of Cyprus, or to the Queen'[38] – to which the Commission replied that 'however, such a remedy, being a measure of grace, is not among those which must be exhausted by virtue of Article 26' of the

Convention.[39] And in the *X* v. *Belgium* case (1960) the Commission stated that the appeal for clemency in the case 'may not be taken into consideration for the application of Article 26 of the Convention because it is not a "remedy" within the meaning of that Article'.[40]

It is therefore clear that the remedies covered by the local redress rule are those of a *legal nature,* the characterization being that they should have their exercise governed by certain principles and according to law, ensuring impartiality and fairness in the examination of the case by the organ concerned. It may well be that the remedy is a 'special' one (see *infra,* pp. 89–94), that it is not available through the regular or ordinary courts of law, or that there is a rather limited discretion in its exercise; where local remedies are determinable and exercisable not according to law but on pure and arbitrary discretion, they need *not* be exhausted. Such remedies lack a judicial or legal nature, and fall outside the scope of application of the local remedies rule.

Expert writers have lent support to the criterion of the legal nature of the remedies to be exhausted embraced by the Commission, even though they have displayed some different views as to the exact importance of it. Amerasinghe, for example, deems the criterion of the judicial nature of the remedies to be of fundamental relevance for the very determination of the kinds of remedies encompassed by the local redress rule.[41] On the other hand, Danelius points out that:

the Commission does not find it necessary to define the concept of 'legal remedies', since, in any event, it has to distinguish between such legal remedies as have to be exhausted according to Article 26 and such other remedies as do not have to be exhausted. The Commission's primary concern is therefore to elaborate this distinction, and the question as to whether a certain action is a legal remedy or not is, generally speaking, of a merely theoretical interest.[42]

The full *extent* of the duty of exhaustion can be properly realized by surveying the numerous decisions of the Commission concerning different kinds of appeal to be exhausted. As remarked by Castberg, 'no State is obliged under the Convention to set up courts of appeal with competence to review decisions made by courts of first instance. However, if such instances of appeal exist, the applicant must take advantage of them before his case is dealt with in Strasbourg'.[43] The terminological equivalences found in English, French, and German are shown on p. 64.[44]

Appeal on fact, or on mixed fact and law	Appel	Berufung
Appeal on law	Pourvoi en cassation	Revision
Application for new trial	Révision	Wiederaufnahme des Verfahrens

Thus the Commission has on two occasions held that the applicants concerned had not exhausted the remedies available to them under Netherlands law for failure to appeal to the Appeal Council[45] and to the Court of Appeal[46] respectively. In another case the Commission declared an application inadmissible for non-exhaustion, as the applicant had not made use of the possibility of lodging a hierarchical appeal (*Dienstaufsichtbeschwerde*) to the president of the competent Court of Appeal, therefore not exhausting the remedies available to him under German law.[47] In the *X* v. *Sweden* case (1967) it was open to the applicant to appeal (from a decision of the Expropriation Court), to the Court of Appeal (and possibly, further on, to the Supreme Court), but as he failed to do so he was found not to have complied with the local remedies rule, and his application was declared inadmissible.[48] In the *Hopfinger* v. *Austria* case (1960) the applicant failed to lodge with the Supreme Court a *recours en annulation*, and part of his complaint was thereby rejected for non-exhaustion.[49] The same happened in the recent *X* v. *Belgium* case (1974), as the applicant had not brought his case either before the *officier van justitie* or – subsequently, if necessary – before the Gerechts-hof (Court of Appeal).[50]

In a complaint lodged against Austria, because the applicant had not exercised his right to appeal to a higher Court (against the rejection of his request that a medical expert should be called to give evidence during the proceedings before the Regional Court of Vienna), part of his application was rejected for non-compliance with the local remedies rule.[51] Similarly, in a case against Belgium, the applicant had his complaint rejected for failure to exercise his right of appeal.[52] In another case an application was rejected for non-exhaustion because the applicant had not taken up his case before the *Cour de Cassation*[53] in Belgium. Likewise, part of an application against Austria was rejected on the same ground, because the applicant had not pursued until the end his *appel* (*Berufung*) and his *pourvoi en cassation* (*Nichtigkeitsbeschwerde*).[54] In a decision of 1970, in the same line, the

Commission rejected another application for non-exhaustion of a *pourvoi en cassation*.[55] (But in the *De Becker* v. *Belgium* case, as already seen above, where the applicant had 'la faculté de se pourvoir en cassation' before the military court of Brussels, the Commission found that in the particularities of the case De Becker needed not exercise the remedy concerned before the *Cour de Cassation* and that the local remedies rule had in the case been duly complied with).[56]

In its recent decision (of 29 May 1974) in the *Monika Berberich* v. *F.R. Germany* case (the applicant's sole complaint being that the period of her detention on remand constituted a violation of Article 5(3) of the Convention), the Commission stated:

The term 'all remedies' in the text of this provision [Article 26 of the Convention] refers to the case where the domestic law provides against some measure or decision a single series of remedies at various levels, such as appeal to a court of appeal, further appeal to a supreme court and, possibly, a constitutional appeal. In such a case where there is a single remedy it should be pursued up to the highest level. The position is not so certain where the domestic law provides a number of different remedies. In such cases the Commission tends to admit that Article 26 has been complied with if the applicant exhausts only the remedy or remedies which are reasonably likely to prove effective.[57]

Having pointed this out, one may now turn to the next set of considerations concerning the local remedies to be exhausted.

3. Constitutional appeals

Attention should be drawn to the 'special' situation of appeals to a constitutional court in countries (parties to the Convention) where such organs exist: the Federal Republic of Germany and Austria. Very early in its life the Commission ruled that the constitutional appeal was a remedy to be exhausted. By 1959 the Commission had already formed a *jurisprudence constante* to that effect (in seven different decisions).[58] And in its decision of 8 January 1959 the Commission invoked its own *jurisprudence* in support of its view that 'il ressort expressément ou implicitement de cette jurisprudence que, dans les matières relevant de la compétence de la Cour Fédérale Constitution-nelle, le recours constitutionnel est un recours interne qui tombe en principe dans le champ d'application des dispositions de l'article 26 de la Convention'.[59]

In the fifteen years between 1960 and 1975, the Commission applied this principle systematically, and on several occasions the applicants' failure to appeal to the Constitutional Court in Austria or in the Federal Republic of Germany led the Commission to reject the applications as inadmissible on the ground of non-exhaustion of local remedies. Throughout this period, on no less than six occasions did the Commission declare inadmissible complaints lodged against Austria, for failure of the applicants to seize the Constitutional Court (*Verfassungsgerichtshof*), thereby not exhausting remedies available under Austrian law.[60] In one of those six decisions (dated 18 December 1967), the Commission observed that the applicant had in fact 'appealed against the decision of the town authorities to the ordinary courts and eventually to the Supreme Court [...] and thereby exhausted the remedies available before the ordinary courts', but – the Commission added categorically – 'this does not absolve him from pursuing the remedy available for an alleged breach of his human and constitutional rights by means of a direct appeal to the Constitutional Court within the time prescribed; [...] therefore, the condition as to the exhaustion of domestic remedies laid down in Articles 26 and 27(3) of the Convention has not been complied with by the applicants'.[61] The Commission added that its decision on the applicants' failure to exhaust local remedies 'is conclusive on the question of the admissibility of the application',[62] which was accordingly declared inadmissible. However, in one particular instance, the *Ringeisen* v. *Austria* case (1968), the Commission found otherwise: here the Commission held that the applicant needed not exhaust a remedy before the Austrian Constitutional Court (invoked by the Austrian government) on the ground that he did not have in that recourse an effective remedy with regard to a particular complaint.[63]

In the same period under consideration (1960–75) the examples of constitutional appeals to be exhausted in the Federal Republic of Germany in compliance with the local remedies rule under the Convention have been even more numerous. In the decade of the sixties one can refer to ten Commission decisions concerning constitutional appeals in Germany: of those, eight led to rejection of the applications for non-exhaustion of a constitutional appeal,[64] one to the Commission's assertion that the *right* of appeal to the Constitutional Court (claimed by the applicant) was 'not one included among the rights and freedoms guaranteed by the Convention',[65] and one to the Commission's statement that the applicant had not complied with the local remedies rule for failure to exercise a constitutional appeal after examining the possible circumstances that could have absolved him from the need to exhaust that remedy (the application being declared partly admissible).[66] As for the first half of the seventies (1970–75) one can refer to seven more decisions of the Commission touching on the need of exhaustion of constitutional appeals in Germany, six of which led to the inadmissibility of the complaints for non-exhaustion of that remedy[67] (one somewhat reluctantly)[68] and the seventh to the applicant – following information received from the Commission – making use of the constitutional appeal and the Commission accordingly restoring the application to its list of cases.[69] Therefore, there have been no fewer than seventeen such cases (concerning Germany)[70] in the Commission's practice in the period considered.[71]

A special case was that of *Retimag S.A.* v. *F.R. Germany* (1961). *Retimag* was a Swiss company holding properties in Germany whose confiscation (on the ground of their use for illegal purposes) had been ordered by the Federal Court of Justice (*Bundesgerichtshof*). *Retimag*, challenging the Federal Court's decision, argued that as a legal person it was entitled to compensation, since it was incapable of being held guilty of (or an accessory to) a criminal offence.[72] The German government raised an objection of non-exhaustion by *Retimag* of the remedy of constitutional appeal.[73] The applicant, on the other hand, contended that it had in fact exhausted local remedies and raised the problem whether a *foreign* corporate body (or other legal person) was entitled to lodge such a constitutional appeal.[74] In its decision of 16 December 1961, the Commission stated that this was:

une question de droit constitutionnel allemand sur laquelle la Cour Fédérale Constitutionnelle allemande a en principe compétence pour se prononcer; [...] il n'appartient pas à la Commission de statuer sur cette question non encore décidée en droit allemand, mais [...] elle doit se borner à constater que la requérante n'a pas clairement établi qu'il ne lui était pas possible de saisir la Cour Constitutionnelle.[75]

In the same decision the Commission further stated that 's'il existe un doute quant à la question de savoir si une voie de recours déterminée peut être ou non de nature à offrir une chance réelle de succès, c'est là un point qui doit être soumis aux tribunaux internes eux-mêmes, avant tout appel au tribunal international'.[76] The position on this last point, of which the rigour is questionable, has been reiterated in other cases.[77]

But it seems exaggerated, if not contrary to the spirit and purposes of the Convention, to leave this matter to the ultimate determination of domestic courts, rather than to the Commission itself. This seems to be an additional obstacle or difficulty for the applicant, who is already under the duty of exhausting all remedies up to the Constitutional Court. This process in itself may prove to be not only costly, but also very time-consuming. But the Commission, as seen *supra*, pp. 65–6, early and readily assumed that a remedy before the Constitutional Court should be exhausted as well. The question thereby acquired constitutional aspects, and assumed relevance to the very relationship between international law and municipal law.

Yet, the excesses which this practice of the Commission may lead to can be more clearly realized in countries with a federal system, and with a highly structured hierarchy of judicial organs, like the Federal Republic of Germany. In certain cases this may aggravate the already inherent difficulty of applying the local remedies rule in cases concerning less justiciable matters (e.g., freedom of information, ill-treatment, and so forth): the applicant must indeed be strongly determined (and have the (material) means to be so) to pursue his appeals until the final stage before the constitutional instance. The question is to some extent intermingled with that of the role played by the criterion of *effectiveness* in the determination of the local remedies to be exhausted (a problem dealt with *infra*, pp. 71–80). But in most cases under the present category, as seen above, constitutional appeals were held to fall within the scope of the local remedies rule, and their non-exhaustion led to the inadmissibility and rejection of the application.

A working-paper released by the Directorate of Human Rights of the Council of Europe on 13 January 1964 observed that, following the Commission's decision of 17 March 1957,[78] it was understood that 'si, dans un État fédéral, le système judiciaire comporte, à côté de la Cour Constitutionnelle Fédérale, une Cour Constitutionnelle dans un des États fédérés, compétentes toutes deux pour examiner le grief du requérant, celui-ci doit s'addresser à l'une et à l'autre'.[79] In fact, this happened in the *Nazih-Al-Kuzbari* v. *F.R. Germany* cases (1963), where the applicant's lawyer lodged constitutional appeals at the Federal Constitutional Court *as well as* at the Bavarian Constitutional Court (in Munich).[80]

Among writers, there has been some reaction to this feature of the practice of the Commission, expressed in brief comments of disapproval.[81] This is not so surprising. This *concurrent* exercise of constitutional appeals before the Federal Constitutional Court *and* the Constitutional Court of the State of the Federation makes of the local remedies rule a severe requirement. By ascribing to the rule such an extensive interpretation, the Commission paves the way for an application which, rather than following a balanced approach according to the generally recognised rules of international law to which Article 26 refers, shows itself as impractical and cumbersome, envisaging the rule as a somewhat formal and mechanical condition of admissibility of international claims.

4. Remedies adequate for the object of the claim

It goes almost without saying that the remedies to be exhausted include those which are adequate for the object of the claim. One of the earliest and most illustrative cases of the condition of *adequacy* of the remedies to be exhausted is the *Lawless* v. *Ireland* case (1958). The applicant at first claimed for his release (from an internment camp) as well as compensation and damages; later on he stated that, notwithstanding his release, he wished to maintain his application with respect to the claim for compensation and damages. The Commission found that in such conditions the right of recourse to the Internment Commission was 'not an effective domestic remedy with respect to the applicant's demand for compensation and damages',[82] as the Internment Commission was entitled only to recommend his release, and not to grant compensation and damages.

In another (unpublished) decision delivered in that same year, the Commission was of the view that 'lorsqu'un requérant condamné considère que le rejet de sa demande en révision de son procès constitue une violation de la Convention, il doit, avant de saisir la Commission, introduire le recours, s'il en existe un, contre la décision de rejet'.[83] On another occasion, in the *X* v. *F.R. Germany* case (1958), the applicant's lawyer complained that the Public Prosecutor had submitted to the judges dealing with the case, without notifying the applicant or his representative, documents containing unfavourable secret information respecting the applicant, in what constituted – he contended – a 'flagrant violation of the rights of the defence'.[84] The Commission held that it was incumbent upon the applicant to lodge a disciplinary action (*Dienstaufsichtsbeschwerde*) with regard to the submission by the Public Prosecutor of the unfavourable secret information which he had no opportunity to see or contest;[85] but as he failed to do so, he was held not to have satisfied the condition of exhaustion of local remedies, and this led to the inadmissibility of his application.

The question of the *adequacy* of the local remedies to be exhausted again came to the fore in two subsequent decisions on applications directed against Sweden. In the first of these cases (1964), the applicant had on several occasions lodged petitions for the re-opening of the proceedings, but the Commission held that such petitions were not in the case, under Swedish law, 'effective and sufficient remedies' falling under the scope of the local remedies rule, and could not therefore be taken into consideration. Thus the final decision regarding the applicant's civil actions was rather a decision rendered by the Supreme Court (in 1956).[86] In the second case (1970), the applicant had attempted to obtain a review of his dismissal from his post, either by challenging before the Supreme Administrative Court an initial decision (of 1968) of the Court of Appeal, or by his appeals and complaints to the King-in-Council and Supreme Court respectively.[87] The Commission, however, ruled that 'such proceedings could not have rectified the wrong of which he now complains and therefore cannot be considered as in any way being equivalent remedies to a duly lodged appeal to the Supreme Administrative Court such as would, under international law, relieve him from the obligations of making such appeal'.[88] And with regard in particular to the applicant's application to the Supreme Administrative Court for a re-opening of the proceedings or a *restitutio in integrum*, the Commission once again found that such remedies 'could not be regarded as effective and sufficient remedies as the proceedings relating to these remedies do not, until successful, affect the validity of the final decision impugned'.[89] Accordingly, the Commission held that the condition as to the exhaustion of domestic remedies was not complied with by the applicant.[90]

More recently, in the *X* v. *Austria* case (1971), the Commission was seized of a case in which the domestic courts had declared that 'les mesures incriminées par le requérant ne constituent pas une expropriation, mais une limitation de la propriété'[91] according to provisions of municipal law. The matter had in fact been taken up to the Austrian Supreme Court. After examining the elements of the case, the Commission found that:

la procédure non contentieuse que le requérant a intentée après l'arrêt du juin 1966 [de la Cour Suprême] n'était pas pertinente en l'espèce étant donné que dans la procédure antérieure les tribunaux avaient constaté que les mesures dont se plaint le requérant ne constituaient pas une expropriation. Ceci a été d'ailleurs confirmé par le tribunal de district de Z. devant lequel le requérant intenta la procédure en question. Cette procédure n'était donc pas nécessaire pour satisfaire à la condition de l'épuisement des voies de recours internes.[92]

5. Effective remedies

The remedies to be exhausted ought to be effective: this is one of the most salient features of the practice of the Commission concerning the rule of exhaustion of local remedies. This condition has also attracted the attention of expert writers, one of whom expressed its importance in the following terms:

La jurisprudence de la Commission en ce qui concerne les voies de recours internes exigibles avant de se porter devant la Commission est dominée par la notion d'efficacité. Elle peut se résumer de la façon suivante: tout recours interne prévu par la loi doit être épuisé à condition qu'il soit efficace et suffisant. Dans chaque cas d'espèce, la Commission recherche cette efficacité, exigeant ou négligeant tel recours ou telle action prévus par la loi. La notion d'efficacité suppose un examen plus approfondi que celui de la simple recevabilité d'une requête.[93]

The Commission's examination of this condition in each *cas d'espèce* is illustrative of the difficulties surrounding the determination of effectiveness. It is intuitive that an *a priori* criterion would prove unworkable here. That determination, it seems, can only be properly carried out by a thorough investigation of the circumstances and factors accompanying each application. This investigation may at times lead to a certain approach to the merits of the case[94] at the stage of examination of the condition of exhaustion of local remedies.

The problem of the determination of effectiveness of local remedies was the object of some attention at a recent colloquium, where one of the members of the Commission, F. Ermacora, characterizing the local redress rule as 'the major concession to the sovereignty of States', observed:

L'expérience montre que l'application de cette règle doit être determinée selon les circonstances de chaque cas concret et la jurisprudence de la Commission enseigne que cette application connaît beaucoup de nuances. Un élément décisif est de savoir si un recours interne est effectif ou non. Pour répondre à cette question il faut non seulement soigneusement examiner le cas concret, mais aussi connaître la situation politico-juridique, pour apprécier si un recours peut être considéré comme effectif dans une situation d'espèce.[95]

On the other hand, one need not delve into an excessive relativism as to the determination of the effective remedies to be exhausted, which may well lead to scepticism towards the whole matter. Attempts have in fact been made to single out certain factors or situations conducive to the characterization of remedies as ineffective, for example, when the organ seized of the complaint lacks the power to grant the claimant the relief or damages sought, when the appellate system lacks the power to review the errors allegedly committed in the lower courts, or when the complainant is for various reasons prevented from having recourse to the remedies.[96] The question of the effectiveness of local remedies is therefore intrinsically connected with the judicial organization and the operation of the organs capable of affording proper means of redress in the country concerned. Thus it is possible that one specific remedy which exists in different countries with similar judicial systems may prove effective in one country and ineffective in another. Likewise, one and the same remedy in a specific country may prove effective in a certain period and ineffective in another period in that same country (e.g., in times of crisis, emergency or exceptional measures, and so forth). Remedies may be subject to spatial as well as temporal contingencies.

So there does not seem to be any simple answer to the problem of effectiveness of local remedies. Yet it remains a key condition in the application of the local remedies rule. The effectiveness of remedies may be properly examined in the light of the circumstances of the *cas d'espèce*, the problem involved being basically not a uniform one. That examination may at once encounter difficulties, for the applicant may complain against the respondent State 'in highly different capacities, e.g., as a defendant in criminal trials, as user of utilities, as taxpayer, as owner of property; and the same means of legal protection is not always suitable for all of these legal relationship'.[97] There are distinct ways whereby the effectiveness of local remedies may be placed in question: for example, when proceedings are too long, when the relief to be afforded is insufficient or inadequate for redressing the situation complained of, when domestic courts are not independent of executive interference,[98] and so forth.

Because the ascertainment of the effectiveness of local remedies cannot be undertaken by abstract criteria, but only by an examination of the practical conditions of application of those remedies within the framework of the domestic legal system at issue, it is clear that a comparative study of local remedies for individual protection in the various national legal systems would provide useful material for such an examination. It would, for example, render it possible, in

Jaenicke's observation, 'to develop objective standards for evaluating the practical effectiveness of a legal remedy, i.e., for judging whether and to what extent a legal remedy will normally compel the executive to comply with the rules prescribed for its conduct'.[99] When the term 'effective remedy' is enshrined in a treaty, as in Article 13 of the European Convention on Human Rights, it seems also possible and valid to attempt to identify the component elements of the term, within the context and scope of the Convention.

In this connection it has been proposed at another colloquium that the expression 'effective remedy', under Article 13 of the European Convention, comprises, for the person concerned:

the right to obtain information concerning an interference with his fundamental freedoms since if this condition is not fulfilled his right to a remedy is meaningless from the beginning; – the right to bring his case before an authority which is legally in a position to provide him with effective redress; – the possibility to reply to the statements of fact and arguments of law put forward by the opposing party.[100]

Recently an attempt was made to extend the question of the effectiveness of the remedies to be exhausted to the very contents of the complaint: it was suggested that one and the same remedy may show itself as effective or ineffective depending on which juridical argument the complaint is based upon.[101] This view seems untenable: of course an applicant stands in a better position if he has a thorough knowledge of the remedies open to him in a given country, and better still if he has the kind of expert assistance as to enable him to draft his application in proper and adequate language. This is, however, far from being the most frequent case in the numerous complaints brought before the Commission. The chances of success of an application will certainly vary accordingly. But it is one thing to question the effectiveness of remedies, and another to question whether the complaint itself is or is not well-founded.[102] After all, 'non-exhaustion of local remedies' and 'manifestly ill-founded' are two distinct grounds of inadmissibility of applications under the Convention.

The Commission itself espoused this view in the *23 Inhabitants of Alsemberg and of Beersel* v. *Belgium* case (1963), where it stated that:

la Commission relève en outre que, pour se prononcer sur le caractère 'vraisemblablement efficace et suffisant' du recours en question, elle ne peut apprécier le bien-fondé de l'argumentation des requérants [...]; à ce stade de la procédure, elle doit accepter l'exactitude de cette argumentation, à titre strictement provisoire et comme une pure hypothèse de travail.[103]

The Commission had earlier taken the same view in the *X and Y* v. *Belgium* case (1963),[104] in language reminiscent of arbitrator Bagge's words in his award in the *Finnish Vessels* case (*supra*).[105]

For the purposes of the application of the local redress rule under the Convention, what counts as a remedy is thus 'a question of substance, not of form. On the one hand, a remedy which is formally open to the applicant does not have to be exhausted if there is no prospect of its giving him satisfaction. On the other hand, there is no formal limit to what counts as a remedy, if it is capable of giving satisfaction as of right.[106]

If a remedy is *likely* to be an effective means of redressing the grievances in question, it ought to be resorted to. Such was the Commission's view in the *Austria* v. *Italy* case (1961), where it declared that 'the rule of local redress confines itself to imposing the normal use of remedies likely to be effective and adequate'.[107] This ruling inspired the Commission in subsequent decisions. In the *X* v. *United Kingdom* case (1970), for example, where the Commission itself admitted that 'there might arise doubts as regards the effectiveness of an appeal to the Court of Appeal',[108] it went on to state:

The exhaustion of a given domestic remedy does not normally cease to be necessary, according to the generally recognised rules of international law, unless the applicant can show that, in these particular circumstances, this remedy was unlikely to be effective; [. . .] furthermore, it is established under international law that if there is any doubt as to whether a given remedy is or is not intrinsically able to offer a real chance of success, that is a point which must be submitted to the domestic courts themselves before any appeal can be made to the international court.[109]

In the *Gussenbauer* v. *Austria* case (1972 – see also *infra*, pp. 85–6), the Commission asserted that, since the remedies to be exhausted comprise 'the entire system of legal protection established by the *corpus* of municipal law', the fact that no appeal in a formal sense was open to the applicant 'does not necessarily mean that the applicant did not have at his disposal a remedy which required to be exhausted'.[110] In the case, the possibility that counsel could request his release from his obligations as a legal aid counsel was found by the Commission to constitute 'a remedy which theoretically might provide an effective and sufficient means of redressing the alleged wrong' complained of.[111] The Commission added that 'the rule of local redress confines itself to imposing on the applicant the normal use of remedies likely to be effective, and [. . .] the exhaustion of a given remedy ceases to be necessary if the applicant can show that in the particular circumstances this remedy was unlikely to be effective and adequate in regard to the grievances in question.[112] (Reference could be made to other illustrative decisions of the Commission.)[113]

Having pointed this out, one may now turn to the practice of the Commission, in which it found remedies to be either effective or ineffective, without considering margins of doubt. There have in fact been some cases where the Commission reached the conclusion that the remedies at issue were *effective*, thereby falling under the scope of application of the local redress rule. Thus, in the X v. *Ireland* case (1961), the Commission found that 'application to the Detention Commission was a legal remedy which offered to the applicant in the present case an effective means of establishing promptly after his arrest the absence of any reasonable grounds for his detention without trial under the 1940 Act and of securing his early release from detention'.[114] (The Commission reached this decision in the light of the facts and circumstances of the case, as in the previous *Lawless* v. *Ireland* case it had found otherwise that recourse to the Detention Commission 'was not an effective domestic remedy with respect to the applicant's demand for compensation and damages' – cf. *supra*, p. 69.)[115] And in the subsequent X v. *Ireland* case (1971) the Commission held that the remedy in question was an effective remedy in respect of the matters complained of.[116]

Again, in 1972, the Commission declared that 'all domestic remedies must be exhausted which appear to be capable of providing an effective and sufficient means of redress for the alleged wrong',[117] and the exhaustion of a given remedy only ceases to be necessary if it is shown that the remedy was 'unlikely to be effective';[118] in the case before it, the Commission found that 'a request for the application for leave to appeal to be restored to the list was an effective remedy which, in principle, required to be exhausted under Article 26 of the Convention'.[119] In two further decisions in that same year, the Commission found that an action before the Labour Court in Sweden,[120] and an appeal to the Court of Appeal in the Netherlands[121] were both effective remedies for the purposes of the application of the local redress rule under the Convention.

There is, on the other hand, a considerable body of case-law of the Commission declaring certain remedies *ineffective*, for the purposes of application of the local remedies rule. Thus, on different occasions, the Commission has ruled that, *in the circumstances of the cases at issue*, a *pourvoi en cassation* before the Supreme Court (in Austria),[122] a petition to the Home Secretary (in the United Kingdom),[123] an appeal of the Court of Appeal (in the United Kingdom),[124] appeal proceedings before the Bavarian Constitutional Court (in Germany),[125] and a *recours en annulation* (in Belgium),[126] did not constitute effective remedies (remedies capable of providing effective redress in the cases at issue), and thereby needed not be exhausted, the local redress rule having thus been complied with.

Likewise, in a case concerning an application for an order of *habeas corpus*, the Commission found, upon examination *ex officio* of the matter, that the situation in question appeared to exclude any chance of success of such an application for a *habeas corpus* order: accordingly, the Commission ruled that the complaints at issue were not to be rejected on the ground of non-exhaustion of local remedies.[127] In fact, the question of the ineffectiveness of remedies is intermingled with that of the unlikelihood of success in the pursuance of the remedies (a point dealt with *infra*, pp. 94–7). Local remedies will thus be ineffective if there is a *jurisprudence constante* against the result sought by the applicant before the domestic courts; as early as 31 May 1956, the Commission maintained that a *jurisprudence bien établie* may constitute a particular circumstance absolving the applicant from the duty under Article 26 of the Convention of exhausting a remedy before the Federal Constitutional Court of Justice (*Bundesverfassungsgericht*) in the Federal Republic of Germany,[128] a decision later re-taken by the Commission (9 March 1962), when it found that in the case at issue there was clear legal precedent whereby the applicants' endeavours seemed doomed to failure.[129] Similarly, in the *X* v. *Austria* case (1960), the Commission stated that:

il n'est pas nécessaire de recourir aux tribunaux internes si le résultat doit être la répétition d'une décision déjà rendue; [...] en l'espèce, comme la situation n'a pas été modifiée par un fait nouveau, les décisions rendues ne font que reprendre les jugements prononcés à la suite de la première demande.[130]

Later, in the *Ringeisen* v. *Austria* case (1968), the Commission observed that the local redress rule encompassed 'remedies which seem effective and sufficient' and, further, that 'remedies which do not offer a possibility of redressing the alleged damage cannot be regarded as effective or sufficient and there is, therefore, no need for them to be exhausted according to the generally recognised principles of international law'.[131] After examining the recent jurisprudence of the

Austrian Constitutional Court on that Court's interpretation of Article 6(1) of the Convention, the Commission remarked that 'the Constitutional Court considered itself as being the proper tribunal having competence to review decisions taken by administrative authorities'; and as 'under Austrian law, there is no possibility of appeal against decisions of the Constitutional Court, [...] it follows that in the present case, even if the applicant had invoked Article 6(1) by alleging that he had been denied access to a tribunal, he would not have been heard on this submission; [...] therefore, he did not have an effective remedy with regard to his aforesaid complaint'.[132]

In the *Neumeister* v. *Austria* case (1964) the Commission again held that 'it was not necessary to have recourse to domestic tribunals if the result must inevitably be the repetition of a decision already pronounced';[133] in the circumstances of the case, the Commission added, the remedy at issue – a renewed request for release on bail – 'cannot be considered an effective and sufficient remedy which under Article 26 of the Convention was bound to be exhausted by the applicant'.[134] And in the *Isop* v. *Austria* case (1962), the Commission declared that 'it would in no way have been an effective remedy for the applicant to invoke Article 6 [of the Convention] in proceedings before the Austrian courts', because earlier, on 27 June 1960, the Austrian Constitutional Court itself had expressly held that:

the lack of precision of certain notions contained in Article 6 which is to be compared with a detailed judicial system of civil procedure and criminal procedure, leads to the idea that Article 6 contains only a declaration of principles which the legislator certainly must carry out and respect, but which in themselves do not constitute immediately applicable rights.[135]

For this reason, the Commission found that under Article 26 of the Convention the applicant was not obliged to invoke Article 6 of the Convention in proceedings before the Austrian courts, before introducing his application to the Commission.[136]

In the *Kornmann* v. *F.R. Germany* case (1966), the Commission indicated that when an applicant, in exhausting remedies, finds it impossible to prove before the authorities concerned certain allegations which are fundamental to the success of his application, this factor creates a presumption to the effect that those remedies had no chance of giving the applicant satisfaction and, therefore, 'cannot be considered as sufficient or effective in the circumstances of the present case and the applicant was not obliged to exhaust them in order to comply with Article 26 of the Convention'.[137] Reference could be made to other decisions where the Commission found the remedies at issue to be ineffective.[138]

The problem of the ineffectiveness of remedies came to the fore in complaints lodged with the Commission by some Danish citizens against their government concerning the introduction (through the 1970 Act) of the system of compulsory sex education in Danish public schools. The complainants deemed that this measure infringed Article 2 of Protocol n. 1 to the Convention, which provides for the parents' right to have children educated in conformity with their religious and philosophical convictions. After examining those complaints – in the *Kjeldsen* v. *Denmark* case (1972) as well as the *Pedersen* v. *Denmark* case (1973) – the Commission concluded *inter alia* that 'there was no effective remedy available with regard to the provisions of the 1970 Act embodying the principle of compulsory sex education';[139] it followed that, *in that respect*, the applications could not be rejected as inadmissible under Article 26 of the Convention.

When for one reason or another the complainant is prevented from having recourse to domestic remedies, these latter may well be held ineffective so as to fall outside the scope of the local redress rule. In fact, in the *Greece* v. *United Kingdom* case (1957) in respect of Cyprus (the so-called 'second Cyprus case'), the Commission found that the applicant had established that the respondent had displayed 'no readiness' to indicate the names of the perpetrators of the alleged ill-treatment, despite an express request for such information: consequently, because of this absence of identity of the accused, the alleged victims did not institute civil or criminal proceedings against them; but where some of the perpetrators of ill-treatment had already been identified, the Commission stated that the local remedies ought first to have been exhausted.[140]

Later, in the *Denmark/Norway/Sweden/Netherlands* v. *Greece* case (1968), the Commission faced a situation where, for example, administrative authorities were under the control of the government and a number of constitutional guarantees relating to the institution and functioning of the ordinary courts and to the procedural rights of individuals had been suspended for an indefinite period of time; the Commission was thus led to the conclusion that in that particular situation at that time the local remedies indicated by the respondent government could not be considered as effective and sufficient.[141] More recently the Commission again remarked, in another case, that in cases of an alleged administrative practice of ill-treatment incompatible with the Convention, local remedies tend to be rendered ineffective (e.g., difficulty of securing probative evidence).[142]

Undue or excessive slowness or delays in the procedure may well render a remedy ineffective for the purposes of the application of the local redress rule (not to speak of the six-month rule enshrined in Article 26 of the Convention). Thus, in the *De Becker* v. *Belgium* case (1958), the Commission held that an *action en réhabilitation* under Belgian law did not seem to constitute an ordinary remedy to be exhausted, because *inter alia* it could not be taken until five years after the claimant's final release, thus proving in any event inadequate in the case.[143] But shortly afterwards the Commission warned in another case that the applicant's subjective appreciation as to the alleged excessive slowness of a particular remedy was immaterial to its own decision on the matter:

en ce qui concerne les allégations du requérant relatives à la lenteur de la procédure devant la Cour Fédérale Constitutionnelle, les deux exemples cités par lui ne sauraient, de l'avis de la Commission, être considérés comme preuves d'une lenteur excessive permettant à la Commission de conclure que le recours constitutionnel doit être tenu pour inefficace ou insuffisant selon les principes de droit international généralement reconnus et applicables à l'épuisement des voies de recours internes; [...] il s'ensuit que le requérant n'a pas établi que la prétendue lenteur de la procédure constitue une circonstance particulière le relevant de l'obligation d'épuiser le recours constitutionnel, conformément aux principes de droit international généralement reconnus.[144]

Such was the Commission's finding in the case. Rather than specifying the length of delay to render remedies ineffective, the Commission seemingly preferred to leave this point to the examination of the circumstances involving each particular case.

In a series of decisions, the Commission indicated that certain domestic remedies were ineffective in the circumstances of the cases at issue. Thus, in the *Becker* v. *Denmark* case (1975), the Commission held that where a breach of the Convention could be brought about by putting into effect a measure for a person's removal from a State's territory, a court action without suspensive effect could not be considered as effective.[145] Similarly, in another case, the Commission held that if an individual claimed that the execution of an expulsion measure taken against him might violate the Convention, a remedy without suspensive effect would be ineffective.[146] On yet another occasion, the Commission maintained that in the absence of a reaction by the competent authorities to an appeal against detention on remand, a hierarchical complaint to a higher court (*Aufsichts-beschwerde*) could not be considered as an effective remedy to secure release from detention on remand.[147]

Not so categorically, the Commission held in the *De Weer* v. *Belgium* case (1977) that in proceedings instituted for the prosecution of an infringement of price regulations, an appeal aiming at the annulment of the decree on which the offence is based would not appear to constitute an effective and adequate remedy.[148] In the *Ph. Agee* v. *United Kingdom* case (1976),[149] the Commission stated *inter alia* that neither the request to an authority to reconsider a decision taken by it, nor the representations to a body of an advisory character could be considered as effective remedies.[150]

Not only the Commission, but also the European Court of Human Rights, have pronounced on the requirement of effectiveness of the remedies to be exhausted. In its judgment of 10 November 1969 on the *Stögmüller* v. *Austria* case, the Court remarked that 'international law, to which Article 26 refers explicitly, is far from conferring on the rule of exhaustion the inflexible character which the government seems to attribute to it. International law only imposes the use of the remedies which are not only available to the persons concerned but are also sufficient, that is capable of redressing their complaints.'[151] And shortly afterwards, in its judgment of 18 June 1971 in the '*Vagrancy*' cases, the Court again recalled that 'under international law, to which Article 26 makes express reference, the rule of exhaustion of domestic remedies demands the use only of such remedies as are available to the persons concerned and are sufficient, that is to say capable of providing redress for their complaints'.[152]

6. Substance of the complaint to be raised before domestic courts

The Commission has strictly and consistently applied the principle that the substance of a complaint ought to be raised before the domestic courts prior to its being raised on the international level before the Commission itself. The principle is in keeping with the rationale of the local redress rule (i.e., granting the respondent State the opportunity of redressing the alleged wrong through its own domestic legal system), and it indicates the full extent of the duty of exhaustion of local remedies prior to international action. Here, once again, the principle is reminiscent of arbitrator Bagge's *dictum* in the *Finnish Vessels* case (*supra*, pp. 57–8) that 'all the contentions of fact and propositions of law which are brought forward by the claimant government [...] must have been investigated and adjudicated upon by the municipal courts up to the last competent instance'.[153] Whether these courts have or have not thoroughly examined those contentions is immaterial, the test remaining that the substance of the complaint ought first to have been submitted at full length before domestic courts.

The Commission adhered to this principle early in its life.[154] On one particular occasion the applicant complained before the Commission that the proceedings before a Regional Court (*Landgericht*) in Germany had allegedly been conducted in a manner which constituted a violation of certain provisions of the Convention. He had not, however, raised the issue on appeal before the Federal Court (*Bundesgerichtshof*).[155] For this reason the Commission concluded that he had not complied with the local remedies rule laid down in Article 26 of the Convention, and, accordingly, his application was declared inadmissible.[156] Another application was rejected on the same ground in 1962, since the applicant had not submitted all the points of his complaint first to a *tribunal correctionnel*, then to a court of appeal and at last to the *Cour de Cassation* (in Belgium).[157]

Later, in the *X* v. *Austria* case (1968), the Commission declared that:

the mere fact that the applicant has, in pursuance of Article 26, submitted his case to the various competent courts does not constitute compliance with this rule; [...] it is also required that any complaint made before the Commission and relating to lower courts or authorities should have been substantially raised before the competent higher court or authority.[158]

In the present case, the applicant had seemingly not availed himself of the possibility, in his plea of nullity and appeal to the Austrian Supreme Court, of invoking his right to a fair hearing and, in this connection, of relying upon the relevant provisions in domestic law (including possibly Article 6 of the Convention).[159] For that reason his application was declared inadmissible for non-compliance with the local remedies rule.[160]

The principle was again applied by the Commission in the *Samer* v. *F.R. Germany* case (1971), where the applicant had in fact submitted his case to the Federal Court and the Federal Constitutional Court, but had not raised in the proceedings before this latter one question concerning his commercial transactions; it followed that he had 'to that extent failed to exhaust a remedy which was available to him under German law'.[161] And in the *X* v. *Belgium* case (1972), the application was likewise rejected for non-exhaustion of domestic remedies, as the applicant had not raised either in form or in substance, in the proceedings before the Court of Appeal (at Ghent) or subsequently in the cassation proceedings before the Supreme Court, the complaints made before the Commission.[162]

In the *Kamma* v. *Netherlands* case (1972), a district court had been called upon to decide issues 'substantially different' from those raised by an appeal to the Court of Appeal (in the Netherlands) against a decision that detention on remand should be ordered or that such detention should continue.[163] The Commission therefore declared that in respect of that complaint it could not be said that the applicant had in fact exhausted domestic remedies.[164] More recently, in the *X* v. *Austria* case (1973), the Commission, referring to its *jurisprudence constante* on the problem at issue, affirmed that the local remedies rule 'requires the applicant to raise, in the appeals' proceedings before the national court, the substance of any complaint subsequently made before the Commission'.[165] Because in the case the applicant was found not to have raised, either in form or in substance, in the proceedings before the Austrian Supreme Court, the complaint which he then brought before the Commission, this latter ruled that his complaint should be rejected for his failure to comply with the condition as to the exhaustion of domestic remedies.[166] Reference could be made to other such decisions of the Commission.[167]

In one particular case (the *Ringeisen* v. *Austria* case, 1968), however, the Commission found that the applicant had in fact exhausted all remedies available to him under Austrian law. The decision read *inter alia* that:

'the Commission has consistently held that the mere fact that the applicant has, in pursuance of Article 26, submitted his case to the various competent courts does not constitute compliance with this rule, but that it is also required that any complaint made before the Commission and relating to lower courts or authorities should have been substantially raised before the competent higher court or authority.[168]

An examination of the case, however, disclosed that, in respect of one complaint, the applicant had in fact brought the issues (under Article 6(1) of the Convention) in substance before the Constitutional Court, and that it was this latter that had refused on formal legal grounds to deal with the question; in this way, the Commission ruled that the applicant had exhausted all remedies available to him under Austrian law according to the generally recognised principles of international law.[169]

It may be asked whether an applicant may be excused from raising a particular issue before the domestic courts, relying upon the duty of those courts to examine that issue *ex officio*. This problem was raised in two cases concerning Belgium. In the *X* v. *Belgium* case (1967) the applicant complained of the refusal of a Court of Appeal to hear a certain witness, even though he did not raise that particular point in his *pourvoi en cassation* before the *Cour de Cassation*, which was under the duty of examining the issue (respect for the rights of defence) *ex officio*. In spite of this, the Commission ruled that by his failure to raise the point before the *Cour de Cassation* the applicant had not exhausted local remedies, and his application was thereby declared inadmissible.[170] But in the *Delcourt* v. *Belgium* case, in the same year, the Commission rendered a different decision: here the applicant complained that he had not had the assistance of an interpreter (as he did not know the Flemish language) in proceedings before the Court of Bruges (first instance) as well as before the Court of Appeal of Ghent. Although the applicant did not raise this particular point in his appeal to the *Cour de Cassation*, which was under the duty of dealing with the question *ex officio*, the Commission this time did not declare the application inadmissible for non-exhaustion, but rather preferred to state that it was not prepared at that stage to tackle the question.[171] This decision was rendered on 7 February 1967; shortly afterwards, the *Delcourt* v. *Belgium* case came again before the Commission, which again considered the issue (the complaint concerning the lack of free assistance of an interpreter). This time the Commission rejected that complaint under the local remedies rule, despite the duty to act *ex officio* of the domestic courts, because the applicant was found not to have raised the issue either in first instance, or on appeal, or in cassation.[172]

This position was confirmed by another decision of the Commission, in the *X* v. *Norway* case (1964). The applicant had not raised in her appeal to the Norwegian Supreme Court the complaint which she then brought before the Commission, namely that the decision of the City Court (of Oslo) had not been handed down in public session, allegedly in violation of the Convention. The fact that the applicant had raised *other* questions in her appeal, and the competence of the Supreme Court to take up the question *ex officio*, were both immaterial; the Commission stated that:

in order to comply with the provisions of Article 26 it is not enough that the applicant should have submitted her case to the various competent courts to which, as requested by the said Article, the case should be referred – the applicant should also plead before the higher court the rights which she alleges were violated by the lower court.[173]

Her application was accordingly rejected for non-exhaustion of the remedies available to her under Norwegian law.[174]

The general trend on the present problem is thus discernible. Despite some hesitation or reluctance displayed in the *Delcourt* case (first decision), the practice of the Commission affords sufficient evidence to corroborate the following proposition: a cautious applicant should not identify in the duty of domestic courts to investigate matters *ex officio* a factor relieving him of the obligation to raise the issues of his case (the substance of his complaint) before the domestic courts. If he does not want to have his chances of applying successfully to the Commission jeopardized, he ought to invoke all the issues – which he might subsequently bring to the Commission – before the national courts, irrespective of any duties of *ex officio* investigation incumbent upon these latter.

This being so, it is beyond doubt that the applicant ought to raise all issues of his case (previously raised before the domestic courts) for which he is seeking redress before the Commission itself, despite this latter's power to examine them *ex officio*. Thus, in the *X v. F.R. Germany* case (1970), the Commission once again asserted that 'any complaint made before the Commission and relating to lower courts and authorities should have been substantially raised before the competent higher court or authority'.[175] In that case the applicant had not availed himself of the possibility of invoking his rights in a constitutional appeal to the Federal Constitutional Court (*Bundesverfassungsgericht*). The Commission, after proceeding to an examination made *ex officio* of the particulars of the case, concluded that the condition as to the exhaustion of domestic remedies had not been complied with by the applicant.[176] The same conclusion was reached by the Commission in another case, directed against Austria, after a similar examination made *ex officio* of the elements of the case.[177]

The practice of the Commission on the problem under study may possibly reveal itself exceedingly rigorous in certain situations, namely when the applicant has not raised an issue before the domestic courts which, if raised, might have been prejudicial to his case,[178] and when the applicant has not done so as those courts were already under the duty of investigating it *ex officio*. In a system of protection of human rights, the presumptions must not necessarily be expected to operate always against the complaints.

7. The problem of procedural remedies

It is clear from the survey thus far that the Commission's conception of the local remedies rule is a *strict* one,[179] i.e., one of a strict application. It may then be asked whether the operation of the rule under the Convention encompasses procedural remedies as well. The problem is directly related to the question previously examined, that of the duty to raise the complaint as a whole (all related issues) before the domestic courts before taking it up to the Commission. But on a few occasions the Commission has tackled the problem of procedural remedies in a more specific way.

On one of those occasions, the applicant, an Italian citizen, complained of his deportation from the Netherlands. Although Dutch law 'does not provide for any specific procedure by which he might have challenged the deportation order as such', the Commission observed:

> however, the applicant had, according to the general principles of Dutch law, the possibility of taking action before the courts on the ground that his detention and subsequent deportation from the Netherlands constituted an abuse of power on the part of the authorities which were responsible for the measures taken against him; [...] the applicant has not availed himself of this possibility and therefore has not exhausted the remedies available to him under Dutch law.[180]

In an earlier decision, the Commission was faced with an applicant complaining of his condemnation; the Commission deemed that he had not exhausted local remedies 'du fait qu'il n'a pas soulevé devant la juridiction supérieure le moyen concernant la composition de la juridiction inférieure, alors même que ce moyen aurait dû être soulevé d'office par la juridiction supérieure'.[181] In the *Gussenbauer* v. *Austria* case (1972), the Commission significantly stated that the remedies to be exhausted 'comprise the entire system of legal protection established by the *corpus* of municipal law';[182] this time, however, the Commission concluded that the means in question (a request for release from obligations as a legal aid counsel) did 'not in reality offer any chance of redressing the damage alleged', and therefore needed not be exhausted.[183] The Austrian government alleged that the Austrian courts might possibly have changed their practice (on the matter at issue) if the applicant had drafted his application in a certain way (relying on other provisions of the Convention); but the Commission nevertheless maintained its decision that the local remedies rule had been complied with and declared the application as a whole admissible.[184]

This did not happen, however, in other cases. In a complaint lodged with the Commission by twenty-three inhabitants of Alsemberg and of Beersel against Belgium, concerning the linguistic regime in Belgian schools, the respondent government argued that the applicants had not availed themselves of the faculty of attacking the decision concerned before the Belgian *Conseil d'État*, while the applicants contested that the decision in question was a 'decision' in the 'legal and procedural' sense of the term, and susceptible of appeal.[185] The Commission, faced with a 'retrait d'une décision d'ouvrir des classes de transmutation' at a certain school, found that such a 'retrait' constituted undoubtedly an *acte* or *règlement administratif* under Belgian law and could thus be the object of a *recours en annulation* before the *Conseil d'État*.[186] To that the applicants objected that the *Conseil d'État* would inevitably recognize its 'absolute incompetence' on the subject, and that such a *recours* before it would have been 'perfectly vain'.[187] The Commission found, however, that 'it seems probable [. . .] that if the *Conseil d'État* had been seized of the matter, it would have annulled the decision' at issue.[188] The Commission went further, remarking that if, by any chance, the Minister of Education refused to comply with such a decision of the *Conseil d'État* and to open the 'classes de transmutation', another remedy would be open to the applicants, who could then demand indemnity before the courts.[189] The Commission finally remarked – repeating what it had already stated on other occasions (cf. *supra*, p. 67)–that a simple doubt as to the existence or effectiveness of a given remedy did not constitute a particular circumstance authorizing the non-exercise of that remedy, for this is a problem upon which the domestic courts themselves should have had an opportunity to pronounce, before recourse is made to the Commission; the complaint was accordingly declared inadmissible for non-exhaustion of local remedies.[190]

In another case against Belgium, the *Delcourt* case (1967), the Commission indicated that the applicant should make use of certain procedural facilities before the *tribunal correctionnel* of Bruges (first instance), so as to invoke them subsequently before the Court of

Appeal (of Ghent) and the *Cour de Cassation*; but as he had not done so, he had not exhausted the local remedies available to him under Belgian law.[191] Moreover, as the applicant complained of a lack of impartiality towards himself on the part of the judges (particularly throughout the debates before the Court of Appeal of Ghent), he should have requested the registration of the allegedly partial declarations of the judges in the written *compte rendu* of the session, so as to enable him to complain of them before the *Cour de Cassation*. But as Delcourt had not made use of such *moyens de recours*, the Commission once again found that in that respect he had not exhausted the local remedies available to him under Belgian law.[192]

In the *X* v. *Ireland* case (1961), the applicant complained before the Commission of his allegedly wrongful detention under the 1940 Act. He had not, however, instituted any proceedings to contest the order for his detention, either before the Detention Commission (provided for in the 1940 Act) or before the ordinary courts, and he had apparently taken no other action to challenge the propriety of the order.[193] Even though the Detention Commission was an administrative rather than a judicial tribunal and recourse to it was an exceptional remedy (under the 1940 Act),[194] the Commission found that (unlike in the *Lawless* case) application to that Detention Commission 'was a legal remedy which offered to the applicant in the present case an effective means of establishing promptly after his arrest the absence of any reasonable grounds for his detention without trial under the 1940 Act and of securing his early release from detention'.[195] Although a remedy applicable only in exceptional circumstances, it was however 'the legal remedy specifically provided by the Irish Parliament for the case of persons detained under the 1940 Act',[196] and which fell within the scope of the local remedies rule. The applicant's failure to exhaust it led to the rejection of his application.[197]

More recently, in a case concerning Switzerland, the Commission held that where the domestic court has a choice between a public hearing or a non-public hearing, the applicant who has not expressly asked for a public hearing has not exhausted local remedies.[198] The Commission further held, in another case, that an accused, in the Federal Republic of Germany, who complains that his legal aid lawyer neglects his defence (on the ground that he does not receive an advance on his fees), must make a request to be given another legal aid counsel.[199] Likewise, in a case concerning the United Kingdom, the Commission ruled that in case of non-compliance with a court order granting access (to a child of a former marriage), the interested party ought to apply for modification of such an order.[200]

A further illustration is provided by the *X* v. *Austria* case (1966). The applicant alleged *inter alia* that the president of a Regional Court (in Austria) had not been impartial in his case. The Commission observed that the applicant could have raised this point in a plea of challenge (Ablehnung) of the judge concerned. But as he apparently failed to do so in the domestic proceedings, he was held not to have exhausted in that regard the domestic remedies within the meaning of Article 26 of the Convention.[201]

In its practice the Commission seems thus to have adhered to,[202] or at least to have been considerably influenced by, the *Ambatielos* principle (*supra*, p. 58 and *infra*, p. 321). This seems to be a regrettable step, which paves the way for a far too rigorous application of the rule. Applicants, in most cases average citizens, may thus be placed under the duty of exhausting successively various means of redress, rendering the application of the rule almost an unsurmountable obstacle. This can be hardly in keeping with a system destined to safeguard and protect human rights. Some practical difficulties may well arise, as indicated by the Directorate of Human Rights of the Council of Europe: it may not be always easy to distinguish between a grievance and the *means* to relieve that grievance, or between a legal means of redress to be utilized and a legal argument.[203]

If procedural means are definitely included in the scope of the rule under the Convention, the English term 'local redress' will prove more appropriate than the French notion of *voie de recours interne*. Anyhow, those means of redress should never be confused with legal arguments, which the applicant is perfectly entitled to use or to omit.[204] Assuming, for the sake of the argument, that the practice of the Commission has to date furnished sufficient evidence for the inclusion of procedural remedies in the application of the local remedies rule under the Convention, even then this view stands in need of some qualification. The requirement would then have to be interpreted in the light of the Convention as a whole, and in conjunction with the other conditions under present review. In this way, an applicant would be under the duty of exhausting only those *procedural means* which are *essential* for redressing the wrongful situation complained of (*supra*, pp. 85–7), and, in doing so, he would only be required to make *normal use* of those means of redress (*infra*, pp. 97–9).

8. The problem of extraordinary remedies

One thus comes to the problem of extraordinary remedies in the practice of the Commission. An appropriate starting-point for the examination of this question is afforded by the *Nielsen* v. *Denmark* case. This was a criminal case, in which the Danish Supreme Court had upheld the judgment of the High Court of Eastern Denmark condemning the applicant.[205] The latter then decided to file a petition with the Special Court of Revision for the re-opening of the case.[206] The Danish government, however, argued before the Commission that:

> the Special Court of Revision is an extraordinary Court outside the ordinary system of the Danish Courts of Law and [. . .], consequently, a petition to the Special Court is not a domestic remedy according to the generally recognized rules of international law; [. . .] in particular, a petition to the Special Court cannot be described as an appeal and [. . .], in regard to the filing of petitions with that Court, the law does not impose any time-limit.[207]

The applicant contested such assertions, arguing that the petition to the Special Court of Revision was a domestic remedy.[208]

The Commission was thus called upon to decide whether a remedy which, in the view of the Danish government, was an extraordinary one, fell within the scope of application of the local remedies rule. The Commission began by observing that the right of recourse to the Special Court of Revision offered to the applicant the possibility of an effective and adequate legal remedy with regard to some of the matters of which he complained in his present application before the Commission.[209] The Commission then immediately turned to the position in general international law, where some authorities had sought to distinguish between ordinary and extraordinary remedies and to maintain that legal remedies needed not be exhausted if they were to be considered extraordinary remedies.[210] In particular in the *Salem* case (*infra*, p. 322), the Commission realled, it had been held that a *recours en requête civile* (in Egypt) needed not be exhausted because it was not a regular legal remedy, but rather was intended to re-open a process which had already been closed by a judgment of last resort.[211] The Commission, however, did not subscribe to that view, even though it admitted that in the present *Nielsen* case the petition to the Special Court of Revision was *also* aimed at re-opening a process which had become *res judicata* with the decision of the Danish Supreme Court.[212]

Instead, the Commission recalled the rationale of the local remedies rule as stated in the *Interhandel* case (*supra*, pp. 57–8), and also invoked the decisions in the *Finnish Vessels* and the *Ambatielos* cases (both *supra*, pp. 57–8 and *infra*, p. 321), to substantiate its view that the respondent State was entitled to insist upon the prior exhaustion of all those domestice remedies of a legal nature which appeared to be capable of providing an effective and sufficient means of redress *without differentiating between ordinary and extraordinary remedies*.[213] The Commission further relied upon the *Electricity Company of Sofia* case (*supra*, p. 58), where, in its view, the Permanent Court of International Justice likewise showed a disinclination to exclude from the duty of exhausting local remedies *any* legal remedy capable of affording adequate and sufficient redress.[214]

The position of the Commission was therefore quite clear: the determining criterion of identification of the remedies to be exhausted was that of the *effectiveness* and *adequacy* of the remedies, and in the present case the right to petition the Special Court of Revision for the re-opening of the proceedings (and an order for a new trial) satisfied those requirements, as it was capable of constituting an effective and adequate means of redress.[215] In the Commission's own words, 'in applying the local remedies rule the crucial question is not the ordinary or extraordinary character of a legal remedy but whether it gives the possibility of an effective and sufficient means of redress'.[216] This was the test embraced and applied by the Commission. Moreover, in the present case, the Commission noted that the right of recourse to the Special Court of Revision appeared to be 'an integral and regular part of the Danish system of administration of justice in criminal cases'.[217] Hence its falling – in the Commission's view – within the scope of application of the local remedies rule.[218]

Even though the decision of the Commission in the *Nielsen* case (with regard to the particular problem under study) was later met with some reservations in that it seemed to constitute to a large extent a *décision d'espèce*,[219] a decision *in concreto* rather than a statement of principle, one factor remains clear: the Commission's indication that, in so far as the remedies to be exhausted are concerned, the decisive test lies in their possibility of affording an effective and sufficient means of redress, rather than on their ordinary or extraordinary character.

The Commission's option for the application of this test, as well as its inclination not to distinguish between ordinary and extraordinary remedies, can be detected by an examination of its case-law. In the

Ringeisen v. *Austria* case, for example, the Commission based its decision (on one point raised) on its finding that the remedy in question (a constitutional appeal) would have been in the case *ineffective*, and *not* because it constituted an extraordinary remedy, as contended by the applicant.[220] Earlier, in the *X* v. *F.R. Germany* case (1960), the Commission began by stating that notwithstanding the opinion in the *Salem* case (*supra*, p. 89) in general international law, 'proceedings for the re-opening of a case are, in principle, remedies which require to be taken into account'[221] in applying the local remedies rule (as held in the *Nielsen* case); however, the Commission added significantly:

in all the circumstances of the present case the Commission does not consider that the petitions to the Federal Constitutional Court and to the Federal Court [in Germany] for the re-opening of the case were effective remedies for the purposes of the generally recognized rule of international law concerning the exhaustion of domestic remedies.[222]

In another case against Germany the Commission held that a *recours en révision* – extraordinary remedy as it was – ought to be effective and offer reasonable chances of success[223] for the purposes of application of the local redress rule; in the present case the application could not constitute an effective remedy 'dans la mesure où le requérant invoquait son grief du caractère non contradictoire de l'audience devant la Cour Fédérale de Justice, c'est-à-dire soulevait une question de pur droit dont la justice allemande n'avait pas à s'occuper dans le cadre d'une instance en révision'.[224] In the *X* v. *Sweden* case (1964) the Commission stated that 'the applicant's petitions, under the provisions of Swedish law, for a re-opening of his cases were not effective and sufficient remedies and do not, therefore, constitute domestic remedies under the generally recognized rules of international law'.[225] Later, in another case against Sweden, decided in 1970, the Commission, faced with the question of the applicant's application to the Swedish Supreme Administrative Court for a re-opening of the proceedings or a *restitutio in integrum*, referred to its view (in the previous *Swedish* case of 1964) on the matter according to which the extraordinary remedies in question (mentioned in chapter 58 of the Swedish Code of Procedure) 'could not be regarded as effective and sufficient remedies as the proceedings relating to these remedies do not, until successful, affect the validity of the final decision impugned'.[226]

And in the recent *Brückmann* v. *F.R. Germany* case (1974) the Commission noted that, after a decision of the German Federal Constitutional Court, the applicant had filed with the Court of Appeal a petition to re-open the proceedings of the case. Referring to its own case-law concerning applications for re-trial under the German Code of Criminal Procedure, the Commission held that that extraordinary remedy did not in the circumstances of the case constitute an effective and sufficient remedy which the applicant was required to exhaust under Article 26 of the Convention before applying to the Commission.[227]

These six cases, just referred to, constitute flagrant illustrations of the application by the Commission of the test of effectiveness and adequacy of the remedies to be exhausted, overriding any distinction between ordinary and extraordinary remedies as a possible criterion. This distinction becomes therefore immaterial for the purposes of the determination of the scope of the local remedies rule. This case-law of the Commission shows that certain extraordinary remedies, in the Commission's view, needed not be exhausted, not because they were extraordinary, but because they happened to be ineffective.

Conversely, while applying the same test of effectiveness and adequacy, the Commission concluded, on other occasions, that certain extraordinary remedies needed to be exhausted, not because they were extraordinary, but because they happened to be effective. An illustration is afforded by the *X* v. *Ireland* case (1961), where the Commission found that recourse to a Detention Commission, although a remedy applicable only in exceptional circumstances, was in the case capable of affording to the applicant an effective means of redress, and therefore was a domestic remedy which it was incumbent upon him to exhaust before submitting his complaint to the Commission.[228] On another occasion, in the *Boeckmans* v. *Belgium* case, the Commission stated that, *a priori*, there was nothing impeding a *demande de renvoi* ('pour suspicion légitime') from constituting an effective and adequate means of redress, notwithstanding its extraordinary character.[229] (Upon examination of the case, however, the Commission concluded on that point that no such problem actually arose because the local remedies rule had been duly complied with in the case.)[230]

At the end of the present section on the so-called 'extraordinary' remedies, it is possible to see that, despite the Commission's ruling in the *Nielsen* case, there have been several instances where the

Commission subsequently held that, for example, an application for a re-opening of the case (and a re-trial) needed not be exhausted (normally on the ground of ineffectiveness). Besides some of the cases already referred to *supra*, pp. 89–92, one could in addition recall in this respect a decision of the Commission – not too long after the *Nielsen* case – whereby it ruled that in the case at issue the applicant's numerous petitions for the re-trial of his case (in Germany) could not be taken into consideration because they did not constitute effective and sufficient remedies within the meaning of the generally recognized rule of international law regarding the exhaustion of local remedies.[231]

More recently, in the *X* v. *Denmark* case (1971), the Commission has gone even further, and also given an indication as to a likely new trend it may pursue in the near future. The case, like the *Nielsen* case, concerned the right of recourse to the Danish Special Court of Revision (for a re-opening of criminal proceedings and a re-trial of the case). On this problem the Commission stated:

In the present case the Commission has once more examined the whole question as to whether an application to the Special Court should in principle be regarded as a remedy for the purposes of Article 26 of the Convention. [...] In making this examination, the Commission has in particular taken into account its extensive jurisprudence, subsequent to the decision in the *Nielsen* case, concerning the relevance, for the purposes of Article 26, of an application for re-trial made according to the laws of other Contracting Parties; [...] in the light of this jurisprudence the Commission has considered the question whether or not to maintain the principle expressed in the *Nielsen* case as regards recourse to the Special Court of Revision; [...] however, in the present case, the Commission has found it undesirable to base its decision on an interpretation of Article 26 different from the one adopted in the *Nielsen* case and has decided, while leaving the question open for consideration in any future case, to pursue its examination of the present application on the basis that recourse to the Special Court could, in principle, be regarded as an effective and sufficient remedy for the purposes of Article 26 of the Convention.[232]

However, the result of that examination led the Commission to the conclusion that – unlike in the *Nielsen* case – 'insofar as the applicant's application to the Special Court was based on alleged procedural errors committed during the proceedings before the trial court [...] that application virtually lacked any prospect of success and can therefore not be regarded as an effective and sufficient remedy under the generally recognized rules of international law'.[233] Therefore, the

Commission added, the decision of the Special Court of Revision in respect of those matters could not be taken into consideration[234] in applying Article 26 of the Convention.

One last remark remains to be made, under the present heading, on what the Commission terms 'informal remedies'. The question arose in the recent *X* v. *F.R. Germany* case (1974), where the respondent government alleged that the applicant had failed to exhaust local remedies as she had the possibility of lodging a *Dienstaufsichts-beschwerde* (hierarchical complaint) against the presiding judge.[235] The Commission found however that 'the informal remedy called *Dienstaufsichtsbeschwerde* in German law cannot be considered a remedy in the sense of Article 26 if directed against judges. Judges are independent and can only be supervised (*Dienstaufsicht*) to such an extent as this independence is not being encroached upon'.[236] The Commission further found that in the circumstances of the case 'a *Dienstaufsichtsbeschwerde* would not have been an effective remedy'.[237] To the respondent government's further contention that the applicant failed to lodge a disciplinary action against the Senator for Construction and Housing, the Commission replied that 'the Senator, being a minister, is the highest organ in the administrative hierarchy and therefore not subject to supervision.[238] The Commission concluded that the applicant was therefore 'not bound to lodge a *Dienstaufsichts-beschwerde* even if such action had at all been possible'.[239] Accordingly, the Commission declared that the application could not be declared inadmissible on the ground that the applicant had failed to exhaust domestic remedies.[240]

9. The 'likelihood of success' test

In determining the local remedies to be exhausted, the Commission has frequently applied the 'likelihood of success' test. This is shown, for example, by its decision in the *X* v. *F.R. Germany* case (1961), where the Commission asserted, in relation to a *recours en révision*, that 'encore faut-il que cette voie de recours extraordinaire soit efficace et offre des chances raisonnables de succès; [...] il appartient à la Commission de rechercher elle-même à la lumière des faits de la cause si tel est ou non le cas'.[241] The test was applied by the Commission in that same year in the *Austria* v. *Italy* case.[242] Earlier, in the *Lawless* v. *Ireland* case (1958), the Commission had found that further *habeas corpus* proceedings open to the applicant in the ordinary courts of the country (concerning his detention under the 1940 Act) 'did not offer him a reasonable prospect of success and must be regarded as ineffective remedies', and, consequently, 'it was not necessary for the applicant to have recourse to such further domestic remedies before submitting his case to the Commission'.[243] On the other hand, in a decision on a complaint against Germany, the Commission found that the personal opinion of the applicant as to the chances of success of an eventual appeal to a superior Administrative Court (*Oberverwaltungsgericht*) could not be taken into consideration, because it was not supported by any element capable of proving that that appeal would have been truly ineffective or insufficient.[244] His application was therefore rejected for non-exhaustion of local remedies.[245]

In the *X* v. *United Kingdom* case (1970), the Commission rejected the applicant's contentions that his complaint and his application for legal aid concerning the institution of civil proceedings would not have been successful.[246] Likewise, in the *X* v. *Luxembourg* case (1973), where a complaint under Article 8 of the Convention (respect for family life) was advanced, the Commission:

a constaté que la jurisprudence des tribunaux luxembourgeois témoigne depuis plusieurs années, en ce domaine, d'une tendance libérale et qu'il n'est en tout cas nullement certain qu'une demande formée par le requérant devant ces tribunaux eût été vouée à l'échec par l'effet de dispositions luxembourgeoises d'ordre public. La Commission estime donc que le requérant disposait, en droit luxembourgeois, d'un recours présentant des chances raisonnables de succès et constate qu'il n'en a pas fait l'usage.[247]

Accordingly, his application was declared inadmissible for non-exhaustion of local remedies.[248]

There have been, on the other hand, cases where the Commission reached the opposite conclusion.[249] In the *Gussenbauer* v. *Austria* case (1972), for example, the Commission was of the opinion that the applicant had clearly shown that the means of redress at issue, 'although theoretically capable of constituting a remedy, does not in reality offer any chance of redressing the damage alleged, and therefore need not be exhausted'.[250] Accordingly, the Commission dismissed the objection of non-exhaustion and declared the application as a whole admissible.[251] Similarly, in the *Handyside* v. *United Kingdom* case (1974), the Commission found *inter alia* that 'an appeal by the applicant to the Court of Appeal would not have redressed the situation of which he complained to the Commission and [. . .] he has therefore satisfied the requirements of Article 26 of the Convention. It follows that the application cannot be rejected under Article 27(3) of the Convention'.[252]

It has also happened that in one and the same case the Commission has reached one conclusion (as to the likelihood of success of local remedies) in relation to one part of the application, and a different and opposite conclusion in relation to another part of the same application. This situation is illustrated by the *Kjeldsen* v. *Denmark* case (1972). The complaints related to the introduction of compulsory sex education in Danish public schools (1970 Act). The Commission began by recalling that 'in order to comply with the requirements of Article 26 of the Convention, an applicant is obliged to exhaust every domestic remedy which cannot clearly be said to lack any prospect of success'.[253] The Commission found that, in so far as the present application related to certain directives issued by the Danish Ministry of Education and other administrative measures taken by the Danish authorities regarding the manner in which the sex education referred to in the 1970 Act should be carried out, it could not be said that the remedy indicated by the respondent government would clearly have been without any prospect of success. It followed that in that respect the applicants had not exhausted local remedies, and that part of their application was therefore rejected.[254] But the applicants had also argued that they could take no proceedings against an Act of Parliament. This assertion was not contested by the Danish government. The Commission, thus, further concluded that there was no effective domestic remedy available to the applicants with regard to the principle of compulsory sex education as embodied in the 1970 Act. It followed that, in that respect, the application could not be rejected as inadmissible under Article 26 of the Convention.[255]

A problem arising in practice is the ill-advice given to the applicant by his lawyer as to the alleged unlikelihood of success of a given domestic remedy, so that, acting perhaps in good faith, the applicant does not exhaust that remedy in the belief that its alleged or assumed uselessness constitutes a special circumstances absolving him from the duty of exhausting it. In such cases the Commission's position has been quite consistent and has left no margin for doubt. In a case against Belgium, the Commission rejected the applicant's contention that his lawyers had convinced him of the uselessness of a *pourvoi en cassation*;[256] he was held not to have exhausted local remedies. Later, in the *Soltikow* v. *F.R. Germany* case (1968), to the applicant's submission that he had been advised by several lawyers that a constitutional appeal would have no prospect of success, the Commission categorically replied that 'advice by lawyers as to the possibility of success on appeal does not constitute a valid excuse for not exhausting a particular remedy'.[257] And again in the *Simon-Herold* v. *Austria* case (1971) the Commission affirmed that neither the Investigating Judge's advice nor the applicant's lawyers advice to him that a further appeal would most likely be unsuccessful and useless constituted a special circumstance which, under the rules of international law within the meaning of Article 26, absolved the applicant from exhausting that remedy.[258]

The criterion most widely applied by the Commission remains, however, that of the *reasonable prospect of success* in the remedies to be exhausted. Of course the Commission has applied this test with a certain margin of appreciation, and, in some cases, it may have displayed more rigour than in others; on this last point, reference has already been made to the *Retimag* case (*supra*, p. 67), where the Commission stated that 's'il existe un doute quant à la question de savoir si une voie de recours déterminée peut être ou non de nature à offrir une chance réelle de succès, c'est là un point qui doit être soumis aux tribunaux internes eux-mêmes, avant tout appel au tribunal international'.[259] Here the Commission embraced a principle held by the Permanent Court of International Justice in the *Panevezys–saldutiskis Railway* case, in general international law (cf. *supra*, p. 58 and *infra*, p. 321). But in other cases, as seen above, the Commission applied the test with more flexibility. In so doing, the Commission seems to have correctly apprehended the law as to be applied in a system of protection of human rights. While, under general international law, remedies ought to be *obviously futile* (cf. Bagge's award in the *Finnish Vessels* case, *supra*, p. 58 and *infra*, p. 321) to fall outside the scope of application of the local remedies rule, in its practice the Commission has clearly replaced that criterion by the one of the *reasonable likelihood of success* of the remedies to exhaust (also applied in general international law), in what appears to be an appropriate trend.

10. The 'normal use' of remedies

As in general international law,[260] the Commission has subscribed to the view that 'the rule of local redress confines itself to imposing the *normal use* of remedies likely to be effective and adequate' (*Austria* v. *Italy* case).[261] In the *Ringeisen* v. *Austria* case (1968) the Commission explained that:

the question whether or not a domestic remedy must be exhausted before the Commission may deal with a case is to be determined according to the generally recognized principles of international law; [...] this means that, if remedies which seem effective and sufficient are open to an individual within the legal system of the responsible State, he must use and exhaust such remedies *in the normal way*.[262]

And again in the *Simon-Herold* v. *Austria* case (1971) the Commission supported the test of the *normal use* of the seemingly effective and adequate remedies to be exhausted.[263]

As indicated by the Commission itself on those occasions, the question of the 'normal use' of the means of redress is intrinsically connected to that of the effectiveness and adequacy of the remedies to exhaust. (Reference may here be made to the survey above.) But at the present stage there remain a few other observations to be made. The normal use of remedies may comprise certain *material* or *substantial* conditions of exhaustion, such as the applicant's duty to raise the substance of his complaint before the domestic courts prior to taking it up to the international level (a problem already examined). But there are likewise certain *formal* conditions of exhaustion, such as *the proper use of local remedies within the time-limits under municipal law*, as well as the applicant's *capacity* to make use of those remedies.[264] The Commission has taken care to ensure compliance with those *formal* conditions as well.

As to the applicant's capacity to exercise remedies in a *valid* way, the Commission held in an early decision that 'pour agir en justice, un interdit doit être représenté par son tuteur' (the application in question was rejected for non-exhaustion of local remedies).[265] But the application of the condition of observance of local time-limits has occurred more frequently. In a complaint lodged with the Commission by a Swiss citizen against Germany, the Commission decided to declare the application inadmissible because the applicant had not utilized a constitutional appeal 'dans le délai fixé par la législation nationale applicable'.[266] Later, in another case against Germany, the applicant claimed that he had exhausted all local remedies; but the Commission found out that he had unduly delayed in seizing the jurisdiction of first instance, and for that reason his application was rejected for non-exhaustion of local remedies.[267]

On another occasion where an application was rejected on the same ground, the Commission observed *inter alia* that the applicants had no excuse for not respecting the time-limit of sixty days to seize the

Belgian *Conseil d'Etat*.[268] Similarly, in the *X* v. *Norway* case (1964), although the applicant had taken up his complaint before the Norwegian Supreme Court, his second appeal had been lodged out of time, according to Norwegian law. He was therefore held not to have complied with the local remedies rule, with the Commission categorically stating that 'time-limits laid down in domestic law for the introduction of appeals must be observed by applicants to the Commission.[269] More recently, in three successive cases, failure by the applicants to lodge a constitutional appeal within the time-limit prescribed by municipal law led to rejection of their respective applications by the Commission.[270]

As the Commission applies so meticulously this formal condition of the exhaustion of local remedies, and as applicants have to abide strictly by *local* time-limits (a question distinct from the six-month rule enshrined in Article 26 *in fine*), one may wonder whether, conversely, the Commission could display a similar concern in cases where the applicants have to wait a long time until the final decision is rendered under municipal law (e.g., in cases of constitutional appeals) before they can take up their cases before the Commission. One may thus wonder whether certain remedies (such as some constitutional appeals, and procedural remedies) do really fit into the test of the 'normal use' of remedies by the applicants as applied by the Commission. After all, the Directorate of Human Rights of the Council of Europe has indicated that, in exhausting local remedies, the applicant 'doit faire un usage *normal* des recours internes et se comporter comme un plaideur raisonnable et non comme un jurisconsulte expérimenté...'.[271] This leads one to consider the question of the notion of final decision.

11. The notion of 'final decision'

Under the local remedies rule an applicant is under the duty of applying to *all competent* domestic courts. Until he has reached the final decision of the highest competent domestic tribunal he cannot take his case to the Commission. The notion of final decision is therefore inherent in the local remedies rule. Besides that, its application under the Convention assumes a particular importance in view of the six-month rule contained in Article 26 *in fine* of the Convention, whereby the Commission may only deal with a matter after the exhaustion of all domestic remedies and within a period of six months from the date on which the final decision was taken. The *final decision* constitutes thus the point from which the six-month period will run.

In the *X* v. *F.R. Germany* case (1960) the Commission explained that the term 'final decision' in Article 26 must be considered

as referring exclusively to the final decision resulting from the exhaustion of all domestic remedies according to the generally recognized rules of international law; [...] the preparatory work of the Convention, in particular the report prepared in June 1950 by the Conference of Senior Officials, confirms this interpretation.[272]

Naturally, the final decision, for the purposes of application of Article 26 of the Convention, will vary from case to case. On different occasions the Commission has held that, in the cases before it, the internal final decisions to be taken into account were those of the German Federal Constitutional Court;[273] of the Supreme Court in Sweden,[274] in Austria,[275] in Denmark;[276] of the Court of Criminal Appeal in the United Kingdom;[277] of the Swedish Labour Court;[278] of a Court of Appeal in Austria;[279] of Regional Courts in Germany.[280]

Within the present context of the notion of 'final decision', the test of effectiveness of the remedies plays an important role as well. The *X* v. *United Kingdom* case (1968) affords a good illustration. In that case the applicant was serving a prison sentence after conviction and after having unsuccessfully appealed to the Court of Criminal Appeal. The Commission noted that:

no further right of appeal was available to the applicant, there being no indication that there was in the present case any issue of public interest, for the determination of which leave to appeal to the House of Lords would have been given. [...] Furthermore, his subsequent application for an order of *habeas corpus* cannot be considered as part of the normal appeal procedure in the United Kingdom judicial system; [...] indeed, where the object of an application for an order of *habeas corpus* is to enable a detained person to have determined the legality of his detention, such order would be inapplicable in the case of a person in detention following conviction by a court of competent jurisdiction.[281]

It followed that, in the circumstances of the case, the Commission concluded, an application for an order of *habeas corpus* did not constitute an effective and sufficient remedy which needed to be taken into consideration and, therefore, 'the final decision regarding the applicant's conviction and sentence is the [earlier] decision of the Court of Criminal Appeal',[282] for the purposes of application of Article 26 of the Convention.

Likewise, in the *X* v. *F.R. Germany* case (1970), the Commission held that in the circumstances of the case the applicant's petition for a re-trial of his case was not an effective and sufficient remedy which needed be exhausted; it followed that 'the decisions regarding this petition cannot be taken into consideration' for the purpose of applying Article 26 of the Convention. Instead, the Commission found in this connection that the final decision regarding the applicant's conviction and sentence was the [earlier] decision of the Federal Court (in Germany).[283]

The Commission has given further indications of its consideration of the notion of final decision. It has, for example, hinted that an applicant should state the date of the internal final decision in his application to the Commission (e.g., for the counting of the six-month period).[284] Perhaps a more important point was the Commission's indication on repeated occasions[285] that by 'final internal decision' Article 26 of the Convention designates exclusively the final decision rendered in the *normal* framework of the exhaustion of local remedies according to generally recognized principles of international law.

Having pointed this out, one may at last turn to the difficult problems the Commission has had to face in its interpretation and application of the notion of final decision. The first of these problems is illustrated by cases where there may be doubts as to the effectiveness of the remedies to be exhausted. In these situations not only may the determination of the final decision become temporarily uncertain, but also the applicant may have his chances of success jeopardised. If he decides, deeming the remedy at issue ineffective, not to exhaust it, the Commission may declare his application inadmissible for non-exhaustion of that remedy (considered effective by the Commission). On the other hand, if he decides to exhaust it anyway, and the Commission decides that the remedy need not be exhausted, then the time spent on that matter may prove fatal to the applicant. The final decision for the purposes of the local remedies rule will have been a previous one, from which the six-month period will have already started running, thus leaving the applicant in considerable risk of lodging his complaint with the Commission out of time.

Fortunately, the incongruencies which such a situation could lead to have been to a large extent overcome by both the Commission and the Court. Thus, in its judgment of 16 July 1971 in the *Ringeisen* v. *Austria* case the Court, following earlier indication of the Commission in the same case,[286] held that the last stage of the exhaustion of local remedies 'may be reached shortly after the lodging of the application but before the Commission is called upon to pronounce itself on admissibility'.[287] In this way, although the applicant remains under the duty of exhausting all domestic remedies before applying to the Commission, he may, nowadays, in cases of doubt, lodge his application with the Commission while at the same time pursuing the last domestic proceedings. It is likely[288] that the Commission, after the ruling in the *Ringeisen* case, will accept that position.

The *Ringeisen* case also illustrates the second difficulty related to the determination of the final internal decision in the exhaustion of local remedies, in cases of a *continuing* situation (e.g., cases of detention on remand).[289] In the *Ringeisen* decision the Commission expressed its view that the purpose of the local remedies rule:

is clearly accomplished where the international tribunal is seized of a complaint by an applicant whose proceedings before the domestic courts terminate in a reasonable time *thereafter* with a final decision by the competent court; [. . .] further, it is clear that such final decision must have been given at the latest when the international authority comes to deal with, namely to decide upon, the application.[290]

The crucial point – the 'deadline' for the exhaustion – is thus the Commission's decision on admissibility rather than the lodging of the application.

Coming to the problem of the final internal decision in a so-called *continuing* situation, the Commission stated (in the same case) that:

it is sufficient for the purposes of the rule requiring the exhaustion of domestic remedies under Article 26 of the Convention that the Commission should have been seized of the applicant's complaint within a reasonable time after the proceedings before the domestic courts have been terminated with a final decision by the competent court, but before the Commission, in fact, deals with, that is to say decides upon, the application. [. . .] The same reasoning applies both to complaints relating to a continuing situation and those concerning single isolated events; [. . .] the Commission finds that a question under Article 26 of the Convention might arise where the period between the date on which the application was lodged with the Commission, and the date on which the final decision was taken by the domestic judicial or other authorities was extremely long; [. . .] however, in the present case, less than three months have elapsed between the introduction of the application and the decision of the Constitutional Court; [. . .] consequently, the Commission finds that the applicant has exhausted the domestic remedies in accordance with Article 26 of the Convention.[291]

Accordingly, the Commission rejected the objection of non-exhaustion of local remedies raised by the respondent government.[292]

More recently, in the *X* v. *Belgium* case (1973), the Commission was called upon to determine which final internal decision was to be taken into account for the purposes of application of Article 26 of the Convention. The circumstances were likewise those of an alleged *continuing* situation. After remarking that Article 26 of the Convention designated exclusively the final internal decision rendered in the *normal* framework of the exhaustion of local remedies,[293] the Commission went on to observe that in the case 'le requérant ne se plaint pas d'un acte instantané, mais s'en prend à une situation qui dure depuis dix ans. Or, le problème du délai de six mois de l'article 26 ne pourrait surgir que quand cette situation aura pris fin.'[294]

One comes finally to the third difficulty the Commission has had to face in the present context, namely that presented by situations where the applicant challenges the 'final' internal decision and attempts to re-open the case. In the *Nielsen* case (1959) the respondent government maintained before the Commission that it was the judgment of the Danish Supreme Court which, in the case, constituted the 'final decision' within the meaning of Article 26 of the Convention,[295] while the applicant contended that it was the decision of the Special Court of Revision (on his petition lodged with it immediately after the Supreme Court judgment) which constituted the final decision within the meaning of Article 26.[296] On this problem the Commission began by observing that the term 'final decision' in Article 26 must be considered as 'referring exclusively to the final decision resulting from the exhaustion of all domestic remedies according to the generally recognised rules of international law'.[297] The Commission contended that international courts had displayed a certain 'disinclination to exclude from the obligation to exhaust local remedies any legal remedy capable of affording adequate and sufficient redress'.[298] After asserting its own competence to appreciate in the light of the facts the effectiveness of any given remedy, the Commission concluded that in the case the decision of the Special Court of Revision – an effective and sufficient means of redress – and not that of the Supreme Court was to be regarded as the 'final decision'.[299] As a consequence the application could not be said – as contended by the Danish government – to have been lodged out of time (i.e., not complying with the six-month rule).[300]

This decision was not confirmed by the Commission's subsequent case-law. A few years later, in an application brought against Sweden, for example, the Commission categorically stated that in the case of criminal proceedings 'a request for revision, being an extraordinary remedy, can [...] not be taken into account for the calculation of the six months time-limit'.[301] (In the present case the final decision concerning the applicant's civil actions was held to have been that of the Swedish Supreme Court.)[302] But a more emphatic illustration of the Commission's new trend on the matter was provided in 1971 by its decision on the *X* v. *Denmark* case. As in the *Nielsen* case, the respondent government argued that the decision of the Danish Supreme Court constituted the final decision within the meaning of Article 26 of the Convention, whereas the applicant submitted that it was the (subsequent) decision of the Special Court of Revision (whereby his application for resumption of the case was rejected) which should be regarded as the final internal decision for the purposes of the six months' time-limit (and accordingly – he added – his present application to the Commission was lodged in time).[303] After considering both arguments, the Commission espoused the view that, as the applicant's application to the Special Court of Revision virtually lacked any prospect of success and could thus be regarded as an ineffective remedy, the decision of the Special Court of Revision[304] could not be taken into consideration in determining the final decision for the purpose of applying the six months time-limit.[305]

The Commission reached this decision notwithstanding a reference it made to its previous position in the *Nielsen* case.[306] Once again the test of effectiveness of the remedies proved decisive. But this time, unlike in the *Nielsen* case, the Commission displayed no readiness to accept the inclusion of a petition for the re-opening of a case within the scope of the local remedies rule. The position nowadays seems to be that such a means of applying for a re-trial does not constitute a remedy for the purposes of Article 26 and cannot re-open the period of time at issue. Anyway, reference has already been made to some of the scepticism with which the *Nielsen* decision was received; the new development initiated by the Commission on the particular problem presently under review seems to point in a sensible direction, for decisions such as that in the *Nielsen* case, as has been remarked, 'if generalized would have the effect of depriving the six months rule of any real significance'.[307] Although the test of effectiveness is bound to remain always a useful and decisive one, in interpreting and applying

Article 26 of the Convention attention ought to be paid to the whole of the principles determining what actually constitutes a remedy to be exhausted.

12. Conclusions

One may now attempt a few concluding remarks. The first, which hardly needs further explanation, is that those conditions of exhaustion examined above do not apply isolated from each other, but rather are in constant and close interplay. Some of the more conspicuous illustrations of this point are the Commission's innumerable invocations of the test of effectiveness of the remedies to be exhausted in connection with, for example, extraordinary remedies and the determination of the final internal decision, and the test of essentialness in connection with, for example, procedural remedies.

It may at this stage be asked to what extent has the Commission's practice on the subject itself conformed with the practice of other international organs and tribunals on the subject in general international law? Because of the Commission's reliance upon the reference of Article 26 to general international law the answer seems to be, not surprisingly, that the human rights experiment conforms to a large extent with the experience and activity of international courts and tribunals in general international law. A comparison between the two preceding sections corroborates this view.

However, if a general approximation of the practice of the Commission to that of other international organs does exist in the present context, there appear to be also some nuances of differences between the two. There seems to be, for example, a certain vagueness or uncertainty in general international practice as to what is meant by an *effective* remedy, as compared with the practice of the Commission on the matter. This is probably because the Commission, operating *continuously* under the Convention, has been called upon to pronounce on this particular point much more frequently than have other international organs. In the numerous cases it was seized of, the Commission had to examine in some depth certain particular domestic remedies of the countries concerned in the course of the proceedings at issue, thus being enabled to ascribe more precision to the matter of the effectiveness of local remedies.

Likewise, when one comes to the problem of extraordinary remedies one is confronted with a great amount of inconclusiveness on the part of international tribunals. The distinction between ordinary and extraordinary remedies, if at all relevant in domestic law, becomes a somewhat unsettled and troublesome matter at the international level for the purposes of the application of the local remedies rule. In this regard, the Commission seems to have approached the matter in a more realistic way, displaying a stronger determination to do away with the distinction between ordinary and extraordinary remedies and to apply the overriding criterion of effectiveness and adequacy, regardless of whether the remedy in question is 'extraordinary' or not.

In trying to secure a proper application of the local remedies rule, the Commission has, in some respects, gone beyond other international organs, thus making an advance in the matter, and, in other respects, it has kept behind them, thus making some retrograde steps. As for the former position, it may be pointed out that, even though the 'likelihood of success' test has been applied in both general international law and in the human rights experiment, some credit ought to be given to the Commission on this particular point: deliberately disregarding the more rigorous test of the 'obvious futility' of remedies (suggested by arbitrator Bagge in the *Finnish Vessels* case), the Commission has insisted on the *reasonable likelihood of success* of the remedies to be exhausted, thus operating a certain relaxation of the application of the local remedies rule, which seems to be well in keeping with a system of international protection of human rights. Equally flexible has been the position of the Commission in recent years towards certain 'special' remedies aiming at the re-opening of the case and re-trial. The more recent practice suggests a tendency of the Commission to reverse its earlier case-law and not to include such remedies necessarily within the scope of the local remedies rule.

On the other hand, the Commission's practice is open to criticism in its strict application of the local remedies rule, at times extending it – regrettably – to certain procedural means of redress in such a way as to render the rule an almost unsurmountable obstacle to the applicant. The same can be said of the time-consuming exhaustion of constitutional appeals in countries like Austria and the Federal Republic of Germany, which not only poses certain constitutional law problems but also makes of the local remedies rule thus extensively interpreted a somewhat formal and mechanical requirement, if not an impractical one.

The Commission has been similarly rigorous in its application in certain situations of the principle that the substance of a complaint of which it has been seized ought to have been previously raised before the domestic courts. There are certain situations in which the Commission could possibly relax the rigidity with which it has applied this principle, such as when the Commission *itself* is under the duty of investigating the matter *ex officio*, or perhaps also when certain allegations regarding the complaint could clearly be prejudicial to the applicant.

Having pointed this out, one may now turn to the question of the *general conformity* of the law concerning the international protection of human rights with general international law, in so far as the question of the conditions of exhaustion of local remedies (remedies to be exhausted) is concerned. It comes as no surprise that in a great many decisions the Commission has expressly relied upon cases of general international law in order to substantiate its reasoning. No surprise because, first, a large body of that case-law had already been formed even years before the Commission came into being (e.g., the *Finnish Vessels, Panevezys – Saldutiskis, Electricity Company of Sofia* cases), and some of it not too long afterwards (e.g., the *Interhandel* and *Ambatielos* cases); and, secondly, because the Commission is expressly authorized to do so under the terms of the Convention, where, for example, Article 26 expressly refers to general international law in providing for the application of the local remedies rule under the Convention.

There have thus been countless occasions on which the Commission recalled *dicta* from cases decided by other tribunals (mainly the ones just referred to) in support of its views. For example, when in the *Retimag* case the Commission ruled that when, in case of doubt as to the effectiveness of remedies (their real chances of success), an applicant should submit the matter previously to the domestic courts themselves,[308] the Commission was in fact applying *mutatis mutandis* a view earlier expressed by the Permanent Court of International Justice in the *Panevezys – Saldutiskis Railway* case. And when in the same case the Commission held that it was the whole system of legal protection, as provided by municipal law, which ought to have been previously exhausted,[309] the Commission was in fact applying the argument maintained by the Commission of Arbitration in the *Ambatielos* case. And in both the *Nielsen*[310] and the *Austria v. Italy*[311] cases the Commission recalled the rationale of the local remedies rule as described by the International Court of Justice in the *Interhandel* case, as it again did in the *Ringeisen* case[312] and in one of the 'Belgian linguistic' applications.[313]

These are only a few examples taken from the vast practice of the Commission on the matter; those cases mentioned above occurred particularly in the Commission's earlier years. Later on, after having formed a considerable body of case-law of its own, the Commission proceeded whenever it saw fit to refer to its own previous leading cases to substantiate its subsequent decisions. This seems to be the position nowadays.

But what is possibly more significant is that more recently the general conformity between general international law and the international law on human rights protection began to show itself as working the other way round as well. Thus, in the 1969 oral hearings in the *Barcelona Traction* case before the International Court of Justice, *both* contending parties invoked in argument the case-law of the European Commission of Human Rights. Citing *inter alia* the *Nielsen* and the *Austria* v. *Italy* cases, Professor Rolin (counsel for Belgium) confessed that he did 'not see any difference between the principles affirmed in the opinions of the Commission in the field of exhaustion of remedies, and those of general international law, to which, furthermore, the Commission is bound to conform'.[314] Although Professor Rolin did not elaborate much on the point, he nevertheless insisted that the practice of the Commission on the matter did not diverge from traditional international law: 'there is no doubt', he remarked, 'that, in the application of the rule, the European Commission has shown itself relatively exacting, but this is understandable, inasmuch as it had to decide more often than not on claims brought by individuals against their own State'.[315]

This view was contested by Professor Guggenheim (counsel for Spain), who replied that 'contrary to what Mr Rolin believes, this exacting attitude [of the Commission] corresponds to the state of general international law, to which the Strasbourg Convention explicitly refers'.[316] Not surprisingly, counsel for Spain upheld a rigorous interpretation of the local remedies rule by the Commission, applying 'not only in respect of proceedings before the ordinary courts, but also to the whole system of legal remedies available in the State in question'.[317] Professor Guggenheim further remarked that Professor Rolin's observations 'fail to upset the fact that the system of exhaustion of legal remedies is nowadays, particularly since the

Ambatielos decision, more developed than in the more or less recent past'.[318]

In the same line of reasoning, Professor Malintoppi (counsel for Spain) declared:

The Spanish government has stressed that the practice of the European Commission of Human Rights furnishes a typical instance of the development of international control ensuring respect for the domestic judicial organization of States and verifying the previous exhaustion of local remedies. Professor Rolin also admitted [...] that the European Commission has shown itself 'relatively exacting' [*supra*, p. 108] in its application of the rule underlying our objection. [...] In point of fact the European Commission has been much more exacting even than Professor Rolin believed. What in any case I have difficulty in accepting is that this attitude is due to the fact that the European Commission is most often called upon to decide claims put forward by individuals against their own State. My difficulty arises from the fact that, under Article 26 of the Rome Convention, application cannot be made to the European Commission until local remedies have been exhausted under 'the generally recognized rules of international law'. I therefore do not see how the scope of the international rule can be altered by the fact that in certain cases the Rome Convention opens the way to direct recourse by individuals against their own State.[319]

In actual practice, however, such cases occur more often than counsel for Spain seems to allow. Further on in his oral argument, Professor Malintoppi repeatedly relied upon the Commission's decision in the *Retimag* case, to illustrate the view that the applicant is under the duty of raising previously all the points of his complaint before the domestic courts[320] and that in case of doubt as to the likelihood of success of the remedies this point ought also to be submitted previously to the domestic courts.[321]

As can be inferred from the survey above, none of these statements – on the part of counsel for Spain or of counsel for Belgium – reflects the whole truth of the matter. None of them seems to have been made after a thorough and meticulous examination of the Commission's jurisprudence on the subject. Some of them were made *in passim*, and all of them were certainly made in order to substantiate the arguments of the two contending parties. Yet the fact that the *two* parties concerned saw fit to consult the Commission's practice on the rule of exhaustion of local remedies and to invoke that practice before the International Court of Justice[322] should not pass unnoticed. Operating with a certain amount of continuity, and frequently pronouncing on the matter, the Commission may well be paving the way for new developments in the application of the local remedies rule, with particular reference to the international protection of human rights.

Section B

The so-called 'exceptions' to the rule
I. In general international law

International practice affords no evidence for treating the local remedies rule as an absolute dogma or sacrosanct principle always to be applied. Having grown out of customary international law, the rule has admitted 'exceptions' also recognized in general international law. Such 'exceptions' may possibly be regarded as a necessary implication of the rule itself, the rationale of which is to afford the State an opportunity to redress the alleged wrong through its own domestic legal system before its international responsibility can be invoked at international level: it thus follows that where remedies are incapable of redressing the wrongful situation the rule does not apply. Its rationale ceases to exist, and there is thereby no reason for further recourse to local remedies. Hermann Friedmann prefers to speak of *limitations* rather than 'exceptions' to the local remedies rule, because the term 'exceptions' presupposes a 'mechanical' outlook of the application of the rule, hardly acceptable to any realistic study of it.[323]

With this in mind, the present study will designate as 'exceptions' those situations which for one reason or another are found to fall outside the scope of application of the local remedies rule, or those situations where special circumstances relieve the applicant from the duty of exhausting domestic remedies. Here, again, the role played by the test of effectiveness of remedies is of paramount importance: it would require little demonstration that if remedies are ineffective or insufficient or inadequate for the object of the claim (even if they seem to be still formally open to the claimant), if they are in sum unable to redress the wrong, the local remedies rule then has no application (cf. *supra*, pp. 57–8 and 71–80).

Even though attempts at enumeration of exceptions to the rule are bound not to be exhaustive, an investigation of the matter remains necessary and useful for better and more precise understanding of the subject. A logical starting-point for the study of the topic appears to be the assumption, confirmed by State practice, case-law and expert writing, that the local remedies rule is in principle a *necessary* condition for the interposition of an international claim, *unless* it can be shown that there are special circumstances absolving the claimant from complying with the principle.

There has been some judicial recognition of the fact that the local remedies rule is far from being a sacrosanct or rigid principle, but admits of many exceptions.[324] The alleged non-application of the rule has in practice been relied upon in argument against preliminary objections of non-exhaustion.[325] There have been cases where the rule was held *not* to apply when there had already been an actual denial of justice[326] and the futility of further proceedings had been fully demonstrated,[327] or when the act charged had been taken by the government itself or the authorized high organs of the State against which 'there hardly exist local remedies',[328] or when courts have no jurisdiction to afford relief or the result is bound to be a repetition of an (adverse) decision already given.[329] A contention of non-application of the local remedies rule may thus be directed not only against a *remedy itself*, but also against the conditions of *its exercise*.[330]

On the other hand, certain arguments have been dismissed by international organs and tribunals as constituting mere excuses not relieving the claimant from the duty of exhausting local remedies. This has happened with regard to contentions based on the applicant's alleged lack of pecuniary means[331] and on his alleged ignorance as to the existence of the remedies to be exhausted.[332] Other excuses which likewise have *not* been accepted as constituting circumstances excluding the application of the local remedies rule include: bad advice by lawyers or counsel as to the exhaustion;[333] impossibility of procuring counsel[334] or of communicating with counsel;[335] too short a time for having recourse to and exhausting local remedies.[336] Similarly, the complainant's personal opinion as to the (assumed) uselessness of a given domestic remedy is no ground for absolving him from the obligation of exhaustion.[337]

On few occasions did the question of the so-called 'exceptions' to the local remedies rule receive so much attention as during the work of the Hague Conference for the Codification of International Law (1929–30).[338] Expert writing has likewise devoted much attention to the issue,[339] in general admitting exceptions to the rule or special circumstances authorizing or justifying its non-application. At this stage, one lesson can be drawn from the instances of non-application of the local remedies rule in international law. Classical writers like

Borchard[340] and Eagleton[341] have maintained that the exhaustion of local remedies ought to be pursued up to the point of a denial of justice before an international claim can be presented and diplomatic interposition become proper. However, in the light of the international practice of exceptions to the rule, this view seems inaccurate. It might be a good description of principle, but it is certainly not a good prescription for claimants.[342] It is surely *not* necessary that judicial irregularities tantamount to a technical denial of justice (once remedies have been exhausted) should be superadded to a previous wrong in violation of international law[343] – as correctly pointed out by Freeman – and least of all if no adequate redress is obtained.

Diplomatic action remains of course and as a matter of principle contingent upon the exhaustion of available local remedies by the aggrieved party. Yet the local remedies rule is not one of an unlimited scope or mechanical application requiring the occurrence of a denial of justice for diplomatic interposition to become proper. It may well be that, as hinted by Ago, the so-called 'exceptions' to the rule would be more adequately regarded as logical and necessary consequences of the application (itself) of the principle upon which the rule is based.[344] Exceptions may already be implicit in the rule, the most adequate being the one provided by the rationale of the local remedies rule itself; where redress proves not to be possible, that rationale disappears, and there remains no reason to keep insisting on further recourse to local remedies.

II. In the practice of the European Commission of Human Rights

1. Introduction

If exceptions or limitations to the local remedies rule exist in its application relating to the law of State responsibility for injuries to aliens, all the more reason for their applying in disputes governed by the law concerning the international protection of human rights. The starting-point is of course Article 26 of the European Convention, which stipulates that 'the Commission may only deal with the matter after all domestic remedies have been exhausted, according to the generally recognised rules of international law, and within a period of six months from the date on which the final decision was taken'.[345] The *ratio legis* of the rule was recalled by the Commission in a recent decision in the following terms:

As shown by the rule of the exhaustion of domestic remedies laid down in Article 26 of the Convention, it first falls to the national authorities to redress any violation of the Convention. In many cases, the violation itself cannot be wiped out with retroactive effect. (No *restitutio in integrum* can be made.) Only reparation can be made and constitute the redress. Such redress is thus, in the Convention system, a means whereby a State can avoid scrutiny by the organs of the Convention.[346]

But Article 26 of the Convention makes no express reference whatsoever to exceptions to the local remedies rule. Nor does Article 27(3) of the Convention. Possibly those exceptions are already implicit in the formulation of the local redress rule, but this is a point which has been left entirely to the Convention organs to develop in their practice. The case-law of the Commission is rich in that respect. The survey of that case-law that follows is of course a natural extension or complement of the survey *supra*, pp. 59–110, of the Commission's practice on the question of the remedies to be exhausted.

The factors which can constitute exceptions to the rule of exhaustion of local remedies may pertain to the *nature of the remedies* to be exhausted or else to the *conditions of their exercise*. The former category has already been studied above (cf. Section A above): the most decisive element in the determination of those factors has been the application of the test of effectiveness. There have been several cases where the local remedies rule was deemed to have been complied with and local remedies were held not to require exhaustion because they were found to be ineffective and insufficient, or inadequate for the object of the claim – in sum, unable to redress the alleged wrong (cf. *supra*, pp. 69–80). This exception has been regarded as implicit in the local redress rule itself, even though no express provision to that effect is found in Article 26 of the Convention.

Conversely, no exception exists if a remedy is found to be effective, i.e., capable of redressing the situation complained of. Here there can be no question that the local remedies rule applies, as of principle. If the effectiveness of a given remedy can be 'unfolded' into its constituent elements, the following are found to be present: a remedy before a local court regularly instituted according to the provisions of municipal law, and which is competent to examine the matter which forms the object of the claim, and which is competent to render a binding decision on the subject. If one of those elements is missing, the Commission will tend to consider the remedy as incapable of redressing the alleged wrong and to regard the situation as one which calls for an exception to the local remedies rule.[347]

But as such situations – pertaining to the character of the remedies themselves – have already been dealt with, the pages that follow are more particularly concerned with the factors entailing the non-application of the rule which are related to the *conditions of exercise* of the remedies to be exhausted. With this preliminary observation in mind, one may pursue the inquiry along the following lines: as the Commission has considered certain factors as constituting exceptions to the rule, and has rejected others as not excusing the applicant from the duty of exhaustion, one may take this twofold categorization as a useful and convenient means of studying the whole problem.

2. Circumstances relieving the applicant from the duty of exhausting local remedies

The Commission has on repeated occasions stated that there are indeed certain special circumstances which may, according to the generally recognised rules of international law, absolve the applicant from the obligation to exhaust domestic remedies.[348] There have been occasions on which the Commission has proceeded to an examination *ex officio* of this question.[349] There have been two main grounds on the basis of which the Commission has been prepared to accept certain circumstances as demanding an exception to the local remedies rule. The first one is the existence of over-lengthy proceedings or unreasonable delays in the procedure. The problem was discussed in more detail in the *X* v. *F.R. Germany* case (1959). The applicant's lawyer argued before the Commission that a constitutional appeal was not a remedy to be exhausted, not only because the Federal Constitutional Court was – in his words – 'une juridiction internationale', but also in view of the undue delay ('la lenteur anormale') of the procedure before the Federal Constitutional Court which, he argued, amounted to a true denial of justice.[350] As for the first part of the argument, the Commission replied that the constitutional appeal was in principle a remedy which fell within the scope of application of the local remedies rule.[351] Having said that, the Commission, turning to the problem of slowness of procedure, admitted that there could here exist special circumstances calling for the non-application of the rule:[352]

la Commission a constaté que [...] l'avocat du requérant avait invoqué subsidiairement les lenteurs de procédure devant la Cour Fédérale Constitutionelle qui équivaudraient à 'un véritable déni de justice' et que pourraient rendre le recours constitutionnel inefficace ou insuffisant; [...] la Commission a noté que de telles circonstances pourraient, le cas échéant, relever le requérant de l'obligation d'exercer ce recours.[353]

After that statement of principle, however, the Commission found that in the instant case the applicant had not established that the alleged slowness of the procedure constituted a special circumstance relieving him of the obligation of exhausting the constitutional appeal.[354] Even though the Commission stated that in principle over-lengthy proceedings may operate an exception to the local remedies rule, in practice its position on the matter, in the present case as in other similar cases (see *supra*, pp. 65–9), is not very convincing. In several applications coming from Austria and the Federal Republic of Germany the Commission has consistently held – as already seen – that recourse ought to be made to constitutional appeals, however time-consuming that might prove to be.

In the *De Becker* v. *Belgium* case (1958), the respondent government objected that the applicant had not sued for re-instatement. This time, however, the Commission replied that that remedy needed not be exhausted according to the generally recognised rules of international law, not only because its purpose was 'to obtain a favour and not to vindicate a right', but also because according to Belgian municipal law the applicant would not be entitled to take that action until five years after his release, thus rendering such a course inadequate in the case.[355] The Commission concluded, accordingly, that local remedies had in the case been exhausted according to the generally recognised rules of international law.[356]

It is difficult to apply a single test for determining what period of time may become an unreasonably long delay. The practice of the Commission is inconclusive on the subject. It may well be that this is a question to be examined in the *cas d'espèce*. The draftsmen of the UN International Convention on the Elimination of All Forms of Racial Discrimination, unlike those of the European Convention on Human Rights, preferred to include in the text of their formulation of the local remedies rule an exception whereby the rule does not apply 'where the application of the remedies is unreasonably prologned'.[357] The same happens with Article 41 of the UN International Covenant on Civil and Political Rights[358] and with Article 5(2)(b) of the Optional Protocol to that Covenant,[359] both stating that the local remedies rule shall not apply 'where the application of the remedies is unreasonably prolonged'. Thus, when one comes to this particular ground of non-application of the rule, the UN texts show themselves more explicit than that of the European Convention.

A few suggestions have been made for the assessment of this exception to the local remedies rule: first, an applicant could be allowed to attempt to demonstrate the alleged excessive delay in the handling of his case by comparing it with that incurred in other similar cases (the applicant not being required to undergo the same lengthy procedure); second, this exception could be considered in combination with other circumstances which might be adverse to the applicant (state of health, advanced age, etc. – but see *infra*, pp. 119–20); third, in determining the delay, account could be taken of the gravity of the situation, and perhaps of the continuing nature of the wrong inflicted upon the applicant, not to speak of the likelihood of success of the remedies to be exhausted; fourth, the presumptions could be made to operate more directly in favour of the allegedly aggrieved party (see n. 360); fifth, the condition of the applicant himself could be taken into account in the examination of the delay (e.g., when the complaint is lodged by a large corporation and the case is rather complicated, delays are bound to be longer than in comparatively simple complaints lodged by individuals).[360]

The other ground for non-application of the local remedies rule seems in this respect to have been regarded by the Commission perhaps in a more coherent way. On some occasions to date the Commission has taken the view that an adverse well-established jurisprudence by domestic courts may constitute a special circumstance relieving the applicant of the duty to exhaust a domestic remedy before those courts.[361] Thus in the *X* v. *Austria* case (1960) the Commission declared that 'il n'est pas nécessaire de recourir aux tribunaux internes si le résultat doit être la répétition d'une décision déjà rendue; [. . .] en l'espèce, comme la situation n'a pas été modifiée par un fait nouveau, les décisions rendues ne font que reprendre les jugements prononcés à la suite de la première demande';[362] as the absence of *fait nouveau* rendered the appeal without any chances of success, being rather a simple repetition of remedies utilized previously, the Commission added that 'dans ces conditions, la circonstance que la troisième procédure est encore pendante devant la Cour d'Appel [. . .] n'empêche pas la requérante de prétendre avoir épuisé toutes les voies de recours internes tel qu'il est entendu selon les principes de droit international généralement reconnus'.[363]

Again in the *A et al.* v. *F.R. Germany* case (1962) the Commission declared that 'une *jurisprudence bien établie* peut constituer une circonstance particulière de nature à dispenser un requérant, selon les principes de droit international généralement reconnus, d'épuiser les voies de recours internes'.[364] The Commission found *inter alia* in the instant case that one of the applicants seemed to have established that there existed in Germany a 'jurisprudence constante vouant d'avance à l'échec les efforts' of the individuals concerned, and that 'il s'avère, dès lors, que les requérants ont rempli les deux conditions définies à l'article 26' of the Convention.[365]

Later on, in the *Neumeister* v. *Austria* case (1964), the Commission asserted in relation to the remedy at issue (a request for release on bail) that 'it was not necessary to have recourse to domestic tribunals if the result must inevitably be the repetition of a decision already pronounced'.[366] Accordingly, the Commission rejected the objection of non-exhaustion of local remedies raised by the respondent government.[367] In another case against Austria the Commission found that it could not arrive at the conclusion that the applicant had not observed the rule of Article 26 of the Convention, as in its view there were in the case special circumstances rendering truly ineffective or insufficient the remedies in question.[368] But for other reasons the Commission ended up by declaring itself incompetent to carry on an examination of the application.[369]

Besides those two major grounds of exceptions to the local redress rule, the Commission, in the so-called *Second Cyprus* case (*Greece* v. *United Kingdom*, 1957), considered it impossible in practice to exercise local remedies due to the absence of any information as to the identity of the accused.[370] And more recently the Commission has displayed its readiness not to apply the local remedies rule in cases of *prima facie* substantiated administrative practices incompatible with the provisions of the Convention.[371]

3. Circumstances not relieving the applicant from the duty of exhausting local remedies

There have been several occasions when the Commission has rejected certain allegations as being nothing more than excuses which do not constitute special circumstances justifying the non-application of the local remedies rule. The Commission has thus apparently distinguished between factors which may directly affect the possibility of a remedy affording adequate redress (*supra*, pp. 114–17) from factors which in its eyes constitute merely excuses or attempts to circumvent the application of the rule or to justify the non-compliance with it (*infra*, pp. 118–20).

Thus, on several occasions the Commission has stressed that ignorance of the existence of a remedy or of the conditions of its exercise does not constitute a special circumstance absolving the applicant from the duty of exhausting it.[372] In one particular case the Commission employed emphatic language, as follows: 'the ignorance of the applicant as to the existence of this remedy at his disposal can in no way relieve him from obligations established by the rules of international law'.[373] The Commission has based such decisions on the general principle that ignorance of the law cannot be relied upon for not complying with the local remedies rule. *Ignorantia juris non excusat.*

It is therefore not surprising that the Commission has ruled that ignorance as to dates and time-limits for taking action before domestic courts does not constitute a circumstance to relieve the applicant of the obligation of exhausting local remedies.[374] Moreover, alleged lack of facilities for the purpose of exhausting local remedies does not, in the Commission's view, excuse an applicant from the duty of exhaustion; in the *Wiechert* v. *F.R. Germany* case (1964), where difficulties to lodge within due time-limit a request (e.g., for legal aid) were alleged,[375] as well as in the *X* v. *Belgium* case (1972), where lack of translation facilities was complained of,[376] the Commission took the view that such allegations, based on alleged lack of facilities in exhausting local remedies, could not be a sufficient reason for the failure to exhaust the remedies at issue, and, therefore, in both cases the Commission rejected the complaints as inadmissible for non-exhaustion.[377]

But the Commission has gone further than that. In the *23 Inhabitants of Alsemberg and of Beersel* v. *Belgium* case as well as in the *X and Y* v. *Belgium* case (both decided in 1963)[378] the Commission stressed that a simple *doubt* as to the existence or the effectiveness of a domestic remedy does not constitute a special circumstance authorizing the non-exercise of that remedy; in such cases, despite the doubt, recourse ought to be made to the domestic courts. This is a similar position to that taken by the Commission in the *Retimag* case (*supra*, pp. 67 and 86). Reference has already been made to the rigidity of this view, and to the fact that, in a more recent case, where the Commission itself had its doubts as to the effectiveness of a given remedy, it decided to declare the application inadmissible on another ground – that it was 'manifestly ill-founded'.[379]

On some occasions submissions have been made of bad advice given by lawyers as to the exhaustion, and the Commission has likewise rejected such excuses.[380] In the *Kornmann v. F.R. Germany* case (1966), for example, it stated:

In regard to the circumstances of the present case, the Commission observes that the applicant has submitted that it would have been impossible for him to find a lawyer willing to assist him, but that, on the other hand, he has in no way shown that he made any attempts to obtain the assistance of a lawyer in the proceedings concerned; and [...] moreover, he has not shown that he applied to the Kammergericht for legal aid in respect of these proceedings. [...] The Commission finds no special circumstances which dispensed the applicant from exhausting this particular remedy; [...] consequently, in this particular respect, the applicant has not exhausted the domestic remedies within the meaning of Article 26.[381]

In a decision rendered in 1973 the Commission remarked that the wrong information given by a court official is not a circumstance absolving the applicant from the duty of raising previously before the German Supreme Court (Bundesgerichtshof) the substance of his complaint:

En l'espèce, la Commission estime que ne saurait être considérée comme dispensant le requérant de porter ces griefs devant la Cour Suprême, l'information verbale qui lui aurait été donnée par un fonctionnaire du tribunal et selon laquelle le pourvoi déposé par son avocat en son nom rendait superflu tout nouveau développement de sa demande en cassation.[382]

Likewise, the Commission has held that the applicant's personal opinion as to the probability of success of a given remedy is not to be taken into account when not supported by any probative element.[383] In one of its earlier decisions, the Commission further indicated that the lack of financial resources of the applicant did not in the case constitute *per se* a special circumstance relieving him of the duty of exhaustion of local remedies.[384] Social assistance is no task of the Commission, but the fact remains that here the Commission could have displayed some degree of flexibility, particularly as no provision for the award of costs is made by the Convention. Finally, the Commission has taken the view that the applicant's ill health[385] or advanced age[386] are not excuses for not exhausting domestic remedies. Not surprisingly, the Commission has indicated in the

Austria v. *Italy* case that 'arguments concerning expediency and the tactics which it was or was not in the accused's interests to adopt' cannot establish the ineffectiveness and hence the non-application of a given domestic remedy.[387]

The fact that an applicant is being held under detention is not sufficient *per se* to exclude the application of the local remedies rule. There have in fact been numerous applications to the Commission coming from persons detained in prison, or otherwise interned. Of the more than five thousand individual applications lodged with the Commission by the middle of July 1971, almost forty per cent of that total fell into that category.[388] And in several of those cases (some well known for having been before both the Commission and the Court, like the *Wemhoff, Neumeister, Stögmüller* and *Matznetter* cases, studied *infra*, pp. 255–8) the local remedies rule has been applied.

But the Secretariat of the Commission has itself admitted that the definition of standards to be applied by the Commission in such cases remains 'extremely fragmentary';[389] after all, most of the applications coming from persons detained in prison are 'finally declared inadmissible'.[390] It can be reasonably expected, therefore, that in such cases the Commission, in applying Article 26 of the Convention, should show itself attentive to a larger extent to certain circumstances surrounding the exhaustion of local remedies by applicants under detention: for example, the fact that the applicant may well expose himself to certain risks by lodging a complaint, in the process of exhaustion, against certain officials. The matter may also be connected with administrative practices, and in this case, in the light of the more recent jurisprudence of the Commission, as already indicated, there is a stronger likelihood that an exception to the local remedies rule will prevail, if those practices incompatible with the Convention are substantiated.

4. Conclusions

From the aforesaid it is clear that the Commission has admitted that there are certain circumstances which amount to a legal or factual impossibility of exhausting local remedies or a justified impediment calling for an exception to the local redress rule. In the *X* v. *Belgium* case (1962) the Commission referred to the 'existence de circonstances particulières, telles qu'une *impossibilité matérielle ou juridique* ou un *empêchement légitime*, de nature à dispenser le requérant, selon les principes de droit international généralement reconnus, d'exercer les recours dont il disposait'.[391] The Commission's interpretation of such circumstances and impediments has been met with a certain amount of disagreement between expert writers.

Some would seemingly have one believe that the Commission's practice on the matter is a natural and expected application of Article 26 of the Convention;[392] others suggest that it might be a rigid application but that rigidity is 'ampiamente giustificata proprio dal fatto che essa nell'applicare l'art. 26 mira a difendere la dignità degli Stati',[393] without of course detracting from the rights of the individuals; others consider the Commission's practice on the subject as being strict, but prudent;[394] others have been more critical of it,[395] sometimes in an outspoken way.[396]

Without necessarily subscribing to any of those views (largely a matter of opinion), there remain a few points to be made about the Commission's practice on the exceptions to the local remedies rule. That practice does not seem to have expanded the general international law rule, as recently suggested;[397] or if it has done so it was only quantitatively (in view of the Commission's numerous decisions, operating with continuity under the provisions of the Convention). The Commission seems rather to have conformed to a large extent to the practice on the matter of other international organs and tribunals in general international law.

This may have been due to a perhaps too literal and strict interpretation by the Commission of the reference made by Article 26 of the Convention to the 'generally recognised rules of international law'. Yet some of the problems the Commission has had to face in practice seem to indicate that the rule of exhaustion of local remedies cannot possibly be understood as an *absolute* condition preceding any international action in the field of protection of human rights,[398] and should not in this area be interpreted *ipsis literis* as it has in other and distinct contexts. The rule is by no means one of a generally unqualified and automatic application.[399]

Thus, the Commission has repeatedly ruled that an adverse well-established jurisprudence may constitute an exception to the local remedies rule. It has stated the same in respect of unreasonably long delays of procedure, but here the Commission has displayed some vacillation. In assessing undue delays, the Commission could work on a comparative basis, assembling similar cases into groups for determining the length of proceedings and their reasonableness, for the purposes of application of Article 26 of the Convention. This would not affect the prerogative attributed to municipal law of setting up time-limits for the exercise of local remedies. In assessing undue delays the Commission could also, *concomitantly*, take into account other factors pertaining to the applicant himself and, more objectively, to the situation he finds himself in and the other concrete elements of the case (such as, for example, the gravity of the alleged wrong, the complexity of the case, and so forth).

In this way, the Commission could tip the balance more in favour of the applicant whenever necessary, or could make the presumptions operate on his behalf, thus relieving him of possibly excessive negative handicaps he faces in trying to comply with the local remedies rule, and applying the rule more properly, in a more balanced way. There have in fact been some occasions when the Commission could have done so but did not. For example, the Commission interpreted the applicant as having 'approved' of undue delays of procedure because he proceeded to exhaust further remedies;[400] it has required the applicant to raise issues before a domestic court which he deemed prejudicial to his case;[401] it has required the applicant to appeal against refusal of grant of free legal assistance and to bring action for damages at his own expense;[402] it has insisted on the exhaustion of certain domestic remedies whose existence or effectiveness was being questioned by the applicant;[403] it has maintained that domestic remedies should be exhausted even though the applicant had been deported from the country concerned, prevented from entering it, and consequently forced to initiate any action from outside its territory.[404] In yet another case, the applicant had apparently been denied justice by a lower court, which seemed to have acted improperly and committed certain procedural irregularities (on hearing of witnesses and delays); nevertheless the Commission rigorously ruled that the applicant had failed to comply with the local remedies rule for not having raised before the German Federal Court of Justice (*Bundesgerichtshof*) the complaints he had against the lower court (*Landgericht*).[405]

At least some of these cases could certainly have been held to call for the non-application of the local remedies rule, if that rule is not to be regarded as an unsurmountable obstacle aimed deliberately at the rejection of complaints. It is disappointing, moreover, to see an insistence upon the duty of exhaustion despite both the applicant's poverty and the refusal to him of free legal assistance, when the Convention makes no provision for the award of costs,[406] an attitude which can only discourage people even to attempt to lodge with the

Commission complaints which may well be deserving of attention.

As for the rejection by the Commission of such 'excuses' as ignorance of the existence of remedies and the conditions of their exercise, lack of facilities for utilizing them, non-exhaustion resulting from alleged incompetence or negligence of counsel, wrong information obtained from officials, the applicant's own personal opinion as to the effectiveness of the remedies, his ill health or advanced age – that rejection seems to be in principle well in conformity with the general international law practice on the matter of exceptions to the local redress rule (cf. *supra*, pp. 110–12).

The application of exceptions to the local remedies rule by the Commission should be weighed against the background of the overall practice of the Commission throughout the whole period of its existence, so as to enable one to verify with more clarity what its significance has been. The figures can be illuminating. By 1 October 1975, about one month before the Council of Europe convened in Rome (5–8 November 1975) its fourth international colloquy on the European Convention on Human Rights to mark the twenty-five years of the Convention's existence, a total of 140 applications had been declared *admissible*, out of a total of 6,847 applications registered with the Commission (until the end of 1974).[407] The statistics are impressive: out of 5,975 decisions taken, 5,598 applications were rejected *de plano* or struck off the Commission's list,[408] and several others were likewise rejected after further consideration and communication to the respondent governments.[409]

Of course the local remedies rule has played and has been playing – expectedly – a most prominent role in the rejection of such an overwhelming majority of applications; but concerning the *exceptions* to the rule, rather should one turn to those 140 applications which, from 2 June 1956 until 27 May 1975, have been declared *admissible* by the Commission. One could, out of those 140 applications which have survived the barriers of inadmissibility, indicate not less than twenty-eight applications where the objection of non-exhaustion of local remedies was discussed or dismissed by the Commission, in seven inter-State cases[410] and in twenty-one cases initiated by individuals.[411]

The figures speak for themselves: the cases in which the exceptions to the local remedies rule prevailed in the end, correspond to a very tiny proportion of the applications of which the Commission has been seized; as likewise the total of complaints declared admissible by the

Convention is minimal in comparison with the total of decisions rendered to date. To that another factor should be added: as the local remedies rule is not the only ground of inadmissibility under the Convention,[412] it may well happen that the Commission may find in a case special circumstances relieving the applicant of the obligation of exhausting local remedies, and yet the case may after all be dismissed on a ground other than non-exhaustion of local remedies.

One could refer to three cases[413] in which this somewhat curious but perfectly possible situation has occurred, of which the most illustrative is the *Kaiser* v. *Austria* case (1971): in that case the Commission rejected the objection of non-exhaustion of local remedies *three times*, first in relation to a *pourvoi en cassation*, secondly in respect of a disciplinary action, and thirdly with regard to an action – *recours en responsabilité* – for damages (all three remedies held to be incapable in the case of redressing the alleged wrong),[414] but in the end the Commission nevertheless decided to declare the application inadmissible on a different ground, that of its being 'manifestly ill-founded' (Article 27(2) of the Convention).[415]

It may finally be asked whether these factors and statistics suggest that there may be something wrong with the Commission's interpretation of the local remedies rule? Here a broader outlook seems desirable, to avoid the danger of simply quantifying results. In many cases the Convention as a whole has had an impact in member countries favourable to human rights promotion and protection, by urging those countries to modify legislation and administrative practice and to adjust them to the provisions of the Convention, and to co-operate with the Convention organs in securing friendly settlement of the cases.

But here one is not concerned with an assessment of the Convention as a whole, however beneficial its overall impact upon the domestic legal systems of the member countries might have been in providing indications and standards for the improvement of their internal administration of justice. The problem here is of a more technical nature, even though its assessment could only be made realistically and with a sense of proportion against the background of the larger framework of the possible impact of the Convention briefly depicted above. In so far as the Commission's application of the exceptions to the local remedies rule is concerned, the figures referred to above strongly suggest that the Commission's interpretation and application of the principle that there are special circumstances which according to the generally recognised rules of international law relieve the applicant of the duty of exhaustion of local remedies, were very narrow indeed.

Against that it can be argued that the Commission *needed* to be rigorous with the application of the local remedies rule (as well as the other grounds of inadmissibility of complaints), in order to gain and secure the confidence of the governments concerned, whose support is so essential for the existence of the system of individual applications (Article 25 of the Convention on the right of individual petition being optional) and for the success of the Convention as a whole. In fact, the cautious attitude of the Commission in the process of admissibility of applications has even recently been praised as having succeeded in its purpose, as reflected in the fact that, for example, 'the number of States prepared to accept the right of individual petition has gradually increased, and, despite hesitations, no State which has once made a declaration accepting this right has yet failed to renew it'.[416]

But the point here is not the Commission's general policy and the general aims pursued, nor the *existence* itself of the local remedies rule, which for the time being seems to remain in safe place within the system of the Convention. Once one turns to the *scope* ascribed to the rule within that system by the Commission, and looks closer into the matter, certain features of the Commission's practice become more visible and lead one to the view that it could in fact have proceeded to a more appropriate application of the rule in some respects.

Cases have been indicated in which the Commission could have reasonably concluded that the local remedies rule should not apply, and in which nevertheless the Commission saw fit to insist on further exhaustion. Furthermore, the Commission could have elaborated more on undue delays and lengthy proceedings as exceptions to the rule, and been less hesitant in deciding on this ground. A particular set of cases where the Commission can do much to improve its application of the rule is that category of applications emanating from applicants under detention. Here the Commission's practice is somewhat inflexible: it is not rare to see the Commission being confronted with the applicant's complaints of alleged ill-treatment during his detention and yet declaring the application inadmissible for non-exhaustion of local remedies because the applicant had not shown that he had seized a higher domestic court of those complaints.[417]

The Commission could also improve its application of the rule when the complainant's point at issue amounts to an alleged denial of justice due to different kinds of procedural irregularities (for example, improper handling of evidence or questioning of witnesses). The Commission has declared that 'it is not competent to deal with an application alleging that errors of law or fact have been committed by domestic courts except where the Commission considers that such errors might have involved a possible violation of any of the rights and freedoms limitatively listed in the Convention'.[418] But this is precisely the point. In some cases this attitude of the Commission led to rejection of the applications for non-exhaustion of local remedies,[419] when perhaps a *more thorough* use of its *ex officio* investigatory powers could have detected the occurrence of a procedural irregularity and a denial of justice. This would possibly be a sounder attitude than insisting on further exhaustion, i.e., on the applicant's duty to raise previously before the domestic courts the substance of all his complaints taken to the Commission.

This is not the same as saying that complaints of alleged denials of justice should receive more attention from the Commission than others, or preferential treatment, thus opening the way for circumvention of the rule. The Commission would rather keep within the confines of its powers, taking due account of the gravity of the wrongs complained of. The Commission has shown its preparedness to draw analogies with the practice on the matter in general international law, possibly by virtue of the reference to generally recognised rules of international law found in Article 26 of the Convention. But it seems that other international organs have, at times, when an alleged denial of justice was at stake, displayed considerably less hesitation to invoke the lack of a certain international or minimum standard of justice in order to justify the non-application of the local redress rule, however controversial this might have been.

Neither this position, nor, conversely, an excess of concern for member States' susceptibilities, appear as proper guides for the Commission's practice on the matter. As the Commission gradually reduces or abandons the apparent pre-disposition to insist on further exhaustion of local remedies, and becomes more prepared, by the operation of presumptions, to tip the balance in favour of the aggrieved party, when this appears *prima facie* the proper course to be taken (for example, when the State concerned does not *prima facie* seem prepared to afford the complainant a fair chance of seeking and effectively obtaining redress), then a categorization of exceptions to the local remedies rule will perhaps prove less necessary than seems to be the position today. After all, bearing in mind the normal use of remedies, the so-called 'exceptions' are *implicit* in the proper operation of the local redress rule itself.

Section C
Waiver or exclusion of the rule

I. Express waiver and waiver in general

The local remedies rule, primarily a prerogative of the sovereignty of the territorial State, has in practice been on some occasions waived by the sovereign will of States. A notorious example of such waiver was afforded by the practice of Mixed Arbitral Tribunals and Mixed Claims Commissions in the inter-war period.[420] One of the immediate implications was that, in order to overcome a general waiver of the local remedies requirement, resort was made to the Calvo clause commitment, effectively binding on the individual, though not on his State, and thus preventing the submission of claims otherwise admissible.[421] More recently, further instances of waiver of the local redress rule are found in the *Gut Dam* arbitration (Canada and the United States, 1965–8),[422] and in the 1958 arbitration award between Saudi Arabia and the Arabian American Oil Company (*Aramco*).[423]

A great many post-war international claims on account of nationalizations of alien property (an estimated 95 per cent) have been followed by compensation by lump-sum agreements, thus apparently depriving the local remedies rule of much practical significance.[424] On the other hand, successive post-war economic co-operation agreements have contrasted sharply with lump-sum agreements in expressly providing for the requirement of exhaustion of local remedies.[425] Even in lump-sum agreements the practice of waiver has given rise to distinct interpretations and has not passed without reservations.[426]

In two particular areas of international law – adjustment of environmental disputes and settlement of investment disputes – current discussion on waiver of the local remedies rule is highly inconclusive. In the context of environmental regulation the more marked tendency is towards waiver of the rule, and this can be explained by various factors in relation to different kinds of environmental disputes. Suffice it here to point out that in general, the historical context of application of the local remedies rule in alien treatment and individualistic diplomatic protection on a State-to-State basis has apparently become too narrow for international environmental protection. In the past heavy emphasis was laid on the interests of the territorial State (as a 'self-sufficient' entity), whereas in the new context one is less concerned with purely individual redress than with trans-frontier solutions benefiting collectivities of people (for example, cessation of polluting activities) on the basis of States' obligations (rather than interests). Here, as in general human rights protection, and perhaps to an even greater extent, there is a shift of emphasis from insistence on formal requirement of exhaustion of local remedies (for individual redress) to the general duty to provide effective remedies – though with the persisting dilemma between public or private treatment of the matter – and to prevent environmental harm.[427]

In the settlement of investment disputes the matter is quite debatable,[428] and is further complicated when intermingled with implied waiver of the local remedies rule, as in the construction of the local remedies requirement found in the 1965 World Bank Convention on Settlement of Investment Disputes (Article 26),[429] which can be interpreted as a non-mandatory or permissive rule which is excluded unless expressly invoked, or else as an implied renunciation of the requirement – the presumption operating to this effect (see *infra*, pp. 131–3, on implied waiver).

In the distinct context of the international protection of human rights, by expressly providing for the inclusion of the local remedies rule[430] amongst the conditions of admissibility of human rights communications, human rights instruments have avoided and dismissed the possibility of expressly waiving the rule of exhaustion of local remedies.

This does not mean, however, that the problem of the waiver of the rule does not arise in practice. The European Commission of Human Rights, for example, is of the view that it can examine *ex officio* whether the local remedies requirement has been satisfied. Thus, when a State refused to avail itself of the objection of non-exhaustion of local remedies, the Commission has interpreted this attitude as amounting to a waiver of the (benefit of the) local remedies rule. In the *57 Inhabitants of Louvain and Environs* v. *Belgium* case (1964), for example, throughout the oral hearing (same date) counsel for the respondent government declared that he did not intend to invoke the objection of non-exhaustion of local remedies because the application was directed not against a ministerial decision, but rather against the Belgian legislation as such.[431] The Commission found that the respondent government had thereby waived the local remedies rule,[432] and therefore, the Commission concluded on the point that there was no question of examining whether the applicants could or should have had resort to the Belgian *Conseil d'État* before seizing the Commission.[433]

This practice may lead to some inadequacies, especially when the renunciation of the rule by the respondent State is not made in clear terms. In fact, an implied waiver, by the State, of the local remedies rule has not necessarily precluded the Commission from examining *ex officio* whether or not the rule has been complied with. But the Commission has gone rather too far in extending that examination even to local remedies not invoked or mentioned by the respondent State. This happened in the *X* v. *Austria* case (1966). The Austrian government raised an objection of non-exhaustion of local remedies with regard to the first and second instances (the Regional Court and the Court of Appeal of Innsbruck).[434] The Commission, in declaring the application inadmissible for non-exhaustion of local remedies, went further by noting that, although it had not been submitted by the respondent government, it was open to the applicant to apply to the Constitutional Court.[435]

The case may serve as an illustration of some of the problems which an implied waiver of the rule or an implied restriction of its field of application may entail. This question will be more appropriately and thoroughly dealt with *infra*, pp. 131–3. As for the express waiver of the rule (as distinct from the question of the implied waiver), from the survey above it was seen that it may happen, and it does happen in practice. In its 1956 resolution on the local remedies rule, the *Institut de Droit International* categorically stated that 'the rule does not apply [...] in cases where its application has been waived by agreement of the States concerned'.[436]

It is not difficult to visualize situations where it might be in the interest of a State to waive the local remedies rule. The State may deem that direct reference of certain claims to international organs may be more adequate or convenient or advantageous for various reasons; it may prove more economical in saving time and reducing costs, under certain circumstances (just as in other cases the same may apply to adjudication by domestic courts); it may also be alleged that international courts are better equipped than domestic courts to deal with certain categories of disputes. In such cases the local remedies rule, a prerogative of State sovereignty, may be waived by the same sovereign will of the States concerned. This shows that the rule of customary international law providing for the exhaustion of local remedies is to a large extent a *rule of compromise*.

In fact, even though not necessarily for any of the reasons stated above, in the *Christian Müller* v. *Austria* case before the Commission the objection of non-exhaustion of local remedies was expressly waived by the Austrian government. On 11 October 1974 the Austrian government submitted their observation to the effect that they considered that 'the formal conditions of admissibility set out in Articles 25 and 26 of the Convention were satisfied', and accordingly they considered it 'desirable to waive their right of contesting the admissibility of the application while reserving that of submitting objections on the merits during the subsequent procedure'.[437] In its decision of 16 December 1974, the Commission, after taking note of the Austrian government's position on the matter and its waiver of admissibility objections (under Articles 25 and 26),[438] decided that the application was to be declared (in part) admissible.[439]

There has been some hesitation as to whether the local remedies rule applies in conciliation procedures: the 'non-juridical' or extra-judicial character of conciliation proceedings (based on the consent of the parties) has been invoked by both opponents and supporters of the application of the rule in this context, either to dispense with the rule because of that non-judicial character, or, for precisely the same reason, not to circumvent the rule and thus to insist on local courts' decisions.[440]

The question does not actually arise in the system of human rights protection under the European Convention, for it would be inaccurate to consider the European Commission as a simple organ of conciliation. In pronouncing on the admissibility of applications the Commission is performing a *judicial function*. The right of individual petition has a jurisdictional character, and the Commission's decision on it is a jurisdictional act taken at the end of a *procédure contradictoire régulière* (even though the applicant does not become a 'party' to the case). There is, therefore, as Virally remarks, a certain 'effacement de la fonction conciliatrice', contrasting with the prominence of the jurisdictional function of the Commission's decisions on individual applications: 'l'aspect juridictionnel tend décidément à l'emporter sur l'aspect de conciliation, au moment où s'établit une confrontation entre ces deux possibilités de solution'.[441] In short, the problem of the application of the local remedies rule in conciliation proceedings does not arise in the context of the Commission's application of the rule under the European Convention, as this application is generally recognized as being vested with an essentially judicial character.

II. Implied waiver (the problem of application of the rule in the absence of express provision)

So far, international law has not provided a satisfactory answer to the question whether the local remedies rule is applicable to the settlement of claims or disputes in the absence of an express provision to that effect. The practice of international tribunals and legal writing have been contradictory and remain divided on the problem, some supporting the *non-application* of the rule,[442] some pointing in the opposite direction in support of the *application* of the rule in the absence of express provision (possibly the majority of international decisions touching on the problem).[443]

It may in fact be argued that in such absence of express provision the rule, as one of *customary* international law, is nevertheless in principle and by necessary implication applicable. It is not only the interests of the respondent State in having the dispute settled within the framework of its own internal legal system which are taken into account; the elements of redress to the aggrieved party and of quick, effective and peaceful settlement in the interests of all concerned are also always present. Bearing this in mind, a few points may be submitted concerning the waiver of the local remedies rule in particular relation to the international protection of human rights.

The practice of States which originally helped to shape the rule was primarily concerned with the protection to be accorded to nationals living or operating abroad. Within this context it came to be recognized as a customary rule of international law. The more recent systems of international protection of human rights appear at variance with the earlier practice of States in that they extend protection to nationals against their own State and to stateless persons. This has been done by means of international agreements and conventions. It may thus be asked whether, in case those instruments chose not to include any provision expressly requiring the exhaustion of local remedies, the requirement should nevertheless apply.

The answer here is perhaps not so clear as in general international law. Unlike the position in customary international law, the presumptions in the conventional international law on human rights are or should be made to work in favour of the aggrieved individuals to be protected. This would entail the non-application of the local remedies rule in the absence of an express provision, on the presumption that, for example, an alleged violation of human rights could be immediately examined by the international organ, without further delay.

This, however, does not happen in practice. Human rights instruments have opted for an *express* requirement of the prior exhaustion of local remedies. This is the case, for example, of the European Convention on Human Rights (Articles 26 and 27(3)), the UN Convention on the Elimination of All Forms of Racial Discrimination (Articles 11(3) and 14(1)(a)), the American Convention on Human Rights (Article 46(1)(a), with the limitations contained in Article 46(2)); this is also the case of the procedures set forth in resolution 1(XXIV) of the UN Sub-Commission on Prevention of Discrimination and Protection of Minorities, and in Article 9 (*bis*) of the Statute and Articles 54 and 55 of the Regulations of the Inter-American Commission on Human Rights – procedures concerned with the admissibility for examination of communications on human rights violations. In all these cases the local remedies rule is expressly provided for. The same is true of the UN Covenant on Civil and Political Rights (Article 41(1)(c)) and its Protocol (Articles 2 and 5). However, the UN Covenant on Economic and Social Rights – its counterpart – is silent on the requirement of exhaustion of local remedies. The silence in this particular case and in view of the circumstances (same draftsmen, same time of preparation and adoption) may well be interpreted, it may be submitted, as constituting an implied waiver of the local remedies rule.

Were the rule not provided for in those instruments, it would be difficult to say that that amounted to a general policy of implied waiver. For it could be argued, against the presumption in favour of the individual, that precisely because the protective system included cases of individuals complaining against their own countries, there would thereby be all the more necessity for the application of the general rule of exhaustion of local remedies.

But the systems of international protection of human rights comprise not only the possibility of complaints lodged by individuals (e.g., Article 25 of the European Convention), but also complaints brought by States themselves under the notion of a 'collective guarantee' (e.g., Article 24 of the European Convention). If the position is uncertain and unclear in the former in the absence of express provision on the local remedies rule, it need not be so in the latter. Here the applicant State complains of a prevailing condition which exists in violation of human rights and which affects many individuals.

It may thus be argued that in such case, in the absence of express provision, the local remedies rule does not apply. This position has had some support both in State practice and in legal writing. Among writers, Amerasinghe has advocated it.[444] In international practice the position was espoused by the Austrian government in the *Austria* v. *Italy* case before the European Commission of Human Rights. There the Austrian government submitted that 'save for complaints made in exercising diplomatic protection, exhaustion of domestic remedies would appear, then, to be irrelevant to the admissibility of applications from States, which would be based on concepts of collective guarantee and general interest'.[445]

In such cases the argument for the application of the local remedies rule appears certainly less forceful (in the hypothetical silence of an international instrument) than in cases of complaints brought by individuals. A closer look at the argument shows, however, that the desirable non-application of the rule in such cases derives less from the absence of express provision than from the prevailing situation in which it would be unwise to have to wait until one of the many affected individuals had exhausted his local remedies, before examining the case. The question seems to be closer to that of the very effectiveness of domestic remedies (for example, in a prevailing situation or condition in violation of human rights, or in certain widespread practices or measures in violation of human rights) than to the more technical question of the so-called implied waiver. The problem remains, thus, inconclusive and open to doubts and uncertainties.

The lesson to be drawn, it may be submitted, is that implied waiver of the local remedies rule is not properly to be followed as a general policy of treaty-making and interpretation. It may lead to uncertainties and perhaps to undesirable results. Where it is made possible (for example, in the UN Covenant on Economic and Social Rights), it should be restrictively interpreted. Consequently, if the States concerned choose not to have the local remedies rule applied – a rule which ultimately exists primarily for their own benefit – they would do better to opt not for silence, but for an *express* waiver of the rule as a wiser policy and one which might possibly lead to more concrete results.

3

THE BURDEN OF PROOF WITH REGARD TO THE EXHAUSTION OF LOCAL REMEDIES

I. Introduction

The burden of proof is an important question of international legal procedure, for on its allocation will ultimately depend the equality of arms. An improper handling of the question may have the result of leaving one of the contending parties in a given case in a weaker position, despite formal procedural equality. The notion of the burden of proof means that a party ought to adduce evidence to prove the necessary facts, so that on the basis of that evidence the judge may form his own representation of the facts.[1] Ultimately, thus, it has been suggested, 'what has to be proved will depend on who has to prove it'.[2] The question therefore has an important bearing on the outcome of litigation, particularly when certain facts are considered not proven.

The principle *onus probandi incumbit actori* presents certain delicate problems. First, it may be asked whether it applies in international law as it does in municipal law. Does the assertion that the burden of proof rests with the *actor* mean that it always rests with the plaintiff? What is then the extent of the burden? In this chapter it is proposed to deal with these problems, examining them in the light of general international law before embarking on an investigation of the question in the jurisprudence of the European Commission of Human Rights and the practice of United Nations organs, with particular reference to the burden of proof concerning the objection of non-exhaustion of local remedies.

II. The burden of proof in general international law

1. International law reliance upon analogies from municipal law

In 1933 Ripert observed that the general principle – common to all legislations – of the *onus probandi incumbit actori* did *not* mean that the burden of proof was incumbent on the claimant by virtue of his position in the procedure, but rather because of his allegation of the existence of a right or a fact. Accordingly, the burden also rested upon the defendant to prove his contentions: *reus in exceptione fit actor*. The two propositions could be summed up in the formula: *onus probandi incumbit ei qui dicit*.[3]

The term *actor* in the principle *onus probandi incumbit actori* is not to be taken to mean the plaintiff from the procedural standpoint, but rather the claimant in view of the issues involved: the burden of proof rests upon the claimant who asserts to prove his assertion.[4] This principle has been admitted without hesitation by international organs. After all, a party cannot simply assert or deny a proposition, and then rest his case upon a technical rule throwing the burden of proof on the other party, without 'running the risk of adverse inference being drawn from his failure to produce evidence'.[5]

International legal practice reflects certain nuances which can be attributed to both the common law and the civil law systems. A general principle common to both those systems is that whichever party makes an allegation must always adduce some evidence to support it.[6] Sandifer speaks in this connection of a *procedural* burden of proof which 'continually shifts during the process of the trial'.[7]

The common law influence on international legal procedure is reflected in the free presentation of proof, the cross-examination of witnesses by the contending parties, and the use of affidavits. The continental influence is manifested by the adoption of the principle of inquisition (the *ex officio* powers of the court) and the almost total absence of restrictions concerning the receivability of evidence.[8]

A notion deriving particularly from the common law and later taken into international arbitrations is that of the *prima facie* evidence. The claimant's duty is hereby limited only to adducing some *prima facie* evidence (*commencement de preuve*) in support of his contentions, rather than fully proving them. To Witenberg this *prima facie* evidence operates a shifting in the burden of proof.[9] In the *L.S. Kling (U.S.)* v. *Mexico* case (1930), the Mexican–U.S. General Claims Commission, after referring to the influence of domestic law rules of evidence upon the procedure before international tribunals, defined *prima facie* evidence as 'evidence which, unexplained or uncontradicted, is sufficient to maintain the proposition affirmed'.[10]

The judicial determination of facts upon which a court bases its decision in a given case can proceed by the presentation or instigation of the parties or on the basis of *ex officio* inquiries. Hence the accusatory or adversary system, and the inquisitorial or investigatory system, respectively. As to the burden of proof in either system, it is significant to note that in a fairly recent colloquium sponsored by the Max-Planck-Institut it was assessed that a distribution of the burden of proof occurred in one way or another in virtually all (municipal) legal systems examined. Conversely, none of them afforded evidence for the view that one of the contending parties would always carry the burden of proof.[11]

There is in fact conclusive evidence for the distribution of the burden of proof not only in different municipal legal systems but also in international law,[12] and with particular reference to the objection of non-exhaustion of local remedies (see *infra*, pp. 138–43) before international tribunals.[13] It has been argued that a further compelling reason in support of the distribution lies in the fact that in international litigation it is frequently not easy to distinguish between plaintiff and defendant and to determine with finality which party is the *actor*[14] for the purposes of application of the principle *onus probandi incumbit actori*.

Consequently, the burden of proof in general international law is far from being a detailedly regulated technical system clearly applicable to any case.[15] The frequent lack of distinction in the position of the contending parties as plaintiff and defendant, with the pleadings 'going forward simultaneously', may render difficult the determination of the division of the burden of proof, and cause it to occur only 'late in the proceedings'.[16] This absence of strict international law rules or criteria gives prominence to decisions on the matter by international courts and tribunals.

It is recalled that in the *W.A. Parker (U.S.)* v. *Mexico* case (1926) the Mexican–U.S. General Claims Commission stated that 'municipal restrictive rules of adjective law or of evidence' could not be erected into 'universal principles of law'. The Commission supported 'the greatest liberality' in the admission of evidence, and expressly denied the existence in international procedure of rules governing the burden of proof borrowed from municipal procedure.[17] The Commission further stated that:

the absence of international rules relative to a division of the burden of proof between the parties is especially obvious in international arbitrations between governments in their own right, as in those cases the distinction between a plaintiff and a respondent often is unknown, and both parties often have to file their pleadings at the same time.[18]

It seems, however, that this argument, relying upon the insufficiency of international procedure on the matter at issue, cannot be pushed too far. Five years later, in the *Chevreau* case (France v. United

Kingdom, 1931), to a contention that the burden of proof was affected since the proceedings had been brought about by a *compromis* of arbitration, there being neither plaintiff nor defendant, the umpire replied that the application of the usual rules concerning the evidence had its place, since (according to the *compromis*) the two parties had a duty to prove to the satisfaction of the arbiter the authenticity of all points of fact invoked to establish or deny the responsibility.[19]

In the *Island of Palmas* case (Netherlands v. United States, 1928), arbitrator Max Huber held that 'the dispute having been submitted to arbitration by special agreement, each party is called upon to establish the arguments on which it relies in support of its claim to sovereignty over the object in dispute'.[20] And in the *Lighthouses* arbitration (1956) between France and Greece (claim n. 14), the Permanent Court of Arbitration applied the principle of 'a reasonable sharing of the burden of proof'.[21]

Where remedies have not been exhausted, it is incumbent upon the claimant to prove his contentions. This view was taken by umpire Ralston in the *Sambiaggio* case (Venezuelan Arbitrations, 1903), in which he asserted that 'the burden of proving want of diligence rests upon the claimants' and particularly so as local remedies had not been exhausted:

the claimants, so far as the evidence shows, never made any appeal to the government for protection, as it was their right to do if they desired to obtain it, and although such appeal, if made, might have had an important effect upon the question of liability.[22]

In the *La Guaira Electric Light and Power Co.* case (Venezuelan Arbitrations, 1903–5), commissioner Bainbridge held that in order to bring the claim within the jurisdiction of the Commission it was 'incumbent upon the claimant to show a sufficient excuse for not having made an appeal to the courts of Venezuela open to it, or a discrimination or denial of justice after such appeal had been made'.[23] And in the *Queen* case (Brazil v. Sweden/Norway, 1872), the umpire stated that it was incumbent upon the claimant to prove his assertions.[24]

By the same token, in the *Gill (U.K.) v. Mexico* case (1931), the British–Mexican Claims Commission, holding the respondent government responsible for injuries suffered by a British subject, found that there was 'strong *prima facie* evidence' of a fault on the part of the local authorities, as the agent of the Mexican government had 'not shown a single proof' that redress was given to the injured individual.[25]

It seems that international arbitrations – a discontinuous system anyway – do not provide a conclusive answer to the problem of the administration of proof.[26] But this is far from meaning that there are in international law no rules governing the burden of proof. The matter is governed by the principle *onus probandi incumbit actori* to the effect that 'the burden of proof rests upon the party who raises the issue'.[27] Accordingly, the general absence of a strict plaintiff–defendant relationship in international litigation cannot be pressed too far to challenge or undermine the principle of distribution of the burden in international law: as the burden rests upon the claimant not in his capacity as such but by virtue of his allegations of a fact, the distinction between claimant and respondent then becomes not very relevant for the question under discussion.[28]

In some instances where the Permanent Court of International Justice allocated the burden of proof to one or another of the contending parties,[29] it avoided submitting fixed criteria for the distribution of that burden, although its jurisprudence displayed a general tendency to stability.[30] In the practice of the International Court of Justice, the *Minquiers and Ecrehos* case (United Kingdom v. France, 1953) may be recalled, where the ICJ, called upon to appraise the relative strength of the opposing claims, espoused the view that the burden of proof rested equally upon both parties. The ICJ thought it was for itself to decide upon the burden of proof, and it stated that each party had to prove its alleged title (to the disputed territory) and the facts upon which it relied.[31] In several other cases the ICJ has touched upon the distribution of the burden of proof.[32]

2. The burden of proof in respect of exhaustion of local remedies

In general international law the principle of distribution of the burden of proof has been applied on several occasions with regard to objections of non-exhaustion of local remedies. In the *Ambatielos* case (1956), for example, the Commission of Arbitration held that 'in order to contend successfully that international proceedings are inadmissible the defendant State must prove the existence, in its system of internal law, of remedies which have not been used'.[33]

The distribution of the burden of proof was confirmed by the Permanent Court of International Justice in the *Panevezys–Saldutiskis*

Railway case (1939). Lithuania fielded an objection on the ground of non-exhaustion of local remedies by the Estonian company. Estonia argued (without contesting the existence of the local remedies rule) that in the case, first, Lithuanian courts could not entertain a suit, and second, on one particular point the Lithuanian highest court had already given a decision 'adverse to the Estonian company's claim'. The Court pondered that if either of those points 'could be substantiated', it would be bound to overrule the Lithuanian objection.[34] To Estonia's further argument that the Lithuanian courts had no jurisdiction to entertain a suit by the Estonian company to establish its title to the Panevezys–Saldutiskis railway, the PCIJ replied that the question depended on Lithuanian law and the local courts alone could pronounce a final decision. It finally added that until it had been 'clearly shown' that the Lithuanian courts had no jurisdiction to entertain the company's suit, the Court could not accept the Estonian contention that the local remedies rule did not apply in the case because Lithuanian law afforded no means of redress.[35]

In the *Norwegian Loans* case (1957), France argued with regard to Norway's (fourth) preliminary objection on the ground of non-exhaustion of local remedies that it did not have to prove the 'caractère inutile du recours aux tribunaux norvégiens. Le gouvernement norvégien est demandeur dans cette exception, il revendique une compétence nationale, et c'est à lui de prouver l'utilité d'un recours à son organisation judiciaire.'[36] Norway, on the other hand, replied that the French contention had no foundation and that the burden of proof rested on France. ·Although it admitted to be the claimant in the objection, it recalled that its claim was based upon a general and uncontested rule of international law by virtue of which local remedies should have been previously exhausted as a condition for the admissibility of the French application to the International Court of Justice. Norway argued that 'si le gouvernement français soutient que le principe n'est pas applicable, c'est à lui d'établir la raison pour laquelle il en est ainsi'.[37] It added that it was not incumbent upon the Norwegian government to prove that 'les voies de recours ouvertes aux porteurs francais par son droit interne offrent à ces derniers des possibilités suffisantes pour que la règle de l'épuisement préalable ne puisse pas être écartée. C'est au gouvernement de la République qu'il incomberait de prouver le contraire.'[38]

At a certain stage of the pleadings, Norway's counsel, Mr

Bourquin, advanced the argument that the burden of proof as to the *existence* of domestic remedies is incumbent upon the State which raises the objection of non-exhaustion of local remedies,[39] but the existence of local remedies ought to be distinguished from their *effectiveness*. As to this latter, the burden of proof is incumbent upon the claimant State:

Une fois l'*existence* des recours internes établie, la règle de l'épuisement préalable devient applicable. Et si l'État demandeur veut échapper aux conséquences de cette règle, c'est à lui qu'il incombe alors de prouver que la règle ne joue pas en raison de l'*inefficacité* des recours existants.[40]

In reply, the agent for the French government, Professor Gros, insisted on the constant collaboration of the parties in the presentation of evidence throughout the proceedings. Thus, he stated, it was not sufficient for Norway to rely on the alleged impartiality of local tribunals, as it was further incumbent upon it to prove or to contribute to prove that, in view of legislation and governmental decisions, there still was a 'reasonable possibility of redressing the situation'. This, he remarked, had not been proved by Norway. In international legal procedure, Professor Gros submitted, there is always collaboration between the parties in the presentation of evidence to the judge. This system was adopted in the Hague Conventions 1899–1907 and in the Statutes of the PCIJ and ICJ (cf. also Rule 62 of the Rules of Court), one of its essential principles being 'l'obligation des parties de collaborer à la preuve'.[41]

The problem was not settled by the Court's decision in the *Norwegian Loans* case, which concerned itself with Norway's first preliminary objection without going into the fourth objection (on non-exhaustion of local remedies). Although the Court found it had no jurisdiction in the case,[42] in his Separate Opinion Judge Lauterpacht touched on the problem at issue. He argued that there was in general a degree of unhelpfulness in the argument concerning the burden of proof, but added:

However, some *prima facie* distribution of the burden of proof there must be. This being so, the following seems to be the accurate principle on the subject: (1) As a rule, it is for the plaintiff State to prove that there are no effective remedies to which recourse can be had; (2) no such proof is required if there exists legislation which on the face of it deprives the private claimants of a remedy; (3) in that case it is for the defendant State to show that, notwithstanding the apparent absence of a remedy, its existence can nevertheless reasonably be assumed; (4) the degree of burden of proof thus to be adduced ought not to be so stringent as to render the proof unduly exacting.[43]

In this connection, reference could also be made to the public hearing of 1 April 1959 before the ICJ in the *Aerial Incident* case (Israel v. Bulgaria). On the occasion, the advocate of the respondent government, Professor Cot, declared that by virtue of the well-known rule *reus in excipiendo fit actor*, 'il appartenait au gouvernement d'Israel de prouver l'inexistence ou l'inefficacité des recours de droit interne. Il nous suffisait donc de dire que les recours de droit interne n'ayant pas été épuisés, nous demandions le bénéfice de cette règle.'[44] On the following day, Professor Cot, having cited the legal provisions whereby local Bulgarian courts were largely open and accessible to aliens, insisted further that it was incumbent upon the government of Israel to prove the alleged ineffectiveness or non-existence of (Bulgarian) local remedies.[45]

And in the public hearing of 11 November 1958 before the ICJ in the *Interhandel* case, Professor Guggenheim, co-agent for the Swiss government, discussing the 'neutral character' of *Interhandel* as well as the non-application of the local remedies rule in the case (the Swiss submissions), observed that the 'repartition du fardeau de la preuve' occurred not only in international law but also in the municipal law of the two countries concerned (Switzerland and the United States). The only difference was, he argued, that in the case before the U.S. Supreme Court the distribution of the burden of proof occurred *d'avance* (before thorough examination of the merits of the case) while in Swiss practice it occurred *en cours de procédure*.[46] But in one case and another, in international law as well as in the 'jurisprudence des cours de prise des pays belligérants' (mainly during the Second World War), the established principle of the distribution of the burden of proof remained unchallenged.[47]

In his award in the *Finnish Vessels* case (Finland v. Great Britain, 1934), arbitrator Algot Bagge held *inter alia* that a State's opportunity to do justice by its own domestic courts (in case of an alleged initial breach of international law) ought to refer only to a claim based upon contentions of fact and propositions of law put forward by the claimant government in the international procedure. The disadvantage would be on the side of the claimant government if it did not maintain certain of the contentions advanced and rejected in the municipal courts. The respondent government, the arbitrator proceeded, had no reasonable interest to insist that contentions repudiated by the claimant government and not put forward as a basis of their claim should be subject to the decision by the municipal courts, as a prior condition to further international proceedings. It seemed unreasonable to ask the claimant government in the international procedure to advance and defend propositions which they held to be wrong.[48]

To arbitrator Bagge, thus, the local remedies rule pertained only to contentions of fact and propositions of law advanced by the claimant State in the international procedure. The international organ would consider only those contentions which ought to have been previously examined by the local courts of the respondent State; in the international procedure they were to be regarded as hypothetically true and correct[49] for the determination of the question of exhaustion of local remedies. The respondent State ought not to insist upon contentions rejected or not advanced by the claimant government, and this latter did not have to defend propositions which it deemed incorrect.

Fawcett has observed that in cases where the act complained of is (first case) a breach of municipal law but not of international law, and then (second case) both of municipal law and of international law, the local remedies rule is applicable. While in the first case it operates as a substantive bar to any international claim, in the second it is a procedural bar (to claims for damages but not to a declaratory judgment). In both cases

the burden of proof rests upon the respondent State, if it relies upon the rule as a preliminary objection or defence, to show that local remedies were available; if it discharges this burden, the burden of proof falls on the claimant State to show that the local remedies indicated were not in the circumstances of the case effective.[50]

The shift or distribution of the burden of proof with regard to the exhaustion of local remedies has also been maintained by Amerasinghe,[51] and Miaja de la Muela,[52] as well as by several other expert writers on the subject.[53]

Writing on the local remedies rule, Gaja regarded the burden of proof as a practical rather than a technical rule.[54] And Charles de Visscher contended that, in international law as in *droit civil*, the fundamental principle governing the allocation of the burden of proof is that 'la charge de la preuve s'impose à celui qui avance un fait contraire à l'état normal et habituel des choses'.[55] The burden of proof is thus incumbent on whichever party submits an exceptional situation.[56]

Before proceeding to an examination of the matter in experiments on the international protection of human rights, one point remains to be made at this stage. It should not be overlooked that the principle governing the burden of proof with regard to exhaustion of local remedies evolved in general international law within the context of litigation between sovereign independent States. The fact was well stressed in the *W.A. Parker (U.S.)* v. *Mexico* case, where the Claims Commission stated that 'the parties before this Commission are sovereign nations who are in honour bound to make full disclosures of the facts in each case so far as such facts are within their knowledge, or can reasonably be ascertained by them'.[57] Such is not necessarily the situation in the scope of international experiments on human rights protection.

III. The burden of proof with regard to exhaustion of local remedies in experiments on the international protection of human rights

In international practice a very distinct situation is found in the ambit of the international law on human rights protection. Here inter-State applications have been rather rare, in contrast with the vast number of applications brought before international organs by individuals, private groups or non-governmental organizations (for example, under Article 25 of the European Convention on Human Rights). We may now turn to the practice of those organs, surveying first the jurisprudence of the European Commission of Human Rights and then the work of United Nations organs on the problem at issue.

1. The practice of the European Commission of Human Rights

(a) *From substantial evidence to* prima facie *evidence*

Rule 41(2) of the rules of procedure of the European Commission of Human Rights, adopted at Strasbourg on 2 April 1955, provided for the burden of proof in applications before the Commission in the following terms: 'In pursuance of Article 26 of the Convention a party shall provide evidence to show that all domestic remedies have been exhausted'.[58]

In a decision of 17 December 1957 the Commission found that the individual applicant had failed to demonstrate that he had exhausted judicial remedies available to him.[59] In another case of 15 July 1957, the Commission again rejected an application as inadmissible for failure by the individual applicant to demonstrate that he had exhausted a remedy that was open to him.[60] In yet another decision (of 8 January 1959) the Commission declared the application inadmissible on the ground that the applicant had not sufficiently proved that the alleged delay in the local procedure constituted a special circumstance relieving him of the obligation to exhaust a *recours constitutionnel* according to generally recognized principles of international law.[61]

These examples[62] show that in its earlier years, pursuant to Rule 41(2) of the rules of procedure, the Commission consistently applied the principle that it was incumbent upon the applicant to prove that he had exhausted all remedies available to him. As the great majority of cases was and is brought before the Commission by individuals and private groups (rather than States), it was incumbent upon these latter not only to exhaust all local remedies but also to provide substantial evidence of their compliance with the requirement.

The rigour of Rule 41(2) of the Commission's rules of procedure was evident. Too heavy a burden lay upon the individual applicants. The situation was somewhat paradoxical in a system set up to accomplish a collective enforcement[63] in European countries of certain of the human rights enshrined in the UN Universal Declaration of 1948. By the terms of the European Convention itself (Article 26) the requirement of exhaustion of local remedies is envisaged in the light of generally recognized rules of international law. This being so, one can only subscribe to the view that the duty to provide information and prove *is divided* between the contending parties.[64] In general international law, to which Article 26 of the Convention expressly refers, the burden of proof – as seen *supra*, pp. 134–43 – rests upon the party alleging a fact. There is a division or shifting of that burden from 'plaintiff' to 'defendant', it being upon the one who makes an assertion to prove it. *Onus probandi incumbit actori, onus probandi incumbit ei qui dicit.*

In fact, in its sitting of 12 October 1957, the European Commission affirmed, as a matter of principle, at the admissibility stage of the *Greece* v. *United Kingdom* case in respect of Cyprus (more commonly known as the *Second Cyprus* case)[65] that:

under Article 26 of the Convention the Commission may only deal with a matter after all domestic remedies have been exhausted, according to the generally recognized rules of international law; and [. . .] in accordance with the said generally recognized rules of international law it is the duty of the government claiming that domestic remedies have not been exhausted to demonstrate the existence of such remedies.[66]

This *dictum* was pronounced by the Commission in an inter-State case. Why then the rigidity in the application of Rule 41(2) of the rules of procedure in applications lodged by individuals? The draftsmen of the rules soon realized the need for change towards a more liberal and realistic approach of the problem of the burden of proof.

The need for a *general revision* of the rules of procedure was felt by the Commission itself (which existed from 18 May 1954 but actually started operating after 5 July 1955) not much later than the adoption of the original text of the rules on 2 April 1955. The Commission started facing the problems contained in individual applications brought before it under Article 25 of the Convention and, with the creation of the Court on 21 January 1959, it had before itself another unexplored field of activity: that of its relations with the Court (Articles 47 and 48 of the Convention).[67]

The modification of the provision on the burden of proof was accomplished in 1960.[68] The general revision of the rules of procedure took place at the twenty-second[69] and twenty-fourth[70] plenary sessions of the Commission. The amended Rule 41(2) read: 'The applicant shall provide information enabling it to be shown that the conditions laid down in Article 26 of the Convention have been satisfied.'[71]

As compared with the original text, the change was remarkable. Previously, the applicant had to prove that he had exhausted all domestic remedies; after the amendment of the rule, the applicant had to provide only *prima facie* evidence (*commencement de preuve*) that that requirement had been duly complied with. This was certainly a turning-point for the practice of the Commission on the problem of the burden of proof.

In the years following this modification, writers began more openly to criticize the practice of the Commission on the determination of the burden of proof in its earlier phase (the period extending from 1955 until 1959).[72] And, with the new text of Rule 41(2) in force, the prevailing view (as indicated by the text itself of the amended rule) lends support to the shifting or division of the burden of proof between the contending parties before the Commission.[73]

Thus, with regard to Article 26 of the Convention, it lays upon the respondent party the initial burden of proving the existence of local remedies to be exhausted; the burden then shifts to the applicant to prove either that local remedies have been exhausted, or that they are not adequate and effective for redress, or else that there are special circumstances relieving him from the duty to exhaust local remedies.

Four years before the amendment of Rule 41(2) of the Commission's rules of procedure, Henri Rolin called for a more active role of the Commission, whose task, he remarked, rather than being limited to the redress of a tort, was to ensure the observance of the Convention.[74] As shown by the powers granted to the Commission (under Articles 30 and 31 of the Convention), the procedure to be followed had the character of an *action publique*. By virtue of its power to bring a case before the Court (Article 48), the Commission appeared in particular as a true *instance d'instruction*,[75] with the right and duty to examine thoroughly the facts brought before it, *without being limited by the evidence adduced by the claimant*.[76]

Analogies with procedures of municipal law should be made with internal criminal procedure rather than with *procès civil*.[77] After remarking that in the absence of a *Ministère Public*[78] it was desirable that the *instruction* should proceed regularly with information received from both contending parties, plaintiff and defendant,[79] Rolin anticipated:

Je vois bien qu'à cette conception certains auront tendance à opposer l'adage *actori incumbit probatio*. Mais encore une fois il ne vaut pas en matière de responsabilité délictuelle en tant qu'on prétendrait en déduire qu'il appartient au lésé de faire la preuve du délit. Sans doute l'inculpé bénéficie-t-il [...] d'une présomption d'innocence – *in dubio pro reo*. Mais c'est le Ministère Public, organe de la société, qui devant les tribunaux d'ordre interne a en principe la responsabilité des poursuites. Et il est dans la logique de la sauvegarde collective des droits de l'homme, que la collectivité des États, c'est-à-dire la Commission qui en est l'organe, assume la charge de vérifier la réalité des violations de la Convention qui lui seraient signalées.[80]

As early as 1956, Rolin depicted as one of the obstacles to the activity of the Commission the 'conception civiliste de "litige" que la Commission Européenne semble s'être faite des affaires dont elle sera saisie',[81] with an important bearing upon the problem of the burden of proof.

One may now turn to an examination of the Commission's jurisprudence (after the 1960 alteration of its rules or procedure) under amended Rule 41(2), on the question of the *onus probandi* as related to the local remedies rule.

(b) *The duty of the contending parties*

The European Commission has espoused the view that any allegation by the individual applicant that resort to local remedies would be futile and fruitless must be accompanied by some evidence or proof in its support. The Commission so stated in categorical terms in its decision of 17 March 1970.[82] The applicant alleged that an application for legal aid towards the institution of civil proceedings would have been unsuccessful, and that in the circumstances of the case his complaint would not have been treated fairly by the courts,[83] while trying to comply with the requirement of exhaustion of local remedies. The Commission recalled that it had constantly held that in order to establish the existence of such special circumstances it was 'for the applicant to show conclusively that his allegations are true'; in the case, he had adduced 'no proof of his suggestions that he would have been refused legal aid in order to institute civil proceedings or that he would not have been treated fairly by the courts'.[84] The Commission having found that no such special circumstances were present and that the applicant had failed to comply with the local remedies rule, the application was ultimately declared inadmissible.[85]

In an earlier decision the Commission likewise found that there were in the case no special circumstances relieving the interested party from the obligation to exhaust available remedies according to generally recognized principles of international law.[86] Not only did the applicant fail to comply with the local remedies rule, but further, in relation to other issues raised in the case, he failed to produce the least *prima facie* evidence ('le moindre commencement de preuve') in support of his assertions;[87] the application was accordingly declared inadmissible.

The reference to the least *commencement de preuve* should not pass unnoticed. In another case the Commission was faced with the applicants' allegation that resort to a remedy in question would have been futile;[88] the Commission refused to accept this view, observing that 'pareille affirmation ne saurait cependant équivaloir à la preuve indispensable, car elle ne s'appuie sur aucun élément de nature à la corroborer'.[89] The applicants having failed to exhaust domestic remedies, their application was therefore declared inadmissible.[90]

In *Second Cyprus* case, as seen above, the Commission stated that according to general international law it was 'the duty of the government claiming that domestic remedies have not been exhausted to demonstrate the existence of such remedies'.[91] The principle was later confirmed by the Commission in the *Austria* v. *Italy* case, where it unequivocally stated: 'According to the generally recognized rules of international law to which Article 26 of the Convention refers, it is incumbent on the respondent government, if they raise the objection of non-exhaustion, to prove the existence, in their municipal legal system, of remedies which have not been exercised.'[92] The Commission further asserted that 'the exhaustion of a given domestic remedy does not normally cease to be necessary, according to the generally recognized rules of international law, unless the applicant can show that, in these particular circumstances, this remedy was unlikely to be effective and adequate in regard to the grievance in question'.[93]

The duty under international law of the respondent State to prove the existence in its domestic legal system of allegedly non-exhausted remedies whenever that objection is raised, was confirmed by the Commission not only in inter-State cases (such as the ones referred to above). In the *Alam and Khan* case, for example, two individual applicants brought a complaint before the Commission alleging that the refusal to allow the latter (Alam's son) to enter the United Kingdom had brought about an alleged violation of the right to family life (Article 8 of the Convention) and of the right to receive a fair and public hearing by an independent and impartial tribunal in determination of their civil rights (Article 6(1) of the Convention).[94]

The Commission's decision on the problem of the burden of proof as related to the local remedies rule began by observing that the applicants' complaint under Article 8 also had regard to the question whether they had exhausted all available local remedies (as required under Article 26 of the Convention). In this connection, the Commission stated that 'according to the generally recognized rules of international law to which Article 26 refers, it is incumbent upon the respondent government, if they raise the objection of non-exhaustion, to prove the existence in their municipal legal system of a remedy which has not been exhausted'.[95]

As to the question whether there was in the domestic legal system concerned an effective remedy against the refusal of the immigration authorities to allow the entry of the complainant into the country, the Commission deemed it to be, in the circumstances of the case, closely linked with the question under Article 6(1), whether or not the applicants had access to an independent and impartial tribunal for the determination of their right to respect for family life. In such circumstances the Commission found that the issue under Article 26 could not be decided without an examination of questions concerning the merits of the applicants' complaint.[96] Accordingly, the Commission found it appropriate to join to the merits the issue of the exhaustion of domestic remedies,[97] and so it did.

Once again, in the *X* v. *Belgium* case (decision of 1963), the Commission declared that in accordance with the generally recognized rules of international law to which Article 26 of the Convention refers, 'it is incumbent upon the respondent government, if they raise the objection of non-exhaustion, to prove the existence in their municipal law system of remedies which have not been exercised'.[98] The Commission's dictum in the same year in the *23 Inhabitants of Alsemberg and of Beersel* v. *Belgium* case was to the same effect.[99]

The distribution of the burden of proof with regard to the exhaustion of local remedies has also been advocated by the Commission in proceedings before the European Court of Human Rights. Throughout the public hearings of 16–18 November 1970 before the European Court in the '*Vagrancy*' cases, the principal delegate of the European Commission, Mr M. Sørensen, advanced the view that:

it lies with a government which raises the objection of non-exhaustion of remedies to prove the existence of a remedy. If the respondent government, or the government which makes such an objection, has proved or at any rate put forward serious evidence that such a remedy exists, it lies with the other party to show either that the remedy has been exhausted or that there were special circumstances which absolved it from exhausting the remedy. But as far as the actual existence of a remedy is concerned, the burden of proof lies on the government which raises the objection.[100]

This new trend in the position taken by the Commission on the problem of the burden of proof seems to be well in accordance with the generally recognized rules of international law. It marks a sensible development, in the years following the amendment of Rule 41(2) of the rules of procedure (1960 onwards), when compared with the stricter case-law of its earlier period of activity (1955–9). The Commission seems to have embraced the view that the burden of proof in respect of the local remedies requirement rests upon the claimant not because he is in the position of a 'plaintiff', but because of the allegations he advances. Thus, the individual applicant has the duty to prove[101] that he has exhausted local remedies, or else that he has not exhausted them because he was relieved by special circumstances from doing so, or because remedies did not exist, or were ineffective, as much as the respondent government is bound to prove that local remedies existed and had not been exhausted, and that they were adequate and effective.

Pursuant to the principle laid down in the *Second Cyprus* case and in the *Austria* v. *Italy* case (*supra*, pp. 147–8), the Commission has in this connection on another occasion made it clear that the exercise of a given local remedy does not normally cease to be necessary, according to the generally recognized principles of international law, except if the applicant succeeds in establishing that, in the circumstances of the case, that remedy was not truly effective and sufficient to redress the alleged wrong.[102] By the same token, the Commission also stated that 'according to the generally recognized rules of international law to which Article 26 refers, it is incumbent upon the respondent government, if they raise the objection of non-exhaustion, to prove the existence in their municipal legal system of a remedy which has not been exhausted'.[103] And the Commission had in mind remedies which are 'essential' or 'likely to be effective and adequate'.[104]

There does not seem to be any contradiction or incongruency in the practice of the Commission on this particular point. What the Commission has done is to have acknowledged and applied the principle of the division of the burden of proof between the contending parties, by virtue of which in the course of the proceedings the party who makes an assertion is bound to prove it. The Commission, unlike in its first years, no longer adheres to the view that it is always incumbent upon the individual applicant to prove his exhaustion of local remedies. This development is a sensible one. The shifting of the burden of proof was originally admitted in general international law in cases where sovereign States were contending parties. There seems therefore to be all the more reason to have the same principle applied to cases where one of the parties is a sovereign State and the other an individual or a private group: the rationale behind the local remedies rule, according to which, before resort may be had to an international court, the State where the violation occurred should have an opportunity to redress it by its own means within the framework of its own domestic legal system,[105] already favours to a great extent the respondent State. If, furthermore, the burden of proof in respect of exhaustion of local remedies is placed entirely upon the much weaker party (the individual applicant), at variance with general international law itself, one can hardly see how a regional system designed collectively to enforce certain human rights – and into which States parties have entered in full exercise of their sovereignty – would not be doomed to become innocuous and superfluous. The very principles and purposes underlying the system would thereby be seriously undermined, if not defeated.

It seems therefore that the post-1960 practice of the Commission has been particularly wise in this regard. It has not however been clearly conclusive on the overall position of the Commission on the many aspects of the problem at issue. One cannot go well beyond the constatation of the liberal tendency towards the distribution of the burden of proof, as pointed out above. Beyond that, there is a certain ambiguity and confusion in the practice of the Commission.

(c) *Remedies of doubtful effectiveness*

In the *Retimag S.A.* v. *Federal Republic of Germany* case,[106] for example, the Commission recalled *inter alia* that it was the whole system of municipal protection as provided by municipal law which should be exhausted before the case was brought to the international level.[107] With regard to the burden of proof in that respect, it was further stated that the Commission in the case 'doit se borner à constater que la requérante n'a pas clairement établi qu'il ne lui était pas possible de saisir la Cour Constitutionnelle'.[108]

The Commission affirmed that the rule of exhaustion of local remedies was 'strict', and consequently it ought to be interpreted as such:

il suffit donc, pour qu'un requérant n'ait pas épuisé les voies de recours internes, qu'il ait omis d'user sur un point déterminé d'une des voies de recours qui lui étaient ouvertes, à supposer qu'en soulevant ce point devant les juridictions internes, il eût eu quelque chance de faire aboutir l'ensemble de sa demande critiquant une seule et même mesure.[109]

As Retimag had failed to lodge a *recours constitutionnel*, and thereby to comply with the local remedies rule, the application was therefore declared inadmissible.[110]

Here the Commission opted for a strict application of the local remedies rule. What, however, was most surprising in its decision in the *Retimag* case was that, although it conceded that according to generally recognized principles of international law an individual was to exhaust 'normally' those remedies 'which seem to be effective and sufficient',[111] it went on to say that 's'il existe un doute quant à la question de savoir si une voie de recours déterminée peut être ou non de nature à offrir une chance réelle de succès, c'est là un point qui doit être soumis aux tribunaux internes eux-mêmes, avant tout appel au tribunal international'.[112]

In subsequent decision (of 24 September 1963), the Commission again stated that a simple doubt about the existence or effectiveness of an internal remedy did not constitute a special circumstance authorizing the non-exercise of that remedy, as that was a problem upon which the competent domestic courts themselves ought to have had the occasion to pronounce before any recourse was had to the Commission.[113]

One may well understand the Commission's concern for prudence in the performance of its delicate task,[114] and its endeavours to maintain the confidence of the governments concerned and not to hurt susceptibilities. But here, it is submitted, the Commission seems to have gone too far. By rigidly extending the application of the local remedies rule to remedies of doubtful effectiveness the Commission seems to have overlooked what it had stated so categorically on several other occasions: that, for the purposes of the application of the rule, *the remedy to be exhausted ought to be adequate and effective* (see *dicta* to this effect in the *Nielsen* case,[115] the *Lawless* case,[116] the *De Becker* case,[117] two *X* v. *Austria* cases,[118] the *Simon-Herold* v. *Austria* case).[119]

The Commission's *dictum* in the *Retimag* case seems hard to reconcile with the notion of effectiveness[120] prevailing in its case-law with regard to the application of the local remedies rule. What seems to be in keeping with the principles and purposes of the Convention is that, in case of doubt as to the effectiveness of a particular domestic remedy, the ultimate determination of the question should rest with the Commission itself[121] rather than with the national authorities. Otherwise the local remedies rule would be carried to such an extreme that it would shake the very foundations of the system of protection of human rights.

The *renvoi* of the problem to the national authorities can hardly lead to a sensible and fair application of the local remedies rule. A doubt about the effectiveness of a local remedy, however well-founded it may seem to be, is usually regarded as not relieving the applicant from the duty of exhausting it. Thus interpreted, the rule runs the risk of becoming a procedural means allowing the State to evade the system of human rights protection, particularly in view of the *renvoi* of the matter on behalf of the internal legal order.[122]

(d) *The Commission's examination* ex officio *and related problems*

This discussion leads to the question whether the Commission may in a given case examine *ex officio* the exhaustion (or not) of local remedies. The position here is clear: as a matter of principle, it may, it ought to. The Commission itself stated in the *Nielsen* case that 'it is the duty of the Commission, *ex officio*, to satisfy itself in every case that it has jurisdiction to entertain the application under the powers conferred upon it by the Convention'.[123] In the same sense, in the *X* v. *Austria* case (appl. n. 3591/68), the decision read that 'the Commission has both the competence and, indeed, the duty to examine, either *ex officio* or at the request of the applicant concerned, a situation which gives rise to a question of undue interference with the effective exercise of the right of petition' (Article 25 of the Convention).[124] And, more particularly, in the *De Becker* case the Commission asserted that it was incumbent upon itself to verify whether the requirement of the exhaustion of local remedies according to generally recognized principles of international law had in the case been complied with.[125] Likewise, in the *X* v. *Austria* case (appl. n. 514/59), when dealing with the problem of exhaustion of local remedies, the Commission stated that it was its duty to verify if that condition of admissibility had been fulfilled in the case.[126]

In the *Helga and Wilhelm Gericke* v. *F.R. Germany* case the Commission went as far as initially to refuse to accept a withdrawal of the case by the applicants, declaring on the occasion (decision of 23 September 1965, from which an assertion of its *ex officio* competence can be deduced) that 'the interests served by the protection of the human rights and fundamental freedoms guaranteed by the Convention extend beyond the interests of the persons concerned' and 'have led the member Parties to the Convention to establish standards forming part of the public law of Europe'; both the Commission and the Court having been set up to ensure the observance of the engagements undertaken by the Parties to the Convention, 'the withdrawal of an application and the respondent government's agreement thereto cannot deprive the Commission of the competence to pursue its examination of the case'.[127]

A difficult problem arises when the respondent government expressly renounces the invocation of the objection of non-exhaustion of local remedies. Is the Commission then bound to proceed to an examination of the problem? It seems that the Commission has tended to opt for the negative. In the *Isop* v. *Austria* case, for example, as the government chose not to rely on Article 26 of the Convention,[128] the Commission did not delve into a detailed examination of the question, and the application was later rejected as inadmissible on another ground, that it was 'manifestly ill-founded'.[129] In the case of *57 Inhabitants of Louvain and Environs* v. *Belgium*, the respondent party having similarly renounced the benefit of the local redress rule, the Commission found that 'in such a case the generally recognized rules of international law in the matter dispense the Commission from pronouncing on the exhaustion of domestic remedies'.[130]

If one considers that the local remedies rule favours the respondent State in the sense that, as stated by the Commission in the *Nielsen* case, it is 'founded upon the principle that the respondent State must have an opportunity to redress by its own means within the framework of its own domestic legal system the wrong alleged to be done to the individual',[131] then, if the respondent State renounces the objection of non-exhaustion, there does not seem to be any reason why the rule should apply in that case at all. In this way, the position taken by the Commission in the above cases seems to be a sensible and accurate one.

The problem, however, does not end there. The Commission may (or may not) ask a respondent government for its observations on the admissibility of an application. The Commission may (or may not) have a respondent government's observations at the time of deciding a case. A respondent government may renounce the objection of non-exhaustion of local remedies, or it may simply omit or refrain from invoking it. Can the Commission, in this latter hypothetical situation, apply *ex officio* the requirement of Article 26 of the Convention, to see that local remedies (even if not invoked by the respondent government) have been duly exhausted?

On one occasion, in the *Boeckmans* case, the Commission answered that 'rien n'aurait empêché la Commission de s'assurer d'office, comme elle le fait très fréquemment, que les conditions de l'article 26 se trouvaient remplies en l'espèce, sauf peut-être si le gouvernment belge avait clairement renoncé au bénéfice de cet article'.[132] But its case-law on this particular problem seems to be far from conclusive.[133] Thus there co-exist, on the one hand, the power of the contending parties to intervene in the course of the proceedings and, on the other hand, the Commission's *ex officio* powers, in a combination representing what has been called 'a blend of the accusatorial and inquisitorial systems'.[134]

The criticism has been made that:

it is difficult to reconcile the conception whereby the Commission could, by virtue of its *ex officio* powers, take the place of a respondent State which has not adduced the objection of non-exhaustion, with the other conception whereby it could be exempted by waiver of the respondent from investigating the question of exhaustion. In view of these two possibilities, it is difficult to understand whether, in the procedural system in question, the inquisitorial system (as the first case would imply) or the accusatorial system (as the second case would suggest) prevails. The Commission itself was aware of this ambiguity and in one of its decisions[135] qualified the affirmation that its *ex officio* powers could be blocked by a respondent's waiver with a very significant 'perhaps', thus pointing more to the inquisitorial interpretation.[136]

What is the bearing of that problem upon that of the burden of proof concerning the exhaustion of local remedies? As has been seen above, the Commission has taken the view that, if the respondent government raises the objection of non-exhaustion, it is incumbent upon it to prove the existence of the alleged non-exhausted remedies in its domestic legal system.[137] Accordingly, as was once observed:

it is slightly surprising to find that, although the burden of proof regarding the existence of a remedy lies with the government, the Commission feels free, in certain cases, to reject a complaint for non-exhaustion of a remedy which has not even been invoked by the government. It is also surprising to find that, after taking the position that it is free to examine the exhaustion question without being bound by the government's submissions, the Commission still considers that it should not examine the question of exhaustion in cases where the government expressly refrains from raising an objection in this regard.[138]

Upon whom will the burden of proof then lie if the respondent government fails to raise the objection of non-exhaustion of local remedies when requested by the Commission to express its views on the admissibility of the application? The question came to the fore in the case of *57 Inhabitants of Louvain and Environs* v. *Belgium*. In its written observations on the admissibility of the application the respondent government alleged that the condition of exhaustion of local remedies had not been fulfilled in the case. However, at a previous hearing in the presence of the parties (5 March 1964), counsel for the respondent government had not dealt with this point and had confined himself to saying that the applicants' complaints were 'outside the scope of the Convention', and, replying to a question by the Commission's president, had stated that he 'did not propose to enter a plea of non-exhaustion of domestic remedies' since the application was 'not directed against a ministerial decision but against the Belgian legislation as such'.[139] The respondent government consequently withdrew the plea in bar originally entered under Article 26 of the Convention.[140]

In its decision of 5 March 1964 the Commission, after recalling the basic rationale of the local remedies rule, stated that the Contracting States were 'best qualified to judge the expediency of availing themselves of this opportunity, the main purpose of Article 26 being to protect their domestic legal system'.[141] The Commission asserted its competence *ex officio* to establish whether the rule had been strictly observed, so long as the application had not been referred to the respondent government;[142] the same did *not* apply when the respondent government, invited (as in the present case) to express its opinion on the admissibility of an application,[143] manifestly declined to avail itself of that opportunity and protection.[144] In such a case, the decision proceeded, the generally recognized rules of international law in the matter dispensed the Commission from pronouncing on the exhaustion of domestic remedies; there was in the case, therefore, 'no need to enquire whether the applicants could or should have appealed to the Belgian Council of State before seizing the Commission'.[145]

The decision in the 57 *Inhabitants of Louvain* v. *Belgium* case marks a development in the practice of the Commission on the subject. Here the Commission's position was qualified with detail and precision: the burden of proof did *not* lie upon the individual applicants if the respondent government had not raised the objection of non-exhaustion of local remedies when expressly invited by the Commission to express its opinion on the admissibility of the application.

To a possible objection that the ground of 'manifestly ill-founded' applications as laid down in Article 27(2) of the Convention perhaps stresses the burden of proof on the applicant, it may be replied that the point could not be pushed too far in the light of the prevailing trend of the Commission's jurisprudence after the general revision of its rules of procedure: in fact, Article 27(2) may indicate that the *initial* burden of proof is incumbent on the applicant, as the ground of 'manifestly ill-founded' applications has in practice served to reject complaints which are not substantiated by any or sufficient evidence or which do not on the facts disclose an appearance of a violation of the Convention;[146] but once the applicant has satisfied the Commission with initial *prima facie* evidence of exhaustion of local remedies, the burden of proof then shifts to the respondent.[147]

(e) *Contentions of legislative measures and administrative practices*[148]

The problem of the burden of proof has also been dealt with by the Commission in relation to the question of the application of the local remedies rule when an application raises the general compatibility of certain alleged 'legislative measures and administrative practices' with the Convention. One such example was the Commission's decision of 31 May 1968 in the *Greek* case.[149] The Commission stated *inter alia* (with regard to Article 3 of the Convention) that as the remedies indicated by the respondent government could not, in its view, be considered effective and sufficient, allegations under Article 3 could not therefore be rejected for non-exhaustion of domestic remedies.[150]

The respondent government argued that those allegations (submitted by the applicant governments) were inadmissible because no *prima facie* proof had been established.[151] The Commission rejected the Greek contention by recalling that when, in a previous case,[152] it considered the admissibility of allegations under Article 3 of the Convention, it stated that it 'could not ascertain whether the applicant Contracting Party establishes *prima facie* proof of its allegations since enquiry into such matters relates to the merits of the case and cannot therefore be undertaken at the present stage of the proceedings'.[153] Thus, in the present *Greek* case, the Commission found that the applicant governments' allegations could *not* be rejected on the ground that no *prima facie* proof had been established.[154]

It is significant that the discussions on the problem in the *Greek* case (*supra*) concerned *prima facie* proof rather than 'substantial evidence'. This point came to the fore in the Commission's decision of 1 October 1972 on the *Ireland* v. *United Kingdom* case. It was there alleged that 'in the present case the Commission, having taken into account the submissions of both Parties, does not find that the applicant government have offered substantial evidence to show that an administrative practice exists as alleged by the applicant government'.[155] In such circumstances, the Commission upheld the requirement of exhaustion of domestic remedies[156] and declared that part of the application inadmissible[157] for non-compliance with that requirement.[158] On the other hand, shortly afterwards, in its decision of 5 April 1973 in the *G. Donnelly and Others* v. *United Kingdom* case, the Commission, 'taking into account the evidence submitted by the applicants jointly and by each of them individually', found that 'the applicants have provided evidence which *prima facie* substantiates their allegations of the existence of an administrative practice in violation of Article 3 [of the Convention] and of their being victims of that practice. It therefore follows', the Commission proceeded, 'that the domestic remedies rule does not apply to this part of the present applications and the Commission finds that the applicants' complaint in this respect raises issues of law and fact whose determination should depend upon an examination of the merits of the case.'[159]

While the *Ireland* v. *United Kingdom* case was an inter-State case, the *Donnelly* case was moved by individuals; in this respect the Commission, in its decision on the *Greek* case (of 31 May 1968), stressed the difference between inter-State and individual applications (as shown by the wording of Articles 24 and 25 of the Convention) with a direct bearing on the matter of proof. Thus, while under Article 24 of the Convention any High Contracting Party may refer to the Commission 'any alleged breach of the provisions of the Convention by another High Contracting Party', under Article 25 'only such individuals may seize the Commission as claim to be "victims" of a violation of the Convention'.[160] As the condition of 'victim' is not mentioned in Article 24, proceeded the Commission, a High Contracting Party, consequently, when alleging a violation of the Convention under that provision, 'is not obliged to show the existence of a victim of such violation either as a particular incident or, for example, as forming part of an administrative practice'.[161]

(f) *Applicants under detention*

A particular problem the Commission has faced is that of the burden of proof in respect of the local remedies requirement when the burden falls upon an applicant in a special situation, namely, when he is in prison. An illustration is afforded by the *Heinz Kornmann* v. *F.R. Germany* case, where the applicant alleged ill-treatment in prison (in breach of Article 3 of the Convention).

In the first application introduced by Kornmann, the Commission observed in connection with Article 26 of the Convention that 'the applicant has submitted that it would have been impossible for him to find a lawyer willing to assist him, but that, on the other hand, he has in no way shown that he made any attempts to obtain the assistance of a lawyer in the proceedings concerned';[162] furthermore, 'he has not shown that he applied to the *Kammergericht* for legal aid in respect of

these proceedings'.[163] As the Commission found no special circumstances dispensing the applicant 'from exhausting this particular
remedy', he consequently failed to comply in that particular respect
with the rule of Article 26 of the Convention, and the Commission
declared the application inadmissible.[164]

In a second and new application brought shortly afterwards by
Kornmann (appl. n. 2686/65), containing the same complaint of an
alleged breach of Article 3 of the Convention for alleged ill-treatment
in prison, the Commission took a different position on the question of
the burden of proof concerning exhaustion of local remedies. This
time the Commission observed that 'the present case concerns
primarily a question of evidence and that the reason why the applicant
was unsuccessful in lodging a criminal charge was that the authorities
did not find that there was sufficient evidence to support his
allegations'.[165] To the Commission, it was 'clear' that the applicant, if
he had lodged an application or had instituted civil proceedings,
'would have been faced with the same problem of proving that he had
in fact been ill-treated'.[166]

The Commission went on to state that 'consequently, his failure to
prove his allegations in connection with his criminal charge creates a
presumption to the effect that neither an application [...] nor civil
proceedings would have had any chance of giving the applicant
satisfaction'.[167] Therefore, the Commission added, 'these two remedies cannot be considered as sufficient or effective in the
circumstances of the present case and the applicant was not obliged to
exhaust them in order to comply with Article 26 of the
Convention'.[168]

The Commission thus concluded that the conditions laid down in
Article 26 of the Convention had been satisfied in the present case,
and – having regard to another partial decision on the case[169] –
decided, on 13 December 1966, to declare admissible and accept the
remainder of the application.[170]

Decisions of this kind assume a particular importance in view of the
situation involved: an application pending before the Commission,
with the individual applicant detained in prison, yet bound to exhaust
local remedies in such difficult circumstances and to prove that he had
done so. As an illustration of the difficulty in such cases one may
recall, for example, the Commission's decision of 14 July 1970,
whereby it declared an application inadmissible on the ground of
non-exhaustion of local remedies, because the applicant 'failed to

complain to the competent court of the alleged failure of the prison authorities to forward his letter' containing an appeal.[171]

Such cases are far from negligible and present a real challenge to the system of protection of human rights, particularly in view of the fact that, for example, out of more than five thousand individual applications lodged under Article 25 of the Convention and registered by the Commission by the middle of July 1971, almost forty per cent of them came from 'persons detained in prison, or otherwise interned'.[172] Most of such applications have been declared inadmissible,[173] sometimes because the prisoners' complaints fell outside the scope of the Convention,[174] but, in cases of alleged ill-treatment in prison, because 'the Commission, on enquiry into these complaints, has very often found that the applicant's allegations could not be corroborated by the evidence taken'.[175] The problem has thus a direct bearing upon the question of the burden of proof, since in most of such cases 'applicants have failed to exhaust their remedies under the national law or their allegations were not found to be corroborated by the evidence submitted'.[176]

Although the Commission, in its examination of an application, expressly limits itself to deciding on the facts of the particular case, its decision (while being a precedent in its own case-law) not going outside the particular case to deal with related cases, on the other hand the Commission needs (as admitted by its own Secretariat) some indication of *standards* in dealing with cases brought before it by individual applicants detained in prison, since the determination of those standards still remains 'extremely fragmentary'.[177]

This task is all the more important and urgent, if the Commission is to maintain its *dictum* in the *Ilse Koch* case, where it asserted that even though 'the applicant is imprisoned in execution of a sentence imposed on her for crimes against the most elementary rights of men, [. . .] this circumstance does not however deny her the guarantee of the rights and freedoms defined in the Convention'.[178]

In those delicate cases where the individual applicants are detained in prison, a 'mere' procedural question such as that of the burden of proof concerning exhaustion of local remedies may be invested with the utmost importance[179] for the very determination of the existence of the right impugned. An improper handling of that procedural question may well render the rights set forth in the Convention a dead letter. In this way, it may be argued that the existence of effective remedies is just as important (if not more so) than the assumed existence of rights. By the same token, the old and often debated question whether individuals are subjects of international law loses ground to the more relevant question whether individuals are endowed with procedural capacity in international law.[180] As once observed, 'le langage étant l'unique véhicule de la pensée, en Droit comme en science de Droit, il n'y a pas une question de fond, dans la besogne du juriste, qui ne soit pas à la fois question de forme'.[181]

The effectiveness of a given domestic remedy for the purpose of the application of the local redress rule in connection with the problem of the burden of proof was one of the issues raised in the *Simon-Herold* v. *Austria* case. The Commission there recalled *inter alia* that the local remedies rule confined itself to imposing 'the normal use of remedies likely to be effective and adequate', and that the exhaustion of local remedies ceased to be necessary according to the generally recognized rules of international law 'if the applicant can show that, in the particular circumstances, this remedy was unlikely to be effective and adequate in regard to the grievances in question'.[182]

The Commission found in the case that the applicant's complaints regarding his treatment while being detained on remand could not be rejected under Article 26 of the Convention, since the domestic remedy in question (an appeal against the decision of an investigating judge), in the particular circumstances of the case, 'would almost certainly have been ineffective'.[183] Accordingly, the part of the application relating to the applicant's treatment in prison during the period of his detention on remand was declared admissible by the Commission,[184] while the remainder of the application was for various reasons[185] declared inadmissible.[186]

(g) *Presumption of innocence*

When considering the burden of proof, the general principle of law should be borne in mind that 'everyone charged with a criminal offence shall have the right to be presumed innocent until proved guilty according to law'.[187] A study of equality in the administration of justice undertaken by the UN Sub-Commission on Prevention of Discrimination and Protection of Minorities has shown that virtually all legal systems surveyed observed the principle of the presumption of innocence; many required proof of guilt 'beyond reasonable doubt', and the burden of proof rested usually upon the accused when he pleaded the defences permitted under the laws concerning the alleged offence or when he claimed the existence of extenuating circumstances (see also *infra*, p. 168).[188]

In fact, in the *Simon-Herold* v. *Austria* case, the applicant complained *inter alia* that he had been treated as a criminal while being detained on remand and that such treatment amounted to a breach of Article 6(2) of the European Convention, which provided for the principle of the presumption of innocence. The Commission found, however, that that allegation was 'not corroborated by any evidence submitted to it by the applicant';[189] as there had been no appearance of a violation of the provisions of Article 6(2) of the Convention, that part of the application was rejected as being manifestly ill-founded (under Article 27(2) of the Convention).[190]

The Commission has at times faced the question of the burden of proof with regard to the observance of the principle of presumption of innocence *in the process of exhaustion of local remedies*. The principle laid down in Article 6(2) of the European Convention whereby 'everyone charged with a criminal offence shall be presumed innocent until proved guilty according to law' was discussed in the *Austria* v. *Italy* case. The Commission held that the principle required 'firstly that court judges in fulfilling their duties should not start with the conviction or assumption that the accused committed the act with which he is charged. In other words, *the onus to prove guilt falls upon the Prosecution, and any doubt is to the benefit of the accused*. Moreover, the judges must permit the latter to produce evidence in rebuttal. In their judgment they can find him guilty only on the basis of direct or indirect evidence sufficiently strong in the eyes of the law to establish his guilt.'[191] *In dubio pro reo*.

The Commission then turned to the problem in cases brought before several domestic courts in the process of exhausting local remedies:

If the lower court has not respected the principle of presumption of innocence, but the higher court in its decision has eliminated the consequences of this vice in the previous proceedings, there has been no breach of Article 6(2) [of the Convention]. On the other hand, such a breach may be found to exist if the failure of the lower court to observe the principle of presumption of innocence has so distorted the general course of proceedings that the higher court has failed to give redress although it has not itself committed any breach of the Article in question.[192]

The Commission next asserted that it was 'not competent to

substitute its own assessment of the evidence for that of the national courts but can only pronounce as to whether the domestic courts have committed any abuse or procedural irregularity'.[193] In the present *Austria* v. *Italy* case, as the defence had not resorted to a remedy provided in Article 55 of the Italian Code of Penal Procedure (application for the case to be referred to another court on grounds of legitimate suspicion), the Commission found that it was not established that the Italian court in question had committed a breach of the principle of presumption of innocence enshrined in Article 6(2) of the European Convention.[194]

A recent study shows that the distribution or shifting of the burden of proof is upheld by the law of the remedy of *habeas corpus*: 'once the applicant overcomes the initial burden of adducing evidence which casts doubt upon the propriety of his detention, the legal burden of proof is cast upon the party detaining'.[195] A significant analogy is found in the principle in the law of false imprisonment whereby 'once the plaintiff establishes the imprisonment, the burden of proving justification lies with the defendant'.[196] Here, one is ultimately concerned with personal freedom, and the principle of general application is that, while the initial burden of adducing evidence to impugn the order rests with the prisoner, the ultimate burden of satisfying the judge rests with the respondent.[197] The basic assumption underlying this shifting in the burden of proof is that 'the restraint of freedom should only be permitted where the party restraining can clearly show justification'.[198] The shift in the legal burden comes into play where the facts are 'evenly balanced', for where these latter are too uncertain, and personal liberty is at stake, 'the prisoner is to be given the benefit of any doubt'.[199]

2. The practice of United Nations organs

(a) *Work of the Sub-Commission on Prevention of Discrimination and Protection of Minorities*

Following ECOSOC resolutions 75(V) of 1947 (and subsequent discussions and amendments) and 728 F(XXVIII) of 1959, both concerning the treatment to the accorded to communications addressed to the UN Commission on Human Rights, the matter again came to the fore in 1966 with a special impetus, with particular regard to colonialism and the racial situation in southern Africa.[200] New resolutions[201] and discussions followed on procedures for dealing with communications relating to situations 'revealing a consistent pattern of gross violations of human rights' until the adoption of ECOSOC resolution 1503(XLVIII) of 27 May 1970.[202]

Although this latter referred once to the local remedies rule[203] in setting up a procedure for dealing with complaints, it did not however take into account criteria for their admissibility. ECOSOC preferred to entrust this matter to the Sub-Commission on Prevention of Discrimination and Protection of Minorities[204] of the UN Commission on Human Rights. In 1971 the Sub-Commission concluded its work on the subject, and the standards and criteria for *admissibility* of complaints were set up in its resolution 1(XXIV), adopted by the Sub-Commission on 14 August 1971.

The issue of the burden of proof concerning the exhaustion of local remedies was the object of much discussion before the adoption of resolution 1(XXIV). Although the discussion proved helpful for the clarification of other procedural points as well, we shall here concentrate on the debates which touched specifically upon the problem under examination.

On 9 August 1971 the Sub-Commission decided, pursuant to ECOSOC resolution 1503(XLVIII), to appoint a working group[205] consisting of not more than five of its members, with due regard to geographical distribution, to consider all human rights communications received by the UN Secretary-General under ECOSOC resolution 728 F(XXVIII). Petitions would then be sent by the Secretary-General to the Sub-Commission's working group, from this latter to the Sub-Commission itself, and at last to the Commission on Human Rights, which would decide whether or not to make a recommendation to ECOSOC; throughout this process petitions would of course be 'screened'.

As to their admissibility, two proposals were initially considered: one whereby communications should be admissible if they appeared to reveal a consistent pattern of gross and reliably attested violations of human rights (presumption of ineffectiveness of local remedies);[206] the other whereby clear proof and evidence of exhaustion of all national recourse procedures should be required.[207] The differences between these two proposals were evident. The second proposal, requiring 'clear proof' of exhaustion, was met with some opposition from the start,[208] though it was pointed out that communications coming in particular from non-governmental organizations should be based on first-hand information as a condition for their admissibility.[209]

Thus, as the Chilean expert summed up, 'there were two possibilities open to the Sub-Commission: either to accept all communications – even where there was insufficient evidence for investigation by the working group – or to adopt more restrictive criteria which would enable the Sub-Commission to be certain that it was acting with full knowledge of the facts'.[210] The different views and proposals on the problem were then assembled in a report of the chairman-*rapporteur* (Mr E. Nettel).[211]

The crucial debates on the question of the burden of proof concerning exhaustion of local remedies were held on 11 August 1971. Several proposals were put to the discussion, among them the Romanian expert's to the effect that 'communications must provide clear proof that all national recourse procedures have been exhausted'.[212] This proposal faced immediate opposition from the experts from Upper Volta, France and Italy, who considered it unreasonable and too demanding (particularly when applicable to persons of little or no financial means), especially bearing in mind that the underlying idea embodied in the texts under discussion was that only those communications relating to 'serious and flagrant violations of human rights' would be taken into account.[213] On the other hand, the proposal under discussion was backed by the Russian expert, for reasons of expediency (to avoid the Sub-Commission being inundated with 'trivial' communications) and of principle (to ensure prior exhaustion of domestic remedies as a matter of respect for the internal legal order).[214]

The expert from Romania insisted on his proposal, because of the 'exceptional' nature of appeals to the United Nations, but agreed to delete the world 'clear' from the requirement that communications must provide 'clear proof' of the exhaustion of local remedies.[215] The expert from the Philippines proposed an amendment to the effect that a communication should be inadmissible 'only if, after consideration thereof together with the reply, if any, of the government concerned, it may be reasonably inferred that there appears to be a consistent pattern of gross and reliably attested violations of human rights'.[216] At that stage of the debates it seemed that the prevailing view among the Sub-Commission members was that not too heavy a burden should be laid upon the individual complainant to prove that he had exhausted local remedies. The expert from Canada then observed that 'some members of the Sub-Commission were attempting to introduce rigid rules into the draft resolution; apparently they thought that the authors of communications were generally lawyers or had lawyers helping them'.[217] That was not the case, he proceeded, and complainants (including some assisted by lawyers unfamiliar with international procedures) would be 'unlikely to know of the existence of rules such as the one requiring the exhaustion of national remedies'.[218] Another expert pondered in this connection that certain complainants would face great difficulty in proving to the working group that they had exhausted all domestic remedies.[219]

The Romanian expert, with the support of the Russian expert,[220] replied that 'in a spirit of compromise' he could accept the idea that 'an individual need not prove that he had exhausted national recourse procedures'[221] although he insisted upon the retention of the local remedies rule.[222]

A draft resolution then submitted by six of the experts and revised on 12 August 1971 provided that communications should be admissible 'only if, after consideration thereof, together with the replies, if any, of the governments concerned, there are reasonable grounds to believe that they may reveal a consistent pattern of gross and reliably attested violations of human rights'.[223] Furthermore, communications should be inadmissible 'if domestic, regional or other international remedies have not been exhausted, unless it appears that such remedies would be ineffective or unreasonably prolonged. Any failure to exhaust remedies should be satisfactorily established.'[224]

On the same day the Romanian expert changed slightly the wording of his earlier proposal and suggested a provision to the effect that 'communications must be accompanied by the clearest possible evidence supporting the allegations made therein'.[225]

In the last discussion on the matter (12 August) before it was put to the vote, the Austrian expert stressed the difficulties that the local remedies rule could present to some complainants.[226] The Canadian expert stated that 'it would be wiser to omit any rule' relating to the exhaustion of local remedies, since 'it was difficult to see how the working group could possibly know whether all other remedies had been exhausted'.[227] The communication itself 'should state whether such was the case', he added, 'but the working group would not be dealing with persons with legal expertise; the complainants included simple people and it would be most unfair to reject all communications which failed to comply with certain formal requirements'.[228]

Another expert, likewise stressing 'the difficulties of establishing' that domestic remedies had been exhausted, suggested that 'at the preliminary stage, in the matter of the burden of proof, the procedure should work in favour of the complainant'.[229] To that end, he further suggested that the following provision should be adopted: 'Any failure to exhaust such remedies should be established to the satisfaction of the working group.'[230] In this way, 'if it was not clear from a communication that other remedies had been exhausted, the working group would proceed to measure the communication against other criteria, leaving the question of the exhaustion of other remedies for consideration at a subsequent stage'.[231]

This proposal was met with criticisms by the expert from Romania, who could not accept other criteria 'without the inclusion of a rule on the exhaustion of other remedies'.[232] Once again backed by the Russian expert,[233] he recalled the exceptional character of recourse to the United Nations, and stated that the local remedies rule should be observed lest there should be undue interference in the domestic affairs of a State.[234] He then proposed the insertion into the revised draft resolution (*supra*) of the following provision: 'Communications must contain a description of the facts and must indicate the purpose of the petition and the rights which have been violated. They should be accompanied by evidence as clear as possible of the allegations referred to.'[235]

The revised draft resolution was put to the vote (13 August), line by line. The Austrian expert asked for a separate vote on the second sentence of the provision proposed by the expert from Romania.[236] The Chairman, Mr Gros Espiell (Uruguay), accordingly invited the Sub-Commission's members to vote on the second sentence of the Romanian expert's proposal.[237] The second sentence was rejected by 8 votes to 7, with 5 abstentions,[238] while the remainder of the proposal was adopted by 19 votes to none, with 3 abstentions.[239]

By rejecting by a narrow majority the second sentence, the members of the Sub-Commission opted for avoiding the laying of too heavy a burden upon the individual complainant to prove his allegations as clearly as possible. The majority of the members preferred to restrict that requirement to a description of the facts, the purpose of the petition, and the allegedly violated rights.

The local remedies rule was inserted into the Sub-Commission's resolution 1(XXIV).[240] But it should be noted that earlier, ECOSOC resolution 1503 had – improperly – assigned the rule to the Commission on Human Rights for consideration.[241] As has been seen above, the Commission only deals with the complaints after they have gone through the Sub-Commission's working group and the Sub-Commission itself. Thus, resolution 1(XXIV) shifted the rule to its proper place, at the *preliminary* stage of examination of communications, thus rendering to a large extent superfluous that same examination by the Commission.[242]

In his 1972 study of equality in the administration of justice, the Sub-Commission's special *rapporteur*, Mr Abu Rannat, properly qualified the problem of the burden of proof (see *supra*, pp. 161–2), rather than simply asserting it to be always incumbent upon the individual complainant.[243]

(b) *Other instruments and procedures*

The outcome of the work of the Sub-Commission just described seems to have been in keeping with other United Nations instruments on human rights. These instruments, where they contain provisions governing the right of petition, are not particularly rigid over the burden of proof as to the exhaustion of local remedies. In fact, the sharing or distribution of the burden of proof is provided for in at least two of them.

The first is the Optional Protocol to the International Covenant on Civil and Political Rights, which states that the Human Rights Committee (set up in part IV of the Covenant) 'shall not consider any communication from an individual unless it has ascertained that the individual has exhausted all available domestic remedies. This shall not be the rule where the application of the remedies is reasonably prolonged'.[244] The Committee shall consider communications 'in the light of all written information made available to it by the individual *and* by the State Party concerned' (my italics).[245] In its application of the local remedies rule, the Committee has so far proceeded with a flexibility comparable to that of the Inter-American Commission on Human Rights.[246]

Another example is afforded by the International Convention on the Elimination of All Forms of Racial Discrimination, which provides that the Committee on the Elimination of Racial Discrimination (set up by Article 8(1) of the Convention) 'shall consider communications in the light of all information made available to it by the State Party concerned *and* by the petitioner [my italics]. The Committee shall not consider any communication from a petitioner unless it has ascertained that the petitioner has exhausted all available domestic remedies. However, this shall not be the rule where the application of the remedies is unreasonably prolonged.'[247]

As to other existing UN procedures on human rights, the rules of procedure of the Trusteeship Council provide *inter alia* that 'normally, petitions shall be considered inadmissible if they [...] lay before the Council a dispute with which the courts [of the administering authority] have competence to deal [...]'.[248] Express references are not made to the burden of proof, and the rules in general do not seem rigid. (Reference is not made to ILO procedures in the present chapter, as exhaustion of local remedies is not strictly required under them; the position in the inter-American system is referred to *infra*, pp. 185, 287 and 366.)[249]

IV. Conclusions

The proper allocation of the burden of proof is of fundamental importance to the observance of the principle of the equality of parties in the administration of justice. In determining the burden of proof with regard to exhaustion of local remedies, international law has to a large extent relied upon analogies from municipal law. General international law (arbitral and judicial practice) provides ample and strong evidence in support of the sharing or distribution of the burden of proof between the contending parties in inter-State litigation. Thus applying the principle of *onus probandi incumbit actori*, by virtue of which the party who makes an assertion is bound to prove it, international practice embodies and reflects a principle common (with distinct nuances) to both the common law and the civil law systems.

In international law experiments in human rights protection the contending parties are not necessarily sovereign States as is the case in general international law. In most cases one of the parties consists of individuals or private groups. Accordingly, there seems to be in this context all the more reason for the proper application of the division of the burden of proof, since the local remedies rule *per se* already favours the much stronger party, the sovereign State.

However, despite the blatant weakness of one of the parties and the consequent risk of inequality in the administration of justice, in the earlier years of its activity (1955–9) the European Commission of Human Rights seems to have laid the burden of proof systematically upon the individual applicants. But the draftsmen of the Commission's rules of procedure soon realized that the burden had been too heavy upon the individuals, and the general revision of the rules in 1960 marked a new phase in the application of the principle. From then onwards, individual applicants have been required to provide only *prima facie* evidence (*commencement de preuve*) of their assertions, in accordance with recognized rules of international law.

Individual applicants have to prove that they have exhausted local remedies, or that they have not exhausted them either because they were relieved from doing so by special circumstances or because remedies did not exist or were ineffective. On the other hand, the respondent government is bound to prove that local remedies existed and were adequate and effective. Such has been the principle upheld by the Commission's subsequent practice to date.

Another turning-point in that practice occurred in 1964, when the Commission expressly ruled that the burden of proof did *not* lie upon the individual applicants if the respondent government had not raised the objection of non-exhaustion of local remedies when expressly invited by the Commission to express its opinion on the admissibility of the application.

Yet the Commission's practice has displayed a certain amount of inconclusiveness and ambiguity in the application of standards in cases involving remedies of doubtful effectiveness, and contentions of 'legislative measures and administrative practices' allegedly incompatible with the provisions of the Convention. The Commission still needs some indication of clear standards to deal with the particular kind of application lodged by individuals detained in prison. For the determination of the burden of proof concerning exhaustion of local remedies in such particular cases there is ample room for equity.[250]

The Commission's determination of facts has reflected a combination representing a blend of the accusatorial (presentation by the parties) and the inquisitorial (*ex officio* inquiries) systems, sometimes with a marked preference for the latter.

United Nations procedures governing the right of petition in human rights matters likewise support the distribution of the burden of proof between the individual complainants and the governments concerned. In 1971, for example, while devising standards and criteria for the admissibility of complaints addressed to the UN Secretary-General, the UN Sub-Commission on Prevention of Discrimination and Protection of Minorities expressly rejected a proposal which intended to lay too heavy a burden upon individual complainants to prove their exhaustion of local remedies, and opted for the adoption of less rigid and more equitable provisions on the matter. Other UN procedures have followed a similar course. In doing so, United Nations organs, like the European Commission of Human Rights in recent years, have provided a sensible interpretation of the principle of international legal procedure: *onus probandi incumbit actori, onus probandi incumbit ei qui dicit.*

4

THE EXTENT OF APPLICATION OF THE RULE OF EXHAUSTION OF LOCAL REMEDIES

It is especially in the context of the international protection of human rights that the question of the extent of application of the rule of exhaustion of local remedies has evolved and been debated in recent years. In this respect the contribution of the case-law of the European Commission of Human Rights is far from negligible, particularly on such items as the application of the rule – *ratione personae* – in inter-State cases under the European Convention, and – *ratione materiae* – in relation to contentions of legislative measures and administrative practices allegedly incompatible with the provisions of the Convention. The Commission's jurisprudence on such problems, examined *infra*, pp. 172–212, may pave the way for a more adequate and clearer delimitation of the extent of application of the local remedies rule, particularly in the system of human rights protection.[1]

I. Exhaustion of local remedies in inter-State cases: the practice under the European Convention on Human Rights

1. Introduction: statement of the problem

The European Convention on Human Rights provides for a system of complaints which may be lodged with the European Commission of Human Rights either by individuals, private groups or non-governmental organisations (Article 25), or by States Parties to the Convention (Article 24). But while acceptance of the Commission's competence in inter-State cases is entailed automatically upon ratification of the Convention, acceptance of its competence is made optional in applications coming from individuals, which require an express declaration to that effect under Article 25 of the Convention.[2] There can be little doubt that the rule of exhaustion of local remedies applies to applications from individuals (Article 27(3)), but there has been some controversy as to whether the local remedies rule applies or should apply to applications coming from the States Parties themselves.

Surely a sovereign State cannot be made to exhaust domestic remedies in the courts of another State. *Par in parem non habet imperium, non habet jurisdictionem.* But this is assuming that the injury complained of is done *directly* to the claimant State. The fundamental question, the answer to which will be decisive for the determination of the applicability or not of the local remedies rule to complaints brought by one State against another, can be formulated thus: do all claims advanced by States concern directly and immediately the States themselves? The *Mavrommatis* principle provides a negative answer, by describing the espousal by the State of the case of its subject as the action whereby the State, *acting on his behalf,* asserts its own right and tries to ensure in the person of its subject respect for the rules of international law.[3] Hyde's categorization of international claims was in this respect straightforward, by distinguishing two broad classes of claims, namely, 'first, those which are based upon private complaints of individuals whose government acts as their representative in espousing their cause; secondly, those which "concern the State itself considered as a whole" '.[4] It is thus apparent that the starting-point for the study of the problem at issue resides in the *nature of the claim*.

The oral arguments in the *Aerial Incident* case (1959 – *infra*, p. 180) focused *inter alia* on the notion of 'direct injury', whereby a State complains of a direct breach of international law by another State causing immediate injury to itself. This instance is clearly different from cases of diplomatic protection. Acts concerning certain subjects are bound to constitute direct injuries to the State itself, for example, injuries caused by one State to another State's diplomatic or consular representatives in the exercise of their public functions (or injuries to State property, or treaty violations, and so forth). The classification of a case as one of direct injury to a State may leave it outside the scope of the local remedies rule.

It has been suggested that the classification of a case as one of direct injury or as one of diplomatic protection should be made to depend on those elements which seem to be *preponderant*, taking the case as a unity (undivided in its constituent elements) once classified in one way or another. Thus, a test for the classification of a case can be found in the 'real interests and objects' pursued by the claimant State: this latter can be found either to be seeking to secure objectives mainly of its own, or else to be espousing the cause of its subject and thus exercising diplomatic protection.[5] In this latter case the preponderant element would be the interest of the national whose cause was espoused, rather than any other distinct interest of the State apart from the espousal;[6] it goes virtually without saying that it is the international organ's appreciation and decision, rather than the contending parties' formulation, that will ultimately count for the classification of a case into one category or another.

This classification or distinction is of paramount importance for the study of the problem under review. The *locus classicus* of the application of the local remedies rule is afforded by the situation where a dispute of a *private* origin between a State and an alien is 'internationalized' by virtue of the State's espousal of the claim of its national abroad. This suggests *prima facie* that only applications lodged with an international organ by individuals can be made subject to the local redress rule, unless applicant States choose to act on behalf of individuals (not necessarily their nationals) by virtue of express provisions of the Convention. This situation may at times give rise to uncertainties, as will be seen.

2. Non-application of the local remedies rule in inter-State cases

In the *First Cyprus* case (Greece v. United Kingdom, 1956), the Commission declared that 'the provision of Article 26 concerning the exhaustion of domestic remedies according to the generally recognized rules of international law does not apply to the present application, the scope of which is to determine the compatibility with the Convention of legislative measures and administrative practices in Cyprus'.[7] The Greek application was thus declared admissible by the Commission.[8] Even though the Commission declared the local remedies rule inapplicable in that inter-State case, its decision did not shed much light upon the crux of the problem under examination; for the decision was taken on account of the incompatibility with the Convention of certain emergency laws and regulations then in force in Cyprus. The problem of the inapplicability *per se* of the local remedies rule in inter-State case *as such*, irrespective of the existence of wrongful domestic measures or practices, remained unsolved.

For reasons similar to those in the *First Cyprus* case, the Commission, in the *First Greek* case (Denmark/Norway/Sweden/Netherlands v. Greece, 1968), declared that the Convention provisions on the exhaustion of domestic remedies did not apply to those applications, the object of which was 'to determine the compatibility with the Convention of legislative measures and administrative practices in

Greece'.[9] Here, again, the existence of those measures and practices appeared to have been the decisive factor in the Commission's decision to waive the application of the local remedies rule.

It would therefore be more appropriate to examine inter-State cases where the problem at issue was debated *without* the invocation of any generalized wrongful legislative measures or administrative practices: this would enable identification of the Commission's position on the matter in principle. First, however, it is pertinent to notice a relevant doctrinal contribution to the study of the problem, proposed by Eustathiades, who added to his knowledge of the drafting of the European Convention his experience as one of the draftsmen of the UN Covenants on Human Rights. In 1953–5 Eustathiades admitted that the local remedies rule as incorporated in Article 26 of the European Convention applied to individual complaints as well as inter-State ones.[10] However, in a study published in 1957,[11] looking more closely into the question, he reached the opposite conclusion.

To him, both the historical background and the content itself of Article 26 supported the view that this provision was directed in particular to applications emanating from individuals. This could be seen first from the reference contained in Article 26 to the 'generally recognized rules of international law': it resulted from international practice prior to the Convention that the exhaustion of local remedies was required in cases of diplomatic protection where States acted on behalf of their subjects by espousing their claims. The reference made by Article 26 to general international law embodied a certain analogy between individual applications under the Convention and the exercise of diplomatic protection by States in traditional international law. This analogy was maintained despite the fact that the Convention substituted for that exercise of diplomatic protection the right of individual petition under the Convention. And by that reference to general international law, Article 26 tried to avoid derogating from prior international practice which conditioned the exercise of diplomatic protection to previous exhaustion of local remedies.[12]

On the other hand, Eustathiades went on, when a Contracting State brought a complaint in accordance with Article 24 of the Convention, it was not simply demanding reparation for damages suffered by individuals, but rather attempting to ensure respect for the obligations ensuing from the Convention, and, therefore, the rule of exhaustion of local remedies did not apply.[13] Furthermore, the author added significantly:

en plus de la lettre, l'esprit et le but de la Convention conduisent – réserve faite de la protection diplomatique – à ne point devoir considérer l'épuisement des recours internes comme une condition de recevabilité des requêtes étatiques. En effet, les recours en vertu de l'article 24 de la Convention ne constituent pas une extension de la protection diplomatique. Ils appliquent l'idée de garantie collective qui domine l'ensemble du mécanisme de mise en oeuvre établi de façon obligatoire par la Convention. À l'article 24 ce n'est pas la lésion qui, comme à l'article 25, se trouve à la base de la requête, mais bien l'intérêt général, l'observation de la Convention. [...] Le requérant de l'article 25 devant prouver qu'il est victime d'une violation alléguée afin qu'il puisse être admis à présenter un recours, il est compréhensible qu'avant l'épuisement des recours internes on ne pourrait dire que l'ordre interne s'est montré défaillant, dans un cas particulier, à offrir réparation à la 'victime' de la violation de la Convention. Par contre, il n'est pas exigé du requérant de l'article 24 qu'il soit directement ou indirectement (en la personne de ses ressortissants) lésé par l'inobservation de la Convention. Le seul fait de l'existence d'une mesure législative, administrative ou judiciaire contraire à la Convention, autorise toute Partie Contractante d'exercer une action en vue de garantir le respect des droits de l'homme, action qui, sous la forme d'un recours conformément à l'article 24, réalise une garantie collective et n'est pas liée à la lésion d'un intérêt propre de l'État requérant, mais vise à la protection de l'intérêt de la collectivité, à savoir de l'intérêt qu'il y a à voir la Convention respectée au sein de cette collectivité.[14]

Eustathiades' inevitable conclusion was that the local remedies rule constituted a condition of admissibility of applications coming from individuals, but *not* of complaints taken to the Commission by States.[15]

Other authors, while not necessarily subscribing to these views, have nevertheless displayed some sympathy for them.[16] Support has been given, for example, to the view that it is of the essence of the notion of 'collective guarantee' underlying the Convention that a State is and should be entitled to intervene even if the victims are not its own nationals, since what ultimately counts here is the *general interest* in securing the observance and respect *erga omnes* of the obligations deriving from the Convention.[17]

The problem of the non-application or otherwise of the local remedies rule in inter-State cases under the Convention came neatly to the fore throughout the proceedings before the Commission of the *Austria* v. *Italy* case. The case was lodged with the Commission by Austria in July 1960; it concerned criminal proceedings leading to the conviction of six young men for the murder of an Italian customs officer in the German-speaking part of South Tyrol. The applicant government alleged that those proceedings were in breach of the

Convention provisions (Article 6) which laid down rules concerning the proper administration of justice and the protection of an accused person's rights. But in the admissibility proceedings of 1961, the Italian government raised an objection of non-exhaustion of local remedies, maintaining that the local remedies rule 'covered a considerably wider field in the European Convention than in general international law' (i.e., the Convention 'extended' the rule to nationals and stateless persons), applying 'equally to individual applications and to those by Contracting States'.[18]

The Austrian government, on the other hand, defended the thesis that individual applications differed from applications from States in that the local remedies rule applied to the former but *not* to the latter. The Austrian government explained:

Articles 26 and 27(3) of the Convention appeared in quite a different light in the case of individual applications and in the case of applications from States. Persons, non-governmental organizations and groups of individuals could only apply to the Commission under Article 25 if they complained that they were *victims* of a violation of their rights and freedoms; this they could not validly do unless they had exhausted all domestic remedies. On the other hand, Article 24 authorized any Contracting State to refer to the Commission without having suffered any prejudice and even without any individual having been harmed simply because it felt justified as asserting that another State had committed some breach of the provisions of the Convention, perhaps merely by promulgating a law or decree. Unlike individuals, States had not the right to plead violations of the Convention before the courts of other States. Save for complaints made in exercising diplomatic protection, exhaustion of domestic remedies would appear, then, to be irrelevant to the admissibility of applications from States, which would be based on concepts of collective guarantee and general interest.[19]

The Commission, however, rejected this view, and, for reasons stated below, took the opposite standing, namely, that the local remedies rule under the Convention applies to individual as well as inter-State applications.

3. Application of the local remedies rule in inter-State cases

An early indication of the Commission's application of the local redress rule in inter-State cases was afforded by the *Second Cyprus* case (Greece v. United Kingdom, 1957), where the Commission required the exhaustion of local remedies from the alleged victims at least for some of the complaints (those where the perpetrators of the alleged ill-treatment – or some of them – had been identified).[20] It was not until four years later, however, that the Commission dealt with the matter at length and clarified its position on the issue, in deciding on the *Austria* v. *Italy* case (admissibility stage).

Against the contentions of the Austrian government, the Commission began by observing that the local redress rule incorporated in Article 26 of the Convention did 'not, in express terms, make any distinction between matters referred to the Commission by a High Contracting Party under Article 24 and matters referred to it by an individual, non-governmental organization, or group of individuals under Article 25'.[21] Some of the uncertainties were due to the clumsy placement of paragraph (3) of Article 27; while paragraphs (1) and (2) of that provision expressly limited the grounds of admissibility contained therein to applications from individuals under Article 25, paragraph (3), in contrast with the two preceding paragraphs of the same Article, did not so limit the requirement of prior exhaustion of domestic remedies.

Could it then be inferred that this requirement was thereby extended not only to individual but also to inter-State applications? The Commission believed so; it deemed that this had been the intention of the Contracting States, and, furthermore, it felt unable to find in the reference made by Article 26 to 'generally recognized rules of international law' any indication that the High Contracting Parties intended to limit the operation of the rule to matters submitted to it in applications by individuals. The Commission explained:

If it is true that under the generally recognized rules of international law the domestic remedies rule has no application to international claims presented in respect of non-nationals of the claimant State, it is equally true that it has no application to claims presented to international tribunals by individuals. [...] In both types of case the reason is simply that the claims themselves are inadmissible under general international law, irrespective of the exhaustion of domestic remedies. [...] It follows that if the insertion of the words 'according to the generally recognized rules of international law' were to be taken as indicating an intention to exclude the operation of the domestic remedies rule in case of applications brought by States under Article 24, it would equally be necessary to interpret them as excluding its operation in the case of applications brought by individual, non-governmental organization, or group of individuals under Article 25.[22]

It was however beyond question that the rule operated in the case of applications from individuals;[23] it followed that likewise it operated *a fortiori* in the case of applications from States. Thus, while paragraphs (1) and (2) of Article 27 applied only to applications from individuals

(Article 25), paragraph (3) of Article 27 together with Article 26 applied *prima facie* to *all* applications under the Convention (Articles 24 and 25), inter-State as well as individual. This has been the position of the Commission on the matter. More recently, in the *Ireland* v. *United Kingdom* case (1972), *part* of the application was rejected for non-exhaustion of local remedies;[24] and in the *Cyprus* v. *Turkey* case (1975) the waiver of the local remedies rule was due *not* to the inter-State character of the case, but rather, as the Commission made it clear, to its characterization as a case involving large-scale human rights violations relating to a military action by a foreign power.[25] The Commission's support for the principle of application of the local remedies rule to individual as well as inter-State cases seems to have gained general support from expert writers in recent years.[26]

4. General assessment and conclusions

The rule of exhaustion of local remedies under the European Convention on Human Rights is applicable *in principle* to all applications, whether coming from individuals (Article 25) or from States (Article 24). This results from the provisions of the Convention. Article 26 contains no limitation of the rule to applications from individuals; and paragraph (3) of Article 27, however misplaced it might be in the *corpus* of the Convention, coming after paragraphs (1) and (2) that are expressly limited to applications from individuals, is also applicable to '*any* petition' under the Convention. Moreover, the draftsmen of the Convention seem to have recognized this position as being the correct one: on 24 September 1953, after the Convention had come into force, the *rapporteur* of the Committee on Legal and Administrative Questions, Mr Teitgen, stated the opinion that 'cases may not be brought before the Commission, *whether they concern a member State, a private individual or group or a non-governmental organization*, until all local remedies have been exhausted. I refer you to Article 26.'[27] And furthermore, the Commission itself has in its practice lent support to the applicability of the local remedies rule in inter-State cases as well (*supra*, pp. 177–9).

But having laid down the principle, one may now turn to some of its qualifications or related problems. It has been observed at the beginning of this section that the nature of the claim and the wrong complained of should constitute the starting-point of the study of the problem presently under examination. It is clear, for example, that the local remedies rule does not apply when one State inflicts an injury directly and immediately upon another. Thus, throughout the oral hearings in the *Norwegian Loans* case (1957), counsel for Norway, Mr Bourquin, tried to dispose of one of the French contentions whereby the Norwegian government could arguably no longer raise an objection of non-exhaustion of local remedies because it had not done so at the time when diplomatic negotiations had *transformed the case* into an inter-State dispute.[28] And while relying on the strictly State-to-State character of the *Aerial Incident* case (1959), counsel for Israel, Mr Rosenne, contended that there had been a direct injury to the State, and that therefore the local remedies rule – which applied 'solely to the case of so-called diplomatic protection' – did not apply to the present case.[29]

There does not seem to be any reason to believe that cases of alleged 'direct injury' might be relevant to the application of the local remedies rule under the European Convention. The Convention simply is not concerned with direct injuries to States. It is concerned with the basic rights of the human person, and not with the rights of States. Thus, the hypothesis of direct injury could be rejected *de plano* from the present considerations.

Nor could it be inferred, conversely, that cases moved by States under the Convention would then necessarily fit into the category and pattern of cases of diplomatic protection. They may and they may not resemble them, and herein lies the remarkable distinction of the Convention as a system of international protection of human rights, which cannot be equated with the more traditional exercise of diplomatic protection; this suggests certain nuances in the application of the local remedies rule in one system and another.

Under the Convention, for example, a Contracting Party may raise a complaint against another Contracting Party for a breach of certain obligations deriving from the Convention. Here the applicant State could hardly be made to pursue the case before the domestic courts of the respondent State. The claimant State is setting in action the 'collective guarantee' of the Convention, without primarily aiming at any form of redress for a breach of the Convention against specific individuals. Here any analogy with traditional general international law would prove inadequate, *notwithstanding the reference to it contained in Article 26 of the Convention.*

But the applicant State may also be seeking redress for a breach of the Convention against persons subject to the jurisdiction of the respondent State, *irrespective of their nationality*. Here an analogy with diplomatic protection would be *prima facie* possible, but only *on condition* that the persons concerned possessed the nationality of the claimant State, or were its subjects. Thus, even in such cases any analogy with traditional general international law would be of a very limited value, *notwithstanding the reference to it contained in Article 26 of the Convention*.

These situations are illustrative of the risks of false analogies in attempting to approach the system of international protection of human rights under the Convention with the same conceptual apparatus that was once proper to the law and practice of diplomatic protection. But there is another difficulty arising from what has just been pointed out. Two kinds of situations in inter-State cases under the Convention have been distinguished: firstly, an alleged breach of the Convention relating to a *general prevailing situation* and not any particular individual or group of individuals aggrieved (for example, a complaint of one Party against another Party for a breach of its obligation, under Article 3 of the First Protocol to the Convention, to hold free elections at reasonable intervals by secret ballot); secondly, an alleged breach of the Convention in respect of a *particular* individual or group of individuals. In this latter case the local remedies rule applies, in the former it does not.[30]

In the latter case the individuals concerned ought to exhaust local remedies before the claim on their behalf can be pursued by the State Party (whether their own State or any other Contracting State) which decided to take the case to the Commission. In the former case, concerning a general prevailing situation in breach of the Convention, recourse need not be had to local remedies. But not necessarily because this is a dispute *between* Contracting Parties, since inter-State cases under the Convention fall *in principle* within the scope of application of the local remedies rule (*supra*, pp. 177–9). The decisive test here is not the inter-State character of the dispute, but rather – coming back to the initial consideration above – the *nature* of the claim and the wrong complained of: as no individual or group of individuals is particularly aimed at, complaints concerning a general prevailing situation do not fall within the scope of application of the local remedies rule. Furthermore, the test of effectiveness of remedies would most likely render the local remedies rule inapplicable in such complaints concerning a general prevailing situation.

The fact that the complaints are lodged by a Contracting State is not the decisive factor for the application of the rule as of principle: it is a precondition for the lodging of the claim with the Commission, since individuals can only complain of violations of the Convention of which they themselves are *victims* (Article 25), whereas States Parties are entitled to refer to the Commission *any* alleged breach of the Convention by another State Party (Article 24). But once a claim is lodged with the Commission, it is immaterial for the purposes of application of the local remedies rule whether the applicant is a State or an individual, since that condition of admissibility extends to all complaints under the Convention.

In the words of the Commission, in its decision in the *Austria* v. *Italy* case (1961), '*by including the words "according to the generally recognized rules of international law" in Article 26 the authors of the Convention intended to limit the material content of the rule and not its field of application* ratione personae'.[31] Thus, in inter-State cases, it is submitted, attention ought to be paid to whether the complaint is related to a general prevailing situation or to specific injuries suffered by a determined individual or group of individuals. In the former case there will be no room for application of the local remedies rule and presumptions can be made to work in favour of potential or actual victims of the violation of the Convention perpetrated by the general prevailing situation.

The nature of the claim and the wrong complained of thus constitutes the determining factor for the non-application of the rule in such a case; the inter-State character of the complaint is immaterial, for if an inter-State complaint seeks redress for particular wrongs suffered by certain individuals, the local remedies rule will apply. The reference to general international law contained in Article 26 is no basis for the non-application of the rule (in the case above) either, since – as recalled by the Commission in the *Austria* v. *Italy* case – customary or general international law does not normally know of individual applications to an international organ such as those contemplated in Article 25 (i.e., applications extended to non-nationals and stateless persons as well).

The proposition may therefore be advanced that in the systems of international protection of human rights (European Convention and others),[32] as far as *complaints lodged by States* are concerned, the local remedies rule applies in cases of *violation of the guaranteed rights*, where the individual victims ought first to seek local redress; on the other hand, the local remedies rule does not apply in cases of a breach of an obligation of a general order, amounting to a *general prevailing situation*, of which individual victims are not indicated or identified in the inter-State complaint. Significantly, this conclusion can be reached without reliance on misleading analogies with the law and practice of diplomatic protection in general or customary international law.

It may be argued that the case of a general prevailing situation of the kind referred to above may be equivalent to a case of legislative measures and administrative practices incompatible with the Convention provisions. This can be accepted only to a certain extent, and there is a tendency in the Commission's jurisprudence *not* to apply the local remedies rule in inter-State cases when such legislative measures and administrative practices are properly substantiated (of which a conspicuous example is afforded by the *Greek* cases).[33] It seems preferable, however, not to rely solely on contentions of legislative measures and administrative practices in examining inter-State cases of non-application of the local remedies rule, not only because those contentions remain the object of a still evolving case-law of the Commission under Article 26 of the Convention, but also for two main reasons: firstly, because those contentions may, as already indicated (*supra*), render obscure the essence of the problem at issue, and secondly, because although cases of 'legislative measures and administrative practices' may present similarities with inter-State cases relating to a 'general prevailing situation' in breach of conventional obligations, they may not necessarily amount to one and the same thing. A complaint of a State Party to the Convention of a breach of a conventional obligation by another State Party reflected in a certain prevailing situation (for example, an omission on the part of the State) may not necessarily amount to a generalized administrative practice or a series of legislative measures incompatible with the provisions of the Convention[34] – the difference being one of degree and not of nature.

The concepts of 'collective guarantee' and 'general interest' underlying the Convention system help to explain the condition of inter-State applications within the framework of the Convention as a whole. But once one comes to the particular problem of exhaustion of local remedies under the Convention and specifically in inter-State cases, one ought to be careful not to oversimplify the matter on the basis of the notions of 'collective guarantee' and 'general interest'. Although they *explain* the condition of inter-State complaints under Article 24, they do not suffice *per se* to justify the non-application of the rule if what is being sought by the complaint is redress for a wrong inflicted upon certain individuals. There does not seem to be any inherent incompatibility between the incidence of the local remedies rule in *such* inter-State cases and the concepts of 'collective guarantee' and 'general interest' underlying the protective system of the Convention.[35]

These two concepts call for further consideration in the present context. They undoubtedly constitute the novelty of the Convention system and this latter's advance in the protection of individual rights *vis-à-vis* the old law and practice of diplomatic protection in State responsibility for injuries to aliens. But there is a certain limit beyond which they cease to be useful concepts and become rather fictitious: the history of inter-State cases under the European Convention to date shows that applicant States have been prepared to exercise the duty of collective guarantee in the general interest of having human rights preserved and protected, but that exercise has not been entirely devoid of unstated and underlying political motives. This may be a handicap of inter-State applications as an instrument for securing the observance of human rights: the implicit political motives may threaten to overlay the legal issues involved,[36] and thus create an atmosphere where States may deem fit to safeguard themselves behind their own sovereign attributes, as reflected in their insistence upon such conditions of admissibility of complaints as the local remedies rule being strictly applied.

But even here one ought to be careful not to oversimplify. The extent of political motivation (intermingled with humanitarian grounds) seems to vary from case to case, even though seemingly present in all. One could hardly place on the same footing, for example, the two cases moved by Denmark, Norway and Sweden (together with the Netherlands in the earlier case) against Greece (the two *Greek* cases, 1968 and 1970), and, in a possibly different degree, the *Austria* v. *Italy* case (1961) with the two countries' larger dispute over the Tyrol, the *Ireland* v. *United Kingdom* case (1972 onwards) with the two countries' major troubles over the status of Northern Ireland, and the *Cyprus* v. *Turkey* case (1975 onwards) with the broader disputed situation stemming from Turkish intervention in Cyprus.[37] The unstated political motives seem to be always present, though admittedly to a varying degree.

This fact can only emphasize the prominence in the system under the Convention of individual applications under Article 25, where the individuals concerned ought to claim to be *victims* of a violation of the Convention by a Contracting State. The 'politicization', if it may so be termed, of inter-State cases can also be made to militate in favour of the maintenance of the *principle* of the application to them of the local remedies rule, with the qualifications and reservations *supra*, pp. 177–9. The maintenance of the principle itself in the system of the European Convention seems to be corroborated by the parallel regional experiment on human rights protection enshrined in the 1969 American Convention on Human Rights: this latter has gone a step further by providing for the Inter-American Commission's *automatic* competence to receive applications from individuals upon ratification of the Convention (Article 44), and its *optional* competence to receive inter-State applications (Article 45), with the local remedies rule applying to *all* applications, either from individuals (Article 44) or from States (Article 45), by express provision of Articles 46 and 47 of the Convention.[38]

By and large, it seems that the aspect of the European system considered in this section, leaving aside the inconvenience surrounding inter-State applications just referred to, constitutes an advancement in international law in the protection of the human person, in allowing States to act on the basis of the fundamental notions of collective guarantee and general interest in securing respect for the obligations ensuing from the Convention. Precisely because that inter-State action cannot necessarily be equated with traditional forms of diplomatic protection, the local remedies rule, applicable in principle, should be interpreted in the light of the ultimate purposes of the human rights system itself and applied with *less severity* than in the traditional law and practice of diplomatic protection. The reasons for this have already been discussed (*supra*, pp. 6–56), it being submitted in this connection that particular inter-State instances revealing a *general prevailing situation* would fall outside the scope of application of the local remedies rule.

This flexibility in the application of the local redress rule by the Commission in inter-State cases under the Convention could be accomplished through distinct means. One would be the limitation of the material scope of the rule (as advocated above). Another would be the 'softening' of the rule by means of procedural devices. Thus, rule 44 of the rules of procedure of the Commission stipulates: 'Where, pursuant to Article 24 of the Convention, an application is brought before the Commission by a High Contracting Party, the president of the Commission shall through the secretary-general of the Council of Europe give notice of such application to the High Contracting Party against which the claim is made and shall invite it to submit to the Commission its observations in writing on the admissibility of such application.'[39] The State concerned is thus formally granted an opportunity to raise objections to the admissibility of such application, or to remedy the alleged wrong within the framework of its own internal legal system (local redress).

However, it might well happen, even in applications from individuals (Article 25), where admissibility issues can be dealt with in a 'swifter' manner by the Commission itself without necessarily a notification to the respondent government, that this latter may not wish to invoke the local remedies rule on its own initiative. It might well happen that it may be in the State's interest to have the matter decided by an international organ and to have the international law issues thus clarified, however theoretical this situation might be. In fact, in a case where fifty-seven inhabitants of Louvain and its environs lodged complaints with the Commission against Belgium, the respondent government raised an objection of non-exhaustion of local remedies in its *written observations* on the admissibility issues to the Commission;[40] but subsequently, in the *oral hearings* (of 5 March 1964), for whatever reason,[41] counsel for the Belgian government expressly declared before the president of the Commission that he did not want to pursue the objection of non-exhaustion and had therefore decided to withdraw it.[42]

This was a case lodged by a group of inhabitants of a city and its environs (Article 25). In the case of applications lodged by States (Article 24) and of rule 44 of the Commission's rules of procedure in particular, it seems fair and reasonable to maintain that, if the respondent State in a given case fails to avail itself of the opportunity of raising an objection of non-exhaustion of local remedies upon notification of the application by the Commission, there does not seem to be any compelling reason why the Commission should subsequently insist *motu proprio* on the requirement of exhaustion.[43] If the proposition can be accepted, it may result in some flexibility in the handling of certain inter-State cases by the Commission, in so far as application of the condition of admissibility set forth in Articles 26 and 27(3) – common to all applications under the Convention – is concerned.

II. Exhaustion of local remedies in relation to legislative measures and administrative practices: the practice under the European Convention on Human Rights

1. Introduction: statement of the problem

In cases where individual rights are claimed to have been disregarded in violation of international law, the State where the violation occurred should have the opportunity to redress the wrong by its own means and within the framework of its own domestic legal system before resort may be had to an international organ. The incorporation of this well-established rule of international law in the system under the European Convention on Human Rights has been met with innumerable problems of interpretation in the handling of concrete cases. One of the most difficult problems that the organ entrusted with the admissibility of complaints (the European Commission of Human Rights) has faced in this connection has been that of the application of the local redress rule when a whole pattern of administrative practices or of legislative measures is complained of before the Commission as being incompatible with the provisions of the Convention. In such cases is there room for the application of the local remedies rule as enshrined in Article 26 of the Convention? The main difficulty lies in the fact that, in situations of the kind, even though local remedies may exist or be alleged to exist, it may be forcefully argued that their availability or effectiveness may be rendered questionable by the existence of certain administrative practices or legislative measures.

A related problem which has arisen in the Commission's practice has been the notion of the 'victim'. In cases of legislative measures and administrative practices, must an individual applicant be a victim of a specific act already perpetrated, or may he complain of administrative and legislative acts that may in the near future be very likely to violate his rights as set forth in the Convention? In a useful indication for a study of the problem, the Commission has approached the question in applications both from States (Article 24) and from individuals (Article 25). It is necessary, therefore, to survey inter-State and individual applications before proceeding to an assessment of the matter. Special issues developed by the recent practice of the Commission will further be considered.

2. Inter-State cases

In the early days of the Commission, in the *First Cyprus* case, the applicant government brought charges against the respondent government (in May 1956) on account of the latter's legislative measures and administrative practices in Cyprus.[44] In its decision on the admissibility of the application (of 2 June 1956), the Commission declared that 'the provision of Article 26 concerning the exhaustion of domestic remedies according to the generally recognized rules of international law does not apply to the present application, the scope of which is to determine the compatibility with the Convention of legislative measures and administrative practices in Cyprus'.[45] The Greek application was accordingly declared admissible and retained by the Commission.[46]

In the following year the Commission was seized of the *Second Cyprus* case, concerning cases of alleged ill-treatment by officials in Cyprus.[47] This time there was no explicit mention of an 'administrative practice' as such, but rather references to instances of individual cases – classified into three separate categories – of maltreatment.[48] The Commission decided (12 October 1957) that in all those cases where the perpetrators (or some of them) of the alleged ill-treatment had already been identified, domestic remedies ought first to have been exhausted in conformity with Article 26 of the Convention.[49] Accordingly, in all those particular instances the Commission upheld the plea of inadmissibility on the ground of non-exhaustion of local remedies[50] and, without prejudice to the merits, declared the application admissible with regard to certain facts and inadmissible with regard to other facts.[51] It is to be noticed, however, that in the *First Cyprus* case, where 'legislative measures and administrative practices' were as such being complained of before the Commission, the latter held the application admissible and declared that in such a particular situation the rule of exhaustion of local remedies did not apply.

This decision was relied upon by the Commission while examining the *Austria* v. *Italy* case (11 January 1961), but it immediately added that the situation in the present case was manifestly not the same as in complaints concerning the compatibility with the Convention of legislative measures and administrative practices regardless of any individual or specific injury.[52] It was therefore made clear that the local remedies rule would in principle not apply only when the complaints related to the alleged incompatibility of 'legislative measures and administrative practices' with the Convention, as distinguished from complaints of individual specific injuries, in which the rule applied.

Years later, in the *First Greek* case brought before the Commission in September 1967, the applicant governments complained of some constitutional acts as well as 'legislative and administrative measures' incompatible with the Convention, 'regardless of any individual or specific injury'.[53] The three Scandinavian governments in particular submitted that, on the basis of the Commission's finding in the *First Cyprus* case (*supra*), Article 26 did not apply to the present case.[54] In its admissibility decision of 24 January 1968, the Commission began by rejecting the respondent government's objection to its competence as 'unfounded',[55] and added that 'in determining the question of admissibility, the provisions of Article 26 and Article 27(3) of the Convention concerning the exhaustion of domestic remedies according to the generally recognized rules of international law do not apply to the present applications, the object of which is to determine the compatibility with the Convention of legislative measures and administrative practices in Greece'.[56] Accordingly, the Commission declared the applications admissible.[57]

Thus, the Commission again stated that legislative measures and administrative practices did *not* fall within the scope of application of the local remedies rule in international law. The applicant governments insisted that Article 26 of the Convention did not apply to further allegations they raised in the course of the proceedings, also relating to administrative practices of the respondent government;[58] alternatively, should the Commission deem the local remedies rule applicable on the ground that an administrative practice had not been established, they submitted that local remedies alleged to be available were in fact 'inadequate and ineffective'.[59] The Greek government, maintaining that the new allegations should be rejected for non-exhaustion of domestic remedies, argued further that 'an essential element of an "administrative practice" is that the practice concerned should be based on specific legislation, executive authority express or implied, or finally on established custom', and that in Greece no such ground existed on which existence of the alleged administrative practice could be based.[60]

The Commission considered (decision of 31 May 1968) the meaning of the term 'administrative practice' (first with regard to allegations under Article 3 of the Convention). Assuming that an 'administrative practice' might exist in the absence of, or contrary to, specific legislation, the Commission stated, the applicants had not adduced at that stage of the proceedings substantial evidence that such a practice existed in Greece (with particular reference to ill-treatment within the meaning of Article 3 of the Convention); therefore, it added, the application of the local remedies rule (Article 26) to the present allegations could not be excluded on the above ground.[61] But after examining the domestic remedies to be exhausted in the case, the Commission did not find that they could be considered as effective and sufficient, concluding therefore that the present allegations could *not* be rejected for non-exhaustion of local remedies.[62]

As to the other set of allegations (under Article 7 of the Convention and Article 1 of the First Protocol), the Commission categorically stated that the local remedies rule did *not* apply to them, 'the object of which is to determine the compatibility with the Convention and the Protocol of legislative measures of the respondent government'.[63] The Commission, therefore, without prejudice to the merits, finally declared admissible the new allegations of the applicants[64] in the *First Greek* case.

In its report on the case, adopted on 5 November 1969, the Commission observed that 'the Convention does not in terms speak of administrative practices incompatible with it, but the notion is closely linked with the principle of exhaustion of domestic remedies'.[65] The local remedies rule (Article 26) was based on the assumption[66] that for a breach of the Convention there was a domestic remedy available and effective. However, where an administrative practice of ill-treatment existed, the Commission considered:

the remedies prescribed will of necessity be side-stepped or rendered inadequate. Thus, if there was an administrative practice of torture or ill-treatment, judicial remedies prescribed would tend to be rendered ineffective by the difficulty of securing probative evidence, and administrative enquiries would either be not instituted, or, if they were, would be likely to be half-hearted and incomplete.[67]

On 10 April 1970, the governments of Denmark, Norway and Sweden filed with the Commission a further application against Greece on account of a trial in alleged violation of Articles 3 and 6 of the Convention[68] – the *Second Greek* case. The Commission invited the respondent government to submit within a four-week time-limit its observations in reply to the applicants' submission that the local remedies rule did not apply to the present allegations (partial decision of 26 May 1970),[69] and examination of the case was adjourned.[70] The respondent government failed to make any submissions,[71] whereas, on the other hand, the applicants insisted that the local remedies rule did not apply to the present application, 'the object of which is to have determined the compatibility with the Convention of certain administrative practices and legislative measures'.[72] The Commission's final decision on the admissibility of the application (16 July 1970) was rendered in particularly emphatic terms: 'It is true that, according to the Commission's constant jurisprudence, the condition of exhaustion of domestic remedies does not apply where an application raises, as a general issue, the compatibility with the Convention of "legislative measures and administrative practices".'[73]

In the instant case, the Commission dealt first with allegations of administrative practices and then with contentions of legislative measures. As to the former (under Article 3 of the Convention), as they concerned an administrative practice of the respondent government (which in the *First Greek* case the Commission had found to exist), if further substantiated they would not be subject to the local remedies rule, in accordance with the Commission's jurisprudence; therefore, they could not be rejected for non-exhaustion of local remedies.[74] As to the latter submissions (under Article 6 of the Convention), relating to a trial before an extraordinary court martial and to the special legislation creating such courts, the Commission added that as the applicants' object was 'to have determined the compatibility of this legislation with the Convention',[75] the condition of exhaustion of domestic remedies 'again does not apply'.[76] These allegations concerning the special legislative measures in force in the field of the administration of justice could not therefore be rejected for non-exhaustion of domestic remedies, and the application was accordingly declared admissible by the Commission.[77]

Possibly one of the most remarkable features of the Commission's final admissibility decision in the *Second Greek* case was its express and reiterated reliance upon its own *jurisprudence constante* to the effect of placing the question of the compatibility with the Convention of 'legislative measures and administrative practices' outside the scope of application of the rule of exhaustion of local remedies in international law.

The matter was further discussed in the *Ireland* v. *United Kingdom* case. In its written and oral submissions, the applicant government maintained that the local remedies rule in Article 26 did not apply to *any* part of the application 'whose object and purpose was to seek a determination of the compatibility of certain legislative measures and administrative practices with the respondent government's obligations under the Convention'; it further pointed out that the application was 'neither in form nor in reality concerned with compensation for, or reparation of, wrongs committed in respect of individual persons', and that 'there was no domestic remedy available in respect of such a claim by a High Contracting Party and no question of exhausting any domestic remedies could arise'.[78] The present application was a 'breach of treaty claim', as such not subject to the local remedies rule, as it was 'only concerned with ensuring the observance by the respondent government of the obligations undertaken by them in the Convention', thus seeking to obtain a determination of the compatibility with those obligations of certain 'legislative measures and administrative practices'.[79] The respondent government replied that the applicant's allegation of an administrative practice was 'unsupported by any assertion of law or fact from which such practice was to be deduced'; as the burden of proof in this connection was incumbent on the applicant government, 'in the absence of such supporting material the issue of exhaustion of domestic remedies was not to be excluded' at the present admissibility stage.[80]

The Commission's admissibility decision of 1 October 1972 in the *Ireland* case concerned itself with four major items. The Commission first examined allegations under Article 2 of the Convention (failure, as a matter of administrative practice, to protect right to life by law): while it was true that the local remedies rule did not apply where an application raised as a general issue the compatibility with the Convention of 'legislative measures and administrative practices', the Commission held, it was not sufficient on the other hand that the existence of such measures and practices should be 'merely alleged'. In order to exclude the application of the local remedies rule, it was also necessary that their existence should be 'shown by means of substantial evidence'.[81] As this was lacking in the present case, those allegations (under Article 2) could not be dealt with until local remedies had been exhausted. And with regard to the argument that the local remedies rule did not apply where breaches of treaty were alleged (*supra*), the Commission replied that it was required by Article 27(3) of the Convention to apply the rule (as set out in Article 26) to *any* application, whether brought under Article 24 or Article 25 of the Convention. Accordingly, the Commission found that it must declare under Article 27(3) that part of the application inadmissible.[82]

Secondly, the Commission considered the applicant's allegations under Article 3 of the Convention (certain interrogation techniques and other forms of ill-treatment of persons in custody, constituting an 'administrative practice'). The Commission had 'no doubt' that the employment of certain interrogation techniques amounted to an 'administrative practice'; therefore, in accordance with its own jurisprudence, those allegations (under Article 3) could not be declared inadmissible for non-exhaustion of local remedies, and were thus retained for further examination on the merits.[83]

Thirdly, allegations in connection with Articles 5, 6 and 15 of the Convention (relating to internment without trial and detention under special regulations) were examined; the issue of exhaustion of local remedies was not raised in this regard, and the Commission found the matters complained of admissible.[84] Fourthly, the Commission considered the applicant's allegations that detention and internment under special regulations had been and were carried out 'with discrimination on grounds of political opinion in violation of Article 14 of the Convention'.[85] As the complaints were very closely related to the previous items, the Commission found that they should likewise be retained for further examination of the merits.[86]

Thus, except for the applicant's initial allegations under Article 2 of the Convention (*supra*, p. 192), which were declared inadmissible, all its other allegations were declared admissible by the Commission and retained for further examination without pre-judging the merits of the case,[87] in conformity with the Commission's case-law on the matter. As for the exception indicated above (complaints relating to Article 2 of the Convention), those allegations in particular were declared inadmissible for the sole reason that the applicant had not sufficiently demonstrated the existence of the 'legislative measures and administrative practices' complained of. But once this proves to be the case, it is the Commission's *jurisprudence constante* that the rule of exhaustion of local remedies does not apply.

3. Applications by individuals[88]

The problem of the application of the local remedies rule in cases of alleged wrongful 'legislative measures and administrative practices' has also been raised before the European Commission in applications lodged by individuals. Thus, in an application concerning Ireland lodged with the Commission as early as 20 March 1957, in which the applicant complained against domestic legislation allegedly incompatible with the provisions of the Convention, the Commission remarked that it could properly receive an application only from an individual who claimed to be the *victim* of a violation by one of the High Contracting Parties of the rights set forth in the Convention.[89] It followed that it could examine the compatibility of domestic legislation with the Convention *only* with respect to its application to an individual and *only* in so far as its application was alleged to constitute a violation of the Convention *in regard to the individual applicant*.[90] The Commission was thus not competent to examine *in abstracto* the question raised in an individual application under Article 25 of the conformity of domestic legislation with the provisions of the Convention.[91] Furthermore, in the present case, even if the applicant had claimed to have been a victim of violations of the Convention, as he did not avail himself of his right to appeal to a higher court against his convictions, his application had to be rejected for non-exhaustion of local remedies; the application was therefore declared inadmissible on that ground.[92] It should not pass unnoticed, however, that the legislation complained of in the case consisted of a law and its amendment,[93] and that at no moment did the applicant seem to complain of a *pattern* of legislation, still less of administrative practices. But the case remains useful for the light it sheds on the notion of 'victim', a notion which subsequently, as it will be seen, was to assume vital importance in cases brought by individuals complaining against 'legislative measures and administrative practices' as such.

One complaint of this sort, questioning the compatibility with the Convention of certain legislative measures, was properly raised in the *Kjeldsen* v. *Denmark* case. The two applicants complained that, by making sex education compulsory in Danish public schools, the Danish government failed to respect the parents' right to ensure that the education of their children should be in conformity with their religious and philosophical convictions (Article 2 of the First Protocol to the Convention). Referring also to the manner in which that education was carried out by the various authorities concerned, they pointed out that the introduction of compulsory sex education in the only school available in the locality where they lived might oblige them to keep their daughter away from school and thereby amount to 'a denial of her right to education'.[94] The Danish government, in their turn, first remarked that by the country's Constitution (Article 76)

Danish parents were *not* obliged to send their children to public schools, but only to ensure that they received an elementary education; sex education had been compulsory in the whole country since 1970, the educational policies lying ultimately in the hands of the Minister of Education, even though the administration of public schools was decentralized.[95] The respondent government added that the applicants had made 'no attempt to take their complaint before the Danish courts'.[96]

Elaborating on the question of exhaustion of domestic remedies, the Danish government, after dwelling upon the proper relationship between international law and municipal law in the circumstances of the case,[97] indicated that Article 63 of the Danish Constitution authorized domestic courts 'to decide any question bearing upon the scope of the authority of the administration'.[98] In the Danish government's submission, moreover, 'the applicants were at liberty to bring an action against the Minister of Education claiming that the Minister be ordered to recognize the applicants' right to have their daughter exempted from obligatory sex education': the application should thus be rejected on the ground of non-exhaustion of available domestic remedies.[99]

The applicants, on their part, stated that they had in fact written a letter to the Danish Parliament (in May 1971), which had not been answered, and thus the government was 'not justifiable' in declaring that the applicants had failed to exhaust domestic remedies 'which the government had failed to point out to them when it had had the opportunity'.[100] Alternatively, the applicants submitted, Article 63 of the Danish Constitution entitled domestic courts to decide any question bearing upon the scope of the authority of the administration, but the present case was not about the authority of the administration, but rather about an Act of Parliament 'which had itself laid down the basic rule, i.e. compulsory sex education, and authorized the Minister of Education to issue regulations to implement this rule'.[101] Besides, a decision of the Danish Supreme Court of 26 September 1972 showed that 'Article 63 of the Constitution could not be invoked against an Act of Parliament'.[102] The applicants, thus, although conceding that they had brought no proceedings before the Danish courts regarding the matters complained of, submitted that a legal action of the kind suggested by the respondent government 'would not be an effective remedy for the purposes of Article 26 of the Convention'.[103]

In its decision of 16 December 1972 on the *Kjeldsen* v. *Denmark* case, the Commission considered two questions in connection with the issue of the exhaustion of local remedies. First, with regard to the possibility of challenging administrative regulations, the Commission began by recalling that in order to comply with Article 26 of the Convention an applicant was obliged to exhaust 'every domestic remedy which cannot clearly be said to lack any prospect of success'.[104] Although in the present case the respondent government had not been able to show that the Danish courts, in proceedings brought under Article 63 of the Constitution, had ever ruled on 'the question whether the Convention could be invoked in judging the legality of administrative regulations', on the other hand the government explained that 'it is a widely accepted view in Danish legal theory that a valid treaty, such as the Convention, imposes on the domestic authorities an obligation to apply and interpret national law in a manner to ensure that, wherever possible, Denmark's treaty obligations are fulfilled'.[105] The Commission found that, in regard to administrative measures concerning the manner in which the sex education should be carried out, it could not be stated that the remedy indicated by the respondent government would clearly have been without any prospect of success.[106] It followed that, in this respect, this part of the application should be rejected for non-exhaustion of local remedies.[107]

Secondly, the Commission considered the question whether there was any remedy against the Danish Act of 27 May 1970 which laid down the principle of compulsory sex education and authorized the Minister of Education to issue regulations on the manner in which the instruction should be given. As the respondent government did not contest the applicants' assertion that no proceedings could be taken (under Article 63 of the Constitution) against an Act of Parliament, and as it did not suggest that any other specific remedy might be available, the Commission thereby concluded that 'there was no effective domestic remedy available to the applicants with regard to the principle of compulsory sex education as embodied in the Act', and that therefore, in this respect, the application could not be rejected for non-exhaustion of local remedies.[108]

The Commission thus declared the application admissible in so far as it complained of the 1970 Act on compulsory sex education in the public schools as violating Article 2 of the First Protocol, and declared the application inadmissible in so far as it related to the directives issued and other administrative measures taken by the Danish authorities regarding the manner in which such sex education should be carried out.[109]

This decision served as basis for the Commission's subsequent partial decision (of 29 May 1973) in the *Pedersen* v. *Denmark* case, which involved similar complaints and allegations.[110] The examination of the part of the application not declared inadmissible was adjourned until 19 July 1973, the date of the final decision on the case; the Commission confirmed that the reasons it had given for declaring the *Kjeldsen* v. *Denmark* case partly admissible applied 'with equal force' to the corresponding part of the *Pedersen* v. *Denmark* case.[111] As in the view of the Commission, determination of the issues raised depended on an examination of the merits of the case, the *Pedersen* application was declared admissible in so far as the applicants complained that the Act of Parliament (of 27 May 1970) providing for compulsory sex education in Danish public schools constituted a violation of Article 2 of the First Protocol to the Convention.[112]

One of the most illustrative cases for the problem under study has been that of *Donnelly and Others* v. *United Kingdom,* concerning ill-treatment of the applicants – while in custody – by the security forces in Northern Ireland (in April and May 1972) contrary to Article 3 of the Convention.[113] The seven applicants maintained that the maltreatment practices and procedures complained of constituted 'part of a systematic administrative pattern' permitting and encouraging violence, incompatible with the Convention, and rendering inapplicable the local remedies rule.[114] To the respondent government's argument that an *individual* application (under Article 25), unlike an inter-State application, could not advance such a general claim regarding the compatibility of domestic legislation with the Convention,[115] the applicants replied that their present application, whereby they sought to have the Commission protect them, had no connection with the government which had initiated the inter-State application (cf. the *Ireland* case, *supra*, pp. 191–3); their claim pertained to 'the direct application to each of them' of an administrative practice of ill-treatment which 'violated their rights under Article 3', directly affecting them as victims.[116]

The British government argued that the application was inadmissible as each of the applicants had failed to exhaust remedies available under domestic law, and had further failed to show that he had been impeded in the access to available local remedies.[117] On their part, the applicants submitted that the exception to the local remedies rule relating to administrative practices (in the context of Article 3), previously elaborated by the Commission (*supra*, pp. 189–90), was *not* limited to inter-State applications (under Article 24), but applied also to their present application, as they claimed to be individual victims of an administrative pattern against which they had 'no adequate or effective domestic relief'.[118] They added that they would be bound to exhaust local remedies only in 'normal circumstances' (for example, an 'isolated incident' of ill-treatment), but not in the present case, where a systematic practice of ill-treatment in detention and interrogation was being complained of.[119]

Thus, in the applicants' view, to hold that the exception to the local remedies rule did not apply to their case would run 'counter to the purpose of the Convention which was *to provide full protection not to States but to individuals*'[120] and would also be 'contrary to normal rules of interpretation of treaties generally'.[121] It would thus be 'unreasonable' if an 'administrative pattern' could not be questioned by an individual applicant.[122] Claiming that in the circumstances of the case 'domestic remedies were not adequate and effective', the applicants stated that the existence of the administrative practice of which they had offered 'substantial evidence' was the primary factor in rendering any 'theoretically available domestic remedy' ineffective.[123]

Such were the main contentions of the two parties before the Commission. In its admissibility decision of 5 April 1973 on the *Donnelly* case, the Commission began by observing that the Convention provisions did *not* prevent an individual applicant from raising before it a complaint in respect of an alleged 'administrative practice' in breach of the Convention, provided that he brought '*prima facie* evidence of such a practice and of his being a victim of it'.[124] Recalling its previous opinions whereby the local redress rule did not apply in cases raising as a general issue the compatibility with the Convention (Article 3) of an administrative practice, the Commission added in particular that where there was 'a practice of non-observance of certain Convention provisions, the remedies prescribed will of necessity be side-stepped or rendered inadequate'; thus, if there was an administrative practice of maltreatment, 'judicial remedies prescribed would tend to be rendered ineffective by the difficulty of securing probative evidence, and administrative enquiries would either not be instituted or, if they were, would be likely to be half-hearted and incomplete'.[125] By similar reasoning, the Commission considered, where an applicant under Article 25 submits evidence, *prima facie* substantiating both the existence of an administrative practice [...contrary to Article 3], and his claim to be a victim of acts part of that practice, the domestic remedies' rule in Article 26 does not apply to that part of his application'.[126]

The Commission examined the allegations made in the present *Donnelly* case in the light of its previous admissibility decision of 1972 in the *Ireland v. United Kingdom* case (cf. *supra*, pp. 189–93). After drawing a parallel between the issues involved in the two cases, the Commission found that the present applicants:

> have provided evidence which *prima facie* substantiates their allegations of an administrative practice in violation of Article 3 and of their being victims of that practice. It therefore follows that the domestic remedies' rule does not apply to this part of the present applications and [...] the applicants' complaint in this respect raises issues of law and fact whose determination should depend upon an examination of the merits of the case.[127]

The Commission then turned to the question whether each applicant was himself a victim of specific acts – as distinct from an administrative practice – in violation of Article 3. In principle, the Commission observed, the applicants must comply with the local remedies requirement before complaining of such acts; however, the Commission recalled in this connection its own case-law to the effect that 'the exhaustion of a given remedy ceases to be necessary if the applicant can show that, in the particular circumstances of his case, this remedy was unlikely to be effective and adequate in regard to the grievances in question'.[128] In the present case the question of the effectiveness of available remedies was 'closely linked with the alleged existence of an administrative practice in breach of Article 3'.[129] In such circumstances, the issue under Article 26 could not be examined without an examination of questions concerning the merits of the applicants' complaint with regard to the alleged administrative practice. As with the previous part of the present application, the Commission found it appropriate to join to the merits also the issue whether each individual applicant had himself been a victim of specific acts in breach of Article 3 and exhausted local remedies under Article 26 of the Convention. The Commission, in conclusion, declared admissible and retained (without pre-judging the merits of the case) the issue raised by the applicants that they were victims of an 'administrative practice' in violation of Article 3 of the Convention, and joined to the merits 'any question relating to the remedies to be exhausted by each applicant as the alleged victim of specific acts, as distinct from an administrative practice, in violation of Article 3'.[13?]

4. Assessment

The relatively little writing to date on the problem under examination[131] may possibly be explained by the fact that only recently did the problem of the exhaustion of local remedies in relation to legislative measures and administrative practices undergo some of its most important developments in the experiment of the Council of Europe. There has been a consistent tendency of the Commission to dispense with the requirement of the exhaustion of domestic remedies when an application (inter-State or individual) raises the compatibility with the Convention of alleged 'legislative measures and administrative practices'. Examination of this problem has compelled the Commission to elaborate on related questions of relevance for the interpretation of Article 26, and indeed of the Convention as a whole – for example, the proper relationship between international law and municipal law (in connection with the application of the local remedies rule), often involving examination of constitutional law issues (as in the *Kjeldsen* and *Donnelly* cases), and the Commission's elaboration on the notion of 'victim'. This may in the long run prove beneficial to the jurisprudence of the Convention organs as a whole.

Consideration of the notion of 'victim' was by no means restricted to applications by individuals; although it was in the *Donnelly* case that the Commission had possibly the best opportunity so far to develop that notion in relation to an administrative practice, the question has attracted the Commission's attention in a series of decisions in the course of several years. Earlier, in the *Austria* v. *Italy* case in 1961, the Commission stated that the local remedies requirement of the Convention 'appeared in quite a different light in the case of individual applications and in the case of applications from States': individuals could apply to the Commission (under Article 25) only if they claimed to be *victims* of a violation of their rights as set forth in the Convention and if they had exhausted all domestic remedies, whereas States could refer to the Commission (under Article 24) 'without having suffered any prejudice and even without any individual having been harmed'.[132] Thus, a State Party to the Convention could claim that another High Contracting Party had committed some breach of the Convention's provisions by, for example, promulgating a law or decree. This had the necessary implication of rendering apparently irrelevant the requirement of exhaustion of local remedies under the Convention to the admissibility of applications *from States* based on 'concepts of collective guarantee and general interest'.[133]

As was remarked by the Commission in the *First Greek* case, while under Article 25 of the Convention 'only such individuals may seize the Commission as claim to be "victims" of a violation of the Convention', the condition of 'victim' was not however mentioned in Article 24 on inter-State applications; consequently, the Commission added, 'a High Contracting Party, when alleging a violation of the Convention under Article 24, is not obliged to show the existence of a victim of such violation either as a particular incident or, for example, as forming part of an administrative practice'.[134] In their turn, individual applicants must claim to be *victims* of a violation of the Convention as a condition of receivability of their applications (cf. the *X* v. *Ireland* and *X* v. *Norway* cases, *supra*, pp. 193–4, and *infra*, p. 374). The Commission elaborated on the notion of 'individual victim' in its decision of 13 July 1970 in the *X* v. *F.R. Germany* case, in which it stated that the term 'victim' meant 'not only the direct victim or victims of the alleged violation but *also any person who would indirectly suffer prejudice* as a result of such violation or who would have a valid personal interest in securing the cessation of such violation'.[135] This notion of '*indirect* victim' was also relied upon or upheld by the Commission in at least two other decisions.[136]

This new element gave more precision to the conception of 'victim' under the Convention, which, however, remained nonetheless construed in rather strict terms. Hence the great significance of decisions such as those in the *Kjeldsen* and the *Donnelly* cases. In the *Kjeldsen* case the Commission allowed the two applicants, *prospective* or *future* victims, to raise the general issue of the compatibility with the Convention (and Protocol) of the introduction of compulsory sex education in public schools. When the Commission declared their application admissible in so far as it was directed against the Danish Act providing for that compulsory education, the Commission was implicitly but clearly recognizing, it may be submitted, that individuals could raise the issue of the compatibility of legislative measures with the Convention, measures whose general and widespread effects (like those of administrative practices) might well go far beyond the immediate requests and interests of the individual applicants in particular. The way would be paved, in this manner, for the Commission to be concerned with the protection not only of victims of past violations of the Convention, but also of those who may in the future, in circumstances such as those described in the *Kjeldsen* and *Pedersen* cases, be the object of likely violations of rights.

The significance of the *Donnelly* case, for its part, was a distinct one. The exception to the local remedies rule on account of 'legislative measures and administrative practices' had until then been developed by the Commission only in inter-State cases (*First Cyprus, First Greek, Second Greek* and *Ireland* cases). In the *Donnelly* case the Commission was called upon for the first time to state whether an individual victim could also rely on that exception to the local redress rule recognized in inter-State cases. The Commission found that if the individual concerned submitted *prima facie* evidence of the existence of an administrative practice in breach of the Convention and of acts of which he was a victim, the local remedies rule would not then apply to that part of the application.

This is *not* therefore, it is submitted, merely a question of subjective appreciation by the applicant of the existence of an administrative practice of maltreatment for the purpose of waiving the local remedies rule. As early as 6 September 1957, in a case against Germany, the Commission categorically stated that the personal opinion of the applicant (unsupported by evidence) on the ineffectiveness of remedies shall not be taken into consideration for the determination of the application or not of the local remedies rule.[137] Moreover, the lack of evidence cannot be an objection *in particular* to a claim of wrongful administrative practice, but possibly to any claim under the Convention. A claim against an administrative practice does *not* differ from a claim of ineffectiveness of local remedies, in that *it is the Commission and not the applicant* that ultimately examines it for the purpose of rejecting or upholding it for further investigation. The applicant's subjective appreciation uncorroborated by evidence seems altogether irrelevant in this context.

In the European experiment under the Convention, it has been suggested that, by lodging an application under Article 25, the individual concerned is initiating an *action publique* (set forth in the Convention) rather than strictly pursuing a *droit subjectif*.[138] The whole procedure can in this way be approached on the basis of rights as well as *duties*. Writing in 1957, before the Commission had developed its case-law on the problems raised by legislative measures and administrative practices, Eustathiades observed that individual applications certainly aimed at reparation to the victims, but served also a general interest, particularly when they concerned legislative measures and judicial or administrative practices independently of their application *vis-à-vis* the individual applicants; inter-State applications were even more closely related to the *general interest* of seeing the Convention observed *vis-à-vis* all persons concerned.[139]

Henri Rolin identified in individual applications a point of coincidence between the individual and the general interest: complaints of individual violations in a way helped to secure respect *erga omnes* for the provisions of the Convention. The *action publique* initiated by the individual complainant worked not only as a means to obtain *reparation* for particular injuries, but also – in cases of legislative measures and administrative practices – as a *preventive measure of protection*, in an identification between the individual and the general interest. Furthermore, once seized of a case, the Commission's task was not limited to that of redressing a tort, but of ensuring the observance of the engagements undertaken by the High Contracting Parties under the Convention (in the terms of its Article 19).[140]

The Commission itself stressed the '*objective* character' of the engagements undertaken by the States Parties to the Convention (Article 19) in the *Austria* v. *Italy* case. The Commission emphasized that an application from a State referring to an alleged breach of the Convention was 'not to be regarded as exercising a right of action for the purpose of enforcing its own rights, but rather as *bringing before the Commission an alleged violation of the public order of Europe*'.[141] The Commission, as the international organ seized of the applications under the Convention, has a *duty* and not only a faculty of examining the complaints and giving continuance to the procedure for the settlement of the cases.

The application of the local remedies rule and related problems can first be approached on the basis of the different kinds of *interests* involved, for example: the individual's interest in having the international wrong judicially settled and remedied as quickly and efficiently as possible; the respondent State's interest in having a chance of doing justice in its own way and by its own domestic courts in order to discharge its responsibility; the international community's interest is seeing that local remedies work efficiently in order to have the dispute settled in the quickest, most effective and least expensive way.[142] But the whole question can also be approached on the basis of the *duties* of the parties concerned, for example, the individual's duty to exhaust local remedies, the respondent State's duty to provide local remedies.[143]

In cases concerning legislative measures and administrative practices, the individual, having shown that such a practice exists, is *not* under the duty of exhausting local remedies, and is entitled to raise the question of the compatibility with the Convention of those measures or practices. The Commission's findings in, for example, the *Kjeldsen* and *Donnelly* cases may have the effect of strengthening the status of individual applicants under the Convention. In instances of wrongful legislative measures and administrative practices the respondent State would be placed under the duty to forbid legislative or administrative acts which may encourage or allow or tolerate systematic practices of ill-treatment (in breach of Article 3 of the Convention). Thus, in the context of cases of legislative measures and administrative practices the issue of the exhaustion of local remedies should preferably be approached on the basis of duties rather than interests.

The Commission may at times go further than upholding contentions of administrative practices in breach of the Convention. In the *Cyprus* v. *Turkey* case, for example, the applicant government complained of large-scale violations of human rights by Turkish authorities in Cyprus, while the respondent government raised an objection of non-exhaustion of local remedies (based mainly on Article 114 of the Turkish Constitution). The applicant retorted that the multiple complaints in the case related to 'an "administrative practice" in the sense of the Commission's case-law', forming part of a government policy which rendered domestic remedies ineffective in the circumstances. In its admissibility decision of 26 May 1975 the Commission found that it had *not* been established that remedies available in domestic courts in Turkey or before Turkish military courts in Cyprus were practicable and normally functioning. As they could not be considered as effective and sufficient within the meaning of Article 26 of the Convention, the Commission concluded that the complaints could *not* be rejected for non-exhaustion of local remedies. In so deciding, the Commission regarded the case not as one of 'administrative practice', as suggested by the applicant government, but expressly as one relating to 'a military action by a foreign power' and to 'the period immediately following it'.[144]

The waiver of the local remedies rule by the Commission in cases of wrongful administrative practices (endorsed by the *Donnelly* decision) should *not* be interpreted as a means of unduly strengthening the procedural status of individuals under the European Convention. There does not seem to be any strong reason for supposing that by invoking an alleged administrative practice the individuals concerned could pursue their case with considerably better prospects of success and circumvent procedural obstacles. Besides the fact that the admissibility decision rests with the Commission alone, even if the local remedies rule is dispensed with the applicants would still have to face the other grounds of inadmissibility of applications set forth in Article 27 of the Convention. It thus remains unlikely that a successful contention of administrative practice would *ipso facto* and automatically entirely clear the way for a subsequent consideration of the merits of the case.

Besides that, the local remedies rule in Article 26 of the Convention was never meant to be an *absolute* ground of inadmissibility of complaints, as is sometimes inaccurately assumed. A most important point, often overlooked and misinterpreted, was clarified by the Commission itself when, in the *Austria* v. *Italy* case, it stressed that, by formulating the local remedies rule in Article 26 by reference to general international law, '*the authors of the Convention intended to limit the material content of the rule*' rather than to extend it.[145] International law recognizes exceptions to the local remedies rule, notably, for example, when domestic remedies do not exist or are manifestly ineffective or inadequate for the object of the claim.

The Commission's exclusion of the local remedies rule in cases of substantiated administrative practices also meets the requirements of common sense. Without that exclusion, and in face of the usually slow process of domestic litigation, individuals would have little – if any – protection against certain practices amounting to systematic violations of human rights. Moreover, by granting remedies in the form of, for example, monetary compensation to the individual victims, a government could forestall indefinitely any inquiry upon the international plane into its larger policies.[146] If one considers that out of a total of 6,847 applications registered with the Commission until the end of 1974 only 127 were declared admissible,[147] and that of the overwhelming majority of rejected applications a considerable number was declared inadmissible for non-exhaustion of domestic remedies, one can hardly avoid the apprehension that unless the Commission sets standards for a more flexible application of the local remedies rule the very foundations of the European system of human rights protection are likely to be undermined. In this way, the Commission's exclusion of the rule in cases of legislative measures and administrative practices may well render a valuable service to the cause of human rights in the European regional context.

The Commission's tendency to accord what appears to be an increasingly wider meaning to the notion of 'victim' (of legislative measures and administrative practices) – as seen in the *Kjeldsen* case – seems to be well in keeping with the parallel experience and developments in the United Nations. Pursuant to ECOSOC resolution 1503(XLVIII) of 1970, the UN Sub-Commission on Prevention of Discrimination and Protection of Minorities set forth in its resolution 1(XXIV), adopted on 13 August 1971, procedures on the admissibility of communications concerning human rights violations addressed to the UN Secretary-General. Those procedures not only expressly exclude the application of the local remedies rule where domestic remedies are 'ineffective or unreasonably prolonged',[148] but also provide *inter alia* that, in cases disclosing 'reasonable grounds to believe that they may reveal a consistent pattern of gross and reliably attested violations of human rights', admissible applications may originate not only from individuals who are 'reasonably presumed' to be victims of those violations but also from individuals and non-governmental organizations having 'direct and reliable knowledge of such violations'.[149]

Thus, by ascribing to the notion of 'victim' an increasingly broader interpretation and by excluding the application of the rule of exhaustion of local remedies in cases of substantiated legislative measures and administrative practices incompatible with the provisions of the Convention, the European Commission of Human Rights seems to be slowly but steadily moving into the right direction, towards an effective accomplishment of the ultimate goals of the European experiment on human rights protection.

5. Special issues

Subsequently to the Commission's admissibility decision of 1 October 1972 on the *Ireland* v. *United Kingdom* case and its admissibility decision of 5 April 1973 on the *Donnelly and Others* v. *United Kingdom* case, both already examined (cf. *supra*, pp. 191–3 and 197–200), the Commission elaborated on special issues of importance to the subject now under examination, in its handling of those two cases. One may largely distinguish two such issues, namely, the relationship between administrative practices and the requirement of exhaustion of local remedies, and consideration of contentions of administrative practices and the adequacy of local remedies. At the close of this section it is thus convenient to examine the later views of the Commission on those particular issues, as raised in the *Ireland* inter-State and the *Donnelly* cases.

(a) The relationship between administrative practices and exhaustion of local remedies

As a preliminary to the question of the proper relationship between the concept of administrative practice and the requirement of exhaustion of local remedies, it may be asked why the Commission has combined 'legislative measures and administrative practices' from the early case-law (for example, the *First Cyprus* case) onwards. The Commission provided an answer in its *Report* on the *Ireland* v. *United Kingdom* case, adopted on 25 January 1976. The Commission stated that the reason for repeatedly combining the two notions 'for purposes of exemption from Article 26 is that when the practice itself is admitted, such cases amount to a challenge of "the law of the land" and thus the normal assumption that domestic remedies could be effective does not apply' (for example, difficulty of proof before national courts).[150]

Earlier, in the *First Greek* case (1969), the Commission laid down as constituent elements of an 'administrative practice', necessary to its existence, those of *repetition of acts* and *official tolerance*.[151] The Commission explained that 'administrative practice' was not 'administrative' in the sense of being a repetition of administrative decisions, but consisting rather of repeated factual events which were tolerated, i.e., passed unchecked.[152] This point was again made by the Commission in the *Ireland* v. *United Kingdom* case.[153] In the *First Greek* case, the Commission further traced the relationship between administrative practices and the local remedies rule by observing that the notion of administrative practice 'is closely linked with the principle of the exhaustion of domestic remedies. The rule in Article 26 is based on the assumption, borne out by Article 13, that for a breach of a Convention provision there is a remedy available in the domestic system of law and administration, even if the provision is not directly incorporated in domestic law, and that that remedy is effective.'[154] However, the Commission added, where there is:

a practice of non-observance or certain Convention provisions, the remedies prescribed will of necessity be side-stepped or rendered inadequate. Thus, if there was an administrative practice of torture or ill-treatment, judicial remedies prescribed would tend to be rendered ineffective by the difficulty of securing probative evidence, and administrative enquiries would either be not instituted, or, if they were, would be likely to be half-hearted and incomplete.[155]

The relationship between the notion of administrative practice and the local remedies rule was further developed by the Commission in its *Report* on the *Ireland* v. *United Kingdom* case. The applicant government argued that the respondent government could not rely on the objection of non-exhaustion of local remedies as, if an administrative practice of ill-treatment was established, it would tend to make judicial remedies ineffective and the local remedies rule inapplicable; furthermore, the fact that some claims had been settled and some people paid damages proved only that *some* people had been able to get damages, and a strong inference remained that a great many people had not been able to get damages.[156] On its part, the respondent government submitted (hearing of December 1973 on the merits) that effective remedies (civil remedies) existed and were being pursued before domestic courts.[157] The parties agreed that, in order to establish whether an administrative practice of ill-treatment existed, the Commission was to rely on the criteria it laid down in the *First Greek* case (*supra*, pp. 189–90), namely, the two requirements of 'repetition of acts' and 'official tolerance'.[158]

The issue of the effectiveness of remedies was much disputed by applicant and respondent governments, in connection with the proper meaning to be ascribed to the notion of 'administrative practices'.[159] In the Commission's view, the essential feature of the 'repetition of acts' as a constituent element of an administrative practice was that 'the acts complained of form a pattern or system in the sense that some link or connection exists in the circumstances surrounding the particular acts, e.g. time and place where the acts occur and the attitude of the persons involved, and that they are not simply a number of isolated acts'; and as for the element of 'official tolerance', the Commission continued, it might be found to exist 'on alternative levels: namely that of the direct superiors of those immediately responsible for the acts involved, or that of a higher authority'.[160] In this way, the Commission expressly dismissed the respondent government's argument that a State could only be responsible if 'official tolerance' was shown 'at the level of the State', and held that the responsibility of a State under the Convention may arise for acts of all its organs, agents and servants (irrespective of their rank), imputed to the State.[161]

The Commission concluded that it was necessary to distinguish between

an administrative practice tending to render domestic remedies ineffective, and a practice in breach of the Convention. Thus:

(a) the role of an administrative practice is, for the Commission, procedural in that it involves the rule of exhaustion of domestic remedies and its applicability;

(b) the role of a practice in breach of the Convention belongs essentially to the merits and where such a practice is found, involving acts in breach of Article 3, the violation of the Convention is that much more serious;

(c) there can be circumstances where a practice in breach of the Convention constitutes also an administrative practice tending to render domestic remedies ineffective.[162]

(b) *Contentions of administrative practices and adequacy of local remedies*

The Commission's admissibility decision of 5 April 1973 on the *Donnelly and Others* v. *United Kingdom* case, already examined (cf. *supra*, pp. 197–200), did not present the Commission's final views on the issue of exhaustion of local remedies as raised in the case. The Commission elaborated on the matter in its subsequent decision of 15 December 1975 on the same case, in which, having considered the parties' submissions as to the local remedies requirement under Article 26 of the Convention,[163] it initially warned that, procedurally, the issue relating to exhaustion of local remedies, while joined to the merits, 'must still be considered as affecting the admissibility of the applications'.[164]

While the applicants complained of ill-treatment (in breach of Article 3 of the Convention) and of being victims of an administrative practice necessarily rendering local remedies ineffective or inadequate, the respondent argued that that was a case of an emergency situation and not of an administrative practice, and that the applicants should make use of the available remedies unless they were shown to be ineffective.[165] The Commission was thus confronted with the issue of the nature of the remedies available; these were action for damages under the common law,[166] claim against the State for compensation,[167] and complaints against members of the security forces.[168]

After considering that 'the possibility of obtaining compensation may, in normal circumstances, be an adequate and sufficient remedy in respect of a complaint of ill-treatment in violation of Article 3 of the Convention',[169] the Commission recalled the steps taken by the applicants to exhaust local remedies: each of them had in fact instituted civil proceedings in order to obtain damages; four of the actions had been settled on the agreed terms,[170] the applicants also receiving their legal costs; the actions by the three remaining applicants were at the time of the Commission's decision still pending.[171] The question then before the Commission was thus that of the effectiveness in practice of the machinery of compensation; having examined in detail the facts and circumstances of each applicant's case,[172] the Commission took the view that the applicants had failed to show that the machinery for compensation did not, or was unlikely to, work effectively in practice.[173]

The Commission remained however faced with the applicant's objection that compensation was not an adequate remedy, since it did not operate so as to prevent the administrative practice complained of.[174] The Commission, recalling the State's duty to provide individuals with effective remedies, drew the following distinction: where a State took reasonable steps to comply with its obligations under Article 3 of the Convention (even though a contravention had occurred), compensation constituted in general an adequate remedy, 'since it is likely to be the only means whereby redress can be given to the individual for the wrong he has suffered'; but where a State did not take reasonable steps to comply with its obligations under Article 3 of the Convention, compensation could not be deemed to have rectified the violation complained of. The Commission thus laid down the principle that 'compensation machinery can only be seen as an adequate remedy in a situation where the higher authorities have taken reasonable steps to comply with their obligations under Article 3 by preventing, as far as possible, the occurrence or repetition of the acts in question'.[175]

In the present case, however, the Commission, on the basis of the evidence examined, was of the opinion that that evidence did not disclose that the applicants had been victims of a policy or administrative practice of ill-treatment tolerated by the higher authorities, 'which could have had the effect of rendering compensation inadequate as a remedy for any wrong they suffered'; on the contrary, it disclosed that the higher authorities had not reacted with indifference to their allegations, which had been reasonably investigated.[176] In fact, in the light of steps taken by the respondent government to fulfil its duty towards the applicants to prevent the occurrence or repetition of the acts complained of, the Commission considered that in the circumstances of the case 'the possibility of obtaining compensation through a civil action for damages constituted an adequate remedy for the specific violations of the Convention alleged by each of the applicants'; and the Commission had already found that it had not been established in any of the present cases that this remedy did not work effectively in practice.[177]

The legal consequences of the Commission's findings as to remedies were thus not hard to anticipate. As to the three applicants whose domestic civil proceedings were still pending, the Commission held that in so far as they claimed to have been victims of specific acts (as distinct from an administrative practice) in breach of Article 3, their applications were to be rejected under Article 27(3) for non-exhaustion of local remedies. As to the four applicants who had received reasonable compensation by using remedies available, they could no longer claim to be victims of any violation of the Convention, and their applications were thus inadmissible on the ground that they had accepted compensation by using available remedies and had renounced further use of local remedies.[178]

As in the *Ireland* inter-State case (*supra*, pp. 208–9), the Commission explained, in the *Donnelly* case, that theoretically the notion of administrative practice – in its component elements of repetition of acts and official tolerance – was closely linked with the requirement of exhaustion of local remedies, rendering remedies ineffective or inadequate where there was definitely a practice of non–observance of the Convention provisions. But where tolerance of ill-treatment had been shown to exist possibly only at the middle or lower level of the chain of command, and not by higher authorities, the Commission had to ascertain the effectiveness of remedies in practice in the light of steps taken by authorities to fulfil their duties *vis-à-vis* the individuals concerned and to prevent the occurrence or repetition of acts of ill-treatment. Thus, not every alleged practice in breach of the Convention would necessarily have the effect of rendering remedies ineffective or inadequate.[179]

In the *Donnelly* case the Commission had already found that the possibility of obtaining compensation in a civil action constituted an adequate and effective remedy for alleged breaches of Article 3 of the

Convention (cf. *supra*, pp. 209–11). Even though such findings did 'not exclude the possibility that at some place or level a practice in violation of the Convention existed', the Commission did 'not find it necessary to examine this question since in its view the same grounds of inadmissibility apply to this part of the application as apply to the applicants' allegations that they have each been the victim of specific acts in violation of Article 3'.[180] The Commission therefore unanimously took the view that that part of the applications 'should be rejected under Article 29 of the Convention since the grounds for the inadmissibility of the applicants' allegations that they have been victims of specific acts in violation of Article 3 are equally applicable in relation to their allegations that they have been victims of an administrative practice'.[181]

In view of the Commission's findings no precise relationship was drawn between the concept of administrative practice and the *adequacy* of local remedies in the *Donnelly* case. This would perhaps be possible if it had been established that an administrative practice of ill-treatment did in fact exist and called for a closer scrutiny on the part of the Commission for the purposes of application of the local remedies rule, which was not exactly the case. It remained, however, clear, both from the Commission's decision in the *Ireland* inter-State case (*supra*, pp. 208–9) and from its decision in the *Donnelly* case, that the notion of 'administrative practice' (constituted by repetition of acts and official tolerance) is, theoretically at least, closely related (procedurally) to the requirement of exhaustion of local remedies under the Convention.

5

THE TIME FACTOR IN THE APPLICATION OF
THE RULE OF EXHAUSTIONS OF
LOCAL REMEDIES

I. Introduction

One procedural problem virtually unexplored so far is that of the application of the rule of exhaustion of local remedies *ratione temporis*. Before embarking on such an examination of the time factor in the application of the rule, a few preliminary remarks are necessary. It must first be noted that the question of *undue delays* in the process of exhaustion of remedies more properly belongs to the domain of the so-called 'exceptions' to the local remedies rule (i.e., the circumstances relieving the claimant or applicant from the duty of exhausting local remedies), already examined.[1] It is, accordingly, left outside the scope of the present chapter. The following questions may then be considered: firstly, special problems related to the time of exhaustion (such as, for example, the proper time of pursuance of domestic remedies and the problem of their exhaustion in so-called 'continuing situations'); secondly, the time of the raising of, and of decision on, objections (the local remedies rule in relation to other preliminary objections); thirdly, the six-month rule enshrined in Article 26 of the European Convention on Human Rights.[2]

In fact, it is under this Convention that the time factor in the application of the local remedies rule has been receiving careful attention. Thus, in the examination of the six-month rule[3] in Article 26 of the Convention, besides the origin of such rule, the following practical procedural problems may be investigated in the light of the jurisprudence of the European Commission of Human Rights on the matter: the determination of the notion of 'final decision' (for the running of the six-month period); the correlation between the six-month rule and the local remedies rule proper; the normal process of exhaustion and the problem raised by certain remedies (for example, petitions for the re-opening of the case and re-trial) in relation to the time factor; the application of the time factor when the complaint is directed not against an isolated act but rather against a permanent state of affairs or a continuing situation; the time factor in the application of the six-month rule itself; the interruption or suspension of the running of the six-month period; and the relation of this latter to the notion of 'unreasonable delay' under Article 5(3) of the Convention.

II. Time of exhaustion

In considering the time of exhaustion of local remedies, attention will be directed to the experiment of the European Convention on Human Rights, under which some special problems have arisen in this respect. This has been one of the relatively rare areas in which the European Court of Human Rights has been able to offer a valuable contribution (in contrast with the vast case-law of the Commission on the exhaustion of local remedies). Two particular points can be conveniently examined under the present heading, namely: the question whether under the Convention an individual applicant must have exhausted local remedies before the filing of the application with the Commission, or whether he may pursue the final stage of exhaustion before domestic courts shortly after the lodging of the application but before the Commission's decision on admissibility; and the problem of exhaustion of local remedies in an alleged 'continuing situation' (particularly in cases of detention while on remand).

1. Exhaustion of local remedies: before the lodging of the application or before the decision on admissibility?

The Court had an opportunity to tackle the problem in the *Ringeisen* case: the application was lodged with the Commission on 3 July 1965, while the final judgment of the Austrian Constitutional Court was not given until 27 September 1965. The Austrian government inferred therefrom that the applicant had not exhausted all local remedies at the time when the application was made and, consequently, 'the Commission was not competent to deal with the complaint'.[4] The government's representatives relied basically on the French text of Article 26 to argue that all domestic remedies ought to have been exhausted before the Commission could deal ('la Commission ne peut être saisie') with the case.[5] On the other hand, the Commission's delegates, relying on the 'equally authentic' English text of Article 26 ('the Commission may only deal with'), took the view that 'non-exhaustion of domestic remedies did not prevent the lodging of the application, but solely its examination by the Commission'.[6] The Commission further argued – leaving the English text aside – that 'common sense' itself showed that the requirement contained in Article 26 'cannot oblige the applicant to do more than exercise all the remedies available to him; it would be hard to imagine that, before petitioning the international organs, he was bound to await the final domestic decision given at the close of a procedure the length of which did not depend exclusively on him'.[7] The Commission expressed the belief that such an interpretation was the only one in conformity with the *ratio legis* of the local remedies rule, which, the Commission added, 'doubtless implied that no international verdict should be given before the final decision of the national courts but not that such a final decision must be prior in point of time to the lodging of the international application'.[8]

Such was the heart of the controversy between the Commission and the Austrian government regarding the substance of the submission of inadmissibility of the complaint on the ground of non-exhaustion of local remedies, which the Court was called to pronounce upon.

The Commission's delegates (Mr G. Sperduti and Mr J.E.S. Fawcett) requested the Court to decide that the objection of the Austrian government under Article 26 of the Convention against the Commission's decision on admissibility (of 18 July 1968) was inadmissible before the Court, and in the alternative, that it was ill-founded.[9] The agent for the Austrian government (Mr E. Nettel), on the other hand, requested the Court to find that it had jurisdiction to interpret Article 26 of the Convention and to decide on the admissibility of the individual application (within the meaning of Article 26 and 27(3) of the Convention), to reject part of the application in question as inadmissible for non-exhaustion of local remedies, and to declare that in the case there had been no violation of the Convention.[10]

The Court's decision was delivered on 16 July 1971. In a Separate Opinion, Judge Verdross, without commenting on the 'common sense' argument made by the Commission, affirmed, as to the position it had taken, that 'the Commission may not select the text which seems to it to be the most practical but must endeavour to find an interpretation which, having regard to the object and purpose of the treaty, best "reconciles" these texts (Article 33(4) of the Vienna Convention on the Law of Treaties)'.[11]

The Court itself began by stating that it did not consider that it could adopt 'either of these extreme positions' (i.e., the Austrian government's or the Commission's)[12] on the problem at issue. It continued:

on the one hand, it would certainly be going too far and contrary to the spirit of the rule of exhaustion of domestic remedies to allow that a person may properly lodge an application with the Commission before exercising any domestic remedies. On the other hand, international courts have on various occasions held that international law cannot be applied with the same regard for matters of form as is sometimes necessary in the application of national law. Article 26 of the Convention refers expressly to the generally recognized rules of international law. The Commission was therefore quite right in declaring in various circumstances that there was a need for a certain flexibility in the application of the rule.[13]

The Court then recalled that, in actual practice, the original applications lodged with the Commission are often followed, shortly afterwards, by additional documents for the purpose of clarification of some points (indicated by the Commission's secretary to the applicant during a preliminary examination carried out). There was no reason, added the Court in this connection:

why this supplement to the initial application should not relate in particular to the proof that the applicant has complied with the conditions of Article 26, even if he has done so after the lodging of the application. When the Commission decides whether or not a case is inadmissible, its examination is directed necessarily to the application and the later documents considered as a whole.[14]

Accordingly, the Court found that 'while it is fully upheld that the applicant is, as a rule, in duty bound to exercise the different domestic remedies before he applies to the Commission, it must be left open to the Commission to accept the fact that the last stage of such remedies may be reached shortly after the lodging of the application but before the Commission is called upon to pronounce itself on admissibility'.[15]

But the Court did not stop there. It went further, recalling in support of its view the fact that 'individual applications often come from laymen who, in more than nine cases out of ten, address themselves to the Commission without legal assistance. A formalistic interpretation of Article 26 would therefore lead to unfair consequences'.[16] The Court satisfied itself that the facts of the case[17] showed that 'no legitimate interest of the respondent State could have been prejudiced in the present case through the fact that the application was lodged and registered a short while before the final decision of the Constitutional Court'.[18] The Court therefore rejected as 'unfounded' the submission of inadmissibility on the ground of non-observance of Article 26.[19]

It is difficult not to endorse the development inaugurated by the Court in its *Ringeisen* decision.[20] After all, the rule of exhaustion of local remedies evolved, in general international law (to which Article 26 refers), within the context of inter-State disputes – or, more properly speaking, of disputes of a private origin *ab initio* (an alien against the State of residence), but subsequently internationalized by the intervention of the alien's State on his behalf (espousal of his claim by his State), thus becoming inter-State disputes.[21] This was the *locus classicus* of application of the local remedies rule in general international law, i.e., within the context and meaning of State responsibility for injuries to aliens and for the purpose of the exercise of diplomatic protection. Another aspect to be borne in mind is that, as exemplified by so many such cases (for example, the *Canadian Hay Importers* case in 1925, the *Losinger* case in 1936, the *Norwegian Loans* case in 1957, the *Interhandel* case in 1959, the *Aerial Incident* case in 1959, the *Barcelona Traction* case in 1964 and 1970, among many others) 'the traditional rule of domestic exhaustion was established for litigants with substantial resources who were involved in complex financial litigation or for aliens who are disfavoured plaintiffs in international litigation'.[22] In fact, 'most international cases on exhaustion concerned merchants and aliens who were expected to be solvent and knowledgeable about their trade'.[23]

This is not at all the case in the application of the rule of local remedies in the international law on human rights protection. As pointed out by the European Court in its *Ringeisen* decision, here individual applicants are most often laymen who 'in more than nine cases out of ten' resort to the Commission without legal assistance (see *supra*, p. 216). It is hard to conceive that in these cases, however serious the political implications might be, the individual applications might constitute a real threat to the sovereignty of States, which the local remedies rule was historically designed to serve and protect[24] as possibly its primary aim.

Quite consistently, the European Commission has made it clear, in a *dictum* acknowledged by the Court in its judgment on the *Matznetter* case ('as to the facts'), that there is 'no complete parallelism' between the system of diplomatic protection and the 'new system' of human rights protection inaugurated by the European Convention.[25] The 'transplantation' of the local remedies rule from one system into another, it may be submitted, cannot operate mechanically and without reconsideration of the matter in the light of the distinct fundamental premises of the two systems, diplomatic protection and human rights protection. The fact should be borne in mind for the proper application of the local remedies rule in cases brought before an international organ in charge of rendering decisions on the ground of the body of law developed – by treaty or custom – for the particular purpose of the international protection of fundamental rights.

In this context one may regard the European Court's finding in the *Ringeisen* case that the Commission is entitled to accept that the last stage of the exhaustion of local remedies can be accomplished shortly after the lodging of the application but before the decision on admissibility (cf. *supra*, pp. 214–16) as a sound and sensible development in the application of the rule. The Court's interpretation, for reasons indicated by the Court itself, operates ultimately on behalf of the individual applicant a certain relaxation of a principle *per se* existing primarily to the benefit of the respondent State, thus remedying to some extent the factual inequality of status between the individual applicant and the respondent State.

Judge Verdross, in his Separate Opinion on the *Ringeisen* case, felt unable to accept the interpretation given in the Court's judgment to Article 26.[26] Judge Verdross recalled that Article 26 of the Convention, as well as all other provisions marking out the 'limits of an international body's jurisdiction' with regard to the exhaustion of local remedies, were 'designed to protect the States from finding themselves arraigned at international level *before* they have had an opportunity to redress a violation which may possibly have been committed by an organ of lower rank. Consequently, every provision in this category must be interpreted strictly.'[27] Judge Verdross cautiously added:

I am not unaware that it would perhaps be more appropriate to amend Article 26 in the way in which the Chamber has interpreted it, but the Commission and the Court must apply the Convention as it has been drafted by the High Contracting Parties. Like the International Court of Justice, 'it is the duty' of our Court 'to interpret the Treaties, not to revise them' (Advisory Opinion of 18 July 1950 on the *Interpretation of Peace Treaties*, [1950] *Reports*, p. 229).[28]

However, the judicial function may be interpreted in distinct ways by the judges of the International Court as well as of the European Court: 'where one judge might in his practice on the Court see a matter as falling within the scope of legitimate interpretation, another may see only an alleged departure from an existing "rule", and a "revision" '.[29] Some judges may be more in favour of judicial innovation than others; what to one magistrate may appear to be a 'revision' of Article 26 of the European Convention, may be interpreted by others to constitute a reasonable and cogent interpretation by the Court of Article 26, particularly after this latter's finding the question of admissibility as falling within the terms of the instrument conferring jurisdiction upon it[30] and thereby rendering it competent to deal with the objection of non-exhaustion of local remedies.

As to the International Court's decision quoted by Judge Verdross, it may be recalled that in a more recent Advisory Opinion (1971) the International Court of Justice stated that it could not tenably be argued that the clear meaning of an institution 'could be ignored by placing upon the explicit provisions embodying its principles a construction at variance with its object and purpose'.[31] In the present case, that object and purpose – referred to in the Judge's Opinion, *supra* – are clearly to ensure a proper observance of human rights pursuant to Article 19 of the Convention. But the 1971 *Advisory Opinion on Namibia*, whose *dictum* above seemed to be well in keeping with the general rule of treaty interpretation embodied in Article 31(1) of the 1969 Vienna Convention on the Law of Treaties,[32] went further than that. The International Court held that:

an international instrument has to be interpreted and applied within the framework of the entire legal system prevailing at the time of the interpretation. [...] In this domain,[33] as elsewhere, the *corpus juris gentium* has been considerably enriched, and this the Court, if it is faithfully to discharge its functions, may not ignore.[34]

And years earlier, in 1958, a former Judge of the International Court of Justice maintained on the problem at issue that:

in all these spheres judicial responsibility, in its quest for justice, has full scope. That quest can derive no decisive assistance from exclusive reliance upon one single doctrine, or tendency, or formula. Unavoidably, in the zeal of forensic effort which it is their business to display, parties will rely upon some such exclusive consideration – just as they will often appeal to what may be no more than an argumentative stratagem. Thus they will assert that it is the business of the Court to interpret treaties and not to rewrite them, or that its task is to apply the law and not to change it. That brand of argument, which depicts the judicial function as obvious and automatic, may be no more than a piece of dialectics which begs the question. For the point is what the treaty, properly interpreted, means; the question is what the law is. That question is not answered by the assertion that the interpretation contended for by the other party would amount to rewriting the treaty or changing the law.[35]

It was not the first time that a problem of the kind raised in the *Ringeisen* case (i.e., institution of international proceedings *before* final domestic decision) was brought and discussed before an international court. In 1939, in the *Electricity Company of Sofia and Bulgaria* (Preliminary Objection) case, for example, the Bulgarian government alleged that the Belgian application to the Permanent Court of International Justice had been introduced before a decision with *final* effect (the judgment of the Bulgarian Court of Cassation) was rendered, and was therefore 'premature and irregular' for non-exhaustion of local remedies, as provided for in Article 3 of the 1931 treaty of conciliation, arbitration and judicial settlement between Belgium and Bulgaria.[36] The Permanent Court found that the local remedies rule enshrined in Article 3 of the treaty implied the exhaustion of all appeals, including appeals to the Court of Cassation which alone could render the judgment final,[37] and that therefore the objection was well-founded. But the domestic decision referred to had not been rendered at the date when the Belgian application was filed; moreover, the irregularity of the Belgian application had not been removed by the judgment rendered on 16 March 1938 by the Bulgarian Court of Cassation, for in the meantime (on 4 February 1938) the 1931 treaty had expired and been denounced by the Bulgarian government.[38] Accordingly, the PCIJ concluded, since the Belgian application had not been submitted in accordance with the conditions laid down by the 1931 treaty, the Belgian government could not found the jurisdiction of the Court on that treaty.[39]

In his Dissenting Opinion on the case, Judge Van Eysinga held that the objection of non-exhaustion of local remedies should not be accepted by the Court. The Bulgarian objection was in fact an objection to the admissibility of the application (rather than to the Court's jurisdiction). The local remedies rule based on Article 3 of the treaty meant that the Belgian government could at once re-submit its application (on the basis of the declarations of Article 36 of the Statute), since by then all local Bulgarian remedies would have been exhausted sometime previously. In these circumstances, Judge Van Eysinga added, it would be a 'pure formality' to uphold the objection based on the local remedies rule, since local remedies had in fact been exhausted in the meantime.[40]

Judge Anzilotti, in his Separate Opinion on the case, deemed that the PCIJ should have accepted the Bulgarian objection based on the local remedies rule and disclaimed jurisdiction. He disagreed with the Belgian view that the local remedies requirement found in Article 3 of the treaty would be fulfilled by the mere submission of the case to the Bulgarian Court of Cassation without waiting for the actual judgment. He further disagreed with the view that the Bulgarian denunciation of the treaty released the Belgian government from the duty of awaiting the judgment.[41] In a passage of his Opinion Judge Anzilotti conceded that the local remedies rule could have a *suspensory* character, serving to suspend the proceedings as an objection to the merits, but in this case the local remedies rule was not one of common or general international law but rather a treaty-based rule.[42]

But from the above it is clearly seen that the local remedies rule cannot be regarded today as a requirement of strict or mechanical application in time. As the European Court itself acknowledged (*supra*, pp. 216–18), a complaint may be accepted by the Commission even if the process of exhaustion is still at its last stage by the time of the lodging of the application, but that process ought anyway to have been completed before the Commission's decision on admissibility of the application.

2. Exhaustion of local remedies in cases of an alleged 'continuing situation' (particularly in cases of detention while on remand)

In three of the so-called 'detention cases'[43] the Court had an opportunity to pronounce on the problem of exhaustion of domestic remedies in a *situation continue*. In the *Neumeister* case, the Court noted that in his application of 12 July 1963 the applicant had complained 'not of an isolated act but rather of a situation in which he had been for some time and which was to last until it was ended by a decision granting him provisional release, a decision which he sought in vain for a considerable time'.[44] In the light of such a situation, the Court took the view that:

> it would be excessively formalistic to demand that an applicant denouncing such a situation should file a new application with the Commission after each final decision rejecting a request for release. This would pointlessly involve both the Commission and the Court in a confusing multiplication of proceedings which would tend to paralyse their working.[45]

With particular reference to the requirement of exhaustion of local remedies, the point was further developed by the Court in the

Stögmüller case. There, the Court was faced with a controversy on the subject between the Austrian government and the Commission. The government challenged the Court's previous *dictum* in the *Neumeister* case (*supra*), stating that 'it would be contrary to Article 26 if we were to adopt the opinion that an application alleging a violation of Article 5(3) related to a situation and not to an isolated act'.[46] The Austrian government explained that if that was the case:

> it would be enough for the person concerned to have exhausted the domestic remedies immediately after the beginning of his detention while on remand in order to be entitled to question the legality of the whole period of detention by applying to the Commission; the respondent State would thus be prevented from taking steps to remedy within the framework of its domestic legal system a supposed violation which might very well not have occurred until after the lodging of the application. In the government's opinion, such a result would be contrary to a rule of customary international law and Article 26 was purely and simply a reproduction of this rule.[47]

Further on, the government conceded that 'it did perhaps fail to raise before the Commission the objection based on Article 26', but it nevertheless considered that it was 'entitled to raise the matter before the Court'.[48]

On the other hand, the Commission remarked that 'if the government's argument was to be accepted, it would lead to the conclusion that a person held in detention while on remand would have to make incessant applications in order to exhaust the domestic remedies with respect to the whole period of his detention: such a large number of applications would not only be likely to be considered as an obstruction of the normal course of criminal procedure but even as an abuse of the right of appeal'.[49] In the view of the delegates of the Commission, 'a person alleging the violation of Article 5(3), with respect to the length of his detention while on remand complains of a continuing situation which should be considered as a whole and not divided up in the manner suggested by the government'.[50] If the government's argument were to be accepted, the Commission went on to say, 'the effect of Article 5(3) of the Convention would be gravely impaired: it would dissuade detained persons from petitioning the Commission until they had endured a long period of detention while on remand'.[51] To the Commission, 'once the application was declared admissible and Article 26 of the Convention had been respected at the stage of examination of admissibility, the Commission and the Court were competent to judge whether the length of the detention while on remand in issue was reasonable without this competence being in any way limited as to time'.[52]

In the public hearings of 10 and 11 February 1969, counsel for the Austrian government (Mr W.P. Pahr) insisted on the principle of general international law that one State could not be sued by another for an alleged violation of international law until it had been given an opportunity to take action itself to remedy the violation in its own domestic legal system.[53] In the present case, he went on, the time element was decisive for the proper weighing-up of the application; the answer to the question whether the Convention had been violated, he contended, depended entirely upon the *moment* at which the question was put. The subject of such proceedings was therefore not so much a situation as a particular fact (i.e., the actual duration of detention which, he alleged, in itself was in accordance with Article 5(1)(c) of the Convention).[54] Therefore, counsel for Austria maintained, the Commission and the Court were entitled and authorized to decide 'only whether the length of the detention against which the application, the starting point of the proceedings, is in fact directed, was excessive in the light of Article 5(3)'.[55]

One of the Commission's delegates (Mr F. Ermacora) remarked that there was no limitation under Austrian law concerning the number of petitions for release which a detained person might introduce; if one adopted the Austrian view advanced in the pleadings, he continued, one might arrive at the conclusion that 'a person detained pending trial would be obliged under Article 26 of the Convention continuously to file petitions for his release in order to exhaust domestic remedies for the entire period of his detention'.[56] The introduction of such a great number of petitions might be considered 'not only to interfere with the proper course of the criminal proceedings but also to constitute an abuse of the right of petition'.[57] He further contended that 'when a person brings a complaint under Article 5(3) of the Convention concerning the length of his detention on remand he refers to a continuing situation. The period of this situation must be considered as a whole, and not in separate parts determined by the dates of the domestic decisions rejecting petitions for release.'[58]

Another of the Commission's delegates (Mr C.T. Eustathiades) asserted that precisely because the matter at issue was not the legality of the *original* detention but rather the *length* of the detention, the period could not be divided into compartments as proposed by the

Austrian government.[59] Acceptance of this latter's argument would lead to one of two extremes: either the prisoner would have to lodge a large number of appeals, or, conversely, detained persons would be discouraged from making new applications for release, an object which could not otherwise be attained until very much later as a result of proceedings before the Commission (or later still in certain cases coming before the Court or the Committee of Ministers).[60] The delegate of the Commission opposed the Austrian government's argument that the critical period of detention to be considered by the Commission and the Court would come to an end when the application was lodged with the Commission; in that case, he argued, 'the effect of such a fundamental provision of the Convention as Article 5(3) would be gravely impaired, for such a thesis would mean that the prisoner would have to wait for a long period of detention to pass before deciding to lodge his application with the Commission with a greater chance of success'.[61] In conclusion, he stated that:

whatever decision may be taken on new request by the prisoner for release, and whatever procedure domestic remedies may follow, once the application is declared admissible on the basis of Article 5(3) of the Convention – Article 26 having been observed at the admissibility stage – both the Commission and the Court have power to judge the reasonableness of the period of detention; if necessary up to the stage at which the organ in question reaches its findings.[62]

The agent for the Austrian government (Mr E. Nettel) recalled the rationale of the local remedies rule (the State should first be given an opportunity to right the alleged wrong before an international authority might concern itself with the case), a rule which was a 'strict one'.[63] He further argued that the Commission's decision on admissibility was not infallible, and the Commission could possibly consider an application admissible which was in fact inadmissible. By Article 45 the jurisdiction of the Court was extended to all cases referred to it concerning the interpretation and application of the Convention.[64] Austria's agent did not consider that the obligation to adduce every argument *in limine litis* arose in such cases (before the Court); to him, in proceedings before the Court there was no ban on introducing new material; he maintained that the fact that he did not raise a certain objection in the proceedings before the Commission did not prevent him from doing so now before the Court, which should also consider whether the application was admissible.[65]

In its judgment of 10 November 1969 on the *Stögmüller* case, the Court found that it was:

in accordance with national and international practice that a court should hold itself competent to examine facts which occurred during the proceedings and constituted a mere extension of the facts complained of at the outset. This is clearly the case in matters of detention while on remand, as courts seized of an application for release take their decisions in the light of the situation which exists at that time.[66]

Having said so, the Court moved on to its interpretation of Article 26 of the Convention within the context and in the light of the circumstances of an alleged continuing situation:

As to the point whether the proceedings instituted ('saisine') may embrace complaints concerning facts which occurred after the lodging of the application, international law, to which Article 26 refers explicitly, is far from conferring on the rule of exhaustion the inflexible character which the government seems to attribute to it. International law only imposes the use of the remedies which are not only available to the persons concerned but are also sufficient, that is to say capable of redressing their complaints. Thus, in matters of detention while on remand, it is in the light of the circumstances of the case that the question is, in appropriate cases, to be assessed whether and to what extent it was necessary, pursuant to Article 26, for the detained applicant, who had exhausted the remedies before the Commission declared his application admissible, to make later on further appeals to the national courts in order to make it possible to examine, at international level, the reasonableness of his continued detention. But such question only arises if the examination of the reasons given by the national courts in their decisions on the appeals made before the lodging of the application has not led to the conclusion that, at that date, the detention had exceeded a reasonable time. Indeed, if the opposite be the case it is clear that the detention while on remand which is held to have exceeded a reasonable time on the day when the application was lodged must be found, except in extraordinary circumstances, to have necessarily kept such character throughout the time for which it was continued. As this is the conclusion which the Court has reached in the present case, there is no need for the Court to examine separately the applicant's complaints concerning the period of detention which followed the lodging of the application.[67]

There seems to have been general agreement as to the Court's finding, no Judge dissenting from the *dictum* above. In fact, in their Separate Joint Concurring Opinion, Judges Verdross and Bilge were even more emphatic in stating that the Court could not entertain a question of exhaustion of domestic remedies which had not been previously submitted to the Commission.[68] Why then did the Court take the trouble of pronouncing on Article 26 when it could apparently have more readily disposed of the matter (i.e., the period of detention subsequent to the lodging of the application) with other arguments? It has been suggested that it did so 'perhaps by courtesy to the Austrian government which seems to have very liberally contributed to the *bonne marche* of the proceedings in the *Neumeister, Stögmüller* and *Matznetter* cases'.[69]

In fact, in the *Matznetter* case as well, the Court was faced with a similar basic disagreement between the Austrian government and the Commission's delegates. The government, although making clear that 'it did not intend to dispute the admissibility of Matznetter's application',[70] strongly relied on Article 26 (in its French text), apparently to a large extent on the basis of the arguments developed by Judge Verdross in his Separate Opinion in the *Ringeisen* case (cf. *supra*, p. 215); the government's representatives added that in any case 'one appeal was still pending at the time the Commission declared the application admissible (16 December 1964)',[71] and they conceded that they 'did not raise before the Commission the question of the period to be considered'.[72]

The Commission, arguing on the basis of the English text of Article 26, repeated arguments previously made (*supra*, pp. 214–15) and recalled its finding in the *Ringeisen* case,[73] later confirmed by the Court's decision (cf. *supra*, pp. 215–17) that 'an applicant has the right to apply to the Commission before exhausting the domestic remedies; it was sufficient if this condition had been fulfilled when the Commission takes its decision on the admissibility of the application'.[74] In the present case, the Commission's delegates proceeded,

the domestic remedies with respect to Matznetter's first application for release were exhausted on 4 March 1964, i.e. a few weeks before the lodging of his application and several months before the decision on admissibility of 16 December 1964. The delegates doubted whether applications made after a long period of detention while on remand had elapsed amounted to true domestic remedies within the meaning of Article 26.[75]

On this occasion, unlike in the *Stögmüller* case, the Court did not delve into a thorough interpretation of Article 26 in the light of the circumstances of the *Matznetter* case. It briefly stated that the Austrian government's arguments 'were not submitted to the Commission'; although the Court would not categorically refuse to examine new submissions by the government on the ground of Article 26, it could however 'only accept them to the extent indicated in its judgment given this day in the *Stögmüller* case ("as to the law", paragraphs 9 to 12)' (see *supra*).[76]

The *Matznetter* case gave rise to an illustrative debate on related points as well, between the Commission's delegates (Mr C.T. Eustathiades and Mr J.E.S. Fawcett) and the Austrian government's agent (Mr E. Nettel), in the public hearings of 11 and 12 February 1969. One of the Commission's delegates (Mr J.E.S. Fawcett), explaining the position taken by the Commission, observed that this latter

has taken into account the fact of the exhaustion of remedies which may be subsequent to the date of an application to it, though of course such a fact cannot be subsequent to its decision on admissibility [as in the *Ringeisen* decision]. In other words, an applicant may make an application which, if it were examined on the date of application, would show that remedies were not exhausted. Remedies may then be pending, an appeal may be pending. When it is determined, remedies are then exhausted. Then comes the decision on admissibility. So in that period, there is a new fact which the Commission will take into account in arriving at its decision on admissibility, though it is a fact subsequent to the date of application to the Commission.[77]

Pursuant to the *Ringeisen* decision, the Commission's delegate proceeded, the fact that the Commission might not go into the substance of an application if remedies had not been exhausted did not mean that it might not take into account facts subsequent to the date of application which might be relevant to its decision on admissibility.[78]

To the Austrian government's agent, the Commission's construction seemed 'unique in judicial practice', as the local remedies rule should be interpreted 'in a formal manner'.[79] He recalled the rationale of the local remedies rule and the need for some degree of protection for States, particularly in the present case, where the right of intervention by an international body was acknowledged in principle:

Any State that has accepted such encroachment on its rights by another sovereign power or by some organisation will wish to ensure that proceedings are not instituted against it before it has had every opportunity to find its own remedy to a wrong alleged to have been done to some person.[80]

The Commission's delegate (Mr J.E.S. Fawcett) insisted that the sense of Article 26 of the Convention could not be limited to mean that an application could not be lodged; to his mind, 'an application must be lodged in order for the Commission to investigate whether domestic remedies have been exhausted'.[81] To the agent for Austria, Article 26 of the Convention had a parallel in the principles underlying intervention in the exercise of diplomatic protection. This latter was inconceivable before exhaustion of local remedies and the *final* domestic judgment. Article 26, he contended, was to be interpreted in the same manner as in several international law decisions in connection with the law of diplomatic protection, which stressed the need to await the *final* domestic decision before appealing to an international body.[82]

This analogy was strongly opposed by the Commission's principal delegate (Mr C.T. Eustathiades), who emphatically rejected the parallel between the local remedies rule in the practice of diplomatic protection for nationals abroad and in the practice of the Convention's supervisory organs, in the following terms:

Here [in the Convention system] we have private individuals. The whole system [...] is based on a Commission which sifts individual applications by persons who cannot be certain whether they have exhausted domestic remedies within the meaning of Article 26. While that Article refers to the recognised principles of international law, this does not mean that any absolute parallel exists between diplomatic protection of individual applications; all that is necessary is to prove that domestic remedies have been exhausted. The individual applies to the Commission, and it is in fact the Commission's task to verify this point. This is not always easy to do, either for the individual or for the Commission. The question of exhaustion of domestic remedies gives rise to lengthy discussion, and the uncertainty is sometimes so great that [...] we join the question to the merits. With regard, then, to the construction placed by the government on the Article, I do not know what force it would have in the case of State applications to the Commission, but in the case of individual applications it would destroy the whole idea underlying the system. I should like to add something else. I must point out that our entire practice since the Commission began would be called into question, for we have proceeded on a different basis.[83]

The agent for Austria nevertheless insisted on the parallel drawn by his government, on the ground that Article 26 of the Convention would not have come into being without the generally recognised rule of international law to which theory and precedents of international law were related.[84] In the present case, he added, as the final domestic decision had not been pronounced and (domestic) proceedings were still pending, the application was therefore inadmissible.[85] One of the Commission's delegates (Mr J.E.S. Fawcett), however, brought into the discussion 'a certain nuance' to be taken into account of the problem of exhaustion of local remedies in cases of detention on remand, like the *Matznetter* case: in the present case, when the Commission admitted the complaint after the applicant had been for the first time up to the court of appeal, the final court (March 1964), he had *already* been eleven months in detention.[86]

III. Time at which to raise objections and time of decision on objections: the objection of non-exhaustion of local remedies in relation to other preliminary objections

1. In general international law

The Statute of the International Court of Justice does not pronounce on the question of preliminary objections.[87] Originally the Rules of Court (of 24 March 1922) were also silent on the treatment of objections, even though the topic was discussed at the preliminary session of the Permanent Court. The 1926 revision of the Rules led to the inclusion of a new Article 38 providing for preliminary objections. The question was again discussed in the 1934–6 work of revision of the Rules, and subsequently, in the 1946 version, the following principle was enshrined in Article 62(1): 'A preliminary objection must be filed by a party at the latest before the expiry of the time-limit fixed for the delivery of its first pleading.' That was the one formal condition *ratione temporis* for the filing of preliminary objections. It has generally been regarded as a flexible and undogmatic attitude of the Court towards preliminary objections.[88]

But amendments adopted on 10 May 1972 modified some provisions of the Rules of 1946, including Article 62, which became new Article 67.[89] The new provision read:

Article 67(1) – Any objection by the respondent to the jurisdiction of the Court or to the admissibility of the application, or other objection the decision upon which is requested before any further proceedings on the merits, shall be made in writing within the time-limit fixed for the delivery of the counter-memorial. Any such objection made by a party other than the respondent shall be filed within the time-limit fixed for the delivery of that party's first pleading.[90]

There has been, in this connection, some urge for uniformity in the time of *raising* preliminary objections – a point once pressed by Hambro. The ICJ Rules of Court are quite clear as to the time when a preliminary objection should be raised: a preliminary objection (for example, to the Court's jurisdiction) is to be filed by a party at the latest before the expiry of the time-limit fixed for the delivery of its first pleading. Hambro argued that, 'it would be better if the State wishing to raise the preliminary objection did so straight away. It might indeed be considered bad faith and almost contempt of Court if the State waited until the very last moment and permitted the other party or parties to present the memorial on the merits before it raised its preliminary objections.'[91]

In his monograph on the time factor in the jurisdiction of the International Court of Justice, Rosenne was very clear on the preliminary objection of non-exhaustion of local remedies: the local remedies rule is examined in the light of '*the premature filing of the case leading to a dilatory temporal objection*, which would normally be an objection to the admissibility rather than an objection to the jurisdiction' (my italics).[92] Thus, Rosenne added:

in an examination in general of the effect of time on the jurisdiction of the Court, an objection based on the rule regarding the non-exhaustion of local remedies, which has been said to be 'of a temporary and relative character', may therefore be regarded as a dilatory objection *ratione temporis*. If accepted it puts an end, on grounds of prematurity, to the case, but implies the possibility of a renewal of the legal dispute when the temporary obstacle is removed.[93]

Once the *preliminary* character of an objection is established, the Court will have to decide whether it ought to deal with all objections raised or only with one of them. In the former hypothesis, the question arises which preliminary objection will have priority in time over the others. There seems to be some uncertainty over this.

A first important doctrinal trend has stressed the Court's freedom of appreciation of preliminary objections, raised either simultaneously or successively.[94] This is the view upheld by Judge Morelli in his Dissenting Opinion in the *Barcelona Traction* (Preliminary Objections) case (1964), where he asserted that if a certain order in the objections raised before the Court is not imposed by any logical necessity, then 'it is for the Court to determine the order that may most suitably be followed. In this connection, the Court may be guided by various criteria and these [. . .] might even be criteria of economy.'[95] Judge Morelli added that:

the Court's freedom to determine the order to be followed, when the order between the different questions is not imposed by any logical necessity, cannot be removed or restricted by the attitude of the parties, still less by the attitude of one of the parties. It would be inconceivable that [. . .] one of the parties should be able to compel the Court to give a prior decision on a certain question, when such prior decision is not called for by any logical necessity.[96]

Such was also the view espoused by Charles de Visscher:[97] firstly, the Court is not obliged to follow the order of objections as submitted by the parties; and secondly:

la diversité presque infinie des liens que peuvent présenter entre elles les exceptions concevables ne permet pas de fixer *a priori* et dans l'abstrait un ordre de priorité auquel la Cour serait tenue de se conformer. C'est de la confrontation des diverses exceptions soulevées simultanément que se dégage la marche à suivre. La question est affaire d'espèce et de coup d'oeil judiciaire.[98]

There has also been, however, a distinct trend of opinion displaying preference for a discernible and constant order in the examination of objections. Thus, in the *Interhandel* case (1959), Judges Armand-Ugon (Dissenting Opinion)[99] and Sir Percy Spender (Separate Opinion)[100] would have liked to see the questions of jurisdiction dealt with *before* that of the exhaustion of local remedies, and they expressly stated so. Likewise, Judge Klaestad, in his Dissenting Opinion, observed that an adjudication by the Court on the objection of non-exhaustion of local remedies would presuppose that the Court has *first* established its jurisdiction – when that jurisdiction is challenged – to deal with the case.[101] Judge Lauterpacht, too, espoused the view that a decision on the objection of non-exhaustion would imply an assumption of the jurisdiction of the Court over the case.[102]

This view, whereby objections to jurisdiction have priority over objections to the admissibility of applications in the order of examination, has found support in juristic writing.[103] Two major tendencies in the jurisprudence of the International Court on the question of the order of examination of preliminary objections have been suggested: the first, examination of the *exceptions péremptoires* before the *exceptions dilatoires*, in order to dispose first of the more radical grounds of objection,[104] leaving for a subsequent stage the objections which admit the possibility of further examination of the case (admittedly a tendency not without exceptions);[105] the second tendency, not exclusive of the first one, amounts to examination of objections to jurisdiction before objections to admissibility, on the ground that questions of jurisdiction should always come first in an international court whose jurisdiction depends on the consent of the parties, and, moreover, that conditions of admissibility are generally more closely linked to the merits than questions of jurisdiction, and an examination of questions of admissibility implies to some extent an exercise by the Court of its own jurisdiction.[106]

But these two main tendencies of the Court as to the order of consideration of preliminary objections remain only a 'représentation approximative de la jurisprudence',[107] and the Court's treatment of preliminary objections can hardly be made to fit squarely into those categorizations. They appear rather as general trends or guidelines of the practice of the International Court on the matter.[108]

2. In the practice under the European Convention on Human Rights.

When an inter-State application (Article 24 of the European Convention) is brought before the Commission, the president of the Commission, through the Secretary-General of the Council of Europe, notifies the 'respondent' State of the application and invites it to submit to the Commission its written observations on the admissibility of the application.[109] An application submitted by an individual (Article 25 of the Convention) is referred by the president of the Commission to one of its members who, as *rapporteur*, examines the application and reports to the Commission on its admissibility; the *rapporteur* may request information relating to the application from the applicant or the State concerned.[110] The Commission then considers the report of the *rapporteur*, and it may at once declare the application inadmissible, or strike it off its list. Alternatively, it may, through the Secretary-General of the Council of Europe, request further information from the applicant or the State concerned (communicating such information to the other party concerned), including written observations. Before deciding upon the admissibility of the application, the Commission may invite the parties to submit further observations, either in writing or at an oral hearing.[111] Throughout this process of gathering information, time-limits are fixed by the *rapporteur* or the Commission itself.[112]

Proceedings before the Commission are mainly in writing, and it is only when the Commission orders a hearing that the parties concerned are invited to appear before it.[113] In practice, the Commission has apparently never declared an application admissible without inquiring of the parties (particularly of the respondent) whether they wished to make further submissions at a hearing.[114] Thus there appears to be under the European Convention, as in general international law, a certain flexibility in the determination of time-limits for the raising of preliminary objections. In fact, under the Convention, there do not seem to be any *fixed* time-limits or expiry dates with regard to the stage at which the objection of non-exhaustion of local remedies is to be raised in the course of the examination of admissibility.[115] The only broad requirement seems to be that the local remedies rule is to be raised some time during the admissibility stage, in accordance with the general principle in international law that 'all points must be pleaded at the proper time'.[116]

In practice, in the *Retimag S.A.* v. *F.R. Germany* case (1961), for example, the Commission accepted the objection of non-exhaustion of local remedies raised later in the proceedings in the course of the *oral* hearings of 20–1 September 1961.[117] Shortly afterwards, in the *Boeckmans* v. *Belgium* case (1963), the Commission was again faced with a contention of non-exhaustion of local remedies, raised not in the written proceedings, but later, in the *oral* hearing of 28 October 1963;[118] the Commission held that nothing obliged the respondent States under the Convention to present all possible submissions as to the admissibility of the application at the stage of the 'written proceedings', it being possible for the local remedies rule to be raised later, during the oral explanations.[119]

Normally, however, the local remedies rule is raised earlier, during the proceedings in writing. It may also happen that, once raised in the written submissions, it ceases to be pursued in the oral hearing, as in the *57 Inhabitants of Louvain* v. *Belgium* case (1964);[120] it may also be raised both at the written and oral proceedings, as in the *23 Inhabitants of Alsemberg and of Beersel* v. *Belgium* case (1963).[121] The possibility open to the respondent State to raise an objection of non-exhaustion later in the oral proceedings, not having raised it in the preceding written phase, seems to strengthen its position *vis-à-vis* the applicant. The respondent State is seemingly given an 'extended' chance to avail itself of an objection which already exists primarily on its behalf. This is surprising in a system designed for the protection of human rights. Here there seems to be room for tipping the balance in favour of the applicant, without necessarily detracting from general international law.

Besides the objection of non-exhaustion of local remedies, the Convention lists some other grounds of inadmissibility (all applicable to applications from individuals under Article 25): they concern applications that are anonymous, or substantially the same as a previously examined matter, or incompatible with the provisions of the Convention, or manifestly ill-founded, or an abuse of the right of petition (Article 27). If two or more of such objections are raised in the same application, the problem may arise as to which objection should be given priority over the other(s) by the Commission. The Convention and the rules of procedure of the Commission are silent on this particular problem.

A President of the Commission, Mr J.E.S. Fawcett, has made two suggestions for dealing with the problem. First, where the Convention in issue forms part of the domestic law of the respondent State, the complaint may be examined in the order it is made, and compliance with the local remedies rule may be examined before going into the other grounds of inadmissibility under Article 27 of the Convention. However – and secondly – it may by and large be contended that the ground of 'manifestly ill-founded' in particular takes precedence over the local remedies rule in the order of examination, 'for if the application discloses on its facts no appearance of a breach of the Convention, then the rule is irrelevant; for, though for the facts complained of there may be a domestic remedy, that cannot involve the Convention'; furthermore, 'to invite the applicant to exhaust domestic remedies for a complaint which the Commission considers manifestly ill-founded under the Convention is futile'.[122]

IV. The six-month rule in Article 26 of the European Convention on Human Rights

In laying down the rule of exhaustion of local remedies, Article 26 of the European Convention on Human Rights prescribes one time-limit: an application will be declared inadmissible if it is not brought before the Commission within the period of six months from the date on which the final domestic decision was taken. Article 26 of the Convention reads that 'the Commission may only deal with the matter after all domestic remedies have been exhausted, according to the generally recognised rules of international law, and within a period of six months from the date on which the final decision was taken'.[123] The origin of the six-month rule will first be considered; then its development through the jurisprudence of the Commission.

1. Origin

Not all international organs granting direct access to individuals have always known of such time-limits as that in Article 26 of the Convention. The Arbitral Tribunal for Upper Silesia, for example, originally had no such rule, and exercised much tolerance in the matter of time-limits, in view, for example, of the difficulties in collecting documents; it was only towards the end of its scheduled period of activity that, in order to prevent a flood of applications, and having found 'repeated proof of abuse', it established time-limits which 'were applied with lenience'.[124]

During the preparatory work of the European Convention on Human Rights the six-month rule was proposed at the Conference of

Senior Officials, held in Strasbourg between 8 and 17 June 1950. The initiative came from the representative of Italy, Mr Perassi, who, at the meeting of 11 June 1950, suggested the introduction of a delay of six months for the seizure of the Commission after the exhaustion of local remedies.[125] The Italian delegation in fact presented a proposal for the inclusion of the six-month rule in the provision on the local remedies rule.[126] On 19 June 1950, *rapporteur* A. Struycken presented his report of the Conference of Senior Officials, where he stated *inter alia* that the Conference had decided to add the six-month rule to the Article on the local remedies rule because it considered it useful 'to fix a time-limit during which recourse to the Commission should be formulated, in accordance with the provision to this effect in Article 31(2) of the General Act of Geneva' of 1928.[127]

The six-month rule was also included in the corresponding provision – Article 46(1)(b) – of the 1969 American Convention on Human Rights.[128] When in 1950 the six-month rule was first inserted into the draft European Convention on Human Rights, the *ratio legis* of the rule was to avoid much discussion of the past and thus a certain amount of uncertainty; for if such a time-limit did not exist, the Commission could be overwhelmed with a mass of complaints relating to past situations; the six-month period was deemed to constitute a reasonable time for applicants to prepare their applications to the Commission.[129] In laying down the six-month rule, the Convention entrusted the Commission with the administration of the rule. In its practice the Commission has had numerous occasions to apply the rule and to develop a body of jurisprudence on the matter.

2. Development

The first fundamental problem in the application of the six-month rule is the determination of the notion of *final decision*, from which the six-month time-limit will run. A leading case on the matter was that of *De Becker* v. *Belgium*. The Belgian government raised an objection based on the expiry of the period of six months, and argued that as Mr De Becker had not appealed to the Cour de Cassation, the final decision in his case was a judgment rendered by a Military Court in 1947.[130] The applicant objected that for persons in his position 'no internal remedy was available, nor was there any final decision from which a given period could be dated'; furthermore, he submitted, 'any time-limit involved had to be regarded as running from the date of the incorporation of the Convention in Belgian law'.[131]

In its decision of 9 June 1958, the Commission held that the 1947 judgment of the Brussels Military Court did not constitute the 'final decision' for the purpose of Article 26 of the Convention and could not mark the beginning of the six-month period, because it had been given prior to the date when the Convention began having binding effect with regard to Belgium (14 June 1955).[132] In fact, the Commission declared, the six-month rule could apply only to the period subsequent to the entering into force of the Convention in the country concerned *and* the acceptance by the country of the right of individual application to the Commission under Article 25 of the Convention (in the present case, 5 July 1955).[133]

The Commission then stressed the *intimate correlation between the local remedies rule and the six-month rule* in the following terms:

The two rules contained in Article 26 concerning the exhaustion of domestic remedies and concerning the six months' period are closely inter-related, since not only are they combined in the same Article but they are also expressed in a single sentence whose grammatical construction implies such correlation. [...] The term 'final decision', therefore, in Article 26 refers exclusively to the final decision concerned in the exhaustion of all domestic remedies according to the generally recognised rules of international law, so that the six months' period is operative only in this context; [...] furthermore, the preparatory work of the Convention, in particular the report prepared in June 1950 by the Conference of Senior Officials, confirms this interpretation.[134]

This correlation between the two rules was again maintained by the Commission in the *X* v. *F.R. Germany* case (1960), where the Commission further added that the remedies to be taken into account for the application of the local remedies rule are

those which are capable of providing an effective and sufficient means of redressing the wrongs which are the subject of the international claim; [...] it is for the Commission itself to appreciate in the light of the particular facts of each case whether any given remedy at any given date appears to have offered to the applicant the possibility of an effective and sufficient remedy for the wrong of which he complains and, if not, to exclude it from consideration in applying the six-months time-limit in Article 26.[135]

In deciding on another application against Germany (1961), the Commission reiterated that 'il existe une étroite corrélation entre les deux règles de l'article 26, à savoir celle de l'épuisement des voies de recours internes et celle du délai de six mois; [...] par décision interne définitive, l'article 26 désigne exclusivement la décision final qui implique l'épuisement de toutes les voies de recours internes, conformément aux principes de droit international généralement reconnus'.[136]

In the *X* v. *United Kingdom* case (1968), the applicant was serving a prison sentence after conviction and an unsuccessful appeal to the Court of Criminal Appeal. Recalling that the 'final decision' within the meaning of Article 26 (the six-month rule) refers solely to the 'final decision involved in the exhaustion of all domestic remedies according to the generally recognised rules of international law', the Commission decided that in the present case the complainant's application for an order of habeas corpus subsequently to an unsuccessful appeal was *not* to be taken into consideration in determining the 'final decision' for the purpose of applying the six-month rule laid down in Article 26 of the Convention.[137] The final decision was therefore that of the Court of Criminal Appeal, given more than six months before the application to the Commission, which was thereby held to have been lodged out of time.[138] The same conclusion was reached by the Commission in the *X* v. *Austria* case (1971) in regard to a *procédure non-contentieuse* pursued by the applicant after an adverse decision by the Austrian Supreme Court (concerning land expropriation); the application was likewise deemed to have been lodged out of time, and the Commission once again pointed out the inter-relationship between the local remedies rule and the six-month rule and its *jurisprudence constante* to the effect that by 'final decision' Article 26 aims exclusively at the final decision rendered in the *normal* framework or scope of the exhaustion of local remedies according to the generally recognized principles of international law.[139]

With the outlook of the *normal* framework of exhaustion constantly in mind, the Commission has in several cases determined the 'final decision' for the purpose of application of the six-month rule in Article 26 of the Convention. On different occasions the Commission has held the final domestic decision in this context to have been the one rendered by the Belgian *Conseil d'État*,[140] by the German Federal Constitutional Court (at Karlsruhe),[141] by the German Court of Appeal (at Celle),[142] by the German Federal Social Court (Bundessozialgericht),[143] by the German Federal Court (Bundesgerichtshof),[144] by a Regional Court in Germany,[145] by Austrian Courts of Appeal,[146] by the Swedish Labour Court,[147] and by the U.K. Court of Criminal Appeal.[148] In several other cases[149] the Commission held that there had *not* been compliance with the six-month rule in Article 26 of the Convention.

On some of those occasions the Commission specifically stated that one or other local remedy was not to be taken into account for the purposes of application of the six-month rule; the Commission has proceeded in this way particularly when finding that the remedy in question is *not* one that would necessarily have to be resorted to in the *normal* exhaustion of local remedies. Thus, for example, in the *X* v. *Sweden* case (1970) the Commission found that a *recours au procureur parlementaire* 'ne constituait point, en l'espèce, une voie ordinaire de recours interne efficace et suffisant; [...] il s'ensuit que les décisions de cet organe ne peuvent entrer en ligne de compte pour le calcul du délai de six mois'.[150] As a consequence, the application was deemed to have been lodged out of time.[151] But, on the other hand, the Commission has also on some occasions[152] taken the view that the six-month rule had been complied with.

A particular problem the Commission has been faced with is whether a decision on revision or on the re-opening of a case for re-trial constitutes a 'final decision' for the purposes of application of the six-month rule in Article 26 of the Convention. In the *Nielsen* v. *Denmark* case (1959) the respondent government raised an objection based on the expiry of the six-month time-limit, while the applicant submitted that the 'final decision' in the case was that of the Special Court of Revision rather than that taken earlier by the Danish Supreme Court.[153] The Commission found in the case that it was in fact the subsequent decision of the Special Court of Revision, and not that of the Supreme Court, that was to be regarded as the 'final decision', so far as concerned 'all those matters with respect to which the remedy before the Special Court of Revision must be deemed to have offered the applicant the possibility of an effective and sufficient means of redress'.[154] The Commission thus rejected the Danish government's objection of non-compliance with the six-month rule.[155]

On subsequent occasions, however, the Commission took a different stand. Thus, in the year following the decision in the *Nielsen* case, the Commission held in an application against Germany that petitions to the Federal Constitutional Court and to the Federal Court for the re-opening of the case were not effective remedies for the purposes of the application of the local remedies rule, and decisions on them could not be considered the 'final decision' of the case in applying the six-month rule in Article 26 of the Convention.[156] In another application against Germany in 1961 the Commission declared that the applicant's numerous petitions for the re-trial of his case did not constitute effective and sufficient remedies within the meaning of the local remedies rule and therefore decisions rejecting those petitions could not be taken into consideration in determining the 'final decision' for the purpose of applying the six-month rule laid down in Article 26.[157] In yet another case concerning Germany in the same year, the Commission concluded that it was the decision on a constitutional appeal – and not on a *recours en révision* – that counted for the purpose of application of the six-month rule.[158]

Likewise, in the *X* v. *Sweden* case (1964) the Commission held that the 'final decision' in the case was one rendered by the Swedish Supreme Court, because the applicant's petitions under the provisions of Swedish law for a re-opening of his case did not constitute effective remedies under the generally recognised rules of international law.[159] Moreover, the Commission expressly stated that in the case of criminal proceedings, a request for revision, being an extraordinary remedy, could *not* be taken into account for the calculation of the six-month time-limit.[160] Again in the *X* v. *Austria* case (1970) the Commission declared that, as the applicant's petitions for a re-trial of his case were not an effective and sufficient remedy under the generally recognised rules of international law, decisions regarding those petitions could not be taken into consideration in determining the 'final decision' for the purpose of applying the six-month rule laid down in Article 26;[161] the final decision in the case was one rendered by the Austrian Supreme Court in 1967.[162] In yet another case against Austria, also in 1970, the Commission once again held the final decision for the calculation of the six-month period to have been one rendered by the Austrian Supreme Court (Oberster Gerichtshof) in 1967, rather than decisions relating to the applicant's *demande en révision*, which did not in the case constitute an effective and sufficient remedy under the generally recognised rules of international law.[163]

In the *X* v. *Denmark* case (1971), the respondent government objected that the applicant had not complied with the six-month time-limit laid down in Article 26 of the Convention, while the applicant submitted that the decision of the Special Court of Revision should in the case be regarded as the 'final decision' for the purposes of the six-month time-limit, in which case his application had been lodged in time.[164] Recalling its decision in the *Nielsen* case (*supra*), the Commission pointed out that the decision of the Special Court of Revision 'could only be regarded as the "final decision" concerning those matters in respect of which that Court offered the applicant the possibility of an effective and sufficient means of redress'.[165] In the present case, however, unlike in the *Nielsen* case, the Commission, after considering the arguments put forward by the parties, concluded that in so far as the complainant's application to the Special Court of Revision was based upon alleged procedural errors committed during the proceedings before the trial court:

> that application virtually lacked any prospect of success and can therefore not be regarded as an effective and sufficient remedy under the generally recognised rules of international law; [...] therefore, the decision of the Special Court of Revision in respect of these matters cannot be taken into consideration in determining the final decision for the purpose of applying the six-month time-limit.[166]

As a result, that part of the application was held to have been lodged out of time.[167]

Thus, in considering decisions on petitions for the re-opening of cases for re-trial, for the purpose of the application of the six-month rule, the Commission has consistently applied the test of effectiveness of the local remedies at issue. With regard to petitions for re-trial in particular, the tendency of the Commission is *not* to regard them as constituting the 'final decision'. This trend of the Commission's jurisprudence is inspired by the test of effectiveness of remedies together with the notion of the *normal* exhaustion of local remedies. Consequently, the rigours of the six-month rule seemingly cannot be pushed too far: the principle is limited, firstly, as already pointed out, to applications concerning States which have not only ratified the Convention but also recognized the right of individual petition under Article 25 of the Convention (optional ratification); and secondly, it is limited to decisions regarding remedies deemed to be effective and adequate.

In this connection, the Commission carefully acknowledged in the *De Becker* case that 'by specifying that application must be made to the Commission within a certain period, Article 26 introduces an exception to the two preceding Articles, namely 24 and 25, which confer competence; [...] *restrictive provisions of this kind do not lend themselves to a broad interpretation*' (my italics),[168] and this applies with 'special force', in the field covered by the Convention, that of the international protection of human rights.[169] This interpretation of the local remedies rule *stricto sensu* has been clearly and consistently adopted by the Commission with regard to a particular group of cases:

those where the applicant complains not of an isolated act, but of an allegedly permanent state or continuing situation.

In this respect as well, the Commission's decision in the *De Becker* case appears as a leading one. Mr De Becker claimed in the case that 'the inability freely to express himself constituted a permanent state of affairs which could not give rise to any separate internal decision from which a specific period could be regarded as running'.[170] The Belgian government, on the other hand, contended that the obligation to observe the six-month time-limit applied in the present case as it does in all applications under the Convention; final domestic decisions in appeals under municipal law 'should not be allowed to be challenged indefinitely', and the insertion of the six-month rule in Article 26 of the Convention showed that the Convention organs were concerned 'essentially with the future and with the past only in respect of decisions of not more than six months' standing on the date on which the Convention came into force. If this rule were not observed, the Commission would soon be overwhelmed with individual applications, a risk which Article 26 was intended to eliminate or at least minimise.'[171]

In its decision of 9 June 1958, the Commission initially recalled the two main points, namely, that the applicant was complaining not of an isolated act but rather of a legal provision giving rise to a constant state of affairs against which no domestic remedy was available to him; and that the existence of the six-month rule specified in Article 26 of the Convention was 'justified by the wish of the High Contracting Parties to prevent the past judgments being constantly called into question'.[172] But the Commission immediately added that in the present case the state of affairs complained of was 'not a thing of the past, but still continues and, in the present state of the Belgian legislation, will continue in principle' indefinitely, without any domestic remedy being available to the applicant.[173]

With this factor in mind, the Commission added categorically that:

since there is no justification for the application of the rule in the present case, there can be no question of the applicant being debarred by lapse of time; [. . .] when the Commission receives an application concerning a legal provision which involves a permanent state of affairs for which there is no domestic remedy, the problem of the six months' period specified in Article 26 *can arise only after this state of affairs has ceased to exist*; [. . .] in the circumstances, it is exactly as though the alleged violation was being repeated daily, thus preventing the running of the six months' period.[174]

The Commission went even further, by declaring that:

> there is no justification for invoking *ratio legis* [that the six-month rule should prevail] if, as in the present case, the state of affairs complained of is still in existence at the time when the Commission is asked to consider it, since it cannot reasonably be assumed that the Contracting Parties, by including the six months' rule in Article 26, intended to exclude the present or, *a fortiori*, the future.[175]

It followed from the foregoing, the Commission concluded, that 'the six months' period referred to in Article 26 of the Convention is inapplicable to the present case'.[176]

This view was strongly confirmed by the Commission's subsequent jurisprudence. Thus, in its two decisions rendered in 1963, in the *23 Inhabitants of Alsemberg and of Beersel* v. *Belgium* case[177] and in the *Charlent et al.* v. *Belgium* case,[178] the Commission, after finding out that the legislation complained of gave rise to a *continuing situation* leaving the applicants without any domestic remedy to attack it, declared that the six-month rule in Article 26 of the Convention did not apply in cases of this sort.[179] Another case in question was that of *Huber* v. *Austria*: in its partial decision of 19 December 1970 in the case, the Commission found that the applicant's complaints concerning his detention pending trial in Austria and the length of that detention had been lodged out of time, not observing the six-month rule in Article 26 of the Convention;[180] but with regard to further criminal charges in the case, the Commission found in its final decision of 14 July 1971 that as the situation complained of by the applicant was a *continuing* one, the application was *not* inadmissible for non-observance of the six-month time-limit laid down in Article 26 of the Convention.[181]

The problem at issue arose in the inter-State case of *Denmark/ Norway/Sweden/Netherlands* v. *Greece* (1968), where the Commission stated that, as the means of redress indicated by the respondent government could not be considered effective within the meaning of Article 26 of the Convention, it followed that 'the term "final decision" has no relevance' in regard to the allegations raised in the case, 'even to the extent that they concern facts occurring more than six months' before the date of the filing of the joint memorial with the Commission (25 March 1968), that 'cannot be rejected for non-observance of the six-month rule' in Article 26 of the Convention.[182] The Commission added that the local remedies rule did not apply to the applicants' complaints, the object of which was to determine the campatibility with the Convention of legislative measures of the respondent government. And as the local remedies rule did not apply, the Commission went on, the term 'final decision' in Article 26 could itself 'have no application in connection with the present legislative measures; [. . .] further, the provisions of Constitutional Act"G" gave rise to a permanent state of affairs which is still continuing and *the question of the six months' rule could only arise after this state of affairs has ceased to exist*' (my italics).[183] It followed, the Commission concluded, that the applicant governments' allegations concerning Constitutional Act 'G' in Greece could *not* be rejected under Articles 26 and 27(3) of the Convention as having been lodged out of time.[184]

More recently, in the *X* v. *Belgium* case (1973), the Commission again asserted:

Compte tenu du lien étroit entre les deux règles qu'énonce l'article 26, on peut dire que par décision interne définitive, l'article 26 désigne exclusivement la décision définitive rendue dans le cadre normal de l'épuisement des voies de recours internes tel qu'il est entendu selon les principes de droit international généralement reconnus de sorte que le délai de six mois ne peut fonctionner que dans ce cadre. Le requérant ne se plaint pas d'un acte instantané, mais s'en prend à une situation qui dure depuis dix ans. Or, le problème du délai de six mois de l'article 26 ne pourrait surgir que quand cette situation aura pris fin.[185]

In the *X* v. *F.R. Germany* case (1974) the problem of the application of the six-month rule was discussed in relation to a *continuing situation*. The respondent government, even though conceding that the applicant had exhausted local remedies, argued – with regard to a *recours constitutionnel* – that the applicant had not complied with the six-month time-limit laid down in Article 26 of the Convention.[186] The applicant, in his turn, invoked a *continuing* violation of Article 3 of the Convention, consisting of the 'persistent refusal of the authorities to suspend the execution of the sentence' (for health reasons); this situation, he argued, rendered inapplicable in the present case the six-month rule enshrined in Article 26 of the Convention.[187]

In its decision of 5 October 1974 the Commission noted that during his dentention the applicant had seemingly exhausted available local remedies under German law: thus, he had introduced the *recours hiérarchique (Dienstaufsichtsbeschwerde)* against the prison authorities, he had several times used the *recours* provided in Articles 23 *et seq* of the Law of Introduction to the Law on Judicial Organization (*Antrag auf gerichtliche Entscheidung*), he had twice introduced a constitutional appeal against judicial decisions rejecting his demands for interruption of the sentence, and he had finally introduced a constitutional appeal against the decision of the Court of Appeal of Frankfurt refusing to grant him suspension of the execution of the sentence.[188] As a consequence, the Commission rejected the objection to the admissibility of that part of the application, raised by the respondent government on the basis of Article 26 of the Convention.[189]

Thus, there appears to be in the Commission's jurisprudence a marked tendency to consider cases involving a *continuing situation* as falling outside the scope of application of the six-month rule in Article 26 of the Convention. In this latter case (*X* v. *F.R. Germany*, 1974), apart from the fact that the complaint was directed against a continuing situation, the applicant had sufficiently established his exhaustion of local remedies. The Commission, therefore, did not have much difficulty in promptly rejecting the respondent government's objection of non-exhaustion.

But that such rejection does not automatically follow was shown by the decision of the Commission on the *X* v. *Austria* case (10 July 1975). The applicant tried to excuse his delay on the ground of his bad state of health and morale in the period at issue; the Commission, finding that his excuse was not supported by any substantial evidence (such as, for example, medical reports), did not accept the excuse as a valid ground that would justify the interruption or suspension of the six-month period laid down in Article 26 of the Convention.[190] Furthermore, the applicant was deemed not to have effectively introduced his complaint, as he had failed to provide the information requested by the Commission's Secretary after a first letter of a general character.[191] In the circumstances it came as little or no surprise that the Commission held the application to have been introduced out of time and thus rejected it as inadmissible under Article 27(3) of the Convention.[192]

In a series of subsequent decisions, the Commission has dwelt upon the running of the six-month period prescribed in the rule. The Commission has held that the six-month rule starts running from: the date of dismissal of a claim for compensation (if the latter would lead to redress of the alleged violation);[193] the date of the decision on the last appeal against conviction (where the complaints relate to criminal proceedings), and not from a subsequent decision in civil proceedings for damages instituted against the State;[194] the date of the decision complained against, when there is no remedy; and the date of delivery of judgment (in open court in the presence of the applicant's lawyer) if the applicant would understand from the spoken judgment that he was not in receipt of a remedy for his grievance.[195]

In its decision of 10 December 1976 in the *X* v. *United Kingdom* case, the Commission explained that in the absence of any remedy against a decision or an act of a public authority, the six-month period runs from the moment the decision or the act takes effect; the Commission further clarified that the act which deprives someone of his property does not give rise to a continuing situation (of lack of property), which would prevent the running of the six-month period.[196]

The remaining problem to be examined pertains to the time factor in the application of the six-month rule itself. Rule 48(2) of the Commission's rules of procedure states that 'for the purpose of determining any time-limits, the date of the filing of the pleading with the Secretariat General of the Council of Europe shall alone be taken into consideration'.[197] This rule was expressly recalled and applied by the Commission with regard to the six-month time-limit laid down in Article 26 in the *X* v. *Norway* case (1963).[198] In the *Engel/Dona/Schul* v. *Netherlands* case (1973), the Commission found that the complaints were *not* out of time, and that the complete facts had been submitted within the prescribed time-limit, even though the provisions of the Convention which the applicants deemed to have been violated were only later specified.[199] On that occasion the Commission declared that:

Article 29 of the Convention confers upon it the power to examine at any stage of the proceedings on the merits, *ex officio* and irrespective of any plea by the parties, the question whether or not one of the grounds provided for in Article 27 had been established. This competence of the Commission is complementary to the Commission's established competence *ex officio* to examine the facts of a given case with a view to determining its admissibility under the Convention irrespective of any specific provisions of the Convention invoked by the applicant. Its object is to enable the Commission to halt, in the circumstances set out above and on condition that the Commission is unanimous, the procedural machinery contemplated by the Convention in the event of the Commission accepting a petition referred to it.[200]

It may at this stage be asked whether the running of the six-month period may be interrupted or suspended. The Commission has proceeded on the basis that it may. In cases where the Commission found that the six-month rule had not been complied with, for example, it normally examined whether there were any circumstances that would have justified or called for an interruption or suspension of the period.[201] In one particular instance, in the *X* v. *Austria* case

(1970), it was the applicant himself, rather than the Commission acting *ex officio*, who raised the issue, with his allegations giving rise to the question whether in the special circumstances of his case the running of the six-month period should be regarded as having been interrupted or suspended.[202] In this case, however, the Commission found it unnecessary to rule on the question, as its examination of the case did not disclose any appearance of a violation of the Convention and especially of the Articles invoked by the applicant.[203]

A further consideration remains to be made on the application of the six-month rule in Article 26 of the Convention to cases under Article 5(3) of the Convention. This last provision stipulates that persons lawfully arrested or detained shall be brought promptly before a competent judge or other officer authorized by law to exercise judicial power and shall be entitled to trial *within a reasonable time* or to release pending trial.[204] In such cases, it has been suggested, a strict application of the six-month rule in Article 26 would be illogical, for an applicant complaining of a prolonged and unreasonably excessive delay in the period of his detention (a substantiated complaint) cannot be reproached for not trying to obtain a 'final' domestic decision before applying to the Commission; it is only after he is sure to have been the victim of a violation of a right enshrined in the Convention that he can be reasonably expected to pursue his case up to a final decision before taking his case to the Commission within the period of six months.[205]

Finally, one could not complete this section without pointing out that there remain some problems pertaining to the six-month rule which have not been solved by the Commission. Thus, in its decision of 11 July 1977 in the *X* v. *Switzerland* case, the Commission did not provide an answer to the question whether a remedy of doubtful effectiveness could be considered as the starting-point for calculating the six-month time-limit.[206] Earlier, in its decision of 2 October 1975 in the *X* v. *Austria* case, the Commission, likewise, did not solve the problem whether the six-month period should start running from the date when the applicant himself was informed of the final domestic decision, pronounced in his absence, notwithstanding its previous communication to the counsel appointed *ex officio* for his defence.[207] And in the *H. Huber* v. *Austria* case (decision of 5 July 1976), the Commission did not solve the problem whether it could, without infringing the six-month rule, examine an application concerning the compatibility of a detention with Article 5(1)(4) of the Convention, when the only final domestic decision of less than six months was a decision rejecting a plea for damages for an allegedly illegal detention.[208]

V. Conclusions

The old rule of general international law, whereby local remedies should be exhausted before a State's international responsibility can be called into question at international level, has undergone significant developments under the European experiment on human rights protection in so far as its application *ratione temporis* is concerned. To start with, in the *Ringeisen* case in 1971, the European Court of Human Rights inaugurated a new trend in the application of the local remedies rule under the Convention by ruling that the European Commission might accept the fact that the last stage of the exhaustion of local remedies may be accomplished shortly after the lodging of the application but anyway before the Commission's decision on admissibility. In this way the Court secured a remarkable flexibility and relaxation in the application of the local remedies rule, thus tipping the balance in favour of the individual and reducing to some extent the factual inequality between applicant and respondent.

In the so-called 'detention cases' (*Stögmüller*, *Matznetter* and *Neumeister* cases, 1968–9), the European Court was faced with complaints relating not to an isolated act, but rather to a 'continuing situation' throughout the period of detention on remand. The Court ruled that in cases of detention exceeding a reasonable time the question of exhaustion of local remedies in the period of detention subsequent to the lodging of the application did *not* arise. Otherwise, if the Court was to require the applicant to file a new application with the Commission (after each final decision rejecting a request for release), such a formalistic attitude could only lead to a pointless multiplication of proceedings tending to paralyse the working of the Convention organs.

In general international law (in cases before the International Court of Justice) it has been normally accepted that a preliminary objection of non-exhaustion of local remedies is to be filed by the party concerned at the latest before the expiry of the time-limit fixed for the delivery of its first pleading. As to the order of examination of objections (the relationship in time between the objection of non-exhaustion and other preliminary objections), it is generally accepted that in principle the International Court has freedom of appreciation when a certain order is not imposed by any logical necessity (Morelli, Ch. de Visscher). Yet trends in the Court's jurisprudence are discernible, to the effect of examining objections to jurisdiction, before an objection to admissibility on the ground of non-exhaustion of local remedies.

Under the European Convention on Human Rights, an objection of non-exhaustion may be raised at some point at the admissibility stage, usually in the proceedings in writing, though in practice it has also been raised at the subsequent stage of oral hearings. Such an objection may be examined before objections on other grounds of admissibility (listed in Article 27 of the Convention), especially if the Convention forms part of the domestic law of the member State, even though there is a case for examining the ground of 'manifestly ill-founded' prior to the local remedies rule.

The six-month time-limit in the application of the rule under the Convention avoids not only uncertainty as to past events but also an otherwise possible overwhelming of the Commission with a mass of complaints relating to past situations. The Commission itself has repeatedly acknowledged the intimate correlation between the six-month requisite and the local remedies rule proper. Of fundamental importance then becomes the notion of *final* (domestic) decision, from which the six-month time-limit will run. As this question is appreciated in the *normal* framework of exhaustion, a final domestic decision may be the one rendered by distinct organs in different cases at issue; it has even occurred that certain local remedies were not taken into account for the purposes of application of the six-month rule. Thus, in considering decisions on petitions for the re-opening of cases for re-trial, the Commission has consistently applied the test of effectiveness of the local remedies at issue.

Where complaints pertain not to an isolated act, but to an allegedly permanent state or continuing situation, the Commission has repeatedly and sensibly stated that the question of the six-month rule can only arise after such a state of affairs has ceased to exist. The marked tendency of the Commission's jurisprudence is, not surprisingly, to leave cases involving a *continuing situation* outside the scope of application of the six-month rule (in Article 26 of the Convention).[209]

The Commission is competent *ex officio* to determine the admissibility of applications under the Convention, and it has proceeded on the basis that the running of the six-month period may be interrupted or suspended. Finally, in detention cases under Article 5(3) of the Convention, it has been argued that a strict application of the six-month rule would be illogical. Admittedly, an applicant complaining of an unduly prolonged and excessive detention could hardly be expected to try to obtain a 'final' domestic decision before applying to the Commission while that situation still persists. The solutions found so far by the European Convention organs to such problems in the application *ratione temporis* of the local remedies rule disclose not only the relevance of the time factor in the incidence of the rule within the context of human rights protection, but also some of the developments of the subject-matter under this latter context when compared with general international law.

6

FURTHER PROBLEMS IN THE APPLICATION OF THE LOCAL REMEDIES RULE

I. Exhaustion of local remedies as related to the internal structure of the international jurisdictional body

As was indicated in the preceding chapter, as compared with the vast case-law of the European Commission of Human Rights on the issue of exhaustion of local remedies, the European Court has so far had but few occasions to pronounce on the matter. This is not surprising, as the Commission is the organ properly entrusted with the task of pronouncing on the admissibility of applications under the Convention. This probably also accounts for the large body of expert comment on the Commission's practice on the subject, in contrast with the comparatively less attention given to the Court's corresponding practice. Yet, on those occasions where the Court has dealt with the matter, it has made a valuable contribution towards clarification of some of the problems surrounding the application of the rule of exhaustion of local remedies under the Convention. One particular problem which has been widely discussed by the Court is that of the application of the rule as related to the internal structure of the international jurisdictional body. This has a direct bearing upon the question of the relationship between the Commission and the Court regarding the admissibility of applications. It thus touches the very foundations of the structural system set up by the Convention, and becomes quite relevant for a proper understanding of the distribution of competences between the organs of the Convention.

A study of the nature of those organs and their functions would go far beyond the present purposes, and the problem has anyway been the object of much attention and writing in past years; suffice it here to indicate the distinct functions of the Commission throughout proceedings under the Convention (admissibility, Article 26 and 27, and friendly settlement, Articles 28 and 30), and to recall the originality of the system established by the Convention in relation to previous experiments of the kind in international law. The 'co-existence' or relationship between the Commission and the Court, for example, promptly raises the important problem of the competence for the determination of the admissibility of applications.

The problem may be stated in the following terms: the Commission, acting under Article 26 and 27 of the Convention, is competent to declare an application inadmissible if it does not comply with the conditions of admissibility contained in those provisions. In accomplishing this task, the Commission performs a *judicial function*.[1] And, as the Court itself has acknowledged or recognized in express terms, whenever the Commission, in accomplishment of that task of sifting applications assigned to it by those provisions of the Convention, decides to reject applications which it considers inadmissible, its decisions are final and 'without appeal'.[2] That is, they cannot be reviewed by the Court, being final. Hence the general agreement to qualify this function of the Commission as *jurisdictional*. But would the same apply in cases where the Commission declares applications admissible? In other words, would a decision of admissibility of the Commission be binding upon the Court, or could the Court again take the issues of admissibility previously examined by the Commission and 'review' them, and possibly reach a conclusion different from that of the Commission?

As the text of the Convention does not seem to provide an answer to this problem, one may well assume that the matter was left for the Convention organs to examine in the course of their subsequent practice, and in the evolution of their jurisprudence in relation to the particular circumstances and issues of the cases brought before them.[3] In fact, in the '*Vagrancy*' cases (judgment of 18 June 1971), the problem was raised before the Court whether it had jurisdiction to examine the objections of delay and non-exhaustion of local remedies made by the Belgian government against the applications which had already been accepted by the Commission. The Court had thus to determine whether it had jurisdiction *ratione materiae* to deal with a preliminary ground of inadmissibility of applications.

The problem, as already mentioned, pertains to the very foundations of the whole mechanism of the Convention and the distribution of competence between the two organs.[4] The question at issue was much debated in the public hearings before the Court on 16–18 November 1970.[5] In its decision of 18 June 1971, the majority of the Court (twelve judges) recalled that Article 45 of the Convention, which determines the Court's jurisdiction *ratione materiae*, specifies that 'the jurisdiction of the Court shall extend to all cases ("toutes les affaires") concerning the interpretation and application of the Convention which the High Contracting Parties and the Commission shall refer to it in accordance with Article 48'.[6] Thus, although one would first have to observe the conditions laid down in Articles 47 and 48 regarding cases which had been duly brought before the Court,[7] the phrase 'cases concerning the interpretation and application of the Convention' contained in Article 45 was, stated the Court's majority, 'remarkable for its width'.[8] And that was confirmed by the English text of Article 46(1), 'drafted in even wider terms ("all matters") than Article 45 ("all cases")'.[9]

Accordingly, it was relatively easy for the Court's majority to reach the conclusion that once a case is duly referred to it, 'the Court is endowed with full jurisdiction and may thus take cognisance of all questions of fact and of law which may arise in the course of the consideration of the case'.[10] Therefore, it went on, it was 'impossible to see how questions concerning the interpretation and application of Article 26 raised before the Court during the hearing of a case should fall outside its jurisdiction'.[11]

The majority of the Court finally observed that the Commission's decision to accept an application had the effect of leading the Commission to perform its functions (laid down in Articles 28 to 31 of the Convention) and of 'opening up the possibility that the case may be brought before the Court';[12] but, it added significantly, 'it is not binding on the Court any more than the Court is bound by the opinion expressed by the Commission in its final report "as to whether the facts found disclose a breach by the State concerned of its obligations under the Convention" (Article 31)'.[13] For those reasons, the Court concluded that it had jurisdiction to examine the questions of delay and of non-exhaustion of local remedies raised in the '*Vagrancy*' cases.[14]

Four judges dissented from this view and upheld the opposite thesis, namely that the Court had no jurisdiction regarding the admissibility problem of non-exhaustion of local remedies. All four judges (Ross, Sigurjónsson, Bilge and Wold) delivered an interpretation of Article 45 different from that of the Court's majority. According to this latter, that provision endowed the Court with ample jurisdiction to ensure that all parts of the Convention were duly observed, whether they were substantive or procedural (see *supra*). The minority judges started from a different standpoint. To

Judges Ross and Sigurjónsson, the word 'cases' (in Article 45) meant 'whether the facts found by the Commission [in its report] disclose a violation of the Convention'.[15] In the same sense, Judge Wold maintained that the 'case' 'is the "report on the facts" and the Commission's opinion "whether the *facts found* disclose a breach by the State concerned of its obligations under the Convention" (Article 31). It is in respect of this report that the Court has jurisdiction to interpret and apply the Convention. In other words it is the merits which the Court shall try.'[16] Likewise, to Judge Bilge, 'according to Articles 31 and 32 what is referred as an "affaire" ("case") by the Commission to the Committee of Ministers or to the Court is the question whether there has or has not been a violation of the Convention. [...] This meaning of the word "affaire" is also confirmed by the general plan of the Convention.'[17]

As to the Court's majority view that the Commission's decision to accept a case 'is not binding on the Court any more than the Court is bound by the opinion expressed by the Commission', Judge Bilge replied that 'the decision of admissibility taken by the Commission and the opinion expressed by it on the merits are of a different nature. An opinion, by its very nature, does not bind anyone. There is no need to cite it alongside the decision of admissibility for the purpose of making an argument against the latter.'[18]

Perhaps the central point in Judge Bilge's reasoning was his view that the Commission and the Court, the two organs set up by the Convention (Article 19) to ensure the observance of human rights, had 'defined powers' to accomplish that aim: 'Competence to accept an application and to check its admissibility belongs to the Commission. Jurisdiction to decide whether there has been a violation of the Convention belongs to the Court. It is within this field that the Court enjoys full jurisdiction.'[19] Judge Bilge pondered that 'it is not reasonable to declare that the decision of refusal binds the Court while that of admissibility does not, for the two aspects of the same jurisdiction cannot be separated'.[20] To him, 'the rule of exhaustion of domestic remedies is not concerned with the internal organisation of a given international jurisdictional body. As stated above, the Convention set up two organs to ensure the observance of human rights. The aim of the rule in question is achieved if the rule is observed by one of these organs and, above all, by the organ entrusted with the task of checking the observance of the conditions of admissibility.'[21] For those reasons, Judge Bilge deemed that the Court had 'no jurisdiction to entertain submissions of non-exhaustion of domestic remedies'.[22] Similarly, to Judges Ross and Sigurjónsson 'the admissibility or inadmissibility of the petition is a *preliminary* (procedural) question which is left to the "powers" of the Commission (Article 25(4))'.[23]

In his Separate Opinion, Judge Wold added significantly:

> The individual has to abide by a decision of non-admissibility. [...] If the Court nevertheless exercises its own jurisdiction in regard to admissibility and decides against the Commission's decision, the inequality between the applicant and the State in proceedings before the Court will be more aggravated, which can only harm the cause of human rights.[24]

He recalled that the Court was not conceived as a court of appeal in relation to the Commission, the whole task (under Article 19) being *divided* between those two organs.[25] To him, the Court's jurisdiction was 'limited to *cases* referred to it by the Commission or a State'; as the question of exhaustion of local remedies was not part of the case (since it was finally decided by the Commission 'exercising a judicial function against which no appeal lies'), it followed that the interpretation and application of Article 26 did 'not therefore fall within the jurisdiction of the Court. The Court has competence to decide its own jurisdiction, but it is not competent to make decisions regarding the jurisdiction of the Commission.'[26] Even with regard to the rationale behind the local remedies rule, since the State had every opportunity to remedy a decision while the application was under examination by the Commission, it seemed 'unreasonable' that, under such circumstances, a State should have the right to pursue this issue of local remedies further and take it up before the Court; after all, the State had every opportunity to look after its interest concerning the exhaustion of local remedies *before the Commission*, its interests also being duly protected.[27]

On the basis of the review of this particular problem, it is difficult to avoid the impression that the four minority Judges did in fact deal with it more thoroughly – or at least more extensively – than the twelve majority judges. It seems likewise that the arguments put forward in support of the dissenting view (*supra*, pp. 252–4) present more logical cogency than the somewhat summary or not fully explored view espoused by the majority judges on the problem at issue. The sparse literature that has so far appeared on the problem (as discussed in the '*Vagrancy*' cases) has tended in the same sense, apparently favouring the views advanced by Judges Ross and

Sigurjónsson,[28] or by Judge Wold,[29] or by the four minority judges in general.[30]

It is pertinent to recall that, over a decade earlier, in the *Lawless* case, the Court itself had acknowledged that 'the Commission's chief function is to carry out an *independent*[31] inquiry, to seek a friendly settlement and, if need be, to bring the case before the Court'.[32] (After all, one of the main concerns throughout the *travaux préparatoires* of Articles 26 and 27(3) of the Convention was to assign to the Commission the task of sifting petitions.) But the *Lawless* judgment went further on the point at issue: once that task had been accomplished, the Court stated, the Commission's main function would be 'to assist the Court', and it was associated with the proceedings.[33] The Court added that even at that stage, however, its action was determined 'not by a decision of the Court, but directly by the terms of the Convention'.[34] Thus, referring to Article 45, the Court itself very significantly asserted that 'the exact meaning of this clause is defined in other Articles of the Convention', such as, for example, 'Article 47, according to which "the Court may only deal with a case after the Commission has acknowledged the failure of efforts for a friendly settlement and within the period of three months provided for in Article 32"'.[35]

In the same sense, it is recalled that in the *De Becker* case the Court simply acknowledged that the Commission had recognized that all domestic remedies in the case had been exhausted.[36] And subsequently, in the *Stögmüller* case, the Court stated that 'as to the admissibility of the application, it was accepted by the Commission in its decision of 1 October 1964; the Court notes that the correctness of that decision has not been contested'.[37]

Thus the earlier practice of the Court itself seems not to provide support for the position it took on the problem at issue in the '*Vagrancy*' cases. The doctrine according to which the Court would be entitled to re-examine or review a Commission's decision on admissibility on the ground that local remedies have been exhausted seems unsatisfactory and inconsistent, if not contradictory.[38] The Court's judgment in the '*Vagrancy*' cases on this particular point appears to be a reflection of that state of confusion, for while on the one hand it holds that the Commission's 'decisions to reject applications which it considers to be inadmissible are without appeal as are, moreover, also those by which applications are accepted',[39] on the other hand, it states that a Commission's decision on admissibility 'is not binding on the Court',[40] even though the jurisdiction exercised by the Commission is the same.

It seems to be in accordance with general international law that an objection of non-exhaustion of local remedies is to be raised *in limine litis*.[41] It is clear that the local remedies rule is *not* concerned with the internal structure of an international jurisdictional body (cf. Judge Bilge, *supra*, p. 253). The purpose it serves is of a different nature. As a preliminary objection, it is meant to afford the respondent State an opportunity to remedy the alleged wrong before the complaint can be dealt with in its merits by the international organ.

In this connection, it may be submitted that the view supported by the minority Judges on the problem at issue in the '*Vagrancy*' cases seems to satisfy the requirements of pure logic, the general plan of the Convention, and common sense: pure logic, because of the unity and indivisibility of jurisdiction (Judges Ross and Sigurjónsson, *supra*, pp. 253–4); the general plan of the Convention, because it is one of the originalities of the system it inaugurated that a case cannot be directly referred to the Court (unlike other international tribunals) without first being examined by the Commission, and, moreover, the *travaux préparatoires* indicate that the Commission was endowed with the task of sifting cases so that the Court would not be 'flooded' by them; common sense because it balances (or at least it attempts to diminish) the existing factual inequality of status between the individual applicant and the State in the proceedings before the Court (Judge Wold, *supra*, p. 254)[42] and, in so doing, pursuant to a well-recognized principle of treaty interpretation, it accords with the object and purpose of the Convention,[43] which could be summarized as providing for a system of effective protection of human rights.[44]

In the cases brought before it so far, the Court has dealt with yet another problem relating to exhaustion of local remedies which has a direct bearing upon the internal structure of the international jurisdictional body. In the *Stögmüller* case (1969) the Austrian government maintained that the local remedies rule (Article 26) not only applied to the admissibility of applications (Article 27) before the Commission, but also prevented both the Commission and the Court (organs mentioned in Article 19) from 'taking account of complaints concerning subsequent facts in respect of which the exhaustion of domestic remedies has not been verified'.[45] As has been seen *supra*, pp. 222–5, the question is of great relevance to cases of detention while on remand (of which the *Stögmüller* case itself was an example). At the present stage, suffice it to notice here that, in reply to the Austrian government's contention, the Court denied the 'inflexible character'[46] which the government seemed to attribute to the local remedies rule as a rule of (general) international law (Article 26). The Court further stated that the problem in question should be examined 'in the light of the circumstances' of each case,[47] and that, in the present case, it had found that there was 'no need for the Court to examine separately the applicant's complaints concerning the period of detention which followed the lodging of the application'.[48]

Similarly, in the *Matznetter* case, to the Austrian government's arguments grounded on Article 26 of the Convention, the Court replied:

While acknowledging the interest of these arguments, the Court notes that they were not submitted to the Commission: quite on the contrary, the government did not cease to participate in the examination, before the Commission, of the period of Matznetter's detention right up to his release [...]. The Court has not felt justified, however, in refusing to examine the new submissions which the government has made on the basis of Article 26 but it can only accept them to the extent indicated in its judgment given this day in the *Stögmüller* case [see *supra*, pp. 222–5].[49]

The Court was very cautious in its decision, even though expressly rejecting an inflexible application of the local remedies rule (see *supra*) in relation to the problem at issue. Yet it seems that the whole question was approached with more logical consistency and precision by Judges Verdross and Bilge in their Separate Joint Concurring Opinion in the *Stögmüller* and *Matznetter* cases (the Opinion having the same text in both cases). For them, the Court simply should not examine the arguments advanced by the Austrian government on the exhaustion of local remedies. They recalled that Articles 45 (on the Court's jurisdiction) and 48 should not be interpreted in isolation, for the Court's jurisdiction was also defined by other provisions, such as that of Article 47, according to which 'the Court may only deal with a matter after the Commission has acknowledged the failure of efforts for a friendly settlement and within the period of three months provided for in Article 32' (see also Article 28). Thus, for Judges Verdross and Bilge, 'a High Contracting Party may not submit to the Court any question it pleases without observing the conditions laid down by the relevant Article of the Convention'.[50]

The local remedies rule, they stressed, 'is a preliminary question relating principally to the admissibility of the application (Article 27(3)). It is for the Commission to decide whether this condition has been fulfilled.'[51]

According to the text of Article 26 of the Convention, they proceeded, 'the question of exhaustion of domestic remedies must be previously raised before the Commission. In the present case that has not been done. Consequently, the Commission has not had an opportunity to take a decision on the point. This conclusion can also find confirmation in the general plan of the Convention and the special features of our jurisdiction.'[52] Judges Verdross and Bilge remarked that to accomplish their aim of ensuring the observance of human rights (Article 19), 'the Commission and the Court have defined powers. Competence to accept an application and to check its admissibility belongs to the Commission. Furthermore, the institution of the Commission and its functions constitute special features of our jurisdiction. One may not therefore interpret Article 45 without taking account of this general plan of the Convention and of the special features we have just mentioned.'[53] Accordingly, the two Judges concluded that 'the Court may not entertain a question of exhaustion of domestic remedies which has not been previously submitted to the Commission. In the present case, the Court should find it sufficient to point out to the Austrian government that the Court is unable to examine the question at this stage.'[54]

II. Exhaustion of local remedies in relation to claims for compensation (under Article 50 of the European Convention on Human Rights)

In the '*Vagrancy*' cases in 1971–2, the European Court of Human Rights was first confronted with the question whether an applicant who lodged with the European Commission a claim for compensation under Article 50 of the Convention was bound to exhaust local remedies as a prior condition for the admissibility of his application. While the Belgian government insisted on the requisite of exhaustion,[55] the Commission's delegates (headed by Mr Max Sørensen) objected to the application of the local remedies rule in the case.[56]

In its decision of 10 March 1972 on the problem, the Court began by noting that Article 26 'relates to the institution of the proceedings which fall within section III of the Convention', while 'the present cases no longer relate to such proceedings but to the final phase of proceedings brought before the Court in accordance with section IV'.[57] The Court made it clear that 'the claims made by the three applicants for compensation are not new petitions; they relate to the reparation to be decided by the Court in respect of a violation adjudged by the Court and they have nothing to do with the introduction of proceedings before the Commission under Articles 25, 26 and 27 of the Convention'.[58] Accordingly, sharing the Commission's view, the Court was thus of the opinion that Article 26 was not applicable in the present matter.[59]

But the Court did not stop there. To the Belgian government's plea of inadmissibility on the ground of non-exhaustion of domestic remedies the Court further replied:

If the draftsmen of the Convention had meant to make the admissibility of claims for 'just satisfaction' subordinate to the prior exercise of domestic remedies they would have taken care to specify this in Article 50 as they did in Article 26, combined with Article 27(3), in respect of petitions addressed to the Commission. In the absence of such an explicit indication of their intention, the Court cannot take the view that Article 50 enunciates in substance the same rule as Article 26.[60]

Moreover, the Court stated, Article 50 had its origin 'in certain clauses which appear in treaties of a classical type[61] [...] and have no connection with the rule of exhaustion of domestic remedies'.[62] In its clarifying judgment the Court added sensibly that 'if the victim, after exhausting in vain the domestic remedies before complaining at Strasbourg of a violation of his rights, were obliged to do so a second time before being able to obtain from the Court just satisfaction, the total length of the procedure instituted by the Convention would scarcely be in keeping with the idea of the effective protection of human rights. Such a requirement would lead to a situation incompatible with the aim and object of the Convention.[63]

Seeing no reason[64] to reject the claims in question as inadmissible, the Court proceeded to examine their merits. The Court's decision to declare the applicants' claims for damages admissible was unanimously adopted.[65]

The Court's second ruling on the problem was delivered in the *Ringeisen* case, on 22 June 1972. The Austrian government maintained that 'even if Ringeisen was entitled to claim other reparation for damage caused by his excessive detention on remand, Austrian law provided him with various means of obtaining it but he confined himself to writing to the Minister of Justice who had no competence to deal with the claim'.[66]

In its reply, the Court referred to its reasoning on the problem in its decision of the same year on the '*Vagrancy*' cases (*supra*, pp. 258–9) to the effect that prior exhaustion of local remedies was not a condition for application of Article 50. 'It is true', the Court added, 'that the government has declared that it is not seeking to rely on Article 26 nor insisting on the exhaustion of domestic remedies prior to any consideration by the Court of a request for just satisfaction. Partial exercise of domestic remedies would, however, serve no purpose and would lead to the same result of preventing the Court from speedily affording reparation for the damage caused by the violation it found.'[67]

Then, embarking on a line of thought somewhat different from that in the '*Vagrancy*' cases, the Court went on to state that 'there can be no doubt that for the Court to be able to give application to Article 50, there should be a need to do so (French: "il y ait lieu"; or, in the English text, "if necessary"); but this necessity exists once a respondent government refuses the applicant reparation to which he considers he is entitled. This is what happened in the present case.'[68] The Court finally added that 'the reason why the applicant wrote to the Minister of Justice rather than to any other authority is apparently because section 4 of the [Austrian] Act of 18 August 1918 on compensation for detention on remand indicated this course for claims based upon that Act'.[69]

The third ruling of the Court (*Neumeister* case, judgment of 7 May 1974) on application of Article 50 of the Convention had apparently no direct bearing on the question of exhaustion of local remedies.[70] It should not pass unnoticed, however, that, in its 1974 *Neumeister* decision, the Court observed that 'the "normative" provisions of section 1 of the Convention' laid down a 'rule of substance', guaranteeing to an individual a right, 'the observance of which is obligatory in the first instance for the authorities of the Contracting States'.[71] For its part, Article 50 'lays down a rule of competence: placed in section IV of the Convention, it authorizes the Court expressly to afford, subject of certain conditions, just satisfaction to the "injured party". One of these conditions is the existence of a national decision or measure "in conflict with the obligations arising from the...Convention" [...]'.[72]

Finally, in a series of decisions rendered in 1975 and 1976, the

Court, having established no failure to comply with the requirements of the Convention, ruled that the question of applicability of Article 50 did not arise;[73] the issue of exhaustion of local remedies in regard to claims for compensation or just satisfaction (not necessarily synonymous) was not discussed in the Court's decisions in these cases.[74]

III. Exhaustion of local remedies in cases of declaratory judgments (requests for interpretation)

In international adjudication the local remedies rule is invoked as a preliminary objection to the admissibility of a claim. The claim usually refers to injuries inflicted upon the alleged victim and contains a demand for reparation. By the operation of the local remedies rule the respondent State is given an opportunity to remedy the wrong within the framework of its domestic legal system, and to the applicant this becomes a condition prior to the institution of international proceedings. It may happen, however, that an applicant lodges with an international organ a request for a declaratory judgment. In that case, no demand for reparation is involved. All the applicant is asking is for a declaration from the court on a given situation, without being concerned with the question of damages. To make such a request, must the applicant first exhaust local remedies (as in the case of a claim for reparation), and, conversely, may the respondent State then raise the objection of non-exhaustion?

There can hardly be any doubt that a request for a declaratory judgment – even though the matter at issue may give rise to distinct and concomitant claims for reparation[75] – is quite different from a request for a judgment aiming at the reparation itself for the injuries suffered by the party concerned. But this does not amount to saying that a demand for a declaratory judgment[76] must necessarily deal with an abstract question. Abstract questions should preferrably be avoided, as was once asserted by the Permanent Court of International Justice itself.[77]

In the *Interhandel* case (1959), Switzerland's position was that the United States third preliminary objection of non-exhaustion of local remedies by *Interhandel* should be rejected on the grounds that the local remedies rule did not apply where only a declaratory judgment was requested, and that one or more of the Swiss alternative submissions constituted such a request for a declaratory judgment.[78] This argument was challenged by the United States on the ground that the local remedies rule should apply to the present case as Switzerland was seeking 'full relief' (not only 'declaratory').[79] In its judgment of 21 March 1959 on the case, the Court, without deciding on the (modified) Swiss request for a declaratory judgment (in its view 'involving the merits of the dispute'), upheld the U.S. third preliminary objection of non-exhaustion of local remedies by nine votes to six, maintaining that the application of the Swiss government was inadmissible.[80]

In the *Ambatielos* case (1953) the International Court characterized its task as one of interpretation of a declaration and deemed that the (British) argument of non-exhaustion was 'entirely outside the terms' of the declaration at issue; consequently, the Court expressed no view on the local remedies rule, and by ten votes to four found that the United Kingdom was under an obligation to submit the matter (i.e., the difference as to the validity of the Ambatielos claim) to arbitration.[81]

In the *Switzerland* v. *F.R. Germany* case (1958) under the Arbitral Tribunal for the Agreement on German External Debts (case n. 1), a similar decision on the matter was reached. The Tribunal, after stating that the general rule of exhaustion of local remedies was applicable (even) in the absence of an express provision, concluded that, as Switzerland was not making a claim for damages against West Germany but rather only requesting a decision by the Tribunal on the interpretation and application of the Debt Agreement (Annex VII), it followed that the local remedies rule did not apply to the present case, and it was therefore unnecessary to examine what domestic remedies – if any – were available to the creditor.[82]

In the *Donnelly and Others* v. *United Kingdom* case (1973), involving complaints of ill-treatment, the applicants requested the European Commission of Human Rights, *inter alia*, for a 'declaratory relief'. In its decision of 5 April 1973, the Commission pointed out that it had at that stage of the proceedings no competence to grant any 'declaratory relief' of the kind requested by the applicants, when its only task was to decide on the question of the admissibility of the applications.[83] But the applicants insisted that their request for a declaratory relief, in the form of a declaration that they had been victims of an illicit administrative practice, in breach of Article 3 of the Convention, was properly before the Commission even if compensation by the respondent government was considered an effective remedy; however, in its subsequent decision of 15 December 1975, the Commission held that 'an applicant under Article 25 of the Convention may not ask that the Commission express any opinion on the merits of his application, other than for the purpose of determining whether it is manifestly ill-founded or not, unless he has complied with the rule as to exhaustion of remedies and failed to obtain adequate remedy'.[84]

Subsequently to the debates of the 1956 Granada session of the *Institut de Droit International* on the question of the exhaustion of local remedies in cases of request for a declaratory judgment,[85] expert writers have been profoundly divided on the matter: while one school of thought opposes the application of the local remedies rule in cases of a declaratory judgment by contrasting such cases with those involving a claim for reparation, where the rule properly applies,[86] another holds that the local remedies rule applies in cases of a declaratory judgment as well, since this latter eventually involves reparation or recovery.[87] In this respect the effects of a declaratory judgment and a *jugement de prestation* do not differ – according to this view – for both affect eventual reparation for injuries suffered by the individuals concerned. Consequently, the non-application of the objection of non-exhaustion in cases of requests for a declaratory judgment would simply be a way of circumventing the local remedies rule.[88]

The grounds for the position just described do not seem, however, very solid. It is at best a position of expediency. The local remedies rule evolved historically within the context of the responsibility of the State for injuries to aliens. Where it applied, one of the ingredients of the dispute was inevitably that of reparation. This element has been maintained in the new and gradually evolving scope of application of the rule, that of human rights protection (cf., for example, applications for 'just satisfaction' or compensation under Article 50 of the European Convention on Human Rights). It is not for an international organ, it may be submitted, to concern itself – in the process of the application of the law – with the intentions of a contending party. A request for a declaratory judgment may be indirectly related to the question of reparation, but if it is really so, the request for a declaration can be accompanied by a claim for reparation. Sometimes the two issues may be brought before the Court in alternative submissions in the same case (as in, for example, the *Interhandel* case). And there is nothing to prevent the Court from pronouncing on the alternative submissions distinctly, even at the admissibility stage. That the situation presents difficulties can be seen by the seeming reluctance of two distinct international organs to dwell upon the question in the cases of *Interhandel* and *Donnelly and Others*. The fact however remains that the rationale behind the local remedies rule pertains to the opportunity accorded to a State to redress the wrong done to an individual, within the framework of its municipal legal system, before international proceedings are instituted. It can hardly be said that the local redress principle should be applied in a distinct situation, not concerned with redressing a wrong,[89] where a request for a declaration is intended only to ensure recognition of a given situation at law.

IV. Other procedural issues

1. Joinder of preliminary objection of non-exhaustion to the merits

In excipiendo reus fit actor: in preliminary objection proceedings the objecting State acts as applicant. The termination of those proceedings can occur not only by judgment of the International Court, but also by the withdrawal of the preliminary objections by the objecting party, the withdrawal of the case itself by both contending parties, the discontinuance of the case by the applicant, or else the joinder of the preliminary objections to the merits of the case by the Court. These cases have all occurred in practice.[90] The reasons for the International Court's joinder have varied from case to case, usually referring to one of the following: to have one and the same judgment on the objection and the merits by agreement of the parties; or because issues (of fact and of law) raised in the objection are too intimately linked to those raised in the merits to allow adjudication on the one without prejudging the latter; or because the Court needs more evidence and a fuller knowledge of the facts to adjudicate on the preliminary objection phase; or because the Court cannot yet determine in that preliminary phase whether the plea was strictly a preliminary objection or a defence to the merits; or because the applicant has submitted a plea for joinder as an alternative submission; or else because in the circumstances of the case it is felt that the joinder is in the interests of the good administration of justice.[91] Under the present heading we shall examine the particular question of the joinder of preliminary objections *to the admissibility* – based specifically on the rule of exhaustion of local remedies – to the merits, in general international law as well as in the practice under the European Convention on Human Rights.

In the *Panevezys – Saldutiskis Railway* (Preliminary Objections) case (1938–9), the Permanent Court of International Justice, after asserting its competence to order the joinder of preliminary objections to the merits in the interests of the good administration of justice, decided that the two Lithuanian objections (one of them on the ground of non-exhaustion of local remedies) should be joined to the merits.[92] Likewise, in the *Losinger* (Preliminary Objection) case (1936), the Court stated that the objection to the admissibility of the application must be joined to the merits, in order that it might adjudicate in one and the same judgment upon the objection and, if need be, upon the merits.[93] More recently, the problem of the joinder of a preliminary objection of non-exhaustion of local remedies was before the ICJ in the *Barcelona Traction* (Preliminary Objections) case (1964),[94] where it became the object of much discussion.[95] In its judgment of 24 July 1964 on the case, the ICJ stated *inter alia* that:

> this is not a case where the allegation of failure to exhaust local remedies stands out as a clear-cut issue of a preliminary character that can be determined on its own. It is inextricably interwoven with the issues of denial of justice which constitute the major part of the merits. The objection of the respondent that local remedies were not exhausted is met all along the line by the applicant's contention that it was, *inter alia*, precisely in the attempt to exhaust local remedies that the alleged denials of justice were suffered. This is so obvious on the fact of the pleadings, both written and oral, that the Court does not think it necessary to justify it further at this stage, by any statement or consideration of the events in question, which can be left until the merits are heard.[96]

Accordingly, by ten votes to six, the Court decided to join the fourth preliminary objection to the merits.[97]

In the *Norwegian Loans* case (Order of 28 September 1956), the ICJ decided to join the Norwegian preliminary objections (the fourth one on the ground of non-exhaustion of local remedies) to the merits, but this time it did so with the *agreement* of the contending parties, France and Norway.[98] In the *Aerial Incident* case (1959), even though the joinder to the merits of a preliminary objection of non-exhaustion of local remedies was discussed in the oral arguments (of counsel for Israel, Mr Rosenne, and counsel for Bulgaria, Professor Cot),[99] the ICJ this time did not touch upon the question, as it found that the Bulgarian acceptance of the Court's jurisdiction did not cover the dispute before it and it was therefore without jurisdiction to adjudicate upon the case.[100]

In case-law as well as juristic writing, the joinder of preliminary objections (of non-exhaustion) to the merits has been the subject of attempts at explanation;[101] and it has not passed without criticism.[102] To sum up, it has been seen that, for a number of reasons, the International Court (PCIJ and ICJ) has deemed it necessary or convenient to join a preliminary objection (to the admissibility, and others) to the merits. In a unique situation, it did so in the *Norwegian Loans* case with the agreement of the parties. And in the *Interhandel* (Preliminary Objections) case (1959), while the Court's majority (nine votes to six) upheld the third preliminary objection of the United States on the ground of non-exhaustion of local remedies and held that the Swiss application was thereby inadmissible,[103] the dissenting Judges Klaestad, Winiarski, Armand-Ugon and Spiropoulos[104] pronounced in favour of joining the third U.S. preliminary objection of non-exhaustion to the merits. Likewise, the co-agent for the Swiss government, Professor Guggenheim, in the public hearing of 11 November 1958, maintained that the examination of that objection touched on the merits of the case, and requested the ICJ (at least) to join it to the merits.[105]

This question of joinder to the merits of the preliminary objection of non-exhaustion of local remedies has also been raised under the system of the European Convention on Human Rights. At the outset, it is pertinent to point out that both the European Commission and the Court have expressed the view that the treatment of international law questions should not be carried out with the same strictness as in municipal law.[106]

In its decision of 30 August 1958 in the *Lawless* v. *Ireland* case, the Commission, having rejected the respondent government's contention of non-exhaustion of local remedies (under Article 26 of the Convention), joined two other questions to the merits and declared the application admissible.[107] In an inter-State case, that of *Greece* v. *United Kingdom* in respect of *Cyprus*, the Commission stated *inter alia* that:

in considering the admissibility of an application lodged pursuant to Article 24 of the Convention it is not the Commission's task to ascertain whether the applicant Contracting Party establishes '*prime facie* proof' of its allegations, since enquiry into such aspects relates to the merits of the case and cannot therefore be undertaken at the present stage of the proceedings.[108]

(The discussions concerned the exhaustion of local remedies in the case under Article 26 of the Convention.)

A different situation arose in the case of the *57 Inhabitants of Louvain and Environs* v. *Belgium*. There the Commission, deeming that the Contracting States were best qualified to judge the expediency of availing themselves of the opportunity accorded to them by the local remedies rule in Article 26, invited the respondent State to express its opinion on the admissibility of the application. As that State declined to avail itself of the opportunity, the Commission found itself dispensed from pronouncing on the exhaustion of local remedies.[109] In the *Greek* case, the applicant governments (Denmark, Norway and Sweden), in submissions to the Commission subsequent to their original application, alleged that for various reasons the condition of exhaustion of local remedies laid down in Article 26 did not apply to their present allegations.[110] In its partial decision of 26 May 1970, the Commission stated that as the respondent government (Greece) had not yet had an occasion to reply to those new submissions of the applicant governments, the Commission considered that before it examined the issue the respondent government should be invited to submit its observations in reply.[111] Accordingly, the Commission decided to invite the Greek government to submit its observations on the question of the exhaustion of local remedies, within a time-limit of four weeks.[112] It also decided, meanwhile, to adjourn its further examination of the application.[113] These examples show that the Commission has resorted to different measures to overcome some of the difficulties presented in some preliminary objections of non-exhaustion of local remedies, other than joining them to the merits.

The joinder of one such objection was carried out by the Commission in the *Alam and Khan* v. *United Kingdom* case (1967). The applicant, a Pakistani citizen, complained *inter alia* of an alleged violation of Article 8 of the Convention, providing for the principle of respect for family life, in connection with refusal of entry of his sons into the country by immigration officials at London airport.[114] The respondent State raised an objection of non-exhaustion of local remedies.[115] In its decision of 15 July 1967, the Commission declared that it had carried out a preliminary examination of the submissions by the parties in regard to the complaint that the refusal by the immigration officer to allow Mohamed Khan to enter the United Kingdom to join his father constituted a violation of the applicant's right to respect for family life as guaranteed by Article 8 of the Convention.[116] The Commission found that this complaint raised issues of law and fact 'whose determination should depend upon an examination of the merits of the case'.[117] The complaint under Article

8 was related to the question whether the applicants had exhausted all domestic remedies available to them as required under Article 26 of the Convention.[118] The Commission went on to state that:

the question whether there was in English law an effective remedy against the refusal of the immigration authorities to allow the entry of Mohamed Alam into the United Kingdom is in the circumstances of the present case closely linked with the question arising under Article 6(1) whether or not the applicants had access to an independent and impartial tribunal for the determination of their right to respect for family life; [...] in these circumstances the Commission finds that the issue under Article 26 cannot be decided without an examination of questions which concern the merits of the applicants' complaint.[119]

Accordingly, the Commission found it 'appropriate to join to the merits the issue under Article 26 of the Convention'.[120] Later the case resulted in a friendly settlement.[121]

The issue of the joinder of local remedies submissions to the merits arose again in the *Donnelly and Others* v. *United Kingdom* case (1973). The individual applicants complained of alleged torture and ill-treatment while in custody contrary to Article 3 of the Convention at the hands of security forces (army and police) in Northern Ireland responsible to the respondent government in April and May 1972.[122] The seven individual applicants jointly submitted that they had been subjected to 'practices and procedures [...] in flagrant breach' of Article 3 of the Convention, which constituted 'a systematic administrative pattern' which permitted and encouraged violence and was incompatible with the Convention.[123] The applicants also brought extensive arguments to show that the applications 'should not be rejected for failure to satisfy the rule of exhaustion of domestic remedies in Article 26 of the Convention'.[124] They requested the Commission *inter alia* to investigate the situation for the purpose of determining whether or not such acts and administrative practices were incompatible with the Convention.[125]

In their written observations and oral submissions on admissibility, the respondent government denied that there had been in Northern Ireland such administrative practice of ill-treatment contravening Article 3 of the Convention, or any official tolerance of such conduct, and further denied that the applicants had been treated in any way amounting to a violation of Article 3.[126] The respondent government submitted that there were adequate and sufficient local remedies in respect of the treatment of which the applicants complained, that those remedies were freely available to each applicant, and that the application was inadmissible because each of the applicants had failed to exhaust the remedies available to him under domestic law.[127] Moreover, such remedies had been and were being pursued against the authorities in Northern Ireland.[128] The government also denied that there was any evidence of an administrative practice in Northern Ireland 'which would prevent the effective pursuit of domestic remedies'.[129]

In reply to the applicants' suggestions that the Commission should, if necessary, join the question of exhaustion of domestic remedies to the merits of the application, the respondent government submitted that 'the situation in the present case was unlike the situation in previous cases' where the joinder was carried out. In previous cases 'the issue under Article 26 had been practically identical with one of the substantive issues raised by the applicants', while in the present case 'there was no such connection', and, 'if the case were to proceed to an examination of the merits, there would no longer be any issue of an administrative practice'.[130] The government, bearing in mind the circumstances of the case, therefore asked the Commission 'to hesitate before taking a course which might involve the parties in an investigation of the merits which in the ultimate issue would prove to be unwarranted'.[131]

In their written observations, the applicants denied that their application was inadmissible on the ground of non-exhaustion of domestic remedies,[132] and further submitted that 'no adequate or effective domestic relief existed'.[133] At the hearing, the applicants' representatives pointed out that the present situation, where an administrative pattern was complained of, was different from a situation where, in normal circumstances, an isolated incident could be brought before the Commission only where local remedies had been exhausted.[134]

In its decision of 5 April 1973 in the *Donnelly and Others* v. *United Kingdom* case, the Commission stated:

In the present case, the question of the effectiveness of the remedies available to the applicants is, for the reasons set out above, closely linked with the alleged existence of an administrative practice in breach of Article 3. In these circumstances, the Commission finds that the issue under Article 26 cannot be examined without an examination of questions which concern the merits of the applicants' complaint concerning the alleged administrative practice. The Commission has already found that the determination of the part of the application relating to such administrative practice should depend upon an examination of the merits. Accordingly, the Commission finds it appropriate to join to the merits the issue under Article 26 of the Convention relating to the applicants' allegations that each of them was a victim of specific acts in breach of Article 3.[135]

Thus the Commission declared admissible and retained – without prejudging the merits of the case – the issue raised by the applicants that they were victims of an administrative practice in violation of Article 3 of the Convention, and joined to the merits 'any question relating to the remedies to be exhausted by each applicant as the alleged victim of specific acts, as distinct from an administrative practice, in violation of Article 3'.[136]

In the *Ireland* v. *United Kingdom* case (the *Ireland* inter-State case), the applicant government argued that the question whether an inter-State application under Article 24 of the Convention was well founded or not was 'solely a question relating to the merits', and that the issues arising from the application could not therefore be considered by the Commission at the stage of admissibility.[137] In its decision of 1 October 1972, the Commission stated that a thorough examination of certain questions regarding the extent of the administrative practice complained of and its consistency with the provisions of the Convention related to the merits and could not be considered by the Commission at the stage of admissibility.[138] The Commission therefore retained for an examination of the merits the applicant government's allegations that the treatment of persons in custody (particularly the methods of interrogation of such persons) constituted an administrative practice in breach of Article 3 of the Convention.[139] Likewise, the Commission reserved for an examination of the merits the question whether the measures concerned (internment without trial and detention under special legislation) were or were not justified under Article 15 of the Convention (right of derogation in time of public emergencies) – a question which could not be considered at the stage of admissibility.[140] Some other arguments submitted by the parties (in conjunction with the question of the exhaustion of local remedies) were also retained, and reserved to an examination of the merits.[141]

In another inter-State case, that of *Austria* v. *Italy*, the Commission, asserting its power to join a preliminary objection to the merits, decided to join to the merits one point of the application concerning its admissibility for exhaustion of domestic remedies. The decision was rendered on 24–5 August 1962.[142] Earlier, in the *Lawless* v. *Ireland* case (1958), the Commission rejected the respondent's objection of non-exhaustion of local remedies and joined other submissions to the merits.[143]

In a case concerning a Swedish trade union, the *Svenska Lotsförbundet* v. *Sweden* case, the Swedish Pilots' Association lodged an application in February 1970 which was declared admissible on 24 May 1971, after written observations had been obtained from the parties. In deciding on its admissibility, the Commission found that the application raised an issue of such complexity that its determination should 'depend upon an examination of the merits of the case'.[144] Furthermore, the Commission also found that the question whether the applicant had complied with the six-month rule laid down in Article 26 of the Convention[145] was likewise closely linked with the substance of the case; the Commission therefore decided to join the question to the merits, and declared the application admissible.[146]

The Commission then obtained from the parties written submissions on the merits of the *Svenska Lotsförbundet* case, and held a hearing in July 1972. In its second decision on the case, rendered on 13 July 1972, the Commission reached the conclusion that the condition of the six-month rule laid down in Article 26 of the Convention had not been fulfilled and, accordingly, the Commission rejected the application as inadmissible under Article 27(3) of the Convention.[147]

It may at first sight seem surprising that the merits of a case can be examined before it is clearly known whether the formal preliminary requisites have been duly complied with. Yet the Commission has on a few occasions found the joinder a useful device to deal with certain cases raising complex problems. On such occasions the Commission has preferred to adjourn its decision on the question of the exhaustion of local remedies, so that it may consider that question in the light of its report on the case covering also the merits of the case. In fact, the joinder, as has been seen above, is not an innovation of the Commission, and has at times been applied by other international tribunals.

Nor is the joinder the only device under the Convention whereby preliminary questions are intermingled with the substance of cases. The joinder to the merits of a preliminary objection of non-exhaustion of local remedies, in particular, has been here considered. But, still at the admissibility stage, a different ground of inadmissibility of applications under the Convention, that of 'manifestly ill-founded' applications as laid down in Article 27(2) of the Convention, may also entail examination of questions touching the merits of the case. It may be slightly surprising to find this requirement listed among the conditions of *admissibility* of complaints. Perhaps to an even greater extent than the local remedies rule, the often utilized objection of 'manifestly ill-founded' involves an examination at the preliminary stage of problems touching on the merits of the case, in this way interweaving preliminary issues to the merits. Conceived, like the local remedies rule, as a device to screen petitions, the ground of 'manifestly ill-founded' has in practice served to reject applications whose allegations do not necessarily constitute a violation of the Convention – i.e., which on the facts (in the light of Convention provisions) do not disclose an appearance of violation of the Convention – or which are not substantiated by any or sufficient evidence. That its application at the admissibility stage involves an examination of the merits of the case is beyond reasonable doubt, and it possibly constitutes a particularity of the Convention.[148]

2. Exhaustion of local remedies in cases of declaration of withdrawal of applications

The issue of exhaustion of local remedies has at times been discussed in conjunction with the withdrawal of the application by the applicant.[149] The jurisprudence of the European Commission of Human Rights on this particular problem seems to emphasize the general observance of the Convention as a whole rather than the individual interests of the applicant concerned. Thus, in a case concerning Germany decided in 1964, the Commission, considering a declaration of withdrawal of the application, declared that 'cette déclaration ne reflète pas la libre volonté de son auteur', but nevertheless found that no reasons of a general character affecting the observance of the Convention necessitated a further examination of the complaint.[150] Three years later, in a case against Austria, as the applicant had declared that he wished to withdraw his application because of a settlement of the case reached with the Austrian government, the Commission struck the application off its list after considering that there appeared to be no reasons of a general character affecting the observance of the Convention which would necessitate a further examination of the application.[151]

However, in the *Heinz Kornmann* v. *F.R. Germany* case (1966), for example, not only did the Commission question the soundness of the applicant's declaration of withdrawal of the application (as on many occasions he had made it clear that he wished to pursue the proceedings before the Commission), but it also found that the application raised problems under the Convention which might extend 'beyond the interests of the particular applicant'.[152] The Commission considered that there were 'sufficient reasons to examine the admissibility of the application irrespective of the possible existence of a declaration of withdrawal on the part of the applicant'.[153] The Commission then embarked on a close examination of the require- ment of exhaustion of local remedies, deciding finally to declare the application inadmissible for non-compliance with the requirement.[154] The Commission's ruling that 'an application cannot be withdrawn without its agreement' was relied upon by the agent for the Austrian government (Mr E. Nettel), in the public hearings of March 1971 (touching on the local remedies rule) before the European Court in the *Ringeisen* v. *Austria* case.[155]

A further decision of the Commission to the same effect was rendered in the case of *Helga and Wilhelm Gericke* v. *F.R. Germany* (1965). The Commission ruled that as the application raised problems extending beyond the interests of the particular applicants, the withdrawal of the application (requested by one of the applicants on behalf of both) and the respondent government's agreement thereto could not deprive the Commission of the competence to pursue its examination of the case.[156] The Commission thus did not accept the withdrawal of the application and adjourned *sine die* its examination of the complaint at issue.[157]

Shortly afterwards, in the *Heinz Kornmann* v. *F.R. Germany* case (1966), the Commission again found that the application raised problems under the Convention extending beyond the interests of the applicant, and that, consequently, there were sufficient reasons to examine the admissibility of the application 'irrespective of the possible existence of a valid declaration of withdrawal on the part of the applicant'.[158] In that case the applicant complained of ill-treatment by prison officers allegedly constituting criminal offences under German law, while the respondent government, on the basis of Article 26 of the Convention, submitted that the principal domestic remedy available to the applicant was the remedy by means of lodging a criminal charge (*Strafanzeige*) with the competent Public Prosecutor, and that, in case of refusal by the Public Prosecutor to institute criminal proceedings, the applicant was obliged to use all remedies available under German law against such decision by the Public Prosecutor (in order to comply with Article 26 of the Convention.)[159]

In the present case the applicant had in fact lodged a criminal charge which, however, he subsequently withdrew. In view of this withdrawal the Public Prosecutor first decided to discontinue the proceedings, but subsequently re-opened the investigation *ex officio*; however, for the second time the Public Prosecutor decided to discontinue the proceedings (15 April 1966). The applicant appealed from this decision, but his appeal was rejected by the Senior Public Prosecutor (18 July 1966). The applicant also lodged an application with the *Kammergericht* (under the German Code of Criminal Procedure, Article 172), but this application was also rejected (29 August 1966).[160]

The Commission therefore found that the applicant had exhausted those particular remedies as required by Article 26 of the Convention. As to the question whether the applicant was obliged to exhaust any further remedies in order to comply with Article 26, the Commission observed that the case concerned 'primarily a question of evidence and the reason why the applicant was unsuccessful in lodging a criminal charge was that the authorities did not find that there was sufficient evidence to support his allegations'.[161] Use of further remedies[162] would thus have been faced with the same problem of proving that he had in fact been ill-treated, the presumption being therefore that they would have had no chance of giving the applicant satisfaction. Consequently, those further remedies could 'not be considered as sufficient or effective in the circumstances of the present case and the applicant was not obliged to exhaust them in order to comply with Article 26 of the Convention'.[163] The Commission therefore concluded that the conditions laid down in Article 26 had been satisfied, thus accepting the application and declaring it admissible.[164]

In conclusion, the Commission's jurisprudence on withdrawal of applications – as related to examination of the local remedies rule – is guided by the general philosophy inspiring the Convention as a whole. Where the Commission has found that there were no reasons of a general character affecting the observance of the Convention, it has acquiesced with the declarations of withdrawal and struck the cases off its list; but where it has found that there were fundamental issues extending beyond the interests of the individual applicants, it has proceeded with an examination of the admissibility of the applications irrespective of the declarations of withdrawal.

Thus a request for withdrawal of a case raising general problems under the Convention is *not* likely to deter the Commission from examining the conditions of application of the rule of exhaustion of local remedies in the case. The *Gericke* and *Kornmann* cases are striking illustrations in this respect. In the *Gericke* case the Commission rejected a declaration of withdrawal to which the respondent government itself had agreed (*supra*, p. 273); the Commission proceeded with its examination of the issues raised in the case *irrespective* of the alleged wishes of *both* the applicants *and* the respondent. In the *Kornmann* case it did not accept the applicant's declaration of withdrawal, and examined his exhaustion of local remedies, deciding in his favour and declaring his application admissible (*supra*, pp. 272–4).

The Commission itself summed up in unequivocal terms, in the *Gericke* case, the basis of its approach to the problem at issue: member Parties to the Convention agreed to establish 'standards forming part of the public law of Europe', and under Article 19 of the Convention both the Commission and the Court are set up to ensure the observance of the engagements undertaken by them in the Convention. Consequently, the applicant's withdrawal of an application, even with the respondent's agreement thereto, cannot deprive the Commission of the competence to pursue its examination of the case, always bearing in mind that 'the interests served by the protection of the human rights and fundamental freedoms guaranteed by the Convention extend beyond the individual interests of the persons concerned'.[165]

3. Exhaustion of local remedies and cases restored to the Commission's list

In the *X* v. *F.R. Germany* case (1969) the Commission first considered whether or not the applicant was entitled to a re-opening of his case and an examination by the Commission of the admissibility of his application; it ruled that 'an applicant may have his application restored to the Commission's list of cases where the circumstances of the case as a whole so justify such restoration'.[166] But having restored the application to its list, it found that the applicant had not on a number of points exhausted the remedies available to him under German law, and it accordingly declared the application inadmissible.[167]

The restoration of a case to the list, on account of proceedings pending before a domestic court, was considered by the Commission in the *X* v. *United Kingdom* case (1972). The Commission held that a request for the application for leave to appeal (to the English Court of Appeal) to be restored to the list was an effective remedy which required to be exhausted; as the applicant failed to show that he had taken any step to bring his complaint before the appropriate domestic authorities, his application was accordingly rejected under Article 27(3) of the Convention.[168]

In another case concerning the United Kingdom, the Commission re-stated that an applicant might have his application restored to its list of cases where the circumstances of the case as a whole justified such restoration. Since in the case the delay in transmitting certain documents in support of the application was attributable not to the applicant himself but to a person acting on his behalf, the Commission found that there was a justification for restoring the application to its list.[169] But upon closer examination the Commission found that the applicant had not complied with the six-month time-limit laid down in Article 26 of the Convention, and his complaints were thus declared inadmissible.[170]

In the *X* v. *F.R. Germany* case (1970) the Commission confirmed its position that 'where an application has been struck off its list of cases on the ground that the applicant appeared to have lost interest in its maintenance, it will restore that application to its list where the circumstances as a whole so justify'.[171] The Commission found that the circumstances of the case justified restoration; the application was accordingly restored to its list and joined with another complaint by the applicant.[172] This case, and other cases listed herein which were restored to the Commission's list, do not disclose a direct correlation between the restoration and the requirement of exhaustion. Usually the latter is examined by the Commission after the former has been accomplished. This is as far as the Commission's practice has gone on this particular point to date.

More recently, after the completion of the present study, the issue of exhaustion of local remedies has been raised in some cases before the Commission.[1] It is pertinent to observe that, just as governments have relied on Article 26 of the Convention to raise an objection of non-exhaustion, there have been recent cases in which the applicants have invoked Article 13 of the Convention to argue that the respondent governments failed to provide an effective local remedy before a national authority (in breach of that provision).[2]

Not only the Commission, but also the Court, had occasion to pronounce on the issue of the exhaustion of local remedies in recent cases under the Convention. That issue was crucial in the Court's judgment of 6 November 1980 in the *Van Oosterwijck* v. *Belgium* case. Even though the Court rejected the application for non-exhaustion of local remedies (application for authorization to change forenames, and appeal to the Court of Cassation and reliance on the Convention),[3] being unable to take cognisance of the merits of the case, it nevertheless clarified two interesting points. First, it pondered that 'the only remedies which Article 26 of the Convention requires to be exercised are those that relate to the breaches alleged and at the same time are available and sufficient [. . .]. In order to determine whether a remedy satisfies these various conditions and is on that account to be regarded as likely to provide redress for the complaints of the person concerned, the Court does not have to assess whether those complaints are well-founded: it must assume this to be so, but on a strictly provisional basis and purely as a working hypothesis.'[4]

Secondly, the Court, finding that the applicant 'did not plead the Convention at first instance or on appeal, neither did he appeal further to the Court of Cassation', added significantly: 'the Convention forms an integral part of the Belgian legal system in which it has primacy over domestic legislation, whether earlier or subsequent. [. . .] Furthermore, Article 8 of the Convention is directly applicable, as has been held by this Court [. . .] and by courts both in Belgium [. . .] and in other States [the Netherlands, Luxembourg]. The applicant could thus have relied on Article 8 in his own country and argued that it had been violated in his respect.'[5] The Court, thus, made it clear that, where the Convention has been incorporated into domestic law, the applicant has to invoke it before domestic courts in the process of utilizing local remedies (as a pre-requisite of admissibility of his application).

Further indications were provided by the Court in its decision of 6 September 1978 in the *Klass and Others* v. *Federal Republic of Germany* case, where, even though it found that there had been no breach of Articles 13 or 6(1) of the Convention, it clarified that Article 13 of the Convention 'must be interpreted as guaranteeing an "effective remedy before a national authority" to everyone who *claims* that his rights and freedoms under the Convention have been violated'; thus, the Court endorsed the Commission's view that it could not be a pre-condition for the application of Article 13 that the Convention had in fact been violated.[6] The Court, furthermore, stated that Article 25 (on the right of individual petition) 'does not institute for individuals a kind of *actio popularis* for the interpretation of the Convention; it does not permit individuals to complain against a law *in abstracto* [...]; it is necessary that the law should have been applied to his detriment'.[7]

In a significant passage of its judgment (of 6 November 1980) in the *Guzzardi* v. *Italy* case, the Court declared in unequivocal terms: 'Admittedly, it is for each Contracting State to establish appropriate courts and tribunals, to set the limits on their jurisdiction and to lay down the conditions for bringing cases before them. However, Article 26, which refers to "the generally recognised rules of international law", should be applied with a certain degree of flexibility and without excessive regard for matters of form.'[8] The Court, after consideration of the matter, rejected the Italian government's objection of non-exhaustion of local remedies.[9]

Likewise, in the *Airey* v. *Ireland* case (judgment of 9 October 1979), the Court rejected the Irish government's objection of non-exhaustion of local remedies.[10] Earlier, before the Commission, the applicant had alleged that she had been deprived of an effective local remedy,[11] and the Commission had found that the failure of the State to ensure her effective access to a court to enable her to obtain a judicial separation (case of dissolution of marriage) amounted to a breach of Article 6(1) of the Convention, and it was thus unnecessary to pursue an examination of the issue under Article 13.[12] This view was endorsed by the Court.[13]

CONCLUSIONS: PERSPECTIVES OF THE LOCAL REMEDIES RULE

At this final stage, it remains to consider the rule of exhaustion of local remedies in international law in relation to the role of national courts. This touches on the interaction between international law and municipal law with regard to the application of the rule.[1] A useful approach to the matter is possible if attention is directed to, for example, the domestic status of international provisions, the interpretation of domestic provisions by international organs, the relevance of municipal law in international legal procedure, or the implementation of international judicial decisions by domestic courts. The local remedies rule is primarily a prerogative (right of priority) of municipal law (local redress), applied by an international organ; the application of the rule in international law implies the existence of remedies under municipal law. In this example, afforded by the application of the rule, of interaction between international law and municipal law, the complementary nature of rights and duties can be clearly identified.

International organs pay regard to decisions of domestic courts to verify the conformity of a State's internal acts with its conventional international obligations; this has a bearing on the application of the rule, by, for example, placing in the right perspective the State's international duty to provide effective local remedies. Difficulties surrounding this duty and the role of domestic courts can be reduced (when compared with general international law) when conditions for the application of the local remedies rule are set forth in a duly ratified treaty. In fulfilling the State's international duty it is important, for the effectiveness of local remedies, that domestic judicial organs be independent from executive influence. In a system of collective guarantee (for example, inter-State complaints under the European Convention on Human Rights), the international organ may be called upon by one member State to verify whether another member State's internal normative, administrative or judicial acts are in conformity with the international provisions of the Convention.

279

The general impact of a system such as that of the Convention on the domestic law of member States is thus important for its effect in entailing internal legislative changes to bring domestic laws of member States into harmony with the Convention system; conversely, municipal law may for its part influence the system of the Convention. The organs of this system are not courts of appeal or cassation from national courts, or substitutes for national courts, even though they control the compatibility of the application of domestic law with the Convention, and establish the factual elements to be evaluated in the application of a Convention provision; conversely, national-court decisions as implementations or reviews of decisions of international organs are made even more important in an 'integrated' system, in which respect for the obligations ensuing from the Convention is made a *common concern* of member States.[2]

Whatever the formal domestic status of the Convention, the local remedies requirement shows that it is primarily before domestic courts that respect must be sought for the guaranteed rights. Thus, in this 'positive' outlook, the local remedies requirement appears as an instance of the application of domestic law or remedies in the international legal procedure. The international organ will certainly refrain from deciding questions of municipal law, but will nevertheless proceed, on the basis of the evidence available, to a factual determination as to whether the local remedies rule (as enshrined in the Convention) has been complied with.[3]

The possibility of the Commission investigating compliance with the rule *ex officio* shows the mandatory character of the rule under the Convention. The test of effectiveness of local remedies plays an important role, as in, for example, the numerous cases concerning arrest or detention and the right to liberty and security of person (Article 5) and the right to a fair hearing before an independent and impartial tribunal (Article 6). But real difficulties are more likely to arise in complaints relating to less justiciable matters, where it is not so certain that local remedies do exist capable of redressing the situations complained of (for example, regarding the right to proper education, freedom of information, certain instances of ill-treatment, and so forth).

The European Court itself has been careful enough to acknowledge expressly the subsidiary nature of the Convention's international enforcement machinery, a notion which has been generally invoked – in connection with the local remedies rule – since the early thirties.

The rationale of this subsidiary nature[4] has found support in State practice, case-law, treaties and doctrine, but it does not follow therefrom that the scope of the local remedies rule is unlimited. A misunderstanding of the rationale of the subsidiary role may unduly stress the formal requirement of exhaustion of local remedies. It may be submitted that the subsidiary character of international proceedings, while offering an explanation for the *existence* of the local remedies rule, cannot properly be invoked as a justification for an enlargement of the *scope* of application of the rule as generally recognized in international law.

The practice of the European Commission itself does not warrant exaggeration of this explanation of the local remedies rule in the subsidiary character of the international proceedings, which however, is acknowledged by the Commission itself,[5] and is implicit in the general economy of the Convention itself. The existence of the local remedies rule in the Convention's provisions bears witness of that subsidiary position, and to argue on the basis of it for a rigid application of the rule would be unwarranted and would beg the question, because it is ultimately the international organ which is competent to determine the proper scope of application of this condition of the admissibility of the complaints addressed to it.

The manifest impact of the Convention on the domestic law of Contracting States can be appreciated not only in the light of the operation of its international machinery but also – and mainly – through national judicial organs. Some of the decisions of domestic courts concerning the Convention provisions have touched on the local remedies rule. Possibly the most important feature of those decisions has concerned the material content of the duty to exhaust local remedies: this appears as a rule requiring actual local redress and not mere judicial exercise or exhaustion *per se* of remedies until the occurrence of a denial of justice.[6]

A matter raised before the Commission indirectly concerning the application of the local remedies rule, and on which expert writers seem to be divided,[7] is whether the rule applies when Convention provisions from part of the law of the land (i.e., the municipal law of the respondent State), or, in other words, when the Convention has the force of *ordre public* in municipal law, and domestic courts are empowered to supervise *ex officio* the application of the Convention provisions.[8] In this connection, it appears that the particular duty to exhaust local remedies is to be considered solely in respect of the applicant, whether or not domestic courts apply the Convention provisions *ex officio*. The rationale behind the rule is to afford the respondent State an opportunity of prior redress within the framework of its own domestic legal system; the duty of domestic courts to apply the Convention *ex officio*, where it exists, derives, for its part, from the fact that it is a matter of *ordre public* that human rights protection must be guaranteed (in municipal law); the two rules have thus clearly distinct foundations.[9]

The applicant's duty to exhaust local remedies has as its necessary counterpart the State's duty to provide local remedies. While an analysis of the local remedies rule from the viewpoint of the underlying *interests* at stake may have been adequate in the traditional context of State responsibility for injuries to aliens, in the field of international human rights protection[10] an approach to the rule stressing the complementary *rights and duties*[11] would seem more appropriate. This approach is followed both in the European Convention and in the UN Covenant on Civil and Political Rights (and its Optional Protocol),[12] when they expressly refer to the State's duty to provide local remedies as a necessary and natural counterpart of the local remedies requirement. The individual's right of individual petition is granted on condition *inter alia* of compliance with that requirement, and it is the State's right to rely on it provided that it has afforded individuals effective local means of redress. The matter is thus directly related to the measures of implementation of human rights protection. Domestic courts themselves have acknowledged the fact that the Convention entrusts human rights protection (also) to municipal law organs and procedures, even though domestic-court decisions touching on the matter have not always displayed a uniform interpretation of the duty to provide local remedies (Article 13 of the European Convention), and have been concerned with upholding existing domestic legislation (in complaints invoking Convention provisions on the ground of the alleged insufficiency of domestic legislation to provide local redress). On the other hand it is reassuring to note that they appear to be more often concerned with the State's duty to provide local remedies than with formal technicalities in the operation of the local remedies rule.

The Commission's prevailing jurisprudence holds that the duty to provide remedies (Article 13) relates to remedies in respect of violations of the rights set forth in other provisions of the Convention. The procedural guarantee of Article 13 operates as a safeguard against denial of justice or undue delays throughout the process of exhaustion of local remedies. This close inter-relationship between the individual's duty of exhaustion and the State's duty to provide local remedies illustrates a modern shift of emphasis towards improvement of national systems of judicial protection, thus rendering historical categories for the determination of denial of justice obsolescent and no longer satisfactory in respect of the application of the local remedies rule.

In human rights protection in particular, it would hardly be necessary that judicial irregularities tantamount to denial of justice should be superadded to a previous wrong in violation of international law, before international proceedings become proper. This view presupposes that the local remedies rule operates as one of procedure, i.e., as a condition of admissibility of international complaints, which is normally the case in human rights protection. This is not the same as saying that complaints of alleged denials of justice should receive preferential treatment on the part of organs such as the European Commission of Human Rights compared with others. The Commission has shown its preparedness to refer to practice in general international law (possibly by virtue of its relevance to the formulation of the local remedies rule); but, perhaps paradoxically, when a denial of justice has been alleged, other international organs seemed to have displayed considerably less hesitation to invoke the lack of a certain international or minimum standard of justice in order to justify the non-application of the local redress rule (however controversial this might have been). On the other hand, it is reassuring to note that the Commission, in more recent years, has appeared less prepared simply to reject applications as inadmissible for non-exhaustion, and more determined to scrutinize local remedies more closely, thus making the presumptions work more in favour of the allegedly aggrieved applicants. If this trend continues, and States cease to rely too heavily on formal objections to admissibility of complaints, then categorizations not only of denials of justice but of exceptions to the local remedies rule in general may prove less necessary in the days to come than they seem to be today.

The traditional conception of the local remedies rule, found in such writers as Borchard and Eagleton, making international proceedings contingent upon exhaustion of local remedies until the occurrence of a denial of justice, if it was adequate in the context of diplomatic protection, is not necessarily an accurate statement of the function of the rule in human rights protection. In this latter context its function is hardly a preventive one, and a subsequent denial of justice need not be superadded to the original violation of human rights to warrant examination of the complaint at international level; what is stressed here is that the operation of local remedies should terminate in *redress*, and in this process of implementation of law a more active role is reserved to domestic courts. This is in line, for example, with the Commission's greater involvement with broader issues under the European Convention in recent years, as compared with its concern, formerly, with relatively minor questions.

Particularly in recent cases involving contentions of legislative measures and administrative practices, the Commission has disclosed a certain inclination to approach the local remedies rule with due regard to underlying duties rather than interests. But the Commission has also cautiously warned that the State's duty under the Convention to provide local remedies is not without limits, i.e., it comprises remedies exercisable before ordinary tribunals but does not extend to special kinds of remedy (for example, constitutional appeals). While it remains true that under the Convention the primary or main task of securing respect for human rights is reserved to national courts, the situation would be somewhat different in those specific cases of conformity of legislative acts with the Convention, where, in view of the very question at issue, the primary task would seem to lie more appropriately with the Convention organs rather than the national courts.

Recognition that the duties of exhausting and of providing local remedies (Articles 26 and 13 of the Convention, respectively) are complementary may open a new trend in the application of the local remedies rule in the context of human rights protection.[13] One may go yet a step further in considering the guarantee of access to domestic courts and the right to judicial hearing (Article 6) as allocating a fundamental role to national courts in ensuring respect for and observance of the State's international obligations of protecting human rights.[14]

The role of domestic courts in the implementation of international provisions is made important by the 'horizontal' and decentralized structure of international law,[15] a fact which may as a result expose their inadequacies in their administration of justice. When those courts operate pursuant to, for example, the European Convention, a certain uniformity of practice – in the present case, on the local remedies

284

rule – can be expected notwithstanding variations in the domestic legal systems concerned.[16] The role of domestic courts in their horizontal interaction (as organs for implementation of international provisions) in a way transcends the boundaries of their own respective national legal systems; in the application of the local remedies rule in this new perspective, classical abstract definitions of denial of justice (or its component elements) give way to an objective examination of domestic procedures. While traditional international law was perhaps predominantly influenced by the classical notion of the executive arm of the State (concerned with inter-governmental relations, mainly through diplomatic means, leaving the legislative and judicial branches insulated from international contacts, and unconcerned for the most part with the domestic legal realities of the State), in human rights protection – as under the European Convention – rules are meant to apply between the States Parties primarily in their judicial aspect (in so far as the operation of the local remedies rule is concerned); and here it may well be expected that national courts will not proceed on the basis of exclusive sovereignty with regard to the provisions addressed to them in the ratified international instrument.

This would appear to be a natural course in cases of treaties which require municipal action for their implementation, as does the European Convention,[17] with the result that States Parties cannot plead municipal law deficiencies as an excuse for non-performance.[18] In the application of the local remedies rule, it is ultimately through domestic court action that the complementary nature of rights and duties is objectively realized. In the past twenty-five years, a great many applications under the European Convention have been rejected for non-compliance with the rule,[19] but a new attitude towards the rule may make States more inclined more frequently to waive formal objection to the admissibility of human rights applications. A key role would be reserved to the over-riding test of the effectiveness of local remedies, with criteria for the determination of effectiveness to be set up and applied by the Commission itself, thus avoiding a *renvoi* of the issue to national authorities.

Thus, States where the Convention lacks the status of domestic law and where the duty to provide local remedies can thereby only be checked by reference to an alleged violation of a guaranteed right (other than Article 13 *per se*) can only employ an objection of non-exhaustion if they prove that local remedies would have been effective, while it remains for the applicant to prove that they exist or that he is relieved by the circumstances of the case from the duty of exhausting them. The over-riding test of effectiveness remains possibly the most adequate test for ascertaining their 'reality', in constant awareness of the concomitant duties in the application of the local remedies rule; in fact, emphasis on the complementarity of judicially enforceable rights and duties in the process of exhaustion of local remedies can pave the way for a more balanced application of that requirement.

In this connection, a particular group of cases deserves special attention, namely: complaints of allegedly wrongful 'legislative measures and administrative practices' under the European Convention on Human Rights; so-called 'general cases' before the Inter-American Commission on Human Rights; communications revealing a 'consistent pattern of gross violations of human rights' before the UN Sub-Commission on Prevention of Discrimination and Protection of Minorities, as well as complaints under the UN International Convention on the Elimination of All Forms of Racial Discrimination. If at all applicable in such graver cases, the local remedies rule can here only be approached adequately in terms of rights and duties (rather than interests); particularly the duty to provide local redress and to develop the possibilities of judicial remedies. In such special complaints relating to a whole pattern of domestic measures and practices the inevitable implication would be a closer scrutiny on the part of the international organ of the real conditions for exhaustion in each instance and of the reasons and circumstances for non-exhaustion. Now that a few decades have passed since acceptance by States of the right of individual petition, and some international experience in this area has been accumulated, it may well happen that the original apprehensions which States had with regard to the recognition of procedural status to individuals upon the international level will gradually fade away, and they will come to recognise that there is no compelling logical or practical reason preventing the application of the local remedies rule from being limited in scope in the cases concerning general practices.

These conclusions are meant to take account of the different contexts in which the local remedies rule applies; they are not meant to be absolute propositions, as the rule itself is not a principle of absolute and immutable value irrespective of the context of its incidence. Perhaps surprisingly, this point seems hitherto to have been largely overlooked. The local remedies rule, commonly regarded as a 'pre-condition of international proceedings', has thus enjoyed, in classical diplomatic protection and State responsibility for injuries to aliens, a 'negative' or preventive character, with emphasis on the process of exhaustion prior to international interposition on a discretionary State-to-State basis. This approach to the rule is hardly adequate for human rights protection, where the role of local courts and remedies is regarded as a component part of the international system of protection, and where the insertion of the rule in international instruments as a mandatory condition makes it possible to accord it detailed treatment. In a system of protection fundamentally victim-oriented, concerned with the rights of individual human beings rather than of States, an outlook of the issue which is more positive than the one by and large followed so far seems appropriate; and is likely to lead to more reassuring results than the ones ensuing from an essentially negative or formalistic approach leading to systematic, if not mechanical, rejection of applications for non-exhaustion of local remedies.

NOTES

Introduction

1. Cf. A.A. Cançado Trindade, 'Origin and Historical Development of the Rule of Exhaustion of Local Remedies in International Law', 12 *Revue belge de Droit international* [1976] pp. 499–527.

2. See A.A. Cançado Trindade, 'Exhaustion of Local Remedies in International Law Experiments Granting a Procedural Status to Individuals in the First Half of the Twentieth Century', 24 *Nederlands Tijdschrift voor internationaal Recht/Netherlands International Law Review* [1977] pp. 373–92, esp. p. 391.

3. Those earlier experiments granting procedural status to individuals further demonstrate that it is possible to regulate the matter at issue by means of detailed rules and procedures, rather than by a vague and ambiguous reference to 'generally recognized rules of international law', as is done today. *Inclusio unius est exclusio alterius*. But even where that general reference is found, it is meant to draw attention to the recognized limitations of the local redress principle rather than warrant its rigid application, particularly when fundamental rights are at stake. Cf. *ibid.*, pp. 391–2.

4. From 1947 to 1950, the work was undertaken by the UN Commission on Human Rights virtually on its own, on the basis of documents provided by the UN Secretary-General and specialized agencies (e.g., governments' replies to questionnaires); from 1950 to 1954 the Commission proceeded with its work together with the Economic and Social Council (ECOSOC) as an intermediary or reviewing organ, and the General Assembly as the ultimate 'decision-making' organ. From 1954 (date of conclusion of the Commission's draft) until the adoption of the Covenants and the Optional Protocol in 1966, the work was mainly undertaken by the Third Committee of the General Assembly. The clauses on the local remedies rule are Article 41(c) of the UN Covenant on Civil and Political Rights, and Articles 2 and 5(2)(b) of the Optional Protocol to that Covenant. On the preparatory work of those provisions, see UN docs. E/600, E/800, E/1371, E/1681, E/1732, E/1992, E/2256, E/2447, E/2573, ECOSOC *Official Records* [1950–1], GA *Official Records* [1950–4, 1963, 1965–6] (Third Committee debates), 5–6 *UN Yearbook on Human Rights* [1950–1], and in particular, UN docs. E/CN. 4/SR. 209–15, A/1384, A/C. 3/534–5, A/2714, A/2686 (ch. v sect. 1), A/2929, A/C. 3/574, E/CN. 4/524, E/CN. 4/474, E/CN. 4/SR. 190, E/L. 68, E/C. 2/259/Add. 1, E/CN. 4/530/Add. 1.

5. The Convention provisions on the local remedies rule are Articles 26 and 27(3), whose *travaux préparatoires* stretched from 1948 to 1950, undertaken by the European Movement, the Council of Europe's Consultative Assembly and its Legal Committee, the Committee of Experts, the Conference of Senior Officials and the Committee of Ministers. See mainly the *Collected Edition of the 'Travaux Préparatoires'* [of the Convention], C. of E. doc. H(61)4, vols. I–VI, and see further C. of E. docs. DH(55)11, H(64)1, H(70)7 and CDH(70)30.

6. An interaction or mutual influence occurred at distinct stages between the preparatory works of the pertinent provisions of the Covenants and the European Convention. The draftsmen of the local remedies clauses of the 1965 UN International Convention on the Elimination of All Forms of Racial Discrimination – Articles 11(3) and 14(7) (a) – were to benefit from that, as they were given some basis to work upon: cf. UN doc. ST/HR/1, and GA *Official Records* [1965], 20th session, pp. 370–85.

7. The relevant provision is Article 4(b) of resolution 1(XXIV) of 13 August 1971 of the UN Sub-Commission, pursuant to ECOSOC resolution 1503(XLVIII) of 27 May 1970, Article 6(b)(1). See mainly, on that provision, UN docs. E/CN. 4/Sub. 2/SR. 536–627 and 710–11, and E/CN. 4/Sub. 2/L. 539/Rev. 1–617.

8. On the distinctions between the pleas of domestic jurisdiction and non-exhaustion of local remedies, cf. A.A. Cançado Trindade, 'Domestic Jurisdiction and Exhaustion of Local Remedies: A Comparative Analysis', 16 *Indian Journal of International Law* [1976] pp. 187–218, and see A.A. Cançado Trindade, 'The Domestic Jurisdiction of States in the Practice of the United Nations and Regional Organisations', 25 *International and Comparative Law Quarterly* [1976] pp. 715–65.

9. On the local redress principle see also Rule 81 of the Rules of Procedure of the UN Trusteeship Council, and, at the inter-American regional level, the local remedies clauses in Article 9(*bis*)(d) of the Statute of the OAS Inter-American Commission of Human Rights, Article 54 of the Regulations of the Inter-American Commission, and Articles 46(1)(a) and (2)(b) of the American Convention on Human Rights. Reference may here be made to the experience, in some respects unique, of the Inter-American Commission of Human Rights with regard to the local remedies rule. The Commission's decisions have resembled administrative acts rather than judicial decisions *stricto sensu*, and particularities in the application of the rule have been reflected in the variety of solutions found for the issue of exhaustion of local remedies: filing of applications or their postponement for non-exhaustion, filing without prejudice to re-opening examination thereof, requests for further information on exhaustion; in this way declaration of inadmissibility has at times been avoided. Cf. OAS docs. OEA/Ser. L/V/II. 1–29 (and further appended documents), and see OAS docs. OEA/Ser. L/V/II. 23–doc. 21, OEA/Ser. L/V/II. 29. doc. 41–Rev. 2. The 1969 American Convention on Human Rights has expressly acknowledged exceptions to the application of the local remedies rule (cf. provision *supra*).

10. Some practical problems of importance in the application of the rule had

likewise to be omitted from the present study. Such is the case of, e.g., the issue of exhaustion and the law of international organizations; cf. A.A. Cançado Trindade, 'Exhaustion of Local Remedies and the Law of International Organizations', 57 *Revue de droit international de sciences diplomatiques et politiques* [1979] pp. 81–123.

It is appropriate to indicate at this stage that, in the present study, by *'local'* remedies it is meant specifically domestic, i.e., national remedies. The question of exhaustion of regional (e.g., European remedies) and international remedies (an issue recently debated at the UN Sub-Commission on Prevention of Discrimination and Protection of Minor-ities – cf. UN doc. E/CN. 4/Sub. 2/L. 549–Rev. 1) is excluded, and so is the topic of exhaustion of [diplomatic] means of negotiation prior to (diplomatic) settlement (as in, e.g., *United Nations Treaty Series*, vol. 161, p. 65, and vol. 373, p. 101). Specific problems relating to the application of the local remedies rule in arbitral settlement are left outside the scope of the present study.

By 'individual' (and 'individual rights') is meant generally natural or physical persons (even though at times corporate persons have lodged international claims on human rights violations); problems relating to juridical or moral persons are thus not dealt with, as 'individual' is taken to mean generally 'any person, non-governmental organization or group of individuals' (as under human rights treaties and instruments, e.g., Article 25 of the European Convention on Human Rights). Diplomatic protection is considered to the extent that it provides a framework for the rationale and operation of the local remedies rule; related problems (e.g., *inter alia,* the nationality of claims rule, the Calvo clause) are not considered or only briefly referred to *passim.*

Chapter 1

1. Text in European Convention on Human Rights, *Collected Texts,* 9th edn, Council of Europe, Strasbourg, March 1974, p. 8.
2. See Council of Europe doc. H(61)4, *Collected Edition of the 'Travaux Préparatoires'* [of the European Convention], Vol. II, p. 442.
3. *Ibid.*
4. In accordance with the proper meaning ascribed to that provision by the draftsmen of the Convention as well as the object and purpose of this latter (Article 31(1) of the 1969 Vienna Convention on the Law of Treaties – text in UN doc. A/CONF. 39/27, 23 May 1969).
5. Cf. A. Makarov, 'Consideraciones sobre el Derecho de Protección Diplomática', 8 *Revista Española de Derecho Internacional* [1955] pp. 511 and 536–41; C.F. Amerasinghe, *State Responsibility for Injuries to Aliens,* Oxford, Clarendon Press, 1967, p. 37.
6. E. Vattel, *Le droit des gens,* 1758, book II, para. 71.
7. E. Vattel, *The Law of Nations or the Principles of Natural Law* (1758: *Classics of International Law* (trans. C. Fenwick, 1916), p. 136). See also H. Grotius, *De Jure Belli ac Pacis* (1625), book II, ch. 17, para. 20, and ch.

21, para. 2: Hugonis Grotii, *De Jure Belli ac Pacis* (extract by B.M. Telders), The Hague, M. Nijhoff, 1948, pp. 79–82 and 88.

8. Cf. P.P. Remec, *The Position of the Individual in International Law According to Grotius and Vattel*, The Hague, M. Nijhoff, 1960, pp. 157–82; F.S. Ruddy, *International Law in the Enlightenment* (The Background of Emmerich de Vattel's *Le droit des gens*), Dobbs Ferry/New York, Oceana, 1975, pp. 1–95, 212–16.

9. E.g. G.F. de Martens, *Précis du droit des gens moderne de l'Europe*, new edn, vol. 1, Paris, Aillaud Libr., 1831, pp. 224–5, para. 96 (on local redress). The first edition of the *Précis* by de Martens is dated 1788.

10. As exemplified by the works on the subject (prior to Borchard's, in the period ranging from 1878 to 1914) of, e.g., Pradiere-Fodéré, Calvo, Rivier, Heilborn, Tchernoff, Triepel, Moore, Anzilotti, Arias, Goebel; and, from 1916 onwards, Borchard, Décencière-Ferrandière, Eagleton, Dunn, Salvioli, Freeman; cf. also below.

11. H.W. Halleck, *International Law, or Rules Regulating the Intercourse of States*, San Francisco, H.H. Bancroft & Co., 1861, vol. II, ch. XII, pp. 297–303.

12. Sir Robert Phillimore, *Commentaries upon International Law*, 3rd edn, vol. II, London, Butterworths, 1882, pp. 3–5.

13. H. Wheaton, *Elements of International Law* (ed. J.B. Scott), Carnegie Endowment for International Peace, 1936, pt IV, pp. 309–11 n. 151, para. 209–2 (literal reproduction of the text of 1866).

14. F. de Martens, *Traité de droit international* (transl. A. Léo), vol. 1, Paris, Libr. Marescq. Aine, 1883, pp. 444–5.

15. Th. Funck-Brentano et A. Sorel, *Précis du droit des gens*, Paris, E. Plon et Cie, 1877, pp. 226–7 and 229.

16. A.-G. Heffter, *Le droit international public de l'Europe* (trans. J. Bergson), Berlin/Paris, Schroeder/Cotillon, 1866, pp. 115–26, para. 58–62, esp. para. 59a; and cf. also M. Bluntschli, *Le Droit international codifié* (transl. M.C. Lardy), Paris, Guillaumin, 1870, p. 25.

17. Pasquale Fiore, *Trattado di Diritto Internazionale Pubblico*, 3rd edn, vol. 1, Torino, Unione Tipografico-Editrice, 1887, pp. 412–13, para. 620.

18. J. Westlake, *International Law*, pt I, Cambridge, University Press, 1904, pp. 313–20; J. Westlake, *The Collected Papers of John Westlake on Public International Law* (ed. L. Oppenheim), Cambridge, University Press, 1914, ch. VI, pp. 78–85.

19. P. Fauchille, *Traité de droit international public*, 8th edn, vol. 1, part 1, Paris, Rousseau et Cie, 1922, pp. 884 and 922–45, para. 440 and 442.

20. L. Oppenheim, *International Law*, 1st edn, vol. 1 London, Longmans, 1905, pp. 375–6, para. 320.

21. T.E. Holland, *Lectures on International Law* (ed. Walker), London, Sweet and Maxwell, 1933, pp. 165–6.

22. A.A. Cançado Trindade, 'Origin and Historical Development of the Rule of Exhaustion of Local Remedies in International Law', 12 *Revue belge de Droit international* [1976] pp. 511–13.

23. *Ibid.*, pp. 514–24.

24. Cf. Remec, *op. cit.*, p. 56 n. 3; and see Ruddy, *op. cit.*, ch. IX, pp. 281–310.
25. PCIJ, Series A, n. 2, 1924, p. 12; the Court added that the private origin of the case was immaterial, as with the espousal of the claim by the State, the latter had become the sole claimant.
26. PCIJ, Series A/B, n. 76, 1939, p. 16.
27. PCIJ, Series A, n. 17, 1928, pp. 27–8; and see also PCIJ, *Serbian Loans* case, Series A, n. 20, 1929, pp. 41–2, 44 and 46–7.
28. Cf. *Interhandel* (Preliminary Objections) case, *ICJ Reports* [1959] p. 27.
29. Cf. C.G. Ténékidès, 'L'épuisement des voies de recours internes comme condition préalable de l' instance internationale', 14 *Revue de droit international et de législation comparée* [1933] pp. 518 and 531–2.
30. Cf. F.S. Dunn, *The Protection of Nationals*, Baltimore, Johns Hopkins Press, 1932, pp. 33–6 and 53 (on the intensified economic competition following the industrial revolution, and the disparities among States at different levels of economic development); Ch. de Visscher, *Théories et réalités en Droit international public*, 4th rev. edn, Paris, Pédone, 1970, pp. 299–300 n. 1; P. de Visscher, 'Cours général de Droit international public', 136 *Recueil des Cours de l'Académie de Droit International* [1972] ch. II, p. 155; F. Przetacznik, 'The Protection of Individual Persons in Traditional International Law (Diplomatic and Consular Protection)', 21 *Österreichische Zeitschrift für öffentliches Recht* [1971] pp. 77–80; E. Staley, 'Une critique de la protection diplomatique des placements à l'étranger', 42 *Revue générale de Droit international public* [1935] pp. 541–2; J. Castañeda, 'The Underdeveloped Nations and the Development of International Law', 15 *International Organization* [1961] pp. 38–40; R.A. Falk, 'Historical Tendencies, Modernizing and Revolutionary Nations, and the International Legal Order', in *International Law* (series 'The Strategy of World Order', ed. Falk and Mendlovitz), vol. II, New York, World Law Fund, 1966, ii, 175–6; S. Prakash Sinha, *New Nations and the Law of Nations*, Leiden, Sijthoff, 1967, ch. vi, pp. 91–6.
31. Dunn, *Protection of Nationals*, pp. 36 and 52–3. Notable examples of this practice were the U.S. – Mexican arbitration conventions of 1839, 1848, 1868 and 1923; the Venezuelan arbitrations of 1903; the U.S. – British arbitration conventions of 1853, 1871 and 1908; the arbitration conventions of the United States with Spain (1871), France (1880), Colombia (1864 and 1874), Chile (1892), Costa Rica (1860), Ecuador (1862), Peru (1863 and 1868) and Venezuela (1888); in the great majority of cases arbitrations were conducted as judicial proceedings; *ibid.*, pp. 58–9.
32. Cf. *ibid.*, p. 55.
33. E.g., the publication in 1898 of J.B. Moore's six-volume *History and Digest of International Arbitrations* (Dunn, *Protection of Nationals*, pp. 58–9). Dunn perspicaciously points out that by the close of the nineteenth century, while writers of the natural law school and their successors of the historical school were chiefly concerned with fundamental doctrines and concepts inherited from classical writers, they failed to perceive the growing body of problems arising out of

industrialization and related phenomena and their implications for normal international relations; on the other hand, the positivists, even though taking into account actual cases and decisions on the subject of protection of citizens abroad, continued to think within the parameters of classical concepts and doctrines, thus insufficiently treating the emerging body of law under a separate category sometimes titled 'claims'; see *ibid.*, pp. 59–60. In Dunn's assessment, it was with Borchard's treatise of 1916 that diplomatic protection became recognized as 'a separate and important branch of international jurisprudence' (*ibid.*, p. 60).

34. *Ibid.*, p. 55; for a comparison of modern practice of diplomatic protection with Vattel's world of a fairly homogeneous 'international society' composed of European Christian States, cf. *ibid.*, pp. 49–52. Not only did Vattel's times not witness modern intensive international trade and frequent changes of alliance (*ibid.*), but also, it should be noted, Vattel had in mind wrongs inflicted by private individuals upon private individuals (aliens), rather than maltreatment of foreigners at the hands of officials of the State of reception; C. Parry, 'Some Considerations upon the Protection of Individuals in International Law', 90 *Recueil des Cours de l'Académie de Droit International* [1956] p. 657.

35. J.C. Witenberg, 'La recevabilité des réclamations devant les juridictions internationales', 41 *Recueil des Cours de l'Académie de Droit International* [1932] p. 51.

36. E.M. Borchard, *The Diplomatic Protection of Citizens Abroad*, New York, Banks Law Publ. Co., 1916, pp. 28 and 354.

37. Cf. *ibid.*, pp. 29, 178 and 350–2; and see, similarly, Borchard, 'Rapport sur la protection diplomatique', I, p. 260; Root, 'The Basis of Protection to Citizens Residing Abroad', 4 *American Journal of International Law* [1910] pp. 520–1; Dunn, *Protection of Nationals*, pp. 41 and 55; Przetacznik, *op. cit.*, p. 113; E.J.S. Castrén, 'Some Considerations upon the Conception, Development, and Importance of Diplomatic Protection', 11 *Jahrbuch für Internationales Recht* [1962] p. 41.

38. Ch. de Visscher, 'La responsabilité des Etats', 2 *Bibliotheca Visseriana* [1924] – II, pp. 115–16; and see Ch. Rousseau, *Droit international public*, Paris, Rec. Sirey, 1953, ch. VI, pp. 356–86.

39. Ch. de Visscher, 'Le déni de justice en droit international', 52 *Recueil des cours de l'Académie de Droit International* [1935] pp. 421, 427 and 431; and cf. Ch. de Visscher, *Théories et réalités*, p. 299.

40. A.V. Freeman, *The International Responsibility of States for Denial of Justice*, London, Longmans, 1938, pp. 404–7, 410, 432–4, 443, 446, 452 and 456–69.

41. For a recent study of the *birth* of State responsibility and the nature of the local remedies rule (excluded from the present work), as distinguished from the *enforcement* of State responsibility, herein considered, see A.A. Cançado Trindade, 'The Birth of State Responsibility and the Nature of the Local Remedies Rule', 56 *Revue de droit international de sciences diplomatiques et politiques* [1978] – III, pp. 157–88.

42. C. Eagleton, *The Responsibility of States in International Law*, New York, University Press, pp. 95, 97–8; C. Eagleton, 'Denial of Justice in International Law', 22 *American Journal of International Law* [1928] pp. 557–8.

43. Eagleton, *Responsibility*, pp. 96–7, 103; C. Eagleton, 'Une théorie au sujet du commencement de la responsabilité de l'État', 11 *Revue de Droit international et de législation comparée* [1930] pp. 647–8, 654–5, 657, 659.

44. Dunn, *Protection of Nationals*, pp. 156–9, esp. p. 158.

45. R. Ago, 'La Regola del Previo Esaurimento dei Ricorsi Interni in Tema di Responsabilità Internazionale', 3 *Archivio di Diritto Pubblico* [1938] pp. 182 and 242–3.

46. *N. Russell (U.S.)* v. *Mexico* case (U.S. – Mexican General Claims Commission, 1931), 4 *Reports of International Arbitral Awards*, p. 811; *Dickson Car Wheel Co. (U.S.)* v. *Mexico* case (U.S. – Mexican General Claims Commission), 4 *R.I.A.A.*, p. 678.

47. G. Scelle, 'Règles générales du droit de la paix', 46 *Recueil des Cours de l'Académie de Droit International* [1933] pp. 656–61; G. Scelle, *Précis de droit des gens – Principes et systématique*, pt 11, Paris, Rec. Sirey, 1934, pp. 252–5.

48. S. Séfériadès, 'Le problème de l'accès des particuliers à des juridictions internationales', 51 *Recueil des Cours de l'Académie de Droit International* [1935] pp. 24–32; and see, likewise, Staley, *op. cit.*, pp. 546–58; Castrén, *op. cit.*, pp. 39–40.

49. J.L. Brierly, 'Le fondement du caractère obligatoire du droit international', 23 *Recueil des Cours de l'Académie de Droit International* [1928] p. 531; and see, likewise, subsequently, J.L. Brierly, *The Law of Nations*, 6th edn (ed. H. Waldock), Oxford, Clarendon Press, 1963, p. 276.

50. Ch. de Visscher's statement in 37 *Annuaire de l'Institut de Droit International* [1932] pp. 484–5; and see Borchard, *op. cit.*, pp. 352–3, and see *supra*, pp. 00–0.

51. Parry, 'Some Considerations', pp. 657–8, 686–8, 696–702 and 722–3; and see also Lord McNair, 'The Expansion of International Law', in *Lord McNair: Selected Papers and Bibliography*, Leiden, Sijthoff/Oceana, 1974, pp. 333–4.

52. Cf., e.g., Castrén, *op. cit.*, pp. 47–8; Przetacznik, *op. cit.*, p. 113. On the more recent tendency to regulate, by means of multilateral agreements, the status of persons devoid of diplomatic protection, of refugees and stateless persons, in international law, see P. Weis, *Nationality and Statelessness in International Law*, London, Stevens, 1956, pp. 246–7 and 259–60. For further criticisms of the *discretionary* character of diplomatic protection, see S.N. Guha Roy, 'Is the Law of Responsibility of States for Injuries to Aliens a Part of Universal International Law?', 55 *American Journal of International Law* [1961] pp. 872–5 and 886–90; I. Brownlie, *Principles of Public International Law*, 2nd edn, Oxford, Clarendon Press, 1973, p. 572; and cf., *a contrario sensu*, C.F. Amerasinghe, *op. cit.*, pp. 4–27 and 284, where the position of inequality between nationals at home and abroad is openly conceded.

53. See Cançado Trindade, 'Origin and Historical Development of the Rule', pp. 499–527.

54. A. Miaja de la Muela, 'El Agotamiento de los Recursos Internos como Supuesto de las Reclamaciones Internacionales', 2 *Anuario Uruguayo de Derecho Internacional* [1963] p. 16; Amerasinghe, *op. cit.*, pp. 172–4.

55. See the debates of the UN International Law Commission on State responsibility in 1957 and in 1969, in *Yearbook of the International Law Commission* [1957]–I, pp. 165–6, and *ibid.* [1969]–I, pp. 104–17 and 266–7; and, on the shift of emphasis from responsibility for treatment of aliens to responsibility for 'acts likely to endanger international peace', see R. Ago, 'First Report on State Responsibility', *Y.I.L.C.* [1969]–II, pp. 137 and 139–41, para. 79 and 90; and see Ch. de Visscher, *Théories et réalités*, 1970 edn, p. 306; R. Quadri, 'Cours général de droit international public', 113 *Recueil des Cours de l'Académie de Droit International* [1964] ch. IV, pp. 453–77; P. Reuter, 'Principes de droit international public', 103 *R.C.A.D.I.* [1961] ch. V, pp. 583–619; and similarly, among writers from socialist countries, G.I. Tunkin, *Droit international – problèmes théoriques*, Paris, Pédone, 1965, pp. 191–227; Y.A. Korovin *et al.*, *International Law*, Moscow, Academy of Sciences of the USSR (Institute of State and Law), pp. 130–5 and 159–62; P. Kouris's book review of D.B. Levine, *La responsabilité des États dans le droit international contemporain* (in Russian), Moscow, 1966, in 72 *Revue générale de Droit international public* [1968] pp. 269–72.

56. Przetacznik, *op. cit.*, p. 113.

57. Cf. Castrén, *op. cit.*, p. 48.

58. The extension of the scope of diplomatic protection has been objected to on the ground that the existing rules of international law represent 'the essential conditions, historically developed, on which the territorial State is prepared to accept claims presented by another State on behalf of persons residing or having interests in it', and further constitute 'a *modus vivendi*, a well-balanced compromise, gradually and peacefully evolved and accepted both by States interested in extending the scope of diplomatic protection and States interested in restricting it': E. Jiménez de Aréchaga, 'International Responsibility', in *Manual of Public International Law* (ed. M. Sørensen), London, Macmillan, 1968, p. 581.

59. H. Lauterpacht, *International Law and Human Rights*, London, Stevens, 1950, p. 27.

60. Borchard, *Diplomatic Protection*, p. 351, and see pp. 351–4 for his reliance on the Vattelian theory.

61. Dionisio Anzilotti, 'La responsibilité internationale des États à raison des dommages soufferts par des étrangers', 13 *Revue générale de Droit international public* [1906] pp. 8–10; hence the fundamental importance of nationality as a *vinculum juris* for the exercise of diplomatic protection. Like Anzilotti, Salvioli distinguishes the position of the individual in international law as subject to his State's power from his position in municipal law with his actionable subjective rights therein: G. Salvioli, 'Variazioni su una vecchia questione di sistematica nel Diritto interna-

zionale', 16 *Archiv für Rechts – und Wirtschaftsphilosophie* [1922–3] pp. 440–7. In his turn, Weis maintains that the right of protection and the individual's right are on different planes, the former being a right under international law and the latter under municipal law; P. Weis, *op. cit.*, pp. 41–2. The implications of this view, however, do not seem to differ much from those ensuing from Anzilotti's views.

62. On this question, as related to the local remedies rule, see further remarks on the exhaustion of local remedies in international law and the role of national courts, *supra*, pp. 277–85.

   At this stage, suffice it to point out that much of the polemic between monists and dualists has proved to be sterile. To give one example in the present context: to assume, as did the PCIJ in the *Mavrommatis Palestine Concessions* case, that, by taking up its national's case, the State is in reality asserting its own right 'to ensure, in the person of its subjects, respect for the rules of international law' (PCIJ, Series A, 1924, n. 2, p. 12), is arguably to assume that 'the subjects of the State are "entitled" to be respected under the rules of international law or are in legal relation under such rules'; Joseph Lazar, *The Status of the Leasehold in International Law* (thesis, University of Minnesota), University Microfilms, Ann Arbor, Michigan, 1965, p. 30 n. 31. The Court's dualist position (right of the State under international law as distinct from right of the individual under municipal law) could thus be objected to with equal force from the viewpoint of a monist approach (cf. *ibid.*, p. 30 n. 31).

63. Paul Guggenheim, *Traité de Droit international public*, vol. I, Geneva, Georg Cie, 1953, p. 311 n. 2; Makarov, *op. cit.*, p. 518.

64. The 'orthodox' view, as espoused by the Permanent Court of International Justice in the *Mavrommatis Palestine Concessions* case.

65. In this sense, D.P. O'Connell, *International Law*, vol. II, 2nd edn, London, Stevens, 1970, p. 1031. Similarly, García Amador has pointed out the 'incoherence' of the traditional view (rights vesting upon the State) reflected in the fact that it is upon the injured individual that it is incumbent to exhaust local remedies; F.V. García Amador, 'Le sujet passif de la responsabilité et la capacité d'être demandeur en Droit international', 34 *Revue de Droit international, de sciences diplomatiques et politiques* [1956] p. 270; see also, p. 276.

66. In an attempt to remedy some of the inconsistencies of traditional diplomatic protection, Charles de Visscher suggested *two* distinct legal relationships in that context, namely: first, the original relation between the alien and the responsible State, and secondly, after the espousal of the claim, the relation between the alien's State and the responsible State. But Ch. de Visscher admitted that the two relationships remained dependent on each other, possessing the same object and arising out of the same fact, the injury inflicted to a national. Charles de Visscher, 'Notes sur la responsabilité internationale des États et la protection diplomatique d'après quelques documents récents', 8 *Revue de Droit international et de législation comparée* [1927] pp. 245–72, esp. pp. 258–9.

67. Borchard, *Diplomatic Protection*, p. 352.

68. On the question, see mainly the *Administrative Decision n. V* case (U.S. – Germany Mixed Claims Commission, 1924), 2 *Reports of International Arbitral Awards*, pp. 151–3; see further the *L.M.B. Janes (U.S.)* v. *Mexico* case (U.S. – Mexican General Claims Commission), 3 *Annual Digest of Public International Law Cases* [1925–6] p. 256; cf. the *I'm Alone, Carthage* and *Manouba* cases, in Jessup's statements in 46 *Annuaire de l'Institut de Droit International* [1956] p. 301. As to the case-law under the European Convention on Human Rights on reparation or just satisfaction *to the injured party* (Article 50), see the *Ringeisen* (1972), *Neumeister* (1974), and *'Vagrancy'* (1972) cases, *supra*. For a doctrinal study of the question, see G. Berlia, 'Contribution à l'étude de la nature de la protection diplomatique', 3 *Annuaire français de droit international* [1957] pp. 65–72; Borchard *Diplomatic Protection*, p. 178; Guha Roy, *op. cit.*, p. 878; Brownlie, *op. cit.*, pp. 572–3; O'Connell, *op. cit.*, pp. 1029–30.

69. See, in this sense, Ch. de Visscher's statement in 37 *Annuaire de l'Institut de Droit International* [1932] p. 482; and, similarly, Eagleton, 'Une théorie au sujet du commencement...', p. 647; Guhu Roy, *op. cit.*, p. 878; umpire Parker's *dicta* in the *Administrative Decision n. V* case (1924), 2 *R.I.A.A.*; and see further C. Parry, 'Some Considerations', pp. 701–2; O'Connell, *op. cit.*, pp. 1030–1.

70. See, in this connection, the remarks by the International Court of Justice on diplomatic protection, in its decision in the *Barcelona Traction* (Second Phase) case, *ICJ Reports* [1970] p. 33 para. 37, p. 44 paras. 78–9, pp. 48 and 50 paras. 94 and 99, pp. 36–8 paras. 46, 51 and 54, pp. 45–6 paras. 85 and 87, p. 47 para. 89; cf. Judge Ammoun's Separate Opinion, *ibid.*, pp. 301, 315–16, and 293 n. 12. And see Berlia, 'Contribution', p. 65; O'Connell, *op. cit.*, pp. 1030–1.

71. O' Connell, *op. cit.*, pp. 1030–1. And cf. the 1961 UN Convention on the Reduction of Statelessness (not in force as of 31 December 1972) and the 1954 UN Convention relating to the Status of Stateless Persons (which entered into force on 6 June 1960), in *Human Rights – a Compilation of International Instruments of the United Nations*, UN doc. ST/HR/1, of 1973, pp. 57–66.

72. Cf., e.g. A.A. Cançado Trindade, 'Exhaustion of Local Remedies in International Law Experiments Granting Procedural Status to Individuals in the First Half of the Twentieth Century', 24 *Netherlands International Law Review* [1977] pp. 391–2; Cancado Trindade, 'The Birth of State Responsibility', pp. 175–6.

73. Articles 26 and 27(3) of the European Convention on Human Rights.

74. Resolution 1(XXIV) of 13 August 1971 of the UN Sub-Commission on Prevention of Discrimination and Protection of Minorities, Article 4(b), pursuant to ECOSOC resolution 1503(XLVIII) of 27 May 1970, Article 6(b)(1); Article 41(c) of the UN Covenant on Civil and Political Rights; Articles 2 and 5(2)(b) of the Optional Protocol to the Covenant on Civil and Political Rights; Articles 11(3) and 14(7)(a) of the UN International Convention on the Elimination of All Forms of Racial Discrimination; Rule 81 of the Rules of Procedure of the UN Trusteeship Council.

75. Article 9(bis)(d) of the Statute of the OAS Inter-American Commission

of Human Rights; Article 54 of the Regulations of the Inter-American Commission of Human Rights; Article 46(1)(a) and (2)(b) of the American Convention on Human Rights.

76. Compare, e.g., Article 13 of the European Convention on Human Rights with Article 2(3) of the UN Covenant on Civil and Political Rights, and with Article 6 of the UN International Convention on the Elimination of All Forms of Racial Discrimination.

77. Appl. n. 788/60, *Austria* v. *Italy* case, decision of 11 January 1961, *Report of the Plenary Commission* (adopted on 31 March 1963), Council of Europe, Strasbourg, 1963, doc. A–84–548, p. 37.

78. European Court of Human Rights, *Wemhoff* case, judgment of 27 June 1968, Series A, p. 23, para. 8.

79. European Court of Human Rights, *Belgian Linguistics* case, judgment of 23 July 1968, Series A, p. 32, para. 5.

80. Appl. n. 4451/70, *S.E. Golder* v. *United Kingdom* case, *Report of the Commission* (adopted 1 June 1973), Council of Europe doc. D–60–355, Strasbourg, 1973, pp. 23–36. On the Commission's previous decision (of 30 March 1971) of non-compliance by the applicant with the local remedies rule, cf. *ibid.*, Appendix II, pp. 74–5.

81. Appl. n. 4451/70, *Golder* case, *Report*, p. 25; and see pp. 26–9 for references to the rules of interpretation contained in the 1969 Vienna Convention on the Law of Treaties (e.g., preparatory work as a *supplementary* means of interpretation). One of the main objects and purposes of the Convention, the Commission's report added, was the idea of the *rule of law* (*ibid.*, p. 30).

82. *Ibid.*, p. 31.

83. European Court of Human Rights, *Golder* case, judgment of 21 February 1975, pp. 9–12, paras. 29–36.

84. Not in conflict with generally accepted methods of interpretation; M. Sørensen, *Do the Rights Set Forth in the European Convention on Human Rights in 1950 Have the Same Significance in 1975?*, Report to the 4th International Colloquy on the European Convention on Human Rights (Rome, 5–8 November 1975), Council of Europe doc. H/Coll. (75)2, Strasbourg, 1975, pp. 4–5.

85. Cf., in this sense, e.g., F.G. Jacobs, *The European Convention on Human Rights*, Oxford, Clarendon Press, 1975, pp. 15–20; H. Golsong, 'International Treaty Provisions on the Protection of the Individual Against the Executive by Domestic Courts', in *Gerichtsschutz gegen die Exekutive/Judicial Protection Against the Executive*, vol. 3, Max-Planck-Institut für ausländisches öffentliches Recht und Volkerrecht, Köln, Carl Heymanns Verlag/Oceana, 1971, p. 252.

86. For a recent reassertion of the rationale of the rule, cf. appl. n. 5964/72, *X* v. *F.R. Germany* (1975), European Commission of Human Rights, *Decisions and Reports*, vol. 3, pp. 57 and 60.

87. Text in European Convention on Human Rights, *Collected Texts*, 9th edn, Strasbourg, March 1974, p. 1 (my italics).

88. And see Article 32 of the Convention, for attributions of the Committee of Ministers.

89. Appl. n. 788/60, *Austria* v. *Italy* case, *Report*, pp. 36–7.
90. *Ibid.*, p. 37.
91. Text in *Collected Texts*, 9th edn, p. 8.
92. See, in this respect, e.g., the Commission's decision in the *A* v. *Norway* case (appl. n. 867/60). The Commission found, *inter alia*, that, in the case, the applicant had not pretended to have been himself in any way a victim of the violation complained of, and, since the Commission was 'not competent to examine *in abstracto*' the conformity of an internal law with the provisions of the Convention, the application was declared inadmissible; cf. *Collection of Decisions of the European Commission of Human Rights*, vol. 6, p. 38. And see, to the same effect, appl. n. 7045/75, *X* v. *Austria* case, decision of 10 December 1976, European Commission of Human Rights, *Decisions and Reports*, vol. 7, pp. 87–9; appl. n. 6742/74, *X* v. *F.R. Germany* case, decision of 10 July 1975, *Decisions and Reports*, vol. 3, p. 102; appl. n. 6853/74, *40 Mothers* v. *Sweden* case, decision of 9 March 1977, *Decisions and Reports*, vol. 9, pp. 27–32.
93. C.Th. Eustathiades, 'Les recours individuels à la Commission européenne des droits de l'homme', in *Grundprobleme des Internationalen Rechts – Festschrift für Jean Spiropoulos*, Bonn, Schimmelbusch & Co., 1957, p. 121. See also C.Th. Eustathiades, 'La Convention européenne des droits de l'homme et le Statut du Conseil de l'Europe', 53 *Die Friedens-Warte* [1955–6] pp. 68–9.
94. M. Virally, 'L'accès des particuliers à une instance internationale: la protection des droits de 1'homme dans la cadre européen', in 20 *Mémoires Publiés par la Faculté de Droit de Genève* [1964] pp. 67–89.
95. E. Müller-Rappard, 'Le droit d'action en vertu des dispositions de la Convention européenne des droits de l'homme', 4 *Revue belge de Droit International* [1968] – 11, pp. 491–2.
96. Müller-Rappard, *op. cit.*, p. 503; H. Rolin, 'Le rôle du requérant dans la procédure prévue par la Commission européenne des droits l'homme', 9 *Revue Hellénique de Droit International* [1956] pp. 3–14, esp. p. 9; K. Vasak, *La Convention européenne des droits de l'homme*, Paris, LGDJ, 1964, pp. 96–8; C.P. Economopoulos, 'Les éléments politiques et judiciaires dans la procédure instaurée par la Convention européenne des droits de l'homme', 22 *Revue hellénique de Droit international* [1969] pp. 125–6; F. Durante, *Ricorsi Individuali ad Organi Internazionali*, Milano, Giuffrè, 1958, pp. 125–52, esp. pp. 129–30.
97. H. Mosler, 'The Protection of Human Rights by International Legal Procedure', 52 *Georgetown Law Journal* [1964] p. 818.
98. Müller-Rappard, *op. cit.*, pp. 497–8.
99. M. Pilotti, 'Le recours des particuliers devant les juridictions internationales', in *Grundprobleme des internationalen Rechts – Festschrift für Jean Spiropoulos*, Bonn, Schimmelbusch & Co., 1957, p. 351.
100. Mosler, 'Protection of Human Rights', p. 819. The question of the actual position of individuals in proceedings before the Court is considered in Ch. 6 on further problems in the application of the local remedies rule, *supra*.

101. And this is probably the reason why the Commission – an international organ – charged with the task of pronouncing on the admissibility of all applications (individual and inter-State), plays a central role in the mechanism of collective protection, having thereby been referred to as the 'pierre angulaire de l'édifice de la Convention'. See N. Antonopoulos, *La Jurisprudence des organes de la Convention européenne des droits de l'homme*, Leiden, Sijthoff, 1967, p. 256; cf. also Müller-Rappard, *op. cit.*, pp. 486 and 515.

102. M.G. Cohn, 'La théorie de la responsabilité internationale', 68 *Recueil des Cours de l'Académie de Droit International* [1939]–II, pp. 250, 301–2 and 313–14.

103. Cohn, *op. cit.*, p. 312.

104. *Ibid.*, p. 312.

105. *Ibid.*, p. 312, and authorities quoted therein; see also A.N. Mandelstam, *Les Droits internationaux de l'homme*, Paris, Les Éditions Internationales, 1931, pp. 45–57 and 95–107.

106. C. Parry, *The Sources and Evidences of International Law*, Manchester, University Press/Oceana, 1965, p. 38; see also C. Parry, 'Some Considerations upon the Protection', pp. 687–8 and 698.

107. See Francisco de Vitoria, *Obras* (1538–1539) – *Relecciones Teologicas: De Indiis* (ed. T. Urdanoz), Madrid, B.A.C., 1960, pp. 491–726; Association Internationale Vitoria-Suarez (ed.), *Vitoria et Suarez – Contribution des théologiens au Droit international moderne*, Paris, Pédone, 1939, pp. 31 seq. and 161 seq.; Hugonis Grotii, *De Jure Belli ac Pacis* (extract by B.M. Telders), The Hague, M. Nijhoff, 1948, pp. 10 and 54; B.A. Wortley, 'Idealism in International Law: a Spanish View of the Colonial Problem', 24 *Transactions of the Grotius Society* [1938] p. 147.

108. See, e.g., C. Th. Eustathiades, 'La Convention européenne des droits de l'homme et le Statut du Conseil de l'Europe', 53 *Die Friedens-Warte* [1955–6] p. 66.

109. Mosler, 'Protection of Human Rights', pp. 814–15; he added that this was 'apparent especially in cases of State succession. After the numerous annexations of territory within the last centuries, protection would theoretically have been required only to those persons in the annexed territory who were neither nationals of the ceding State nor of the annexing State. In reality, as a rule, the entire population of the annexed territory was treated in accordance with that standard.'

110. Cf. Paris Peace Treaty of 10 February 1947, with Italy, Romania, Bulgaria, Hungary and Finland; and 'State Treaty for the Establishment of an Independent and Democratic Austria' of 15 May 1955, in Mosler, 'Protection of Human Rights', p. 815.

111. *Ibid.*, pp. 815–17, and cf. Articles 1 and 57 of the European Convention; on Article 25 of the Convention, cf. *ibid.*, pp. 817–19.

112. A.-Ch. Kiss, 'La condition des étrangers en droit international et les droits de l'homme', *in Miscellanea W.J. Ganshoff van der Meersch*, vol. 1, Brussels/Paris, Bruylant/LGDJ, 1972, pp. 499–509; for a similar view of an 'élargissement' of the scope of diplomatic protection brought about by the machinery of the European Convention on Human Rights, see

Michel Virally, 'L'accès des particuliers à une instance internationale: la protection des droits de l'homme dans la cadre européen', 20 *Mémoires Publiés par la Faculté de Droit de Genève* [1964] pp. 76–7.

113. See, *a contrario sensu*, A.V. Freeman, 'Human Rights and the Rights of Aliens', 44 *Proceedings of the American Society of International Law* [1951] p. 123, for the view that 'international law does not confer "political" rights on the alien'.

114. Kiss, 'La condition des étrangers', pp. 499–509.

115. *Ibid.*, pp. 509–10.

116. C. Th. Eustathiades, 'Les sujets du Droit international et la responsabilité internationale: nouvelles tendances', 84 *Recueil des Cours de l'Académie de Droit International* [1953]-III, pp. 586–7, 608 and 610.

117. *Ibid.*, pp. 405–28 and 611; on determination of civil and penal responsibility, see *ibid.*, p. 601, and further, e.g., G. Berlia, 'De la responsabilité internationale de l'État', in *La Technique et les principes du Droit public – Etudes en l'honneur de Georges Scelle*, vol. II, Paris, LGDJ, 1950, pp. 875–94.

118. C. Th. Eustathiades, 'Les sujets du Droit', p. 611; and, on this 'double capacity' of the individual – 'capacité au délit et à la mise en application de responsabilités internationales' – see *ibid.*, pp. 611–14.

119. Cf. Cançado Trindade, 'Exhaustion of Local Remedies in International Law Experiments Granting Procedural Status to Individuals', pp. 373–92; and cf. comments in W.P. Gormley, *The Procedural Status of the Individual before International and Supranational Tribunals*, The Hague, M. Nijhoff, 1966, pp. 32–44.

120. H. Lauterpacht, *International Law and Human Rights*, London, Stevens, 1950, p. 48.

121. C. Th. Eustathiades, 'Les sujets du Droit', p. 550.

122. *Ibid.*, p. 550.

123. *Ibid.*, pp. 552–3.

124. *Ibid.*, p. 538, and see pp. 540–1 for his comments on nationality as basis of an international claim being completed by other notions equally regarded as being capable of providing ground for an international claim (e.g. 'general collective interest', 'guarantee of the functioning of an international public service', 'lien de service' upheld by the ICJ in 1949 in the *Reparation for Injuries* case). Raestad maintains that diplomatic protection affords a 'solution transactionnelle' between respect for territorial sovereignty and 'respect du droit' (i.e., protection of aliens); his study is useful mainly for detecting legal rules 'de caractère plutôt formel, portant sur la capacité et la compétence', concerning diplomatic protection; cf. A. Raestad, 'La protection diplomatique des nationaux à l'étranger', 11 *Revue de Droit international* [1933] pp. 494 and 544; see, more recently, e.g., Paul de Visscher, *op. cit.*, pp. 165–6; O'Connell, *op.cit.*, pp. 1032 seq; R.Y. Jennings, 'General Course on Principles of International Law', 121 *Recueil des Cours de l'Académie de Droit International* [1967]-II, pp. 474–80, and see pp. 480–6. Although not espousing Scelle's and Duguit's views of the individual as the ultimate subject of the law of nations, Eustathiades nevertheless conceded that

Duguit and Scelle rendered a great service to international legal theory for reacting against the excesses of the traditional doctrine whereby only States were subjects of international law; on this particular question Eustathiades's systematization was *à mi-chemin* between traditional doctrine and individualistic theories; cf. C. Th. Eustathiades, 'Les sujets du Droit', pp. 604–5 and 607. For an approach of State responsibility starting from the basic premise that individuals are the ultimate subjects of the law of nations, see Hans Kelsen, *General Theory of Law and State*, Cambridge, Mass., Harvard University Press, 1949, pp. 341–63; Léon Duguit, *Law in the Modern State* (transl. H. Laski), London, G. Allen & Unwin Ltd., 1921, ch. VII, pp. 206–7; and, for the views on the matter of Kelsen's 'first-generation disciples' (mainly Verdross and Kunz), see, e.g., J.J. Lador-Lederer, 'Some Observations on the "Vienna School" in International Law', 17 *Nederlands Tijdschrift voor internationaal Recht* [1970] pp. 140–2 and 135–6.

125. C. Th. Eustathiades, 'Les Sujets du Droit', p. 549; and, in the same sense, Paul de Visscher, *op. cit.*, p. 155; Sir Humphrey Waldock, 'General Course on Public International Law', 106 *Recueil des Cours de l'Académie de* [1962]–II, pp. 194–5.

126. C. Th. Eustathiades, 'Les sujets du Droit', p. 549; earlier experiments granting procedural status to individuals, such as those under the League of Nations, had been 'partial' or limited experiments, with protection extended to certain individuals under certain conditions.

127. For an extension of protection *ratione personae* to all individuals within the jurisdiction of the High Contracting Parties, cf. Article 1 of the European Convention on Human Rights, and for an enforcement of protection collectively by the High Contracting Parties, cf. Article 24 of the Convention; on this 'generalization' of protection, cf. C. Th. Eustathiades, 'La Convention européenne des droits de l'homme et le Statut', pp. 68–9.

128. C. Th. Eustathiades, 'Les sujets du Droit', p. 571, and see pp. 553–66 and 583–93.

129. Cf. *ibid.*, p. 586, for his further remarks.

130. See O'Connell, *op. cit.*, vol. II, p. 1031; Freeman, 'Human Rights', pp. 120–1, 123 and 125–7.

131. C. Th. Eustathiades, 'Les sujets du Droit', pp. 606–7 n. 2, and see pp. 594–5; Freeman, 'Human Rights' pp. 128–9.

132. C. Th. Eustathiades, 'Les sujets du Droit', pp. 607–8 and 610–11, and see pp. 595 and 600.

133. The *summa divisio* naturally leading to the dualist view of the relationship between municipal law and international Law.

134. M. Virally, 'Droits de l'homme et théorie générale du droit international', in *René Cassin Amicorum Discipulorumque Liber*, vol. IV, Paris, Pédone, 1972, pp. 327–9 (also for the author's monist approach), and see pp. 323–6 for traditional forms of protection (e.g., humanitarian intervention, humanitarian law).

135. E.g., by treating the 'older' system in preliminary chapters, in method

of periodization or chronological sequence; see L.B. Sohn and T. Buergenthal, *International Protection of Human Rights*, New York, Bobbs – Merrill Co., 1973, pp. 8 seq., and pp. 87–96 for references; M. Ganji, *International Protection of Human Rights*, Geneva, Droz, 1962, p. 1; G. Ezejiofor, *Protection of Human Rights under the Law*, London, Butterworths, 1964, pp. 25–6 and 32; H. Lauterpacht, *International Law and Human Rights*, pp. 3–72; K. Vasak, 'La protection internationale des droits de l'homme', *Documentation française: problèmes politiques et sociaux* [1973] pp. 6–14 nn. 203–4; D. Uribe Vargas, *Los Derechos Humanos y el Sistema Interamericano*, Madrid, Ed. Cultura. Hispánica 1972, pp. 149–50; P.N. Drost, *Human Rights as Legal Rights*, Leiden, Sijthoff, 1965, pp. 15–16 and 21–7.

136. E.g. relations between tribes, clans, families, cities, States. On *group* protection, cf. J.J. Lador-Leaderer, *International Group Protection*, Leiden, Sijthoff, 1968, pp. 16–23; A. Rigo Sureda, *The Evolution of the Right of Self-Determination*, Leiden, Sijthoff, 1973, p. 356.

137. N. Politis, *The New Aspects of International Law*, Washington, Carnegie Endowment for International Peace, 1928, p. 24. And see J. Spiropoulos, 'L' individu et le droit international', 30 *Recueil des Cours de l' Académie de Droit International* [1929] pp. 256–66. It was thus no surprise that, at a time when diplomatic protection was commonplace and prestigious for the beneficiaries, when the Statutes of the Permanent Court of International Justice were being drawn up, the idea of granting direct recourse to individuals was dismissed and encountered general hostility on the part of the Hague's Committee of Jurists; cf. critical remarks by N. Politis, *op. cit.*, pp. 28–30; and cf. further, Ch. de Visscher, Report on 'Les droits fondamentaux de l'homme, base d'une restauration du droit international', 41 *Annuaire de l'Institut de Droit International* [1947] pp. 1–13; H. Lauterpacht, *International Law and Human Rights*, pp. 273–393.

138. For a recent example, expressly recalling the Vattelian principle, see Opinion of the Law Officers of Northcutt Ely, *International Law Applicable to Deep-Sea Mining*, 14 November 1974, pp. 32–43, and cf. further on the case: 'Deep-Sea Ventures Inc.: Notice of Discovery and Claim of Exclusive Mining Rights, and Request for Diplomatic Protection and Protection of Investment' (filed with the U.S. Secretary of State on 15 November 1974), 14 *International Legal Materials* [1975] pp. 51–68 and 795–6.

139. E.g., States inadequately insisting on certain procedural hurdles (e.g., the local remedies rule) to be applied to the same (or to a greater) extent under the treaty as normally in traditional diplomatic protection, thereby undermining the principles and purposes of the treaty.

140. Virally, for example, at the end of his optimistic description of the fundamental change brought about in contemporary international law by the new system of human rights protection, concedes that diplomatic protection is nowadays probably even more important than in the past in view of the growing importance of economic problems in contemporary

international relations ('la montée de l'économique dans le politique'), and displays some concern for the possibility of political interests dominating in the future the system of protection of the individual as such; see M. Virally, 'Droits de l'homme et théorie générale', pp. 326 and 330. One may thus wonder whether these points would not tend to dismiss the denial of the existence of two 'spheres' operated by human rights protection which he emphatically advocated.

141. C. Th. Eustathiades, 'Les sujets du Droit', pp. 600–1.

142. As, e.g., upon optional ratification, under Article 25 of the European Convention on Human Rights.

143. Cf. G. Dahm, 'Die Subsidiarität des internationalen Rechtsschutzes bei Völkerrechts widriger Verletzung von Privatpersonen', in *Vom deutschen zum europäischen Recht – Festschrift für Hans Dölle*, vol. 11, Tübingen, J.C.B. Mohr (P. Siebeck), 1963, pp. 3–33, esp. pp. 6–23 on the local remedies rule and the subsidiary character of international procedures in general international law, and pp. 23–33 on the scope and conditions of the application of the rule (in the context of injuries to private persons contrary to public international law).

144. Much of the controversy concerned the nationality of claims rule in relation to the position of the individual in international law; the discussion polarized in opposite arguments raised by Politis and Borchard. Cf. statements in 36 *Annuaire de l'Institut de Droit International* [1931]–II, p. 202, and 37 *Annuaire I.D.I.* [1932] p. 236.

145. 37 *Annuaire de l'Institut de Droit International* [1932] p. 237.

146. *Ibid.*, pp. 242–3. Cf. Politis's and Dumas's remarks in *ibid.*, p. 265, and De La Barra's remarks in *ibid.*, pp. 264–5.

147. *Ibid.*, pp. 486–7.

148. *Ibid.*, p. 489, and see p. 490; as an example of that 'apparition' he referred to the *Serbian Loans* case (*ibid.*, pp. 489–90). Earlier, in 1926, he spoke of 'the status of the individual in international law': see N. Politis, *The New Aspects*, pp. 18–31 (and cf. French edition, N. Politis, *Les Nouvelles Tendances du Droit international*, Paris, Libr. Hachette, 1927).

149. See 37 *Annuaire de l'Institut de Droit International* [1932] pp. 490–1, and pp. 492–3; and see Séfériadès's remarks in *ibid.*, p. 493.

150. *Ibid.*, p. 492; for his criticism of the Vattelian principle and his support for the granting to individuals (as recognized subjects of international law) of direct access to international tribunals, see: A. De La Pradelle, 'La place de l'homme dans la construction du Droit international', 1 *Current Legal Problems* [1948] pp. 146–7, and see pp. 140–51. 151. Cf., e.g., *ibid.*, pp. 517 and 522; and see also Borchard's comments in *ibid.*, p. 523.

152. For criticisms of De La Pradelle and Politis's presentation of their views, see H.W. Briggs, *The Law of Nations*, 2nd edn, New York, Appleton – Century-Crofts, 1952, p. 735. For Borchard's subsequent comments on the discussions at the *Institut*, see E.M. Borchard, 'The Protection of Citizens Abroad and Change of Original Nationality', 43 *Yale Law Journal* [1934] pp. 359–92; and also E.M. Borchard, 'La protection des nationaux à l'étranger et le changement de la nationalité d'origine' 14

Revue de Droit international et de législation comparée [1933] pp. 421–67. And see also A. De La Pradelle, 'La place de l'homme', pp. 140–51.

153. Those were the relations between the State of sojourn and the injured alien (territorial supremacy), between the injured alien and his home State, which was usually the protecting State (personal supremacy), and between the said two States, based on international law (custom or treaty); see E.M. Borchard, 'Les principes de la protection diplomatique des nationaux à l'étranger', 3 *Bibliotheca Visseriana* [1924], pp. 3–52, esp. pp. 7–17; see also Borchard, *Diplomatic Protection*, pp. 3–32.

154. In 36 *Annuaire de l'Institut de Droit International* [1931]–II, p. 210. On the prominence of the interests of the claimant State, see Borchard, *Diplomatic Protection*, pp. 351–4, and pp. 384–8 (for the distribution of awards and indemnities).

155. In 36 *Annuaire de l'Institut de Droit International* [1931]–II, p. 210. And see A. De La Pradelle, 'La place de l'homme', p. 147 (for the distribution of awards and indemnities).

156. Session of 1900, 'State responsibility for damages to aliens', 'règlement' voted by the *Institut*, in 18 *Annuaire I.D.I.* [1900] pp. 254–6; session of 1927, 'State responsibility for injuries to aliens' (see also elsewhere), resolutions voted by the *Institut*, in 33 *Annuaire I.D.I.* [1927]–III, pp. 330–5; session of 1936, 'Juridical status of stateless persons and refugees', *Institut*'s resolutions in 39 *Annuaire I.D.I.* [1936]–II, pp. 292–9; session of 1956, 'The rule of exhaustion of local remedies' (see also elsewhere), *Institut*'s resolutions in 46 *Annuaire I.D.I.* [1956] pp. 358–9; session of 1967, 'The legal conditions of capital investment in countries in course of development and agreements relating thereto', *Institut*'s resolutions in 52 *Annuaire I.D.I.* [1967] pp. 560 and 565.

157. Cf. 37 *Annuaire de l'Institut de Droit International* [1932] p. 529: 'l'incident est clos' (final words).

158. Cf. Cançado Trindade, 'Exhaustion of Local Remedies in International Law Experiments Granting Procedural Status to Individuals', pp. 373–92.

159. What, e.g., Cavaré terms 'protection by delegation', would correspond to the international protection of human rights. See L. Cavaré, 'Les transformations de la protection diplomatique', 19 *Zeitschrift für ausländisches öffentliches Recht und Völkerrecht* [1958] pp. 55–8 and 61–8; see also Staley, *op. cit.*, pp. 542–3; Castrén, *op. cit.*, p. 37; E. Kaufmann, 'Règles générales du droit de la paix', 54 *Recueil des Cours de l'Académie de Droit International* [1935] pp. 420–35; J. Puente Egido, 'Algunas Consideraciones en torno a la Situación Procesal de los Particulares ante Instancias Internacionales', 20 *Revista Española de Derecho Internacional* [1967] pp. 277–98. Accordingly, it would seem inaccurate to deal with the new protective system of human rights under the framework of diplomatic protection (based on distinct premises) and to consider it merely as a 'transformation' or 'development' of this latter. For a more cautious approach by Cavaré himself, cf. L. Cavaré, *Le Droit international public positif*, vol. I, 3rd. ed., Paris, Pédone, 1967, pp. 280–96. See also F.S.

Dunn, *The Diplomatic Protection of Americans in Mexico*, New York, Columbia University Press, 1933, pp. 428–30.

160. The 'international standard of justice', apart from its vagueness and imprecision, had its origin traced back to the sort of reasoning which 'gave rise to the system of capitulations or extraterritoriality that was for so long imposed upon the peoples of Asia and Africa', with 'the consequent discrimination in favour of the foreign groups of the population, and the infringement of the principle of equality among nations'; the standard thus became seen as 'a distinctly imperfect rule and one which is only of very relative usefulness'. On the other hand, the principle of 'equality between nationals and aliens' seemed likewise 'inadmissible in its extreme form conflicting with international law'; although aliens could not rationally 'expect a privileged status as compared with nationals', the fact that nationals suffered from a situation in which their State did not provide for or respect safeguards for their rights could not constitute a valid excuse for a State 'to evade its international responsibility' (with respect to its treatment of aliens). F.V. García Amador, First Report on International Responsibility, *Yearbook of the International Law Commission* [1956]–II, p. 203, paras. 154–5, and see pp. 199–203. Borchard, a strong advocate of the 'minimum standard' of alien treatment, attacked the doctrine of absolute equality on the ground that aliens' rights could only be disregarded by a State 'at the peril of international responsibility'; this body of law, 'fashioned empirically', operated as 'a check on arbitrariness'. E.M. Borchard, 'The "Minimum Standard" of the Treatment of Aliens', 33 *Proceedings of the American Society of International Law* [1939] pp. 53, 56 and 60. For a fuller discussion of the 'minimum' standard and the 'national treatment' standard in the framework of the law on alien treatment, see A.H. Roth, *The Minimum Standard of International Law Applied to Aliens*, Leiden, Sijthoff, 1949, pp. 62–123.

161. F.V. García Amador, First Report, p. 199, para. 135.

162. *Ibid.*, p. 203, para. 156.

163. *Ibid.*, p. 203, paras. 156–7.

164. *Ibid.*, p. 203, para. 158 (my italics) García Amador remarked that all instruments for human rights protection accorded a measure of protection going 'well beyond the *minimum* protection which the rule of the "international standard of justice" was meant to ensure to aliens'; moreover, *equality of rights* (of all individuals) constituted their very essence (*ibid.*, p. 203, para. 158; and see p. 202, para. 153, for his criticisms of some of the shortcomings of diplomatic protection).

165. In *Yearbook of the International Law Commission* [1957]–II, pp. 112–16.

166. In *Yearbook of the International Law Commission* [1958]–II, pp. 49–50.

167. In *Yearbook of the International Law Commission* [1959]–II, pp. 3–10.

168. See, e.g., Articles 1 and 3(2), in *Yearbook of the International Law Commission* [1961]–II. pp. 46–7, and explanations on Articles 1 and 3 in *ibid.*, p. 50

169. Cf. F.V. García Amador, 'State Responsibility – Some New Problems', 94 *Recueil des Cours de l'Académie de Droit International* [1958]–II, pp. 435–9.
170. On this particular point, see J.G. Starke, 'Imputability in International Delinquencies', 19 *British Yearbook of International Law* [1938] pp. 104–17, esp. pp. 104–9; a clear understanding of the issue is important, as imputability within the context of State responsibility and the operation of the local remedies rule is closely related to the relationship between international law and municipal law.
171. One may thus speak of a certain 'suspensive condition [for the 'enforcement' of responsibility], which may be procedural or substantive, but to which the right to bring international claims is subordinated'; Garcia Amador, 'State Responsibility', p. 449.
172. García Amador, 'State Responsibility', p. 449; and, in the same sense, F.V. Garcia Amador, Third Report on State Responsibility for Injuries to Aliens, *Yearbook of the International Law Commission* [1958]–II, pp. 55–6.
173. García Amador, 'State Responsibility', p. 471.
174. In *Yearbook of the International Law Commission* [1969]–II, p. 133, para. 50, and see also p. 133, para. 47–9.
175. *Ibid.*, p. 134, para. 54.
176. Particularly those expressed in *Yearbook of the International Law Commission* [1957]–II, pp. 112–16.
177. In *Yearbook of the International Law Commission* [1969]–I, pp. 114–15, para. 11.
178. E.S.C.O.R. [1973], 54th session, *Annexes*, p. 72.
179. Resolution 8(XXV) of the Sub-Commission, and resolution 3(XXIX) of the Commission; see UN docs. E/5265 and E/CN. 4/1127, Commission on Human Rights, *Report of the Twenty-Ninth Session* (1973), pp. 32, 71 and 98.
180. UN doc. E/5265, p. 32.
181. UN doc. E/CN. 4/Sub. 2/SR. 686, p. 185.
182. *Ibid.*, p. 186.
183. UN doc. E/CN. 4/Sub. 2/L. 598, of 8 August 1974, pp. 1–4.
184. UN doc. E/CN. 4/Sub. 2/L. 598, p. 2.
185. UN doc. E/CN. 4/Sub. 2/L. 598, pp. 2–3.
186. *Ibid.*, p. 2.
187. UN doc. E/CN. 4/Sub. 2/L. 600, of 9 August 1974, p. 2.
188. *Ibid.*, p. 2.
189. Un doc. E/CN. 4/Sub. 2/L. 600/Rev. 1, of 16 August 1974, p. 2 (draft resolution submitted by Mr. Gros Espiell, Mrs Warzazi and Mrs Daes). Lady Elles was to be entrusted with the task of preparing a report supplementing a previous study on the subject (UN doc. E/CN. 4/Sub. 2/335, and see UN docs. E/CN. 4/1160 and E/CN. 4/Sub. 2/355); cf. UN doc. E/CN. 4/Sub. 2/L. 619, of 23 August 1974, p. 1.
190. UN docs. E/5464 and E/CN. 4/1154, Commission on Human Rights, *Report on the Thirtieth Session* (1974), p. 39, and see pp. 6–7 and 55.

191. ECOSOC resolution 1871(LVI) of 17 May 1974.
192. Sub-Commission's resolution 10(XXVII), of 1974.
193. UN docs. E/5635 and E/CN. 4/1179, Commission on Human Rights, *Report on the Thirty-First Session* (1975), p. 7.
194. *Ibid.*, p. 7.
195. Commission's resolution 4(XXXI), of 1975, in UN docs. E/5635 and E/CN. 4/1179, p. 73, and see p. 7.
196. Un doc. E/CN. 4/Sub. 2/392 (of 23 June 1977), *The Problem of the Applicability of Existing International Provisions for the Protection of Human Rights to Individuals Who are Not Citizens of the Country in Which They Live* (by Baroness Elles, special *rapporteur*), pp. 1–108 (and annexes), esp. pp. 93 and 99 for the local remedies rule. On the draft declaration on the subject, cf. UN docs. E/CN. 4/1336 (of 5 December 1978), pp. 1–4, and E/CN. 4/Sub. 2/L. 682 (of 20 July 1978), pp. 1–27 (and annex); for the government replies on the draft declaration, cf. UN doc. E/CN. 4/Sub. 2/L. 682/Add. 1 (of 1 August 1978), pp. 1–74.
197. Baroness Elles, 'Aliens and Activities of the United Nations in the Field of Human Rights', 7 *Revue des droits d l'homme/Human Rights Journal* [1974] p. 296.
198. Baroness Elles, *op. cit.*, pp. 296, 304, 313–14 and 316.
199. *Ibid.*, p. 317.
200. *Ibid.*, p. 317. One example referred to was the fairly recent collective expulsion of 55,000 Asians from Uganda, without legal remedies opened to the individuals concerned; the event apparently strongly influenced the Commission to authorize the Sub-Commission to study the problem of the applicability of UN instruments for human rights protection to individuals who are not citizens of the country in which they live (*ibid.*, p. 304). On this point, see also R.B. Lillich, 'The Problem of the Applicability of the Existing International Provisions for the Protection of Human Rights to Individuals who are not Citizens of the Country in which They Live', 70 *American Journal of International Law* [1976] pp. 507–8.
201. Baroness Elles, *op. cit.*, p. 316.
202. Although Article 14 could be said to apply specifically to aliens, political rights were not extended to 'non-citizens', nor intended to be so extended, and the rights contained in the Declaration were those of all individuals, regardless of nationality or citizenship. *Ibid.*, pp. 307–8.
203. See *ibid.*, pp. 308–9.
204. Even though its Article 6 granted to non-nationals effective protection and the right to seek remedies through competent local courts against acts of racial discrimination; *ibid.*, p. 310.
205. See *ibid.*, pp. 310–14; and for alien protection in provisions prohibiting acts contrary to human rights, see *ibid.*, p. 314.
206. *Barcelona Traction* case (Second Phase), *ICJ Reports* [1970] p. 33, para. 37.
207. Dunn, *Protection of Nationals*, pp. 161, esp. pp. 1, 20, 33, 35, 40, 53 and 58; Borchard, *Diplomatic Protection*, p. 350; C. Eagleton, *The Responsibility of States*, pp. 206 and 219/221; C. Parry, 'Some Considerations',

pp. 695–6; Ch. de Visscher, *Théories et réalités*, p. 299; E. Staley, *op. cit.*, pp. 541–2; Falk, *op. cit.*, pp. 175–6.

208. O'Connell, *op. cit.*, 1031.

209. Castrén, 'Some Considerations', p. 40 and n. 19; Przetacznik, *op. cit.*, p. 113.

210. With particular reference to the question of distribution of indemnities; cf. Berlia, 'Contribution', pp. 70 and 72; and, more cautiously than Berlia, Paul de Visscher, *op. cit.*, pp. 158–9.

211. Amerasinghe, *State Responsibility*. pp. 4–6, 12–22 and 25–6, for his advocacy of 'Westernalization' of developing 'uncommitted nations' (through flow of (protected) foreign private investment), reflected in his conclusions (*ibid.*, pp. 270, 279–80 and 284–6). While he concedes that enforceable human rights law may render the law of alien treatment 'theoretically superfluous' (*ibid.*, p. 5), he goes on to state, in an apparent contradiction, that the relation between the minimum standard of alien treatment and human rights is one of 'mutual interaction rather than that the latter determines the former' (*ibid.*, p. 279). It is not made clear whether the relation between the two systems is one of constant mutual interaction or one of gradual subsuming of one system into another. It might be that it is neither, for if it is admitted that the two systems are based upon different premises one can hardly speak of a parallelism between them. Amerasinghe's view that 'the declared conceptions of basic human rights represent a legally binding standard in regard to aliens' (*ibid.*, pp. 279–80) may be objected to on the ground that 'declared conceptions of basic human rights' aim at aliens as well as nationals, irrespective of nationality; furthermore, it is hard to see a 'standard' being 'legally binding', as a 'standard' is usually resorted to in the absence or insufficiency of positive legal rules on a given matter. The author's assertion that 'the position of the alien is somewhat different from that of a national, in that he is an alien and his position brings into play an international or non-national element which *vis-à-vis* the State may properly require special treatment by that very fact' (*ibid.*, p. 284) begs the question. On Amerasinghe's attempted justification of the *status quo* of traditional law on alien treatment, see *ibid.*, pp. 25–6: his reliance on the so-called 'intrinsic nature of all rules of law' does not seem to take into account that legal rules do not exist in the void, as they are a human product and a response to human needs and purposes. Amerasinghe's minimization of diplomatic protection as a product of nineteenth-century economic expansionism (cf. *ibid.*, p. 24), has little support in legal writing (cf. *supra*, particularly, *inter alia*, F.S. Dunn, *Protection of Nationals*, pp. 1–66) and State practice (cf., e.g., OAS doc. OEA/Ser. I/VI. 2 – CIJ–61, Inter-American Juridical Committee, *Contribution of the American Continent to the Principles of International Law that Govern the Responsibility of the State*, Washington, OAS General Secretariat, January 1962, ch. II, pp. 3–5).

212. Castrén, *op. cit.*, p. 45.

213. Amerasinghe, *State Responsibility*, p. 23.

214. A hypothesis envisaged by R.A. Falk, *The Status of Law in International Society*, Princeton, University Press, 1970, p. 427 (in relation to substantive rules of State responsibility for injury to alien interests).

215. As invoked by C.F. Amerasinghe, *State Responsibility*, p. 23.

216. As in *ibid.*, p. 23. In this connection, in the opening paragraph of a report to the *Institut de Droit International*, Borchard referred to the probable 'feudal origin' of diplomatic protection (deriving from reciprocal obligations of protection and allegiance), an institution developed in a period of 'intense individualism and *laisser-faire*', being a consequence not of those two elements, but of 'une forme primitive d'organisation du clan et d'une institution sociale primitive qui considérait un dommage à un membre du clan comme un dommage causé au clan lui-même et justifiant une vengeance collective'. E.M. Borchard, First Draft Report on 'Protection diplomatique des nationaux à l' étranger', 36 *Annuaire de l'Institut de Droit International* [1931]–1, p. 256, and see pp. 257–60 on the Vattelian axiom.

217. In support of the allegedly 'primitive character' of international law, see, for example, H. Kelsen, *Pure Theory of Law* (trans. from 2nd German edn by M. Knight), Berkeley/L.A., University of California Press, 1967, p. 323 (paragraph under the heading 'international law as a primitive legal order'); and, in the same sense, see P. Guggenheim, *Traité de Droit international public*, vol. I, 2nd edn, Geneva, Georg & Cie., 1967, pp. 22–3; and also Georges Scelle, 'Théorie et pratique de la fonction exécutive en Droit international', 55 *Recueil des Cours de l'Académie de Droit International* [1936]–1, p. 164. But, *a contrario sunsu*, contesting or denying the allegedly 'primitive nature' of international law, see, e.g.: M. Virally, 'Sur la pretendue "primitivité" du Droit international', in *Recueil des Travaux* [1969], Assemblée de la Société Suisse des Juristes, pp. 201–13; and also R. Ago, *Scienza Giuridica e Diritto Internazionale*, Milano, Giuffrè, 1950, pp. 106–8 (in relation to his thesis of a 'spontaneous' process of creation of norms of international law). For a general discussion, see, e.g., H. Lauterpacht, *The Function of Law in the International Community*, Oxford, Clarendon Press, 1933, Ch. XX, pp. 399–438; G.A. Walz, *Esencia del Derecho Internacional y Crítica de sus Negadores*, Madrid, ed. Rev. de Derecho Privado, 1943, pp. 1 seq.

218. Amerasinghe's views on State responsibility for injuries to aliens and diplomatic protection (cf., *supra*, p. 307) have met with some opposition (cf., e.g., on the ground *inter alia* of changes in relations between the individual and the State, Guha Roy, *op. cit.*, pp. 871–5, 881, 885 and 888). To sum up, Amerasinghe's assumptions are but a reassertion of the old doctrine of the international or minimum standard of alien treatment, just as much as García Amador's work reflects a certain tendency to favour the standard of equality of treatment between national and aliens (cf. *supra*, p. 304–5). But while García Amador at least takes due account of both standards, Amerasinghe's major work does not. From the start he contends that the objections of some developing countries to the international standard in relation to aliens "in reality amount to a recognition that there is an international standard for

the treatment of aliens which may or may not coincide with the previous content of that international standard, depending on whether the concept of human rights has accepted that or a lower standard" (Amerasinghe, *State Responsibility*, p. 19, and see pp. 43–5). One may only infer that the author's 'concept of human rights' stands on equal footing to the 'international standard' for treatment of aliens. More recently a similar reasoning has been followed by writers concerned with so-called foreign wealth 'deprivations'; see M.S. McDougal, H.D. Lasswell, L.-C. Chen, 'The Protection of Aliens from Discrimination and World Public Order: Responsibility of States Conjoined with Human Rights', 70 *American Journal of International Law* [1976] pp. 432–69; Lillich, 'The Problem of the Applicability', pp. 507–10; R.B. Lillich, 'The Diplomatic Protection of Nationals Abroad: an Elementary Principle of International Law under Attack', 69 *American Journal of International Law* [1975] pp. 359–65. These constructions are insufficiently penetrating, as, while on the substantive level they feel free to invoke 'human rights' of aliens as 'members of the world community', on the procedural level they rely on mechanisms of diplomatic protection, besides being wholly based on distinctions of nationality which are immaterial in human rights protection.

219. H. Lauterpacht, 'Boycott in International Relations', 14 *British Yearbook of International Law* [1933] p. 134; and see pp. 127, 130, 134–5, 138 and 140 for his further remarks on the problem in relation to the topic at issue.

220. W. Friedmann, 'The Growth of State Control over the Individual, and Its Effect upon the Rules of International State Responsibility', 19 *British Yearbook of International Law* [1938] pp. 118–50. The basic assumptions of Amerasinghe's study of 1967 (*supra*) contrast sharply with Friedmann's early warning that 'it is not for the lawyer to determine the political and social structure of the society which provides the basis for legal rules. The law cannot ignore social change beyond a certain point, for no law can command respect which bases its rules on the society of yesterday' (*ibid.*, p. 148).

221. Cf. H. Rolin, 'Les principes de droit international public', 77 *Recueil des cours de l'Académie de Droit International* [1950] pp. 441–53 and 456–7; see also Berlia, 'De la responsabilité internationale', pp. 875–94.

222. P. Weis, 'Diplomatic Protection of Nationals and International Protection of Human Rights', 4 *Revue des droits de l'homme/Human Rights Journal* [1971] pp. 643–78; Weis, *Nationality and Statelessness*, pp. 35–49; C. Joseph, *Nationality and Diplomatic Protection – The Commonwealth of Nations*, Leiden, Sijthoff, 1969, pp. 4–7 and 236/237; H.F. Van Panhuys, *The Role of Nationality in International Law*, Leiden, Sijthoff, 1959, pp. 224–7.

223. P.N. Drost, *Human Rights as Legal Rights*, Leiden, Sijthoff, 1965, pp. 133–4. In the traditional system, the individual enjoyed a larger measure of protection by international law in his capacity as an alien than as a citizen of his own State (however paradoxical that might appear); Lauterpacht, *International Law*, p. 121.

224. Weis, 'Diplomatic Protection', p. 675; G. Sperduti, 'Protezione Interna-zionale dei Diritti Umani', *Enciclopedia del Diritto*, vol. XII, Milano, Giuffrè, 1964, p. 820; K. Vasak, 'Egoisme et droits de l'homme', *Mélanges offerts à Polys Modinos*, Paris, Pédone, 1968, pp. 366–7. Treaties could produce effects *erga omnes* (create objective law) also in areas other than human rights protection; for examples, see A.D. McNair, 'Treaties Producing Effects *"Erga Omnes"*', *Scritti di Dirito Internazionale in Onore di T. Perassi*, vol. II, Milano, Giuffrè, 1957, pp. 23–6; but see, *contra*, Ph. Cahier, 'Le problème des effects des traités à l'égard des États tiers', 143 *Recueil des Cours de l'Académie de Droit International* [1974] pp. 589–736.
225. Ph. C. Jessup, *A Modern Law of Nations – An Introduction*, N. Macmillan Co., 1948, ch. V, pp. 94–122.
226. See Cançado Trindade, 'Exhaustion of Local Remedies in International Law Experiments Granting Procedural Status to Individuals', pp. 373–92.
227. Ph. C. Jesssup, *Modern Law*, pp. 94–122. Koessler tried to approach diplomatic protection not on the ground of the Vattelian dogma (offence to the State), but as a substitute for the individual's inaccessability to an international forum; M. Koessler, 'Government Espousal of Private Claims before International Tribunals', 13 *University of Chicago Law Review* [1946] pp. 180–94; and see also Borchard, First Draft Report on 'Protection diplomatique', p. 256; F.G. Dawson and I.L. Head, *International Law, National Tribunals and the Rights of Aliens*, Syracuse, University Press, 1971, pp. 109–10 (on theories on the accessability of *local* (foreign) tribunals to aliens in particular).
228. Ph. C. Jessup, *Modern Law*, ch. IV, p. 90.
229. See discussion in, e.g., J.E.S. Fawcett, 'General Course on Public International Law', 132 *Recueil des Cours de l'Académie de Droit International* [1971] pp. 530–5; D.R. Shea, *The Calvo Clause*, Minneapolis, University of Minnesota Press, 1955, pp. 119, 223–6, and 282–4; and, in general, H.B. Jacobini, *A Study of the Philosophy of International Law as Seen in the Works of Latin American Writers*, The Hague, M. Nijhoff, 1954, pp. 56–72, 79–86, 98–120 and 140.
230. E.g., the 1966 UN Covenants on Human Rights (and Protocol) only came into force in 1976. The sole effective human rights treaty in force until then, the one producing concrete results, the European Convention on Human Rights, operates regionally among States in homogeneous or approximate degrees of economic development, sharing similar cultural orders and a common heritage of liberal values and principles crystallized throughout centuries of historical and political development. Cf. Introduction, *supra*, pp. 1–5.
231. E.g., contracts of foreign investment; cf. K. Doehring, 'Does General International Law Require Domestic Judicial Protection against the Executive?', in *Gerichtsschutz gegen die Exekutive/Judicial Protection Against the Executive*, vol. 3, Max-Planck-Institut für ausländisches offentliches Recht und Völkerrecht, Köln, Heymanns/Oceana, 1971, pp. 233–4.
232. By virtue of Article 26 of the 1966 IBRD Convention on the Settlement of Investment Disputes between States and Nationals of Other States,

the local remedies rule is excluded unless expressly invoked. Cf. text, and *Report of the Executive Directors*, in 4 *International Legal Materials* [1965] pp. 528–9 and 532–44. The Convention, in accepting the right of the individual (investor) 'to pursue his own independent international remedies', acknowledges the possibility of 'non-parallel' developments in alien treatment and human rights protection. On individual protection under the World Bank Convention, cf. E. Lauterpacht, 'The World Bank Convention on the Settlement of International Investment Disputes', *Recueil d'études de droit international en hommage à Paul Guggenheim*, Geneva, Fac. Dr. Univ. de Genève/I.H.E.I., 1968, p. 664. Furthermore, in the World Bank Convention system the granting of direct access to an international jurisdiction to individual investors operates a considerable mitigation of the exercise by their State of diplomatic protection (Article 27(1) *in fine* of the Convention realistically abandons the Vattelian dogma, virtually in its entirety). But the fact remains that the system is not one of protection of the individual *qua* individual, but rather of the individual in his limited capacity as foreign investor, what may to some extent remain an ironical situation.

233. Application n. 788/60, *Austria* v. *Italy* case, *Report of the Plenary Commission* (adopted on 31 March 1963), Council of Europe doc. A–84–548, Strasbourg, 1963, p. 42.

234. *Ibid.*, pp. 42–3.

235. *Ibid.*, p. 43.

236. The problem is studied in detail in Ch. 4, *infra*, on the extent of application of the rule of exhaustion of local remedies (cf. particularly section 1 of that chapter).

237. Appl. n. 788/60, *Austria* v. *Italy* case, *Report*, p. 44; the Commission thereby rejected the Austrian contention that the local remedies rule was not applicable to applications lodged by States (under Article 24); cf. *ibid.*, p. 45. It should not pass unnoticed that, in the *Golder* case (Commission's Opinion, 1973), the Commission dismissed as 'not particularly relevant' in the context of human rights protection under the Convention the respondent government's arguments on the basis of analogies with commercial treaties intended to guarantee the right of access to domestic courts to aliens and nationals alike. Appl. n. 4451/70, *Golder* case, *Report*, p. 34.

238. While the agent for the government of Israel, Mr Rosenne, argued that the act complained of constituted a direct injury to the State of Israel and that therefore the Bulgarian exception of non-exhaustion of local remedies should be rejected, the agent for the Bulgarian government, Professor Cot, contended that the local remedies rule did apply, as the question of reparation for injury caused to individual victims of the incident should first be submitted to Bulgarian courts. *Aerial Incident of 27 July 1955* case (Israel v. Bulgaria); Pleadings, Oral Arguments, Documents; *ICJ Reports* [1959] pp. 530–1 and 448–9, respectively. As for the so-called 'link theory' invoked in the case, cf. Mr Rosenne's remarks, *ibid.*, pp. 531–2, and Professor Cot's remarks, *ibid.*, pp. 565–74; and cf. further T. Meron, 'The Incidence of the Rule of

Exhaustion of Local Remedies', 35 *British Yearbook of International Law* [1959] pp. 94–6 (on the 'link theory'); *Nottebohm* case, *ICJ Reports* [1955] pp. 22–3 and 26 ('real and effective nationality'); *Mergé* case (1955), *Reports of International Arbitral Awards*, vol. XIV, pp. 246–7 (dominant or effective nationality, in case of dual nationality); F.A. Mann, 'The Doctrine of Jurisdiction in International Law', 111 *Recueil des Cours de l'Académie de Droit International* [1964] pp. 9–158, for criticism of the Huber-Storyan territorial approach to jurisdiction and support for the 'close-connection' approach.

239. On the alien's submission to local law counterbalanced by his State's power over him (allegiance), see Borchard, *Diplomatic Protection*, pp. 817–18 and 354, respectively; D.R. Mummery, 'The Content of the Duty to Exhaust Local Judicial Remedies', 58 *American Journal of International Law* [1964] pp. 390–5. Today, with the increasing vulnerability of the territorial State, which is benefited by the local remedies rule, some changes are expected to be undergone by general rules which helped to shape customary international law. It is not difficult to conceive of injuries inflicted in violation of international law by one State upon nationals of another State who are not in the territory of the former. Would the injured individuals have to exhaust local remedies in the courts of the offending State before a claim could be pursued on their behalf? The local remedies rule would seem to apply, traditionally, only in cases where the *locus* of the injury to the individuals was the territory of the respondent State; C. Parry, 'Some Considerations', p. 688; for the 'dis-localization' of the local remedies rule' cf. T. Meron, *op. cit.*, pp. 97–101. And on this problem, cf. discussion in Ch. 2 on the application or otherwise of the local remedies rule in the adjustment of environmental disputes (*supra*, pp. 127–8).

240. Cf. in this sense statement by Mr Fawcett, Commission's delegate, in European Court of Human Rights, *Matznetter* case, Series B, Pleadings, Oral Arguments and Documents, p. 236. And see further on this particular point the pleadings before the Court in the *Stögmüller* case (1969, Series B).

241. Cf. in this sense statements by Mr Pahr, Austria's counsel, in European Court, *Matznetter*, Series B, Pleadings, pp. 225–6; and statements by Mr Nattel, Austria's agent, *ibid.*, Series B, pp. 239–40. And see further on this point the pleadings in the *Stögmüller* case (1969, Series B).

242. A problem discussed in detail in Ch. 5, *supra*, on the time factor in the application of the rule of exhaustion of local remedies.

243. Mr Nettel's statement in European Court of Human Rights, *Matznetter* case, Series B, Pleadings, pp. 244–5.

244. *Ibid.*, p. 244.

245. Mr Eustathiades's statement, in European Court of Human Rights, *Matznetter* case, Series B, Pleadings, p. 245; in the same sense, cf. the author's statements in *Yearbook of the International Law Commission* [1969]–I, pp. 114–15, para. 11; and C. Th. Eustathiades, 'Les sujets du Droit, pp. 538 and 600.

246. On the joinder of the question to the merits, see, e.g., G. Sperduti, 'La

recevabilité des exceptions préliminaires de fond dans le procès international', 53 *Rivista di Diritto Internazionale* [1970] pp. 461−90.

247. Eustathiades's pleadings, *Matznetter* case, p. 245.

248. Cf. Mr Nettel's pleadings, *Matznetter* case, pp. 245−6.

249. See considerations *infra*, and, for an earlier treatment of this particular question, cf. Witenberg, 'La récevabilité des réclamations', p. 51; see also K. Vasak, *La Convention européenne*, p. 115, para. 220.

250. European Court of Human Rights, *Matznetter* case, Series A, judgment of 10 November 1969, 'As to the facts', p. 26.

251. 'As to the law'.

252. A problem discussed in detail in Ch. 5, *supra*, on the time factor in the application of the local remedies rule.

253. European Court of Human Rights, *Stögmüller* case, Series A, judgment of 10 November 1969, 'As to the law', p. 42, para. 11; *ibid.*, *Matznetter* case, Series A, 1969, 'As to the law', p. 32, para. 6.

254. European Court of Human Rights, *Stögmüller* case, Series A, 1969, 'As to the law', p. 42, para. 12; *ibid.*, *Matznetter* case, Series A, 1969, 'As to the law', p. 32, para. 6.

255. For example, in the so-called *First Greek* case (appls. ns. 3321/67, 3322/67, 3323/67, 3344/67, Denmark/Norway/Sweden/Netherlands v. Greece), the Commission, declaring the applications admissible on 24 January 1968, held that 'the provision of Article 26 of the Convention concerning the exhaustion of domestic remedies did not apply to the present applications, the object of which was to determine the compatibility with the Convention of legislative measures and administrative practices': *Yearbook of the European Convention on Human Rights*, vol. 12, p. 21; but see further discussion on this point in the Commission's second decision on admissibility (of 31 May 1968) in the case, in *ibid.*, vol. 12, pp. 21−4.

256. See Ch. 4 on the extent of application of the rule of exhaustion of local remedies, section II on the local remedies rule in relation to legislative measures and administrative practices (*supra*, pp. 187−212).

257. Appl. n. 5310/71, *Ireland* v. *United Kingdom* case, decision of 1 October 1972, *Collection of Decisions of the European Commission of Human Rights*, vol. 41, p. 84.

258. *Ibid.*, p. 85.

259. E. Spatafora, 'La Regola del Previo Esaurimento dei Ricorsi Interni nella Giurisprudenza della Commissione Europea dei Diritti dell'Uomo', 11 *Rivista di Diritto Europeo* [1971] p. 111. For a critical view of the operation of the 'collective guarantee' under the Convention, see Virally, 'L'accès des particuliers', pp. 76−7 and 86.

260. G. Perrin, 'Organisation judiciaire interne et protection des ressortissants étrangers en Droit international', 24 *Revue juridique et politique − Indépendance et coopération* [1970] pp. 52−3; and see p. 64 for the view that protection of aliens' rights and of human rights lies primarily in the domestic legal system. Years earlier, García Amador remarked that while 'the entire traditional theory of diplomatic protection rests on the

premise that no international action whatsoever could be taken by the individual and that, after the exhaustion of local remedies, the individual was completely without recourse if the State from which he has claimed reparation denied him justice', the situation become a different one when States voluntarily agreed 'to the appearance of their nationals as direct claimants before international bodies'. F.V. García Amador, Third Report on State Responsibility for Injuries to Aliens, *Yearbook of the International Law Commission* [1958]−II, p. 63, para. 9.

261. J.H.W. Verzijl, Preliminary Report on 'La règle de l'épuisement des recours internes', 45 *Annuaire de l'Institut de Droit International* [1954]−I, pp. 5−33, and Definitive Report, 45 *Annuaire I.D.I.* [1954]−I, pp. 84−III, and Supplementary Report, 46 *Annuaire I.D.I.* [1956] pp. 1−20; A. Bagge, 'Intervention on the Ground of Damage Caused to Nationals, with Particular Reference to Exhaustion of Local Remedies and the Rights of Shareholders', 34 *British Yearbook of International Law* [1958] p. 169; Brownlie, *op. cit.*, p. 483; J.H. Ralston, *International Arbitration from Athens to Locarno*, Stanford, University Press, 1929, pp. 60−1.

262. Cf., in this sense, e.g., C.F. Amerasinghe, 'The Rule of Exhaustion of Local Remedies and the International Protection of Human Rights', 17 *Indian Yearbook of International Affairs* [1974] pp. 7−8 and 13.

263. For the view that the reference to general international law contained in Article 26 of the European Convention on Human Rights is rather 'unfortunate' for its ambiguity and the uncertainties it gives rise to, see E. Ruiloba Santana, 'La Regla del Agotamiento de los Recursos Internos a través de las Decisiones de la Comisión Europea de los Derechos del Hombre', in *Estudios de Derecho Internacional Publico y Privado − Libro-Homenaje al Profesor Luis Sela Sampil*, Universidad de Oviedo, 1970, pp. 471−3.

264. Cf., in this sense, e.g., Weis, 'Diplomatic Protection of Nationals', pp. 675−8.

265. ICJ, Advisory Opinion on the *Legal Consequences for States of the Continued Presence of South Africa in Namibia (South West Africa) notwithstanding Security Council Resolution 276 (1970)*, 21 June 1971, *ICJ Reports* [1971] pp. 31, 33, 46, 55 and 57, paras. 53, 59, 92, 122 and 131 (rights of peoples); Dissenting Opinions of Judges Tanaka and Jessup, *South West Africa* cases, *ICJ Reports* [1966], 18 July 1966, pp. 250−324 and 325−442, respectively; ICJ, Advisory Opinion on the *International Status of South West Africa* [1950], 11 July 1950, pp. 136−7; ICJ, Advisory Opinion on the *Admissibility of Hearings of Petitioners by the Committee on South West Africa, ICJ Reports* [1956], 1 June 1956, p. 27; ICJ, Advisory Opinion on *Reservations to the Convention on the Prevention and Punishment of the Crime of Genocide, ICJ Reports* [1951], 28 May 1951, p. 23 (humanitarian principles underlying the Convention being recognized as 'binding on States, even without any conventional obligation'); ICJ, Advisory Opinion on *Reparation for Injuries Suffered in the Service of the United Nations, ICJ Reports* [1949], 11 April 1949, pp. 174−88; *Corfu Channel* case, *ICJ Reports* [1949], judgment of 9 April 1949, p. 22; *North Sea Continental Shelf* cases, *ICJ Reports* [1969], 20 February 1969, pp.

38–45; *Barcelona Traction* (Second Phase) case, *ICJ Reports* [1970], judgment of 5 February 1970, p. 32, paras, 33–5 (obligations *erga omnes* and rights of protection entering the *corpus* of general international law), and Separate Opinions of Judges Gros and Morelli, *ibid.*, pp. 273–4 and 232, respectively. And see comments in, e.g., Sir Hersch Lauterpacht, *The Development of International Law by the International Court*, London, Stevens, 1958, pp. 176 and 182; L. Martínez-Agulló, 'El Agotamiento de los Recursos Internos y el Caso de la "Barcelona Traction"', 23 *Revista Española de Derecho Internacional* [1970] pp. 364–74. In addition, it should not pass unnoticed that in the recent *Nuclear Tests* case (Australia and New Zealand v. France) one of the applicant governments contended *inter alia* that the nuclear testing undertaken by the French government in the South Pacific region violated not only the right of New Zealand that no radioactive material enter its territory, air space and territorial waters *and* those of other Pacific territories but *also* 'the rights of all members of the international community, including New Zealand, that no nuclear tests that give rise to radioactive fallout be conducted'; *Application Instituting Proceedings*, filed in the Registry of the International Court of Justice on 9 May 1973, *Nuclear Tests* case (New Zealand v. France), pp. 4–16, esp. pp. 8 and 15–16. For a recent discussion of this case, with references to principles of traditional diplomatic protection as well as human rights protection, see, e.g., W.P. Gormley, *Human Rights and Environment: the Need for International Co-operation*, Leiden, Sijthoff, 1976, ch. 6, pp. 151–3, 158, 163–4 and 175.

266. Cf. Eustathiades, 'Les sujets du Droit', pp. 594–5 and 606–7 and n. 2.
267. Ivan L. Head, 'A Fresh Look at the Local Remedies Rule', 5 *Canadian Yearbook of International Law* [1967] p. 155.
268. A. Sarhan, 'L'épuisement des recours internes en matière de responsabilité internationale' (thesis), Université de Paris, 1962, pp. 536–42 (mimeographed).
269. In League of Nations doc. C. 75.M.69.1929.V, p. 67. However, it was the same jurist who, on another occasion, took a completely different stand on the matter. In the course of the *Mavrommatis* case, the question arose whether an injury to a Greek national constituted a dispute between the mandatory power for Palestine (Great Britain) and the other member State of the League (for the purposes of the British mandate over Palestine, Article 26). On behalf of the United Kingdom, Sir Cecil Hurst contended that the issue in question was not a dispute between two States but rather one between a State and a private person (cf., for the Court's *dictum,* PCIJ, Series A, n. 2, p. 12). On the other hand, the Greek contention, put forward by Mr Politis, was to the effect that the Greek government had taken up the cause of its national and made of it its own cause (cf. PCIJ, Series C, n. 5–1, p. 51). Mr Politis was *here* quite successful. . .
270. This point is of course related to the nature of the local remedies rule; for a recent discussion, see Cançado Trindade, 'The Birth of State Responsibility', pp. 157–88.
271. Head, *op. cit.*, pp. 142–58, esp. pp. 150 and 156.

272. Drost, *op. cit.*, pp. 87, 90, 117–20 and 122–4 and 133–4; Drost held a minority view. In criticizing diplomatic protection as inadequate for protection of individuals *vis-à-vis* their own government (*ibid.*, p. 133), Drost seems to have taken for granted, as many other writers have done (sometimes reaching opposite conclusions as to the applicability of the local remedies rule), that diplomatic protection and human rights protection were necessarily intermingled.

273. J. Guinand, 'La règle de l'épuisement des voies de recours internes dans le cadre des systèmes internationaux de protection des droits de l'homme', 4 *Revue belge de Droit International* [1968] p. 472, see also pp. 475–6; and, for a doctrinal misconception, see pp. 483–4 and n. 43.

274. Cf. *ibid.*, pp. 483–4.

275. Ténékidès, 'L'épuisement', pp. 514–35, esp. pp. 534–5.

276. H. Friedmann, 'Épuisement des voies de recours internes', 14 *Revue de Droit international et de législation comparée* [1933] pp. 319–23.

277. *Ibid.*, pp. 319–20 and 323.

278. The proposition that the application of the rule ought to be a *proper* one (with due account taken of the context in which it operates) seems largely acceptable, but it does not amount to stating that its application ought to be always a loose or relative one, as H. Friedmann seems to convey (*ibid.*, pp. 319–20), later supported by Chappez (J. Chappez, *La Règle de l'épuisement des voies de recours internes*, Paris, Pédone, 1972, p. 204). H. Friedmann's views may be supported in that the local remedies rule cannot and ought not to have a rigid or mechanical application in any circumstances, but it is hard to endorse his identification of the 'mechanical' conception with the substantive view (*supra*) of the rule, propounded as the rule historically evolved within the system of diplomatic protection. This fact is not pointed out by Chappez, who simply criticizes the extension of the scope of the rule to comprise local *procedural* remedies as well (cf. *Ambatielos* award, *supra*). But perhaps in the context of diplomatic protection that extension was not so objectionable as it is sometimes depicted. What seems to be much more open to criticism is the transposition of that extended scope from the system of diplomatic protection (in which it was formulated) into the system of human rights protection (as the European Commission of Human Rights has done – cf. *supra*, Ch. 2 – in a rather unqualified way).

279. Eagleton, *Responsibility of States*, pp. 95–102; Eagleton, 'Une théorie', p. 658; Eagleton, 'Denial of Justice', p. 558 (the local remedies rule as a means of reconciling State sovereignty and international law).

280. Freeman, *International Responsibility*, p. 452.

281. Ch. de Visscher, 'La responsabilité', p. 115; Ch. de Visscher, 'Le déni de justice', pp. 421–32.

282. Cf. D. Anzilotti, 'La responsabilité internationale des États à raison des dommages soufferts par des étrangers', 13 *Revue générale de Droit international public* [1906] pp. 5–29 and 285–309; D. Anzilotti, *Cours de droit international* (trans. G. Gidel), Paris, Rec. Sirey, 1929, pp. 466–534.

283. Cf. R. Ago, 'Le délit international', 68 *Recueil des Cours de l'Académie de Droit International* [1939] pp. 419–545; R. Ago, 'Observations [sur la

règle de l'épuisement des recours internes]', 45 *Annuaire de l'Institut de Droit International*, [1954]–I, pp. 34–45; Ago, 'La Regola del Previo Esaurimento', pp. 181–249; R. Ago, Second Report on State Responsibility, *Yearbook of the International Law Commission* [1970]–II, pp. 421–32. On Ago's theory, see discussion with regard to the local remedies rule in Cançado Trindade, 'The Birth of State Responsibility', pp. 157–88.

284. See his classical statement, pointing out five 'practical' reasons for the application of the rule, in Borchard, *Diplomatic Protection*, pp. 817–18; E.M. Borchard, 'Theoretical Aspects of the International Responsibility of States', I *Zeitschrift für ausländisches öffentliches Recht und Völkerrecht* [1929] pp. 240–1.

285. Cf., in this sense, the critical remarks by J.E.S. Fawcett, 'The Exhaustion of Local Remedies: Substance or Procedure?', 31 *British Yearbook of International Law* [1954] p. 452; Amerasinghe, *State Responsibility*, pp. 171–2 and 201–2.

286. Those of the alien, of the 'respondent' State, of the alien's State, in sum, the general interests of all concerned in having the dispute settled peacefully, fairly and efficiently, with tensions minimized as much as possible.

287. See, for example, C.H.P. Law, *The Local Remedies Rule in International Law*, Geneva, Droz, 1961, pp. 15–19 and 147–8; C.P. Panayotacos, *La Règle de l'épuisement des voies de recours internes*, Marseille, Moullot, 1952, pp. 21–30 and 113–14; Sarhan, *op. cit.*, pp. 178–91, 287 and 536–42; Chappez, *op. cit.*, pp. 25–9, 72–83 and 239–43.

288. See, for example, Law, *op. cit.*, pp. 19 and 148; Chappez, *op. cit.*, pp. 239–43; somewhat dogmatically, Sarhan, *op. cit.*, pp. 536–42; and, without dwelling upon the human rights system, T. Haesler, *The Exhaustion of Local Remedies in the Case-Law of International Courts and Tribunals*, Leiden, Sijthoff, 1968, pp. 150–6.

289. Cf. Chappez, *op. cit.*, pp. 175, 177 and 232.

290. Cf. *ibid.*, pp. 212 and 226

291. Cf. *ibid.*, p. 234.

292. Cf. *ibid.*, pp. 204 and 206.

293. Cf. *ibid.*, pp. 163–72.

294. Cf. *ibid.*, pp. 175 and 183.

295. Cf. *ibid.*, pp. 173, 177, 179, 185, 202–3 and 214.

296. As in *ibid.*, p. 175 (where the applicant is referred to as 'l'individu', even though not by reference to a case under the European Convention system); the point was made by Vallindas in 46 *Annuaire de l'Institut de Droit International* [1956] p. 273.

297. K. Doehring's statement in *Human Rights in National and International Law* (ed. A.H. Robertson), Manchester, University Press/Oceana, 1970, p. 269.

298. For examples drawn from State practice, see Cançado Trindade, 'Origin and Historical Development', pp. 514–24 (nineteenth – and twentieth-century State practice); for the general practice on the matter, including arbitral and judicial settlement, see Chs. 2 to 6, *supra*.

299. Cf., e.g., L. of N. doc. C 75.M.69.1929. V; on the insertion of the rule in bilateral treaties, cf. Przetacznik, *op. cit.*, p. 106; Makarov, *op. cit.*, pp. 541–4 (non-uniformity of such treaty practice); G. Gaja, *L'Esaurimento dei Ricorsi Interni nel Diritto Internazionale*, Milano, Giuffrè, 1967, pp. 160–4, 172–9 and 219–21 (problems of application of the rule in treaty practice).

300. In this sense, Makarov refers to 'ciertas matizaciones y limitaciones' of the local remedies rule as a pre-condition, in principle, to the exercise of diplomatic protection: Makarov, *op. cit.*, p. 551.

301. E.g., insertion of the local remedies rule in Article 31 of the 1949 Revised General Act for the Pacific Settlement of International Disputes (restoring the General Act of 1928), as well as into Article 7 of the 1948 Inter-American Treaty on Pacific Settlement of Disputes (the so-called Pact of Bogotá); cf. text of those provisions *in* UN GA resolution 268(III) A, and *U.N.T.S.*, vol. 30, p. 55, respectively, both reproduced in van Panhuys (ed.), *International Organisation and Integration*, Leiden, Sijthoff/Kluwer, 1968, pp. 198 and 1064, respectively.

302. Haesler, *op. cit.*, pp. 23–5, esp. p. 24.

303. *Ibid.*, p. 25; and see Przetacznik, *op. cit.*, p. 112. In this connection, Zourek recalled the old practice of consular claims, addressed to local authorities before the taking of a final decision; they likewise had a *preventive* character in the protection of nationals, and consular authorities were 'in no way bound to wait until the party concerned has exhausted all internal remedies'; J. Zourek, 'Some Theoretical Problems of Consular Law', 90 *Journal du droit international* (Clunet) [1963] p. 55. Ch. de Visscher preferred to speak of 'rôle suspensif' rather than preventive character; cf. Ch. de Visscher, 'Observations [sur la règle de l'épuisement des recours internes]', 46 *Annuaire de l'Institut de Droit International* [1956] p. 49.

304. On this question, see A.A. Cançado Trindade, 'Exhaustion of Local Remedies', pp. 388–91 (on the practice of Mixed Arbitral Tribunals and Mixed Claims Commissions); and see also Ch. 2, section C, *supra*, on waiver of the local remedies rule.

305. N. Antonopoulos, *La Jurisprudence des organes de la Convention européenne des droits de l'homme*, Leiden, Sijthoff, 1967, pp. 258–60.

306. *Ibid.*, p. 71; see also p. 68.

307. F. Castberg, *The European Convention on Human Rights*, Leiden, Sijthoff/Oceana, 1974, p. 191. On his part, Weil ponders that the jurisprudence on the exhaustion of local remedies under the Convention is bound to be 'of significant importance not only for the evolution of the Convention itself but for international law in general'; G.L. Weil, *The European Convention on Human Rights*, Leiden, Sijthoff, 1963, p. 212.

308. See remarks in the Introduction *supra*, pp. 1–5, on the place of the local remedies rule in contemporary international law on human rights protection. But a word of caution is here necessary, as the preparatory work of the Convention, undertaken at different stages by different groups, is not clearly conclusive on all related points, also leaving a margin for some element of uncertainty.

309. Cf., e.g., the Commission's decision in the leading *Austria v. Italy* case (*supra*); and see further the chapters *supra* on the Commission's practice on the local remedies rule.

310. For example, in the *Panevezys – Saldutiskis Railway* case the Permanent Court of International Justice stated that 'there can be no need to resort to the municipal courts if those courts have no jurisdiction to afford relief; nor is it necessary again to resort to those courts if the result must be a repetition of a decision already given' (PCIJ, *Panevezys – Saldutiskis Railway* case, Series A/B, n. 76, p. 18; and see PCIJ, *Chorzòw Factory* case, Series A, n. 9, p. 31). And in the *Finnish Vessels* case (1934) arbitrator Bagge asserted *inter alia* that even when remedies are formally open to the parties, they need not be exhausted if recourse to them is 'obviously futile' (*Reports of International Arbitral Awards*, vol. III, p. 1503); exhaustion of local remedies is carried out in a normal rather than mechanical way. But see *supra* , for a study in detail of such problems in subsequent chapters devoted to the application of the local remedies rule in general international law as well as under the European Convention on Human Rights.

311. See *supra*, on the drafting of the local remedies rule provisions (Articles 26 and 27(3)) of the European Convention of Human Rights.

312. As already indicated *supra*, pp. 14–16, the very nature of rights and obligations ensuing from the Convention, for example, has been conceived as *not* implying a reciprocity of rights and duties among the the High Contracting Parties and as serving a general interest transcending the level of contractual relations between the States concerned. Cf., e.g., Commission's *Report* of 1973 of the *Golder* case (*supra*, p. 15), p. 31 of the Opinion; and cf. pertinent remarks, years earlier, in F. Monconduit, *La Commission européenne des droits de l'homme*, Leiden, Sijthoff, 1965, p. 305.

313. For a similar reference to general international law in provisions on the local remedies rule, see Article 41(1)(c) of the UN Covenant on Civil and Political Rights; Article 11(3) of the UN International Convention on the Elimination of All Forms of Racial Discrimination; Article 46(1)(a) of the 1969 American Convention on Human Rights. But that reference is not found in Article 4(b) of resolution 1(XXIV) of the UN Sub-Commission on Prevention of Discrimination and Protection of Minorities (pursuant to ECOSOC resolution 1503(XLVIII) of 1970), also on the application of the local remedies rule, to examination of communications on human rights violations received by the UN Secretary-General.

314. Cf., in this sense, e.g., Amerasinghe, 'The Rule of Exhaustion of Local Remedies and the International Protection', pp. 7–8 and 13.

315. Cf. Cançado Trindade, 'Exhaustion of Local Remedies in International Law Experiments', pp. 388–92, and cf. Ch. 2, section c, *supra*.

316. Article 41(1)(c).

317. Articles 11(3) and 14(7)(a).

318. See *supra*, on the drafting of those provisions. Further steps could well be taken in that direction, as indicated in subsequent chapters on the

application of the local remedies rule (cf. *supra*, Chs. 2–6).

319. E.g., Article 13 of the European Convention on Human Rights; Article 2(3) of the UN Covenant on Civil and Political Rights; Article 6 of the UN International Convention on the Elimination of All Forms of Racial Discrimination.

320. Unlike human rights protection, diplomatic protection 'does not throw a proper light on any obligation of the territorial State to provide remedies for cases of violation of such rights by other private persons, since aliens by the nature of their position in a foreign State do not possess full civil and political rights'; A.J.P. Tammes, 'the Obligation to Provide Local Remedies', in *Volkenrechtelijke Opstellen aangeboden aan Prof. G.H.J. van der Molen*, Kampen, 1962, p. 164; and on this last point, cf., to the same effect, Freeman, 'Human Rights', p. 123.

321. Tammes, *op. cit.*, pp. 164–8, 154 and 157; and, in the same sense, K. Doehring, 'Does General International Law Require Domestic Judicial Protection against the Executive?', in *Gerichtsschutz gegen die Exekutive/ Judicial Protection against the Executive*, vol. 3, Köln, C. Heymanns Oceana, 1971, pp. 242–4.

322. In Tammes's view, this occurs at the cost of diplomatic protection, or 'parallel to the decline of diplomatic protection in its original form'; Tammes, *op. cit.*, pp. 166–8.

323. See, further, Conclusions, *supra*, pp. 277–85.

324. Cançado Trindade, 'Exhaustion of Local Remedies in International Law Experiments', pp. 391–2.

Chapter 2

1. A.J.P. Tammes, 'The Obligation to Provide Local Remedies', in *Volkenrechtelijke Opstellen aangeboden aan Prof. G.H.J. van der Molen*, Kampen, 1962, pp. 152, 161 and 167–8.

2. *Interhandel* (Preliminary Objections) case, *ICJ Reports* [1959] p. 27; British memorial (n. 45) in *Finnish Vessels* case (1934), *Reports of International Arbitral Awards* (R.I.A.A.), vol. III, pp. 1495 and 1498–9; *Ambatielos* case (1956), *R.I.A.A.*, vol. XII, p. 119.

3. Judge Levi Carneiro's Dissenting Opinion in the *Anglo-Iranian Oil Company* case, *ICJ Reports* [1952] pp. 160 and 165; *Panevezys – Saldutiskis Railway* case, PCIJ, Series A/B, n. 76, 1939, p. 18; *Interocean Transportation Company of America* case (1937), *Annual Digest and Reports of Public International Law Cases* (A.D.R.P.I.L.C.) [1935–7] pp. 273–4; *Forests of Central Rhodopia* case (1933), *A.D.R.P.I.L.C.* [1933–4] pp. 94– 5, and R.I.A.A., vol. III, p. 1420; *R.T. Johson* v. *Peru* case (1870), *Moore's Digest*, vol. II, pp. 1656–7; *Robert E. Brown (U.S.)* v. *Great Britain* case (1923), *R.I.A.A.*, vol. VI, p. 129; *Italian Residents in Peru* case (Claim n. 44, 1901), *R.I.A.A.*, vol. XV, pp. 433–4; *Jesse Lewis (U.S.)* v. *Great Britain* case (1921), *R.I.A.A.*, vol. IV, pp. 89–90 and 93; *S.S. 'Segurança'* case (1939), *R.I.A.A.*, vol. III, p. 1869; *Orinoco Steamship Company* case (1903–5), *R.I.A.A.*, vol. IX, pp. 181 and 198. And, as to juristic writing, cf. E.M. Borchard, *The Diplomatic Protection of Citizens*

Abroad, New York, Banks Law Publ. Co., 1916, pp. 821–2; D. Anzilotti, *Cours de Droit International*, vol. i, Paris, Rec. Sirey, 1929, p. 482.

4. Cf. C. Eagleton, 'Denial of Justice in International Law', 22 *American Journal of International Law* [1928] pp. 544–5; F.G. Dawson and I.L. Head, *International Law, National Tribunals and the Rights of Aliens*, Syracuse University Press, 1971, pp. 214–15 n. 102; A. Miaja de la Muela, 'El Agotamiento de los Recursos Internos como Supuesto de las Reclamaciones Internacionales', 2 *Anuario Uruguayo de Derecho Internacional* [1963] pp. 33–4. And, for case-law corroborating the point above, see *El Oro Mining and Railway Company* case (1931), *R.I.A.A.*, vol. v, pp. 197–8; oral arguments in the *Phosphates in Morocco* case, PCIJ, Series C, n. 84, 1938, pp. 212–21, 440–52, 747–82, 696–7, 817–18, 840, and Series C, n. 85, 1938, pp. 1091–8, 1209–17, 1282 and 1330, and Series A/B, n. 74, 1938, pp. 28–9. For support of the above point in the 1930 Hague Conference for the Codification of International Law, see League of Nations doc. C. 75.M.69.1929.V, pp. 136–9, and L. of N. doc. C. 351(c).M.145(c).1930.V, pp. 61–2, 66–7 and 70–81.

5. *Finnish Vessels* case (1934), *R.I.A.A.*, vol. iii, p. 1497; *Marguerite de Joly de Sabla* case (1933), *R.I.A.A.*, vol. vi, pp. 361–3; *Davy* case (1903), J.H. Ralston's *Law and Procedure of International Tribunals* (rev. edn 1926), pp. 87–8 and 338–9; and see Borchard, *Diplomatic Protection*, pp. 824–5.

6. See mainly the *Finnish Vessels* case (1934), *R.I.A.A.*, vol. iii, pp. 1484–504 and 1543. See also *Ambatielos* case (1956) *R.I.A.A.*, vol. xii, pp. 119 ('obviously futile' remedies as the test for their ineffectiveness); France's arguments in the *Norwegian Loans* case, *ICJ Reports* [1957], Pleadings etc., pp. 408–10, and Judge Lauterpacht's Separate Opinion in the case, *ICJ Reports* [1957] p. 39. Among writers, see, e.g., L. Oppenheim, *International Law – A Treatise* (8th edn, ed. H. Lauterpacht), London, Longman, 1955, pp. 361–2; J.C. Witenberg, 'La recevabilité des réclamations devant les juridictions internationales', 41 *Recueil des Cours de l'Académie de Droit International* (R.C.A.D.I.) [1932] pp. 55–6; I. Brownlie, *Principles of Public International Law* (2nd. edn), Oxford, Clarendon Press, 1973, pp. 485–6; D.R. Mummery, 'The Content of the Duty to Exhaust Local Remedies', 58 *American Journal of International Law* [1964] pp. 400–4 and 409–14; Ch. Durand, 'La responsabilité internationale des États pour déni de justice', 38 *Revue générale de Droit international public* [1931] p. 707. And see I. Seidl-Hohenveldern, 'La sentence du Tribunal Arbitral Austro-Allemand concernant la protection diplomatique', 18 *Annuaire français de Droit international* [1972] pp. 323–6.

7. *Eliza* case (1863–4), A. De La Pradelle/N. Politis, *Recueil des arbitrages internationaux*, vol. ii, Paris, Éd. Internationales, 1957, pp. 271–6, and Moore's *Digest*, vol. ii, pp. 1630–7; *Yuille, Shortridge and Company* case (1861), De La Pradelle/Politis, *Recueil*, vol. ii, pp. 103–4 and 111–12; Belgium's argument in *Electricity Company of Sofia and Bulgaria* case, PCIJ, Series C, n. 88, 1939, pp. 427–9; *Interhandel* case, *ICJ Reports* [1959] pp. 26–9.

8. See mainly the *Ambatielos* case (1956), *R.I.A.A.*, vol. XII, pp. 83 *seq.*, esp. pp. 118–24, and see pp. 125–8 for the more cogent minority views of commissioners R. Alfaro and J. Spiropoulos.
9. Cf. the debates of the *Institut de Droit International*, in 45 *Annuaire I.D.I.* [1954]–I, pp. 60–1 and 70 (remarks by M. Bourquin and G.H. Hackworth), and 46 *Annuaire I.D.I.* [1956] pp. 314–15 and 364 (Institute's resolution expressly referring to the 'normal use' standard). As to case-law, see *Leichardt* case (1868), Moore's *Digest*, vol. III, p. 3134, and J.H. Ralston, *op. cit.*, p. 331; oral arguments in the *Norwegian Loans* case, *ICJ Reports* [1957], Pleadings etc., pp. 158, 161, 168, 186 and 188–9. Cf. also R. Ago, Second Report on State Responsibility, *Yearbook of the International Law Commission* [1970]–II, p. 183 para. 21.
10. See mainly the *Electricity Company of Sofia and Bulgaria* (Preliminary Objection) case, PCIJ, Series A/B, n. 77, 1939, pp. 74, 78–9, 135 (Dissenting Opinion Hudson), 107 (Diss. Op. Urrutia), 96–7 (Sep. Op. D. Anzilotti), 114–15 (Diss. Op. Van Eysinga), 144–5 (Sep. Op. Erich), 138–9 (Sep. Op. De Visscher), and Series C, n. 88, 1939, pp. 393, 427–9 and 432–3; see also: *C.G. Pirocaco* case (1923), Hackworth's *Digest*, vol. V, p. 502; *Salem* case (1932), *R.I.A.A.*, vol. II, p. 1189. And see further Article 18(2) of Garcia Amador's Revised Draft on State Responsibility for Injuries to Aliens, *Yearbook of the International Law Commission* [1961]–II, p. 48.
11. As exemplified in particular by the oral arguments in the *Barcelona Traction* case (1964 and 1969–70), ICJ, doc. Series C.R. 64/13, 26, 27, 29, and C.R. 69/20, 21, 40, 41, 63, and *ICJ Reports* [1970] pp. 26–30 and 51, and 57–63 (Sep. Op. Bustamante y Rivero), 143 (Sep. Op. Tanaka), 164 (Sep. Op. Jessup), and further remarks by other Judges on pp. 259–60, 284–5, 286–7, 322–5, 355–7.
12. European Commission of Human Rights, *The Nielsen Case – Report of the Commission* (appl. n. 343/57), decision of 2 September 1959, Council of Europe, Strasbourg, 1961, p. 37; and see p. 35 to the same effect.
13. *X* v. *Ireland* case (appl. n. 493/59), decision of 27 July 1961, *Collection of Decisions of the European Commission of Human Rights* (hereinafter referred to as *Collection*), vol. 7, p. 94, and, to the same effect, see p. 96.
14. *Lawless* v. *Ireland* case (appl. n. 332/57), decision of 30 August 1958, *Yearbook of the European Convention on Human Rights* (hereinafter referred to as *Yearbook*) [1958–9], vol. II, p. 322.
15. *Syndicat National de la Police Belge* v. *Belgium* case (appl. n. 4464/70), partial decision of 28 May 1971, *Collection*, vol. 39, p. 32.
16. Appl. n. 603/59 (1960), *Collection*, vol. 4, p. 5; appl. n. 844/60 (1961), *Collection*, vol. 7, p. 83; appl. n. 2300/64 (1967), *Collection*, vol. 22, pp. 81–2; appl. n. 3040/67 (1967), *Collection*, vol. 22, p. 137; appl. n. 2413 (1966), *Collection*, vol. 23, p. 7; appl. n. 2472/65 (1967), *Collection*, vol. 23, p. 47; appl. n. 2465/65 (1967), *Collection*, vol. 24, p. 62; appl. n. 3843/68 (1969), *Collection*, vol. 32, p. 35; appl. n. 3873/68 (1969), *Collection*, vol. 32, p. 45; appl. n. 3944/69 (1970), *Collection*, vol. 33, p. 6; appl. n. 4186/69 (1970), *Collection*, vol. 33, p. 33; appl. n. 4101/69 (1970), *Collection*, vol. 34, p. 41; appl. n. 4065/69 (1970), *Collection*, vol.

35, p. 120; appl. n. 4436/70 (1970), *Collection*, vol. 35, p. 172; appl. n. 4351/70 (1970), *Collection*, vol. 36, p. 86; appl. n. 4284/69 (1971), *Collection*, vol. 37, p. 76; appl. n. 5564/72 (1972), *Collection*, vol. 42, p. 122; appl. n. 5409/72 (1973), *Collection*, vol. 43, p. 157.

17. Appl. n. 2749/66 (1967), *Collection*, vol. 24, p. 110; appl. n. 3485/68 (1969), *Collection*, vol. 29, pp. 56–7; appl. n. 4036/69 (1970), *Collection*, vol. 32, pp. 74–5; appl. n. 4225/69 (1970), *Collection*, vol. 33, pp. 42–3; appl. n. 3898/68 (1970), *Collection*, vol. 35, p. 99; appl. n. 4133/69 (1970), *Collection*, vol. 36, pp. 63–4; appl. n. 4451/70 (1971), *Collection*, vol. 37, p. 132; appl. n. 4534/70 (1971), *Collection*, vol. 38, pp. 121–2; appl. n. 4471/70 (1972), *Collection*, vol. 39, p. 50; appl. n. 4798/71 (1972), *Collection*, vol. 40, p. 33; appl. n. 5282/71 (1972), *Collection*, vol. 42, p. 104; appl. n. 5197/71 (1972), *Collection*, vol. 42, p. 138; appl. n. 5608/72 (1973), *Collection*, vol. 44, p. 76.

18. Appl. n. 793/60 (1960), *Collection*, vol. 5, p. 3; appl. n. 1006/61 (1961), *Collection*, vol. 6, pp. 67–8; appl. n. 1103/61 (1962), *Collection*, vol. 8, p. 124; appl. n. 1488/62 (1963), *Collection*, vol. 13, p. 96; appl. n. 2322/64 (1967), *Collection*, vol. 24, pp. 41–2, appl. n. 2689/65 (1967), *Collection*, vol. 24, p. 84; appl. n. 4072/69 (1970), Collection, vol. 32, p. 85; appl. n. 4741/71 (1973), *Collection*, vol. 43, p. 18; appl. n. 6115/73 (1974), *Collection*, vol. 45, p. 123.

19. Appl. n. 596/59 (1960), *Collection*, vol. 5, p. 4; appl. n. 617/59 (1960), *Collection*, vol. 5, p. 12; appl. n. 833/60 (1960), *Collection*, vol. 5, pp. 7–8; appl. n. 1599/62 (1963), *Collection*, vol. 10, p. 6; appl. n. 1135/61 (1963), *Collection*, vol. 11, p. 22; appl. n. 1918/63 (1963), *Collection*, vol. 12, p. 119; appl. n. 4622/70 (1972), *Collection*, vol. 40, p. 19.

20. Appl. n. 1449/62 (1963), *Collection*, vol. 10, p. 2; appl. n. 2383/64 (1967), *Collection*, vol. 23, p. 30; appl. n. 5483/72 (1973), *Collection*, vol. 44, pp. 61–2.

21. Appl. n. 2358/64 (1967), *Collection*, vol. 23, p. 153; appl. n. 3788/68 (1970), *Collection*, vol. 35, pp. 71–3; appl. n. 5525/72 (1973), *Collection*, vol. 43, pp. 116–17.

22. Appl. n. 4144/69 (1970), *Collection*, vol. 33, p. 30; appl. n. 5288/71 (1973), *Collection*, vol. 44, p. 28.

23. Appl. n. 4764/71 (1971), *Collection*, vol. 39, p. 90.

24. Appl. n. 4210/69 (1970), *Collection*, vol. 35, pp. 149–50.

25. Appl. n. 4125/69 (1970), *Collection*, vol. 37, p. 41.

26. This was, to the Commission, a 'commonly admitted' position. Appl. n. 788/60, decision of 11 January 1961, *Austria v. Italy case – Report of the Plenary Commission* (adopted on 31 March 1963), Council of Europe, Strasbourg, 1963, p. 57.

27. Appl. 1727/62, *Boeckmans v. Belgium* case, decision of 29 October 1963, *Collection*, vol. 12, p. 47; appl. n. 4459/70, *Kaiser v. Austria* case, decision of 3 April 1971, *Collection*, vol. 38, p. 55.

28. Appl. n. 4802/71, *X v. F.R. Germany* case, decision of 5 October 1972, *Collection*, vol. 42, p. 40.

29. Appl. n. 4349/70, *X v. F.R. Germany* case, decision of 24 May 1971, *Collection*, vol. 38, p. 36.

30. Appl. n. 1197/61, *X* v. *F.R. Germany* case, decision of 5 March 1962, *Collection*, vol. 8, p. 72.
31. Appl. n. 493/59, *X* v. *Ireland* case, decision of 27 July 1961, *Collection*, vol. 7, pp. 94–7.
32. Appl. n. 232/56, *X* v. *F.R. Germany* case, decision of 15 July 1957, *Yearbook* [1955–7] vol. 1, p. 144. More recently, the Commission rejected another application for non-exhaustion, as the applicant, *inter alia*, had failed to appeal to the Danish General Social Welfare Board (*den sociale ankestyrelsen*); appl. n. 6854/74, *X* v. *Denmark* case, decision of 29 September 1976, *Decisions and Reports*, vol. 7, pp. 81–3.
33. J.E.S. Fawcett, *The Application of the European Convention on Human Rights*, Oxford, Clarendon Press, 1969, p. 295, and see pp. 300–1.
34. E. Ruiloba Santana, 'La Regla del Agotamiento de los Recursos Internos a través de las Decisiones de la Comisión Europea de los Derechos del Hombre', in *Estúdios de Derecho Internacional Público y Privado – Libro-Homenaje al Professor Luis Sela Sampil*, Universidad de Oviedo, 1970, p. 481.
35. 'La inclusión de este tipo de recursos', Ruiloba Santana observes, 'es una consecuencia lógica de la de los anteriores si se tiene en cuenta que normalmente en los sistemas jurídico-administrativos se exige que sea recorrida la vía administrativa, previamente al inicio de la acción contencioso-administrativa.' *Ibid.*, p. 481, and references quoted therein.
36. Text in *Human Rights: a Compilation of International Instruments of the United Nations*, UN doc. ST/HR/1, p. 8.
37. Appl. n. 214/56, *De Becker* v. *Belgium* case, decision of 9 June 1958, *Yearbook* [1958–9] vol. II, pp. 236–8, esp. p. 238.
38. Appl. n. 299/57, *Greece* v. *United Kingdom* case, decision of 12 October 1957, *Yearbook* [1958–9] vol. II, p. 192.
39. *Ibid.*, p. 192.
40. Appl. n. 458/59, *X* v. *Belgium* case, decision of 29 March 1960, *Yearbook* [1960] vol. III, p. 234.
41. C.F. Amerasinghe, 'The Rule of Exhaustion of Local Remedies and the International Protection of Human Rights', 17 *Indian Yearbook of International Affairs* [1974] pp. 40–4; C.F. Amerasinghe, 'The Rule of Exhaustion of Domestic Remedies in the Framework of International Systems for the Protection of Human Rights', 28 *Zeitschrift für ausländisches öffentliches Recht and Völkerrecht* [1968] pp. 286–7.
42. H. Danelius, 'Conditions of Admissibility in the Jurisprudence of the European Commission of Human Rights', 2 *Revue des droits de l'homme/Human Rights Journal* [1969] p. 292.
43. F. Castberg, *The European Convention of Human Rights*, Leiden, Sijthoff/Oceana, 1974, p. 42.
44. Fawcett, *Application of the European Convention*, p. 296.
45. Appl. n. 1094/61, *X* v. *Netherlands* case, decision of 4 October 1962, *Collection*, vol. 9, p. 44.
46. Appl. n. 4771/71, *Kamma* v. *Netherlands* case, decision of 30 May 1972, *Collection*, vol. 42, p. 19.

47. Appl. n. 4427/70, *X V. F.R. Germany* case, decision of 24 May 1971, *Collection*, vol. 38, p. 39.

48. Appl. n. 2358/64 *X* v. *Sweden* case, decision of 10 July 1967, *Collection*, vol. 23, p. 153.

49. Appl. n. 617/59, *Hopfinger* v. *Austria* case, decision of 19 December 1960, *Collection*, vol. 5, p. 12. Cf. also appl. 6289/73, *Airey* v. *Ireland* case, decision of 7 July 1977, *Decisions and Reports*, vol. 8, p. 48 (non-exhaustion of remedies under Irish law for failure to institute any civil proceedings against police officers); appl. n. 6694/74, *Artico* v. *Italy* case, decision of 1 March 1977, *Decisions and Reports*, vol. 8, pp. 88–9 (non-exhaustion for failure to claim compensation for alleged damage).

50. Appl. ns. 5351/72 and 6579/74 (joined), *X* v. *Belgium* case, decision of 18 July 1974, *Collection*, vol. 46, p. 83.

51. Appl. n. 596/59, *Pataki* v. *Austria* case, decision of 19 December 1960, *Collection*, vol. 5, p. 4.

52. Appl. n. 793/60, *X* v. *Belgium* case, decision of 21 December 1960, *Collection*, vol. 5, p. 3.

53. Appl. n. 1103/61, *X* v. *Belgium* case, decision of 12 March 1962, *Collection*, vol. 8, p. 124.

54. Appl. n. 1237/61, *X* v. *Austria* case, decision of 5 March 1962, *Collection*, vol. 8, p. 77.

55. Appl. n. 4072/69, *X* v. *Belgium* case, decision of 3 February 1970, *Collection*, vol. 32, p. 85.

56. Appl. n. 214/56, *De Becker* v. *Belgium* case, decision of 9 June 1958, *Yearbook* [1958–9] vol. II, pp. 236–8.

57. Appl. n. 5874/72, *Monika Berberich* v. *F.R. Germany* case, decision of 29 May 1974, *Collection*, vol. 46, p. 159. The Commission added: 'On the other hand, Article 26 does not have the scope attributed to it by the respondent Government in cases where the domestic law provides a single remedy against a particular measure, but allows the person in question to make use of this remedy as often as he feels inclined and at intervals left entirely, or to a great extent, to his discretion throughout the time the measure in question remains in force. Such, in fact, is the position in the present case. Under the rules of criminal procedure in the Federal Republic of Germany persons in detention on remand may at any time apply for provisional release (see Section 117(1) of the Code on Criminal Procedure – StPO). The Code on Criminal Procedure imposes no restrictions on the exercise of this remedy. Nor, on the other hand, does it require the detained person to make a minimum use of the remedy. Furthermore, the competent court of appeal must, in cases where detention on remand exceeds six months, decide *ex officio* and at regular intervals whether that detention should continue. There is no possibility of an appeal or a constitutional appeal against such decision if, as in the present case, it is given by the Berlin Court of Appeal. It follows that the Commission can not accept the respondent Government's submission that the conditions of Article 26 of the Convention are not met simply because the applicant has not appealed against this or that

particular decision ordering her detention on remand or the continuation of such detention. Nor can the Government rely on the fact that the applicant has not taken advantage of the possibility temporarily open to her of bringing the matter before the constitutional court. In fact she was later deprived of this possibility by the retransfer of her case to the West Berlin prosecuting authorities.

It was sufficient for the purposes of Article 26 of the Convention that the applicant exhausted at any time she thought fit the domestic remedies existing at that time. This requirement is entirely satisfied. Prior to the lodging of the present application with the Commission on 9 October 1972, the Berlin Court of Appeal had, in three decisions not subject to appeal, refused to order the applicant's provisional release. The last of those decisions was taken on 6 September 1972 (*ibid.*, pp. 159–60).

58. Decisions on applications ns. 27/55, 188/56, 225/56, 254/57, 272/57, 277/57 and 333/57.

59. Appl. n. 222/56, *X* v. *F.R. Germany* case, decision of 8 January 1959, *Yearbook* [1958–9] vol. II, p. 349. Accordingly, the Commission added that 'le requérant aurait dû, par conséquent, exercer ce recours pour satisfaire aux prescriptions de l'article 26 de la Convention' (*ibid.*, p. 349).

60. Appl. n. 1135/61 (1963), *Collection*, vol. 11, p. 22; appl. n. 2547/65 (1966), *Collection*, vol. 20, p. 83; appl. n. 2370/64 (1967), *Collection*, vol. 22, p. 101; appl. n. 2854/66 (1967), *Collection*, vol. 26, p. 53; appl. n. 4002/69 (1971), *Collection*, vol. 37, pp. 22–3; appl. n. 4511/70 (1971), *Collection*, vol. 38, p. 85.

61. Appl. n. 2854/66, *X and Y* v. *Austria* case, decision of 18 December 1967, *Collection*, vol. 26, p. 53.

62. *Ibid.*, p. 54.

63. Appl. n. 2614/65, *Ringeisen* v. *Austria* case, decision of 18 July 1968, *Collection*, vol. 27, pp. 53–4.

64. Appl. n. 1086/61 (1962), *Collection*, vol. 9, p. 16; appl. n. 1475/62 (1963), *Collection*, vol. 11, pp. 48–9; appl. n. 2038/63 (1964), *Collection*, vol. 13, p. 114; appl. n. 2201/64 (1965), *Collection*, vol. 16, p. 75; appl. n. 2185/64 (1965), *Collection*. vol. 17, pp. 20–1; appl. n. 1191/61 (1965), *Collection*, vol. 17, pp. 77–80; appl. n. 2366/64 (1967), *Collection*, vol. 22, p. 122; appl. n. 2459/65 (1967), *Collection*, vol. 24, p. 49. In one of these cases, there had been undue delay to exercise the constitutional appeal: cf. appl. 1191/61 (1965), *Collection*, vol. 17, pp. 77–80.

65. Appl. n. 778/60, *X* v. *F.R. Germany* case, decision of 4 January 1961, *Collection*, vol. 5, pp. 2–3.

66. Appl. n. 2257/64, *Soltikow* v. *F.R. Germany* case, decision of 5 April 1968, *Collection*, vol. 27, pp. 24–8.

67. Appl. n. 4046/69 (1970), *Collection*, vol. 35, pp. 115–16; appl. n. 4119/69 (1970), *Collection*, vol. 35, pp. 130–1; appl. n. 4124/69 (1970), *Collection*, vol. 35, pp. 134–5; appl. n. 4247/69 (1970), *Collection*, vol. 36, pp. 74–5; appl. n. 4445/70 (1970), *Collection*, vol. 37, pp. 121–2;

appl. n. 5172/71 (1973), *Collection*, vol. 44, p. 125.

68. Appl. n. 4119/69 (1970), *Collection*, vol. 35, pp. 130–1.
69. The application had previously been struck off the list. Appl. n. 2834/66 (1970), *Collection*, vol. 35, pp. 26–8.
70. Two further recent cases could be added to that total. In one of them, the application was rejected for non-exhaustion, firstly, of an appeal against an expulsion order, secondly, of an appeal to the Administrative Court of Appeal (in asylum proceedings), and, finally, of a constitutional appeal. (Appl. n. 6357/73, *X* v. *F.R. Germany* case, decision of 8 October 1974, European Commission of Human Rights, *Decisions and Reports*, vol. 1, Strasbourg, July 1975, pp. 77–8). In the other case, the applicant was found not to have lodged an appeal to the Federal Constitutional Court (*Bundesverfassungsgericht*), even though she had appealed to the Bavarian Constitutional Court; the Commission stated that 'an appeal to the Constitutional Court of a Land is not sufficient where there is, as in the present case, the possibility of appealing to the Federal Constitutional Court'; the application was thus rejected for non-exhaustion of local remedies (appl. n. 6729/74, *X* v. *F.R. Germany* case, decision of 12 December 1974, *Decisions and Reports*, vol. 1, p. 93). On the subject (exhaustion of a constitutional appeal to the Federal Constitutional Court), cf. further submissions of the parties in appl. n. 5078/71, *X* v. *Italy and F.R. Germany* case, final decision of 30 May 1974, *Collection*, vol. 46, pp. 48 and 50.
71. For further decisions of the Commission, in 1976–7, concerning the exhaustion of constitutional appeals, see appl. n. 6830/74, *X* v. *F.R. Germany* case (1977), *Decisions and Reports*, vol. 9, pp. 23–4; appl. n. 6271/73, *X* v. *F.R. Germany* case (1976), *Decisions and Reports*, Vol. 6, pp. 62–4; appl. n. 6965/75, *X* v. *Austria* case (1976), *Decisions and Reports*, vol. 5, pp. 130–1; appl. n. 6452/74, *Giuseppe Sacchi* v. *Italy* case (1976), *Decisions and Reports*, vol. 5, pp. 43 and 49–52.
72. Appl. n. 712/60, *Retimag S.A.* v. *F.R. Germany* case, decision of 16 December 1961, *Collection*, vol. 8, pp. 29–33.
73. *Ibid.*, p. 37.
74. *Ibid.*
75. *Ibid.*, p. 41.
76. *Ibid.*, p. 38.
77. After the *Retimag* case the Commission repeated the view that a doubt as to the availability and effectiveness of a remedy is not a circumstance authorizing the non-exhaustion of that remedy in the following cases: appl. n. 1661/62, *X and Y* v. *Belgium* case, decision of 17 January 1963, *Collection*, vol. 10, p. 19; appl. n. 1474/62, *23 Inhabitants of Alsemberg and of Beersel* v. *Belgium* case, decision of 24 September 1963, *Collection*, vol. 12, p. 28; but more recently, in a case where the Commission itself found doubtful the effectiveness of a remedy, it declared the application inadmissible on another ground, that it was 'manifestly ill-founded': appl. n. 3868/68, *X* v. *United Kingdom* case, decision of 25 May 1970, *Collection*, vol. 34, p. 17.
78. Cf. appl. n. 302/57, decision of 17 March 1957 (unpublished), in Council

of Europe doc. H(64)1, of 13 January 1964, p. 9 (mimeographed).

79. *Ibid.*, p. 9.
80. Appl. n. 1802/63, *Nazih-Al-Kuzbari* v. *F.R. Germany* case, decision of 26 March 1963, *Collection*, vol. 10, pp. 23–6.
81. K. Vasak, *La Convention européenne des droits de l'homme*, Paris, LGDJ, 1964, p. 120; and, somewhat less emphatically, Chappez, *op. cit.*, p. 187.
82. Appl. n. 332/57, *Lawless* v. *Ireland* case, decision of 30 August 1958, *Yearbook* [1958–9] vol. II, p. 326.
83. Cf. appl. n. 324/57, decision of 18 March 1958 (unpublished), in Council of Europe doc. H(64)1, of 13 January 1964, p. 14 (mimeographed).
84. Appl. n. 297/57, *X* v. *F.R. Germany* case, decision of 22 March 1958, *Yearbook* [1958–9] vol. II, p. 210.
85. *Ibid.*, p. 214.
86. Appl. n. 1739/62, *X* v. *Sweden* case, decision of 2 March 1964, *Collection*, vol. 13, p. 102.
87. Appl. n. 3788/68, *X* v. *Sweden* case, decision of 13 July 1970, *Collection*, vol. 35, p. 72.
88. *Ibid.*, p. 72.
89. *Ibid.*
90. *Ibid.*, p. 73–4.
91. Appl. n. 3972/69, *X* v. *Austria* case, decision of 2 April 1971, *Collection*, vol. 37, p. 19.
92. *Ibid.*
93. A.-M. Nay-Cadoux, *Les Conditions de recevabilité des requêtes individuelles devant la Commission européenne des droits de l'homme*, Paris/Torino, LGDJ/Giappichelli, 1966, pp. 97–8.
94. Nay-Cadoux, *op. cit.*, p. 83.
95. F. Ermacora, 'L'accès aux mécanismes juridictionnels de protection des personnes privées dans la Convention européenne des droits de l'homme', (report presented at the Colloquium of Grenoble of 25–6 January 1973 on 'L'efficacité des mécanismes juridictionnels de protection des personnes privées dans le cadre européen'), in 6 *Revue des droits de l'homme/Human Rights Journal* [1973] p. 652.
96. P. Schaffer and D. Weissbrodt, 'Exhaustion of Remedies in the Context of the Racial Discrimination Convention', 2 *Revue des droits de l'homme/Human Rights Journal* [1969] pp. 641–3.
97. A. Bleckmann, 'Summary Report on the Discussions at the Colloquium', in *Gerichtsschutz gegen die Exekutive/Judicial Protection against the Executive*, vol. 3, Max-Planck-Institut für ausländisches öffentliches Recht und Völkerrecht, Köln, Heymanns/Oceana, 1971, p. 185; and see p. 183.
98. In this connection two methods of restricting legal protection were examined in a recent colloquium, namely: firstly, 'the enumeration principle which confines legal protection to those cases in which a judicial intervention is believed to be tolerable' (admittedly a dangerous method), and, secondly, the introduction of 'the general clause, but simultaneously requir [ing] restraint in the judicial review of the exercise of discretion'; see Bleckmann, *op. cit.*, pp. 183–4 and see p. 186.

99. Jaenicke adds that 'in this connection it cannot be assumed *a priori* that courts will guarantee a more effective legal protection than non-judicial authorities in all cases'; G. Jaenicke, 'Judicial Protection of the Individual within the System of International Law', in *Gerichtsschutz gegen die Exekutive*, vol. 3, p. 290. Bleckmann warns that 'comparative jurisprudence, too, should not cling to formalities'; Bleckmann, *op. cit.*, p. 183. And on the question, see, further H. Steinberger, 'Comparative Jurisprudence and Judicial Protection of the Individual against the Executive: A Method for Ascertaining International Law?', in *Gerichtsschutz gegen die Exekutive*, vol. 3, pp. 269–79.

100. H. Golsong, 'International Treaty Provisions on the Protection of the Individual against the Executive by Domestic Courts', in *Gerichtsschutz gegen die Exekutive*, vol. 3, pp. 265–6, esp. p. 266.

101. Chappez, *op. cit.*, p. 225.

102. In this sense: Danelius, *op. cit.*, p. 293.

103. Appl. n. 1474/62, 23 *Inhabitants of Alsemberg and of Beersel* v. *Belgium* case, decision of 24 September 1963, *Collection*, vol. 12, p. 27. The Commission added that 'en partant de cette hypothèse, on arrive nécessairement à la conclusion que le pouvoir quasi discrétionnaire du Ministre de l'Éducation Nationale et de la Culture [...] se trouvait circonscrit par la Convention depuis l'entrée en vigueur de celle-ci a l'égard de la Belgique; [...] il semble probable, dès lors, que s'il avait été appelé à statuer, le Conseil d'État aurait dû annuler la décision litigieuse' (*ibid.*, p. 27).

104. Appl. n. 1661/62, *X and Y* v. *Belgium* case, decision of 17 January 1963, *Collection*, vol. 10, p. 19.

105. Cf. *Reports of International Arbitral Awards*, vol. III, pp. 1503–4.

106. F.G. Jacobs, *The European Convention on Human Rights*, Oxford, Clarendon Press, 1975, pp. 240–1.

107. Appl. 788/60, *Austria* v. *Italy* case, decision of 11 January 1961, *Report of the Plenary Commission*, pp. 54–7, esp. p. 57.

108. Appl. n. 3651/68, *X* v. *United Kingdom* case, decision of 4 February 1970, *Collection*, vol. 31, p. 90. More recently, in the *Baader/Meins/Meinhof/Grundmann* v. *F.R. Germany* case (1975), the respondent government raised an objection of non-exhaustion of local remedies, but the Commission found that the applicants had in fact appealed to the Federal Constitutional Court, and that there might therefore be doubt (only) as to the effectiveness of any *further* appeal; but the Commission did not go further into this question, as it decided to reject the application as inadmissible for being 'manifestly ill-founded' within the meaning of Article 27(2) of the Convention. Appl. n. 6166/73, *Baader/Meins/Meinhof/Grundmann* v. *F.R. Germany* case, decision of 30 May 1975, in European Commission of Human Rights, *Decisions and Reports*, vol. 2, Strasbourg, December 1975, pp. 61–3 (also reported in *Yearbook*, vol. 18, 1975, pp. 142 and 146).

109. Appl. n. 3651/68, p. 90. In the present case, as the applicant failed to show that such appeal to the Court of Appeal was an ineffective remedy, which might have absolved him from the obligation to exhaust it, he

was held not to have complied with the local remedies rule (cf. *ibid.*, p. 91).

110. Appl. n. 4897/71 *Gussenbauer* v. *Austria* case, decision of 22 March 1972, *Collection*, vol. 42, p. 47.
111. *Ibid.*
112. *Ibid.*, p. 48. In the case the Commission found that the applicant had in fact exhausted local remedies, and his application was therefore declared as a whole admissible (cf. *ibid.*, p. 48).
113. Appl. n. 1661/62 (1963), *Collection*, vol. 10, p. 19; appl. n. 4119/69 1970), *Collection*, vol. 35, pp. 130–1.
114. Appl. n. 493/59, *X* v. *Ireland* case, decision of 27 July 1961, *Collection*, vol. 7, p. 95.
115. Cf. *ibid.*, pp. 95–6.
116. Appl. n. 4125/69, *X* v. Ireland case, final decision of 1 February 1971, *Collection*, vol. 37, p. 50.
117. Appl. n. 5006/71, *X* v. *United Kingdom* case, decision of 9 February 1972, *Collection*, vol. 39, p. 93.
118. *Ibid.*
119. *Ibid.*
120. Appl. n. 4475/70, *Svenska Lotsförbundet* v. *Sweden* case, second decision of 13 July 1972, *Collection*, vol. 42, p. 13.
121. Appl. n. 4771/71, *Kamma* v. *Netherlands* case, partial decision of 30 May 1972, *Collection*, vol. 42, p. 20.
122. Appl. n. 4459/70, *Kaiser* v. *Austria* case, final decision of 3 April 1971, *Collection*, vol. 38, p. 55.
123. Appl. n. 4623/70, *X* v. *United Kingdom* case, partial decision of 19 July 1971, *Collection*, vol. 39, pp. 64–5.
124. Appl. n. 5493/72, *Handyside* v. *United Kingdom* case, decision of 4 April 1974, *Collection*, vol. 45, p. 48.
125. Appl. n. 1802/63, *Nazih-Al-Kuzbari* v. *F.R. Germany* case, decision of 26 March 1963, *Collection*, vol. 10, p. 28.
126. Appl. ns. 2551/65, 3155/67, 3174/67 and 3499/68, *W, X, Y and Z* v. *Belgium* case, decision of 17 December 1971, *Collection*, vol. 39, p. 8.
127. Appl. ns. 3435–8/67, *W, X, Y and Z* v. *United Kingdom* case, decision of 19 July 1968, *Collection*, vol. 28, pp. 122–3. Earlier, in the *Lawless* v. *Ireland* case (1958), the Commission declared *inter alia* that further *habeas corpus* proceedings open to the applicant in the ordinary courts of the Republic 'did not offer him a reasonable prospect of success and must be regarded as ineffective remedies; [...] it follows that under the generally recognised rules of international law it was not necessary for the applicant to have recourse to such further domestic remedies before submitting his case to the Commission'. Appl. n. 332/57, *Lawless* v. *Ireland* case, decision of 30 August 1958, *Yearbook* [1958–9] vol. II, p. 318.
128. Appl. n. 27/55, *X* v. *F.R. Germany* case, decision of 31 May 1956, *Yearbook* [1955–7] vol. I, p. 139.
129. Appl. n. 899/60, *A et al.* v. *F.R. Germany* case, decision of 9 March 1962, *Collection*, vol. 9, p. 9.

130. Appl. n. 514/59, *X* v. *Austria* case, decision of 5 January 1960, *Collection*, vol. 2, p. 3.
131. Appl. n. 2614/65, *Ringeisen* v. *Austria* case, final decision of 18 July 1968, *Collection*, vol. 27, pp. 53–4.
132. *Ibid.*, p. 54.
133. Appl. n. 1936/63, *Neumeister* v. *Austria* case, decision of 6 July 1964, *Collection*, vol. 14, p. 48.
134. *Ibid.*, p. 49. The Commission remarked that in the circumstances of the case 'there was no reason to believe that the Austrian courts would [...] order the applicant's release on bail' (*ibid.*, p. 48).
135. Appl. n. 808/60, *Isop* v. *Austria* case, decision of 8 March 1962, *Collection*, vol. 8, p. 88.
136. *Ibid.*
137. Appl. n. 2686/65, *Kornmann* v. *F.R. Germany* case, final decision of 13 December 1966, *Collection*, vol. 22, p. 10. In the present case, the Public Prosecutor had discontinued the proceedings but subsequently re-opened the investigation *ex officio*, and then for the second time discontinued the proceedings; the applicant's appeal against this decision was rejected by the Senior Public Prosecutor, and his application lodged with the Kammergericht was likewise rejected. The Commission thus found that the applicant had exhausted those particular remedies as required by Article 26 of the Convention (*ibid.*, p. 10).
138. Appl. n. 1008/61 (1962), *Collection*, vol. 8, p. 67; appl. n. 1727/62 (1963), *Collection*, vol. 12, p. 48; appl. n. 1706/62 (1966), *Collection*, vol. 21, pp. 60–1. On one occasion, as the Commission had some doubts on the matter, it found otherwise: cf. appl. n. 434/58 (1959), *Collection*, vol. 1, p. 14. On another occasion, however, although it displayed some reluctance at first, the Commission concluded by finding that the applicant was absolved from appealing (an ineffective remedy) against a decision of an Investigating Judge: cf. appl. n. 4340/69 (1971), *Collection*, vol. 38, p. 33.
139. Appl. n. 5926/72, *Pedersen* v. *Denmark* case, partial decision of 29 May 1973, *Collection*, vol. 44, p. 94; appl. n. 5095/71, *Kjeldsen* v. *Denmark* case, decision of 16 December 1972, *Collection*, vol. 43, p. 55. And cf. also appl. n. 5920/72, decision of 29 May 1973, *Busk Madsen* v. *Denmark* case, in *Collection*, vol. 44, p. 93, n. 1.
140. Appl. n. 299/57, *Greece* v. *United Kingdom* case, decision of 12 October 1957, *Yearbook* [1958–9] vol. II, pp. 194–6.
141. Appl. ns. 3321/67, 3322/67, 3323/67, 3344/67, *Denmark/Norway/Sweden/Netherlands* v. *Greece* case, decision of 31 May 1968, *Collection*, vol. 26, pp. 107–8.
142. Appl. ns. 5577–83/72 (joined), *Donnelly and Others* v. *United Kingdom* case, decision of 5 April 1973, *Collection*, vol. 43, p. 147. The problems relating to legislative measures and administrative practices allegedly incompatible with the Convention are more appropriately dealt with under a separate heading elsewhere (cf. Ch. 4, *supra*).
143. Appl. n. 214/56, *De Becker* v. *Belgium* case, decision of 9 June 1958, *Yearbook* [1958–9] vol. II, pp. 237–8.

144. Appl. n. 222/56, *X* v. *F.R. Germany* case, decision of 8 January 1959, *Yearbook* [1958–9] vol. II, p. 351.
145. Appl. n. 7011/75, *H. Becker* v. *Denmark* case (1975), *Decisions and Reports*, vol. 4, pp. 232–3 and 227–8.
146. In the case, the suspension of an administrative order of expulsion or repatriation (to Poland) remained within the discretion of the Ministry of Justice; appl. n. 7465/76, *X* v. *Denmark* case (1976), *Decisions and Reports*, vol. 7, p. 154.
147. Appl. n. 6701/74, *X* v. *Austria* case (1976), *Decisions and Reports*, vol. 5, pp. 78–9 (but the application was declared inadmissible, as 'manifestly ill-founded').
148. Appl. n. 6903/75, *J. de Weer* v. *Belgium* case (1977), *Decisions and Reports*, vol. 8, pp. 100–2.
149. Declared inadmissible as 'manifestly ill-founded' and 'incompatible with the Convention *ratione materiae*'; cf. appl. n. 7729/76, *Ph. B.F. Agee* v. *United Kingdom* case (1976), *Decisions and Reports*, vol. 7, pp. 172–6.
150. Cf. *ibid.*, p. 171. See also appl. n. 7216/75, *X* v. *F.R. Germany* (1976), *Decisions and Reports*, vol. 5, p. 142 (appeals not regarded as effective in the case at issue); appl. n. 6870/75, *Y* v. *United Kingdom* case (1977), *Decisions and Reports*, vol. 10, pp. 50–1 (local remedy presumably ineffective).
151. European Court of Human Rights, *Stögmüller* case, judgment of 10 November 1969, Series A, p. 42, para. 11.
152. European Court of Human Rights, *'Vagrancy'* cases, judgment of 18 June 1971, Series A, p. 33, para. 60. (Other aspects of the Court's case-law on the application of the local remedies rule are properly investigated in Ch. 5 and 6, *supra*.)
153. *Reports of International Arbitral Awards*, vol. III, p. 1502.
154. Cf. the Commission's early decisions on the admissibility of applications ns. 263/57, 309/57, 327/57, 342/57 and 776/60. The question was also raised in the *Austria* v. *Italy* case: cf. appl. n. 788/60 (1961), *Report of the Plenary Commission*, pp. 56–7.
155. Appl. n. 627/59, *X* v. *F.R. Germany* case, decision of 14 December 1961, *Collection*, vol. 8, pp. 23–4. The applicant contended that, if raised, the issue might have been prejudicial to his appeal (cf. *ibid.*, p. 24).
156. *Ibid.*, p. 24.
157. Appl. n. 1103/61, *X* v. *Belgium* case, decision of 12 March 1962, *Collection*, vol. 8, p. 124.
158. Appl. n. 3001/66, *X* v. *Austria* case, decision of 30 May 1968, *Collection*, vol. 26, p. 59. The Commission referred to its 'constant jurisprudence' on the matter (*ibid.*, p. 59)
159. *Ibid.*
160. *Ibid.*, pp. 59–60. That the substance of a complaint is to be raised before domestic courts is also confirmed by the following Commission's decisions: appls. ns. 5573/72 and 5670/72 (joined), *A, B, C, D, E, F, G, H and I* v. *F.R. Germany* case (1976), *Decisions and Reports*, vol. 7, p. 19; appl. n. 5574/72, *X* v. *United Kingdom* case (1975), *Decisions and Reports*, vol. 3, p. 15; appl. n. 6861/75, *X* v. *United Kingdom* case (1975), *ibid.*, pp.

148–50; appl. n. 7238/75, *F. van Leuven/M. de Meyere* v. *Belgium* case (1977), *Decisions and Reports*, vol. 8, pp. 158–9, and see p. 157; appl. n. 7367/76, *M. Guzzardi* v. *Italy* case (1977), *ibid.*, pp. 209–10, and see pp. 202–7; appl. n. 6878/75, *H. Le Compte* v. *Belgium* case (1976), *Decisions and Reports*, vol. 6, pp. 79 and 97–9.

161. Appl. n. 4319/69, *Samer* v. *F.R. Germany* case, decision of 15 December 1971, *Collection*, vol. 39, p. 18. The Commission, once again, referred to its 'constant jurisprudence' on the matter (cf. *ibid.*, p. 18).

162. Appl. n. 4930/71, *X* v. *Belgium* case, decision of 1 June 1972, *Collection*, vol. 40, p. 41. A further reference to its 'constant jurisprudence' on the matter was made by the Commission (cf. *ibid.*, p. 41).

163. Appl. n. 4771/71, *Kamma* v. *Netherlands* case, decision of 30 May 1972, *Collection*, vol. 42, p. 19.

164. *Ibid.*, p. 19, and see pp. 19–20.

165. Appl. n. 5560/72, *X* v. *Austria* case, decision of 31 May 1973, *Collection*, vol. 45, p. 64.

166. *Ibid.*, pp. 64–5.

167. Appl. n. 4681/70, *Murphy* v. *United Kingdom* case, final decision of 3 and 4 October 1972, *Collection*, vol. 43, p. 12; appl. n. 1706/62, *X* v. *Austria* case, final decision of 4 October 1966, *Collection*, vol. 21, p. 43 (failure to raise a certain point in a plea of challenge (*Ablehnung*) of the judge concerned); appl. n. 1661/62, *X and Y* v. *Belgium* case, decision of 17 January 1963, *Collection*, vol. 10, pp. 18–19 (with an express reference to arbitrator Bagge's award in the *Finnish Vessels* case); appl. n. 6173/73, *Société Anonyme X* v. *Belgium* case, decision of 18 July 1974, *Collection*, vol. 46, p. 185 (failure to invoke before the Belgian Cour de Cassation the Convention provisions forming part of Belgian municipal law).

168. Appl. n. 2614/65, *Ringeisen* v. *Austria* case, final decision of 18 July 1968, *Collection*, vol. 27, p. 53.

169. *Ibid.*, p. 55.

170. Appl. n. 2322/64, *X* v. *Belgium* case, decision of 31 May 1967, *Collection*, vol. 24, p. 42.

171. Appl. n. 2689/65, *Delcourt* v. *Belgium* case, partial decision of 7 February 1967, *Collection*, vol. 22, p. 72.

172. Appl. n. 2689/65, *Delcourt* v. *Belgium* case, final decision of 6 April 1967, *Collection*, vol. 24, p. 84. The application was declared inadmissible in part and admissible in part (cf. *ibid.*, p. 84).

173. Appl. n. 2002/63, *X* v. *Norway* case, decision of 2 July 1964, *Collection*, vol. 14, p. 27.

174. *Ibid.*, p. 28.

175. Appl. n. 4124/69, *X* v. *F.R. Germany* case, decision of 13 July 1970, *Collection*, vol. 35, p. 135.

176. *Ibid.*

177. Appl. n. 3001/66 (1968), *Collection*, vol. 26, pp. 59–60.

178. Appl. n. 627/59 (1961), *Collection*, vol. 8, p. 24.

179. In the *Retimag* case, referring to the applicant's failure to introduce a constitutional appeal, the Commission declared that 'la règle de l'épuisement des voies de recours internes est stricte et doit s'interpreter

en conséquence; [...] il suffit donc, pour qu'un requérant n'ait pas épuisé les voies de recours internes, qu'il ait omis d'user sur un point déterminé d'une des voies de recours qui lui étaient ouvertes, à supposer qu'en soulevant ce point devant les juridictions internes, il eût eu quelque chance de faire aboutir l'ensemble de sa demande critiquant une seule et même mesure' (appl. n. 712/60 (1961), *Collection*, vol. 8, p. 41).

180. Appl. n. 1211/61, *X* v. *Netherlands* case, decision of 4 October 1962, *Collection*, vol. 9, p. 48.

181. Appl. n. 342/57, decision of 4 September 1958 (unpublished), quoted in Council of Europe doc. H(64)1 (of 13 January 1964), pp. 19–20.

182. Appl. n. 4897/71, *Gussenbauer* v. *Austria* case, decision of 22 March 1972, *Collection*, vol. 42, p. 47.

183. *Ibid.*, pp. 47–8.

184. *Ibid.*, p. 48.

185. Appl. n. 1474/62, 23 *Inhabitants of Alsemberg and of Beersel* v. *Belgium* case, decision of 24 September 1963, *Collection*, vol. 12, pp. 25–6.

186. *Ibid.*, p. 26.

187. *Ibid.*, p. 27.

188. *Ibid.*

189. *Ibid.*

190. *Ibid.*, p. 28.

191. Appl. n. 2689/65, *Delcourt* v. *Belgium* case, partial decision of 7 February 1967, *Collection*, vol. 22, pp. 67–8.

192. *Ibid.*, p. 68.

193. Appl. n. 493/59, *X* v. *Ireland* case, decision of 27 July 1961, *Collection*, vol. 7, p. 94.

194. *Ibid.*, p. 96.

195. *Ibid.*, pp. 95–6.

196. *Ibid.*, p. 96.

197. *Ibid.*, pp. 96–7.

198. The application was rejected as inadmissible for non-exhaustion; appl. n. 6916/75, *X, Y and Z* v. *Switzerland* case (1976), *Decisions and Reports*, vol. 6, pp. 107 and 113.

199. Application equally rejected as inadmissible for non-exhaustion; appl. n. 7641/76, *X and Y* v. *F. R. Germany* case (1976), *Decisions and Reports*, vol. 10, pp. 224 and 228. In another case, the Commission ruled that a person who complains of the length of his prolonged detention should have drawn up – and at least reasonably renewed – a request for release; appl. n. 7317/75, *W.P. Lynas* v. *Switzerland* case (1976), *Decisions and Reports*, vol. 6, pp. 141 and 167.

200. Appl. n. 7434/76, *X* v. *United Kingdom* case (1977), *Decisions and Reports*, vol. 9, pp. 103–4; application also declared inadmissible for, *inter alia*, non-exhaustion.

201. Appl. n. 1706/62, *X* v. *Austria* case, final decision of 4 October 1966, *Collection*, vol. 21, p. 43.

202. In this sense, Council of Europe doc. H(64)1 (of 13 January 1964), p. 19; and, among writers, e.g. Vasak, *La Convention européenne*, p. 129); Chappez, *op. cit.*, p. 207.

203. Council of Europe doc. H(64)1 (of 13 January 1964), pp. 19 and 21.
204. *Ibid.*
205. Appl. n. 343/57, *Nielsen* v. *Denmark* case, decision of 2 September 1959, *Report of the Commission*, pp. 25–30.
206. *Ibid.*, p. 30.
207. *Ibid.*, pp. 32–3.
208. *Ibid.*, p. 34.
209. *Ibid.*, p. 36.
210. *Ibid.*
211. *Ibid.*
212. *Ibid.*
213. *Ibid.*, pp. 36–7.
214. *Ibid.*, p. 37.
215. *Ibid.*, pp. 37–8.
216. *Ibid.*, p. 37.
217. *Ibid.*, p. 38.
218. *Ibid.* See further observations on the *Nielsen* case *supra*, in relation to the question of the notion of 'final decision'.
219. Vasak, *La Convention européenne*, p. 122; Castberg, *European Convention*, p. 42; Jacobs, *European Convention*, pp. 238–9; Council of Europe doc. H(64)1 (of 13 January 1964) p. 13; Nay-Cadoux, *op. cit.*, p. 93.
220. Appl. n. 2614/65, *Ringeisen* v. *Austria* case, final decision of 18 July 1968, *Collection*, vol. 27, pp. 53–4.
221. Appl. n. 654/59, *X* v. *F.R. Germany* case, decision of 3 June 1960, *Collection*, vol. 7, p. 4.
222. *Ibid.*, p. 5.
223. Appl. n. 968/61, *X* v. *F.R. Germany* case, decision of 14 December 1961, *Collection*, vol. 8, p. 27.
224. *Ibid.*, p. 28. On a *révision* of condemnation, cf. also application n. 1237/61 (1962), *Collection*, vol. 8, pp. 76–9.
225. Appl. n. 1739/62, *X* v. *Sweden* case, decision of 2 March 1964, *Collection*, vol. 13, p. 102. As early as 1959 Wiebringhaus argued that *demandes en révision* (as well as *actions en réhabilitation* and means of redress not provided by law) needed *not* be exhausted under Article 26 of the Convention; cf. H. Wiebringhaus, 'La règle de l'épuisement préalable des voies de recours internes dans la jurisprudence de la Commission européenne des droits de l'homme', 5 *Annuaire Français de Droit International* [1959] p. 695.
226. Appl. n. 3788/68, *X* v. *Sweden* case, decision of 13 July 1970, *Collection*, vol. 35, p. 72. The Commission therefore held that the applicant had not complied with the local remedies rule as regards that part of the application (*ibid.*, p. 73).
227. Appl. n. 6242/73, *Ingrid Brückmann* v. *F.R. Germany* case, decision of 27 May 1974, *Collection*, vol. 46, p. 207. The application was declared admissible (*ibid.*, p. 210).
228. Appl. n. 493/59, *X* v. *Ireland* case, decision of 27 July 1961 *Collection*, vol. 7, pp. 96–7.

229. Appl. n. 1727/62, *Boeckmans* v. *Belgium* case, decision of 29 October 1963, *Collection*, vol. 12, p. 46.

230. *Ibid.*, p. 48. The same test was applied in the *Austria* v. *Italy* case, where the Commission concluded in regard to one of the complaints that 'it has not been established that an application for a change of venue on the ground of legitimate suspicion would not have constituted, in the case at issue, a remedy likely to be effective and adequate'; appl. n. 788/60, decision of 11 January 1961, *Report of the Plenary Commission*, p. 55. It could also be recalled that, in the *Ireland* v. *United Kingdom* case, for example, the applicant government complained of the respondent government's alleged exercise (in Northern Ireland) of their powers to detain and intern persons under the Special Powers Act and Regulations, whereas the respondent government replied that adequate domestic remedies were available and had not been exhausted; appl. n. 5310/71, decision of 1 October 1972, *Collection*, vol. 41, pp. 88–9.

231. Appl. n. 918/60, *X* v. *F.R. Germany* case, decision of 18 September 1961, *Collection*, vol. 7, p. 110.

232. Appl. n. 4311/69, *X* v. *Denmark* case, decision of 1 February 1971, *Collection*, vol. 37, p. 96.

233. *Ibid.*

234. *Ibid.*

235. Appl. n. 6049/73, *X* v. *F.R. Germany* case, decision of 14 December 1974, European Commission of Human Rights, *Decisions and Reports*, vol. 1, Strasbourg, July 1975, p. 56.

236. *Ibid.*, p. 57.

237. *Ibid.*

238. *Ibid.*

239. *Ibid.*

240. *Ibid.*

241. Appl. n. 968/61, *X* v. *F.R. Germany* case, decision of 14 December 1961, *Collection*, vol. 8, p. 27.

242. Appl. n. 788/60, *Austria* v. *Italy* case, decision of 11 January 1961, *Report of the Plenary Commission*, p. 55.

243. Appl. n. 332/57, *Lawless* v. *Ireland* case, decision of 30 August 1958, *Yearbook* [1958–9] vol. II, p. 318.

244. Appl. n. 289/57, *X* v. *F.R. Germany* case, decision of 6 September 1957, *Yearbook* [1955–7] vol. I, p. 149.

245. *Ibid.*

246. Appl. n. 4225/69, *X* v. *United Kingdom* case, decision of 17 March 1970, *Collection*, vol. 33, p. 43.

247. Appl. n. 5288/71, *X* v. *Luxembourg* case, decision of 10 July 1973, *Collection*, vol. 44, p. 28. The Commission proceeded to this examination *ex officio* (cf. *ibid.*, p. 28).

248. *Ibid.* More recently, the Commission has made it clear that a mere doubt as to the likelihood of success of an available remedy does not absolve the applicant from the duty of exhausting it; appl. n. 6861/75, *X* v. *United Kingdom* case (1975), *Decisions and Reports*, vol. 3, pp. 147–50.

249. Reference could be made to a few more recent decisions in which the

Commission, applying the 'likelihood of success test' with regard to domestic remedies, deemed the circumstances relieved the applicants of the duty of exhausting local remedies; cf., to this effect, appl n. 6870/75, *Y* v. *United Kingdom* case (1977), *Decisions and Reports*, vol. 10, p. 66; appl. n. 5613/72, *A. Hilton* v. *United Kingdom* case (1976), *Decisions and Reports*, vol. 4, pp. 186–7; appl. n. 7705/76, *X* v. *F.R. Germany* case (1977), *Decisions and Reports*, vol. 9, p. 203, and see p. 196; and cf. appls. ns. 5573/72 and 5670/72 (joined), *A, B, C, D, E, F, G, H, and I* v. *F. R. Germany* case (1976), *Decisions and Reports*, vol. 7, p. 20.

250. Appl. n. 4897/71, *Gussenbauer* v. *Austria* case, decision of 22 March 1972, *Collection*, vol. 42, p. 48.

251. *Ibid.*

252. Appl. n. 5493/72, *Handyside* v. *United Kingdom* case, decision of 4 April 1974, *Collection*, vol. 45, p. 48.

253. Appl. n. 5095/71, *Kjeldsen* v. *Denmark* case, decision of 16 December 1972, *Collection*, vol. 43, p. 54.

254. *Ibid.*, p. 55.

255. *Ibid.*

256. Appl. n. 1488/62, *X* v. *Belgium* case, decision of 18 December 1963, *Collection*, vol. 13, pp. 96–7, esp. p. 96.

257. Appl. n. 2257/64, *Soltikow* v. *F.R. Germany* case, final decision of 5 April 1968, *Collection*, vol. 27, p. 26. The Commission referred to another decision it rendered to the same effect, on 22 March 1958, on application n. 272/57 (*ibid.*, p. 26).

258. Appl. n. 4340/69, *Simon-Herold* v. *Austria* case, decision of 2 February 1971, *Collection*, vol. 38, p. 33.

259. Appl. n. 712/60 (1961), *Collection*, vol. 8, p. 38. And, later, in the *Soltikow* case, the Commission asserted that 'an applicant is obliged to exhaust every domestic remedy which cannot clearly be said to lack any chance of success'; appl. n. 2257/64 (1968), *Collection*, vol. 27, p. 26.

260. Cf. 1956 resolution of the *Institut de Droit International, supra.*

261. Appl. n. 788/60, *Austria* v. *Italy* case, decision of 11 January 1961, *Report of the Plenary Commission*, p. 57 (my italics).

262. Appl. n. 2614/65, *Ringeisen* v. *Austria* case, final decision of 18 July 1968, *Collection*, vol. 27, p. 53 (my italics).

263. Appl. n. 4340/69, *Simon-Herold* v. *Austria* case, decision of 2 February 1971, *Collection*, vol. 38, p. 33, and further decisions to the same effect referred to therein (*ibid.*, p. 33).

264. F. Monconduit, *La Commission européenne des droits de l'homme*, Leiden, Sijthoff, 1965, p. 315.

265. Appl. n. 225/56, *X* v. *F.R. Germany* case, decision of 18 July 1957, in Council of Europe doc. H(64) 1 (of 13 January 1964), p. 19, and in *Yearbook* [1955–7] vol. I, pp. 145–6.

266. Appl. n. 352/58, *X* v. *F.R. Germany* case, decision of 4 September 1958, *Yearbook* [1958–9] vol. II, p. 344.

267. Appl. n. 945/60, *X* v. *F.R. Germany* case, decision of 10 March 1962, *Collection*, vol. 8, p. 105.

268. Appl. n. 1474/62, *23 Inhabitants of Alsemberg and of Beersel* v. *Belgium*

case, complementary decision of 24 September 1963, *Collection*, vol. 12, pp. 27–8.

269. Appl. n. 2002/63, *X* v. *Norway* case, decision of 2 July 1964, *Collection*, vol. 14, pp. 27–8.

270. Appl. n. 2366/64, *X* v. *F.R. Germany* case, decision of 7 April 1967, *Collection*, vol. 22, p. 122; appl. n. 2854/66, *X and Y* v. *Austria* case, final decision of 18 December 1967, *Collection*, vol. 26, p. 53; appl. n. 3897/68, *X and Y* v. *F.R. Germany* case, partial decision of 5 February 1970, *Collection*, vol. 35, p. 80.

271. Council of Europe doc. H(64)1 (of 13 January 1964), p. 20; and Vasak, *La Convention Européenne*, p. 130.

272. Appl. n. 654/59, *X* v. *F.R. Germany* case, decision of 3 June 1960, *Collection*, vol. 7, p. 4. The Commission further stressed the direct interrelation between the exhaustion of local remedies and the six-month period, as implied by the grammatical construction of the single sentence of Article 26 of the Convention (*ibid.*, p. 4). The six-month rule is under the present heading dealt with only *incidenter tantum*, in so far as it is directly related to the notion of final decision.

273. Appl. n. 653/59 (1960), *Collection*, vol. 3, p. 2 (Federal Constitutional Court at Karlsruhe); appl. n. 968/61 (1961), *Collection*, vol. 8, p. 28 (Federal Constitutional Court). In another case against Germany the final decision was held to be the one rendered by the Federal Court: appl. n. 918/60 (1961), *Collection*, vol. 7, p. 110.

274. Appl. n. 1739/62 (1964), *Collection*, vol. 13, p. 102; appl. n. 3893/68 (1970), *Collection*, vol. 33, p. 10.

275. Appl. n. 3747/68 (1970), *Collection*, vol. 32, p. 21 (Oberster Gerichtshof); appl. n. 3972/69 (1971), *Collection*, vol. 37, p. 20.

276. Appl. n. 4311/69 (1971), *Collection*, vol. 37, pp. 95–6 (in respect of one of the complaints).

277. Appl. n. 3505/68 (1968), *Collection*, vol. 29, p. 63.

278. Appl. n. 4475/70 (1972), *Collection*, vol. 42, p. 13.

279. Appl. n. 1053/61 (1961), *Collection*, vol. 8, pp. 7–8.

280. Appl. n. 654/59 (1960), *Collection*, vol. 7, p. 5 (Supreme Regional Court of C.); appl. n. 4438/70 (1971), *Collection*, vol. 39, pp. 24–5 (Regional Court of K.).

281. Appl. n. 3505/68, *X* v. *United Kingdom* case, decision of 4 October 1968, *Collection*, vol. 29, pp. 62–3.

282. *Ibid.*, p. 63.

283. Appl. n. 3979/69, *X* v. *F.R. Germany* case, decision of 16 March 1970, *Collection*, vol. 33, p. 13. And see also on this point e.g., appl. n. 3893/68, *X* v. *Sweden* case, decision of 16 March 1970, *Collection*, vol. 33, p. 10.

284. Appl. n. 5560/72 (1973), *Collection*, vol. 45, p. 64.

285. Appl. n. 3972/69 (1971), *Collection*, vol. 37, p. 19; appl. n. 3893/68 (1970), *Collection*, vol. 33, p. 10.

286. Appl. n. 2614/65, *Ringeisen* v. *Austria* case, final decision of 18 July 1968, *Collection*, vol. 27, pp. 51–2.

287. European Court of Human Rights, *Ringeisen* case, Series A, judgment of 16 July 1971, p. 38, para. 91. The case is more appropriately examined in Ch. 5 on the time factor in the application of the local remedies rule.
288. It has been remarked that, should the Commission – unlikely as it may seem – reject an application for non-exhaustion on the ground that the final decision has not yet been given, that decision may constitute a 'relevant new fact' – under Article 27(1)(b) of the Convention – entitling the applicant to introduce a fresh application. Cf. Jacobs, *European Convention*, p. 242.
289. Again, such cases are more appropriately dealt with in Ch. 5, on the time factor in the application of the local remedies rule.
290. Appl. n. 2614/65, *Ringeisen* v. *Austria* case, final decision of 18 July 1968, *Collection*, vol. 27, p. 52 (my italics).
291. *Ibid.*, pp. 55–6.
292. *Ibid.*, p. 56.
293. Appl. n. 4859/71, *X* v. *Belgium* case, decision of 9 July 1973, *Collection*, vol. 44, pp. 6–7.
294. *Ibid.*, p. 7.
295. Appl. n. 343/57, *Nielsen* v. *Denmark* case, decision of 2 September 1959, *Report of the Commission*, p. 32.
296. *Ibid.*, p. 34.
297. *Ibid.*, p. 35.
298. In this connection the Commission quoted – but not without some reluctance – the PCIJ's decision in the *Electricity Company of Sofia* case (*supra*); see *ibid.*, p. 37.
299. *Ibid.*, p. 39.
300. *Ibid.* The Commission, further on, maintained the non-severability of an application (different parts of application not severable) for purposes of Article 26; cf. *ibid.*, p. 40.
301. Appl. n. 1739/62, *X* v. *Sweden* case, decision of 2 March 1964, *Collection*, vol. 13, p. 102.
302. *Ibid.*
303. Appl. n. 4311/69, *X* v. *Denmark* case, decision of 1 February 1971, *Collection*, vol. 37, p. 95.
304. Concerning alleged procedural errors committed during the proceedings before the trial court; cf. *ibid.*, p. 96.
305. *Ibid.*
306. See *ibid.*
307. Jacobs, *European Convention*, p. 242.
308. Appl. n. 712/60 (1961), *Collection*, vol. 8, p. 38.
309. *Ibid.*
310. Appl. n. 343/57 (1959), *Report of the Commission*, pp. 36–7.
311. Appl. n. 788/60 (1961), *Report of the Plenary Commission*, p. 43.
312. Appl. n. 2614/65 (1968), *Collection*, vol. 27, p. 52.
313. Appl. n. 1994/63 (1964), *Collection*, vol. 13, p. 109.
314. ICJ doc. C.R. 69/20 (translation), oral hearing of 13 May 1969 (mimeographed), p. 46.
315. *Ibid.*, p. 47.

316. ICJ doc. C.R. 69/24 (translation), oral hearing of 22 May 1969 (mimeographed), p. 32.
317. *Ibid.*, p. 31.
318. *Ibid.*
319. ICJ doc. C.R. 69/40 (translation), oral hearing of 16 June 1969 (mimeographed), p. 24.
320. ICJ doc. C.R. 69/63 (translation), oral hearing of 21 July 1969 (mimeographed), p. 28.
321. ICJ doc. C.R. 69/41 (translation), oral hearing of 17 June 1969 (mimeographed), p. 25.
322. The 1970 judgment of the International Court of Justice on the *Barcelona Traction* case contained the now well-known reference to human rights law in paragraph 34 of the judgment (*ICJ Reports* [1970] p. 32); similar references were made by Judges Morelli (*ibid.*, p. 232) and Gros (*ibid.*, pp. 273–4) in their respective Separate Opinions.
323. H. Friedmann, 'Epuisement des voies de recours internes', 14 *Revue de Droit international et de législation comparée* [1933] pp. 326–7.
324. Dissenting Opinion of Judge Van Eysinga in the *Panevezys – Saldutiskis Railway* case, PCIJ, Series A/B, n. 76, 1939, pp. 40–1; Dissenting Opinion of Judge Armand-Ugon in the *Interhandel* case, *ICJ Reports* [1959] p. 87. And see, on undue delays, the *Administration of the Prince von Pless* (Preliminary Objection) case, Series A/B, n. 52, 1933, p. 16.
325. See the French oral arguments in the *Norwegian Loans* case, *ICJ Reports* [1957], Pleadings etc., pp. 186–9, and cf. *ICJ Reports* [1957] p. 27.
326. *R.T. Johnson* v. *Peru* case (1870), *supra*.
327. *Robert E. Brown* v. *Great Britain* case (1923), *supra*.
328. *Forest of Central Rhodopia* case (1933), *supra*.
329. *Panevezys – Saldutiskis Railway* case (1939), and see the debates between the British and the Greek representatives in the *Don Pacifico* case (1851), La Pradelle/Politis, *Recueil*, vol. 1, 2nd edn, pp. 580–97; and cf. *Neptune* case (1797), *ibid.*, vol. 1, pp. 139 and 159–61.
330. *El Oro Mining and Railway Company* case (1931), *R.I.A.A.*, vol. v, p. 198 (undue delay in judicial proceedings); and see also *Swift and Company* v. *Board of Trade* case (1925), Hackworth's *Digest*, vol. v, pp. 521–4.
331. *Napier* case (1871), Moore's *Digest*, vol. III, pp. 3152–4, and La Pradelle/Politis, *Recueil*, vol. III, p. 123. See several further cases in which such contentions were rejected, reported in Moore's *Digest*, vol. III, p. 3158. But in the *Jesse Lewis* case (1921) the complainant's absence of pecuniary means was taken into account, and the U.S. – British Arbitral Tribunal suggested an allowance to be granted him; *R.I.A.A.*, vol. VI, pp. 92–3.
332. Cf. cases reported in J.B. Moore's *Digest*, vol. III, pp. 3157–8.
333. *Argonaut* case, as reported in Moore's *Digest*, vol. III, pp. 3157–8.
334. *La Guaira Electric Light and Power Company* case (1903–9), Hackworth's *Digest*, vol. v, pp. 510–11.
335. *Amelia* case (but not without hesitation), Moore's *Digest*, vol. III, p. 3157.

336. *M.S. Perry* case (again with some hesitation) and *Matamoras* case, Moore's *Digest*, vol. III, pp. 3158–9.

337. See, e.g., Court's *dictum* in the *Panevezys – Saldutiskis Railway* case, PCIJ, Series A/B, n. 76, 1939, p. 19. In the same way, official statements of a contending party to a dispute on the alleged uselessness of a given domestic remedy are not regarded as constituting *per se* circumstances relieving the applicant of the duty of exhaustion; *Interhandel* case, *ICJ Reports* [1959] p. 27.

338. See League of Nations doc. C.75.M.69.1929.V, pp. 136–9, 171–2, 180, 182, 190, 192–3, 195, 206, 209, 216; L. of N. doc. C. 75(a).M.69(a).1929.V, p. 23; *Acts–Minutes of the Third Committee*, vol. IV, pp. 63, 65, 70–1, 74–6, 78, 162, 164–5, 168–9; L. of N. doc. C.351(c).M.145(c).1930.V, p. 203.

339. See e.g., Witenberg, 'La recevabilité des réclamations', pp. 53–6; M. Bos, 'Les conditions du procès en Droit international public', 19 *Bibliotheca Visseriana* [1957] pp. 232–7; S. Séfériadès 'Le problème de l'accès des particuliers à des juridictions internationales', 51 *R.C.A.D.I.* [1935] pp. 72–82; E.M. Borchard, 'Theoretical Aspects of the International Responsibility of States', 1 *Zeitschrift für ausländisches öffentliches Recht und Völkerrecht* [1929] pp. 241–2; P. Guggenheim, *Traité de Droit international public*, vol. II, Genève, Georg et Cie, 1954, p. 24 n. 1.

340. Borchard, *Diplomatic Protection*, p. 818.

341. C. Eagleton, *The International Responsibility of States in International Law*, New York, University Press, 1928, p. 113; and see H.W. Briggs, *The Law of Nations*, New York, Appleton – Century-Crofts, 1952, p. 648.

342. Cf. in this sense Mummery, 'The Content', p. 413.

343. A.V. Freeman, *The International Responsibility of States for Denial of Justice*, London, Longmans, 1938, p. 406.

344. R. Ago, 'La Regola del Previo Esaurimento, pp. 249 and 182.

345. Text in European Convention on Human Rights, *Collected Texts*, 9th edn, Council of Europe, Strasbourg, March 1974, p. 8.

346. Appl. n. 5575/72, *X* v. *Austria* case, decision of 8 July 1975, European Commission of Human Rights, *Decisions and Reports*, vol. 1, Strasbourg, July 1975, p. 45.

347. Monconduit, *La Commission européenne*, p. 322. In his turn, starting from the criterion of effectiveness of remedies, Ruiloba Santana proposes a twofold classification of exceptions to the application of the local remedies rule in the present context, namely, 'circunstancias de orden técnico y circunstancias procedentes de una defectuosa administración de justicia'; E. Ruiloba Santana, 'La Regla del Agotamiento de los Recursos Internos a Través de las Decisiones de la Comisión Europea de los Derechos del Hombre', in *Estúdios de Derecho Internacional Público y Privado – Libro-Homenaje al Profesor Luis Sela Sampil*, Universidad de Oviedo, 1970, pp. 491–2; and see pp. 492–6 for examples.

348. Appl. n. 225/56 (1957), *Yearbook* [1955–7] vol. 1, pp. 145–6; appl. n. 226/56 (1956), *ibid.*, pp. 142–3; appl. n. 245/57 (1957), *ibid.*, p. 187; appl. n. 165/56 (1956), *ibid.*, pp. 203–4; appl. n. 172/56 (1957), *ibid.*, p. 218;

appl. n. 352/58 (1958), *Yearbook* [1958–9] vol. II, pp. 342–4; appl. n. 424/58 (1960), *Collection*, vol. 2, p. 7; appl. n. 631/59 (1960), *Collection*, vol. 3, p. 5; appl. n. 704/60 (1960), *Collection*, vol. 3, p. 6; appl. n. 5594/72 (1973), *Collection*, vol. 44, p. 133. On all those occasions the Commission, after examining the *dossier* of the cases, concluded that its examination of them did *not* disclose the existence of any special circumstances which could have absolved the applicant, according to the generally recognized rules of international law, from exhausting local remedies (at his disposal). Other such cases could be referred to, e.g., appl. n. 276/57 (1957), *Yearbook* [1955–7] vol. I, pp. 171–4; appl. n. 273/57 (1957), *ibid.*, pp. 207–8; appl. n. 285/57 (1957), *ibid.*, p. 258, amongst others.

349. E.g., appl. n. 297/57 (1958), *Yearbook* [1958–9] vol. II, pp. 213–14; appl. n. 704/60 (1960), *Collection*, vol. 3, p. 6.

350. Appl. n. 222/56, *X* v. *F.R. Germany* case, decision of 8 January 1959, *Yearbook* [1958–9] vol. II, pp. 348–9.

351. *Ibid.*, p. 349.

352. *Ibid.*, pp. 349–50.

353. *Ibid.*, p. 350.

354. *Ibid.*, p. 351. In the same sense (with regard to an appeal): appl. n. 568/59 (1960), *Collection*, vol. 2, p. 3.

355. Appl. n. 214/56, *De Becker* v. *Belgium* case, decision of 9 June 1958, *Yearbook* [1958–9] vol. II, pp. 236–8.

356. *Ibid.*, p. 238.

357. Articles 11(3) and 14(7)(a) of the UN Convention on the Elimination of All Forms of Racial Discrimination, text in *Human Rights – A Compilation of International Instruments of the United Nations*, UN doc. ST/HR/1, pp. 26–7.

358. Text in *ibid.*, p. 13.

359. Text in *ibid.*, p. 16.

360. P. Schaffer and D. Weissbrodt, 'Exhaustion of Remedies in the Context of the Racial Discrimination Convention', 2 *Revue des droits de l'homme/Human Rights Journal* [1969] pp. 639–40. And cf. also H. Wiebringhaus, 'La règle de l'épuisement préalable des voies de recours internes dans la jurisprudence de la Commission européenne des droits de l'homme', 5 *Annuaire Français de Droit International* [1959] p. 698: in the light of two very early dicisions of the Commission – appl. ns. 38/55 (1955) and 115/55 (1956) – the author remarks that the non-exhaustion of local remedies may occur even if the applicant has indirectly 'accepted' the undue delays of procedure by making recourse to further remedies still pending by the time he lodges his complaint with the Commission (*ibid.*, p. 698). It is in situations of this sort that it seems that the presumptions could be made to work more in favour of the individual complainant.

361. Cf. e.g., appl. n. 27/55, *X* v. *F.R. Germany* case, decision of 31 May 1956, *Yearbook* [1955–7] vol. I, p. 139. In the present case the Commission also dismissed, once again, the applicant's contention that

there had been undue delays in the procedure before the domestic court (*ibid.*, p. 139).

362. Appl. n. 514/59, *X* v. *Austria* case, decision of 5 January 1960, *Collection*, vol. 2, p. 3.

363. *Ibid.* Cf. also the Commission's *dictum* in appl. n. 434/58, *X* v. *Sweden* case, decision of 30 June 1959, *Yearbook* [1958–9] vol. II, p. 374.

364. Appl. n. 899/60, *A et al.* v. *F.R. Germany* case, decision of 9 March 1962, *Collection*, vol. 9, p. 9.

365. *Ibid.*

366. Appl. n. 1936/63, *Neumeister* v. *Austria* case, decision of 6 July 1964, *Collection*, vol. 14, p. 48. The Commission's decisions to this effect were reminiscent of the PCIJ's *dictum* to that same effect in the *Panevezys – Saldutiskis Railway* case (cf. Series A/B, n. 76 p. 18).

367. Appl. n. 1936/63 (1964), *Collection*, vol. 14, p. 49.

368. Appl. n. 1008/61, *X* v. *Austria* case, decision of 5 March 1962, *Collection*, vol. 8, p. 67.

369. *Ibid.* And cf. also appl. n. 1706/62, *X* v. *Austria* case, final decision of 4 October 1966, *Collection* vol. 21, pp. 50–4 (no obligation, in the circumstances of the case, to exhaust a civil action in particular).

370. Appl. n. 299/57, *Greece* v. *United Kingdom* case (in respect of Cyprus), decision of 12 October 1957, *Yearbook* [1958–9] vol. II, pp. 194–5.

371. Appl. ns. 5577/72–5583/72 (joined), *Donnelly and Others* v. *United Kingdom* case, decision of 5 April 1973, *Collection*, vol. 43, pp. 147–8.

372. Appl. n. 5006/71, *X* v. *United Kingdom* case, decision of 9 February 1972, *Collection*, vol. 39, p. 93; appl. n. 1404/62, *Wiechert* v. *F.R. Germany* case, final decisin of 3 November 1964, *Collection*, vol. 15, p. 23; appl. n. 1918/63, *X* v. *Austria* case, decision of 18 December 1963, *Collection*, vol. 12, p. 119; appl. n. 512/59, *X* v. *Belgium* case, decision of 29 August 1959, *Collection*, vol. 1, p. 4; appl. n. 1211/61, *X* v. *Netherlands* case, decision of 4 October 1962, *Collection*, vol. 9, p. 48; appl. n. 1094/61, *X* v. *Netherlands* case, decision of 4 October 1962, *Collection*, vol. 9, p. 44. In a recent case, the Commission maintained that the fact of being a mental patient or of lacking legal knowledge does not absolve the applicant from the duty of exhausting remedies (one should instead consider the effectiveness of remedies, applying the 'likelihood of success' test in the 'normal use' of remedies); appl. n. 6840/74, *X* v. *United Kingdom* case (1977), *Decisions and Reports*, vol. 10, pp. 15–20.

373. Appl. n. 1211/61 (1962), *Collection*, vol. 9, p. 48.

374. Appl. n. 6115/73, *X* v. *Belgium* case, decision of 28 March 1974, *Collection*, vol. 45, p. 123.

375. Appl. n. 1404/62 (1964), *Collection*, vol. 15, p. 23.

376. Appl. n. 4930/71 (1972), *Collection*, vol. 40, p. 41. And also, earlier, appl. n. 3040/67 (1967), *Collection*, vol. 22, p. 137.

377. Cf. appl. n. 1404/62 (1964), *Collection*, vol. 15, p. 23; appl. n. 4930/71 (1972), *Collection*, vol. 40, p. 41.

378. Appl. n. 1474/62 (1963), *Collection*, vol. 12, p. 28; appl. n. 1661/62 (1963), *Collection*, vol. 10, p. 19.

379. Cf. appl. n. 3868/68 (1970), *Collection*, vol. 34, p. 17.
380. Appl. n. 1488/62 (1963), *Collection*, vol. 13, p. 96; appl. n. 2257/64 (1968), *Collection*, vol. 27, p. 26; appl. n. 4340/69 (1971), *Collection*, vol. 38, p. 33.
381. Appl. n. 2004/63, *Kornmann* v. *F.R. Germany* case, final decision of 24 May 1966, *Collection*, vol. 20, p. 53. And cf. also appl. n. 1404/62 (1964), *Collection*, vol. 15, p. 23. Fawcett has written, however, that a lawyer's failure may, if proved, constitute a special circumstance excusing compliance with the rule in Article 26, provided the applicant has sought to obtain *restitutio in integrum*; the author quotes Commission's decision in appl. n. 495/59 (1959); Fawcett, *Application of the European Convention*, p. 304.
382. Appl. n. 5594/72, *X* v. *F.R. Germany* case, decision of 6 October 1973, *Collection*, vol. 44, p. 133. In the same sense (with regard to renewal of application to the Court of Appeal in the United Kingdom), see: appl. n. 4133/69 (1970), *Collection*, vol. 36, p. 64.
383. Appl. n. 289/57 (1957), *Yearbook* [1955–7] vol. I, p. 149.
384. Appl. n. 181/56 (1957), *Yearbook* [1955–7] vol. I, pp. 139–41. Cf. also applicant's complaint of not having been given legal assistance, despite his request, in appl. n. 1918/63 (1963), *Collection*, vol. 12, p. 118.
385. Appl. n. 289/57 (1957), *Yearbook* [1955–7] vol. I, p. 149; cf. also appl. n. 181/56 (1957), *ibid.*, pp. 140–1.
386. Appl. n. 568/59 (1960), *Collection*, vol. 2, p. 3.
387. Appl. n. 788/60, *Austria* v. *Italy* case, decision of 11 January 1961, *Report of the Plenary Commission*, p. 55.
388. European Commission of Human Rights, *Case-Law Topics/Sujets de Jurisprudence: Human Rights in Prison*, Strasbourg, 1971, p. 1.
389. *Ibid.*, p. 46.
390. *Ibid.*, p. 2.
391. Appl. n. 1103/61, *X* v. *Belgium* case, decision of 12 March 1962, *Collection*, vol. 8, p. 124. In the case, however, the Commission concluded that no such circumstances or impediments existed (cf. *ibid.*, p. 124).
392. Monconduit, *La Commission européenne*, pp. 327–9; Fawcett, *Application of the European Convention*, pp. 303–4.
393. E. Spatafora, 'La Regola del Previo Esaurimento dei Ricorsi Interni nella Giurisprudenza della Commissione Europea dei Diritti dell 'Uomo', 11 *Rivista di Diritto Europeo* [1971] p. 111–12.
394. Nay-Cadoux, *op. cit.*, pp. 103 and 99. The author sees in the Commission's examination of 'exceptions' to the local redress rule an *approche du fond* of the cases (*ibid.*, pp. 103 and 107).
395. Amerasinghe, 'The Rule of Exhaustion of Local Remedies', pp. 55–8; C.F. Amerasinghe, 'The Rule of Exhaustion of Domestic Remedies in the Framework of International Systems for the Protection of Human Rights', 28 *Zeitschrift für ausländisches öffentliches Recht und Völkerrecht* [1968] pp. 291–7.
396. N. Antonopoulos, *La Jurisprudence des organes de la Convention Européenne des droits de l'homme*, Leiden, Sijthoff, 1967, pp. 63–8, esp. p. 68. The

author considers the practice of the Commission on the matter to be 'extrêmement stricte et rigide, peu satisfaisante aux exigences de la vie pratique et de l'opinion publique européenne' (*ibid.*, p. 68).

397. R. Beddard, *Human Rights and Europe*, London, Sweet and Maxwell, 1973, p. 71.

398. Cf. J. Guinand, 'La règle de l'épuisement des voies de recours internes dans le cadre des systèmes internationaux de protection des droits de l'homme', 4 *Revue belge de Droit international* [1968] pp. 482–4.

399. Spatafora, *op. cit.*, p. 111.

400. Wiebringhaus, *op. cit.*, p. 698.

401. Appl. n. 627/59, *X* v. *F.R. Germany* case, decision of 14 December 1961, *Collection*, vol. 8, pp. 23–4.

402. Fawcett, *Application of the European Convention*, p. 304 n. 6.

403. Appl. n. 1661/62 (1963), *Collection*, vol. 10, p. 19; appl. n. 1474/62 (1963), *Collection*, vol. 12, p. 28.

404. Appl. n. 1211/61, *X* v. *Netherlands* case, decision of 4 October 1962, *Collection*, vol. 9, p. 48. And see also appl. n. 172/56, *X* v. *Sweden* case (1957), *Yearbook* [1955–7] vol. I, pp. 211–19.

405. Appl. n. 263/57, *X* v. *F.R. Germany* case, decision of 20 July 1957, *Yearbook* [1955–7], vol. I, pp. 146–7. Here the Commission held that, despite the apparent denial of justice, the exhaustion of local remedies was not enough, as the applicant had to bring before the higher court (before seizing the Commission) any complaints of a procedural order he might have against the lower domestic court (*ibid.*, p. 147).

406. Also in support of this view, Amerasinghe, 'The Rule of Exhaustion of Local Remedies', p. 57.

407. European Commission of Human Rights (A.B. McNulty, Secretary), *Stock-taking on the European Convention on Human Rights – A Periodic Note on the Concrete Results Achieved under the Convention*, Strasbourg, 1 October 1975, pp. 65–7.

408. *Ibid.*, p. 65.

409. See *ibid.*

410. Appl. n. 176/56, *First Cyprus* case (Greece v. United Kingdom, 1956), *Yearbook* [1958–9] vol. II, p. 184; appl. n. 299/57, *Second Cyprus* case (*idem*, 1957), *ibid.*, p. 194; appl. n. 788/60, *Austria* v. *Italy* case (1961), *Report of the Plenary Commission*, pp. 54–60; appl. ns. 3321–3323/67 and 3344/67, *First Greek* case (Denmark/Norway/Sweden/Netherlands v. Greece, 1968 – January and May), *Collection*, vols. 25 and 26, pp. 112–16 and 101–11, respectively; appl. n. 4448/70, *Second Greek* case (*idem*, 1970), *Collection*, vol. 34, p. 69; appl. n. 5310/71, *Ireland* v. *United Kingdom* case (1972), *Collection*, vol. 41, pp. 84–92; appl. ns. 6780/74 and 6950/75, *Cyprus* v. *Turkey* case, European Commission of Human Rights, *Decisions and Reports*, vol. 2, Strasbourg, December 1975, pp. 137–8.

411. Appl. n. 1474/62, *23 Inhabitants of Alsemberg and of Beersel* v. *Belgium* case (1963), *Collection*, vol. 11, pp. 54–8; appl. n. 1769/63, *Charlent et al.* v. *Belgium* case (1963), *ibid.*, pp. 65–8; appl. n. 1727/62, *Boeckmans* v. *Belgium* case (1963), *Collection*, vol. 12, pp. 39–48; appl. n. 1936/63, *Neumeister* v. *Austria* case (1964), *Collection*, vol. 14, pp. 47–53; appl. n.

2689/65, *Delcourt* v. *Belgium* case (1967), *Collection*, vol. 24, pp. 83–4; appl. n. 2257/64, *Soltikow* v. *F.R. Germany* case (1968), *Collection*, vol. 27, pp. 23–8; appl. n. 2614/65, *Ringeisen* v. *Austria* case (1968), *ibid.*, pp. 50–6; appl. n. 3897/68, *X and Y* v. *F.R. Germany* case (1970), *Collection*, vol. 35, pp. 79–82 and 95–6; appl. n. 4403/70 (25 applications), *Patel and Others* v. *United Kingdom* case (the so-called 'East African Asians' case, 1970), *Collection*, vol. 36, pp. 114–22; appl. n. 4451/70, *X* v. *United Kingdom* case (1971), *Collection*, vol. 37, pp. 131–3; appl. n. 4340/69, *Simon-Herold* v. *Austria* case (1971), *Collection*, vol. 38, pp. 30–4; appl. n. 4517/70, *Huber* v. *Austria* case (1970), *ibid.*, pp. 96–8 and 110–14; appl. ns. 2551/65, 3155/67, 3174/67 and 3499/68. *W, X, Y and Z* v. *Belgium* case (1971), *Collection*, vol. 39, pp. 7–10; appl. n. 4464/70, *Syndicat National de la Police Belge* v. *Belgium* case (1971), *ibid.*, pp. 31–3; appl. n. 5207/71, *X* v. *F.R. Germany* case (1971), *ibid.*, p. 103; appl. n. 4897/71, *Gussenbauer* v. *Austria* case (1972), *Collection*, vol. 42, pp. 46–8; appl. n. 5095/71, *Kjeldsen* v. *Denmark* case (1972), *Collection*, vol. 43, pp. 50–6; appl. ns. 5577/72–5583/72 (joined), *Donnelly and Others* v. *United Kingdom* case (1973), *ibid.*, pp. 132–49; appl. ns. 5100/72, 5354/72, 5370/72, *Engel/Dona/Schul* v. *Netherlands* case (1973), *Collection*, vol. 44, pp. 9–12; appl. n. 5926/72, *Pedersen* v. *Denmark* case (1973), *ibid.*, pp. 93–5 and 100; appl. n. 5493/72, *Handyside* v. *United Kingdom* case (1974), *Collection*, vol. 45, pp. 47–53.

412. Cf. other grounds of inadmissibility listed in Article 27 of the Convention.

413. Appl. ns. 3435–3438/67, *W, X, Y and Z* v. *United Kingdom* case, decision of 19 July 1968, *Collection*, vol. 28, pp. 122–31 (local redress rule excluded for unlikelihood of success and ineffectiveness of domestic remedies, but applications later declared inadmissible on different grounds); appl. n. 4623/70, *X* v. *United Kingdom* case, partial decision of 19 July 1971, *Collection*, vol. 39, pp. 64–5 (local redress rule held inapplicable due to the ineffectiveness and insufficiency of the means of redress, but application later declared inadmissible on another ground, but this time only in part, with the examination of the other part adjourned by the Commission); appl. n. 4459/70, *Kaiser* v. *Austria* case, final decision of 3 April 1971, *Collection*, vol. 38, pp. 52–7 (cf. *infra*).

414. Appl. n. 4459/70 (1971), *Collection*, vol. 38, pp. 54–6.

415. *Ibid.*, pp. 56–7.

416. Jacobs, *European Convention*, p. 275.

417. E.g., appl. n. 2370/64 (1967), *Collection*, vol. 22, p. 101; and see further *supra*.

418. Appl. n. 3001/66 (1968), *Collection*, vol. 26, pp. 58–9; appl. n. 1140/61 (1961), *Collection*, vol. 8, pp. 62–3.

419. Appl. n. 3001/66 (1968), *Collection*, vol. 26, pp. 59–60; appl. n. 263/57 (1957), *Yearbook* [1955–7] vol. I, pp. 146–7; appl. n. 2243/64 (1965), *Collection*, vol. 17, pp. 25–6 (applicant's complaint of having been prevented from submitting evidence).

420. The model provision on waiver of the rule was Article v of the 1923

Convention establishing the U.S. – Mexican General Claims Commission. In fact, all the Conventions instituting the *six* Mexican Claims Commissions rejected the local remedies rule. Cf. A.H. Feller, *The Mexican Claims Commissions* (1923–1934), New York, Macmillan Co., 1935, p. 34; F.K. Nielsen, *International Law Applied to Reclamations*, Washington, J. Byrne & Co., 1933, p. 70; J.G. de Beus, *The Jurisprudence of the General Claims Commission, United States and Mexico*, The Hague, M. Nijhoff, 1938, pp. 21–2, 130–2, 303–4; E.M. Borchard, 'Recent Opinions of the General Claims Commission, United States and Mexico', 25 *American Journal of International Law (A.J.I.L.)* [1931] pp. 735–8; C. Eagleton, 'L'épuisement des recours internes et le déni de justice, d'après certaines décisions récentes', 16 *Revue de Droit international et de législation comparée* [1935] pp. 518–19 and 525–6.

421. D.R. Shea, *The Calvo Clause*, Minneapolis, University of Minnesota Press, 1955, pp. 257 and 260–1.

422. Cf. L. Erades, 'The Gut Dam Arbitration', 16 *Nederlands Tijdschrift voor internationaal Recht* [1969] pp. 161–206.

423. Quoted in American Law Institute, *Second Restatement of the Foreign Relations Law of the United States* (1962), St Paul – Minneapolis, 1965, p. 622.

424. See remarks in F.G. Dawson and I.L. Head, *International Law, National Tribunals and the Rights of Aliens*, Syracuse, University Press, 1971, pp. 52–6; I.L. Head, 'A Fresh Look at the Local Remedies Rule', 5 *Canadian Yearbook of International Law* [1967] p. 156.

425. Those agreements, concluded in mid-1948 between the United States and various European States, are reported in volumes 19–24 and 29 of the *United Nations Treaty Series*.

426. Cf. n. 424 *supra*.

427. See discussion in, e.g., K.B. Hoffman, 'State Responsibility in International Law and Transboundary Pollution Injuries', 25 *International and Comparative Law Quarterly* [1976] pp. 513–41; P.H. Sand, 'The Role of Domestic Procedures in Transnational Environmental Disputes', Bellagio Conference Papers – American Society of International Law, July 1974, pp. 1–4 (mimeographed); S.C. McCaffrey, 'Private Remedies for Transfrontier Pollution Injuries', *Environmental Law, International and Comparative Aspects – A Symposium*, London, British Institute of International and Comparative Law, 1976, pp. 12–13 and 22; A.P. Lester, 'River Pollution in International Law', 57 *A.J.I.L.* [1963] p. 849; S.A. Bleicher, 'An Overview of Environmental Regulation', 2 *Ecology Law Quarterly* [1972] pp. 10, 14–15; A.Ch. Kiss, 'Transnational Pollution Carried in the Medium of Air', Bellagio Conference Papers (1974), A.S.I.L., pp. 11–44 (mimeographed); P.G. Dembling, 'International Liability for Damages Caused by the Launching of Objects into Outer Space – Theory and Applications', UN doc. A/CONF. 34/2, vol. II, 1969, pp. 1116–20; D.M. Poulantzas, 'The Rule of Exhaustion of Local Remedies and Liability for Space Vehicle Accidents', 17 *Revue hellénique de Droit international* [1964] pp. 103–4; C. Wilfred Jenks,

'Liability for Ultra-Hazardous Activities in International Law', 117 *R.C.A.D.I.* [1966] p. 191; A.Ch. Kiss et C. Lambrechts, 'Les dommages causés au sol par les vols supersoniques', 16 *Annuaire français de Droit international* [1970] pp. 773–4 and 769–81.

428. See, e.g., G. Schwarzenberger, *Foreign Investments and International Law*, London, Stevens, 1969, pp. 116–17, 160–1, 166–7; R.B. Lillich, 'The Effectiveness of the Local Remedies Rule Today', 58 *Proceedings of the American Society of International Law (P.A.S.I.L.)* [1964] pp. 102 and 107; D.R. Mummery, 'Increasing the Use of Local Remedies', 58 *P.A.S.I.L.* [1964] pp. 111–16; N.S. Rodley, 'Some Aspects of the World Bank Convention on the Settlement of Investment Disputes', 4 *Canadian Yearbook of International Law* [1966] p. 53 n. 38; S.M. Schwebel and J.G. Wetter, 'Arbitration and the Exhaustion of Local Remedies', 60 *A.J.I.L.* [1966] pp. 484–501; debates on 'Les conditions juridiques des investissements de capitaux dans les pays en voie de développement et des accords y relatifs', 52 *Annuaire de l'Institut de Droit International* [1967]–II, pp. 431–6, 447, 451–4 (oral interventions by Jiménez de Aréchaga, Yasseen, Valladão, Wright and Rolin); C.F. Amerasinghe, 'The Local Remedies Rule in an Appropriate Perspective', 36 *Zeitschrift für ausländisches öffentliches Recht und Völkerrecht* [1976] pp. 728–9, 758.

429. I.B.R.D., *Investment Laws of the World*, New York, Oceana, 1972, p. 10 (for text).

430. See *supra*, p. 132, for reference to pertinent provisions.

431. C.E. doc. A–87.198, p. 21, quoted in 57 *Inhabitants of Louvain and Environs* v. *Belgium* case (appl. n. 1994/63, decision of 5 March 1964), *Collection of Decisions of the European Commission of Human Rights*, vol. 13, p. 109.

432. *Ibid.*, p. 109.

433. *Ibid.*, p. 109. Another example of the respondent government choosing not to rely on the local remedies rule (Article 26 of the Convention) is afforded by the *Isop* v. *Austria* case (application n. 808/60, decision of 8 March 1962, in *Collection*, vol. 8, p. 87). Furthermore, in three subsequent cases, the respondent governments accepted that there were no local remedies to exhaust, and therefore did *not* pursue an objection of non-exhaustion; cf. appl. n. 6232/73, *E. König* v. *F.R. Germany* case (1975), *Decisions and Reports*, vol. 2, p. 82; appl. n. 6833/74, *Marckx* v. *Belgium* case (1975), *Decisions and Reports*, vol. 3, p. 126; appl. n. 6210/73, *G.W. Luedicke* v. *F.R. Germany* case (1976), C. of E. doc. 50.409–06.2 (Commission's report of 18 May 1977, mimeographed), Annex II, pp. 25–32, esp. p. 27.

434. *X* v. *Austria* case (application n. 2547/65, final decision of 14 July 1966), *Collection*, vol. 20, pp. 80–2.

435. *Ibid.*, pp. 83–5.

436. Text in 46 *Annuaire de l'Institut de Droit International* [1956] p. 358.

437. Appl. n. 5849/72, *Christian Müller* v. *Austria* case, decision of 16 December 1974, *Report of the European Commission of Human Rights* (adopted 1 October 1975), Strasbourg, 15 May 1976, p. 20.

438. *Ibid.*, p. 21.

439. *Ibid.*, p. 22.

440. See discussion in *Interhandel* case, *ICJ Reports* [1959], Pleadings etc., p. 573, and *ICJ Reports* [1959] pp. 29, 45 (Sep. Op. Córdova), 121 (Diss. Op. Lauterpacht), 84 (Diss. Op. Winiarski); J.P. Cot, *La Conciliation internationale*, Paris, Pédone, 1968, pp. 233–4; G. Gaja, *L'Esaurimento dei Ricorsi Interni nel Diritto Internazionale*, Milano, Giuffrè, 1967, pp. 159–60.

441. M. Virally, 'L'accès des particuliers à une instance internationale: la protection des droits de l'homme dans le cadre européen', 20 *Mémoires publiés par la Faculté de Droit de Genève* [1964] pp. 79–84 and 88–9, esp. p. 81.

442. Dissenting Opinion of Judge Van Eysinga in the *Panevezys – Saldutiskis Railway* case, PCIJ, Series A/B, n. 76, 1939, pp. 33–9 and 41; *Certain German Interests in Polish Upper Silesia* (Jurisdiction) case, PCIJ, Series A, n. 6, 1925, pp. 13–14; *Lighthouses* arbitration (France v. Greece), 23 *International Law Reports* [1956] pp. 659–82; *R.L. Trumbull v. Chile* case (1889), Moore's *Digest*, vol. IV, pp. 3569/3571; *G. Uzielli v. Italy* case (1963), *R.I.A.A.*, vol. XVI, pp. 270–1; *Young, Smith & Company* case, Moore's *Digest*, vol. III, pp. 3147–8; *Selwyn* case (1903), *R.I.A.A*, vol. IX, pp. 380–1; *Davy* case, *R.I.A.A.*, vol. IX, pp. 468–9; *Aroa Mines* case (1903), *R.I.A.A.*, vol. IX, pp. 435 and 444; *Moses* case (1868), Moore's *Digest*, vol. III, pp. 3128–9; *Manasse & Co.* case (1871), Moore's *Digest*, vol. IV, pp. 3463–4; *Lacaze* case (1864), La Pradelle/Politis, *Recueil*, vol. II, 2nd edn, pp. 297–304; *Inglis* case, La Pradelle/Politis's *Recueil*, vol. I, pp. 23–4; *Central Rhodope Forests* case (1933), *R.I.A.A.*, vol. III, p. 1419; British memorial in the *Anglo-Iranian Oil Company* case (1952), *ICJ Reports* [1952], Pleadings etc., pp. 122–4. And, amongst writers, cf. Borchard, 'Theoretical Aspects', p. 241; Borchard, *Diplomatic Protection*, p. 819 and n. 2; S.M. Schwebel and J.G. Wetter, *op. cit.*, p. 501; C.G. Ténékidès, 'L'épuisement des voies de recours internes comme condition préalable de l'instance internationale', 14 *Revue de Droit international et de législation comparée* [1933] pp. 519–35; G. Gaja, *L'Esaurimento*, pp. 156–7; M. Domke, 'International Commercial Arbitration', International Law Association – *Report of the Fiftieth Conference* (Brussels 1962), pp. 239–41; Ch. Carabiber, 'L' arbitrage international entre gouvernements et particuliers', 76 *R.C.A.D.I.* [1950] pp. 250–1; J.N. Hyde, 'Economic Development Agreements', 105 *R.C.A.D.I.* [1962] p. 352; C.M. Spofford, 'Third Party Judgment and International Economic Transactions', 113 *R.C.A.D.I.* [1964] p. 168.

443. *G. Salem (U.S.) v. Egypt* case (1932), *R.I.A.A.*, vol. II, p. 1189; *Canadian Hay Importers* case (1925), *R.I.A.A.*, vol. VI, pp. 142–7; *Owner of the 'R.T. Roy'* case (1925), *R.I.A.A.*, vol. VI, pp. 147–9; *A.G. Studer* case (1925), *R.I.A.A.*, vol. VI, pp. 149–53; *Mexican Union Railway Ltd* case (1926), *R.I.A.A.*, vol. V, pp. 9 and 123; *Pacific Mail Steamship Co.* case (1866), Moore's *Digest*, vol. II, pp. 1413–15; *Queen* case (Brazil v. Sweden – Norway, 1872), La Pradelle/Politis, *Recueil*, vol. II, pp. 706–12; *Ziat and Ben Kiran* claim (n. 53, 1924), *R.I.A.A.*, vol. II, pp. 731–2; [three] *Bensley* cases, Moore's *Digest*, vol. III, pp. 3016–18; *Baldwin* case (1849), Moore's *Digest*, vol. III, p. 3127; *La Guaira Electric*

*Light and Power Co.*case (1903–5), *R.I.A.A.*, vol. IX, p. 243, Hack-worth's *Digest*, vol. V, pp. 510–11; *Switzerland v. Federal Republic of Germany* case (1958), 25 *International Law Reports* [1958]–I, pp. 42–50; Dissenting Opinion of Judge Urrutia in the *Electricity Co. of Sofia and Bulgaria* (Preliminary Objection) case, PCIJ, Series A/B n. 77, 1939, p. 104; *G. Pinson* case (1928), *R.I.A.A.*, vol. V, p. 351. And, among writers, see Guggenheim, *Traité*, vol. II, p. 22 n. 2; Freeman, *International Responsibility*, p. 414; Witenberg, 'La recevabilité des réclamations, p. 52; A. Makarov, 'Consideraciones sobre el derecho de protección diplomática', 8 *Revista Española de Derecho Internacional* [1955] pp. 541–4 and 547–8; G. Schwarzenberger, *International Law*, 3rd edn, vol. I, London, Stevens, 1957, pp. 610–11; F.V. García Amador, Third Report on State Responsibility for Injuries to Aliens, *Yearbook of the International Law Commission* [1958]–II, p. 60 para. 24; J.H.W. Verzijl, 'Rapport supplémentaire sur la règle de l'épuisement des recours internes', 46 *Annuaire de l'Institut de Droit International* [1956] pp. 3–4.

444. Amerasinghe, 'The Rule of Exhaustion of Domestic Remedies', pp. 268–9; Amerasinghe, 'The Rule of Exhaustion of Local Remedies, p. 11.

445. *Austria v. Italy* case (application n. 788/60), *Report of the Plenary Commission* (adopted on 31 March 1963), Strasbourg, 1963, p. 42.

Chapter 3

1. J.C. Witenberg, '*Onus probandi* devant les juridictions arbitrales', 55 *Revue générale de droit international public* [1951] pp. 321 and 339.
2. C.F. Amerasinghe, *State Responsibility for Injuries to Aliens*, Oxford, Clarendon Press, 1967, p. 265.
3. G. Ripert, 'Les règles du droit civil applicables aux rapports interna-tionaux', 44 *Recueil des Cours de l'Académic de Droit International* [1933]–II, p. 646.
4. In this sense: D.V. Sandifer, *Evidence before International Tribunals*, Chicago, Foundation Press, 1939, pp. 97 and 92–3; J.C. Witenberg, 'La théorie des preuves devant les juridictions internationales', 56 *Recueil des Cours de l'Académie de Droit International* [1936]–II, p. 41; Bin Cheng, *General Principles of Law as Applied by International Courts and Tribunals*, London, Stevens, 1953, p. 332; R. Cassin (arbitrator), award of 10 June 1955 on a matter of diverted cargoes (Greece v. Great Britain), 22 *International Law Reports* [1955] p. 825; Ripert, *op. cit.*, pp. 646–7.
5. Sandifer, *op. cit.*, p. 97.
6. C. Witenberg, 'La théorie des preuves', pp. 41–2; Sandifer, *op. cit.*, pp. 92–3 and 97–8; Bin Cheng, *General Principles of Law*, p. 334. On the influence of private law notions upon international law, cf., e.g., H. Lauterpacht, 'The Grotian Tradition in International Law', in *International Law – The Collected Papers of Hersch Lauterpacht*, vol. II, Cambridge, University Press, 1975, p. 339; U. Scheuner, 'L'influence du droit interne sur la formation du droit international', 68 *Recueil des Cours de l'Académie de Droit International* [1939] pp. 99–206; J.H.W. Verzijl, 'La

base des jugements internationaux au cours de l'histoire', 58 *Revue générale de Droit international public* [1955] pp. 397–405. The administration of proof in international law is flexible, being entirely derived neither from Anglo-American nor from continental rules of evidence; H. Lauterpacht, 'The So-Called Anglo-American and Continental Schools of Thought in International Law', in *Collected Papers*, pp. 462–4. But see, *a contrario sensu*, for a general rejection of municipal law analogies in international adjudication, R. Bierzanek, 'Some Remarks on the Function of International Courts in the Contemporary World', 7 *Polish Yearbook of International Law* [1975] pp. 121–50.

7. Sandifer, *op. cit.*, p. 92. For examples of international law reliance upon analogies from municipal law, see further, in general, H. Steinberger, 'Comparative Jurisprudence and Judicial Protection of the Individual Against the Executive: a Method for Ascertaining International Law?', *Gerichtsschutz gegen die Exekutive/Judicial Protection against the Executive*, vol. 3, Max-Planck-Institut f.a.o.R.u.V., Köln, Heymanns/Oceana, 1971, p. 271 (as applied to the burden of proof). Grossen (*infra*) argues that presumptions are a device of legal technique applicable in branches of municipal law as well as in international law itself, intimately related to questions of evidence. In international law, they can in fact pertain either to the domain of evidence or to that of treaty interpretation. It is the former which is of direct interest here; by means of presumptions the international judge can better appreciate the evidence submitted by the parties in order to establish the factual situation from which he is to determine the legal consequences (p. 153). Grossen supports the distribution of, or collaboration of the parties in, the burden of proof (p. 169), and further observes that presumptions have their place here, considering the uncertainties surrounding the administration of proof in international legal procedure, which can neither be said to be entirely inquisitorial nor accusatorial (pp. 163/168), and which is to a large extent reliant in this domain upon analogies from municipal law (municipal legal systems) (pp. 172–3). As once observed by F. Gény, there is no law which does not suggest 'les moyens propres de sa réalisation' (p. 171): J.-M. Grossen, *Les Présomptions en Droit international public*, Neuchâtel/Paris, Delachaux & Niestlé, 1954, pp. 133–80.

8. J.F. Lalive, 'Quelques remarques sur la preuve devant la Cour Permanente et la Cour Internationale de Justice', 7 *Schweizerisches Jahrbuch für Internationales Recht* [1950] p. 102. See also, in this regard, H. Lauterpacht, *Private Law Sources and Analogies of International Law*, London, Longmans, 1927, pp. 210–11; J. C. Witenberg, *L'Organisation judiciaire, la procédure et la sentence internationales*, Paris, Pédone, 1937, pp. 234 and 236; A.P. Sereni, *Principî Generali di Diritto e Processo Internazionale*, Milano, Giuffrè, 1955, pp. 27–8, 31–2, 75–6 and 91; J.A. Jolowicz, *The Active Role of the Court – General Report to the Ninth Congress of Comparative Law*, International Academy of Comparative Law, 1974, esp. pp. 45 and 50–3 (mimeographed); J.A. Jolowicz, 'The Active Role of the Court in Civil Litigation', section II of M. Cappelletti and J.A. Jolowicz, *Public Interest Parties and the Active Role of the Judge in*

Civil Litigation, Milano, Giuffrè, 1975, pp. 187–91, 199–202, 206–8, 216–19 225–6, 234, 258–65 and 299–301.

9. Witenberg, 'La théorie des preuves', pp. 41–2, 48 and 50.
10. *Reports of International Arbitral Awards*, vol. IV, p. 585, see pp. 575–86.
11. K. Buschbeck, 'Evidence: Procedures of Judicial Discovery and Burden of Proof', *Gerichtsschutz gegen die Exekutive*, vol. 3, Colloquium, Max-Planck-Institut für ausländisches öffentliches Recht und Völkerrecht, Köln, C. Heymanns/Oceana, 1971, pp. 164–6, esp. p. 165.
12. Witenberg, 'La théorie des preuves', pp. 41 and 44–5.
13. C.H.P. Law, *The Local Remedies Rule in International Law*, Geneva, Droz, 1961, p. 56.
14. S. Rosenne, *The Law and Practice of the International Court*, vol. II, Leiden, Sijthoff, 1965, p. 580.
15. In this sense: G. Morelli, 'La théorie générale du procès international', 61 *Recueil des Cours de l'Académie de Droit International* [1937]–III, pp. 360–1; A. Bleckmann, 'Summary Report on the Discussions at the Colloquium', Max-Planck-Institut, vol. 3, p. 181; Brownlie, *Principles of International Law*, pp. 11 and 8; M. Bos, 'Les conditions du procès en droit international public', 19/20 *Bibliotheca Visseriana* [1957] pp. 178 and 271–2.
16. Sandifer, *op. cit.*, p. 91.
17. *Reports on International Arbitral Awards*, vol. IV, pp. 39–40.
18. *Ibid.*
19. *Reports of International Arbitral Awards*, vol. II, pp. 1124–5.
20. *Ibid.*, p. 837.
21. *International Law Reports* [1956] vol. 23, p. 679.
22. Ralston, *The Law and Procedure*, p. 351. The umpire remarked that 'in the *expedientes* now under consideration not a word of affirmative proof is furnished to show negligence on the part of the government' (*ibid*).
23. *Reports of International Arbitral Awards* vol. IX, p. 243. The commissioner added that, as the claim stood, it had 'not the necessary basis for an international reclamation' (*ibid.*, p. 243).
24. La Pradelle/N. Politis, *Recueil*, p. 708.
25. 6 *Annual Digest of Public International Law Cases* [1931–2] pp. 203–4.
26. See Article 21 of the Model Draft on Arbitral Procedure adopted by the International Law Commission at its fifth session, and comments by *rapporteur* Georges Scelle; *Yearbook of the International Law Commission* [1958]–II, pp. 9 and 14; *ibid.*, [1953]–II, p. 210. It seems, however, that Scelle's draft has not so far been much used by goverments, if at all.
27. Ralston, *The Law and Procedure*, p. 102. And Schwarzenberger, *International Law as Applied by International Courts and Tribunals*, 3rd edn, vol. I, London, Stevens, 1957, p. 73.
28. Witenberg, 'La théorie des preuves', pp. 42–4, 47–52 and 97–8; Witenberg, '*Onus probandi*', pp. 323 and 331–8; Sandifer, *op. cit.*, pp. 97 8.
29. PCIJ, *Mavrommatis Palestine Concessions* (Merits) case, 1925, Series A, n. 5, p. 29; PCIJ, *German Interests in Polish Upper Silesia* (Merits) case, 1926,

Series A, n. 7, p. 30; PCIJ, *Lotus* case, 1927, Series A, n. 10, pp. 31 and 28; PCIJ, *Legal Status of Eastern Greenland* case, 1933, Series A/B, n. 53, p. 49; PCIJ, *Lighthouses* case (France v. Greece), Series A/B, n. 62, p. 18.

30. M. Sörensen, *Les Sources du droit international*, Copenhagen, E. Munksgaard, 1946, pp. 207–9.

31. *Minquiers and Ecrehos* case, *ICJ Reports* [1953] pp. 67 and 52.

32. In the *Asylum* case (Colombia v. Peru, 1950), with regard to Colombia's reliance upon an alleged regional custom peculiar to Latin American States, the ICJ stated that 'the party which relies on a custom of this kind must prove that this custom is established in such a manner that it has become binding on the other party'. *Asylum* case, *ICJ Reports* [1950] p. 276. See further *dicta* in *Corfu Channel* case, *ICJ Reports* [1949] p. 18; Judge Read's Dissenting Opinion in the *Anglo-Norwegian Fisheries* case, *ICJ Reports* [1951] p. 189, and Pleadings; *U.S. Nationals in Morocco* case, *ICJ Reports* [1952] p. 200; *Barcelona Traction* (Preliminary Objections) case, *ICJ Reports* [1964] pp. 23–4; *North Sea Continental Shelf* cases, *ICJ Reports* [1969] pp. 28–9; Judge Sir Gerald Fitzmaurice's Separate Opinion in the *Barcelona Traction* (Second Phase) case, *ICJ Reports* [1970] pp. 88–90; Judge de Castro's Separate Opinion in the *Icelandic Fisheries* case (United Kingdom v. Iceland), *ICJ Reports* [1974] pp. 78–9; Judge Dillard's Separate Opinion, *ibid.*, p. 59; *Nuclear Tests* case (Australia v. France), *ICJ Reports* [1974] pp. 257, 265 and 292. And for general comment, cf. J.F. Lalive, *op. cit.*, pp. 83–101; S. Rosenne, *Law and Practice*, pp. 580–4; Bin Cheng, 'Burden of Proof before the ICJ', 2 *International and Comparative Law Quarterly* [1953] pp. 595–6; Sir Hersch Lauterpacht, *The Development of International Law by the International Court*, London, Stevens, 1958, pp. 362–7 and 386–8; L. Favoreu, 'Récusation et administration de la preuve devant la Cour Internationale de Justice', 11 *Annuaire Français de Droit International* [1965] pp. 233–5 and 255–77.

33. *Reports of International Arbitral Awards*, vol. XII, p. 119. Here, again, the principle is that the burden rests upon the party who asserts to prove his assertion.

34. PCIJ, *Panevezys – Saldutiskis Railway* case, 1939, Series A/B, n. 76 , p. 18.

35. *Ibid.*, p. 19.

36. *Norwegian Loans* case, *ICJ Reports* [1957]; Pleadings, Oral Arguments, Documents; vol. I, pp. 183–4.

37. *Ibid.*, p. 280, para. 110.

38. *Ibid.*, p. 281, para. 114.

39. *Ibid.*, public hearing of 22 May 1957, pp. 161–2.

40. *Ibid.*, p. 162.

41. *Ibid.*, public hearing of 24 May 1957, pp. 187–8. Professor Gros stated: 'En droit international, il n'est pas fait appel aux règles de preuves du droit interne car, dans les différends entre États, le juge ne pourrait pas, comme en droit interne, considérer qu'un fait allégué, mais non prouvé, n'est pas existant. L'État qui plaide peut n'être pas en mesure de fournir une preuve que son adversaire fournira facilement. Il y a donc

collaboration des parties pour la présentation des preuves au juge' (*ibid.*, p. 188).
42. *Norwegian Loans* case, *ICJ Reports* [1957], Judgment of 6 July 1957, p. 27.
43. *Ibid.*, Separate Opinion of Sir Hersch Lauterpacht, p. 39.
44. *Aerial Incident* case, *ICJ Reports* [1959]; Pleadings, Oral Arguments, Documents, p. 559. Professor Cot added that counsel for the contending parties should endeavour to help the Court by providing the necessary elements of information (cf. *ibid.*).
45. Cf. *ibid.*, pp. 565–6.
46. *Interhandel* case, *ICJ Reports* [1959]; Pleadings, Oral Arguments, Documents, pp. 562–3.
47. Cf. *ibid.*, pp. 562–3. The Swiss co-agent contested only that the distribution of the burden of proof could occur *before* the competent court had acquired a thorough knowledge of the merits of the case (cf. *ibid.*, p. 563).
48. *Reports of International Arbitral Awards*, vol. III, p. 1502.
49. See *ibid.*, pp. 1503–4.
50. J.E.S. Fawcett, 'The Exhaustion of Local Remedies: Substance or Procedure?', 31 *British Yearbook of International Law* [1954] p. 458.
51. Amerasinghe, *State Responsibility*, pp. 206, 220, 230, 260, 263–9; C.F. Amerasinghe, 'The Exhaustion of Procedural Remedies in the Same Court', 12 *International and Comparative Law Quarterly* [1963] pp. 1319–23; C.F. Amerasinghe, 'The Formal Character of the Rule of Local Remedies', 25 *Zeitschrift für ausländisches öffentliches Recht und Völkerrecht* [1965] pp. 452–3; Amerasinghe, 'The Rule of Exhaustion of Local Remedies, pp. 8 and 58–63.
52. Supporting the 'distribución del *onus probandi* entre ambos litigantes', Miaja de la Muela asserted that 'la carga de la prueba' regarding the exhaustion of local remedies before international tribunals 'no se sujeta a unas normas inflexibles, sino que ha de apreciarse siempre dentro de unas reglas de equidad, en función de las circunstancias de cada caso, que impiden resolver de una manera rigurosamente matemática su distribución entre las partes'. A. Miaja de la Muela, 'El Agotamiento de los Recursos Internos como Supuesto de las Reclamaciones Internacionales', 2 *Anuario Uruguayo de Derecho Internacional* [1963] pp. 40–1; and see further, pp. 41–3.
53. Law, *op. cit.*, pp. 54–61; A. Sarhan, *L'Épuisement des recours internes en matière de responsabilité internationale*, Université de Paris, 1962, pp. 218–23 and 227–30 (thesis, mimeographed); J. Chappez, *La Règle de l'épuisement des voies de recours internes*, Paris, Pédone, 1972, pp. 234–7; Sørensen, *op. cit.*, pp. 207–9; Sereni, *op. cit.*, pp. 30, 40, 76–7 and 90; Guggenheim, *Traité*, p. 81.
54. G. Gaja, *L'Esaurimento dei ricorsi interni nel Diritto internazionale*, Milano, Giuffre, 1967, pp. 227–31.
55. Ch. de Visscher, 'Notes sur la responsabilité internationale des États et la protection diplomatique d'après quelques documents récents', 8 *Revue de Droit international et de législation comparée* [1927] pp. 252–3. He added that 'ce principe, appliqué avec le discernement, avec la souplesse qu'

exige la diversité des espèces, fournit, croyons nous, une solution pleinement satisfaisante à la plupart des difficultés que soulève la responsabilité internationale des États' (*ibid.*, p. 253).

56. Ch. de Visscher, 'Notes', p. 254: 'les principes généraux du droit suffisent donc, a notre avis', De Visscher concludes, 'à justifier la charge, ainsi que le déplacement éventuel du fardeau de la preuve.' Cf. also, similarly, Roger Pinto, 'L'organisation judiciaire internationale – la Cour Internationale de Justice', *Juris-Classeur de Droit International*, Paris, Les Éditions Techniques, 1959, fascicule 217, pp. 26–8, 30–1 and 12; S. Bastid, 'L'organisation judiciaire internationale – l'arbitrage international', *Juris-Classeur de Droit International*, Paris, Les Éditions Techniques, 1961, fascicule 248, p. 9. And on the distribution of the burden of proof between the contending parties, the free administration of proof by the judge, and the collaboration between the parties and the judge in that respect (all in the international legal procedure), cf. A. Cassese, *Il Diritto Interno nel Processo Internazionale*, Padova, Cedam, 1962, pp. 169–76, 191 and 193. On the free administration of proof by the international judge, cf. further J. A. Stoll, *L'Application et l'interprétation du droit interne par les juridictions internationales*, Université Libre de Bruxelles, Institut de Sociologie, 1962, pp. 201–5.

57. *Reports of International Arbitral Awards*, vol. IV, p. 39. And in the same sense, *Georges Pinson (France)* v. *Mexico* case, decision of the Franco-Mexican Claims Commission of 19 October 1928, *Reports of International Arbitral Awards*, vol. V, pp. 413 and 327 seq.

58. Text in [*Yearbook*], European Commission of Human Rights, *Documents and Decisions* (1955–7], vol. I, p. 74.

59. Appl. n. 188/56, *Yearbook*, vol. I, pp. 178–9.

60. Appl. n. 232/56, *Yearbook*, vol. I, p. 144.

61. Appl. n. 222/56, *Yearbook*, vol. II, p. 351.

62. See, in addition, in the same sense, decisions of appl. n. 65/55 (16 December 1955), n. 307/57 (18 March 1958), n. 174/56 (28 September 1956), n. 103/55 (29 September 1956), quoted in H. Wiebringhaus, 'La règle de l'épuisement préalable des voies de recours internes dans la jurisprudence de la Commission Européenne des droits de l'homme', 5 *Annuaire Français de Droit International* [1959] pp. 688–9 and n. 8.

63. Cf. preamble of the European Convention on Human Rights.

64. In this sense, Amerasinghe, 'The Rule of Exhaustion of Domestic Remedies', pp. 298–9.

65. Two cases were brought by Greece against the United Kingdom in 1956/1957: the *First Cyprus* case (appl. n. 176/56) and the *Second Cyprus* case (appl. n. 299/57), here under consideration.

66. Appl. n. 299/57, *Yearbook*, vol. II, pp. 190–2. The Commission further asserted that 'in considering the admissibility of an application lodged pursuant to Article 24 of the Convention it is not the Commission's task to ascertain whether the applicant Contracting Party establishes *prima facie* proof of its allegations, since enquiry into such aspects relates to the merits of the case and cannot therefore be undertaken at the present stage of the proceedings' (*ibid.*, p. 190).

67. M.-A. Eissen, 'Le nouveau règlement intérieur de la Commission européenne des droits de l'homme', 6 *Annuaire Français de Droit International* [1960] p. 774. Article 36 of the Convention stated that the Commission was to draw up its own rules of procedure; it was equally up to the Commission to amend them, taking its decisions by a majority of the members present and voting (Article 34 of the Convention).

68. Some minor modifications of the original rules of procedure had been introduced in 1955 (September), 1957 (July), 1958 (June) and 1959 (January and December), but the *general* revision, modifying *inter alia* the provision on the burden of proof, was carried out in the course of 1960. Cf. Eissen, 'Le nouvean règlement', pp. 774–5.

69. Twenty-second session, 28 March to 2 April 1960, *Yearbook*, vol. III, p. 120.

70. Twenty-fourth session, 1 to 5 August 1960, *Yearbook*, vol. III, p. 120. The process of revision was based upon a draft prepared by a working group composed of Mr Waldock (President), Mr Eustathiades and Mr Petrén, and inspired in suggestions by the Secretariat; cf. Eissen 'Le nouvean règlement', p. 775.

71. Text in *Yearbook*, vol. III, p. 24.

72. See F. Monconduit, *La Commission européenne des droits de l'homme*, Leiden, Sijthoff, 1965, p. 318; A.–M. Nay-Cadoux, *Les conditions de recevabilité des requêtes individuelles devant la Commission européenne des droits de l'homme*, Giappichelli/LGDJ, Torino/Paris, 1966, p. 88; Amerasinghe, 'The Rule of Exhaustion of Domestic Remedies', pp. 297–8; cf. M.-A. Eissen, 'Le nouvean règlement', p. 785; N. Antonopoulos, *La Jurisprudence des organes de la Convention européenne des droits de l'homme*, Leiden, Sijthoff, 1967, p. 68 and n. 124; E. Grillo Pasquarelli, 'The Question of the Exhaustion of Domestic Remedies in the Context of the Examination of Admissibility of an Application to the European Commission of Human Rights', in *Privacy and Human Rights* (ed. A.H. Robertson), Manchester, University Press, 1973, p. 335.

73. In this sense, J.E.S. Fawcett, *The Application of the European Convention on Human Rights*, Oxford, Clarendon Press, 1969, pp. 289–90; Pasquarelli, *op. cit.*, pp. 335–6; Amerasinghe, 'The Formal Character of the Rule', pp. 452–3; P. Schaffer and D. Weissbrodt, 'Exhaustion of Remedies in the Context of the Racial Discrimination Convention', 2 *Revue des droits de l'homme/Human Rights Journal* [1969] pp. 646–7; A.H. Robertson, 'The European Convention on Human Rights and the Rule of Exhaustion of Local Remedies', 4 *Revista de Derechos Humanos* [1974] (Comisión de Derechos Civiles de Puerto Rico), p. 201; K. Vasak, 'Le droit international des droits de l'homme', 140 *Recueil des Cours de l'Académie de Droit International* [1974]–IV, pp. 380–1.

74. H. Rolin, 'Le rôle du requérant dans la procédure prévue par la Convention européenne des droits de l'homme', 9 *Revue hellénique de droit international* [1956] pp. 9–10, and cf. Article 19 of the Convention.

75. Rolin, 'Le rôle du requérant', p. 10.

76. *Ibid.*, p. 11, and cf. Article 28(a) of the Convention and Rules 50(1), 54(1) to (6) and 56 of the Commission's rules of procedure; cf. also

Rolin's criticisms of the procedure concerning the hearing of witnesses and experts, *ibid.*, pp. 11–12. Whether the international organ decides strictly on the basis of the evidence produced or on its own appreciation of it irrespective of the opinion of the parties is a point which may go beyond the distribution of the burden of proof and touch the general question of the function of evidence produced by the parties. This may, however, prove to be no more than an academic question, the only practical implication being the concern for guarantee of acceptance of a decision by the party concerned. The problem hardly seems to have arisen in the Convention system, at least not to the same extent as in general international adjudication (with possible exception of unique cases such as the *Greek* cases, studied in Ch. 4, on the extent of application of the rule of exhaustion of local remedies).

77. And this applied to the question of expenses with evidence (witnesses and experts); cf. Rolin, 'Le rôle du requérant', p. 12.

78. Writing on the Ministère Public (and analogues of other countries) and the 'active role' of the (national) judge, Cappelletti discerns the all-encompassing trend of 'procedural publicization', taking place to a greater or lesser extent surely in many of the civil law countries of Europe. Even though the parties still dispose of the content or subject-matter of the (private) litigation, the judge's active role (his powers and responsibilities) go beyond the 'formal' control of proceedings to comprise also the determination of the scope of litigation and the search for truth. Public control in a way supplements private initiative, and theoretically at least there appears to be a connection between judicial activism and the role of the Ministère Public in civil litigation. But Cappelletti cautiously adds that the existing French model of a 'public party' has not so far been able to assume successfully 'the entire burden of representing public and group interests in civil litigation' (he emphasizes the Ministère Public's role in criminal prosecution and civil matters akin to criminal proceedings). M. Cappelletti, 'Governmental and Private Advocates for the Public Interest in Civil Litigation: a Comparative Study', 73 *Michigan Law Review* [1975] pp. 832–7. See further Cappelletti's report in section 1 of M. Cappelletti and J.A. Jolowicz, *Public Interest Parties*, pp. 73–82.

79. Rolin, 'Le rôle du requérant', p. 12.

80. *Ibid.*, pp. 12–13. To him, some of his remarks seemed to apply even more forcefully to applications coming from Governments; see *ibid.*, p. 13.

81. Ibid., p. 14.

82. Appl. n. 4225/69, *Collection*, vol. 33, pp. 34 seq.

83. Appl. n. 4225/69, *Collection*, vol. 33, p. 43.

84. *Ibid.*, p. 43.

85. *Ibid.*, pp. 43 and 46.

86. Appl. n. 852/60 (19 September 1961), *Collection*, vol. 6, pp. 79 seq., esp. p. 83.

87. Appl. n. 852/60, *Collection*, vol. 6, pp. 83–4. Likewise, in the subsequent *X v. United Kingdom* case (decision of 5 July 1976), the

Commission concluded that the applicant had not substantiated his allegation that he had been prevented from instituting proceedings, and the application was ultimately rejected for non-exhaustion of local remedies under Article 27(3) of the Convention. Appl. n. 6148/73, *Decisions and Reports*, vol. 6, p. 20.

88. Appl. n. 1474/62 (24 September 1963), *Collection*, vol. 12, p. 27, see pp. 18 seq.
89. Appl. n. 1474/62, *Collection*, vol. 12, p. 27.
90. *Ibid.*, p. 28.
91. Appl. n. 299/57, *Yearbook*, vol. II, pp. 190–2.
92. Appl. n. 788/60 (11 January 1961), *Austria v. Italy* case, *Collection*, vol. 7, p. 62; *Report of the Plenary Commission on the Austria v. Italy* case (adopted on 31 March 1963), publ. n. A–84–548, Strasbourg, 1963, p. 54.
93. Appl. n. 788/60, *Collection*, vol. 7, pp. 63–4; *Report*, p. 55. The Commission further stated that only the non-utilisation of an 'essential' recourse could lead to the inadmissibility of an international claim, and that the local remedies rule confined itself to imposing the 'normal' use of remedies 'likely to be effective and adequate'. Cf. appl. n. 788/60, *Report*, p. 57; *Collection*, vol. 7, p. 66.
94. Appl. n. 2991/66, *Alam and Khan v. United Kingdom* case, *Collection*, vol. 24, pp. 116 seq. The case is also illustrative of the meaning of 'civil right' under Article 6(1) of the Convention and of the existence of a 'civil right' in matters of family life; see *ibid.*
95. Appl. n. 2991/66, *Collection*, vol. 24, p. 133.
96. *Ibid.*, p. 133.
97. *Ibid.*, p. 133.
98. Appl. n. 1727/62, decision of 29 October 1963, *Yearbook*, vol. VI, p. 398.
99. Appl. n. 1474/62, supplementary decision of 24 September 1963, *Collection*, vol. 12, p. 25.
100. *'Vagrancy'* cases (1969–71), Publications of the European Court of Human Rights; Series B; Pleadings, Oral Arguments and Documents, p. 293. Agent and counsel for the Belgian government, Mr J. De Meyer, took note of the Commission's principal delegate's view (see *ibid.*, p. 306).
101. On the applicant's general duty see: K. Vasak, *La Convention européenne des droits de l'homme*, Paris, LGDJ, 1964, p. 117; N. Antonopoulos, *op. cit.*, p. 69.
102. Appl. n. 1474/62, *Collection*, vol. 12, p. 27.
103. Appl. n. 2991/66, *Collection*, vol. 24, p. 133.
104. Appl. n. 788/60, *Austria v. Italy* case, *Report*, p. 57. More recently, in its decision of 28 September 1976 in the *X v. United Kingdom* case, the Commission maintained that, as the local remedy at issue (petitioning the Home Office) may have been ineffective and inoperable, the matter required 'the observations of the respondent government on the admissibility of the application including the question of exhaustion of domestic remedies'; appl. n. 7161/75, *Decisions and Reports*, vol. 7, pp. 100–1.

105. *Interhandel* (Preliminary Objections) case, Judgment of 21 March 1959, *ICJ Reports* [1959] p. 27.
106. In short, the case concerned a Swiss company (Retimag) owning property in Germany, whose confiscation was ordered by the Federal Supreme Court on the ground that it was used for illegal purposes. Retimag having filed an application with the Commission, the German government objected *inter alia* that the applicant had failed to exhaust the remedy for constitutional appeal. (It was unclear whether a foreign company could do so under German law.) Although the Commission held that this was a question of German constitutional law to be decided by the Constitutional Court itself, it also found that, as the applicants had not established that it was impossible for them to appeal to the Constitutional Court, the case was to be declared inadmissible for non-exhaustion of domestic remedies. Cf. appl. n. 712/60 (16 December 1961), *Collection*, vol. 8, pp. 29–42.
107. Appl. n. 712/60, *Collection*, vol. 8, p. 38. This principle was first held (as embracing procedural remedies as well) in 1956 by the Commission of Arbitration in the *Ambatielos* claim; *Reports of International Arbitral Awards*, vol. XII, p. 120.
108. Appl. n. 712/60, *Collection*, vol. 8, p. 41.
109. *Ibid.*, p. 41.
110. *Ibid.*, pp. 41–2.
111. *Ibid.*, p. 38.
112. *Ibid.*, p. 38.
113. Appl. n. 1474/62, *Collection*, vol. 12, p. 28.
114. On the nature and characterization of its task and function, see F. Stryckmans, 'La Commission européenne des droits de l'homme et le procès équitable', *Journal des Tribunaux*, Brussels, 1 October 1966, pp. 533–43 and 555–62, esp. p. 537; European Commission of Human Rights, *Case-Law Topics/Sujets de jurisprudence n. 3*, rev. edn, Strasbourg, January 1974, p. 42; Vasak, *La Convention européenne*, pp. 145–7, paras. 275/278; Monconduit, *La Commission européenne*, p. 540; C.C. Morrisson Jr, *The Developing European Law of Human Rights*, Leiden, Sijthoff, 1967, p. 27; G.L. Weil, *The European Convention on Human Rights*, Leiden, Sijthoff, 1963, pp. 194–8; N. Antonopoulos, *op. cit.*, pp. 23–36.
115. Appl. n. 343/57, *B.S. Nielsen v. Denmark* case, *Report of the Commission on the Nielsen case* (dated 15 March 1961), Strasbourg, p. 35.
116. Appl. n. 332/57 (30 August 1958), *Lawless v. Ireland* case, *Yearbook*, vol. II, p. 318; see also p. 326.
117. Appl. n. 214/56 (9 June 1958), *De Becker v. Belgium* case, *Yearbook*, vol. II, pp. 236–8.
118. Appl. n. 514/59 (5 January 1960), *X v. Austria* case, *Collection*, vol. 2, p. 3; appl. n. 3591/68 (5 February 1970), *X v. Austria* case, *Collection*, vol. 31, p. 46.
119. Appl. n. 4340/69 (2 February 1971), *Simon-Herold v. Austria* case, *Collection*, vol. 38, pp. 30–4, esp. p. 33. The case is discussed *supra*, pp. 161–2.

120. What test is to be applied to verify the effectiveness of domestic remedies? The problem seems to depend to a large extent upon the circumstances of each case. Yet there are in the practice of the Commission some indications for the determination of effectiveness. Undue delays and slowness in the procedure, for example, are bound to render remedies ineffective. Fawcett has suggested that 'judicial remedies will be ineffective for purposes of Article 26 if there is clear legal precedent (*une jurisprudence constante*) against the conclusion or order, which the applicant seeks to obtain from the courts; or if, because there is no change in the situation or new evidence to be presented to the courts, further proceedings can only result in repetition'. Fawcett, *Application of the European Convention*, pp. 301—2, esp. p. 301.

121. This is of course quite different from saying that the Commission would be entitled to examine the validity *per se* of national legislation with regard to the Convention. To say that the Commission should pronounce upon the effectiveness of a particular domestic remedy in a given case does not amount to saying that the Commission could embark on an examination *in abstracto* of the conformity of the domestic legal system concerned with the provisions of the Convention. For, it is recalled, in the *X* v. *Norway* case (appl. n. 867/60), the principle was established that the Commission is competent to examine the compatibility of domestic legislation with the Convention '*only* with respect to its application to a person, non-governmental organization or group of individuals, and *only* in so far as its application is alleged to constitute a violation of the Convention in regard to the person, organization or group in question' (my italics); cf. appl. n. 867/60 (29 May 1961), *Collection*, vol. 6, pp. 37—8.

122. K. Vasak, *La Commission interaméricaine des droits de l'homme*, Paris, LGDJ, 1968, p. 146 n. 16 (with regard to the *Retimag* case).

123. Appl. n. 343/57, *Report*, p. 45.

124. Appl. n. 3591/68 (5 February 1970), *Collection*, vol. 31, p. 45.

125. Appl. n. 214/56 (9 June 1958), *Yearbook*, vol. II, p. 237. In its decision in the *X* v. *United Kingdom* case (appl. n. 3898/68), the Commission explicitly referred – twice – to examination of issues of the case (one concerning the applicant's non-exhaustion of local remedies) made *ex officio*; cf. appl. n. 3898/68 (partial decision of 2 February 1970), *Collection*, vol. 35, pp. 99—100.

126. Appl. n. 514/59 (5 January 1960), *Collection*, vol. 2, p. 3.

127. Appl. n. 2294/64 (decision of 23 September 1965 on certain procedural questions), *Yearbook,* vol. VIII, p. 320. On the extension of the Commission's *ex officio* powers by virtue of the text of the new Article 29 of the Convention (as amended in accordance with Article 1 of the Third Protocol to the Convention), see Pasquarelli, *op. cit.*, p. 337 n.114.

128. Cf. appl. n. 808/60 (8 March 1962), *Isop* v. *Austria* case, *Collection*, vol. 8, p. 87.

129. Appl. n. 808/60, *Collection*, vol. 8, pp. 80—90.

130. Appl. n. 1994/63 (5 March 1964), *57 Inhabitants of Louvain and Environs* v. *Belgium* case, *Yearbook*, vol. VII, pp. 260—1.

131. Appl. n. 343/57, *Nielsen* v. *Denmark* case, *Report*, p. 36.
132. Appl. n. 1727/62 (29 October 1963), *Boeckmans* v. *Belgium* case, *Collection*, vol. 12, p. 45; see criticisms in, e.g., N. Antonopoulos, *op. cit.*, p. 69. In the same *Boeckmans* case the Commission further stated that 'selon les principes de droit international généralement reconnus, auxquels renvoie l'article 26, il incombe au gouvernement qui soulève l'exception de non-épuisement de prouver l'existence, dans son système juridique interne, d'un recours qui n'ait pas été exercé'. Appl. n. 1727/62, *Collection*, vol. 12, p. 45.
133. In this sense, K. Vasak has considered the case-law of the Commission 'quite ambiguous' on this point; K. Vasak, *La Convention européenne*, p. 117 and n. 63. On the non-uniformity of the practice of the Commission on this point, Danelius has remarked: 'On the one hand, the Commission has sometimes declared an application inadmissible for failure to exhaust a remedy which had not been invoked by the government. On the other hand, the Commission has taken the position that it should not reject an application for non-exhaustion of domestic remedies if the government has expressly indicated that it does not wish to invoke this ground of inadmissibility.' H. Danelius, 'Conditions of Admissibility in the Jurisprudence of the European Commission of Human Rights', 2 *Revue des droits de l'homme/Human Rights Journal* [1969] pp. 287–9, p. 288.
134. Pasquarelli, *op. cit.*, p. 337.
135. Appl. n. 1727/62, *Boeckmans* case, *supra*.
136. Pasquarelli, *op. cit.*, pp. 337–8.
137. Appl. ns. 2991/66, n. 788/60, n. 299/57, *supra*.
138. Danelius, *op. cit.*, p. 289.
139. Appl. n. 1994/63, *Yearbook*, vol. VII, p. 258; see pp. 252–8.
140. Appl. n. 1994/63, *Yearbook*, vol. VII, pp. 258–60.
141. *Ibid.*, p. 260.
142. *Ibid.*, p. 260, and cf. Rule 45(3a) of the Commission's Rules of Procedure.
143. *Ibid.*, cf. Rules 44 and 45(2) and (3b) of the Commission's Rules of Procedure (the latter amended by the Commission in 1973); cf. new text in European Convention on Human Rights, *Collected Texts*, 9th edn, Strasbourg, March 1974, p. 311.
144. Appl. n. 1994/63, *Yearbook*, vol. VII, p. 260.
145. *Ibid.*, p. 260. Similarly, at a certain stage in the *Isop* v. *Austria* case, the respondent government submitted that the applicant had not exhausted local remedies 'as he had failed to show that he had invoked before the Austrian courts the provisions of the Convention', but anyway the government added that in the case 'it chose not to rely on Article 26 of the Convention'. Appl. n. 808/60, *Yearbook*, vol. V, p. 120; see pp. 120–2.
146. See further remarks in Ch. 5, *supra*.
147. There remains always the possibility of the question being joined to the merits; besides, 'manifestly ill-founded' is, like 'non-exhaustion of local remedies', a ground of inadmissibility of applications, and the Commis-

sion does not seem to have treated the distribution of the burden of proof as to the latter as being incompatible with application of the former. The question of the *order* of appreciation of the two grounds may sometimes assume practical importance, as shown in Ch. 5. The precise interrelationship between the various grounds of admissibility of applications under the Convention is a difficult question, and the Commission tends to tackle each point at a time, aware of the intricacies involved. It is not without significance that, in this chapter, it has been proposed to deal with the burden of proof *with regard to* the ground of exhaustion of local remedies, in particular. Consideration of parallels of general international-al law (*supra*, pp. 134–43) has been dictated by the express reference to them contained in Article 26 of the Convention.

148. This question is here dealt with only in so far as it has a direct bearing on the burden of proof, as it is more appropriately studied, in detail, in section II, on the exhaustion of local remedies in relation to legislative measures and administrative practices under the European Convention, of Ch. 4 on the extent of application of the rule of exhaustion of local remedies'.

149. Appl. ns. 3321/67, 3322/67, 3323/67, 3344/67, *Denmark/Norway/ Sweden/Netherlands* v. *Greece* case, admissibility decisions of 24 January 1968 and 31 May 1968 (this latter containing new allegations considered by the Commission as an extension of the original applications); on this latter decision, see *Yearbook*, vol. XI, pp. 770–8. In the present case the Commission, recalling its previous decision on the *First Cyprus* case, stated that the local remedies rule, likewise, did not apply to such allegations as raised in the present *Greek* case (in relation to Article 7 of the Convention and Article I of the First Protocol); see *ibid.*, p. 778.

150. *Greek* case, *Yearbook*, vol. XI, p. 774.

151. *Ibid.*, p. 768; the respondent government did so without specifically invoking Article 27(2) of the Convention; cf. *ibid.*, p. 768.

152. Appl. n. 299/57, *Second Cyprus* case, *Yearbook*, vol. II, pp. 186 and 190, quoted in *Yearbook*, vol. XI, p. 768.

153. *Greek* case, *Yearbook*, vol. XI, p. 768.

154. Or else on the ground that they were manifestly ill-founded within the meaning of Article 27(2) of the Convention; in *Yearbook*, vol. XI, p. 768.

155. Appl. n. 5310/71 (1 October 1972), *Ireland* v. *United Kingdom* case, *Collection*, vol. 41, p. 85.

156. Appl. n. 5310/71, *Collection*, vol. 41, p. 85, see pp. 84–92.

157. *Ibid.*, pp. 85 and 91.

158. *Ibid.*, p. 85. In the case, in relation to Article 26 the respondent governement argued that the onus of proof (of the existence of an administrative practice) was incumbent upon the applicant (cf. *ibid.*, p. 24), while this latter contended that Article 26 did not apply to the present case, as this was a breach of treaty claim and not a claim of diplomatic protection (cf. *ibid.*, pp. 26–7).

159. Appl. ns. 5577/72–5583/72 (joined), *Donnelly and Others* v. *United Kingdom* case, *Collection*, vol. 43, p. 148.

160. In *Yearbook*, vol. XI, p. 776.

161. *Ibid.*
162. Appl. n. 2004/63 (final decision of 24 May 1966), *H. Kornmann* v. *F.R. Germany* case, *Collection*, vol. 20, p. 53.
163. *Ibid.*
164. *Ibid.*
165. Appl. n. 2686/65 (final decision of 13 December 1966), *Kornmann* v. *F.R. Germany* case, *Collection*, vol. 22, p. 10.
166. *Ibid.*
167. *Ibid.*
168. *Ibid.*
169. Partial decision of 16 December 1965 (not published).
170. Appl. n. 2686/65, *Collection*, vol. 22, pp. 10–11.
171. Appl. n. 4065/69 (14 July 1970), *X* v. *Federal Republic of Germany* case, *Collection*, vol. 35, p. 120.
172. European Commission of Human Rights, *Case-Law Topics/Sujets de jurisprudence n. 1*, Strasbourg, 1971, p. 1.
173. *Ibid.*, p. 2.
174. *Ibid.*, p. 1.
175. *Ibid.*, p. 8.
176. *Ibid.*
177. *Ibid.*, p. 1 and 46.
178. Appl. n. 1270/61 (8 March 1962), *Ilse Koch* v. *Federal Republic of Germany* case, *Yearbook*, vol. v, p. 134.
179. See remarks in F. Castberg, *The European Convention on Human Rights*, Leiden, Sijthoff/Oceana, 1974, p. 191.
180. The two questions, of course, are by no means synonymous; cf. H. Lauterpacht, *International Law and Human Rights*, London, Stevens, 1950, pp. 54–6 and 48.
181. F. Longchamps, 'Sur le problème du droit subjectif dans les rapports entre l'individu et le pouvoir', *Mé langes en l'honneur de Paul Roubier*, vol. I, Paris, Dalloz/Sirey, 1961, p. 319; see also p. 305.
182. Appl. n. 4340/69 (decision of 2 February 1971), *Simon-Herold* v. *Austria* case, *Collection*, vol. 38, p. 33.
183. Appl. n. 4340/69, *Collection*, vol. 38, p. 33.
184. *Ibid.*, p. 34.
185. *Ibid.*, pp. 30–4.
186. *Ibid.*, p. 34.
187. As enshrined in Article 14(2) of the UN International Covenant on Civil and Political Rights.
188. UN doc. E/CN. 4/Sub. 2/296/Rev. 1, *Study of Equality in the Administration of Justice*, by Mohammed Ahmed Abu Rannat, special *rapporteur* of the Sub-Commission, 1972, pp. 24–5, para. 75.
189. Appl. n. 4340/69 (2 February 1971), *Collection*, vol. 38, p. 30.
190. *Ibid.* As early as 1935 Kaufmann related the question of the burden of proof to that of *denial of justice*. He distinguished 'le délit de déni de justice, qui charge l'État réclamant de la preuve d'une attitude arbitraire ou discriminatoire, des délits résultant de lésions d'obligations interna-tionales concrétisées, qui n'exigent pas la preuve des faits arbitraires ou

discriminatoires'. E. Kaufmann, 'Règles générales du droit de la paix', 54 *Recueil des Cours de l'Académie de Droit International* [1935]–IV, p. 432; see his additional remarks on the same page.

191. Appl. 788/60, *Austria* v. *Italy* case, *Report of the Plenary Commission*, p. 208 (my italics).

192. *Ibid.*, p. 209.

193. *Ibid.*, p. 211.

193. *Ibid.*, p. 212. Two years later, in the *X* v. *Belgium* case, where the local remedies rule was also, discussed (cf. *supra*), the Commission took note of the applicant's complaint of the local judge's 'violation of the principle of the presumption of innocence'; cf. appl. 1727/62, decision of 29 October 1963, *Yearbook*, vol. VI, p. 398. And see recently, on presumption of innocence, e.g., appl. n. 6062/73, *X* v. *F.R. Germany* case, decision of 18 December 1974, European Commission of Human Rights, *Decisions and Reports*, vol. 2, Strasbourg, December 1975, pp. 55–6. And for decisions of national courts touching on the principle of presumption of innocence as enshrined in the European Convention, cf. Council of Europe/Directorate of Human Rights, *European Convention on Human Rights – National Aspects*, Strasbourg, January 1975, pp. 45–51.

195. R.J. Sharpe, *The Law of Habeas Corpus*, Oxford, Clarendon Press, 1976, p. 121.

196. *Ibid.*, p. 86.

197. *Ibid.*, p. 87.

198. *Ibid.*, p. 88.

199. *Ibid.*, pp. 87–8.

200. See John Humphrey, 'The Right of Petition in the United Nations', 4 *Revue des droits de l'homme/Human Rights Journal* [1971] pp. 470–5.

201. ECOSOC resolutions 1102(XL) of 1966; 1164(XLI) of 1966; 1235(XLII) of 1967.

202. Cf. 48 ESCOR, suppl. n. 1A, UN doc. E/4832/Add.1, pp. 8–9.

203. Cf. Article 6(b)(1).

204. Cf. Articles 1 and 2 of ECOSOC resolution 1503(XLVII), and previous resolutions 728 F(XXVIII) and 1235(XLII), in the same sense.

205. UN doc. E/CN.4/Sub.2/L.539/Rev.1.

206. UN doc. E/CN.4/Sub.2/L.540, pp. 2–3; UN doc. E/CN.4/Sub.2/SR.614, p. 30; the proposal was advanced in form of a draft resolution submitted by three of the experts.

207. Such was the proposal by the expert from Romania: cf. UN doc. E/CN.4/Sub.2/L.541, pp. 1–2; UN doc. E/CN.4/Sub.22/Sr.613, pp. 23–4.

208. Especially from the experts from the Philippines and Austria: cf. UN doc. E/CN.4/Sub.2/SR. 615, pp. 42 and 45, respectively.

209. Cf. the point of view of the experts from Egypt and France, *ibid.*, pp. 46–7; see also UN doc. E/CN.4/Sub.2/L.542.

210. UN doc. E/CN.4/Sub.2/SR. 615, p. 48; he himself preferred the latter approach. The Russian expert, on his part, submitted a draft resolution to the effect that complaints would be inadmissible if coming from

'persons who have not taken advantage of all opportunities available within the State in order to exercise their rights'; UN doc. E/CN.4/Sub.2/L.543, p. 2; see also UN doc. E/CN.4/Sub.2/SR.620, p. 95.

211. UN docs. E/CN.4/Sub.2/L.544, pp. 1–4, and see Add.1, pp. 1–2, and L.545.

212. UN doc. E/CN.4/Sub.2/SR.623, p. 132; UN doc. E/CN. 4/Sub.2/L.544, p. 4.

213. Cf. UN doc. E/CN.4/Sub.2/SR.623, pp. 132–3, 135, and 138.

214. *Ibid.*, p. 137; to facilitate the task of screening, guided by the principle of expediency, the expert from the Philippines suggested that only those petitions containing 'concrete allegations of specific violations of human rights' should be admissible, and the authenticity of all communications 'should be verified before they were considered by the Sub-Commission' (*ibid.*, p. 137).

215. *Ibid.*, pp. 136, 139 and 141.

216. UN doc. E/CN.4/Sub.2/L.548.

217. UN doc. E/CN.4/Sub.2/SR.623, p. 139.

218. *Ibid.*, pp. 139–40.

219. *Ibid.*, pp. 140–1.

220. *Ibid.*, p. 141.

221. *Ibid.*

222. *Ibid.*

223. UN doc. E/CN.4/Sub.2/L.549/Rev.1, p. 2: Article 1(b); see *ibid.*, pp. 1–3.

224. *Ibid.*, Article 4(a), pp. 2–3; see also Article 5, *ibid.*, p. 3.

225. UN doc. E/CN.4/Sub.2/SR.625, p. 8.

226. *Ibid.*, p. 13.

227. *Ibid.*

228. *Ibid.*

229. *Ibid.*

230. *Ibid.*, pp. 13–14.

231. *Ibid.*, p. 14. Another expert likewise 'did not think that the burden of proof should be placed on the individual complainant'; cf. *ibid.*, pp. 15–16.

232. *Ibid.*, p. 14.

233. *Ibid.*

234. *Ibid.*

235. UN doc. E/CN.4/Sub.2/SR.627, p. 44.

236. *Ibid.*

237. *Ibid.*

238. *Ibid.*

239. *Ibid.*

240. Article 1(b) provides that 'communications shall be admissible only if, after consideration thereof, together with the replies if any of the governments concerned, there are reasonable grounds to believe that they may reveal a consistent pattern of gross and reliably attested violations of human rights [...]'. Article 4(b) provides that 'communications shall be inadmissible if domestic remedies have not been

exhausted, unless it appears that such remedies would be ineffective or unreasonably prolonged. Any failure to exhaust remedies should be satisfactorily established.' And cf. also Article 5 of resolution 1(XXIV) of the Sub-Commission.

241. Article 6(b)(1).
242. A. Cassese, 'The Admissibility of Communications to the United Nations on Human Rights Violations', 5 *Revue des droits de l'homme/ Human Rights Journal* [1972] p. 393 n. 27.
243. Cf. UN doc. E/CN.4/Sub.2/296/Rev. 1, pp. 24–5, para. 75. Cf. also the recent debates of the Sub-Commission on 'The Question of the Human Rights of Persons Subjected to Any Form of Detention or Imprisonment', UN doc. E/CN.4/Sub.2/L.609/Rev.1, UN doc. E/ CN.4/Sub.2)L.610 and L.616–17, UN doc. E/CN.4/Sub.2/SR.710–11, pp. 111–20 August 1974).
244. Article 5(2)(b); text in *Human Rights: A Compilation of International Instruments of the United Nations*, UN doc. ST/HR/1 (1973), p. 16.
245. Article 5(1): text *ibid.*, p. 16.
246. See A.A. Cançado Trindade, 'Exhaustion of Local Remedies under the UN Covenent on Civil and Political Rights and its Optional Protocol', 28 *International and Comparative Law Quarterly* [1979] pp. 734–65; A.A. Cançado Trindade, 'Exhaustion of Local Remedies in the Inter-American System, 18 *Indian Journal of International Law* [1978] pp. 345–51.
247. Article 14(7)(a): text cited in n. 244 p. 27; cf. also Article 11(3) of the Convention, text *ibid.*, p. 26. For a recent study, see A.A. Cançado Trindade, 'Exhaustion of Local Remedies under the United Nations International Convention on the Elimination of All Forms of Racial Discrimination' 22 *German Yearbook of International Law* [1979] pp. 374–83.
248. Rule 81; text in *Rules of Procedure of the Trusteeship Council* (as amended up to and during its 29th session), UN doc. T/1/Rev.6, p. 14. For a study, see, e.g., Jean Beauté, *Le Droit de pétition dans les territoires sous tutelle*, Paris, LGDJ, 1962, pp. 1 seq.
249. On the practice of the Inter-American Commission on Human Rights, see Introduction, n. 9. A further reference can be made, in support of the distribution of the burden of proof, to the position in the system of the proposed International Prize Court (of the Second Hague Peace Conference, 1907); see Cançado Trindade, 'Exhaustion of Local Remedies in International Law Experiments Granting Procedural Status to Individuals', pp. 375–6.
250. In this sense: C.W. Jenks, *The Prospects of International Adjudication*, London, Stevens/Oceana, 1964, p. 423; Ch. de Visscher, *De l'équité dans le règlement arbitral ou judiciaire des litiges de droit international public*, Paris, Pédone, 1972, p. 91 and n. 1. *A contrario sensu: T. Haesler, The Exhaustion of Local Remedies in the Case-Law of International Courts and Tribunals*, Leiden, Sijthoff, 1968, pp. 33–7, esp. p. 35; and generally, M. Akehurst, 'Equity and General Principles of Law', 25 *International and Comparative Law Quarterly* [1976] pp. 801–25.

Chapter 4

1. Problems of application of the local remedies rule *ratione temporis* are more appropriately studied separately, in Ch. 5

2. Another matter likewise made optional is the compulsory jurisdiction of the European Court (Article 46 of the Convention).

3. PCIJ, *Mavrommatis Palestine Concessions* (Jurisdiction) case, 1924, Series A, n. 2, p. 12.

4. C.C. Hyde, *International Law – Chiefly as Interpreted and Applied by the United States*, 2nd rev. edn, vol. 11, Boston, Little – Brown & Co., 1945, p. 888 (as quoted in T. Meron, 'The Incidence of the Rule of Exhaustion of Local Remedies', 35 *British Yearbook of International Law* [1959] p. 84).

5. Meron, *op. cit.*, pp. 86–7.

6. *Ibid.*, pp. 87–8. In his turn, A. de La Pradelle distinguishes *three* kinds of situations, namely: those where a wrong is done to an individual (abroad), those in which an injury is inflicted by a State upon another State, and finally those where 'un tort est fait d'État à État, d'où naissent un ou plusieurs torts individuels'; A. de La Pradelle *et al., Recueil des arbitrages internationaux*, Paris, Les Éditions Internationales, 1954, vol. III, p. 134. Contacts at inter-governmental level may in fact take place between representatives of the private interests: see *Barcelona Traction* case (Preliminary Objections), *ICJ Reports* [1964] pp. 22–3.

7. Appl. n. 176/56, *First Cyprus* case (Greece v. United Kingdom), decision of 2 June 1956, *Yearbook* [1958–9] vol. II, p. 184.

8. *Ibid.*, p. 186.

9. Appls. ns. 3321–3323/67 and 3344/67, *First Greek* case (Denmark/Norway/Sweden/Netherlands v. Greece), decision of 24 January 1968, *Collection*, vol. 25, pp. 114–15.

10. C.Th. Eustathiades, 'La Convention européenne des droits de l'homme et le Statut du Conseil de l'Europe', 52 *Die Friedens-Warte* [1953–5] pp. 355–6.

11. C.Th. Eustathiades, 'Les recours individuels à la Commission européenne des droits de l'homme', in *Grundprobleme des Internationalen Rechts – Festschrift für Jean Spiropoulos*, Bonn, Schimmelbusch & Co., 1957, pp. 111–37.

12. Eustathiades, 'Les recours', pp. 129–30.

13. *Ibid.*, p. 131.

14. *Ibid.*, pp. 131–2.

15. *Ibid.*, p. 132; the author remarked that there is no scope for the application of the local remedies rule when the inter-State application raises the general compatibility or otherwise with the Convention of legislative measures or administrative or judicial practices; in such cases what is requested to the Commission is an interpretation or its declaration as to whether certain measures are contrary to the Convention (cf. *ibid.*).

16. See, for example, N. Antonopoulos, *La Jurisprudence des organes de la Convention européenne des droits de l'homme*, Leyden, Sijthoff, 1967, p. 49 n. 9; K. Vasak, *La Convention européenne des droits de l'homme*, Paris,

LGDJ, 1964, pp. 114–15. More recently Vasak has insisted on the waiver or a more flexible application of the local remedies rule in inter-State cases under the Convention as reflecting not an exercise of classical diplomatic protection but rather an action under the Convention system of collective guarantee of human rights; K. Vasak, 'Le droit international des droits de l'homme', 140 *Recueil des Cours de l'Académie de Droit International* [1974]–IV, pp. 377–8 and 380.

17. H. Rolin, 'Le rôle du requérant dans la procédure prévue par la Commission européenne des droits de l'homme', 9 *Revue hellénique de Droit international* [1956] pp. 8–9.

18. Appl. n. 788/60, *Austria v. Italy* case, decision of 11 January 1961, *Report of the Plenary Commission*, Council of Europe doc. A–84–548, Strasbourg, 1963, pp. 40–1.

19. *Ibid.*, p. 42.

20. Appl. n. 299/57, *Second Cyprus* case (Greece v. United Kingdom), decision of 12 October 1957, *Yearbook* [1958–9] vol. II, pp. 192–6.

21. Appl. n. 788/60, *Austria v. Italy* case, *Report*, p. 44.

22. *Ibid.*, p. 44.

23. *Ibid.*, p. 44.

24. Appls. ns. 5310/71 and 5451/72, *Ireland v. United Kingdom* case, decision of 1 October 1972, *Collection*, vol. 41, pp. 23–7, 51 and 84–92, esp. p. 84.

25. Appls. ns. 6780/74 and 6950/75, *Cyprus v. Turkey* case, decision of 26 May 1975, European Commission of Human Rights, *Decisions and Reports*, vol. 2, Strasbourg, December 1975, pp. 134–8, esp. p. 137.

26. See, in this sense, e.g., H. Danelius, 'Conditions of Admissibility in the Jurisprudence of the European Commission of Human Rights', 2 *Revue des droits de l'homme/Human Rights Journal* [1969] pp. 285–6; A.H. Robertson, 'The European Convention on Human Rights and the Rule of Exhaustion of Domestic Remedies', 4 *Revista de Derechos Humanos* [1974] (Comisión de Derechos Civiles de Puerto Rico), p. 203; F. Monconduit, *La Commission européenne des droits de l'homme*, Leyden, Sijthoff, 1965, p. 303; J.E.S. Fawcett, *The Application of the European Convention on Human Rights*, Oxford, Clarendon Press, 1969, p. 292; A.-M. Nay-Cadoux, *Les Conditions de recevabilité des requêtes individuelles devant la Commission européenne des droits de l'homme*, Paris/Torino, LGDJ/Giappichelli, 1966, p. 88; F. Castberg, *The European Convention on Human Rights*, Leyden, Sijthoff/Oceana, 1974, p. 40. It has in this connection been observed that, whether an application is lodged with the Commission by an individual (or group of individuals) or by a State, the obligation to exhaust local remedies under Article 26 of the Convention exists and ought to be considered in respect of the individuals (i.e., the victims) concerned; W.J. Ganshof van der Meersch, 'Does the Convention Have the Force of *"Ordre Public"* in Municipal Law?', in *Human Rights in National and International Law* (ed. A.H. Robertson), Manchester, University Press/Oceana, 1970, p. 142.

27. Council of Europe doc. DH(55)11, of 5 September 1955, p. 15.

28. *Norwegian Loans* case (France v. Norway), *ICJ Reports* [1957]; Pleadings,

Oral Arguments, Documents; p. 160.

29. *Aerial Incident* case (Israel v. Bulgaria), *ICJ Reports* [1959]; Pleadings, Oral Arguments, Documents; p. 531.

30. Cf. indications in this sense in Directorate of Human Rights, Council of Europe doc. DH(55)11, of 5 September 1955, pp. 15−16; J.M. Glenn, *Le Pacte international relatif aux droits civils et politiques et la Convention européenne des droits de l'homme: une étude comparative*, vol. II, Université de Strasbourg, 1973, p. 370 (mimeographed thesis); Amerasinghe, 'The Rule of Exhaustion of Local Remedies', pp. 24−6. A particular problem arises when a State Party to the Convention injures a national of a State not Party to the Convention in breach of the Convention. Either the individual concerned lodges an application with the Commission (under Article 25), or else his State takes up the case in the exercise of diplomatic protection (Amerasinghe, 'The Rule of Exhaustion of Local Remedies', p. 19); in either case or situation the local remedies rule would apply. Admittedly another State Party to the Convention could always take up the case by lodging an application with the Commission (under Article 24), even though this might not be a satisfactory solution to the problem. It is interesting to point out that in the *Donnelly* case the Commission was particularly careful to distinguish its handling of the case from its handling of the previous *Ireland* inter-State case; compare appls. ns. 5577−5583/72 (joined), *Donnelly and Others* v. *United Kingdom* case, decision of 5 April 1973, *Collection*, vol. 43, pp. 145−9, esp. p. 149; appls. ns. 5310/71 and 5451/72, *Ireland* v. *United Kingdom* case, decision of 1 October 1972, *Collection*, vol. 41, pp. 84−92.

31. Appl. n. 788/60, *Austria* v. *Italy* case, *Report*, p. 44. The inclusion of the reference to 'generally recognized rules of international law' in the local remedies requirement of Article 26 of the Convention has in practice given rise to some uncertainty and ambiguity; E. Ruiloba Santana, 'La Regla del Agotamiento de los Recursos Internos a Través de las Decisiones de la Comisión Europea de los Derechos Humanos', in *Estudios de Derecho Internacional Público y Privado − Libro-Homenaje al Profesor Luis Sela Sampil*, Universidad de Oviedo, 1970, pp. 471−3. In fact, as early as 1930 Karl Strupp warned against the risks of referring to the 'notion assez vague' of 'general principles of international law'; K. Strupp, 'Le droit du juge international de statuer selon l'équité', 33 *Recueil des Cours de l'Académie de Droit International* [1930] p. 447; and see also p. 452. In general international law itself the expression above had already been the object of much attention and debate; see, e.g., K. Wolff, 'Les principes généraux du droit applicables dans les rapports internationaux', 36 *Recueil des Cours de l'Académie de Droit International* [1931] pp. 483−553; A. Verdross, 'Les principes généraux du Droit dans la jurisprudence internationale', 52 *Recueil des Cours de l'Académie de Droit International* [1935] pp. 195−251; Bin Cheng, *General Principles of Law as Applied by International Courts and Tribunals*, London, Stevens, 1953, esp. pt III, pp. 161−253 (on 'General Principles of Law in the Concept of Responsibility'); W. Friedmann, 'The Uses of "General Principles" in the Development of International Law', 57 *American Journal of Interna-*

tional Law [1963] pp. 279–99 (Friedmann distinguishes three types of 'general principles', namely, general principles of interpretation, procedural standards of fairness, and substantive general principles; *ibid.*, pp. 286–90). In the framework of the European Convention on Human Rights, contrary to what seems sometimes to be commonly assumed, the inclusion of the expression at issue was meant to limit, rather than to extend, the scope of application of the local remedies rule: this is confirmed by the *travaux préparatoires* of the Convention provision in question, by the Commission's jurisprudence on the matter (cf. appl. n. 788/60, *Austria* v. *Italy* case, *Report of the Plenary Commission*, Council of Europe doc. A–84–548, decision of 11 January 1961, p. 44), as well as by recent expert writing on the subject; cf. A.H. Robertson, *Human Rights in Europe*, 2nd edn, Manchester, University Press, 1977, pp. 162–3: 'International law has long recognized this limitation on the domestic remedies rule; it was to take account of it that the words "according to the generally recognized rules of international law" were included in Article 26 of the European Convention [. . .] The generally recognized rules of international law release an applicant from the obligation to exhaust domestic remedies if they are clearly ineffective [. . .].'

32. The position taken by the European Commission on the problem of application of the local remedies rule in inter-State cases finds parallels in international experiments on human rights protection under the United Nations. Inter-State communications under the UN International Covenant on Civil and Political Rights are subject to the local remedies rule (Article 41(1)(c) of the Covenant), just as communications from individuals are (Articles 2 and 5(2)(b) of the Optional Protocol to the Covenant); cf. text in: *Human Rights: A Compilation of International Instruments of the United Nations*, UN doc. ST/HR/1, of 1973, pp. 13 and 16. Similarly, under the UN International Convention on the Elimination of All Forms of Racial Discrimination, human rights communications from individuals or groups of individuals (Article 14(7)(a) of the Convention), as well as from States Parties (Article 11(3) of the Convention), are subject to the rule of exhaustion of domestic remedies; cf. text *ibid.*, UN doc. ST/HR/1, pp. 26–7.

33. Appls. ns. 3321–3323/67 and 3344/67, *First Greek* case (Denmark/Norway/Sweden/Netherlands v. Greece), decision of 24 January 1968, *Collection*, vol. 25, pp. 112–16; and decision of 31 May 1968, *Collection*, vol. 26, pp. 101–11; appl. n. 4448/70, *Second Greek* case (Denmark/Norway/Sweden v. Greece), decision of 26 May 1970, *Collection*, vol. 34, pp. 66–9; and decision of 16 July 1970, *ibid.*, pp. 72–5.

34. It is pertinent to point out in this connection that, on its part, the Inter-American Commission on Human Rights has accepted, for purposes of application of the local remedies rule (Article 9(bis)(d) of its Statute and Articles 54 and 55 of its Regulations), a distinction between so-called 'general cases' and so-called 'individual cases'. Characterization of a complaint pertaining to a 'general case' brings about a waiver of the local remedies rule. Cf. G. Fraga, *El Agotamiento de Recursos Internos*

Previo a la Acción Internacional, OAS doc. OEA/Ser.L/V/II.28–doc. 19, of 4 May 1972, p. 10; and for an example in more recent practice, cf. 14 *International Legal Materials* [1975] pp. 115–16.

35. Amerasinghe, 'The Rule of Exhaustion of Local Remedies', p. 26.
36. F.G. Jacobs, *The European Convention on Human Rights*, Oxford, Clarendon Press, 1975, pp. 273–74.
37. Cf. *ibid.*, and, on the latest *Cyprus* v. *Turkey* case, cf. Council of Europe doc. H(76)1, of 19 January 1976, p. 2.
38. For the original text of those provisions, cf. OAS doc. OEA/Ser.L/V/II.23-doc.21 Rev., of 11 June 1970, Inter-American Commission on Human Rights, *Manual de Normas Vigentes en Materia de Derechos Humanos*, OAS General Secretariat, pp. 63–4.
39. Text in European Convention on Human Rights, *Collected Texts*, 9th edn, Council of Europe, Strasbourg, March 1974, p. 311.
40. Council of Europe doc. DH/Misc.(64)1, p. 2, in appl. n. 1994/63, *57 Inhabitants of Louvain and Environs* v. *Belgium* case, decision of 5 March 1964, *Collection*, vol. 13, p. 108.
41. The reason advanced by the Belgian government was that part of one group of the applications in the *linguistic cases* 'was directed not against a ministerial decision but rather against the Belgian legislation as such'; cf. Council of Europe doc. A–87–198, p. 21, *Collection*, vol. 13, p. 109.
42. *Collection*, vol. 13, p. 109. And cf. rule 45 of the Commission's rules of procedure, in *Collected Texts*, p. 311.
43. Cf., for a similar view, Castberg, *The European Convention*, p. 49.
44. Application n. 176/56, *First Cyprus* case (Greece v. United Kingdom), *Yearbook*, vol. 2, pp. 182–4.
45. *Ibid.*, p. 184.
46. *Ibid.*, p. 186.
47. Application n. 299/57, *Second Cyprus* case (Greece v. United Kingdom), *Yearbook*, vol. 2, pp. 188–92.
48. Cf. *ibid.*, p. 194. The Commission found it 'superfluous' to distinguish among the three categories of cases for the purpose of the application of Article 26 of the Convention (*ibid.*).
49. *Ibid.*, p. 196.
50. Article 27(3) of the Convention.
51. Appl. n. 299/57, p. 196.
52. Application n. 788/60, *Austria* v. *Italy* case, *Report of the Plenary Commission*, adopted on 31 March 1963, p. 45. The case concerned certain criminal proceedings (alleged by Austria to be incompatible with the Convention) leading to the conviction of six young men for the murder of an Italian customs officer in the German-speaking part of South Tyrol.
53. Applications ns. 3321/67, 3322/67, 3323/67, 3344/67, *First Greek* case (Denmark/Norway/Sweden/Netherlands v. Greece), *Yearbook*, vol. 11, pp. 710–14, esp. p. 714.
54. *Ibid.*, p. 714, also for reference to similar Dutch submissions. As the respondent government contested the Commission's competence in the case (*ibid.*, and see pp. 714–18), the applicant governments replied that

the Greek government was bound by the whole Convention (to which Greece had been a party since 1953), and that under Articles 19 and 24 of the Convention the Commission was competent to examine the applications and in particular 'the question whether legislative measures and administrative practices of the new Greek government were compatible with the Convention' (*ibid.*, p. 720).

55. *Ibid.*, p. 724.

56. *Ibid.* The Commission further stated that it was bound 'to reserve for an examination of the merits of this case the question whether the legislative measures and administrative practices in Greece, which form the subject of the present applications, were or are justified under Article 15 [of the Convention]' (right of derogation in time of public emergencies); *ibid.*, p. 728.

57. *Ibid.*

58. *First Greek* case, *Yearbook*, vol. 11, p. 748. The respondent government had submitted that the new allegations raised by the applicants were inadmissible as regards their form of presentation and that they should have been filed as new applications (cf. *ibid.*, p. 764). But the Commission took the view that they had been 'properly' introduced as 'an extension of the original applications' of the three Scandinavian governments (cf. *ibid.*, p. 766).

59. *Ibid.*, p. 748. They recalled in this connection that, e.g., 'the constitutional and conventional guarantees of a fair and public trial had been suspended' (cf. *ibid.*).

60. *Ibid.*, p. 770. It further contended that ill-treatment was prohibited by laws the enforcement of which was strictly supervised by 'competent administrative and independent judicial authorities', and that therefore the alleged ill-treatment could not be held to constitute an 'administrative practice' as alleged by the applicant governments (*ibid.*)

61. *Ibid.*, p. 770.

62. *Ibid.*, p. 774.

63. *Ibid.*, p. 778. The same was true of other allegations under Article 3 of the First Protocol, not subject to the local remedies rule for the same reason (cf. *ibid.*, pp. 778–80).

64. Cf. *ibid.*, p. 780.

65. *First Greek* case, *Report of the European Commission of Human Rights* (5 November 1969), *Yearbook*, vol. 12, p. 194.

66. Borne out by Article 13 of the Convention (right to an effective domestic remedy).

67. *Report*, in *Yearbook*, vol. 12, p. 194. The Commission then defined an 'administrative practice' of ill-treatment as necessarily consisting of two elements, namely, *repetition of acts and official tolerance* (see *ibid.*, pp. 195–6).

68. Application n. 4448/70, *Second Greek* case, *Yearbook*, vol. 13, p. 108. While the respondent government submitted that the local remedies rule should be applied in the case, the three Scandinavian governments alleged that there were 'no domestic remedies available' to the individuals concerned (*ibid.*, p. 116).

69. *Ibid.*, p. 122.
70. *Ibid.*
71. *Ibid.*, p. 130.
72. *Ibid.*, p. 128; and see pp. 128–30 for the facts. The applicants, moreover, denied that there were domestic remedies available (cf. *ibid.*, p. 130).
73. *Ibid.*, p. 132.
74. *Ibid.*, p. 134.
75. *Ibid.*
76. *Ibid.*
77. *Ibid.*, pp. 134–6.
78. Application n. 5310/71, *Ireland* v. *United Kingdom* case, *Collection*, vol. 41, p. 25.
79. *Ibid.*, p. 26. The applicant government further argued that generally recognized rules of international law made a distinction between a breach of treaty claim and claims of diplomatic protection, the local remedies rule applying only to the latter category of cases; the same distinction should be made with regard to inter-State claims brought under Article 24 of the Convention (cf. *ibid.*, pp. 26–7).
80. *Ibid.*, p. 24. On the problem of the burden of proof regarding the exhaustion of local remedies in such cases of legislative measures and administrative practices, cf. Ch. 3, *supra*.
81. *Ibid.*, p. 85. While the respondent party submitted that this part of the application should be rejected for non–exhaustion of local remedies, the applicant maintained that Article 26 did not apply where an administrative practice in violation of the Convention was complained of (cf. *ibid.*, p. 84).
82. *Ibid.*, p. 85.
83. *Ibid.*, pp. 85–7.
84. Cf. *ibid.*, pp. 87–8.
85. *Ibid.*, p. 88. The respondent government *inter alia* denied the charge and raised the objection of non-exhaustion of local remedies, whereas the applicant government submitted that this latter did not apply to any part of the application, whose object was 'to seek a determination of the compatibility with the Convention of certain legislative measures and administrative practices' (*ibid.*, p. 89). As a subsidiary argument, the Irish government submitted that even if the local remedies rule was held applicable, there were no adequate and effective remedies for the purposes of Article 26 of the Convention (*ibid.*).
86. *Ibid.*, p. 89. The Commission also reserved to an examination of the merits the question whether there had been a breach of Article 1 of the Convention with regard to those parts of the application found to be admissible (cf. *ibid.*, p. 90).
87. Cf. *ibid.*, pp. 91–2.
88. The term 'individuals' is used in the present sub-section as within the scope and meaning of Article 25 of the Convention, i.e., as comprising 'any person, non-governmental organization or group of individuals' claiming to be the victim of a violation by one of the High Contracting Parties of the rights set forth in the Convention.

89. Application n. 290/57, *X* v. *Ireland* case, *Yearbook*, vol. 3, p. 218.
90. *Ibid.*, p. 220.
91. *Ibid.*
92. *Ibid.*, p. 222.
93. The 'Offences Against the State Act 1939' and the 'Offences Against the State [Amendment] Act 1940'. The Commission's decision in the *X* v. *Ireland* case was delivered on 29 March 1960. Shortly afterwards the same problem arose in the *X* v. *Norway* case (application n. 867/60), in which the applicant's claim was made on behalf of parents who without their own consent or knowledge 'have or will have their offspring taken away by *abortus provocatus*', and on behalf of those 'taken away by such operations'. The applicant requested the Commission to investigate the compatibility of the Norwegian Act of 12 October 1960 with the provisions of the Convention. The Commission, however, noticed that the applicant had not pretended to have been himself in any way a victim of the Norwegian Act of 12 October 1960. As the Commission had already made it clear that it was competent to examine the compatibility of domestic legislation with the Convention only with respect to its application to an individual and only in so far as that application is alleged to constitute a violation of the Convention in regard to the individual concerned, the Commission in the present case did not find itself competent to examine *in abstracto* the question of the conformity of this Act with the provisions of the Convention. The Commission therefore declared the application inadmissible, the issue of the exhaustion of local remedies not having been raised. Cf. application n. 867/60, *X* v. *Norway* case, *Collection*, vol. 6, pp. 37–8.
94. Again under Article 2 of the First Protocol to the Convention. Cf. application n. 5095/71, *Kjeldsen* v. *Denmark* case, *Collection*, vol. 43, p. 46.
95. *Ibid.*, p. 46.
96. *Ibid.*, p. 50.
97. Cf. the two Danish rules of *interpretation* and *presumption*, *ibid.*, p. 50.
98. *Ibid.*
99. *Ibid.*, p. 51, also for the Danish government's further submissions.
100. *Ibid.*, pp. 51–2.
101. *Ibid.*, p. 52.
102. *Ibid.*
103. *Ibid.*, p. 54.
104. *Ibid.*, p. 54.
105. *Ibid.*, pp. 54–5.
106. *Ibid.*, p. 55.
107. *Ibid.*
108. *Ibid.*, p. 55.
109. *Ibid.*, p. 56.
110. Directed against compulsory sex education in public schools introduced by an Act of Parliament, regarding the parents' right to have their children educated in conformity with their religious and philosophical convictions (Article 2 of the First Protocol to the Convention). Cf.

application n. 5926/72, *Pedersen* v. *Denmark* case, *Collection*, vol. 44, pp. 93–5. And cf. also application n. 5920/72, *Busk Madsen* v. *Denmark* case, cited in *Collection*, vol. 44, p. 93 n. 1.

111. Application n. 5926/72, *Pedersen* v. *Denmark* case, *Collection*, vol. 44, p. 100.

112. *Ibid.*

113. Appls. ns. 5577/72 to 5583/72 (joined), *Donnelly and Others* v. *United Kingdom* case, *Collection*, vol. 43, p. 122.

114. *Ibid.*, pp. 124–5.

115. *Ibid.*, pp. 128–9; and see p. 125.

116. *Ibid.*, pp. 131–2. They envisaged, in particular, powers under the Civil Authorities [Special Powers] Act (Northern Ireland) 1922, concerning arrest and detention for interrogation.

117. On the pursuance of local remedies, cf. *ibid.*, pp. 131–3.

118. *Ibid.*, pp. 137–40. On the government's insistence on the application of the local remedies rule, cf. *ibid.*, pp. 134–7, and 132, especially remarks at p. 135.

119. *Ibid.*, pp. 140–1.

120. My italics.

121. *Ibid.*, p. 142.

122. *Ibid.*

123. *Ibid.*, pp. 142–3. The applicants pointed out that the only remedies indicated by the respondent government were directed either to *compensation* or to the *prosecution* of those responsible for causing the injuries. Criminal prosecution, they submitted, 'could not provide an adequate remedy because the applicants had no control over the initiation of such proceedings and any private prosecution might be quashed by the public prosecutor' (*ibid.*, p. 143). For further complaints in this connection, cf. *ibid.*, pp. 143–4. As to compensation, they conceded that the civil actions referred to by the government would constitute adequate remedies for 'isolated cases' of ill-treatment, but in the present case, 'merely awarding damages to a few individuals would have no ameliorative effect on the practice [of ill-treatment] itself' (*ibid.*, p. 143).

124. *Ibid.*, p. 146.

125. *Ibid.*, pp. 146–7.

126. *Ibid.*, p. 147.

127. *Ibid.*, pp. 147–8.

128. *Ibid.*, p. 148. In this connection, the Commission referred to its decision on admissibility in the *Simon-Herold* v. *Austria* case (application n. 4340/69), *Collection*, vol. 39, pp. 18–33, cited in *Collection*, vol. 43, p. 148.

129. *Ibid.*

130. *Ibid.*, pp. 148–9. See further *supra*, on the Commission's final decision (of 15 December 1975) on the *Donnelly* case.

131. Castberg, *The European Convention*, pp. 46–8; K. Boyle and H. Hannum, 'Individual Applications under the European Convention on Human Rights and the Concept of Administrative Practice: the *Donnelly*

case', 68 *American Journal of International Law* [1974] pp. 440–53; E. McGovern, 'The Local Remedies Rule and Administrative Practices in the European Convention on Human Rights', 24 *International and Comparative Law Quarterly* [1975] pp. 119–27. On the *non-application* of the local remedies rule in relation to legislative measures and administrative practices under the European Convention, cf. Sir Humphrey Waldock, 'General Course on Public International Law', 106 *Recueil des Cours de l'Académie de Droit International* [1962]–11, p. 209; E. Müller-Rappard, 'Le droit d'action en vertu des dispositions de la Convention européenne des droits de l'homme', 4 *Revue Belge de Droit International* [1968]–11, pp. 489–90. *A contrario sensu*, cf. H. Danelius, 'Conditions of Admissibility in the Jurisprudence of the European Commission of Human Rights', 2 *Revue des droits de l'homme/Human Rights Journal* [1969] pp. 286–7, esp p. 287.

132. Application n. 788/60, *Austria v. Italy* case, *Report of the Plenary Commission*, p. 42.

133. *Ibid.*

134. *First Greek* case, *Yearbook*, vol. 11, p. 776.

135. Application n. 4185/69, *X v. F.R. Germany* case, *Collection*, vol. 35, p. 142. The applicant in the case was the wife of a person detained in a lunatic asylum, who claimed to be an 'indirect victim' of her husband's detention following decisions of German courts; the Commission found *inter alia* that the condition as to the exhaustion of domestic remedies had not been complied with by the applicant (cf. *ibid.*, pp. 140–2).

136. Application n. 1478/62, *Koolen v. Belgium* case, *Collection*, vol. 13, p. 89; application n. 282/57, *X v. F.R. Germany*, case, *Yearbook*, vol. 1, p. 166. On this question (direct and indirect victims of violations of the Convention), see European Commission of Human Rights, *Case-Law Topics/Sujets de jurisprudence* no. 3, Strasbourg, January 1974, pp. 2–7. And cf. also Fawcett, *Application of the European Convention*, pp. 282–5. rule 36(2) of the Commission's rules of procedure allows individual applicants (under Article 25 of the Convention) to be assisted or represented by lawyers approved by the Commission. On this point, see European Commission, *Case-Law Topics* no. 3, pp. 7–9. On the gradual strengthening of the individual's role in the proceedings before the Commission, see mainly the *Lawless* (1961) and the '*Vagrancy*' (1970) cases. More recently, in its decision of 13 December 1976 in the *X v. Belgium* case, the Commission maintained that the author of the application, brother of the victim, was to be considered as being an indirect victim of the alleged violations; appl. n. 7467/76, *Decisions and Reports*, vol. 8, pp. 220–1.

137. Application n. 289/57, *X v. F.R. Germany* case, *Yearbook*, vol. 1, p. 149.

138. Vasak, *La Convention européenne*, pp. 97–8; C.P. Economopoulos, 'Les éléments politiques et judiciaires dans la procédure instaurée par la Convention européenne des droits de l'homme', 22 *Revue Hellénique de Droit International* [1969] pp. 125–6.

139. C.Th. Eustathiades, 'Une nouvelle expérience en Droit international: les recours individuels à la Commission européenne des droits de l'homme',

in *Grundprobleme des Internationalen Rechts–Festschrift fur Jean Spiropoulos*,
Bonn, Schimmelbusch & Co., 1957, pp. 120–2.

140. Rolin, 'Le rôle du requérant', pp. 8–10.
141. Application n. 788/60, *Austria* v. *Italy* case, *Report*, p. 37 (my italics).
The Commission drew attention not only to the 'objective character of
the obligations and rights established in the Convention', but also to the
'unqualified terms in which the right to refer alleged breaches of the
Convention to the Commission is formulated in Article 24' – a provision
which was the expression of the '*system of collective guarantee*' underlying
the Convention (*ibid.*, p. 38). The Commission then stated that the local
remedies rule applied to inter-State applications in the same way as it
applied to applications from individuals. Although the rule (Article 26)
referred to general international law, in its application regard should be
had to the particularities of the system inaugurated by the Convention,
e.g., the extension of the protection not only to aliens but also to a
State's own nationals, thus embracing claims which would be 'inadmissible under general international law, irrespective of the exhaustion of domestic remedies' (*ibid.*, pp. 42–5 esp. pp. 43–4).
142. Amerasinghe, 'The Rule of Exhaustion of Local Remedies', pp. 5–6;
Amerasinghe, 'The Rule of Exhaustion of Domestic Remedies', pp.
261–3; Fawcett, *The Application of the European Convention*, pp. 293–4.
And see also G. Gaja, *L'Esaurimento dei ricorsi interni nel Diritto
internazionale*, Milano, Giuffrè, 1967, pp. 95–9; A. Miaja de la Muela,
'El Agotamiento de los Recursos Internos como Supuesto de las
Reclamaciones Internacionales', 2 *Anuario Uruguayo de Derecho Internacion-
al* [1963] p. 16.
143. A.J.P. Tammes, 'The Obligation to Provide Local Remedies', in
*Volkenrechtelijke Opstellen aangeboden aan Professor Gesina H.J. van der
Molen*, Kampen, 1962, pp. 152–68; K. Doehring, 'Does General
International Law Require Domestic Judicial Protection against the
Executive?', in *Gerichtsschutz gegen die Exekutive*, vol. 3 (Colloquium,
Max-Planck-Institut für ausländisches öffentliches Recht und Völker-
recht), Köln, C. Heymanns/Oceana, 1971, pp. 240–4.
144. Applications ns. 6780/74 and 6950/75, *Cyprus* v. *Turkey* case, in
European Commission of Human Rights, *Decisions and Reports*, vol. 2,
December 1975, pp. 129–30, 132, 134 and 137–8.
145. Application n. 788/60, *Austria* v. *Italy* case, *Report*, p. 44 (my italics).
146. Boyle and Hannum, 'Individual Applications', p. 452.
147. A.B. McNulty (Secretary to the Commission), *Stock-Taking on the
European Convention on Human Rights*, Council of Europe doc. DH(75)4,
Strasbourg, 1 October 1975, p. 65.
148. Sub-Commission's resolution 1(XXIV) of 1971, Article 4(b).
149. *Ibid.*, Articles 1(b) and 2(a).
150. Appl. n. 5310/71, *Ireland* v. *United Kingdom* case, *Report of the Commission*
(adopted on 25 January 1976), published version, Strasbourg, p. 381; and
see pp. 345 and 404–9.
151. Appl. ns. 3321–3323/67 and 3344/67, *First Greek* case, *Yearbook*, vol. 12,
pp. 195–6.

152. *Ibid.*, pp. 501–4.
153. Appl. n. 5310/71, *Report of the Commission*, p. 381.
154. Appl. ns. 3321–3323/67 and 3344/67, *Yearbook*, vol. 12, p. 194.
155. *Ibid.*
156. Appl. n. 5310/71, *Report of the Commission*, p. 259.
157. *Ibid.*, pp. 270–1.
158. *Ibid.*, p. 335. The Commission drew a distinction between the application of the concept of 'administrative practice' at the *admissibility stage* (a procedural function related to the principle of exhaustion of local remedies in Article 26 of the Convention), and its applications on the *merits* of the application (non-procedural, being rather a 'relevant feature in the description of the breach involved'); *ibid.*, pp. 384–5.
159. For the applicant government's arguments, see mainly *ibid.*, pp. 379–80, 366–8, and 372; for the respondent government's arguments, see mainly *ibid.*, pp. 380 and 372–4. Remarking that the concept of 'administrative practice' might have to cover 'widely different situations of law and fact' (even in relation to Article 3 of the Convention), the Commission promptly drew a line of distinction between the situations in the *First Greek* case (concerning a repressive regime) and in the present *Ireland* case (where efforts were being made towards peaceful settlement); the difference, however, the Commission added, did not affect 'the value of the description of the concept of an administrative practice' (given in the former case), 'whilst it might affect its application in the particular case'; *ibid.*, p. 381.
160. *Ibid.*, p. 382.
161. *Ibid.*, p. 383; procedurally, all complaints of violations ought to be directed against States as responsible. Having set up the principle, the Commission established certain nuances of the significance of 'official tolerance' on the part of direct superiors of the authors of the (wrongful) acts and on the part of higher authorities; cf. *ibid.*, pp. 386–8.
162. *Ibid.*, pp. 388 and 490. The Annexes to the Commission's *Report* on the case (vol. II) contain the admissibility decision of 1 October 1972 (also touching on the local remedies rule), reported in vol. 41 of the *Collection* as well, and already examined *supra*.
163. Cf. European Commission of Human Rights, appls. ns. 5577–5583/72, *Donnelly and Others* v. *United Kingdom* case, (final) decision of 15 December 1975, Council of Europe doc. 43.662–06.2 (mimeographed), pp. 37–42 and 52–60.
164. *Ibid.*, p. 61.
165. *Ibid.*, p. 62.
166. Out of 231 such actions, commenced in the period between 9 August 1971 and 30 September 1975, 220 had been settled and only 11 went to trial (damages assessed by judge or jury); cf. *ibid.*, pp. 63–4.
167. Under the Criminal Injuries to Persons [Compensation] Act (Northern Ireland) 1968; cf. *ibid.*, p. 64.
168. Which investigations could lead to prosecution or disciplinary action; cf. *ibid.*
169. *Ibid.*, p. 65.

170. Two applicants having received each £5,000 damages, a third £6,000 damages, and a fourth applicant £301 (*ibid.*).
171. Cf. *ibid.*
172. Cf. *ibid.*, pp. 65–75.
173. In particular, each of four of the applicants received sums in the settlement of their actions 'which were apparently reasonably proportionate to the injuries they suffered'; and in the cases of three of them 'the sums paid were high' and it had 'not been disputed that they included a substantial element of punitive damages, in the form of aggravated and exemplary damages' (*ibid.*, p. 75).
174. *Ibid.*
175. *Ibid.*, p. 76. The Commission explained that 'the obligation to provide a remedy does not constitute a substitute for or alternative to those obligations [under Article 3], but rather an obligation to provide redress within the domestic system for violations which may, inevitably, occur despite measures taken to ensure compliance with the substantive provisions of Article 3' (*ibid.*).
176. *Ibid.*, p. 77, and see pp. 77–82. The Commission added that it had not been established in the case that 'any ill-treatment which the present applicants may have suffered was condoned or tolerated by persons in authority other than those directly involved with the applicants at the relevant times'; and the fact that ill-treatment may have been tolerated by officers at the middle or lower levels of the chain of command did not necessarily mean, the Commission observed, that the State concerned had failed 'to take the required steps to comply with its substantive obligations under Article 3 of the Convention. Existing remedies which provide redress for the individual victims of ill-treatment are not therefor necessarily rendered inadequate in such a situation' (*ibid.*, p. 82).
177. *Ibid.*
178. *Ibid.*, pp. 83–4.
179. *Ibid.*, pp. 84–5.
180. The Commission added that 'the provisions of Articles 26 and 27 apply to all applications submitted under Article 25, whether the breach in question is alleged to be the result of an administrative practice or not. Only if it had been established in the present applications that the existing remedies had been rendered ineffective or inadequate, whether as the result of an administrative practice or otherwise, could the applicants' allegations that they have been victims of violations of the Convention have been considered admissible' (*ibid.*, p. 85).
181. *Ibid.*, p. 86; thus, the applications were declared inadmissible under Articles 26 and 27 of the Convention (in so far as the applicants alleged to have been victims of specific acts in violation of Article 3), and unanimously rejected under Article 29 of the Convention (in so far as they had already been declared inadmissible) (*ibid.*). This decision contrasts with the earlier Commission's decision on the case (of 1973, *supra*) of (partial) admissibility; the immediate reaction to it has so far been unfavourable, particularly with regard to the 'adequacy' of compensation in cases of the kind and to the rather unusual rejection of

applications under Article 29 (as amended by Protocol n. 3 to the Convention); cf. K. Boyle and H. Hannum, 'The *Donnelly* Case, Administrative Practice and Domestic Remedies Under the European Convention: One Step Forward and Two Steps Back', 71 *American Journal of International Law* [1977] pp. 316–21.

Chapter 5

1. See Ch. 2, section B, *supra*. Examples are afforded by, e.g., the existence of over-lengthy proceedings or unreasonable delays in the procedure, and the presence of an *adverse* well-established jurisprudence by domestic courts to the effect of rendering local remedies ineffective.
2. Cf. text in European Convention on Human Rights, *Collected Texts*, 9th edn, Council of Europe, Strasbourg, March 1974, p. 8.
3. The rule whereby the European Commission of Human Rights may only deal with a matter after exhaustion of local remedies *within a period of six months* from the date on which the *final* (domestic) decision was rendered.
4. European Court of Human Rights, *Ringeisen* case, Series A, judgment of 16 July 1971, p. 36, para. 85.
5. *Ibid.*, p. 36, para. 87. Cf. pleadings of Mr W.P. Pahr (counsel for the Austrian government) in European Court of Human Rights, *Ringeisen* case, Series B – Pleadings, Oral Arguments, Documents [1970–1], vol. II, public hearings of 8 to 10 March 1971, pp. 196–200; and, in the same sense, pleadings of Mr E. Nettel (agent for the Austrian government), *ibid.*, pp. 253–8, and cf. his further remarks at pp. 277–8.
6. *Ibid.*, Series A, p. 36, para. 88; cf. the Commission's report on the case, *ibid.*, Series B, pp. 93 and 114–19 (on the problem at issue); and cf. pleadings by Mr G. Sperduti (Commission's delegate), *ibid.*, pp. 208–19 and 266–70, and cf. his further remarks at pp. 275/277.
7. *Ibid.*, Series A, p. 37, para. 88.
8. *Ibid.*, Series A, p. 37, para. 88. As to the six-month rule (laid down in Article 26 *in fine*), the Commission warned that 'the sole purpose of this provision was to fix clearly a time-limit beyond which matters finally decided by the domestic courts cannot again be put in issue before the Commission' (cf. *ibid.*). At a certain stage of the pleadings, one of the Commission's delegates (Mr Sperduti) stated that 'one must attempt as far as possible to confer on the rule of exhaustion as adopted in Article 26 the same scope and the same legal effects as apply to the rule of exhaustion seen from the point of view of the rules generally applicable to the procedure for the peaceful settlement of international disputes'; he further referred, e.g., to Article 29(1) of the 1957 European Convention on the Peaceful Settlement of Disputes. Cf. *ibid.*, Series B–Pleadings, etc., p. 210.
9. European Convention on Human Rights, *Ringeisen* case, Series B– Pleadings, etc., pp. 222 and 286, respectively.
10. *Ibid.*, pp. 289–90; cf. his further contentions, *ibid.*, pp. 259–61.
11. European Court of Human Rights, *Ringeisen* case, Series A, Judgment of

16 July 1971, Separate Opinion of Judge Verdross, p. 49.

12. *Ibid.*, Series A, Judgment of 16 July 1971, p. 37, para. 89.

13. *Ibid.*, p. 37, para. 89; the Court recalled, for example, the (Commission's) decision of 30 August 1958 on the admissibility of application n. 332/57, *Lawless* case, *Yearbook*, vol. II, pp. 324–26.

14. *Ibid.*, p. 38, para. 90.

15. *Ibid.*, p. 38, para. 91. However, a slight qualification of this principle held in the *Ringeisen* case is suggested by the Commission's more recent decision of 7 October 1976 on the *X* v. *Belgium* case, where it was indicated that when an application has been introduced before the exhaustion of local remedies, the adjournment of the examination of the admissibility for a long period may be inappropriate, if the national authority decision drags on; appl. n. 5024/71, *Decisions and Reports*, vol. 7, pp. 5–7. On Article 26 of the Convention and domestic proceedings, see appl. n. 7050/75, *Arrowsmith* v. *United Kingdom* case, decision of 16 May 1977, *Decisions and Reports*, vol. 8, pp. 123 and 130–1; appl. n. 7629/76, *Krzycki* v. *F.R. Germany* case, decision of 14 July 1977, *Decisions and Reports*, vol. 9, pp. 175 and 178–9.

16. European Court of Human Rights, *Ringeisen* case, Series A, judgment of 16 July 1971, p. 38, para. 92.

17. Domestic and international proceedings listed, with dates, *ibid.*, p. 38, para. 93.

18. *Ibid.*, p. 38, para. 93.

19. *Ibid.*, p. 38, para. 93.

20. In a brief comment on the *Ringeisen* decision, Vallée praises the 'force de dissuasion' of the Court, and sees in its judgment a 'reflet d'une évolution'; but the meaning of this 'evolution' in so far as the problem of exhaustion of local remedies is concerned needs further elaboration; Cf. Ch. Vallée, 'L'affaire *Ringeisen* devant la Cour européenne des droits de l'homme', 76 *Revue générale de Droit international public* [1972] p. 124.

21. C.G. Ténékidès, 'L'épuisement des voies de recours internes comme condition préalable de l'instance internationale', 14 *Revue de Droit international et de législation comparée* [1933] p. 518, and see pp. 516–18; and on this point, for a more recent developed treatment, cf. J. Chappez, *La Règle de l'épuisement des voies de recours internes*, Paris, Pédone, 1972, pp. 33–109.

22. P. Schaffer and D. Weissbrodt, 'Exhaustion of Remedies in the Context of the Racial Discrimination Convention', 2 *Revue des droits de l'homme/Human Rights Journal* [1969] p. 635.

23. *Ibid.*, p. 643.

24. *Interhandel* case, *ICJ Reports* [1959] p. 27; Judge Read's Dissenting Opinion, *Norwegian Loans* case, *ICJ Reports* [1957] p. 97; *Austria* v. *Italy* case (application n. 788/60), European Commission of Human Rights, *Report of the Plenary Commission* (adopted on 31 March 1963), Council of Europe doc. A–84–548, pp. 42–3; A. Sarhan, *L'Épuisement des recours internes en matière de responsabilité internationale*, Université de Paris, 1962, pp. 536–42 (mimeographed thesis); C.P. Panayotacos, *La Règle de l'épuisement des voies de recours internes*, Marseille, Imp. Moullot, 1952, p.

84; F. Durante, *Ricorsi Individuali ad Organi Internationali*, Milano, Giuffrè, 1958, p. 137; C.H.P. Law, *The Local Remedies Rule in International Law*, Geneva, Droz, 1961, p. 19; T. Haesler, *The Exhaustion of Local Remedies in the Case Law of International Courts and Tribunals*, Leiden, Sijthoff, 1968, pp. 23–5; G. Gaja, *L'Esaurimento dei Ricorsi Interni nel Diritto Internazionale*, Milano, Giuffrè, 1967, pp. 95–9; G. Dahm, 'Die Subsidiarität des internationalen Rechtsschutzes bei Völkerrechtswidriger Verletzung von Privatpersonen', *in Vom Deutschen zum Europaischen Recht – Festschrift für Hans Dölle*, vol. II, Tübingen, Mohr/Siebeck, 1963, pp. 3–9; A. Miaja de la Muela, 'El Agotamiento de los Recursos Internos como Supuesto de las Reclamaciones Internacionales', 2 *Anuario Uruguayo de Derecho Internacional* [1963] pp. 56–8; J. Guinand, 'La règle de l'épuisement des voies de recours internes dans le cadre des systèmes internationaux de protection des droits de l'homme', 4 *Revue belge de Droit international* [1968] pp. 482–3; Amerasinghe, 'The Rule of Exhaustion of Domestic Remedies', p. 262; H. Wiebringhaus, 'La règle de l'épuisement préalable des voies de recours internes dans la jurisprudence de la Commission européenne des droits de l'homme', 5 *Annuaire français de Droit international* [1959] p. 687; Chappez, *La Règle de l'épuisement*, pp. 26–8 and 243.

25. Cf. European Court of Human Rights, *Matznetter* case, Series A, Judgment of 10 November 1969, p. 26, para. 3; and, in the same sense, *Austria* v. *Italy* case (application n. 788/60), *Report of the Plenary Commission*, pp. 42–5.

26. To Judge Verdross, only the French version of Article 26 could be reconciled with the English and the French texts; to him, 'the verb "dealt with" ("saisir") refers to the two clauses in Article 26, namely, the exhaustion of domestic remedies and the six-month time-limit. If then one were to accept the interpretation adopted by the Commission whereby the term "deal with" ("saisir") means "concern itself with an application" ("s'occuper d'une affaire") one would reach the absurd conclusion that the Commission could concern itself with a case only within the time of six months from the date of the final domestic decision. My interpretation', Judge Verdross proceeded, 'finds confirmation in the provision contained in Article 27(3), which obliges the Commission to reject any petition contrary to Article 26. The Commission cannot, therefore, decide whether the conditions for the admissibility of an application are fulfilled *ex nunc*, that is at the time it begins to examine the case: the Commission must decide whether the application as such fulfilled *ex tunc* the conditions of Article 26' (European Court of Human Rights, *Ringeisen* case, Series A, Judgment of 16 July 1971, Separate Opinion of Judge Verdross, p. 49). As to the Commission's and the Chamber's invocation of the practice in international judicial precedents, Judge Verdross observed that the reference found in Article 26 to 'the generally recognized rules of international law' was made 'within the framework of the special provisions of Article 26 and this can be done because the rules of general

international law on the exhaustion of domestic remedies do not form part of the *jus cogens*. The special conditions of Article 26 therefore prevail over the general rules of international law. For this reason, it seems to me superfluous to undertake an analysis of international practice in the matter' (cf. *ibid.*, pp. 49–50).

27. *Ibid.*, p. 50.

28. *Ibid.*, p. 50.

29. R. Higgins, 'Policy Considerations and the International Judicial Process', 17 *International and Comparative Law Quarterly* [1968] p. 68.

30. As to its jurisdiction (on admissibility of applications), the Court did not accept the Commission's main submission that the Commission was, under the Convention, the only competent organ to decide on the admissibility of applications; in rejecting the Commission's view, the Court asserted its own jurisdiction to deal with the matter, based upon the reasons it had stated previously in paragraphs 47 to 51 of its judgment of 18 June 1971 on the '*Vagrancy*' cases (cf. *supra*); see European Court of Human Rights, *Ringeisen* case, Series A, Judgment of 16 July 1971, pp. 35–6, para. 84

31. *Advisory Opinion on Namibia, ICJ Reports* [1971] p. 30.

32. Namely, 'a treaty shall be interpreted in good faith in accordance with the ordinary meaning to be given to the terms of the treaty in their context and in the light of its object and purpose' (text in UN doc. A/CONF.39/27, 23 May 1969).

33. I.e., in the domain of the mandates system.

34. *Advisory Opinion on Namibia, ICJ Reports* [1971] pp. 31–2. It may be submitted that the passage may well hold true for the domain of the international protection of human rights, whose body of law has been greatly enriched in the last two or three decades.

35. Sir Hersch Lauterpacht, *The Development of International Law by the International Court*, London, Stevens, 1958, p. 397; see also p. 396. And see *supra*, pp. 258–61, for the issue of exhaustion of local remedies in relation to claim for compensation, also raised in the *Ringeisen* case.

36. PCIJ, *Electricity Company of Sofia and Bulgaria* (Preliminary Objection) case, Series A/B, n. 77, p. 78.

37. *Ibid.*, p. 79.

38. *Ibid.*, p. 80.

39. *Ibid.*, p. 80.

40. PCIJ, *ibid.*, Series A/B, n. 77, Dissenting Opinion of Judge Jonkheer Van Eysinga, pp. 113–15.

41. PCIJ, *ibid.*, Series A/B, n. 77, Separate Opinion of Judge Anzilotti, pp. 95–100. To Judge Anzilotti, the Bulgarian government 'was entitled to denounce the treaty and was sole judge of the expediency or necessity of doing so' (*ibid.*, p. 98).

42. *Ibid.*, p. 98. In yet another case before the Permanent Court of International Justice, that of the *Administration of the Prince von Pless*, the Court proceeded to an extension of the time-limit; cf. PCIJ, Series A/B, n. 52, pp. 16–17. Cf. also, on the matter, European Court of Human

Rights, *Ringeisen* case, Series B – Pleadings, Oral Arguments and Documents [1970–1], vol. II, pp. 216–19, 259–61 and 276–70, and authorities cited therein.

43. Namely, the *Stögmüller* case (10 November 1969), the *Matznetter* case (10 November 1969), and the *Neumeister* case (27 June 1968); in its judgment in the related *Wemhoff* case (27 June 1968), the Court did not expressly dwell upon the problem at issue. The cases raise of course much interest for a study of difficult problems relating to Articles 5 and 6 of the Convention, such as, e.g., that of the 'reasonable delay' of detention while on remand (Article 5(3) of the Convention). Such substantive law problems fall outside the scope and purposes of the present study; as an example of the interest they have raised, cf., e.g., S. Trechsel, 'La durée raisonnable de la détention preventive (Article 5 para. 3 de la Convention européenne des droits de l'homme)', 4 *Revue des droits de l'homme/Human Rights Journal* [1971] pp. 119–52; S. Trechsel, *Die Europäische Menschen-rechtskonvention, ihr Schutz persönlichen Freiheit und die schweizerischen Strafprozessrechte*, Bern, Verlag Stämpfli, 1974; T. Buergenthal, 'Comparison of the Jurisprudence of National Courts with that of the Organs of the Convention as regards the Rights of the Individual in Court Proceedings', in *Human Rights in National and International Law* (ed. A.H. Robertson), Manchester, University Press/Oceana, 1970, esp. pp. 151–94 and 198–200 (for Articles 5 and 6 of the Convention).

44. European Court of Human Rights, *Neumeister* case, Series A, Judgment of 27 June 1968, p. 38, para. 7.

45. *Ibid.*, p. 38, para. 7; and see p. 43, para. 23.

46. European Court of Human Rights, *Stögmüller* case, Series A, Judgment of 10 November 1969, p. 37, para. 11.

47. *Ibid.* The Austrian government further stated that 'the application was not directed against the detention as such but against the length of a period of detention which in itself was compatible with the requirements of the Convention. Consequently, the time factor was of capital importance for the determination of the subject of the dispute which was not so much a continuing situation but a definite fact, that is, the length of a detention which itself complied with the requirements of Article 5(1)(c), (*ibid.*, Series A, pp. 37–8, para. 11).

48. *Ibid.*, p. 38, para. 11.

49. *Ibid.*, pp. 32–3, para. 4.

50. *Ibid.*, p. 33, para. 4.

51. *Ibid.*; but the Commission took account also of the interests of the respondent State, in stating that 'it might in the result be less favourable for the respondent State in cases where a detained person was set at liberty on foot of a request for release subsequent to the lodging of his application' (*ibid.*).

52. *Ibid.*

53. European Court of Human Rights, *Stögmüller* case, Series B – Pleadings, Oral Arguments, Documents [1967–9], p. 190.

54. *Ibid.*, Series B – Pleadings, etc., p. 191.

55. *Ibid.*

56. *Ibid.*, p. 210.
57. *Ibid.*
58. *Ibid.*, pp. 210–11.
59. *Ibid.*, p. 212.
60. *Ibid.*
61. *Ibid.*
62. *Ibid.*, p. 213; he added that the Court's power to consider a period of detention could not 'in any circumstances be limited by the date of either the Commission's decision on admissibility or the adoption of the Commission's report' (*ibid.*).
63. *Ibid.*, p. 217.
64. *Ibid.*, pp. 218–19.
65. *Ibid.*, p. 219.
66. European Court of Human Rights, *Stögmüller* case, Series A, p. 41, para. 7. The Court recalled that it had already had occasion 'to pronounce itself on the question whether or not it could take account of facts which were subsequent to an application but were directly related to the facts covered by the application' (*ibid.*). The Court had answered the question in the affirmative. Thus, in the *Lawless* case, e.g., the Court 'took into account the applicant's internment from 13 July to 11 December 1957 even though the lodging of the application dated from 8 November 1957' (cf. European Court of Human Rights, *Lawless* case, Series A, Judgment of 1 July 1961, p. 51, para. 12, quoted in *Stögmüller* case, Series A, *ibid.*). Similarly, in the *Neumeister* case, the Court 'examined the entire period of detention of Neumeister from 12 July 1962 to 16 September 1964, the date on which he recovered his freedom, that is, more than one year after he had petitioned the Commission (12 July 1963)'; and the Court recalled the reasons it stated in the *Neumeister* decision (European Court of Human Rights, *Neumeister* case, Series A, Judgment of 27 June 1968, p. 38, para. 7), quoted in *Stögmüller* case, Series A, *ibid.*). As to the present *Stögmüller* case, the Court made a point of noting that 'not only did the government not rely on this provision [Article 26] before the Commission, but itself clearly took into consideration, both during the proceedings on admissibility and in the course of the examination of the merits of the case, the period of detention which elapsed between the lodging of the application and the release of Stögmüller' (*ibid.*, Series A, p. 41, para. 8).
67. *Ibid.*, Series A, pp. 42–3, paras. 11 and 12.
68. *Ibid.*, p. 47.
69. R. Pelloux, 'Les arrêts de la Cour européenne des droits de l'homme dans les affaires *Stögmüller et Matznetter*', 16 *Annuaire français de Droit international* [1970] p. 345; although displaying some sympathy for the Court's 'broad interpretation' of Article 26 (*ibid.*), the author saw fit to go even further than did Judges Verdross and Bilge, considering that the Commission has *exclusive* competence to pronounce upon the admissibility of applications; cf. *ibid.*, pp. 344–5. Also criticizing the 'excessive formalism' of the Austrian government's arguments on Article 26 of the Convention (in the *Stögmüller* as well as the *Matznetter* and the

Neumeister cases), see Trechsel, 'La durée raisonnable', pp. 124–6; and see pp. 121–3.

70. European Court of Human Rights, *Matznetter* case, Series A, Judgment of 10 November 1969, p. 28, para. 6.
71. *Ibid.*, pp. 28–9, para. 6. On Austria's reliance on the French text of Article 26, see pleadings of counsel for the Austrian government (Mr W.P. Pahr), in European Court of Human Rights, *Matznetter* case, Series B–Pleadings, Oral Arguments and Documents [1967–9], pp. 225–7; cf. also pleadings to the same effect of the agent for the Austrian government (Mr E. Nettel), *ibid.*, pp. 239–40, and cf. his further remarks, *ibid.*, pp. 230–1 and 237–8.
72. *Ibid.*, Series A, p. 29, para. 6.
73. Application n. 2614/65, *Ringeisen* case, (final) decision of 18 July 1968, *Collection of Decisions of the European Commission of Human Rights*, vol. 27, pp. 51–2.
74. European Court of Human Rights, *Matznetter* case, Series A, Judgment of 10 November 1969, p. 25, para. 3.
75. *Ibid.*, Series A, p. 26, para. 3; both the Commission and the Austrian government referred to their respective submissions made throughout the hearings of the *Stögmüller* case (cf. *ibid.*, p. 26, para. 3, and p. 30, para. 6, respectively).
76. *Ibid.*, Series A, p. 32, para. 6; the Separate Joint Concurring Opinion of Judges Verdross and Bilge in the present case (the same as in the *Stögmüller* case) was to the effect that the Court could not entertain a question of exhaustion of local remedies which had not been previously submitted to the Commission; cf. *ibid.*, Series A, pp. 38–9. The present study was concerned with this problem (*supra*, pp. 250–8) while examining the related issue of the exhaustion of local remedies with regard to the internal structure of the international jurisdictional body.
77. European Court of Human Rights, *Matznetter* case, Series B–Pleadings, Oral Arguments and Documents [1967–9], p. 236; he deemed that this procedure could often be used for the protection of the respondent government as well (cf. *ibid.*, p. 236).
78. *Ibid.*, Series B–Pleadings, etc., p. 236.
79. *Ibid.*, p. 239.
80. *Ibid.*; and cf. further remarks, *ibid.*, pp. 241–2.
81. *Ibid.*, p. 243.
82. *Ibid.*, p. 244.
83. *Ibid.*, p. 245.
84. *Ibid.*, p. 246.
85. *Ibid.*, p. 247.
86. *Ibid.*, p. 248.
87. Article 36(6) is the provision which may be of concern on the matter, stipulating that 'in the event of a dispute as to whether the Court has jurisdiction, the matter shall be settled by the decision of the Court'.
88. S. Rosenne, *The Law and Practice of the International Court*, vol. 1, Leiden, Sijthoff, 1965, p. 451; É. Grisel, *Les Exceptions d'incompétence et d'irrecevabilité dans la procédure de la Cour internationale de Justice*, Berne,

éd. H. Lang & Cie, 1968, pp. 26–7.

89. *Yearbook of the International Court of Justice* [1971–2] pp. 2–3 and 8.
90. Text in *Documents on the International Court of Justice* (ed. S. Rosenne), Leiden, Sijthoff/Oceana, 1974, p. 173. In 1965 Rosenne observed that 'the question whether a party may raise a series of objections in successive phases of a case, and after the original time-limit laid down in Article 62(1) of the Rules [new Article 67(1)], is not regulated by the Statute or Rules of Court, and does not permit an unqualified answer'; Rosenne, *The Law and Practice*, p. 455. Suzanne Bastid writes that objections ought to be presented *in limine litis*, before any defence as to the merits, within the time-limit for the reply or counter-memorial: S. Bastid, 'L'organisation judiciaire internationale – l'arbitrage international', *Juris-Classeur de Droit International*, Paris, Les Éditions Techniques, 1961, fasc. 248, p. 11.
91. E. Hambro, 'The Jurisdiction of the International Court of Justice', 76 *Recueil des Cours de l'Académie de Droit International* [1950]–1, pp. 208–9. But Hambro also concedes that that 'late' interposition of the preliminary objection might possibly be done in good faith, in cases where it might be 'very difficult for a State to decide whether it wants to file a preliminary objection or not, and it might happen that a State would not be in a position to do so before it had read very carefully the memorial of the other party' (*ibid.*, p. 209).
92. S. Rosenne, *The Time Factor in the Jurisdiction of the International Court of Justice*, Leiden, Sijthoff, 1960, p. 70.
93. *Ibid.*, p. 71. For the remark that the 'preliminary character' of the objection of non-exhaustion of local remedies may in fact depend on the arguments raised by the interested party in the case, cf. Grisel, *op. cit.*, p. 159. On his part, Gaja has preferred to concentrate on the *formal* aspect of the 'preliminary character' of the objection of non-exhaustion in the light of the practice of the ICJ; cf. G. Gaja, *L'Esaurimento dei Ricorsi Interni nel Diritto Internazionale*, Milano, Giuffrè, 1967, pp. 209–17.
94. M. Mabrouk, *Les Exceptions de procédure devant les juridictions internationales*, Paris, LGDJ, 1966, p. 270: 'le juge international est libre d'examiner, en premier lieu, telle exception d'incompétence ou d'irrecevabilité qu'il voudra (celle dont l'examen ne lui semble guère trop difficile et qui lui paraît la plus pertinente). Si un ordre d'examen des exceptions s'impose, c'est en toute souveraineté que la juridiction international le détermine, dans chaque cas d'espèce' (cf. further pp. 265–70).
95. *Barcelona Traction* (Preliminary Objections) case, *ICJ Reports* [1964], Dissenting Opinion of Judge Morelli, pp. 98–9.
96. *Ibid.*, p. 99; and cf. further, *Barcelona Traction* (Second Phase) case, *ICJ Reports* [1970], Separate Opinion of Judge Morelli, pp. 226–31.
97. See Ch. de Visscher, *Aspects récents du droit procédural de la Cour internationale de justice*, Paris, Pédone, 1966, pp. 104–5.
98. *Ibid.*
99. *Interhandel* case, *ICJ Reports* [1959], Dissenting Opinion of Judge Armand-Ugon, p. 91.

100. *Ibid.*, Separate Opinion of Sir Percy Spender, p. 54.
101. *Ibid.*, Dissenting Opinion of President Klaestad, pp. 78–9.
102. *Ibid.*, Dissenting Opinion of Sir Hersch Lauterpacht, p. 100.
103. See, in this sense: G. Guyomar, *Commentaire du règlement de la Cour internationale de justice – Interprétation et pratique*, Paris, Pédone, 1973, p. 369; J. Chappez, *La Règle de l'épuisement des voies de recours internes*, Paris, Pédone, 1972, pp. 154–6. See, further, suggestions and propositions on the matter by Rosenne, *Law and Practice*, pp. 458–9. And, in support of the criterion of the economy of procedure, see G. Sperduti, 'La recevabilité des exceptions préliminaires de fond dans le procès international', 53 *Rivista di Diritto Internazionale* [1970] p. 489.
104. *But* it may be recalled that in the *Interhandel* case (1959), for example, the International Court retained the objection of non-exhaustion of local remedies before examining the objection of domestic jurisdiction: *Interhandel* case, *ICJ Reports* [1959] p. 29, and cf. discussion in Cançado Trindade, 'Domestic Jurisdiction and Exhaustion of Local Remedies', pp. 187–218. And two decades earlier, in the *Panevezys – Saldutiskis Railway* case (1939), the Permanent Court upheld the objection of non-exhaustion of local remedies after finding that the objection grounded on the nationality of claims rule did not possess a 'preliminary' character and could not be passed upon at the preliminary stage of the proceedings; PCIJ, *Panevezys – Saldutiskis Railway* case, Series A/B, n. 76, 1939, pp. 15–22.
105. G. Abi-Saab, *Les Exceptions préliminaires dans la procédure de la Cour internationale*, Paris, Pédone, 1967, pp. 229–31.
106. *Ibid.*, pp. 231–2; in addition, proceeded the author, 'les exceptions d'incompétence sont presque toujours des exceptions péremptoires, cependant que les exceptions d'irrecevabilité sont tantôt dilatoires, tantôt péremptoires' (p. 232). It may again be recalled that in the *Interhandel* case the Court decided to reverse the order of the third and fourth U.S. preliminary objections (on non-exhaustion of local remedies and on domestic jurisdiction, respectively), because as the fourth objection related to the Court's jurisdiction, it should be considered before the third objection (to admissibility) of non-exhaustion of local remedies (cf. *Interhandel* case, ICJ Reports [1959] pp. 23–4), even though the Court ended up by upholding this latter; cf. comments in Cançado Trindade, 'Domestic Jurisdiction and Exhaustion of Local Remedies', pp. 188, 190 and 213–18.
107. G. Abi-Saab, *op. cit.*, p. 234.
108. Cf. further remarks, *ibid.*, pp. 237–8; see p. 238 on, *inter alia*, the 'principe de la prudence et de l'économie de la fonction judiciaire'. A kind of objection which would precede even the questions of jurisdiction is that of an objection as to the existence itself of a dispute (pp. 239–40); its examination would normally come before that of the Courts own jurisdiction.
109. Rule 44 of the rules of procedure of the European Commission of Human Rights (text of Rules in European Convention on Human Rights, *Collected Texts*, 9th edn, Council of Europe, Strasbourg, March

1974, pp. 302–17).

110. Rule 45 of the Commission's rules of Procedure (as amended by the Commission on 19 July 1973).

111. Rule 46 of the Commission's rules of procedure.

112. See para. 3 of Article 46 of the Commission's rules of procedure.

113. European Commission of Human Rights, *Case-Law Topics/Sujets de Jurisprudence*, n. 3 (*Bringing an Application before the European Commission of Human Rights*), rev. edn, Strasbourg, January 1974, p. 29.

114. *Ibid.*, p. 28.

115. E. Grillo Pasquarelli, 'The Question of the Exhaustion of Domestic Remedies in the Context of the Examination of Admissibility of an Application to the European Commission of Human Rights', in *Privacy and Human Rights* (ed. A.H. Robertson), Manchester, University Press, 1973, p. 336.

116. C.C. Morrisson Jr, *The Developing European Law of Human Rights*, Leiden, Sijthoff, 1967, p. 86. On the Commission's competence *ratione temporis* see, in general, M.-A. Eissen, 'Jurisprudence de la Commission européenne des droits de l'homme – Décisions en matière de compétence *ratione temporis*', 9 *Annuaire Français de Droit International* [1963] pp. 722–33; A.H. Robertson, 'The Guarantees Afforded by the Institutional Machinery of the Convention', in *Privacy and Human Rights* (ed. A.H. Robertson), Manchester, University Press, 1973, pp. 322–31, esp. p. 331 for proposed timetable (namely, admissibility decision within six months of registration, Commission's report within nine months of admissibility decision, Committee of Ministers' decision within six months of transmission of report, Court's judgment within twelve months of reference to Court; issue of 'manifestly ill-founded' application, unlike that of exhaustion of local remedies, not necessarily needing to be referred by the Commission to respondent government). On the Commission's competence *ratione temporis* and the six-month rule in Article 26 of the Convention, see also, e.g., the *William Posnet Lynas* v. *Switzerland* case (1976) in Council of Europe doc. C(76)32 (Commission's communiqué of 11 October 1976), pp. 1–3.

117. Application n. 712/60, *Retimag S.A.* v. *F.R. Germany* case, decision of 16 December 1961, *Collection*, vol. 8, pp. 36–7.

118. Appl. n. 1727/62, *Boeckmans* v. *Belgium* case, decision of 29 October 1963, *Collection*, vol. 12, p. 45.

119. *Ibid.* The application of the local remedies rule was also debated at the oral hearings of 7 January 1961 in the *Austria* v. *Italy* case (1961); cf. *Yearbook*, vol. IV, pp. 158–78.

120. In this case the Belgian government expressly stated that it intended to pursue no further the objection of non-exhaustion of local remedies (oral hearing of 5 March 1964): cf. appl. n. 1994/63, *Collection*, vol. 13, pp. 108–9.

121. Appl. n. 1474/62, *Collection*, vol. 11, p. 55.

122. J.E.S. Fawcett, *The Application of the European Convention on Human Rights*, Oxford, Clarendon Press, 1969, p. 313 (also for further remarks). Robertson has observed that 'it is necessary to distinguish between

rejection under the six months' rule [Article 26, see *supra*], and a decision of inadmissibility *ratione temporis*. The latter occurs if the respondent government had not ratified the Convention, or not accepted the right of individual petition, at the relevant date; six months' rule only comes into play when these other conditions are satisfied' (A.H. Robertson, 'The European Convention on Human Rights and the Rule of Exhaustion of Domestic Remedies', 4 *Revista de Derechos Humanos* [1974] (Comisión de Derechos Civiles de Puerto Rico) p. 202). And see further, on the relationship between the local remedies requirement and other preliminary objections, more recently, appl. ns. 5577−5583/72, *Donnelly and Others* v. *United Kingdom* case, European Commission of Human Rights, (final) decision of 15 December 1975, Council of Europe doc. 43. 662−06.2 (mimeographed), p. 83.

123. Text in *Collected Texts*, 9th edn, p. 8.
124. G.L. Weil, *The European Convention on Human Rights*, Leiden, Sijthoff, 1963, p. 122; G. Kaeckenbeeck, *The International Experiment of Upper Silesia*, London, Oxford University Press, 1942, p. 501.
125. Council of Europe doc. H(61)4, *Collected Edition of the 'Travaux Préparatoires'* [European Convention on Human Rights], vol. III, Strasbourg, p. 577.
126. *Ibid.*, p. 583.
127. *Ibid.*, p. 654. For a study, see A.A. Cançado Trindade, 'Exhaustion of Local Remedies in the "Travaux Préparatoires" of the European Convention on Human Rights', 58 *Revue de droit international de sciences diplomatiques et politiques* [1980] pp. 73−88.
128. Text in OAS doc. OEA/Ser. L/V/II.23, of 11 June 1970, p. 64.
129. G.L. Weil, *European Convention*, pp. 119 and 121; F. Monconduit, *La Commission européenne des droits de l'homme*, Leiden, Sijthoff, 1965, p. 329.
130. Appl. n. 214/56, *De Becker* v. *Belgium* case, proceedings before the Commission and Commission's decision, in European Court of Human Rights, *De Becker* case, Series B − Pleadings, Oral Arguments and Documents; pp. 52 and 54.
131. *Ibid.*, p. 53.
132. *Ibid.*, pp. 56−7.
133. *Ibid.*, p. 57.
134. *Ibid.*
135. Appl. n. 654/59, *X* v. *F.R. Germany* case, decision of 3 June 1960, *Collection*, vol. 7, pp. 4−5.
136. Appl. n. 968/61, *X* v. *F.R. Germany* case, decision of 14 December 1961, *Collection*, vol. 8, p. 27.
137. Appl. n. 3505/68, *X* v. *United Kingdom* case, decision of 4 October 1968, *Collection*, vol. 29, pp. 62−3.
138. *Ibid.*, p. 63.
139. Appl. n. 3972/69, *X* v. *Austria* case, decision of 2 April 1971, *Collection*, vol. 37, pp. 19−20.
140. Appl. n. 512/59 (1959), *Collection*, vol. 1, p. 4.
141. Appl. n. 653/59 (1960), *Collection*, vol. 3, p. 2; appl. n. 1216/61 (1963), *Collection*, vol. 11, p. 5.

142. Appl. n. 2457/65 (1967), *Collection*, vol. 24, p. 46.
143. Appl. n. 2694/65 (1967), *Collection*, vol. 23, p. 97.
144. Appl. n. 3979/69 (1970), *Collection*, vol. 33, p. 13.
145. Appl. n. 4438/70 (1971), *Collection*, vol. 39, pp. 24–5.
146. Appl. n. 1053/61 (1961), *Collection*, vol. 8, pp. 7–8 (Austrian Court of Appeal of C.); appl. n. 1159/61 (1962), *Collection*, vol. 8, p. 129 (Austrian Court of Appeal of B.).
147. Appl. n. 4475/70 (1972), *Collection*, vol. 42, p. 13.
148. Appl. n. 3827/68 (1969), *Collection*, vol. 32, pp. 28–9.
149. Appl. n. 458/60 (1960), *Collection*, vol. 2, p. 4; appl. n. 613/59 (1960), *Collection*, vol. 3, p. 2; appl. n. 1789/63 (1963), *Collection*, vol. 11, p. 27; appl. n. 2300/64(1967), *Collection*, vol. 22, p. 82; appl. n. 3071/67 (1968) *Collection*, vol. 26, p. 76; appl. ns. 3542/68 and 4099/69 (1970), *Collection*, vol. 35, p. 55; appl. n. 4112/69 (1970), *Collection*, vol. 36, p. 41; appl. n. 4149/69 (1970), *Collection*, vol. 36, p. 67; appl. n. 5560/72 (1973), *Collection*, vol. 45, p. 64; appl. n. 2618/65 (1965), *Yearbook*, vol. VIII, p. 380.
150. Appl. n. 3893/68 (1970), *Collection*, vol. 33, p. 10.
151. *Ibid.*
152. Appl. n. 846/60 (1961), *Collection*, vol. 6, pp. 64–5; appl. n. 4464/70 (1971), *Collection*, vol. 39, p. 33; appl. n. 5207/71 (1971), *Collection*, vol. 39, p. 103.
153. Appl. n. 343/57, *Nielsen* v. *Denmark* case, *Report of the Commission*, pp. 32–9.
154. *Ibid.*, p. 39.
155. *Ibid.*
156. Appl. n. 654/59 (1960), *Collection*, vol. 7, p. 5.
157. Appl. n. 918/60 (1961), *Collection*, vol. 7, p. 110. The Commission held the final decision in the case to be one rendered by the German Federal Court in 1956 (*ibid.*).
158. Appl. n. 968/61 (1961), *Collection*, vol. 8, p. 28. The immediate consequence was that the application was deemed to have been lodged out of time; in this case, once again, the Commission applied the test of effectiveness to the local remedies at issue (cf. *ibid.*).
159. Appl. n. 1739/62 (1964), *Collection*, vol. 13, p. 102.
160. *Ibid.*
161. Appl. n. 3591/68 (1970), *Collection*, vol. 31, p. 46.
162. *Ibid.*
163. Appl. n. 3747/68 (1970), *Collection*, vol. 32, p. 21.
164. Appl. n. 4311/69 (1971), *Collection*, vol. 37, p. 95.
165. *Ibid.*, p. 96.
166. *Ibid.*
167. *Ibid.*
168. Appl. n. 214/56, *De Becker* v. *Belgium* case, in European Court of Human Rights, Series B, Pleadings, decision of the Commission of 9 June 1958, p. 58. In support of this view the Commission recalled the *dicta* by the PCIJ in the *Nationality Decrees in Tunis and Morocco* case (Series B, n. 4, p. 25) and in the *Certain German Interests in Polish Upper*

Silesia case (Series A, n. 27, p. 76); *ibid.*, p. 58.

169. *Ibid.*
170. *Ibid.*, p. 53.
171. *Ibid.*, pp. 54–5.
172. *Ibid.*, p. 57.
173. *Ibid.*
174. *Ibid.*, pp. 57–8 (my italics).
175. *Ibid.*, p. 58.
176. *Ibid.* It might be asked, the Commission pondered, 'whether, in such special circumstances in which the *lex specialis* of Article 26 is no longer applicable, the *lex generalis*, according to which all international appeals must be lodged within a reasonable time, does not again obtain; [...] however, there is no need to consider this question in the present case, as it is sufficient to observe that the claimant has lodged his application within a reasonable time, according to the generally recognised rules of international law' (*ibid.*, pp. 58–9). The application could *not* thus be declared inadmissible as being out of time (*ibid.*, p. 59).
177. Appl. n. 1474/62 (1963), *Collection*, vol. 11, pp. 57–8.
178. Appl. n. 1769/63 (1963), *Collection*, vol. 11, pp. 67–8.
179. In both cases the Commission recalled its previous decision to the same effect in the *De Becker* case: cf. *ibid.*, pp. 57–8 and 67–8, respectively.
180. Appl. n. 4517/70 (1970), *Collection*, vol. 38, p. 96.
181. Appl. n. 4517/70 (1971), *Collection*, vol. 38, p. 113. The Commission referred to its own jurisprudence in that sense, as well as that of the European Court of Human Rights (*ibid.*).
182. Appl. ns. 3321/67, 3322/67, 3323/67 and 3344/67, Commission's sitting and decision of 31 May 1968, *Yearbook*, vol. 11, p. 776. The Commission once again recalled (as it had done in the *De Becker* case) that 'the term "final decision" in Article 26 refers exclusively to the final decision given in the course of the normal exhaustion of domestic remedies and the six months period is operative only in this context' (*ibid.*, pp. 774–6.)
183. *Ibid.*, p. 778.
184. *Ibid.*
185. Appl. n. 4859/71 (1973), *Collection*, vol. 44, p. 7.
186. Appl. n. 6181/73, *X* v. *F.R. Germany* case, decision of 5 October 1974, *Collection*, vol. 46, p. 196.
187. *Ibid.*
188. *Ibid.*
189. *Ibid.*; in the end the application was declared partly admissible and partly inadmissible (cf. *ibid.*, p. 201).
190. Appl. n. 6317/73, *X* v. *Austria* case, decision of 10 July 1975, European Commission of Human Rights, *Decisions and Reports*, vol. 2, Strasbourg, December 1975, pp. 87–8.
191. *Ibid.*
192. *Ibid.*, pp. 88–9.
193. Appl. n. 7629/76, *Krzycki* v. *F.R. Germany* case, decision of 14 July 1977, *Decisions and Reports*, vol. 9, pp. 175 and 178–80.

194. Appl. n. 6930/75, *X* v. *Norway* case, decision of 9 March 1977, *Decisions and Reports*, vol. 9, pp. 37–9.
195. Appl. n. 5759/72, *X* v. *Austria* case, decision of 20 May 1976, *Decisions and Reports*, vol. 6, pp. 15–17.
196. Appl. n. 7379/76, *Decisions and Reports*, vol. 8, pp. 211–13. On the application of the six-month rule, see also the *Hätti* v. *F.R. Germany* case, appl. n. 6181/73, decision of 5 October 1974, C. of E. doc. 48.072–06.2, appendix II, pp. 46–9; and the *Brüggemann and Scheuten* v. *F.R. Germany* case, appl. n. 6959/75, decision of 19 May 1976, C. of E. doc. I.16.284, annexe III, p. 53.
197. Text in European Convention on Human Rights, *Collected Texts*, 9th edn, p. 312.
198. Appl. n. 1468/62 (1963), *Collection*, vol. 12, pp. 104–5, and, for the arguments of the respondent government and the applicant's counsel, cf. *ibid.*, pp. 87–8.
199. Appl. ns. 5100/71, 5354/72, 5370/72 (1973), *Collection*, vol. 44, p. 12.
200. *Ibid.*
201. Appl. n. 613/59 (1960), *Collection*, vol. 3, p. 2; appl. n. 1789/63 (1963), *Collection*, vol. 11, p. 27; appl. n. 3071/67 (1968), *Collection*, vol. 26, p. 76; appl. ns. 3542/68 and 4099/69 (1970), *Collection*, vol. 35, p. 55; appl. n. 4149/69 (1970), *Collection*, vol. 36, p. 67; appl. n. 4112/69 (1970), *Collection*, vol. 36, p. 41.
202. Appl. n. 3591/68 (1970), *Collection*, vol. 31, p. 46.
203. *Ibid.*
204. Cf. text in European Convention on Human Rights, *Collected Texts*, 9th edn, p. 3.
205. S. Trechsel, 'La durée raisonnable de la détention préventive (Article 5(3) de la Convention européenne des droits de l'homme', 4 *Revue des droits de l'homme/Human Rights Journal* [1971] p. 121.
206. Cf. appl. n. 7758/77, *Decisions and Reports*, vol. 9, pp. 217–18.
207. Appl. n. 6814/74, *Decisions and Reports*, vol. 3, pp. 108–10.
208. Appl. n. 6821/74, *Decisions and Reports*, vol. 6, pp. 65 and 69–70.
209. In all cases it is understood that the applicant's allegations are to be supported by evidence; cf. Ch. 3, *supra*.

Chapter 6

1. Cf. mainly, *inter alia*, M. Virally, 'L'accès des particuliers à une instance internationale', 20 *Mémoires publiés par la Faculté de Droit de Genève* [1964] pp. 70–89 (possibly one of the most complete treatments of the problem); M. Søensen, 'La recevabilité de l'instance devant la Cour européenne des droits de l'homme', in *René Cassin Amicorum Discipulorumque Liber*, vol. I, Paris, Pédone, 1969, p. 334; C. Th. Eustathiades, 'Une nouvelle expérience en Droit international: les recours individuels à la Commission européenne des droits de l'homme', in *Grundprobleme des internationalen Rechts – Festschrift für Jean Spiropoulos*, Schimmelbusch & Co., Bonn, 1957, pp. 126–7 ('fonction judiciaire dans la recevabilité'); F. Ermacora, 'L'accès aux mécanismes juridictionnels de protection

des personnes privées dans la Convention européenne des droits de l'homme' (report to the Colloque de Grenoble, 25–6 January 1973), 6 *Revue des droits de l'homme/Human Rights Journal* [1973] pp. 651–3 (judicial function in admissibility); F. Pocar, 'La trattazione dei ricorsi ricevibili davanti alla Commissione europea dei diritti dell'uomo', 55 *Rivista di Diritto Internazionale* [1972] pp. 224–5 ('funzione giurisdizionale nella ricevibilità'), and see pp. 223–52; A.-M. Nay-Cadoux, *Les Conditions de recevabilité des requêtes individuelles devant la Commission européenne des droits de l'homme*, Paris/Torino, LGDJ/Giappichelli, 1966, p. 1 ('pouvoirs d'ordre juridictionnel en matière de recevabilité'); F. Durante, *Ricorsi Individuali ad Organi Internazionali*, Milano, Giuffrè, 1958, p. 143; H. Mosler, 'Organisation und Verfahren des Europäischen Gerichtshofs für Menschenrechte', 20 *Zeitschrift für ausländisches öffentliches Recht und Völkerrecht* [1959–60] pp. 440/441; F Stryckmans, 'La Commission européenne des droits de l'homme et le procès équitable', in *Journal des Tribunaux*, Bruxelles, 1 October 1966, p. 537; G. Sperduti, 'Protezione Internazionale dei Diritti Umani", *in Enciclopedia del Diritto*, vol. xii, Milano, Giuffrè, 1964, p. 817 ('la Commissione esercita poteri strettamente giudiziari allo stadio della ricevabilità [...]'). But notwithstanding the Commission's *judicial function* at the admissibility stage, it does not necessarily follow that the Commission is an international 'tribunal' *stricto sensu*: cf. H. Golsong, 'The Control Machinery of the European Convention on Human Rights', in *The European Convention on Human Rights*, British Institute of International and Comparative Law (International Law Series n. 5, *ICLQ* suppl. n. 11), 1965, pp. 43–4.

2. European Court of Human Rights, '*Vagrancy*' cases, Series A, Judgment of 18 June 1971, p. 30. And see, in the same sense, S. Petrén, 'La saisine de la Cour européenne par la Commission européenne des droits de l'homme', in *Mélanges offerts à Polys Modinos*, Paris, Pédone, 1968, pp. 235–6, and see pp. 233–44 for problems related to the seizure of the Court by the Commission when it is so possible after the establishment of the Commission's report; the author stresses, e.g., the Convention's effect of enlarging the *droit public européen* and of, concomitantly, reducing the scope of domestic jurisdiction of the States concerned (*ibid.*, p. 243).

3. See, in this sense, M. Sørensen, 'La recevabilité', pp. 333–5.

4. On the Belgian government's request to the Court for inadmissibility of the applications for non-exhaustion of local remedies (as an alternative plea), see European Court of Human Rights, '*Vagrancy*' cases, Series B – Pleadings, Oral Arguments and Documents [1969–71] p. 205; on the Commission's request to the Court for inadmissibility of the Belgian request, see *ibid.*, pp. 209–10, 214–15 and 222; on the Belgian government's reply, see *ibid.*, pp. 227–30.

5. Cf. arguments of the Commission's principal delegate, Mr M. Sørensen, *ibid.*, pp. 261–2 and 291, and see p. 400 for the Commission's conclusions; cf. also arguments of the Belgian government's agent and counsel, Mr J. de Meyer, *in ibid.*, pp. 263–6, 269–70 and 280–1.

6. European Court of Human Rights, '*Vagrancy*' cases, Series A, Judgment

of 18 June 1971, p. 29, para. 47. The Court further recalled its previous decision to the effect that 'the basis of the jurisdiction *ratione materiae* of the Court is established once the case raises a question of the interpretation or application of the Convention'; E.C.H.R., '*Belgian Linguistic*' case, Series A, Judgment of 9 February 1967, p. 18.

7. *Ibid.*, p. 29, para. 49.
8. *Ibid.*, p. 29, para. 48.
9. *Ibid.*
10. *Ibid.*, p. 29, para. 49.
11. *Ibid.*, p. 29, para. 50.
12. *Ibid.*, p. 30, para. 51. As to the Commission's decisions on inadmissibility, final, without appeal, and taken 'in complete independence', the Court referred *mutatis mutandis* to its *Lawless* judgment of 14 November 1960, Series A, p. 11.
13. *Ibid.*, p. 30, para. 51.
14. Cf. *ibid.*, p. 30, para. 52. And see, to the same effect, *ibid.*, Separate Opinion of Judge Zekia, pp. 60–1; Sørensen, 'La recevabilité', pp. 342–3 and 345. It is difficult to endorse Sørensen's minimization of procedural problems in human rights protection (see passage *ibid.*, p. 346), particularly if one is speaking *jus constitutum* rather than *jus constituenda*. The fact that, e.g., out of 7740 applications registered with the Commission by the end of 1976, only 142 have been declared admissible (*Stock-Taking on the European Convention on Human Rights*, Council of Europe doc. DH (77)3, Strasbourg, 1977, p. 87), bears witness to the considerable practical relevance of procedural obstacles at the admissibility stage. But *jus constituenda*, of course, admissibility objections should not play such an important role in a system of international protection of human rights.
15. European Court of Human Rights, '*Vagrancy*' cases, Series A, Judgment of 18 June 1971, Joint Separate Opinion of Judges Ross and Sigurjónsson, pp. 49–50.
16. European Court of Human Rights, '*Vagrancy*' cases, Series A, Judgment of 18 June 1971, Separate Opinion of Judge Wold, p. 57.
17. European Court of Human Rights, '*Vagrancy*' cases, Series A, Judgment of 18 June 1971, Separate Opinion of Judge Bilge, p. 52. One may in this connection recall Sørensen's remark that, unlike other international jurisdictional systems, the Court can only be seized of a case after the Commission has completed its examination of it and accomplished its 'triple' function, namely, establishment of facts, attempts to friendly settlement (cf., e.g., Article 47 of the Convention) and opinion as to whether the case amounts to a violation of the Convention (not to speak of the Commission's report to the Committee of Ministers). Cf. Sørensen, 'La recevabilité', pp. 341 and 343. Apparently the question whether or not the Court would be endowed with jurisdiction to deal with problems of admissibility here remains open, however.
18. European Court of Human Rights, 'Vagrancy' cases, Series A, Judgment of 18 June 1971, Separate Opinion of Judge Bilge, pp. 53–4.
19. *Ibid.*, p. 52, and see remarks at p. 53.

20. *Ibid.*, p. 54.
21. *Ibid.*, p. 53, also for further remarks.
22. *Ibid.*, p. 54.
23. *Ibid.*, Joint Separate Opinion of Judges Ross and Sigurjónsson, p. 50, also for their further remarks; see also p. 51, and point made by Judge Wold, to the same effect, *ibid.*, Separate Opinion of Judge Wold, p. 56.
24. *Ibid.*, p. 56.
25. *Ibid.*, p. 55, also for his further remarks.
26. *Ibid.*, pp. 55–6. It is be interesting to note here that, about two years before the Court's judgment in the '*Vagrancy*' cases, the (then) President of the Commission, M. Sørensen, wrote that 'la Cour est compétente en vertu de l'article 49 pour décider en cas de contestation sur sa propre compétence; par contre, elle n'est pas compétente pour statuer sur la compétence des autres organes prévus par la Convention'; Sørensen, 'La recevabilité', p. 337. As for Judge Wold's statement in his Separate Opinion that 'Articles 28 to 31 clearly show that the meaning of the Convention is that the Contracting States shall also abide by a decision of admissibility' (in '*Vagrancy*' cases, Series A, p. 56), it seems to be not quite relevant to the present discussion, since he speaks of the attitude of the Contracting States, not of the Court.
27. *Ibid.*, Separate Opinion of Judge Wold, p. 57; and cf. p. 58, for his further remarks (such as those relating to the competence of the Committee of Ministers and the competence of the Court).
28. Cf. A. Vanwelkenhuyzen, 'Jurisprudence internationale intéressant la Belgique, Cour Européenne des Droits de l'Homme (arrêt du 18 Juin 1971) – Affaires De Wilde, Ooms et Versyp', 6 *Revue belge de Droit international* [1973] p. 354.
29. Cf. R. Pelloux, 'Les arrêts de la Cour Européenne des Droits de l'Homme dans les affaires de Vagabondage', 18 *Annuaire français de Droit international* [1972] p. 445: 'La jurisprudence de la Cour est peu équitable a l'égard du requérant initial, car elle permet à la haute juridiction d'écarter comme irrecevable une requête qui a été déclarée recevable par la Commission, mais elle ne lui permettrait pas, à l'inverse, de déclarer recevable une requête écartée par la Commission, puisque, en pareil cas, personne ne pourrait la saisir.'
30. Cf. Vanwelkenhuyzen, *op. cit.*, p. 357: 'Le souci de la protection efficace des droits de l'homme recommande à notre avis que les questions de recevabilité prévues à l'article 27 de la Convention soient examinées par la seule Commission, expressément chargée de les trancher.' For a discussion of the general background and broader implications of the Court's decision in the '*Vagrancy*' cases, cf. T.E. McCarthy, 'The International Protection of Human Rights – Ritual and Reality', 25 *International and Comparative Law Quarterly* [1976] pp. 261–91.
31. My italics.
32. European Court of Human Rights, *Lawless* case, Series A, Judgment of 14 November 1960, p. 11.
33. *Ibid*
34. *Ibid*

35. *Ibid.*; according to Article 45 of the Convention, the Court's jurisdiction 'shall extend to all cases concerning the interpretation and application of the Convention'.
36. See European Court of Human Rights, *De Becker* case, Series A, Judgment of 27 March 1962, p. 11.
37. See European Court of Human Rights, *Stögmüller* case, Series A, Judgment of 10 November 1969, p. 42. But this appears to be to some extent an ambiguous statement, for it implies that the Commission's decision on admissibility could have been contested by the Court. It is pertinent to note here that in his study mentioned *supra*, n.1., Sørensen observes at one stage that 'la Convention ne prévoit pas d'appel contre les décisions de recevabilité prises para la Convention [at least to date], la Cour n'ayant pas compétence pour annuler les procédures devant la Commission' (Sørensen, 'La recevabilité', p. 341). The author affirms that the whole system of the Convention implies that the Court can only be seized of a case after the Commission has formally concluded its examination thereof (*ibid.*), but subsequently maintains that the Court is not bound by the Commission's findings on admissibility (but earlier he considered that the Commission's prior examination of a case could be regarded as a 'condition of admissibility' of that case by the Court; cf. *ibid.*).
38. See n. 37 above, and *supra*.
39. European Court of Human Rights, '*Vagrancy*' cases, Series A, Judgment of 18 June 1971, p. 30, para. 51; in the same sense (as for the 'independence' of the Commission's decisions), *mutatis mutandis*, European Court of Human Rights, *Lawless* case, Series A, Judgment of 14 November 1960, p. 11.
40. '*Vagrancy*' cases, p. 30, para. 51.
41. Even though if the decision on that preliminary objection is to the effect of joining the question to the merits – as, in general international law, did the International Court of Justice in the *Barcelona Traction* (Preliminary Objections) case, Judgment of 24 July 1964, *ICJ Reports* [1964] pp. 41–7, or as, under the European Convention on Human Rights, did the European Commission in the *Alam and Khan* case, application n. 2991/66, decision of 15 July 1967, *Collection*, vol. 24, p. 133.
42. On the question of the applicant's *locus standi in judicio* under the Convention, see Articles 25(1) and 44 of the Convention; European Court of Human Rights, *Lawless* case, Series A, Judgment of 14 November 1960, p. 15, and Series B – Pleadings Oral Arguments, Documents, pp. 261–2 (statement by the (then) President of the Commission, Sir Humphrey Waldock); European Court of Human Rights, *Lawless* case, Series A, Judgment of 7 April 1961, p. 24; European Court of Human Rights, *De Becker* case, Series A, Judgment of 27 March 1962, p. 26, and Series B – Pleadings etc., pp. 227/228; E.C.H.R., "*Vagrancy*" cases, Series B – Pleadings etc.), pp. 351–4, and Series A, Judgment of 18 November 1970, pp. 7–8. After this last decision, although individuals still remained without *locus standi in judicio* before the Court, their role before that organ had been 'strengthened' by

the fact that their counsel could now assist the Commission (at this latter's request) in the course of its debates before the Court.

43. Article 31(1) of the 1969 Vienna Convention on the Law of Treaties reads that 'a treaty shall be interpreted in good faith in accordance with the ordinary meaning to be given to the terms of the treaty in their context and in the light of its object and purpose' (text in UN doc. A/CONF. 39/27, 23 May 1969). And, in the same sense, cf. the following cases: Advisory Opinion on *Reservations to the Convention on the Prevention and Punishment of the Crime of Genocide, ICJ Reports* [1951] pp. 24–7; Advisory Opinion on *Reparation for Injuries Suffered in the Service of the United Nations, ICJ Reports* [1949] p. 180; Judge Alvarez's Dissenting Opinion in the *Competence of the General Assembly for the Admission to the United Nations* case, *ICJ Reports* [1950] pp. 17–18; *Advisory Opinion on Namibia, ICJ Reports* [1971] p. 30.

44. For another issue related to the local remedies rule, raised in the '*Vagrancy*' cases, and concerning the substance of the Belgian government's contention that the applicants had not exhausted domestic remedies (a contention rejected by the Court), see European Court of Human Rights, '*Vagrancy*' cases, (Series A, Judgment of 18 June 1971, pp. 46–7 and 33–5, and Series B – Pleadings etc., pp. 284–7 and 294 seq.; and cf. Joint Separate Opinion of Judges Balladore Pallieri and Verdross, *ibid.*, Series A, pp. 67–8.

45. European Court of Human Rights, *Stögmüller* case, Series A, Judgment of 10 November 1969, p. 42, para. 9.

46. *Ibid.*, p. 42, para. 11.

47. *Ibid.*, p. 42. para 12.

48. *Ibid.*, p 43, para. 12.

49. European Court of Human Rights, *Stögmüller* case, Series A, Judgment of 10 November 1969, p. 32, para. 6. Likewise, in the *Neumeister* case, in which the applicant had been subjected to two periods of detention on remand, the Court stated that it 'cannot consider whether or not the first period was compatible with the Convention; for even supposing that in 1961 Neumeister availed himself of certain remedies and exhausted them, he did not approach the Commission until 12 July 1963, that is to say after the six-month time-limit laid down in Article 26 of the Convention had expired' (European Court of Human Rights, *Neumeister* case, Series A, Judgment of 27 June 1968, p. 37, para. 6).

50. European Court of Human Rights, *Stögmüller* case, Series A, Judgment of 10 November 1969, Separate Joint Concurring Opinion of Judges Verdross and Bilge, p. 46; European Court of Human Rights, *Matznetter* case, Series A, Judgment of 10 November 1969, Separate Joint Concurring Opinion of Judges Verdross and Bilge, p. 38.

51. *Ibid.*, *Stögmüller* case, p. 46, and *Matznetter* case, p. 38.

52. *Ibid.*, *Stögmüller* case, p. 46, and *Matznetter* case, p. 38.

53. *Ibid.*, *Stögmüller* case, pp. 46–7, and *Matznetter* case, pp. 38–9.

54. *Ibid.*, *Stögmüller* case, p. 47, and *Matznetter* case, p. 39.

55. Cf.: Belgian government's written observations of 27 October 1971, in European Court of Human Rights, '*Vagrancy*' cases, Series B – Pleadings

etc., vol. 12, pp. 21–3 and 26; Belgian complementary observations of 31 January 1972, *ibid.*, pp. 38–42; arguments (of 14 February 1972) of the agent and counsel for the Belgian government, Mr de Meyer, *ibid.*, pp. 53, 57–9, 69–72, 77–8, 86 and 90–1.

56. See *ibid.*, pp. 28–9, and see mainly Mr Sørensen's arguments (as the Commission's principal delegate), *ibid.*, pp. 87 and 89. The applicants themselves (De Wilde, Ooms and Versyp) argued that 'in the present cases Belgian internal law does not allow reparation to be made for the consequences of the violation committed' (*ibid.*, p. 30, and see pp. 30–4).

57. European Court of Human Rights, '*Vagrancy*' cases, Series A, vol. 14, Judgment of 10 March 1972, p. 8, para. 15.

58. *Ibid.*; the Court added that 'while the Commission transmitted them to the Court, it did so without any accompanying report and solely with a view to giving the Court the assistance which, in a general way, it lends to the Court in accordance with Rule 71 of its Rules of Procedure'.

59. *Ibid.*

60. *Ibid.*, p. 8, para. 16.

61. Such as Article 32 of the Geneva General Act for the Pacific Settlement of International Disputes (1928), and Article 10 of the German–Swiss Treaty on Arbitration and Conciliation (1921): cited *ibid.*, pp. 8–9, para. 16.

62. *Ibid.*

63. *Ibid.*, p. 9, para. 16.

64. *Ibid.*, p. 9, para. 17.

65. See *ibid.*, p. 11; but see also comments in the Joint Separate Opinion of Judges Holmbäck, Ross and Wold, *ibid.*, pp. 14–15, and in the Separate Opinion of Judge Mosler, *ibid.*, pp. 19–20, paras. 6 and 7; and see pp. 9–10, para. 20.

66. European Court of Human Rights, *Ringeisen* case, Series A, vol. 15, Judgment of 22 June 1972, p. 9, para. 22. And see observations of the Austrian government (of 24 February 1972), in European Court of Human Rights, *Ringeisen* case [1971–2], Series B, – Pleadings, Oral Argument and Documents, vol. 13, p. 25; and see further statements by counsel for the Austrian government (Mr Pahr) in the public hearings of 26 and 27 May 1972, *ibid.*, Series B, vol. 13, pp. 51–2.

67. *Ibid.*, p. 9, para. 22.

68. *Ibid.*

69. *Ibid.* In the outcome of the case the Court unanimously afforded the applicant compensation in the sum of twenty thousand German marks to be paid by Austria (cf. *ibid.*, p. 11).

70. European Court of Human Rights, *Neumeister* case, Judgment of 7 May 1974, p. 9, para. 29; the Austrian government raised *inter alia* an objection of a different nature, which it is not intended to consider here.

71. As the use 'in the English text of the adjective "enforceable" confirms'; see *ibid.*, p. 10, para. 30.

72. *Ibid.*, p. 10, para. 30; the judgment further recalled 'the aim and object of the Convention', and referred to its *dictum* in this regard, *mutatis*

mutandis, in the '*Vagrancy*' cases (European Court of Human Rights, '*Vagrancy*' cases, Series A, n. 14, Judgment of 10 March 1972, p. 9, para. 16 *in fine*: 'keeping with the idea of the effective protection of human rights'). In the 1974 *Neumeister* decision, the Court held *inter alia* that Austria was to pay to the applicant, in respect of lawyers' costs, the sum of thirty thousand schillings, and that decision was unanimously taken (cf. *ibid.*, p. 17).

73. European Court of Human Rights, *Schmidt and Dahlström* case, Judgment of 6 February 1976, p. 13; *National Union of Belgian Police* case, Judgment of 27 October 1975, p. 18; *Swedish Engine Drivers' Union* case, Judgment of 6 February 1976, p. 13; *Engel and Others* case, Judgment of 8 June 1976, p. 37 (in relation to some of the complaints only). In the *Golder* case, the Court ruled that in the circumstances of the case it was 'not necessary to afford to the applicant any just satisfaction other than that resulting from the finding of a violation of his rights': Judgment of 21 February 1975, p. 16.

74. In the *Golder* case, the Court limited itself to registering the Commission's handling of the question of exhaustion of local remedies: cf., pp. 3 and 5; and see *Engel and Others* case, p. 15, for contentions of non-availability of legal remedies to terminate interim custody. For pertinent criticisms on types of redress of violations of the Convention, with particular reference to 'just satisfaction' under Article 50 of the Convention, see, e.g., Ph. Vegleris, 'Modes de redressement des violations de la Convention européenne des droits de l'homme', in *Mélanges offerts à Polys Modinos*, Paris, Pédone, 1968, pp. 369–88, and authorities quoted therein. On Article 50 of the Convention, see further, e.g., W. Vis, *La Réparation des violations de la Convention européenne des droits de l'homme* (report presented at the Colloquy of Strasbourg of 14–15 November 1960), Council of Europe doc. A–58–036, Strasbourg, 1960, pp. 1–9 (mimeographed); M.-A. Eissen, 'La Cour européenne des droits de l'homme – de la Convention au règlement', 5 *Annuaire français de Droit international* [1959] p. 635.

75. On the duty of reparation, cf. PCIJ, *Chorzów Factory* (Claim for Indemnity – Jurisdiction) case (1927), Series A, n. 9., p. 21.

76. The request for a declaratory judgment was the point in issue in the *Certain German Interests in Polish Upper Silesia* (Jurisdiction) case, PCIJ, Series A, 1925, n. 6; and see further PCIJ, same case (Merits), Series A, 1926, n. 7, p. 12; PCIJ, *Interpretation of Judgments ns. 7 and 8* (*The Chorzów Factory*) case (1927), Series A, n. 13, p. 20; PCIJ, *Chorzów Factory* (Claim for Indemnity – Jurisdiction) case, Series A, 1927, n. 9, p. 12; PCIJ, *Administration of the Prince von Pless* case (1933); Series C, n. 70, Pleadings, Oral Statements and Documents, hearings of 9 November 1932, p. 270 (argument of the German agent, Professor Kaufmann, upholding the non-application of the local remedies rule in case of a request for a declaratory judgment).

77. PCIJ, *Interpretation of the Statute of the Memel Territory* case (1932), Series A/B, n. 49, p. 311.

78. Cf. arguments of the co-agent for the Swiss government, Professor Guggenheim, *Interhandel* case, *ICJ Reports* [1959]; Pleadings, Oral Arguments, Documents, pp. 564–6; and cf. also P. Guggenheim, *Traité de droit international public*, vol. II, Genève, Georg & Cie, 1954, pp. 164–5.
79. Cf. arguments of the North American agent, Mr Becker, *Interhandel* case, *ibid.*, Pleadings etc., pp. 618–22, and see also pp. 475–85.
80. *Interhandel* (Preliminary Objections) case, *ICJ Reports* [1959] pp. 20 and 30.
81. *Ambatielos* case (Merits: Obligation to Arbitrate), *ICJ Reports* [1953], judgment of 19 May 1953, p. 23.
82. 25 *International Law Reports* [1958]–1, pp. 42–50; also reported in 19 *Zeitschrift für ausländisches öffentliches Recht und Völkerrecht* [1958] pp. 770–7. The Tribunal did not seem over-impressed with West Germany's endeavours to try to demonstrate that recent developments in international law amounted to an extension of the applicability of the local remedies rule.
83. Appl. ns. 5577–5583/72 (joined), *Donnelly and Others* v. *United Kingdom* case, *Collection*, vol. 43, p. 149.
84. Appl. ns. 5577–5583/72 (joined), *Donnelly* case, European Commission of Human Rights (final) decision of 15 December 1975, Council of Europe doc. 43.662–06.2 (mimeographed), p. 83.
85. See mainly the interventions by Guggenheim, Badawi, Paul de Visscher, Giraud and Jessup, in 46 *Annuaire de l'Institut de Droit International* [1959] pp. 299–302. And cf., well before the *Institut*'s debates, supporting the non-application of the local remedies rule in the present context, Ch. de Visscher, 'Le déni de justice en droit international', 52 *Recueil des Cours de l'Académie de Droit International* [1935] p. 425; J.E.S. Fawcett, 'The Exhaustion of Local Remedies: Substance or Procedure?', 31 *British Yearbook of International Law* [1954] p. 457. And see, generally, E.M. Borchard, 'Declaratory Judgments in International Law', 29 *American Journal of International Law* [1935] pp. 489 and 492.
86. In this sense, e.g., J. Chappez, *La Règle de l'épuisement des voies de recours internes*, Paris, Pédone, 1972, pp. 94–7.
87. In this sense, C.H.P. Law, *The Local Remedies Rule in International Law*, Geneva, Droz, 1961, p. 110; T. Haesler, *The Exhaustion of Local Remedies in the Case-Law of International Courts and Tribunals*, Leyden, Sijthoff, 1968, p. 120.
88. Law, *op. cit.*, pp. 109–10; Haesler, *op. cit.*, pp. 120–5.
89. The problem is not dissociated from that of implied waiver of the local remedies rule, Ch. 2, section C, *supra*.
90. The International Court has in fact at times, for example, joined preliminary objections to the merits in, e.g., PCIJ, *Administration of the Prince von Pless* case, Series A/B, n. 52, p. 16; PCIJ, *Losinger* case, Series A/B, n. 67, pp. 24–5; *Right of Passage over Indian Territory* (Preliminary Objections) case, *ICJ Reports* [1957] pp. 150–2.
91. On the joinder of preliminary objections to the merits, see, e.g., E.

Grisel, *Les Exceptions d'incompétence et d'irrecevabilité dans la procédure de la Cour Internationale de Justice*, Berne, ed. H. Lang, 1968, pp. 171–84; S. Rosenne, *The Law and Practice of the International Court*, Leyden, Sijthoff, 1965, vol. I, pp. 464–6, and vol. II, p. 551; G. Abi-Saab, *Les Exceptions préliminaires dans la procédure de la Cour Internationale*, Paris, Pédone, 1967, pp. 194–8; J. Lang, 'La jonction au fond des exceptions préliminaires devant la CPJI et la CIJ', 95 *Journal du Droit International (Clunet)* [1968] pp. 5–45.

92. PCIJ, *Panevezys–Saldutiskis Railway* case, 1938–9, Series A/B, Order of 30 June 1938, and see Series A/B, n. 75 (1938), pp. 55–6. On the objection of non-exhaustion, see pleadings by the agent for the Lithuanian government, Professor Mandelstam, *ibid.*, Series C (Pleadings, Oral Statements and Documents, 13–15 June 1938), n. 86, pp. 451–69, and 499–500 and 506–11, and pleadings by the agent for the Estonian government, Baron Nolde, *ibid.*, pp. 478–97 and 518–31. The subsequent developments of the case are discussed elsewhere; see PCIJ, *ibid.*, Series A/B, n. 76 (Judgment of 28 February 1939), pp. 5 seq.

93. PCIJ, *Losinger* case, Series A/B, n. 67 (Order of 27 June 1936), pp. 24–5, and see also pp. 18 and 23; and cf. Series C (Pleadings, etc.), n. 78, pp. 40–1. In the *Borchgrave* case (1937), although Belgium requested the Court either to declare the Spanish objection of non-exhaustion inadmissible or to join it to the merits, the case was later discontinued and removed from the Court's list; cf. PCIJ, Series A/B, n. 72, pp. 160–1, and 169 and Series C (Pleadings etc.), n. 83, pp. 115–17, 119–25; and cf. Series A/B, n. 73 (Order of 30 April 1938), pp. 4–5.

94. *Barcelona Traction* (Preliminary Objections) case, *ICJ Reports* [1964] pp. 12 and 14–16.

95. Cf. arguments by one of the Spanish government's counsel in the case, Professor A. Malintoppi, in ICJ docs. distr. C.R. 64/13–15 (mimeographed – translation), pp. 7–8; arguments by one of the counsel for the Belgian government, Professor H. Rolin, in ICJ doc. distr. C.R. 64/29 (mimeographed), pp. 2, 4–12, 14–17, 24, 26–7 and 29–30; arguments by counsel for Spain, Professor R. Ago, in ICJ doc. distr. C.R. 64/37 (mimeographed), pp. 32–8 and 42–3; Professor Rolin's reply, in ICJ doc. 64/43 (mimeographed), pp. 29–35, 41 and 43.

96. *Barcelona Traction* (Preliminary Objections) case, *ICJ Reports* [1964] p. 46.

97. *Ibid.*, pp. 46–47, and Judge Jessup's declaration, *ibid.*, p. 50; on this step taken by the Court, see also Dissenting Opinion of Judge Armand-Ugon, *ibid.*, pp. 164 and 166; Dissenting Opinion of Judge Morelli, *ibid.*, pp. 100 and 114–15. And see further, on the same point, in the 1970 decision in the case, *Barcelona Traction* case, *ICJ Reports* [1970], Separate Opinion of Judge Tanaka, p. 115; Separate Opinion of President Bustamante y Rivero, p. 57; Separate Opinion of Judge Fitzmaurice, pp. 110–13; Separate Opinion of Judge Jessup, pp. 163–4; Dissenting Opinion of Judge Riphagen, p. 356.

98. *ICJ Reports* [1956] pp. 73–5, and cf. Judgment of 6 July 1957 on the case, in *ICJ Reports* [1957] pp. 11 seq.

99. *Aerial Incident* case, *ICJ Reports* [1959], Pleadings etc., pp. 593 and 523–4 (for Mr Rosenne's arguments), and pp. 564, 445, 559 and 572 (for Professor Cot's pleadings).
100. *Aerial Incident* case (Preliminary Objections), *ICJ Reports* [1959] p. 146.
101. See, e.g., Ch. de Visscher, *Aspects récents du droit procédural de la Cour Internationale de Justice*, Paris, Pédone, 1966, pp. 106–11; Anzilotti's remarks (in 1936) in the course of the work of the elaboration of the rules of Court, PCIJ, Series D (Acts and Documents Concerning the Organization of the Court), n. 2, Addendum 3, p. 647; Joint Separate Opinion of Judges De Visscher and Rostworowski in the *Panevezys–Saldutiskis Railway* case (1939), Series A/B, n. 76, pp. 24–5.
102. Cf. G. Sperduti, 'La recevabilité des exceptions préliminaires de fond dans le procès international', 53 *Rivista di Diritto Internazionale* [1970] pp. 483–4 and 488–9. On his part, Mabrouk sets forth two conditions for the joinder to the merits, namely: first, 'the objection must be *preliminary*', and, secondly, 'knowledge of the merits must be absolutely necessary to pronounce on the objection'; M. Mabrouk, *Les Exceptions de procédure devant les juridictions internationales*, Paris, LGDJ, 1966, pp. 285–6.
103. *Interhandel* (Preliminary Objections) case, *ICJ Reports* [1959] p. 30.
104. *Ibid.*, pp. 81, 84, 89 and 124, respectively.
105. *Ibid.*, Pleadings etc., pp. 553–6; and see also Judge Hudson's Dissenting Opinion in the *Panevezys–Saldutiskis Railway* case, PCIJ, Series A/B, n. 76, p. 47.
106. In its Judgment of 22 June 1972 in the *Ringeisen* case (question of the application of Article 50 of the Convention), the Court considered a 'formalistic attitude' as being 'alien to international law'; European Court of Human Rights, *Ringeisen* case, Series A, vol. 15, p. 7, para. 18. And the Commission, in its decision of 30 August 1958 in the *Lawless* v. *Ireland* case, stated that 'the present Commission, as an international tribunal, is not bound to treat questions of form with the same degree of strictness as might be the case in municipal law' (appl. n. 332/57, *Yearbook*, vol. II, p. 326). In so stating, the Commission recalled the PCIJ's *dictum* in the *Mavrommatis Palestine Concessions* case (1924); 'The Court, whose jurisdiction is international, is not bound to attach to matters of form the same degree of importance which they might possess in municipal law' (PCIJ, Series A, n. 2, p. 34).
107. Appl. n. 332/57, *Lawless* v. *Ireland* case, *Yearbook*, vol. II, pp. 308–40; the two objections joined to the merits were founded on Articles 17 and 15 of the Convention, respectively; cf. *ibid.*, pp. 340, 330 and 334.
108. Appl. n. 299/57, *Greece* v. *United Kingdom* case (in respect of Cyprus), Commission's sitting of 12 October 1957, *Yearbook*, vol. II, pp. 188–96, esp. p. 190.
109. The Commission thus disposed of the matter at that stage; rather than contemplating joining it to the merits, the Commission identified in the respondent government's attitude an instance of waiver of the application of the local remedies rule. Cf. appl. n. 1994/63, 57 *Inhabitants of Louvain and Environs* v. *Belgium* case, decision of 5 March 1964,

Yearbook, vol. 7, p. 260.

110. Appl. n. 4448/70, *Denmark/Norway/Sweden* v. *Greece* case, (partial) decision of 26 May 1970, *Collection*, vol. 34, p. 69.

111. *Ibid.*

112. *Ibid.*

113. *Ibid.*

114. Appl. n. 2991/66, *Alam and Khan* v. *United Kingdom* case, *Yearbook*, vol. X, pp. 478–88.

115. *Ibid.*, pp. 498–500.

116. *Ibid.*, p. 502.

117. *Ibid.*

118. *Ibid.*, p. 504.

119. *Ibid.*, pp. 504–6.

120. *Ibid.*, p. 506. The question of the exhaustion of local remedies was joined to the merits and the application of Mr Alam and Mr Khan was declared admissible and retained for further examination (in accordance with Articles 28*seq.* of the Convention); cf. *ibid.*

121. Cf. Report of the Sub-Commission (adopted on 17 December 1968) on appl. n. 2991/66, *Alam and Khan* v. *United Kingdom* case, *Yearbook*, vol. XI, pp. 788–94.

122. Appl. ns. 5577/72–5583/72 (joined), *Donnelly and Others* v. *United Kingdom* case, *Collection*, vol. 43, p. 122.

123. *Ibid.*, p. 124.

124. *Ibid.*, pp. 124–5.

125. *Ibid.*, p. 125.

126. *Ibid.*

127. *Ibid.*, p. 132; see pp. 132–3.

128. *Ibid.*, p. 132.

129. *Ibid.*, p. 136. The problem of the exhaustion of local remedies in connection with contentions of legislative measures and administrative practices as raised in the present case is more thoroughly discussed in Ch. 4 on the extent of application of the rule of exhaustion of local remedies, *supra*, pp. 187–212.

130. *Ibid.*, p. 137.

131. *Ibid.*

132. *Ibid.*

133. *Ibid.*, p. 139.

134. *Ibid.*, p. 140.

135. *Ibid.*, p. 148.

136. *Ibid.*, p. 149.

137. Appl. n. 5310/71, *Ireland* v. *United Kingdom* case, *Collection*, vol. 41, p. 25.

138. *Ibid.*, p. 87.

139. *Ibid.*

140. *Ibid.*, p. 88.

141. Cf. *ibid.*, pp. 89–92; the allegations thus retained – without prejudging the merits – are listed *ibid.*, pp. 91–2.

142. Appl. n. 788/60, *Austria* v. *Italy* case, *Report of the Plenary Commission*

(adopted on 31 March 1963), Strasbourg, 1963, pp. 64–6, and see pp. 69–70.

143. Appl. n. 332/57, *Lawless* v. *Ireland* case, decision of 30 August 1958, *Yearbook*, vol. 2, pp. 340, 330 and 334.

144. Appl. n. 4475/70, *Svenska Lotsförbundet* v. *Sweden* case, decision of 24 May 1971, *Collection*, vol. 38, p. 76.

145. It reads: 'The Commission may only deal with the matter after all domestic remedies have been exhausted, according to the generally recognized rules of international law, and within a period of six months from the date on which the final decision was taken.' Text in European Convention on Human Rights, *Collected Texts*, 9th edn, Strasbourg, March 1974, p. 8.

146. Appl. n. 4475/70, *Svenska Lotsförbundet* v. *Sweden* case, *Collection*, vol. 38, p. 76.

147. *Ibid.*, vol. 42, p. 13.

148. On this ground of inadmissibility (as related, sometimes, to the local remedies rule), see, e.g. Fawcett, *Application of the European Convention*, pp. 312–13 (and cf. his further comments *supra*); Monconduit, *La Commission européenne*, pp. 346–56; Jacobs, *The European Convention*, pp. 243–6; and, on trends of the Commission's practice on the matter, see, e.g., appl. n. 1468/62, *Iversen* v. *Norway* case, decision of 17 December 1963, *Yearbook*, vol. 6, p. 326, and see pp. 322–4 (on the six-month time-limit under Article 26 of the Convention); and appl. n. 4897/71, *Gussenbauer* v. *Austria* case, decision of 22 March 1972, *Collection*, vol. 42, pp. 47–8, and appl. n. 5219/71, *Gussenbauer* case decision of 14 July 1972, *Collection*, vol. 42, pp. 95–6.

149. It may be recalled, for example, that, in the *Borchgrave* case (Belgium v. Spain, 1937), the PCIJ took into account Spain's express withdrawal of its (second) preliminary objection of non-exhaustion of local remedies and its request that that objection be joined to the merits as a defence; the Court held, however, that the objection having been withdrawn, it could not be joined to the merits; PCIJ, *Borchgrave* case, Series A/B, n. 72, 1937, pp. 169–70. The case was subsequently discontinued and removed from the Court's list; PCIJ, *Borchgrave* case, Series A/B, n. 73, 1938, pp. 4–5.

150. Appl. ns. 2169/64, 2204/64 and 2326/64, *Mme X* v. *F.R. Germany* case, decision of 2 October 1964, *Collection*, vol. 14, pp. 81–3.

151. Appl. n. 2339/64, *X* v. *Austria* case, decision of 6 April 1967, *Collection*, vol. 22, p. 117.

152. Appl. n. 2004/63, *Kornmann* v. *F.R. Germany* case, final decision of 24 May 1966, *Collection*, vol. 20, pp. 50–1.

153. *Ibid.*, p. 51.

154. *Ibid.*, pp. 51–3.

155. European Court of Human Rights, *Ringeisen* case (1970–1); Series B – Pleadings, Oral Arguments, Documents, vol. II, pp. 260–1.

156. Appl. n. 2294/64, *Helga and Wilhelm Gericke* v. *F.R. Germany* case, decision of 23 September 1965, *Collection*, vol. 20, pp. 99–100.

157. *Ibid.*, p. 100.

158. Appl. n. 2686/65, *Kornmann* v. *F.R. Germany* case, final decision of 13 December 1966, *Collection*, vol. 22, p. 9.
159. *Ibid.*
160. *Ibid.*, p. 10.
161. *Ibid.*
162. I.e., those remedies provided for in the Introductory Act to the Judicature Act, Article 23, and also civil proceedings against the Land Berlin (cf. *ibid.*).
163. *Ibid.*
164. *Ibid.*, pp. 10–11.
165. Appl. n. 2294/64, *Helga and Wilhelm Gericke* v. *F.R. Germany* case, decision of 23 September 1965, *Collection*, vol. 20, p. 99.
166. Appl. n. 2840/66, *X* v. *F.R. Germany* case, decision of 19 December 1969, *Collection*, vol. 31, pp. 4–5.
167. *Ibid.*, pp. 4–7.
168. Appl. n. 5006/71, *X* v. *United Kingdom*, decision of 9 February 1972, *Collection*, vol. 39, pp. 93–4. See also, similarly, appl. n. 3075/67, *X* v. *United Kingdom* case, decision of 19 July 1968, *Collection*, vol. 28, p. 108.
169. Appl. n. 3542/68, *X* v. *United Kingdom* case, decision of 13 July 1970, *Collection*, vol. 35, pp. 54–5.
170. *Ibid.*, appl. ns. 3542/68 and 4099/69, p. 55.
171. Appl. n. 2834/66, *X* v. *F.R. Germany* case, decision of 13 July 1970, *Collection*, vol. 35, p. 27.
172. *Ibid.*, pp. 27–8. Subsequently, the two joined applications were declared inadmissible on another ground; cf. appl. ns. 2834/66 and 4038/69, *X* v. *F.R. Germany* case, decision of 13 July 1970, *Collection*, vol. 35, pp. 33–6.

Addendum

1. Cf.: appl. n. 7033/75, *Deutsch* v. *F.R. Germany* case, Council of Europe (C.E.) doc. DH (77) 6, of Oct. 1977, p. 11; appl. n. 7397/76, *Peyer* v. *Switzerland* case, C.E. doc. DH (77) 7, of Dec. 1977, p. 15; appls. ns. 5947/72, 6205/73, 7052/75, 7061/75, 7107/75, 7113/75 and 7136/75, *Seven Prisoners' Correspondence Cases* v. *United Kingdom*, C.E. doc DH (78) 1, of Feb. 1978, p. 6; appl. n. 6871/75, *Caprino* v. *United Kingdom* case, C.E. doc. DH (78) 2, of March 1978, p, 12; appl. n. 7438/76, *Ventura* v. *Italy* case, C.E. doc. DH (78) 2, of March 1978, p. 15; appl. n. 6694/74, *Artico* v. *Italy* case, C.E. doc. DH (78) 6, of Dec. 1978, p. 12; appl. n. 7975/77, *Bonazzi* v. *Italy* case, in *ibid.*, p. 15; appl. n. 7598/76, *Kaplan* v. *United Kingdom* case, in *ibid.*, p. 20; appl. n. 8130/78, *H. and M. Eckle* v. *F.R. Germany* case, C.E. doc. DH (79) 3, of May 1979, p. 11; appl. n. 7907/77, *X* v. *United Kingdom* case, C.E. doc. DH (79) 6, of Oct. 1979, p. 11; appl. n. 7630/76, *Reed* v. *United Kingdom* case, C.E. doc. DH (79) 7, of May 1980, p. 10; appl. ns. 8022/77, 8025/77 and 8027/77, *A, B and C* v. *United Kingdom* case, in *ibid.*, p. 12; appl. n. 8304/78, *Corigliano* v. *Italy* case, C.E. doc. DH (80) 5, of Jan. 1981, p. 14; appl. n. 7653/76, *Agneessens* v. *Belgium* case, C.E. doc. C (80) 22, of May 1980, p. 2; appl. n. 8378/78, *Kamal* v. *United Kingdom* case, C.E. doc. C (80)

23, of May 1980, p. 2; appl. n. 8463/78, *Kröcher and Möller* v. *Switzerland* case, C.E. doc. C (81) 37, of July 1981, p. 2; and cf. further the cases *Kofler* v. *Italy* (1981), C.E. doc. C (81) 39, of July 1981, p. 2; and *De Jong and Baljet* v. *Netherlands* (1981), C.E. doc. C (81) 20, of May 1981, p. 2; and cf. the other cases, referred to *infra*.

2. Cf. appls. ns. 7151/75 and 7152/75, *Sporrong and Lönnroth* v. *Sweden* case, C.E. doc. DH (79) 6, of Oct. 1979, pp. 12–13; appls. ns. 7601/76 and 7806/77, *Young, James and Webster* v. *United Kingdom* case, C.E. doc. DH (79) 4, of July 1979, p. 13, and cf. C.E. doc. DH (78) 2, of March 1978, p. 11 (in respect of appl. n. 7806/77, *Webster* v. *United Kingdom* case); and cf. also C.E. docs. C (81) 7–8, of Feb. – March 1981, p. 2, and C (81) 43, of Aug. 1981, p. 2; appls. ns. 7819/77 and 7878/77, *Campbell and Fell* v. *United Kingdom* case, C.E. doc. DH (81) 2, of April 1981, pp. 10–11; appls. ns. 5947/72, 6205/73, 7052/75, 7061/75, 7107/75, 7113/75 and 7136/75, *Seven Prisoners' Correspondence Cases* v. *United Kingdom*, C.E. doc. DH (78) 1, of Feb. 1978, p. 6. Cf. also appl. n. 7598/76, *Kaplan* v. *United Kingdom* case, C.E. doc. DH (81) 2, of April 1981, p. 14; *Silver and Others* v. *United Kingdom* case (1972–1975 onwards), C.E. doc. C (81) 12, of March 1981, p. 1; *Arrondelle* v. *United Kingdom* case (1979–1980), C.E. doc. H. (81) 1, of Feb. 1981, p. 4; appl. n. 8691/79, *Malone* v. *United Kingdom* case (1981), C.E. doc. C. (81) 41, of July 1981, p. 1.

3. A decision taken by thirteen votes to four; European Court of Human Rights, *Van Oosterwijck* case, Judgment of 6 November 1980, C.E. publ., pp. 9–12 and 14. The Court found that there were no special circumstances dispensing the applicant from exercising those local remedies; *ibid.*, pp. 13–14.

4. *Ibid.*, p. 9; in this respect, the Court referred to the 1934 arbitral award in the *Finnish Vessels* case.

5. *Ibid.*, p. 11 – On the *Van Oosterwijck* case, cf. also C.E. docs. DH (78) 3, of May 1978, p. 14; H (81) 1, of Feb. 1981, pp. 10–11; H (82) 2, of Feb. 1982, p. 12.

6. European Court of Human Rights, *Case of Klass and Others*, Judgment of 6 September 1978, C.E. publ., p. 23, and cf. pp. 23–7.

7. *Ibid.*, p. 13. The Court admitted that in the present case each of the applicants was entitled to claim to be the victim of a violation of the Convention, even though he was unable to prove that he had been subject to measures of secret surveillance; the question whether he was actually a victim of a breach of the Convention involved 'determining whether the contested legislation is in itself compatible with the Convention's provisions'; *ibid.*, p. 15.

8. European Court of Human Rights, *Guzzardi* Case, Judgment of 6 November 1980, C.E. publ., p. 21, and cf. pp. 21–2.

9. A decision taken by ten votes to eight; cf. *ibid.*, p. 35; and, on the matter, cf. also the Dissenting Opinions of Judges Cremona (p. 41) and Bindschedler-Robert (p. 47). The latter ponders that, whilst the flexibility called for by the Court is 'correct' if applied 'to the international rule itself when one is in the process of determining its

scope', on the other hand, 'to apply it to domestic law in order to determine and interpret the conditions laid down thereunder in the matter of remedies amounts to endowing the international court with jurisdiction to interpret that law and, in the final analysis, to make domestic law that does not exist. [...] The principle that the rule of exhaustion of domestic remedies should be flexibly interpreted concerns the scope of the *international* obligation and not the interpretation of domestic law' (. 47). On the case, cf. also C.E. doc. H (82) 2, of Feb. 1982, pp. 13–15.

10. C.E. doc. H (80) 3, of Jan. 1980, p. 12.

11. C.E. docs. C (79) 28, of Sept. 1979, p. 1; C (79) 4, of Feb. 1979, pp. 1–2; C (79) 5, of Feb. 1979, p. 1.

12. C.E. doc. C (79) 31, of Oct. 1979, p. 2.

13. *Ibid.*, pp. 1 and 4; C.E. doc. H (80) 3, of Jan. 1980, p. 13. – Similarly, in its judgment of 13 August 1981 in the *Young, James and Webster* v. *United Kingdom* case, the Court held *inter alia* that in the circumstances it was unnecessary to determine whether there had been a breach of Article 13 of the Convention; C.E. doc. C (81) 43, of August 1981, p. 4. – And, in its judgment of 6 February 1981, again in the *Airey* v. *Ireland* case (this time under Article 50 on 'just satisfaction'), the Court afforded the applicant reparation but rejected the part of her argument whereby her decision to move house was attributed to her lack of effective access to court for petitioning for judicial separation; C.E. doc. C (81) 6, of Feb. 1981, pp. 2–3.

Conclusions

1. In approaching that interaction one no longer needs to venture into the classical irreconcilable antagonism between dualist and monist positions. See, on the former, H. Triepel, *Droit international et droit interne* (trans. R. Brunet), Paris, Pédone, 1920, pp. 11–165; D. Anzilotti, *Corso di Diritto Internazionale*, 3rd edn, vol. I, Padova, Cedam, 1955, pp. 49–110. And, on the monist thesis, cf. H. Kelsen, 'Les rapports de système entre le droit interne et le droit international public', 14 *Recueil des Cours de l'Académie de Droit International* (R.C.A.D.I.) [1926] pp. 231–6; H. Kelsen, 'Théorie du Droit international public', 84 *R.C.A.D.I.* [1953] pp. 182–200; G. Scelle, *Précis de Droit des Gens*, vol. I, Paris, Rec. Sirey, 1932–4, pp. 30–1.

2. Effects of the Convention as a whole upon the domestic law of States Parties have admittedly varied from country to country. But if the Convention's formal domestic status varies in member States, application of Convention provisions by domestic courts illustrates the extent of the Convention's influence upon Contracting States over the years.

3. The European Commission, under Article 19 of the Convention, can be concerned with errors of law or fact committed by domestic courts but only in so far as they appear to have resulted in the violation of one of the guaranteed rights; the same applies to domestic legislation, which cannot be examined *in abstracto*, but only in so far as its application is alleged to constitute a violation of one of the guaranteed rights. The Commission's

examination of an alleged violation of the Convention may be carried out *ex officio*, even if the applicant did not rely on a specific Article of the Convention. Under Article 7, e.g., the Convention itself refers to municipal law, and here in particular it is clear that the Commission is to exercise, however cautiously, its supervisory function.

4. See J.C. Witenberg, 'La recevabilité des réclamations devant les juridictions internationales', 41 *R.C.A.D.I.* [1932] pp. 51–6; G. Dahm, 'Die Subsidiarität des internationalen Rechtsschutzes bei Völkerrechtswidriger Verletzung von Privatpersonen', in *Vom Deutschen zum Europäischen Recht – Festschrift für Hans Dölle*, vol. II, Tubingen, Mohr – Siebeck, 1963, pp. 6–27.

5. Cf. appl. 1852/63 (1965), *Yearbook*, vol. VIII, pp. 198–200; appls. ns. 1420/62, 1477/62 and 1478/62, *X and Y* v. *Belgium* case (18 December 1963), *Yearbook*, vol. VII, p. 626.

6. Cf. *Collection of Decisions of National Courts Referring to the [European] Convention*, Council of Europe – Directorate of Human Rights, and Supplements 1 to 4, Strasbourg, 1969–74: see mainly national courts decisions on Articles 26 and 13 of the Convention (loose-leaf collection, no page references). But this positive feature is also accompanied by a 'negative' feature in that national court decisions have also seemed to reveal a certain tendency to look at precedents of the forum-State's courts of last instance rather than at the vast jurisprudence of the Convention organs themselves in interpreting them. Cf., on this point, C.H. Schreuer, 'The Authority of International Judicial Practice in Domestic Courts', 23 *International and Comparative Law Quarterly* [1974] pp. 693–4.

7. Cf., for different views, on the one hand, Vasak, *La Convention européenne*, p. 249; and, on the other hand, Fawcett, *Application of the European Convention*, p. 302, and W.J. Ganshof van der Meersch, 'Does the Convention Have the Force of "*Ordre Public*" in Municipal Law?', in *Human Rights in National and International Law* (ed. A.H. Robertson), Manchester, University Press/Oceana, 1970, pp. 135–43.

8. The question touches on the conditions for the application of the local remedies rule under the Convention (developed by the Commission's jurisprudence), particularly the one whereby the substance of a complaint lodged with the Commission ought previously to have been raised before domestic courts (cf. *supra*, pp. 80–5). On the problem presently at issue, cf. appl. n. 788/60, *Report*, C. of E. doc. A–84–548, pp. 45–51; appl. n. 1661/62 (1963), *Collection*, vol. 10, p. 18; appl. n. 1488/62 (1963) *Collection*, vol. 13, p. 96; appl. n. 1475/62 (1963), *Collection*, vol. 11, pp. 48–9.

9. In this sense, Ganshof van der Meersch, *op. cit.*, pp. 142–3.

10. The public hearings in the *Matznetter* case (1969) led the European Court of Human Rights to reject inadequate analogies between diplomatic protection and human rights protection for purposes of application of the rule (cf. *supra*, pp. 40–5). Similarly, years earlier, an Opinion of a Committee of Jurists (under the League of Nations) and the oral hearings before the Permanent Court of International Justice in the *Administration of the Prince von Pless* case (1933) provided important elements for a rejection

of analogies between State responsibility for injuries to aliens and minorities protection (this latter, e.g., permanent or continuous and not occasional) for purposes of application of the local remedies rule (cf. *supra*).

11. As already indicated, the correlation between rights and duties is lacking in diplomatic protection (see *supra*).

12. The Covenant goes even further by expressly providing for the duty to develop the possibilities of *judicial* remedies (cf. *supra*).

13. Does not the normal operation of the local remedies rule (with attention to the facts which remain the same throughout the process of pursuance of a common objective) call for a reconsideration of the traditional positivist-dualist assumption that international law and municipal law govern relations between different subjects?

14. A guarantee comprising all legal claims conferred upon the individual by the domestic legal system concerned, distinctly from the duty enshrined in Article 13, which pertains only to the rights guaranteed by the Convention (*supra*). The two provisions are not, however, mutually exclusive, but rather concurrently applicable, and it may well happen that where Convention provisions form an integral part of municipal law, the duty to provide local remedies (Article 13) appears in a way 'absorbed' by the guarantee of access to domestic courts (Article 6).

15. See R.A. Falk, *The Role of Domestic Courts in the International Legal Order*, Syracuse, University Press, 1964, pp. 21–59 and 170–7.

16. Such uniformity ensuing from the co-ordinated activity of domestic courts (under the Convention) may be expected particularly in a system largely inspired by the notions of general interest and collective guarantee, with the local remedies rule operating therein as a procedural device for allocating jurisdiction between the municipal and international legal order.

17. E.g., State's duty to provide local remedies (Article 13).

18. The role of domestic courts decisions under the European Convention is also apparent in taking the Convention as a source of legal duties to all concerned. The notion of 'rule of law', a substratum of legal substantive values, underlies such engagements as the duty to provide local remedies (Article 13) and the right to a fair and public hearing (Article 6). It is surely more important that local remedies can in effect be demanded and enforced than that they are formally open to the individual.

19. By the end of 1976, of 7,740 applications registered with the Commission, 6,293 had been rejected as inadmissible or struck off the list (cf. C. of E. doc. DH (77)3, *Stock-Taking on the European Convention on Human Rights*, Strasbourg, 1977, p. 87), a considerable number of these latter for non-exhaustion of local remedies. Cf. further data in Ch. 2, *supra*.

1. *International Court* (Permanent Court of International Justice and International Court of Justice):*

*Cases in the Court's jurisprudence other than the ones listed herein, even though not touching specifically on the local remedies rule, may have an indirect bearing on, e.g., certain issues of procedure (such as, e.g., the burden of proof, Chapter 3, *supra*) applicable to the local remedies rule; references to such cases are to be found in the notes.

2. European Convention on Human Rights

(a) *European Commission of Human Rights*:*

Applications ns.

*Additional references to other decisions in the Commission's practice (including cases of lesser relevance to, or without a direct bearing on, the local remedies rule) may be found in the notes. These latter also contain references to some *unpublished* decisions of the Commission. Likewise, references to the Commission's *Reports* on some of the cases herein listed, or to individual *Opinions* of some of the Commission's members, may be found in the notes of the present study. Many of the cases listed herein are reported both in the Convention's *Yearbook* and in the Commission's *Collection of Decisions* (and more recently in its *Decisions and Reports*). Whenever this has happened, preference for citation has been given to the texts of decisions as they appeared in the *Collection of Decisions* and the *Decisions and Reports*, for the reason that they were published more promptly (either in English or in French, the language in which they were drafted) than in the *Yearbook*, and they contained a greater number of the Commission's decisions. As many of the cases listed herein contain references to specific remedies and specific courts in the municipal legal systems of States parties to the Convention, reference may here be made to the Council of Europe publication *Judicial Organisation in Europe* (Strasbourg, 1975): this book may prove useful for a fuller appreciation of some of the questions discussed in some of the cases listed herein (e.g., the question of the local remedies to be exhausted, Chapter 2, *supra*), as it contains general indications of the constitutional systems of member States of the Council of Europe, including remedies available before domestic courts, charts portraying the overall picture of the structure and hierarchy of those courts and the machinery of rights of action, and general statistics.

Table of cases

*References to other cases in the Court's jurisprudence, not included in the list which
follows, and thus without a direct bearing on the local remedies rule, may be found in
the notes, particularly to Chapters 5 and 6 of the present study. It is to be noticed that
decisions of *national* courts referring to the Convention have not been included in the
present table of cases, as it was deemed more adequate to refer to the *Collection of
Decisions of National Courts Referring to the Convention* (and *Supplements* 1 to 4) (Council
of Europe – Directorate of Human Rights, Strasbourg 1969−74). (The Collection
being a loose-leaf (mimeographed)publication, page references are not made; consult
in particular national-court decisions in relation to Articles 26 and 13 of the
Convention.)

SELECT BIBLIOGRAPHY

1. *Theses (published and unpublished), books, monographs*

Abi-Saab, G., *Les Exceptions préliminaires dans la procédure de la Cour internationale*, Paris, Pédone, 1967, ch. x

Amerasinghe, C.F., *State Responsibility for Injuries to Aliens*, Oxford, Clarendon Press, 1967

Antonopoulos, N., *La Jurisprudence des organes de la Convention européenne des droits de l'homme*, Leyden, Sijthoff, 1967

Beddard, R., *Human Rights and Europe*, London, Sweet and Maxwell, 1973

Bin Cheng, *General Principles of Law as Applied by International Courts and Tribunals*, London, Stevens, 1953

Borchard, E.M., *The Diplomatic Protection of Citizens Abroad*, New York, Banks Law Publ. Co., 1916

British Institute of International and Comparative Law (ed.), *The European Convention on Human Rights (ICLQ suppl. n. 11)*, London, 1965

Carey, J., *UN Protection of Civil and Political Rights*, Syracuse, University Press, 1970

Cassese, A., *Il Diritto Interno nel Processo Internazionale*, Padova, Cedam, 1962

Castberg, F., *The European Convention on Human Rights*, Leiden, Sijthoff/ Oceana, 1974

Chappez, J., *La Règle de l'épuisement des voies de recours internes*, Paris, Pédone, 1972

*It would be impracticable to list here all works which have been referred to in the course of the present study. The following is a select bibliography, which comprises only those works which have, or may have, a direct bearing on the rule of exhaustion of local remedies in distinct contexts. Thus, treatises and general works and courses in international law touching on the local remedies rule *incidenter tantum* have been excluded from the following list, unless they are illustrative of specific aspects of the rule. Likewise, commentaries of case-law on the local remedies rule have been omitted, unless they contain observations of a general nature going beyond pure reporting and description of the cases at issue. Finally, works on issues related to the local remedies rule (such as questions of procedure) and on cognate concepts have similarly been excluded, unless they have a direct bearing on the operation of the local remedies rule. References to works omitted from the bibliography may be found in the notes to the present study. (On State responsibility in international law in general, cf. bibliography in *Yearbook of the International Law Commission* [1963] – 11, pp. 254–6; on the European Convention on Human Rights in general, cf. *Bibliography Relating to the European Convention on Human Rights*, Council of Europe doc. 1–16.076, Strasbourg, February 1978, pp. 1–173.)

Select bibliography

Dawson, F.G., and Head, I.L., *International Law, National Tribunals and the Rights of Aliens*, Syracuse, University Press, 1971

De Beus, J.G., *The Jurisprudence of the General Claims Commission, United States and Mexico*, The Hague, M. Nijhoff, 1938

De Visscher, Ch., *Aspects récents du droit procédural de la Cour internationale de Justice*, Paris, Pédone, 1966
  De l'équité dans le règlement arbitral ou judiciaire des litiges de Droit international public, Paris, Pédone, 1972
  Théories et réalités en Droit international public (4th rev. edn), Paris, Pédone, 1970

Drost, P.N., *Human Rights as Legal Rights*, Leiden, Sijthoff, 1965

Dunn, F.S., *The Protection of Nationals*, Baltimore, Johns Hopkins Press, 1932
  The Diplomatic Protection of Americans in Mexico, New York, Columbia University Press, 1933

Durante, F., *Ricorsi Individuali ad Organi Internazionali*, Milano, Giuffrè, 1958, esp. pp. 125−52

Eagleton, C., *The Responsibility of States in International Law*, New York, University Press, 1929

Ezejiofor, G., *Protection of Human Rights under the Law*, London, Butterworths, 1964

Falk, R.A., *The Role of Domestic Courts in the International Legal Order*, Syracuse, University Press, 1964

Fawcett, J.E.S., *The Application of the European Convention on Human Rights*, Oxford, Clarendon Press, 1969

Feller, A.H., *The Mexican Claims Commissions (1923−34)*, New York, MacMillan Co., 1935

Freeman, A.V., *The International Responsibility of States for Denial of Justice*, London, Longmans, 1938

Gaja, G., *L'Esaurimento dei Ricorsi Interni nel Diritto Internazionale*, Milano, Giuffrè, 1967

Ganji, M., *International Protection of Human Rights*, Geneva, Droz, 1962

García Amador, F.V., *Principios de Derecho Internacional que Rigen la Responsabilidad − Análisis Crítico de la Concepción Tradicional*, Madrid, Escuela de Funcionários Internacionales, 1963

Giebeler, U., *Die Erschopfung der innerstaatlichen Rechtsbehelfe als zulassigkeitsvoraussetzung der Menschenrechtsbeschwerde zugleich ein vergleich mit der entsprechenden Regel des allgemeinen Volkerrechts und des Verfassungsbeschwerderechts*, University of Marburg, 1972

Gormley, W.P., *The Procedural Status of the Individual before International and Supranational Tribunals*, The Hague, M. Nijhoff, 1966

Grisel, E., *Les Exceptions d'incompétence et d'irrecevabilité dans la procédure de la Cour internationale de justice*, Berne, H. Lang et Cie, 1968

Guradze, H., *Die Europaische Menschenrechtskonvention*, Berlin/Frankfurt, F. Vahlen, 1968

Haesler, T., *The Exhaustion of Local Remedies in the Case-Law of International Courts and Tribunals*, Leiden, Sijthoff, 1968

Hudson, M.O., *International Tribunals − Past and Future*, Washington, Carnegie Endowment for International Peace, 1944

Select bibliography

Jacobs, F.G., *The European Convention on Human Rights*, Oxford, Clarendon Press, 1975

Jenks, C.W., *The Prospects of International Adjudication*, London/New York, Stevens/Oceana, 1964

Joseph, C., *Nationality and Diplomatic Protection – the Commonwealth of Nations*, Leiden, Sijthoff, 1969

Lauterpacht, H., *International Law and Human Rights*, London, Stevens, 1950
  Private Law Sources and Analogies of International Law, London, Longmans, 1927
  The Development of International Law by the International Court, London, Stevens, 1958

Law, C.H.P., *The Local Remedies Rule in International Law*, Geneva, Droz, 1961

Mabrouk, M., *Les exceptions de procédure devant les juridictions internationales*, Paris, LGDJ, 1966

Marie, J.-B., *La Commission des droits de l'homme de l'ONU*, Paris, Pédone, 1975

Max-Planck/Institut fur auslandisches offentliches Recht und Volkerrecht, *Gerichtsschutz gegen die Exekutive/Judicial Protection against the Executive*, vol. 3, Koln, C. Heymanns/Oceana, 1971

Mertens, P., *Le Droit de recours effectif devant les instances nationales en cas de violation d'un droit de l'homme*, University of Brussels, 1973

Monconduit, F., *La Commission européenne des droits de l'homme*, Leiden, Sijthoff, 1965

Morrisson, C.C., Jr, *The Developing European Law of Human Rights*, Leiden, Sijthoff, 1967

Nay-Cadoux, A.-M., *Les Conditions de recevabilité des requêtes individuelles devant la Commission européenne des droits de l'homme*, Paris/Torino, LGDJ/Giappichelli, 1966

Nielsen, F.K., *International Law Applied to Reclamations*, Washington, J. Byrne and Co., 1933

Nørgaard, C.A., *The Position of the Individual in International Law*, Copenhagen, Munksgaard, 1962

Panayotacos, C.P., *La Règle de l'épuisement des voies de recours internes*, Marseille, Impr. Moullot, 1952

Panhuys, H.F. van, *The Role of Nationality in International Law*, Leiden, Sijthoff, 1959.

Parry, C., *The Sources and Evidences of International Law*, Manchester, University Press, 1965

Ralston, J.H., *The Law and Procedure of International Tribunals*, Stanford, University Press, 1926

Reitzer, L., *La Réparation comme conséquence de l'acte illicite en Droit international*, Paris, Sirey, 1938

Remec, P.P., *The Position of the Individual in International Law according to Grotius and Vattel*, The Hague, M. Nijhoff, 1960

Robertson, A.H., *Human Rights in Europe* (2nd edn), Manchester, University Press, 1977
  Human Rights in the World, Manchester, University Press, 1972

Robertson, A.H. (ed.), *Human Rights in National and International Law*, Manchester, University Press/Oceana, 1970
  Privacy and Human Rights, Manchester, University Press, 1973
Rosenne, S., *The Law and Practice of the International Court*, vols. I and II, Leiden, Sijthoff, 1965
  The Time Factor in the Jurisdiction of the International Court of Justice, Leiden, Sijthoff, 1960
Roth, A.H., *The Minimum Standard of International Law Applied to Aliens*, Leiden, Sijthoff, 1949
Sandifer, D.V., *Evidence before International Tribunals*, Chicago, Foundation Press, 1939
Sarhan, A., *L'Épuisement des recours internes en matière de responsabilité internationale*, University of Paris, 1962
Schreiber, A.P., *The Inter-American Commission on Human Rights*, Leiden, Sijthoff, 1970
Schwarzenberger, *International Law as Applied by International Courts and Tribunals*, vol. I (3rd edn), London, Stevens, 1957
Sereni, A.P., *Principî Generali di Diritto e Processo Internazionale*, Milano, Giuffrè, 1955
Shea, D.R., *The Calvo Clause*, Minneapolis, University of Minnesota Press, 1955
Sohn, L.B., and Buergenthal, T., *International Protection of Human Rights*, New York, Bobbs-Merrill Co., 1973
Sørensen, M., *Les Sources du Droit international*, Copenhagen, Munksgaard, 1946
Sperduti, G., *L'Individuo nel Diritto Internazionale*, Milano, Giuffrè, 1950
Stoll, J.A., *L'Application et l'interprétation du droit interne par les juridictions internationales*, Institut de Sociologie/Université Libre de Bruxelles, 1962
Strozzi, G., *Interessi Statali e Interessi Privati nell'Ordinamento. Internazionale*, Milano, Giuffrè, 1977
Ténékidès, G., *L'Individu dans l'ordre juridique international*, Paris, Pédone, 1933
Vasak, K., *La Convention européenne des droits de l'homme*, Paris, LGDJ, 1964
  La Commission interaméricaine des droits de l'homme, Paris, LGDJ, 1968
Verzijl, J.H.W., *International Law in Historical Perspective*, vols. V (Individuals) and VI (International Rights and Obligations), Leiden, Sijthoff, 1973
Weil, G.L., *The European Convention on Human Rights*, Leiden, Sijthoff, 1963
Weis, P., *Nationality and Statelessness in International Law*, London, Stevens, 1956
Witenberg, J.-C., *L'Organisation judiciaire, la procédure et la sentence internationales*, Paris, Pédone, 1937

2. *Articles, courses, contributions to Festschriften, conference reports (published and unpublished)*

Accioli, H., Principes généraux de la responsabilité internationale d'après la doctrine et la jurisprudence, 96 *Recueil des Cours de l'Académie de Droit International* [1959], pp. 353–441
Ago, R., La Regola del Previo Esaurimento dei Ricorsi Interni in Tema di

Responsabilità Internazionale, 3 *Archivio di Diritto Pubblico* [1938], pp. 181–249

Reports on State Responsibility, *Yearbook of the International Law Commission* [1969–76]–II

Observations [sur la règle de l'épuisement des recours internes], 45 *Annuaire de l'Institut de Droit International* [1954]–I pp. 34–45, and 46 *Annuaire de l'Institut de Droit International* [1956] pp. 24–8

Le délit international, 68 *Recueil des Cours de l'Académie de Droit International* [1939] pp. 419–554, esp. pp. 514–21

Diritto positivo e diritto internazionale, *Scritti di Diritto internazionale in onore di Tomaso Perassi*, vol. I, Milano, Giuffrè, 1957, pp. 3–64

Akehurst, M., Settlement of Claims by Individuals and Companies against International Organisations, 37/38 *Annuaire de l'AAA/Yearbook of the AAA* [1967–8] pp. 69–98

Amerasinghe, C.F., The Formal Character of the Rule of Local Remedies, 25 *Zeitschrift fur auslandisches offentliches Recht und Volkerrecht* [1965] pp. 445–77

The Rule of Exhaustion of Domestic Remedies in the Framework of International Systems for the Protection of Human Rights, 28 *Zeitschrift fur auslandisches offentliches Recht und Volkerrecht* [1968] pp. 257–300

The Exhaustion of Procedural Remedies in the Same Court, 12 *International and Comparative Law Quarterly* [1963] pp. 1285–1325

The Rule of Exhaustion of Local Remedies and the International Protection of Human Rights, 17 *Indian Yearbook of International Affairs* [1974] pp. 3–63

The Local Remedies Rule in an Appropriate Perspective, 36 *Zeitschrift fur auslandisches offentliches Recht und Volkerrecht* [1976] pp. 727–59

Anzilotti, D., La responsabilité internationale des Etats à raison des domages soufferts par des étrangers, 13 *Revue générale de Droit international public* [1906] pp. 5–29, 285–309

Arangio-Ruiz, G., L'individuo e il Diritto internazionale, 54 *Rivista di Diritto Internazionale* [1971] pp. 561–608

Bagge, A., Intervention on the Ground of Damage Caused to Nationals, with Particular Reference to Exhaustion of Local Remedies and the Rights of Shareholders, 34 *British Yearbook of International Law* [1958] pp. 162–75

Berlia, G., Contribution à l'étude de la nature de la protection diplomatique, 3 *Annuaire français de Droit international* [1957] pp. 63–72

De la responsabilité internationale de l'État, , *La technique et les principes du Droit public – Études en l'honneur de Georges Scelle*, vol. II, Paris, LGDJ, 1950, pp. 875–94

Bin Cheng, Burden of Proof before the ICJ, 2 *International and Comparative Law Quarterly* [1953] pp. 595–6

Borchard, E.M., Theoretical Aspects of the International Responsibility of States, 1'*Zeitschrift für auslandisches offentliches Recht und Volkerrecht* [1929] pp. 223–50

The Local Remedy Rule, 28 *American Journal of International Law* [1934] pp. 729–33

Les principes de la protection diplomatique des nationaux à l'étranger, 3 *Bibliotheca Visseriana* [1924] pp. 3–52

Rapport sur la protection diplomatique des nationaux à l'étranger, 38 *Annuaire de l'Institut de Droit International* [1931]–I pp. 256–455, and 39 *Annuaire de l'Institut de Droit International* [1931]–II pp. 201–12

Rapport supplémentaire sur la protection diplomatique des nationaux à l'étranger, 40 *Annuaire de l'Institut de Droit International* [1932] pp. 235–62

The Access of Individuals to International Courts, 24 *American Journal of International Law* [1930] pp. 359–65

The 'Minimum Standard' of the Treatment of Aliens, 33 *Proceedings of the American Society of International Law* [1939] pp. 51–63

Declaratory Judgments in International Law, 29 *American Journal of International Law* [1935] pp. 488–92

Bos, M., Les conditions du procès en Droit international public, 19/20 *Bibliotheca Visseriana* [1957] esp. pp. 221–37

Bourquin, M., Observations [sur la règle de l'épuisement des recours internes], 45 *Annuaire de l'Institut de Droit International* [1954]–I pp. 45–62, and 46 *Annuaire de l'Institut de Droit International* [1956] pp. 28–31

Observations [sur la responsabilité internationale des États à raison des dommages causés sur leur territoire à la personne ou aux biens des étrangers], 33 *Annuaire de l'Institut de Droit International* [1927]–I pp. 501–9

L'humanisation du Droit des gens, *La technique et les principes du Droit public-Études en l'honneur de Georges Scelle*, vol. I, Paris, LGDJ, 1950, pp. 21–54

Boyle, K., and Hannum, H., Individual Applications under the European Convention on Human Rights and the Concept of Administrative Practice: the *Donnelly* Case, 68 *American Journal of International Law* [1974] pp. 440–53

The *Donnelly* Case, Administrative Practice and Domestic Remedies under the European Convention: One Step Forward and Two Steps Back, 71 *American Journal of International Law* [1977] pp. 316–21

Briggs, H.W., The Local Remedies Rule: a Drafting Suggestion, 50 *American Journal of International Law* [1956] pp. 921–7

Brownlie, I., The Individual before Tribunals Exercising International Jurisdiction, II *International and Comparative Law Quarterly* [1962] pp. 701–20

Bruegel, J.W., The Right to Petition an International Authority, 2 *International and Comparative Law Quarterly* [1953] pp. 542–63

Buergenthal, T., Comparative Study of Certain Due Process Requirements of the European Human Rights Convention, 16 *Buffalo Law Review* [1966] pp. 18–54

The Effect of the European Convention on Human Rights on the Internal Law of Member States, *The European Convention on Human Rights*, London, British Institute of International and Comparative Law (*ICLQ* suppl. n. 11), 1965, pp. 79–106

The European Convention and Its National Application: Interaction of

National Law and Modern International Agreements: Some Introductory
Observations, 18 *American Journal of Comparative Law* [1970] pp 233–6

Comparison of the Jurisprudence of National Courts with that of the
Organs of the Convention as Regards the Rights of the Individual in
Court Proceedings, *Human Rights in National and International Law*
(ed. A. H. Robertson), Manchester, University Press/Oceana, 1970,
pp. 151–200

Bullinger, M., Comparative Aspects of Judicial Protection against the
Executive, *Gerichtsschutz gegen die Exekutive/Judicial Protection against the
Executive*, vol. 3, Colloquy, Max-Planck-Institut für auslandisches
offentliches Recht und Volkerrecht, Koln, C. Heymanns/Oceana, 1971,
pp. 193–220

Buschbeck, K., Evidence: Procedures of Judicial Discovery and Burden of
Proof, *Gerichtsschutz gegen die Exekutive/Judicial Protection against the
Executive*, vol. 3, Colloquy, Max-Planck-Institut f.a.o.R.u.V., Koln, C.
Heymanns/Oceana, 1971, pp. 153–66

Carabiber, Ch., L'arbitrage international entre gouvernements et particuliers,
76 *Recueil des Cours de l'Académie de Droit International* [1950] pp. 221–317

Cassese, A., The Admissibility of Communications to the United Nations on
Human Rights Violations, 5 *Revue des droits de l'homme/Human Rights
Journal* [1972] pp. 375–93

Cassin, R., La Déclaration Universelle et la mise en oeuvre des droits de
l'homme, 79 *Recueil des Cours de l'Académie de Droit International* [1951]
pp. 241–365

Castberg, F., Observations [sur la règle de l'épuisement des recours internes],
45 *Annuaire de l'Institut de Droit International* [1954]–1 pp. 62–6

Le droit de requête individuelle d'après la Convention européenne des droits
de l'homme, *Multitudo Legum Ius Unum – Festschrift für Wilhelm Wengler*,
vol. 1, Berlin, Inter-Recht, 1973, pp. 51–8

Castrén, E.J.S., Some Considerations upon the Conception, Development,
and Importance of Diplomatic Protection, 11 *Jahrbuch für Internationales
Recht* [1962] pp. 37–48

Cavaré, L., Les transformations de la protection diplomatique, 19 *Zeitschrift
für ausländisches öffentliches Recht und Volkerrecht* [1958] pp. 54–80

La notion de juridiction internationale, 2 *Annuaire français de Droit
international* [1956] pp. 496–509

Cohen-Jonathan, G., Droits de l'homme et pluralité des systèmes européens
de protection internationale, 6 *Revue des droits de l'homme/Human Rights
Journal* [1973] pp. 615–49

Cohn, M.G., La théorie de la responsabilité internationale, 68 *Recueil des Cours
de l'Académie de Droit International* [1939] pp. 209–325

Comte, Ph., The Application of the European Convention on Human Rights
in Municipal Law, 4 *Journal of the International Commission of Jurists* [1962]
pp. 94–129

Dahm, G., Die Subsidiarität des Internationalen Rechtsschutzes bei Volker-
rechtswidriger Verletzung von Privatpersonen, *Vom deutschen zum europäischen Recht – Festschrift für Hans Dölle*, vol. 11, Tubingen, J.C.B. Mohr
(P. Siebeck), 1963, pp. 3–33

Danelius, H., Conditions of Admissibility in the Jurisprudence of the European Commission of Human Rights, 2 *Revue des droits de l'homme/ Human Rights Journal* [1969] pp. 284–336

Dawson, F.G., International Law and the Procedural Rights of Aliens before National Tribunals, 17 *International and Comparative Law Quarterly* [1968] pp. 404–27

Decencière-Ferrandière, Essai critique sur la justice internationale, 41 *Revue générale de Droit international public* [1934] pp. 148–78

De La Barra, F.L., Observations [sur la protection diplomatique des nationaux à l'étranger], 40 *Annuaire de l'Institut de Droit International* [1932] pp. 263–6

De Visscher, Ch., Observations [sur la règle de l'épuisement des recours internes], 46 *Annuaire de l'Institut de Droit International* [1956] pp. 48–9

Le déni de justice en Droit international, 52 *Recueil des Cours de l'Académie de Droit International* [1935] pp. 369–441, esp. ch. III, pp. 421–32

La responsabilité des États, 2 *Bibliotheca Visseriana* [1924] pp. 89–157

Notes sur la responsabilité internationale des États et la protection diplomatique d'après quelques documents récents, 8 *Revue de Droit international et de législation comparée* [1927] pp. 245–72

Les droits fondamentaux de l'homme, base d'une restauration du Droit International, 45 *Annuaire de l'Institut de Droit International* [1947] pp. 1–13

De Visscher, P., Cours général de Droit international public, 136 *Recueil des Cours de l'Académie de Droit International* [1972] ch. II (La protection diplomatique), pp. 154–77

Diena, G., L'individu devant l'autorité judiciaire et le droit international, 16 *Revue générale de Droit international public* [1909] pp. 73–6

Doehring, K., Does General International Law Require Domestic Judicial Protection against the Executive?, *Gerichtsschutz gegen die Exekutive/ Judicial Protection against the Executive*, vol. 3, Colloquy, Max-Planck-Institut f.a.o.R.u.V., Koln, C. Heymanns/Oceana, 1971, pp. 221–44

Durand, Ch., La responsabilité internationale des États pour déni de justice, 38 *Revue générale de Droit international public* [1931] pp. 694–748

Eagleton, C., Denial of Justice in International Law, 22 *American Journal of International Law* [1928] pp. 538–59

Une théorie au sujet du commencement de la responsabilité de l'État, 11 *Revue de Droit international et de législation comparée* [1930] pp. 643–59

L'épuisement des recours internes et le déni de justice, d'après certaines décisions récentes, 16 *Revue de Droit international et de législation comparée* [1935] pp. 504–26

International Organization and the Law of Responsibility, 76 *Recueil des Cours de l'Académie de Droit International* [1950] pp. 323–425

Economomopoulos, C.P., Les éléments politiques et judiciaires dans la procédure instaurée par la Convention européenne des droits de l'homme, 22 *Revue hellénique de Droit international* [1969] pp. 122–39

Eissen, M.A., The European Convention on Human Rights and the Duties of the Individual, 32 *Nordisk Tidsskrift for International Ret (Acta Scandinavica Juris Gentium)* [1962] pp. 230–53

Le nouveau règlement intérieur de la Commission européenne des droits de l'homme, 6 *Annuaire français de Droit international* [1960] esp. pp. 774–5, 783–6

Jurisprudence de la Commission européenne des droits de l'homme – décisions en matière de compétence *ratione temporis*, 9 *Annuaire française de Droit international* [1963] pp. 722–33

Elles, Baroness, Aliens and Activities of the United Nations in the Field of Human Rights, 7 *Revue des droits de l'homme/Human Rights Journal* [1974] pp. 291–320

Ermacora, F., L'accès aux mécanismes juridictionnels de protection des personnes privées dans la Convention européenne des droits de l'homme, 6 *Revue des droits de l'homme/Human Rights Journal* [1973] pp. 645–57

Eustathiades, C. Th., Les sujets du Droit international et la responsabilité internationale: nouvelles tendances, 84 *Recueil des Cours de l'Académie de Droit international* [1953] pp. 401–614, esp. pp. 426–7, 538–40, 547–66, 571, 584–614

Une nouvelle expérience en Droit international – Les recours individuels à la Commission des droits de l'homme, *Grundprobleme des internationalen Rechts – Festschrift für Jean Spiropoulos*, Bonn, Schimmelbusch and Co., 1957, pp. 111–37

La Convention européenne des droits de l'homme et le Statut du Conseil de l'Europe, 52 *Die Friedens-Warte* [1953–5] pp. 332–61, esp. pp. 341–4, 354–6, and 53 *Die Friedens-Warte* [1955–6] pp. 47–69, esp. pp. 65–9

Fabozzi, C., La nozione di controversia giuridica nel Processo internazionale—Note in tema di eccezioni preliminari, 11 *Comunicazioni e Studi* [1963] pp. 157–97

Fachiri, A.P., The Local Remedies Rule in the Light of the *Finnish Ships* Arbitration, 17 *British Yearbook of International Law* [1936] pp. 19–36

Favoreu, L., Récusation et administration de la preuve devant la Cour Internationale de Justice, 11 *Annuaire français de Droit international* [1965] pp. 233–5, 255–77

Fawcett, J.E.S., The Exhaustion of Local Remedies: Substance or Procedure?, 31 *British Yearbook of International Law* [1954] pp. 452–8

The Application of the European Convention on Human Rights, *Transnational Law in a Changing Society – Essays in Honour of Ph. C. Jessup* (ed. W. Friedmann, L. Henkin and O. Lissitzyn), New York, Columbia University Press, 1972, pp. 228–41

Some Aspects of the Practice of the Commission of Human Rights, *The European Convention on Human Rights*, London, British Institute of International and Comparative Law (*ICLQ* suppl. n. 11), 1965, pp. 71–2

Feinberg, N., La pétition en Droit international, 40 *Recueil des Cours de l'Académie de Droit International* [1932] pp. 529–644

Fitzmaurice, G., The Meaning of the Term 'Denial of Justice', 13 *British Yearbook of International Law* [1932] pp. 93–114

Hersch Lauterpacht – the Scholar as Judge – 1 (paragraph 10: Particular Points of International Law: the Exhaustion of Local Remedies Rule), 37 *British Yearbook of International Law* [1961] esp. pp. 53–64

Fix-Zamudio, H., Los Derechos Humanos y su Protección ante las

Juridicciones Nacionales, *Miscellanea W.J. Ganshof van der Meersch*, vol. III, Bruxelles/Paris, Bruylant/LGDJ, 1972, pp. 107–42

Fraga, G., El Agotamiento de Recursos Internos Previo a la Acción Internacional, report, OAS doc. OEA/Ser L/V/II 28–doc. 19, 1972, [mimeographed,] pp. 1–10

Freeman, A.V., Human Rights and the Rights of Aliens, 44 *Proceedings of the American Society of International Law* [1951] pp. 120–30

Friedmann, H., Épuisement des voies de recours internes, 14 *Revue de Droit international et de législation comparée* [1933] pp. 318–27

Friedmann, W., The Growth of State Control over the Individual, and Its Effect upon the Rules of International State Responsibility, 19 *British Yearbook of International Law* [1938] pp. 118–50

Frowein, J. Abr., The Guarantees Afforded by the Institutional Machinery of the [European] Convention, *Privacy and Human Rights* (ed. A.H. Robertson), Manchester, University Press, 1973, pp. 284–304

Ganshof van der Meersch, W.J., Does the Convention Have the Force of 'Ordre Public' in Municipal Law?, *Human Rights in National and International Law* (ed. A.H. Robertson), Manchester, University Press/Oceana, 1970, pp. 135–43

García-Amador, F.V., State Responsibility – Some New Problems, 94 *Recueil des Cours de l'Académie de Droit International* [1958] pp. 369–491

State Responsibility in the Light of the New Trends of International Law, 49 *American Journal of International Law* [1955] pp. 339–46

Le sujet passif de la responsabilité et la capacité d'être demandeur en Droit international, 34 *Revue de Droit international, des sciences diplomatiques et politiques* [1956] pp. 270–6

La doctrine de la protection diplomatique et la reconnaissance internationale des droits de l'homme, 34 *Revue de Droit international, des sciences diplomatiques et politiques* [1956] pp. 353–62

Reports on State Responsibility, *Yearbook of the International Law Commission* [1956–61]

Goldie, L.F.E., *Locus Standi* of Individuals and State Responsibility, 29 *Annuaire de l'AAA/Yearbook of the AAA* [1959] pp. 38–48

Golsong, H., The European Convention on Human Rights before Domestic Courts, 38 *British Yearbook of International Law* [1962] pp. 445–56

The European Convention for the Protection of Human Rights and Fundamental Freedoms in a German Court, 33 *British Yearbook of International Law* [1957] pp. 317–21

Implementation of International Protection of Human Rights, 110 *Recueil des Cours de l'Académie de Droit International* [1963] pp. 7–151

International Treaty Provisions on the Protection of the Individual against the Executive by Domestic Courts, *Gerichtsschutz gegen die Exekutive/Judicial Protection against the Executive*, vol. 3, Colloquy, Max-Planck-Institut f.a.o.R.u.V., Koln, C. Heymanns/Oceana, 1971, pp. 245–67

Grillo Pasquarelli, E., The Question of the Exhaustion of Domestic Remedies in the Context of the Examination of Admissibility of an Application to the European Commission of Human Rights, *Privacy and Human Rights* (ed. A.H. Robertson), Manchester, University Press, 1973, pp. 332–9

Guerrero, J.G., Observations [sur la règle de l'épuisement des recours internes], 45 *Annuaire de l'Institut de Droit International* [1954]–1 pp. 66–8

Guggenheim, M.H., Key Provisions of the New United Nations Rules Dealing with Human Rights Petitions, 6 *New York University Journal of International Law and Politics* [1973] pp. 427–46

Guggenheim, P., Observations [sur la règle de l'épuisement des recours internes], 46 *Annuaire de l'Institut de Droit International* [1956] pp. 31–7

Guha Roy, S.N., Is the Law of Responsibility of States for Injuries to Aliens a Part of Universal International Law?, 55 *American Journal of International Law* [1961] pp. 863–91

Guinand, J., La règle de l'épuisement des voies de recours internes dans le cadre des systèmes internationaux de protection des droits de l'homme, 4 *Revue belge de Droit international* [1968] pp. 471–84

Hackworth, G.H., Observations [on the rule of exhaustion of local remedies], 45 *Annuaire de l'Institut de Droit International* [1954]–1 pp. 69–72

Responsibility of States for Damages Caused in Their Territory to the Person or Property of Foreigners, 24 *American Journal of International Law* [1930] pp. 500–16

Hambro, E., The Jurisdiction of the International Court of Justice, 76 *Recueil des Cours de l'Académie de Droit International* [1950] pp. 125–215, esp. ch. VI, pp. 208–13

Individuals before International Tribunals, 34 *Proceedings of the American Society of International Law* [1941] pp. 22–8

Head, I.L., A Fresh Look at the Local Remedies Rule, 5 *Canadian Yearbook of International Law* [1967] pp. 142–58

Heydte, F. von der, L'individu et les tribunaux internationaux, 107 *Recueil des Cours de l'Académie de Droit International* [1962] pp. 287–358

Huber, M., Observations [sur la règle de l'épuisement des recours internes], 46 *Annuaire de l'Institut de Droit International* [1956] pp. 37–41

Humphrey, J., The Right of Petition in the United Nations, 4 *Revue des droits de l'homme/Human Rights Journal* [1971] pp. 463–75

Irizarry y Puente, J., The Concept of 'Denial of Justice' in Latin America, 43 *Michigan Law Review* [1944] pp. 383–406

Jacobs, F.G., The European Convention on Human Rights in the English Courts, 29 *Europaische Grundrechte-Zeitschrift* [1975] pp. 569–73

Jaenicke, G., Judicial Protection of the Individual within the System of International Law, *Gerichtsschutz gegen die Exekutive/Judicial Protection against the Executive*, vol. 3, Colloquy, Max-Planck-Institut f.a.o.R.u.V., Koln, C. Heymanns/Oceana, 1971, pp. 281–321

Jessup, Ph. C., Responsibility of States for Injuries to Individuals, 46 *Columbia Law Review* [1946] pp. 903–28

Jiménez de Aréchaga, E., International Responsibility, *Manual of Public International Law* (ed. M. Sørensen), London, MacMillan, 1968, pp. 531–603

International Responsibility of States for Acts of the Judiciary, *Transnational Law in a Changing Society – Essays in Honour of Ph.C. Jessup* (ed. W. Friedmann, L. Henkin and O. Lissitzyn), New York, Columbia University Press, 1972, pp. 171–87

Kelsen, H., Les rapports de système entre le droit interne et le droit
international public, 14 *Recueil des Cours de l'Académie de Droit International*
[1926] pp. 231–329

Kiss, A.Ch., La condition des étrangers en droit international et les droits de
l'homme, *Miscellanea W.J. Ganshof van der Meersch*, vol. 1, Bruxelles/Paris,
Bruylant/LGDJ, 1972, pp. 499–511

   La Convention européenne des droits de l'homme et le système de garantie
   du Droit international public, report, C. of E. doc. A–58–159, 1960
   Strasbourg Colloquium, [mimeographed,] pp. 1–16

Koessler, M., Government Espousal of Private Claims before International
Tribunals, 13 *University of Chicago Law Review* [1946] pp. 180–94

Korowicz, M.St., The Problem of the International Personality of Individuals, 50 *American Journal of International Law* [1956] pp. 533–62

Kraus, H., Observations [sur la protection diplomatique des nationaux à
l'étranger], 38 *Annuaire de l'Institut de Droit International* [1931]–1 pp.
455–91

Lalive, J.F., Quelques remarques sur la preuve devant la Cour Permanente et
la Cour Internationale de Justice, 7 *Schweizerisches Jahrbuch für internationales Recht* [1950] pp. 77–103

Lamberti Zanardi, P., Le prime esperienze della Corte europea dei diritti
dell'uomo in materia di eccezioni preliminari, 13 *Comunicazioni e Studi*
[1969] pp. 207–32

Lang, J., La jonction au fond des exceptions préliminaires devant la CPJI et la
CIJ, 95 *Journal du Droit international (Clunet)* [1968] pp. 5–45

La Pradelle, A. de, La place de l'homme dans la construction du Droit
international, 1 *Current Legal Problems* [1948] pp. 140–51

Lillich, R.B., The Effectiveness of the Local Remedies Rule Today, 58
Proceedings of the American Society of International Law [1964] pp. 101–7

   The Diplomatic Protection of Nationals Abroad: an Elementary Principle
   of International Law under Attack, 69 *American Journal of International
   Law* [1975] pp. 359–65

   The Problem of the Applicability of the Existing International Provisions
   for the Protection of Human Rights to Individuals who are not Citizens
   of the Country in which They Live, 70 *American Journal of International
   Law* [1976] pp. 507–10

Lipstein, K., The Place of the Calvo Clause in International Law, 22 *British
Yearbook of International Law* [1945] pp. 130–45

Lissitzyn, O.J., The Meaning of the Term Denial of Justice in International
Law, 30 *American Journal of International Law* [1936] pp. 632–46

Longchamps, F., Sur le problème du Droit subjectif dans les rapports entre
l'individu et le pouvoir, *Mélanges en l'honneur de Paul Roubier*, vol. 1,
Paris, Dalloz/Sirey, 1961, pp. 305–22

Makarov, A., Consideraciones sobre el Derecho de Protección Diplomática, 8
Revista Española de Derecho Internacional [1955] pp. 511–52

Marcus-Helmons, S., The Guarantees Afforded by the Institutional Machinery of the [European] Convention, report, C. of E. doc. H/Coll(70)5/
Com 4, 1970 Brussels Colloquium, [mimeographed,] pp. 1–9

Martínez-Agulló, L., El Agotamiento de los Recursos Internos y el Caso de la

Barcelona Traction, 23 *Revista Española de Derecho Internacional* [1970] pp. 344–74

Meron, T., The Incidence of the Rule of Exhaustion of Local Remedies, 35 *British Yearbook of International Law* [1959] pp. 83–101

Mertens, P., Le droit à un recours effectif devant l'autorité nationale compétente dans les Conventions internationales relatives à la protection des droits de l'homme, 4 *Revue belge de Droit international* [1968] pp. 446–70

Origines et fondements du droit de recours interne en cas de violation d'une norme de Droit international, report, 1975 Brussels Colloquium, [mimeographed,] pp. 26–8

Mertens de Wilmars, J., L'accès aux mécanismes juridictionnels de protection des personnes privées en Droit communautaire, 6 *Revue des droits de l'homme/Human Rights Journal* [1973] pp. 627–44

Miaja de la Muela, A., El Agotamiento de los Recursos Internos como Supuesto de las Reclamaciones Internacionales, 2 *Anuario Uruguayo de Derecho Internacional* [1963] pp. 9–58

Aspectos Jurídicos de las Diferencias entre Estados y Personas Privadas Extranjeras, 22 *Revista Española de Derecho Internacional* [1969] pp. 9–41

Monconduit, F., Bilan des conditions de la recevabilité: les tendances de la jurisprudence, 8 *Revue des droits de l'homme/Human Rights Journal* [1975] pp. 417–30

Moore, J.B., Observations [sur la protection diplomatique des nationaux à l'étranger], 40 *Annuaire de l'Institut de Droit International* [1932] pp. 266–76

Morelli, G., La théorie générale du procès international, 61 *Recueil des Cours de l'Académie de Droit International* [1937] pp. 257–373

Questioni preliminari nel Processo internazionale, 54 *Rivista di Diritto Internazionale* [1971] pp. 5–20

Morgenstern, F., Judicial Practice and the Supremacy of International Law, 27 *British Yearbook of International Law* [1950] pp. 42–92

Mosler, H., Organisation und Verfahren des Europaischen Gerichtshofs für Menschenrechte, 20 *Zeitschrift für auslandisches offentliches Recht und Volkerrecht* [1959–60] pp. 440–1

L'application du Droit international public par les tribunaux nationaux, 91 *Recueil des Cours de l'Académie de Droit International* [1957] pp. 619–710

L'influence du Droit national sur la Convention européenne des droits de l'homme, *Miscellanea W.J. Ganshof van der Meersch*, vol. 1, Bruxelles/Paris, Bruylant/LGDJ, 1972, pp. 521–43

La procédure de la Cour Internationale de Justice et de la Cour européenne des droits de l'homme, *René Cassin Amicorum Discipulorumque Liber*, vol. 1, Paris, Pédone, 1969, pp. 175–84

The Protection of Human Rights by International Legal Procedure, 52 *Georgetown Law Journal* [1964] pp. 800/823

Moussa, A, L'étranger et la justice nationale, 41 *Revue générale de Droit international public* [1934] pp. 441–59

Muller-Rappard, E., Le droit d'action en vertu des dispositions de la Convention européenne des droits de l'homme, 4 *Revue belge de Droit international* [1968] pp. 485–517

Mummery, D.R., The Content of the Duty to Exhaust Local Judicial Remedies, 58 *American Journal of International Law* [1964] pp. 389–414

Increasing the Use of Local Remedies, 58 *Proceedings of the American Society of International Law* [1964] pp. 107–22

Muûls, F., Observations [sur la règle de l'épuisement des recours internes], 45 *Annuaire de l'Institut de Droit International* [1954]–1 pp. 73–5

McDougal, M.S., Lasswell, H.D., and Chen, L.-C., The Protection of Aliens from Discrimination and World Public Order: Responsibility of States Conjoined with Human Rights, 70 *American Journal of International Law* [1976] pp. 432–69

McGovern, E., The Local Remedies Rule and Administrative Practices in the European Convention on Human Rights, 24 *International and Comparative Law Quarterly* [1975] pp. 119–27

McNulty, A.B., and Eissen, M.A., The European Commission of Human Rights: Procedure and Jurisprudence, 1 *Journal of the International Commission of Jurists* [1958] pp. 198–219

Parry, C., Some Considerations upon the Protection of Individuals in International Law, 90 *Recueil des Cours de l'Académie de Droit International* [1956] pp. 657–723

Pelloux, R., L'accès aux mécanismes juridictionnels de protection des personnes privées dans le cadre européen, 6 *Revue des droits de l'homme/Human Rights Journal* [1973] pp. 619–26

Perassi, T., Observations [sur la règle de l'épuisement des recours internes], 45 *Annuaire de l'Institut de Droit International* [1954]–1 pp. 75–7, and 46 *Annuaire de l'Institut de Droit International* [1956] pp. 41–2

Perrin, G., Organisation judiciaire interne et protection des ressortissants étrangers en Droit international, 24 *Revue juridique et politique – Indépendance et coopération* [1970] pp. 51–64

Petrén, S., La saisine de la Cour européenne par la Commission européenne des droits de l'homme, *Mélanges offerts à Polys Modinos*, Paris, Pédone, 1968, pp. 233–44

Pilotti, M., Le recours des particuliers devant les juridictions internationales, *Grundprobleme des internationalen Rechts – Festschrift fur Jean Spiropoulos*, Bonn, Schimmelbusch and Co., 1957, pp. 351–62

Pocar, F., La tratazione dei ricorsi ricevibili davanti alla Commissione europea dei diritti dell'uomo, 55 *Rivista di Diritto Internazionale* [1972] pp. 223–52

Poulantzas, D.M., The Rule of Exhaustion of Local Remedies and Liability for Space Vehicle Accidents, 17 *Revue hellénique de Droit international* [1964] pp. 101–4 (also in I.I.S.L. – I.A.F., *Proceedings – Sixth Colloquium*, pp. 1–6)

The Individual before International Jurisdictions, 15 *Revue hellénique de Droit international* [1962] pp. 375–90

Przetacznik, F., The Protection of Individual Persons in Traditional International Law (Diplomatic and Consular Protection), 21 *Österreichische Zeitschrift für öffentliches Recht* [1971] pp. 69–113

Puente Egido, J., Algunas Consideraciones en torno a la Situación Procesal de los Particulares ante Instancias Internacionales, 20 *Revista Española de*

Derecho Internacional [1967] pp. 269–98

Raestad, A., La protection diplomatique des nationaux à l'étranger, 11 *Revue de Droit international* [1933] pp. 494–544

Reuter, P., Quelques remarques sur la situation juridique des particuliers en Droit international public, *La technique et les principes du Droit public – Études en l'honneur de Georges Scelle*, vol. II, Paris, LGDJ, 1950, pp. 542–3, 550–2

Ripert, G., Les règles du Droit civil applicables aux rapports internationaux, 44 *Recueil des Cours de l'Académie de Droit International* [1933] pp. 569–663, esp. ch. III

Ritter, J.-P., La protection diplomatique à l'égard d'une organisation internationale, 8 *Annuaire français de Droit international* [1962] pp. 427–56

Robertson, A.H., The European Convention on Human Rights and the Rule of Exhaustion of Domestic Remedies, 4 *Revista de Derechos Humanos* (Puerto Rico) [1974] pp. 199–207

Rolin, H., Observations [sur la règle de l'épuisement des recours internes], 46 *Annuaire de l'Institut de Droit International* [1956] pp. 42–4

Le rôle du requérant dans la procédure prévue par la Commission européenne des droits de l'homme, 9 *Revue hellénique de Droit international* [1956] pp. 3–14

Le contrôle international des juridictions nationales, 3 *Revue belge de Droit international* [1967] pp. 1–23, and 4 *Revue belge de Droit international* [1968] pp. 160–206

Root, E., The Relations between International Tribunals of Arbitration and the Jurisdiction of National Courts, 3 *American Journal of International Law* [1909] pp. 529–36

The Basis of Protection to Citizens Residing Abroad, 4 *American Journal of International Law* [1910] pp. 517–28

Ruiloba Santana, E., La Oponibilidad de la Excepción del Inagotamiento de los Recursos Internos en el Arreglo Arbitral de las Diferencias Internacionales, 22 *Revista Española de Derecho Internacional* [1969] pp. 465–84

La Regla del Agotamiento de los Recursos Internos a través de las Decisiones de la Comisión Europea de los Derechos del Hombre, *Estúdios de Derecho Internacional Público y Privado – Libro-Homenaje al Profesor Luis Sela Sampil*, Universidad de Oviedo, 1970, pp. 467–503

Rundstein, S., L'arbitrage international en matière privée, 23 *Recueil des Cours de l'Académie de Droit International* [1928] pp. 436–55

Ruzié, D., Du droit de pétition individuelle en matière de droits de l'homme: à propos de la résolution 1503(XLVIII) du Conseil Économique et Social des Nations Unies, 4 *Revue des droits de l'homme/Human Rights Journal* [1971] pp. 89–101

Salvioli, G., Observations [sur la règle de l'épuisement des recours internes], 45 *Annuaire de l'Institut de Droit International* [1954]–1 pp. 77–8, and 46 *Annuaire de l'Institut de Droit International* [1956] p. 45

Sand, P.H., The Role of Domestic Procedures in Transnational Environmental Disputes, report, 1974 Bellagio Conference, [mimeographed,] pp. 1–21

Scelle, G., Observations [sur la règle de l'épuisement des recours internes], 45

Annuaire de l'Institut de Droit International [1954]–1 pp. 78–81

Schaffer, P., and Weissbrodt, D., Exhaustion of Remedies in the Context of the Racial Discrimination Convention, 2 *Revue des droits de l'homme/ Human Rights Journal* [1969] pp. 632–52

Schreuer, C.H., The Implementation of International Judicial Decisions by Domestic Courts, 24 *International and Comparative Law Quarterly* [1975] pp. 153–83

The Authority of International Judicial Practice in Domestic Courts, 23 *International and Comparative Law Quarterly* [1974] pp. 681/708

Schwebel, S.M., and Wetter, J.G., Arbitration and the Exhaustion of Local Remedies, 60 *American Journal of International Law* [1966] pp. 484–501

Schwelb, E., Complaints by Individuals to the Commission on Human Rights: 25 Years of an Uphill Struggle (1947–71), *The Changing International Community – Essays in Honour of M. Mushkat*, The Hague/ Paris, Mouton, 1973, pp. 119–39

The Abuse of the Right of Petition, 3 *Revue des droits de l'homme/Human Rights Journal* [1970] pp. 313–32

Séfériadès, S., Le problème de l'accès des particuliers à des juridictions internationales, 51 *Recueil des Cours de l'Académie de Droit International* [1935] pp. 5–119

Seidl-Hohenveldern, I., La sentence du Tribunal Arbitral Austro-Allemand concernant la protection diplomatique, 18 *Annuaire français de Droit international* [1972] pp. 323–7

Sibert, M., Contribution à l'étude des réparations pour des dommages causés aux étrangers en conséquence d'une législation contraire au Droit des gens, 48 *Revue générale de Droit international public* [1941] pp. 5–34

Sohn, L.B., and Baxter, R.R., Responsibility of States for Injuries to the Economic Interests of Aliens, 55 *American Journal of International Law* [1961] pp. 545–84

Sørensen, M., La recevabilité de l'instance devant la Cour européenne des droits de l'homme – Notes sur les rapports entre la Commission et la Cour, *René Cassin Amicorum Discipulorumque Liber*, vol. 1, Paris, Pédone, 1969, pp. 333–46

Do the Rights Set forth in the European Convention on Human Rights in 1950 Have the Same Significance in 1975?, report, C. of E. doc.H/Coll (75)2, 1975 Rome Colloquium, [mimeographed,] pp. 1–25

Spatafora, E., La Regola del Previo Esaurimento dei Ricorsi Interni nella Giurisprudenza della Commissione Europea dei Diritti dell'Uomo, 11 *Rivista di Diritto Europeo* [1971] pp. 101–13

Sperduti, G., La recevabilité des exceptions préliminaires de fond dans le procès international, 53 *Rivista di Diritto Internazionale* [1970] pp. 461–90

L'individu et le droit international, 90 *Recueil des Cours de l'Académie de Droit International* [1956] pp. 727–847

La Convenzione europea dei diritti dell'uomo e il suo sistema di garanzei, 46 *Rivista di Diritto Internazionale* [1963] pp. 161–75

Protezione internazionale dei diritti umani, *Enciclopedia del Diritto*, vol. XII, Milano, Giuffrè, 1964, esp. p. 820

Spiegel, H.W., Origin and Development of Denial of Justice, 32 *American*

Journal of International Law [1938] pp. 63–81

Spiropoulos, J., L'individu et le droit international, 30 *Recueil des Cours de l'Académie de Droit International* [1929] pp. 195–269

Staley, E., Une critique de la protection diplomatique des placements à l'étranger, 42 *Revue générale de Droit international public* [1935] pp. 541–58

Steinberger, H., Comparative Jurisprudence and Judicial Protection of the Individual against the Executive: a Method for Ascertaining International Law?, *Gerichtsschutz gegen die Exekutive/Judicial Protection against the Executive*, vol. 3, Colloquy, Max-Planck-Institut f.a.o.R.u.V., Koln, C. Heymanns/Oceana, 1971, pp. 269–79

Strisower, L., Rapport sur la responsabilité internationale des États à raison des dommages causés sur leur territoire à la personne ou aux biens des étrangers, 33 *Annuaire de l'Institut de Droit International* [1927]–1 pp. 455–98, and [Rapport final] *ibid.*, pp. 521–62

Stryckmans, F., La Commission européenne des droits de l'homme et le procès équitable, *Journal des Tribunaux* (Bruxelles) [1966] pp. 533–43, 555–62

Susterhenn, A., L'application de la Convention [européenne] sur le plan du droit interne, report, C. of E. doc. A–58–248, 1960 Strasbourg Colloquium, [mimeographed,] pp. 1–25

Tammes, A.J.P., The Obligation to Provide Local Remedies, *Volkenrechtelijke Opstellen aangeboden aan Professor Dr Gesina H.J. van der Molen*, Kampen, 1962, pp. 152–68

Tardu, M., Quelques questions relatives à la coexistence des procédures universelles et régionales de plainte individuelle dans le domaine des droits de l'homme, 4 *Revue des droits de l'homme/Human Rights Journal* [1971] pp. 589–625

Ténékidès, C.G., L'épuisement des voies de recours internes comme condition préalable de l'instance internationale, 14 *Revue de droit international et de législation comparée* [1933] pp. 514–35

Triepel, H., Les rapports entre le droit interne et le Droit international, 1 *Recueil des Cours de l'Académie de Droit International* [1923] pp. 77–121

Vasak, K., Le droit international des droits de l'homme, 140 *Recueil des Cours de l'Académie de Droit International* [1974] pp. 343/414

Le problème des 'pétitions' individuelles relatives aux droits de l'homme, *La protection internationale des droits de l'homme dans le cadre européen* (Colloque de Strasbourg de 1960), Paris, Dalloz, 1961, pp. 261–78

L'application des droits de l'homme et des libertés fondamentales par les juridictions nationales, *Droit communautaire et Droit national – Semaine de Bruges*, Bruges, De Tempel, 1965, pp. 336–58

La protection internationale des droits de l'homme – 25e anniversaire de la Déclaration Universelle, *Problèmes politiques et sociaux* (*La documentation française*) [1973] ns. 203–4, pp. 6–54

La protection internationale des droits de l'homme dans le cadre des organisations regionales, *Documents d'études – Droit international public* (*La documentation française*) [1973] ns. 3.05–3.06, pp. 3–63

Egoisme et droits de l'homme (esquisse pour un procès), *Mélanges offerts à Polys Modinos*, Paris, Pédone, 1968, pp. 366–7

Velu, J., Voies de droit ouvertes aux individus devant les instances nationales en cas de violation des normes et décisions de droit européen, report, 1975 Brussels Colloquium, [mimeographed,] pp. 14–26

Verdross, A., Observations [sur la règle de l'épuisement des recours internes], 46 *Annuaire de l'Institut de Droit International* [1956] pp. 47–8

Verzijl, J.H.W., Rapport préliminaire sur la règle de l'épuisement des recours internes, 45 *Annuaire de l'Institut de Droit International* [1954]–1 pp. 5–33

    Rapport définitif sur la règle de l'épuisement des recours internes, 45 *Annuaire de l'Institut de Droit International* [1954]–1 pp. 84–111

    Rapport supplémentaire sur la règle de l'épuisement des recours internes, 46 *Annuaire de l'Institut de Droit International* [1956] pp. 1–12, and see pp. 13–20

Vignes, D.H., Sur l'irrecevabilité de certaines requêtes, 2 *Annuaire français de Droit international* [1956] pp. 397–401

Virally, M., L'accès des particuliers à une instance internationale: la protection des droits de l'homme dans le cadre européen, 20 *Mémoires publiés par la Faculté de Droit de Genève* [1964] pp. 67–89

    Droits de l'homme et théorie générale du Droit international, *René Cassin Amicorum Discipulorumque Liber*, vol. IV, Paris, Pédone, 1972, pp. 323–30

    Sur un pont aux anes: les rapports entre droit international et droits internes, *Mélanges offerts à Henri Rolin*, Paris, Pédone, 1964, pp. 488–505

Vis, W., La réparation des violations de la Convention européenne des droits de l'homme, report, C. of E. doc. A–58–036, 1960 Strasbourg Colloquium, [mimeographed,] pp. 1–9

Waldock, C.H.M., The European Convention for the Protection of Human Rights and Fundamental Freedoms, 34 *British Yearbook of International Law* [1958] pp. 356–63

Weil, G.L., Decisions on Inadmissible Applications by the European Commission of Human Rights, 54 *American Journal of International Law* [1960] pp. 874–81

Wengler, W., Réflexions sur l'application du Droit international public par les tribunaux nationaux, 2 *Ottawa Law Review* [1968] pp. 265–319

    Réflexions sur l'application du Droit international public par les tribunaux internes, 72 *Revue générale de Droit international public* [1968] pp. 921–90

Weis, P., Diplomatic Protection of Nationals and International Protection of Human Rights, 4 *Revue des droits de l'homme/Human Rights Journal* [1971] pp. 643–78

Wiebringhaus, H., La règle de l'épuisement préalable des voies de recours internes dans la jurisprudence de la Commission européenne des droits de l'homme, 5 *Annuaire français de Droit international* [1959] pp. 685–704

Wilkoc, A.R., Procedures to Deal with Individual Communications to International Bodies: the Sub-Commission on Prevention of Discrimination and Protection of Minorities, 1 *New York University Journal of International Law and Politics* [1968] pp. 277–301

Witenberg, J.-C., La recevabilité des réclamations devant les juridictions internationales, 41 *Recueil des Cours de l'Académie de Droit International* [1932] pp. 5–135, esp. pp. 50–6

    Onus probandi devant les juridictions arbitrales, 55 *Revue générale de Droit international public* [1951] pp. 321–42

La théorie des preuves devant les juridictions internationales, 56 *Recueil des Cours de l'Académie de Droit International* [1936] pp. 5–105

Wolf, F., Aspects judiciaires de la protection internationale des droits de l'homme par l'O.I.T., 4 *Revue des droits de l'homme/Human Rights Journal* [1971] pp. 773–838

Wortley, B.A., Some Observations on Claims for Violations by a State of the Human Rights of a Citizen, 8 *Rivista di Diritto Europeo* [1968] pp. 103–20

Zotiades, G.B., Some Aspects of the Functions Assigned to the European Commission of Human Rights in the Examination of the Merits of the Case, 22 *Revue hellénique de Droit international* [1969] pp. 65–91

INDEX